Resistencia
Corrientes
Posadas

**ARGENTINIAN
MESOPOTAMIA**

ta Fe
Concordia
Paraná
Rosario

**BUENOS
AIRES**
La Plata

THE PAMPAS

Tandil
Bahía
Blanca
Mar del
Plata
Necochea

0 km | 300
0 miles | 300

**ARGENTINIAN
MESOPOTAMIA**
Pages 156–175

THE PAMPAS
Pages 136–155

BUENOS AIRES AREA BY AREA

**PLAZA DE MAYO AND
MICROCENTRO**
Pages 60–75

**SAN TELMO AND
LA BOCA**
Pages 76–85

**PLAZA SAN MARTÍN
AND RETIRO**
Pages 86–93

RECOLETA
Pages 94–103

**PALERMO AND
BELGRANO**
Pages 104–115

EYEWITNESS TRAVEL
ARGENTINA

EYEWITNESS TRAVEL
ARGENTINA

LONDON, NEW YORK,
MELBOURNE, MUNICH AND DELHI
www.dk.com

MANAGING EDITOR Aruna Ghose
EDITORIAL MANAGER Ankita Awasthi
DESIGN MANAGERS Sunita Gahir, Priyanka Thakur
PROJECT EDITOR Janice Pariat
PROJECT DESIGNER Kavita Saha
EDITOR Jayashree Menon
DESIGNER Kaberi Hazarika
SENIOR CARTOGRAPHIC MANAGER Uma Bhattacharya
CARTOGRAPHER Alok Pathak
SENIOR DTP DESIGNER Vinod Harish
SENIOR PICTURE RESEARCHER Taiyaba Khatoon
PICTURE RESEARCHERS Sumita Khatwani, Shweta Andrews

CONTRIBUTORS
Wayne Bernhardson, Declan McGarvey, Chris Moss

PHOTOGRAPHERS
Demetrio Carrasco, Nigel Hicks, Linda Whitwam

ILLUSTRATORS
Chapel Design and Marketing Ltd, Sanjeev Kumar, Arun Pottirayil, T. Gautam Trivedi

Reproduced in Singapore by Colourscan
Printed and bound by L. Rex Printing Company Limited, China

First American Edition, 2008
10 11 12 13 10 9 8 7 6 5 4 3 2 1

Published in the United States by DK Publishing,
375 Hudson Street, New York, New York 10014

Reprinted with revisions 2010

Copyright © 2008, 2010 Dorling Kindersley Limited, London
A Penguin Company

Published in Great Britain by Dorling Kindersley Limited.

A CATALOG RECORD FOR THIS BOOK IS AVAILABLE
FROM THE LIBRARY OF CONGRESS

ISSN 1542-1554
ISBN 978-0-75666-193-9

Front cover main image: Mount Fitz Roy, Patagonia

MIX
Paper from
responsible sources
FSC
www.fsc.org   FSC™ C018179

**The information in this DK Eyewitness
Travel Guide is checked regularly.**

Every effort has been made to ensure that this book is as up-to-date as possible at the time of going to press. Some details, however, such as telephone numbers, opening hours, prices, gallery hanging arrangements and travel information are liable to change. The publishers cannot accept responsibility for any consequences arising from the use of this book, nor for any material on third party websites, and cannot guarantee that any website address in this book will be a suitable source of travel information. We value the views and suggestions of our readers very highly. Please write to: Publisher, DK Eyewitness Travel Guides, Dorling Kindersley, 80 Strand, London, WC2R 0RL, Great Britain.

The spectacular Quebrada landscape

CONTENTS

INTRODUCING
ARGENTINA

DISCOVERING
ARGENTINA **8**

PUTTING ARGENTINA
ON THE MAP **10**

A PORTRAIT OF
ARGENTINA **12**

ARGENTINA THROUGH
THE YEAR **40**

THE HISTORY
OF ARGENTINA **46**

BUENOS AIRES
AREA BY AREA

BUENOS AIRES AT
A GLANCE **58**

Brightly painted houses in La Boca,
Buenos Aires

◁ Stratified Quebrada de Humahuaca, Córdoba and the Andean Northwest

PLAZA DE MAYO AND
MICROCENTRO 60

SAN TELMO AND
LA BOCA 76

PLAZA SAN MARTÍN
AND RETIRO 86

RECOLETA 94

PALERMO AND
BELGRANO 104

SHOPPING IN
BUENOS AIRES 118

ENTERTAINMENT IN
BUENOS AIRES 122

A couple perform
street tango

BUENOS AIRES
STREET FINDER 126

ARGENTINA
REGION BY
REGION

ARGENTINA AT A
GLANCE 134

THE PAMPAS 136

ARGENTINIAN
MESOPOTAMIA 156

CÓRDOBA AND
THE ANDEAN
NORTHWEST 176

CUYO AND
THE WINE
COUNTRY 202

PATAGONIA 220

TIERRA DEL FUEGO
AND ANTARCTICA
256

TRAVELERS'
NEEDS

WHERE TO STAY 270

WHERE TO EAT 288

SHOPPING IN
ARGENTINA 304

ENTERTAINMENT IN
ARGENTINA 308

OUTDOOR ACTIVITIES
AND SPECIALIZED
HOLIDAYS 310

Horse riding in the countryside
outside Tandil

SURVIVAL GUIDE

PRACTICAL
INFORMATION 318

TRAVEL
INFORMATION 328

GENERAL INDEX 336

ACKNOWLEDGMENTS
348

PHRASE BOOK 350

Mate gourds for sale

Grand old architecture
of Santa Catalina

INTRODUCING
ARGENTINA

THE ANGLO-AMERICAN GAUCHOS CATCHING WILD HORSES, IN THE FALKLAND ISLANDS.

DISCOVERING ARGENTINA 8–9
PUTTING ARGENTINA ON THE MAP 10–11
A PORTRAIT OF ARGENTINA 12–39
ARGENTINA THROUGH THE YEAR 40–45
THE HISTORY OF ARGENTINA 46–55

DISCOVERING ARGENTINA

First-time visitors to Argentina are often surprised by the sheer vastness and variety of its landscape,

Argentinian *fileteado* artwork

which compels people to return time and again and explore a new region. Buenos Aires is a magical city, with the architecture and cosmopolitan air of a European capital, but the vitality and raw energy of Latin America. At its edge are miles of rolling grassland filled with birdsong and gaucho (cowboy) customs. A journey beyond the Pampas takes visitors to the subtropical lushness of Mesopotamia, the shimmering beauty of the high plains and ravines of the Andean Northwest, and the vineyards and soaring peaks of Cuyo. In the distant south is Patagonia, where lakes, glaciers, and endless steppes compete for attention.

BUENOS AIRES

• **Historical architecture of Casa Mínima**
• **Dining in Palermo**
• **Boating in the Paraná Delta**

Argentina's capital was given some splendid French architecture and city parks in the 1920s. San Telmo offers an opportunity to experience how the city was in the period before this. Here visitors will find **Casa Minima** *(see p78)*, a rare example of home-grown Buenos Aires architecture, along with the country's only open-air museum at **El Caminito** *(see p85)*. Palermo barrio houses **Parque 3 de Febrero** *(see p106)*, while the best area for dining and drinking is concentrated around Palermo Viejo. For a green break from the city, hop on a train to **Tigre** *(see pp116–17)* and take a wooden boat through the labyrinthine channels of the wild subtropical delta.

A lively gaucho festival filled with equestrian activity

THE PAMPAS

• **Living on an estancia**
• **Authentic gaucho towns**
• **Atlantic beach resorts**

The great swathe of grasslands that encircles the capital provides wonderful places to relax. Many grand old ranches are now open as hotels or parks, and visitors can check in for a day or two to go horse riding, bird-watching, hiking, or simply to eat plenty of barbecued steak. Across the region are old-style gaucho towns such as **San Antonio de Areco** *(see p145)* and **Santa Rosa** *(see p154)*, ideal for tapping into the laid-back rhythms of life in the countryside. On the eastern edge of the Pampas are the Atlantic resorts that porteños, residents of

Brightly painted walls in La Boca

Buenos Aires, flock to every summer. The well-heeled have houses at **Pinamar** *(see p150)*, but the people's resort of **Mar del Plata** *(see pp148–9)* offers a classic beach town experience.

ARGENTINIAN MESOPOTAMIA

• **Magnificent Iguazú Falls**
• **Gualeguaychú's carnival**
• **Fly-fishing on the Paraná**
• **Wildlife of Esteros del Iberá**

In the north of the fertile Argentinian Mesopotamia region are the magical **Iguazú Falls** *(see pp172–5)*, a huge horseshoe of high waterfalls straddling the border between Argentina and Brazil. A stopover in **Gualeguaychú** *(see p164)* is recommended for the annual carnival, when the whole town paints itself in techni-color makeup and dons vibrant costumes to party into the night and perform traditional street dancing. More relaxing may be a slow weekend angling on the banks of the **Río Paraná** *(see p163)*, where huge dorado fish fight viciously with experienced fly fishermen. In the gleaming wetlands of **Esteros del Iberá** *(see pp166–7)*, nature lovers can catch glimpses of abundant wildlife up close, including caiman and cabybaras, and an array of bird species. Visitors can hire a horse to wade through the deep channels.

◁ Couple dancing the tango on a signboard, La Boca, Buenos Aires

View of surreal mountainscape, Quebrada de Cafayate

CÓRDOBA AND THE ANDEAN NORTHWEST

• Córdoba's Jesuit legacy
• The Quebradas
• Salta's handicrafts

The heart of the province, **Córdoba** *(see pp180–81)* has Jesuit churches and estancias (ranches) which retell their story of settlement, evangelization, Hispanification, and agriculture. Up north is the **Quebrada de Cafayate** *(see p190)*, with beautiful red-rock canyons and slopes covered in candelabra cacti, and the winemaking oasis of **Cafayate** *(see p190)*. The **Quebrada de Humahuaca** *(see pp196–9)* is another deep cleft in the Andean high-plain where the exposed cliffs are a riot of colors. Here, native and mestizo (of mixed race) culture remains strong. In **Salta** *(see pp192–5)* visitors can pick up a folk guitar, panpipes, and other handicrafts – even a traditional scarlet-and-black poncho.

CUYO AND THE WINE COUNTRY

• Cerro Aconcagua
• Mendoza's vineyards
• Skiing in Las Leñas

The Andes range provides an opportunity for plenty of outdoor activity, including climbing **Cerro Aconcagua** *(see p213)*, which is the highest peak in the Americas. The region's other famous attraction is wine. Some of the world's finest malbecs come out of the wineries that surround **Mendoza** *(see pp206–209)*, **San Juan** *(see p216)*, and the small hamlets that cling to the foothills of the mountains. From July through early October, there is some great skiing to be had at **Las Leñas** *(see p219)*.

PATAGONIA

• Argentina's Lake District
• Cueva de las Manos
• Whale-watching in Península Valdés
• Trekking in Parque Nacional Los Glaciares

A popular holiday spot, **Bariloche** *(see p238)* is located in Patagonia's northwest corner, the heart of the Lake District. Nearby **San Martín de los Andes** *(see p236)* offers golf and excellent restaurants. In the far

south is **Cueva de las Manos** *(see p243)*. A UNESCO World Heritage Site, it is the country's finest example of prehistoric cave art. On the other side of the steppe, on the Atlantic coast, is the World Heritage Site of **Península Valdés** *(see pp226–7)*. A quiet, unpopulated place, its calm bays provide an ideal breeding ground for Southern Right whales. The stunning **Parque Nacional Los Glaciares** *(see pp250–5)* is a major draw, attracting both experienced trekkers and those who just want to admire Glaciar Perito Moreno.

TIERRA DEL FUEGO AND ANTARCTICA

• Bustling Ushuaia
• Cruising to Antarctica
• Wildlife-rich Falkland Islands

The island of Tierra del Fuego is located at the mythic *fin del mundo* (end of the world). One of its biggest urban centers, **Ushuaia** *(see p260)* is a port for cruises to **Antarctica** *(see pp264–7)*. The traffic of cruisers and climbers, backpackers and bird-watchers gives the town a unique buzz. Huge Magellanic woodpeckers keep the icy forests all around full of raucous cheer. To the east of the continent are the **Falkland Islands** (Islas Malvinas) *(see pp264–7)*. Remote and unspoilt, these British islands are a great place for wildlife watching.

A large colony of king penguins, Falkland Islands

Putting Argentina on the Map

Argentina occupies most of the triangular southern tip
of South America and shares its borders with Uruguay,
Brazil, Paraguay, Bolivia, and Chile. Covering an area
of 1.08 million sq miles (2.8 million sq km), it is the
eighth largest country in the world. It is more than
3,100 miles (5,000 km) long following the western
frontier down the Andes range, while some 1,900 miles
(3,000 km) of Atlantic coastline stretch between Buenos
Aires and Tierra del Fuego, an island separated from
the continent by the Magellan Strait and shared with
Chile. Argentina has a population of 40 million and
administratively, it is divided into 23 provinces and a
federal district in which stands the bustling capital.

KEY

 International airport	
	Ferry port
	Expressway
	Highway
	Railroad
	International border

0 km	300
0 miles	300

Satellite image of Argentina, where Tierra
del Fuego and Patagonia are clearly visible

*PACIFIC
OCEAN*

Mar Argentin

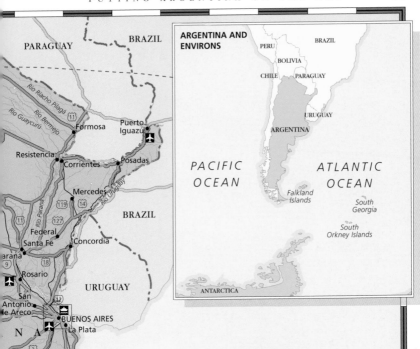

PARAGUAY

BRAZIL

Rio Riacho Pilagá

Rio Bermejo

Rio Guaycurú

Formosa

Puerto
Iguazú

Resistencia

Corrientes

Posadas

Mercedes

Rio Uruguay

BRAZIL

Federal

Santa Fe

Concordia

Paraná

Rosario

San
Antonio
de Areco

URUGUAY

BUENOS AIRES

La Plata

Olavarría

Tandil

Mar del
Plata

ATLANTIC
OCEAN

Mar
Argentino

**ARGENTINA AND
ENVIRONS**

PERU

BRAZIL

BOLIVIA

CHILE

PARAGUAY

URUGUAY

ARGENTINA

PACIFIC
OCEAN

ATLANTIC
OCEAN

Falkland
Islands

South
Georgia

South
Orkney Islands

ANTARCTICA

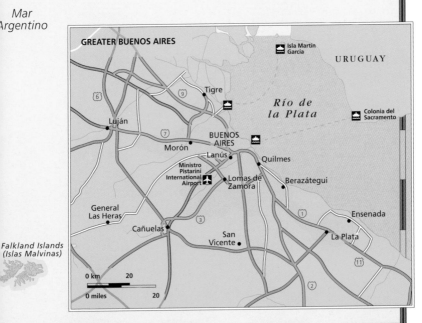

Falkland Islands
(Islas Malvinas)

GREATER BUENOS AIRES

Isla Martín
García

URUGUAY

Tigre

Río de
la Plata

Colonia del
Sacramento

Luján

BUENOS
AIRES

Morón

Lanús

Quilmes

Ministro
Pistarini
International
Airport

Lomas de
Zamora

Berazátegui

General
Las Heras

Ensenada

Cañuelas

San
Vicente

La Plata

0 km   20

0 miles   20

A PORTRAIT OF ARGENTINA

*B*ehind Argentina's European veneer is a colorful, chaotic, and enchanting Latin American nation. Passionate about their music, meat, and politics, the people of the country are fun-loving and friendly. Its breathtaking range of landscapes and distinct historical evolution, both during and since the Spanish conquest, combine to make Argentina the exciting destination it is today.

Bounded by the towering Andes in the west and the waters of the Atlantic to the east, Argentina is the eighth largest country in the world, second in size only to Brazil in Latin America. About a third of the country's population lives in the bustling capital, Buenos Aires, and its sprawling suburbs. The rest of the country is thinly populated, and lonely swathes of the rural interior, especially in Patagonia, are almost devoid of settlement.

Evidence of the country's Spanish past abounds across Argentina. In the 16th century, Jesuits followed in the wake of the conquistadors, converting natives and building

Handcrafted *mate* gourd and straw

magnificent monuments to their faith. Córdoba, Mendoza, and La Plata most strongly reflect their influence. Following land-grabbing military campaigns in the 1870s and 80s in the central and southern provinces, many of Argentina's indigenous peoples were wiped out. A wave of immigrants, mainly from Italy and Spain, swept into the country, making it Latin America's most Europeanized nation. The country's history is intricately linked to the five nations with which it shares its borders. The landscapes and peoples of Argentina, however, are utterly distinct, with most *Argentinos* bearing a strong sense of national identity.

Guanacos in Parque Nacional Perito Moreno against a backdrop of the Patagonian Andes

◁ People passing a life-size mural on a street in Caminito, Buenos Aires

LAND AND CONSERVATION

The absence of human settlement in many areas and the abundance of green spaces makes Argentina in many ways a natural paradise. The Pampas grasslands spill endlessly around the capital city, while subtropical forests characterize Argentinian Mesopotamia. The Andean Northwest offers deep ravines weathered by wind and rain, and Patagonia thrills visitors with its magnificent glaciers. The country's 27 national parks and municipal preserves protect a wide range of environments, including icefields, deserts, and wetlands.

Visitors' center logo, Parque Nacional Chaco

The government has now begun to realize that the booming tourist industry will depend on sustaining this wilderness. For over a century, the country's economy has focused on agriculture, cattle-raising, and sheep-farming, and land in many areas has been damaged by the impact. For example, the plains of Patagonia have been desertified by intensive sheep farming. The growing of wheat and other grains have replaced the original grasslands of central Argentina, and cash crops, such as genetically modified soya and tobacco, have replaced the quinoa and *amaranth* that pre-Columbian farmers planted.

Argentina's growing industrial sector has also had a devastating impact on nature. Native flora and fauna are under threat due to the hydro-electric projects on the Uruguay and Paraná rivers, and the forestry projects in Misiones and Tierra del Fuego. The World Wide Fund for Nature (WWF) estimates that more than 61,775 sq miles (160,000 sq km) of forest cover were lost between 1980 and 2000. Illegal hunting is a problem in all provinces.

The country's main environmental non-governmental organization, Vida Silvestre, works with private organizations and philanthropists to create new protected areas and establish sustainable tourism projects. Recent successes have included the temporary shutdown of a Shell refinery in Buenos Aires for inadequate waste-handling procedures, and the creation of Parque Nacional Monte León through the non-profit Patagonia Land Trust.

The stunning red rocks of Parque Provincial Ischigualasto, a UNESCO World Heritage Site

Gaucho on an estancia near El Calafate, Patagonia

ECONOMY

The Argentinian economy has experienced several booms and melt-downs in the past, and Argentinians have always kept a close watch on economic fluctuations. In the late 1980s, only a few years after the return of democracy, inflation soared to 1,000 percent. During the presidency of Carlos Menem in the 1990s, Argentinians thought a new era had been ushered in: the peso was pegged to the dollar, credit was available, and people were able to afford all kinds of luxuries. No one was prepared for what happened in December 2001, when a run on the banks caused the government to seques-ter private savings, and eventually led to the collapse of the peso. Today, as the country experiences a mod-erate economic revival, confidence is gradually returning. The country is the third largest beef exporter in the world after Brazil and Australia, and the fifth largest wine-producer in the world. Tourism is flourishing and is the

Cristina Fernandez de Kirchner during the presidential elections

third largest source of the country's income. However, poverty has risen since the 1980s, and crime and security worry most Argentinians, as does the "brain drain." After the 2001 banking disaster, many of Argentina's talented young people left the country, and many have stayed away despite the gradual improvement in affairs back home.

POLITICS

For the majority of Argentinians, politics has thrown up more drama and damage than the worst trials and tribulations of the economy. While there have always been *caudillos* (political-military dictators) in Argentina, almost all Argentinians view the generals who ran the country during the 1976–1983 period as tyrants. However, national politics since the military dictatorship has been relatively stable and peaceful, and while democracy has brought its own set of problems for Argentinians, few would exchange today's elected leaders for the dictators of the past.

Today, the country's government is a representative-democratic, federal, and presidential one wherein the president is the head of state and head of government, complemented by a multiparty system. The country is divided into a federal capital and 23 provinces; the federal government is headed by the president and the bicameral national congress, and the provinces by gover-nors. After winning the popular vote in the October 2007 elections, Argentina's First Lady, Cristina Fernandez de Kirchner, became the president of Argentina.

SPORTS AND ARTS

Argentina is well ahead of other Latin American countries in terms of sporting prowess and artistic creativity. It is a world-class nation in soccer and several other sports, including tennis, golf, polo, and hockey. At the 2004 Olympic Games, Argentina took the gold in basketball and in men's soccer. In 2007, Angel Cabrera won the US Open Golf Championship. However, it is in soccer that Argentina's passions spill onto the streets. Past legends such as Alfredo di Stefano, Mario Kempes, Gabriel Batistuta, and Diego Maradona are still revered as demi-gods while Lionel Messi is a current favorite.

Argentinian pop band Miranda at a performance

Buenos Aires's most important cultural institute, Teatro Colón, is where famous classical music artistes, including pianist Martha Argerich, conductor Daniel Barenboim, and composer Osvaldo Golijov, have performed. While there is always a huge turnout for rock concerts by visiting international bands, many young Argentinians prefer their *rock nacional*. Argentinian pop and rock have been politicized since the 1970s when the band Sui Generis recorded anti-establishment songs in the midst of the military dictatorship. International critics often point out that there is, through the influence of tango, a melancholy in all Argentinian music. While very few Argentinians actually dance to the famous rhythm, urbanites enjoy Carlos Gardel, the Bing Crosby of Argentinian tango.

After the heady days of the Latin American boom during the middle of the 20th century, few Argentinian writers have won international acclaim. For many, the works of Jorge Luis Borges and Julio Cortázar remain the benchmarks by which all literature must be measured. Nonetheless, Argentinians are avid readers; the annual Feria de Libro in Buenos Aires attracts huge audiences, and the publishing of new books by contemporary writers such as Ana María Shua, Pablo de Santis, and Tomás Eloy Martínez are major events in the cultural calendar.

Cinema is popular in the country. In the last few years, a new school of cinema verité has developed, which, as well as scooping up prizes in prestigious international film festivals, has given the country a register with which to debate social realities in the post-1983 democratic period.

Lionel Messi playing against the Mexico team

PEOPLE AND SOCIETY

A nation of immigrants since the 19th century, Argentina is today a cultural melting pot comprising people of Italian, Spanish, Jewish, and French ancestry. Buenos Aires's flamboyant, confident residents, the porteños, enjoy many of the same luxuries and suffer the same stresses as the residents of any major world city. Their city also has certain unique characteristics of its own, such as the enduring melodrama of tango, the booming gastronomic scene, and the insomniac nightlife. Porteños often refer to their ring road, Avenida General Paz, as if it were some kind of frontier, and the less-traveled urban working classes are wont to imagine the provincial heartland as a somewhat untamed, impenetrable, and exotic periphery.

A brightly painted café in Caminito, La Boca

However, those who do venture out of the city limits are often charmed by the myriad pleasures of the interior. In the small towns of Misiones, Chaco, and Corrientes, village life goes on much as it has done for 200 years, with locals gathering at the bar in the plaza, and the year-round rhythms of work and family life broken only by major fiestas. In the Andean plains of the Northwest, vestiges of pre-Columbian life still remain, with native residents and mestizos (people of mixed European and indigenous ancestry) still playing the panpipes and flutes and wearing ponchos. Far south in Patagonia, visitors will be surprised to meet descendants of Welsh and German settlers.

An essential bonhomie and zest for life have always endured in the Argentinian soul. For the visitor, it is easy to enjoy the endearing qualities of this colorful and thrilling nation, its abundant wildlife, vast landscapes, and friendly people.

An indigenous ceremony taking place in the Neuquén province

Landscape and Wildlife of Argentina

Despite threats to its environment, Argentina still remains one of the richest countries in the world for its variety of flora and fauna. It has over 1,000 species of birds, many of which are unique to the country, 29 sprawling national parks, and a large number of provincial preserves that protect a fascinating array of mammals. It owes its natural wealth to a highly varied topography that covers a range of climatic zones ranging from arid, harsh environments dominated by steppe, salt pans, and soaring Andean peaks to great swathes of grassy plains and wetlands.

A colorful flamingo

View of Mount Fitz Roy in Parque Nacional Los Glaciares

THE PAMPAS WETLANDS

Seasonal rainfall across the Pampas in Buenos Aires and Entre Ríos leads to the formation of the channels and vast lagoons of Esteros del Iberá (*see pp166–7*). It is home to waders and many other bird species.

The wattled jacana, *with its huge feet, seems to walk on water. It daintily strides over lily pads and is a discreet wader until it flies and flashes its bright yellow underwings.*

The dorado *is king of Río Paraná (see p163). Known for its power, it is the prize catch of anglers in the northeast.*

Yacaré *thrive in the Iberá wetlands, sharing the banks and islands with capybaras and howler monkeys.*

MOUNTAINS AND PUNA

At over 8,000 ft (2,400 m) above sea level, the *puna* (montane grasslands) in Argentina's northwestern provinces is a mixture of semi-arid and desert landscapes. On its western edge, it rises to become the Andes range.

The Andean condor *has a wingspan of over 9 ft (3 m). It can be seen wheeling on the thermals that form in the crevasses and lagoons of the Andes.*

The Royal chinchilla *is a rodent found in the high plains. Hunted for its fur, it is an endangered species.*

The Cardón cactus *grows in abundance across the northwest and is protected inside Parque Nacional Los Cardones in the Valles Calchaquíes area (see p191).*

THE ATLANTIC COAST

The rugged coastline between Buenos Aires and Cape Horn stretches over 1,900 miles (3,000 km). The cold currents of the South Atlantic are the natural habitat of Southern Right whales, seals, and sea lions, all seen at Península Valdés *(see pp226–7)*. Offshore, petrels and albatrosses patrol the waves.

Magellanic penguins *are a common sight along the Patagonian coast. The continent's largest colony is found at Punta Tombo in Chubut (see p228).*

The Southern Right whale *earned its name as the "right" whale for hunters to kill because it floats after being harpooned. It is now protected in Argentinian waters.*

SUBTROPICAL FORESTS

Sizeable protected subtropical forests can be found in Misiones, Corrientes, and Salta. Flora flourishes beneath the dense canopy; the more remote forests provide a habitat for rare species such as harpy eagles and jaguars.

PATAGONIA

Best known for its vast, semi-arid steppes and glaciers, Patagonia also has forests near the Andes and rich marine wildernesses along its coast. Wildlife includes rare species such as the *huemul* and miniature *pudú* deer.

The ceibo *is a carmine-red native arboreal bloom, adopted as Argentina's national flower.*

The Toco toucan *is a raucous forest species, seen at dawn or dusk flitting across the canopy in Parque Nacional Iguazú (see pp172–5).*

The myrtle tree *is found all across northern Patagonia. It is a versatile plant, with a warm fawn color.*

The Magellanic woodpecker *is a large, gregarious bird, easily spotted in Parque Nacional Tierra del Fuego in Ushuaia (see p261).*

The jaguar *is the largest feline in South America. Only a handful are now found in remote corners of protected preserves in the Salta, Jujuy, and Chaco regions.*

The huemul *has been on the endangered list since 1976. It is a shy, solitary woodland deer found mainly in the high Patagonian Andes.*

The Peoples of Argentina

Argentina is the most Europeanized of all Latin American nations and the majority of its 40 million people are of mainly Spanish or Italian descent. There are also small but significant British, German, French, Armenian, and Levantine communities, and Argentina has opened its doors to Jewish refugees from Russia and Poland. Official statistics suggest that only 404,000 Argentinians are indigenous, the majority of whom are the Mapuche, although research by the University of Buenos Aires suggests that up to half the population is mestizo.

A shop in Jujuy selling an array of indigenous handicrafts

INDIGENOUS PEOPLES

Few native tribes remain today, compared to the dozens of sizeable indigenous groups at the time of the Spanish conquest. While most still live in rural communities, the growing impoverishment of their lands have forced many to migrate to cities.

The Mapuche, *estimated to number 250,000, form the country's largest indigenous community. Most of them live in the province of Neuquén.*

Mapuche traditional clothing consists of handwoven ponchos and leather belts.

The Guaraní *speak a language of the same name and are mostly concentrated in Misiones province in the north of Argentina. There are approximately 10,000 Guaranís in the country.*

The Colla *community is the main indigenous group in Jujuy province, with an estimated population of 35,000. Their mother tongue is Quechua and they are famous for their colorful handmade clothes.*

The Tehuelche *were once an important Patagonian tribe. They suffered at the hands of both the Mapuche and the Spanish conquerors. Now, less than 200 people are classified as Tehuelche, though many thousands of mestizos have Tehuelche blood.*

The Wichí *people number about 25,000, with communities in the provinces of Chaco, Salta, and Formosa. Though Wichí land rights are recognized by law, their territory is under constant threat from developers.*

IMMIGRANTS

Mass immigration transformed Argentinian society at the end of the 19th century, bringing much-needed cheap labor while at the same time enriching the country's social and cultural scene.

Buenos Aires *was the favored disembarking point for European immigrants, and although conditions were tough for a majority of the people, they continued to come in their thousands.*

Animal sacrifices are held to ensure a good harvest for the coming year.

The Italian community *in the capital's La Boca area is famous for its tenement buildings painted in primary colors by the first wave of Genoese immigrants. The lively port barrio (neighborhood) still retains something of its original atmosphere.*

Germans *also form a sizeable community. A number of Argentinian towns such as Villa Gesell (see p150) were founded by German immigrants, as is apparent from their architecture and street names. Several have retained their native customs, including the Oktoberfest beer festival.*

The Jews *in Argentina form one of the largest Jewish communities of any country outside Israel. It is estimated to comprise 250,000 people, around 180,000 of whom live in the capital city, which has several synagogues.*

Swiss *immigrants to Argentina made their homes in towns that nestled in the slopes of the beautiful Andes region. Their architectural influence is still evident today, as can be seen in this Swiss-style hotel in Bariloche (see p238).*

The Gaucho: Symbol and Reality

There are macho cowboy figures throughout the Americas, but few are as central to the national culture as the gaucho is to Argentina. The earliest gauchos herded semi-wild Cimarron cattle in the 17th century, often sleeping out in the open pampas and riding into town to trade in leather and tallow. This free-roaming life came to an end when the vast interior was divided up into huge estancias (ranches) in the 19th century. Modern-day gauchos still dress in their traditional garb for major holidays and festivals, and many are first-rate horsemen.

The gaucho and his favorite horse often form a strong lifelong bond

The *asado* is an open-air barbecue for grilling cuts of meat. They are an important community ritual for gauchos and country-dwellers. Here, the griller is grilling al cuero, a method of cooking meat with the skin still attached.

Patagonian gauchos, trained for years, are expert shepherds.

Mate is the traditional, rather bitter green tea of Argentina, Paraguay, Uruguay, and southern Brazil. Gauchos sip this concoction during their leisure hours.

THE GAUCHO WAY OF LIFE

The Argentinian estancia is often located far from any major towns or suburbs. Surrounded by largely unpopulated plains or barren hills, it is the classic gaucho homestead, providing them with solitude and freedom, close to the life they once led.

Sheep are the most commonly raised animal on an estancia, bred and sheared for their wool.

Training horses using boleadoras (heavily weighted lassos) and breaking in willful colts form part of the daily routine for many gauchos, who are often expert horsemen.

The rhythms of the *milonga*, strummed on a guitar and often accompanied by a "call-and-response" story about some popular local drama, are central to Argentina's rich folk tradition.

GAUCHO FESTIVALS

Many towns and cities in the Argentinian interior celebrate their local gaucho and farming heritage with lively parades, folk music concerts, and spectacular equestrian shows. The biggest fiesta in the country is the Día de la Tradición, a festive extravaganza held every November, especially in San Antonio de Areco *(see p145)*.

A gaucho in parade garb *and his smartly dressed* china *(female partner) perform a country dance known as the* chacarera. *Originating in the northwest of Argentina, it is a dance of lively rhythms and pantomimic play.*

Dancers from the northwest *of the country perform a high-spirited* carnavalito *(circle dance) during La Rural (see p43), the annual agricultural fair held in August in Buenos Aires. Here, people celebrate the culture and traditions of the country in the heart of the bustling city.*

GAUCHO GEAR

Gauchos don the full Moorish-influenced costume only for important fiestas. However, their everyday workclothes usually contain a few elements of traditional dress.

The poncho is a simple garment worn usually to keep warm.

The boina is a traditional Basque hat.

Facones *are handy for cutting rope, vegetation, and of course meat; they can also be used as weapons.*

The rastro is a metal belt decorated with equestrian or patriotic symbols.

Bombachas are loose trousers that have a hint of the Arabian about them.

Tough working boots are replaced by *alpargatas drilles* (sandals) for leisure.

THE LEGEND OF JUAN MOREIRA

Poster of the film
Juan Moreira

An outlaw and local folk-hero, Juan Moreira is an important figure in Argentina's gaucho history. He fought against the injustice meted out to gauchos as the military advanced across the country's interior during the late 19th century. The plains were fenced off and handed out to Creole aristocrats, and many gauchos were forced into employment as poorly paid peons and footsoldiers fighting in regional battles between landowners. Moreira was murdered by the authorities in 1874. In 1973, Argentinian director Leonard Favio made a celebrated film in his honor.

Boleadoras *are heavy ball-lassos, effective for capturing the wild flightless rheas that inhabit the Pampas region.*

Religion in Argentina

Argentina's most prominent religion is Christianity, with a large majority of Roman Catholic followers. Native religions were unable to resist the combined force of the Spanish sword and Jesuit teachings, but a certain degree of syncretism took place and a native version of Catholicism evolved, replete with saints, superstitions, and native iconography. Besides traditional religious practices, popular cult or folklore figures such as Difunta Correa, Gauchito Gil, and Ceferino Namuncurá, are still venerated throughout the country.

Statue of Mary, Luján

Statues on the façade of Basílica Nuestra Señora de Luján

CHRISTIANITY

Roman Catholicism is the country's state religion, supported by an article of the Argentinian constitution. This support is both economic and institutional, with the federal state paying salaries to bishops, and with the army setting up special posts for Catholic chaplains. Many schools are also affiliated to the church.

The first major Roman Catholic presence in the country was during the period of the Jesuit Missions (1599–1767), which were established in Córdoba and the northeast with their headquarters at Manzana de las Luces in Buenos Aires. The Jesuits, together with Franciscan and Dominican monks, laid the groundwork for the establishment of the

Catholic faith as the official religion of the country. Roman Catholicism spread to southern Argentina only at the end of the 19th century. Salesian missions were established in Patagonia in the 1890s and played a central

View of crumbling Jesuit ruins, San Ignacio Miní, Misiones

role in evangelizing the indigenous population and creating schools. At the same time, Anglican missionaries from the United Kingdom established an outpost on Canal Beagle.

The Independence movement in the early 19th century, however, was fronted by men fired by secular passions, and the open-door immigration policy that Argentina adopted from the mid-19th century onwards created a tolerant, nondenominational society.

The involvement of Catholic church leaders in the 1955 military coup that overthrew Perón, and in the machinations of the military government between 1976 and 1983, has cast a pall over the religious institution. There have been few left-leaning church leaders in Argentina, and the country has never been a seedbed for revolutionary liberation theology, which focuses on Christ as not only a Redeemer but also a Liberator of the oppressed. The church cannot be said to have fully succeeded in its doctrinal promise to represent the poor. Consequently, Catholicism is losing ground to the Mormon church, which gained prominence in the 1980s, as well as to the evangelical movements in the provinces. Today, Roman Catholicism is largely an element of Argentina's cultural heritage rather than a national faith.

JUDAISM

One of Argentina's famous claims is that Buenos Aires, after New York, is the most Jewish city outside Israel. While this is not strictly true, the Jewish community in Argentina is a significant 2 percent of the population and, more importantly, has a cultural presence and political clout disproportionate to mere numbers. Among those who made up the first waves of migration

Dome of Templo de la Congregación Israelita, Buenos Aires

to the rural interior during the late 1880s were groups of gauchos *judíos* (Jewish cowboys). In Buenos Aires, large numbers of Jewish families arrived between 1880 and 1940 to escape the pogroms in Russia and, later, the growing tide of anti-Semitic feeling across central and eastern Europe. After many decades of peaceful coexistence, the bombings of the Israeli Embassy in 1992, killing 29 people and wounding 242, and of the Argentinian-Israeli Mutual Association (AIMA) in 1994, killing 85 people, sent shock waves through the local community. While these acts of terrorism were largely ignored by the international community at the time, post-9/11 they have been attributed to Al-Qaeda.

Pan Altar exhibit, Museo Xul Solar

WORLD RELIGIONS

Argentina's constitution guarantees freedom of worship for all. A Muslim minority makes up about 1.5 percent of its population and Buenos Aires's King Fahd Mosque is the biggest in Latin America. The country is also home to other groups, including Mormons, Spiritualists, Jehovah's Witnesses, and Buddhists. A few Buddhist temples in the capital serve the descendants

of a Chinese commnity who migrated to Argentina in the mid-19th century as contract laborers.

PRE-COLUMBIAN BELIEFS

Although many indigenous groups were wiped out by war and disease during Spanish rule, several groups remain who still practice their traditional beliefs. The Andean Northwest was on the fringes of the Incan empire, and even today mestizo and native communities in Salta and Jujuy pay homage to Pachamama (Earth Mother) and perform pre-Columbian or syncretistic rituals such Fiesta de Inti-Raymi (winter solstice). Some members of the Mbya-Guaraní-speaking tribes of Misiones also follow a belief system that predates the Spanish conquest, with emphasis on the creation of the world by the supreme god, Tupã, dream narratives, and a strong sense of living in harmony with nature's rhythms.

Argentina's Mapuche community continues to observe their ancient traditions through storytelling and through *Ngillatún,* a major annual fiesta celebrated at different times according to the local sowing and harvesting calendar.

Gathering of native Mapuche women for *Ngillatún*

POPULAR CULTS

Argentinians venerate a number of unorthodox holy figures and even those who profess to no religion often adopt these as part of the national or regional folklore. The three best known quasi-saints are Difunta Correa *(see p216),* a woman who, though deceased, is believed to have continued to breastfeed and nourish her infant son; Gauchito Gil, a Robin Hood figure from Corrientes; and, from the province of Río Negro, Ceferino Namuncurá, son of a Mapuche chief. Ceferino is worshipped across northern Patagonia. Bus drivers often have the Virgin of Luján dangling from their rear-view mirrors alongside the colorful pendants of their football teams, and San Cayetano, the saint who cares for poor people, is a figure whose importance ebbs and flows in correlation to the economic realities of the day.

Largest mosque in South America, the King Fahd Mosque, Buenos Aires

Argentinian Tango

Tango has its roots in the bars and bordellos that
sprung up around Buenos Aires at the turn of the
20th century. From the cultural melting-pot of
European immigrants and Africans, a vibrant music
and dance form evolved. While early tango was
played on flute, violin, and guitar, musicians soon
adopted the *bandoneón* (button accordion) for its
rhythmic energy and melancholic strains. Tango
boomed in Argentina and in Europe in the early 1900s,
but declined during the Perón years. Since the 1980s
a revival has taken place, and a new tango music scene
has emerged inspired mainly by touring tango shows.

**Final of the Tango Metropolitan
Championship in Buenos Aires**

TANGO ON THE STREETS

The age-old tradition of practicing tango on the streets is
kept up by professional street performers who don retro
gear and show off their flicks and kicks to locals and
tourists in Calle Florida, Sam Telmo, and La Boca.

The upper body is usually
stiff, locked in a close
embrace in traditional
Argentinian tango.

The crowd is usually
encouraged to join in
and try a few steps
with the dancers.

Footwork involves
complicated move-
ments and is flexible,
quick, and exquisitely
choreographed.

Tango postures *often suggest that the man is the
stiff central focus and the woman the subjugated
outer flourish of the performance. However, it is
in most respects a dance of equals.*

*La milonga has come to mean a gathering
where people listen to tango music and
dance. Locals and tourists flock to milongas
that are scattered through the capital. On
some evenings shows are put on in which
audience participation is encouraged.*

Fantasia or show tango *is full of clever twirls,
exaggerated kicks, and aerial flights of
fancy. This is in contrast to the milonga style,
in which the feet cling to the floor. Fantasia
gained popularity during the tango revival
in the 1980s.*

TANGO IN POPULAR CULTURE

Buenos Aires is sometimes called a "tangopolis" or tango city. Music plays on taxi drivers' radios, grafitti is on the walls, and even films about contemporary issues often include a track of old tango to conjure up the capital city's ineffable melancholy.

Tango in street art *is popular and seen in murals and graffiti decorating walls all over Buenos Aires, including this brightly colored relief in the La Boca area.*

Tango in film *was first used in Rudolph Valentino's* The Four Horsemen of the Apocalypse *in 1921 to suggest illicit passion.*

Tango in pop art *is usually portrayed as a colorful and vibrant social experience by Argentinian painters, despite the seeming sobriety of the music. This atmospheric work,* La Milonga 2 *was painted in 2004 by Diego Manuel Rodriguez.*

THE BEST OF TANGO

Tangueros (tango fans) all have their own halls of fame. Yet everyone accepts that Carlos Gardel was an inspirational pioneer and that Ástor Piazzolla was the last great revolutionary to pick up a baton and lead tango down a new path. *Bandoneón* legend Aníbal Troilo and singer Roberto Goyeneche are up there in the pantheon too.

Carlos Gardel *was an enormously popular tango singer during the early 1900s. His death in an airplane crash at the height of his career created an image of a tragic hero. For many music fans, Gardel embodies the soul of Argentinian tango.*

Adriana Varela, *with her smoky voice, is a popular contemporary tango singer. She is also outspoken about her left-wing leanings.*

Ástor Pantaleón Piazzolla *is considered the most important tango composer of the late 20th century. His compositions revolutionized traditional tango by adding elements of modern jazz.*

Juan Carlos Copes *is widely recognized as the greatest dancer of the modern age. He is famed for his performances in the 1980s show* Tango Argentino.

Music and Dance

Rock nacional, pop, and tango dominate in the country's capital and other urban areas, where middle-class Argentinians stress their fondness for these genres, while *cumbia* and other Latin rhythms are popular among the working classes. Folk music, known in Castellano as *folklore*, enjoys greater popularity in rural parts. *Chacarera* and *zamba*, both dance and musical forms, are popular in the Pampas and Andean high plains respectively, while from the Mesopotamian provinces comes the lively fusion of *chamame*.

Mapuche women playing traditional ceremonial music

FOLKLORE

Built on the rhythms of pre-Columbian indigenous music, *folklore* exhibits Old World influences and has adopted the guitar as a key instrument. It is an umbrella term for the music that combines traditional indigenous elements with the structures or instrumentation of European folk.

Zamba *is not to be confused with its homonym, samba. The Argentinian* zamba *is an elegant courting dance during which couples tease and taunt each other using a white handkerchief. Lyrics cover all subjects, from love and the countryside to passionate political protest.*

Andean music *is synonymous with the sound of pan pipes,* charango *guitars, and flutes, while lyrics praise Pachamama (Earth Mother). Jaime Torres is the country's best-known* charango *virtuoso.*

Chamame *is a fusion of German schottis, Guaraní ethnic music, Brazilian forms, and Spanish rhythms and has a notably subtropical feel. Leading exponents include Chango Spasiuk.*

URBAN RHYTHMS

In Argentina's major cities there is access to a healthy mix of various genres of music ranging from Western classical and rock to hip hop, pop, and trance. Urbanites love to listen, and to dance, to tango, *marcha*, *cumbia*, *cuarteto*, pop-influenced *folklore*, and different kinds of rhythms that reflect Latin American and traditional indigenous influences.

Argentinian **cumbia** *was originally derived from Colombian cumbia. The term used to refer to songs dealing with love and jealousy set to a tinny beat, but in the late 1990s a scene called* cumbia villera *(shanty town) emerged. Well-known bands include Damas Gratis (right) and Yerba Brava.*

Chacarera *is played on the guitar, violin, and* bombo legüero *(drum), and sometimes with an accordion. It is an upbeat country rhythm with a dance akin to a line-dance with couples moving in and out of the embrace position. Los Chalchaleros are the best-known performers of this popular genre.*

La Nueva Canción *is a pan-national movement that emerged in the wake of the successful Cuban Revolution, when Latin American songwriters began to compose protest songs. Argentina's Mercedes Sosa was an early pioneer and over a span of 30 years has become the best known exponent of the style.*

Bombo legüero, **an Andean skin drum**

A *siku,* **pan pipe made of bamboo**

Quena, **a traditional six-hole bamboo flute**

Folklore *instruments such as the pan flute and* quena *are the essentials of Andean music, and are often combined with the* charango *and violin. Mapuche folk musicians have their own distinctive instruments, including the* trutruka *(horn) and* kultrun *(hide-drum).*

MAPUCHE MUSIC

Although recordings of the musical traditions of the now extinct Tehuelche, Diaguita, and Querandíes cultures are difficult to find, there is still a living Mapuche tradition in Argentina. Artists such as Beatriz Pichi Malen perform songs in the Mapuche tongue, *Mapundungun*, and incorporate native instruments and ancient poetry into their compositions. Mapuche music springs from a tradition of living in close and harmonious contact with nature. Unlike most Western music, it is not codified or written but based on natural melodic patterns and ancestral rhythms that are transmitted orally. Mapuche music influences their poetry, dance, dramatic representations, empirical medicine as well as religious beliefs.

Mapuche singer Beatriz Pichi Malen

Rock nacional *started in Buenos Aires and Rosario in the 1960s. Although initially incorporating many British rock influences, musicians later explored local musical roots and created a distinctive sound. Santa Fe-born León Gieco (left) is a well-loved veteran performer of folk rock music.*

Pop and fusion *thrive in Argentina, as young people are able to explore international musicians as well as listen to major local bands such as Divididos and Bersuit Vergarabat. Soda Stereo, led by Gustavo Cerati (right), is the most successful band to emerge in Argentina in the past 30 years.*

Art and Literature in Argentina

It is difficult to identify a cohesive "Argentinian" culture prior to Independence; neither the descendants of the Spanish settlers nor the indigenous tribes regarded themselves as belonging to a "nation" in the modern sense. In the 1700s, under the Viceroyalty of the River Plate, whose intentions in the region were purely commercial, Buenos Aires remained a cultural back-water. Only gradually, after Independence and spurred by immigration, a growing middle-class, and, later, the explosion of interest in Latin American literature, did Argentina and its vibrant capital begin to export as well as to import arts and culture.

RELIGIOUS AND INDIGENOUS ART

Pre-Hispanic art in what would later become Argentina was mainly pro-duced in the country's north-western regions, particularly in the valleys of Catamarca and Salta where the indige-nous population developed an array of pottery, metal-work, ceramics, and textiles. Noteworthy is the pottery produced during the La Aguada period (AD 650–900), which usually explored animistic themes through geometric representations of fantastic animals and anthro-pomorphic avatars of gods and monsters, reminiscent – on a less sophisticated level – of Hindu and Egyptian art. Cave paintings from much earlier epochs have been discovered in several prov-inces, the most famous being Cueva de las Manos in Patagonia *(see p243)*.

Art in the colonial era was dominated by religious painting, especially of the Cusco School, architecture, and sculpture. The finest works of this period are the altar pieces and pulpits pro-duced by Jesuit sculptors working with indigenous craftsmen. The ruins found in San Ignacio Mini *(see p169)* are a fine example of this. Jesuit architects such as Andrés Bianchi (1677–1740) built temples, schools, and accommodations in the north of the country, the ruins of which still inspire awe for

Colonial religious painting of the Cusco School

their scale and elegance. The watercolors of German Jesuit Florian Pauke (1719–89) show the everyday life and work of both the indigenous population and European travelers, and are striking for conferring the former with the same dignity and strength of purpose as the latter.

SECULAR ART

The War of Independence that Argentina waged against Spain had been fueled by the rationalist ideas of the Enlightenment and the French Revolution, so it is no surprise that the country's postcolonial artists largely ignored religious themes. The first major Argentinian artists were the painter and lithographer Carlos Morel (1813–94) and Prilidiano Pueyrredón (1823–70). The latter's *Retrato de Manuelita Rosas* and *The Bath* docu-ment the era with great clarity. Cándido López (1840–1902) was a painter and soldier famous for his paintings of the War of the Triple Alliance (1864–70).

Buenos Aires produced few significant artists until the late 19th century, when immigration invigorated the city's cultural scene. Well-known painters include Benito Quinquela Martín (1890–1977) and Fortunato Lacámera (1887–1951).

Modernist styles, mainly French cubism and Italian futurism, were imported from Europe's art capitals in the early 20th century. The key artists of this period were Antonio Berni (1905–81) and Xul Solar (1887–1963). Also popular was Florencio Molina Campos (1891–1959), best known for his gaucho caricatures. Major

Painting by Cándido López at Museo Nacional de Bellas Artes

contemporary artists include Antonio Seguí (b.1934), Luis Fernando Benedit (b.1937), and Guillermo Kuitca (b.1961) who is widely exhibited and is the most lauded Argentinian artist of his generation.

INDEPENDENT VOICES: 1810–1880

Postcolonial Argentina was, for most of the 19th century, a divided country where the pens of writers and intellectuals were pitted against the swords of provincial *caudillos* in a battle for the support of the population. In the view of writers such as Esteban Echeverría (1805–80) and Domingo Sarmiento (1811–88), the conflict was between European-style civilization (democracy and secularism) and home-grown barbarism (dictatorship and the law of the jungle). Echeverría's and Sarmiento's *bête noire* was the dictator Juan Manuel de Rosas, whom both writers attack in their best-known works, *El Matadero* (1871) and *Facundo* (1845) respectively.

GAUCHO LITERATURE: 1880–1900

José Hernández's (1834–86) verse epic *El Gaucho Martín Fierro* (1872) is highly lauded for its free-spirited hero drawn from rural folk ballads. It is regarded as the greatest expression of the country's national identity. The other work is Ricardo Güiraldes's (1886–1927) *Don Segundo Sombra* (1926), which casts a sceptical eye on the gaucho myth but still paints a vivid portrait of rural life of the era.

THE MODERNS: 1900–PRESENT DAY

Partially on its own merits and also drawn along in the slipstream of the boom in interest in Latin American writing, Argentinian literature has blossomed in the 20th century. Early talents include Uruguay-born Horacio Quiroga (1878–1937), whose collections of short fables made him one of the precursors of magical realism, while Roberto Arlt (1900–1942) is famous for his surreal, violent stories of alienation and despair. Manuel Puig (1932–90) was another influential author who used pop art techniques such as montage to startling effect. His key novels include *El Beso de la Mujer Araña* (1976), which brought him global fame after it was made into a movie and a Broadway musical. Another

Movie poster of *Blow-up*

Argentinian writer whose fame was bolstered by a silver screen adaptation was Julio Cortázar (1914–84): his story *Las Babas del Diablo* (1959) was the source for Michelangelo Antonioni's movie *Blow-up* (1966).

Julio Cortázar's brilliantly structured short stories, along with his experimental novels, have made him one of the most enduringly popular of all Argentinian writers, although he spent most of his life in self-imposed exile, disgusted at the right-wing and authoritarian drift of his homeland. Another politically committed writer was Rodolfo Walsh (1927–77). Regarded as one of the finest and most well-known Latin American journalists, he was shot on the orders of the Argentinian military dictatorship in 1977.

During the second half of the 20th century, the production and publication of women's writing proliferated in Argentina. Heiress Victoria Ocampo (1890–1979) played a leading role in the intellectual life of Buenos Aires during the 1920s and 30s,

Puig's *El Beso de la Mujer Araña* on stage

working as a critic and publishing the magazine *Sur*, which provided a platform for local writers as well as translating European writers for Argentinian readers. Proto-feminist ideas are evident in the erotically charged writings of poet Alfonsina Storni (1892–1938) and in the anti-patriarchal political works of Latin American playwright and novelist Griselda Gambaro (b.1928).

Other noted contemporary authors include Tomás Eloy Martínez (b.1934), César Aira (b.1949), and Ricardo Piglia (b.1941). No modern writers, however, have come close to matching the reputation of Jorge Luis Borges (1899–1986), the undisputed master of 20th-century Argentinian letters and one of the most influential writers to emerge since World War II. A prolific poet, essayist, and even film critic, Borges is best known for his two collections of short stories, *Ficciones* and *El Aleph*. As elusive as they are allusive, his brilliant works have influenced many major writers of our time.

Jorge Luis Borges, a 20th-century literary genius and icon

Cinema and Theater

A vibrant dramatic arts scene, especially in Buenos Aires, has existed since the late 1700s, while the Argentinian cinematic tradition dates back to the late 19th century. During the 1920s, the capital was one of the major Latin American centers of film production, a time when theater also peaked with the *sainete criollo* (musical comedy). Although artistic growth was curbed by the military dictatorship from 1978 to 1983, today over 200 films are made in Argentina every year, and the country is also enjoying an exciting and experimental theater boom.

Theater poster on Avenida Corrientes, Buenos Aires

CINEMA

The Argentinian film industry boomed between the 1920s and 50s when tango musicals and gaucho-themed films drew huge audiences. Art house cinema took off after World War II but was cut short by the dictatorship of 1978–83. Cinema flourished again during the mid-1990s, when a new generation of directors emerged, working with limited budgets to address social issues.

Art house and National cinema *of the 1950s and 60s had directors who responded to the country's turbulent political scene, including Armando Bo who directed* El Trueno Entre Las Hojas *(1956), Pino Solanas, Leopoldo Torre Nilsson, and Héctor Olivera.*

Films on tango and romance *in the 1930s and 40s were very popular. Gaucho and other local themes were often thrown into these movies, which usually featured a beautiful woman and a romantic rival to the lead. In* The Big Broadcast of 1936 *(1935), Carlos Gardel played himself – a singer-songwriter.*

THEATER

The iconic status of Teatro Colón in Buenos Aires is ample evidence of the importance of the dramatic arts in Argentina. Theater peaked in the first decades of the 20th century, when plays began to address national issues and feature gauchos and tango dancers. Corrientes is the Broadway of Argentina; the more serious drama is performed at Teatro General San Martín.

During the early 20th century *Argentinian theater progressed from light musical comedy focused on national issues to more absurdist, social realistic, and grotesque plays. The "neo-grotesque" plays of Griselda Gambaro (left) brought together these traditions and gave a voice to women.*

In 1981, a powerful cultural movement began *against the military dictatorship. The organizers of* Teatro Abierto *(Open Theater) were a group of writers, actors, and directors, including Roberto Cossa, Osvaldo Dragún, and Carlos Gorostiza, who performed anti-establishment plays.*

The brutality of the Dirty War *inspired Luis Puenzo's* La Historia Oficial *(1985), which deals with the military junta kidnappings during the 1970s and 80s. He is the first Argentinian to win an Academy Award for Best Foreign Film.*

FOREIGN FILMS

Argentinians have catholic tastes when it comes to foreign films, and love Woody Allen and Disney as much as French auteurs or their local cineastes. The films of Spanish director Pedro Almodóvar have a loyal following, particularly in Buenos Aires, as many of them star local actor Cecilia Roth. Argentina has also become a popular location for directors shooting feature films, such as Alan Parker's *Evita* (1996). More recently Brazilian director Walter Salles's *The Motorcycle Diaries* (2004) was enjoyed by Argentinians for its familiar locations and for reminding the world that Che Guevara was one of their compatriots.

Madonna in Alan Parker's popular musical *Evita*

New Argentinian cinema *developed in the 1990s, when a group of young directors made films on shoestring budgets, often employing non-actors to give a social realist feel to their stories. The movement was started by Adrián Caetano and Bruno Stagnaro's* Pizza, Birra, Faso *(1998).*

Contemporary Argentinian cinema *showcases directors who have evolved a subtle, home-grown approach that deals with local subjects. Lucrecia Martel's acclaimed* La Niña Santa *(2004), was nominated for the Palme d'Or at Cannes.*

Popular theater *in the 1980s, in some respects, heralded the return of democracy. La Boca's popular theater troupe, Grupo Teatro Catalinas Sur, performs plays that offer audiences a grotesque take on modern urban reality with underlying political and social themes.*

The latter-day legacy of Teatro Abierto *is the thriving off-Corrientes scene, where radical actors perform in small venues. Formerly an underground street theater company, De La Guarda toured their dialogue-free show* Villa Villa *round the world in the late 1990s to huge acclaim.*

Architecture

There is no single architectural style that can be called Argentinian. Porteño architects have always borrowed from European styles and the capital is characterized by eclecticism, with French mansards, Art Deco cupolas, and glass-walled skyscrapers. Across the provinces, the most interesting buildings are often small colonial churches and low-slung 19th- and 20th-century townhouses which, with their patios and wrought-iron gates, pay homage to Andalucia and the Old World. Occasionally, a modernist masterpiece or brutalist warehouse rises in the Pampas, remnants of earlier, wealthier periods in Argentinian rural history.

The ornate Casa Rosada on Plaza de Mayo, Buenos Aires

EARLY COLONIAL

Few buildings of the 16th to 18th centuries remain, as most of the fortresses, ranches, and ordinary residences erected then were improvised adobe constructions made of fibrous material.

Iglesia de San Pedro *in Salta was built in the 1770s. Its whitewashed adobe and local brick walls, plain façade, and twin bell-towers are typical of Spanish colonial churches.*

El Zanjón (see p78) *in Buenos Aires has arches made of slim, rustic bricks which can be seen in the remnants of many early civic buildings.*

BAROQUE

Popular in the 18th and mid-19th centuries, the baroque style was introduced by Jesuit scholars who combined it with Moorish and indigenous elements, giving church exteriors a rich, varied character and imposing façades.

The Iglesia de la Compañía *in Córdoba* (see p180) *is a 17th-century Jesuit-built church with a richly decorated interior. Most noteworthy is the baroque panel, which is the work of Catamarca-born painter Emilio Caraffa.*

Details are picked out in braid-like golden yellow

The church has distinctive terracotta walls

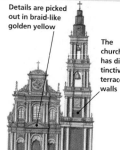

Iglesia y Convento San Francisco *in Salta* (see p195) *was built in 1858, and has a wide and elegant baroque façade.*

IMMIGRANT ARCHITECTURE

Argentina's architectural eclecticism derives from the native penchant for copying all things European, and also from the fact that many architects are descendants of immigrants. Across the country are dotted British-style railway stations, grand estancias modeled after French rural chateaux, and Bauhaus-influenced urban dwellings.

Truncated dome on the mansard roof

Beaux-arts grandeur of Correo Central

MODERNIST

Modern styles, including Art Deco, Art Nouveau, and expressionism were popular between 1900 and 1940. This new architecture provided tangible proof that Buenos Aires was a cosmopolitan city.

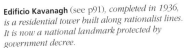

Edificio Kavanagh (see p91), *completed in 1936, is a residential tower built along rationalist lines. It is now a national landmark protected by government decree.*

The best apartments have open-air terraces

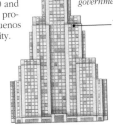

Palacio Barolo (see p68), *commissioned by a local textile magnate, was completed in 1923. This bulbous, 22-story edifice is full of allegorical references to Dante's Divine Comedy.*

VERNACULAR ARCHITECTURE

By taking elements from various traditions and schools, Argentinian architects evolved a native style suited to the country's culture and climate.

Narrow chorizo *houses allow for dense housing suited to the gridblock layout of the cities.*

Estancias *in the far south of the country need to be low slung to cope with the gusting westerlies.*

CONTEMPORARY

The predominant model for dwellings and commercial property in Argentina is the mid- to high-rise tower. There has been a surge in skyscrapers over 30 stories tall with gardens, pools, gyms, and social spaces on site.

Torre le Parc, *a residential tower located in upscale Palermo, is the ultimate dwelling for television personalities, footballers, and the nouveaux riches.*

The building stands at 51 stories high

The structure is designed along plain rationalist lines

Museo de Arte Latinoamericano de Buenos Aires (see pp110–11) *has a striking design that stands out in a neighborhood of high-rise towers. The interior is designed to allow natural light to pour in onto the sculptures and public spaces.*

Ersatz Swiss buildings in Bariloche

British-style Puerto Madero docks

German-style chalet, Huapi

Argentina's Equestrian Sports

Although the horse is not indigenous to the country, it has become an intrinsic part of Argentina's national culture and identity. Feats of horsemanship and the traditions that go with equestrian pursuits are taken very seriously in all the provinces. This is most evident in the popularity of equestrian sports, ranging from gauchos competing in *sulky* races on the Pampas plains to the exciting horse races that take place in Buenos Aires's famous hippodromes. It is in polo, however, that Argentina dominates at an international level. Its polo team has produced some of the top *polistas* (polo players) in the world.

Young rider in a show jumping competition in Córdoba

POLO

Introduced by English immigrants in the 1800s, polo is one of the most popular equestrian sports in Argentina. Its polo team has been the uninterrupted world champion since 1949 and the annual Argentina Polo Open is one of the world's most important polo competitions.

A player's wrist movement has to be quick and flexible while hitting the ball.

The mallet has a rubber-wrapped grip and a leather thumb sling.

Adolfo Cambiaso *is regarded by many to be the best polo player in the world. With his 10-goal handicap (the highest rank possible), good looks, and commercial savvy, he is often referred to as the "David Beckham" of polo.*

PATO

Argentina's official sport, *pato* is also known as "horseball" and has been practiced since the 17th century. *Pato* is Spanish for "duck" and, originally, games used a live duck inside a basket instead of a ball. The modern version is played with a ball that has six leather handles, which the two teams try to insert into hoops placed on poles located at each end of a field.

A horseball player *needs a great deal of practice to skilfully pick up a* pato. *The game requires players to be excellent riders with a great sense of balance and stability. They also need to be able to move swiftly around the field.*

The annual Argentinian Pato Championship *is usually held in November. Games are played at a number of locations across Buenos Aires province and the final is held at Campo Argentino de Polo de Palermo (see p109).*

GAUCHO SPORTS

Horsemanship is an essential component of the gaucho tradition and lives on in the modern era. There are a number of gaucho sports, the majority of which involve doing dangerous stunts with untamed horses.

The *sulky* competition *is a popular traditional pursuit in the rich pampas of Buenos Aires province. The sulky refers to the cart that is attached to the horse.*

Tradition Day *in San Antonio de Areco offers a chance for gauchos to show off their equestrian skills. Various competitions, such as taming wild horses, keep the traditions of rural Argentina alive.*

RACING AND SHOW JUMPING

Horse racing, known as *el turf*, is hugely popular in the country, and the best race tracks can be found in Buenos Aires. Introduced by immigrant European communities in the 19th century, show jumping competitions throughout the country attract thousands of enthusiasts.

Argentinian rider Matías Albarracín *is a popular contender at show jumping events. Horse shows are staged at numerous clubs in Buenos Aires and other major cities, and take place weekly from March to December.*

The Hipódromo Argentino *in Palermo, which can accommodate more than 10,000 spectators, is Argentina's most important turf venue. The biggest draw of the year is the Gran Premio Nacional, held annually in November.*

THE ARGENTINIAN THOROUGHBRED

Argentina has always had a reputation for breeding top racehorses, a reputation that was bolstered in 2007 when Argentinian-bred Invasor won the Dubai World Cup, the world's richest horse race with prize money of over US$6 million. Argentinian thoroughbreds, a distinct breed of horse, not to be confused with the more general term "purebred," are usually bred for racing, though they may also be used for show jumping, while smaller horses are used for polo. Naturally athletic and with a good temperament and plenty of staying power, Argentinian thoroughbreds are in demand all over the world, with around 200 registered sales in 2006 to destinations all across the world, from Singapore to Sydney.

Argentinian thoroughbred Invasor trains for the Breeders' Cup Classic, Kentucky

Soccer in Argentina

The AFA coat of arms

British immigrants brought soccer to Argentina in the late 19th century. The fanaticism for the sport has only grown since then and every schoolboy's dream is to be the next *fútbol* legend. Spare patches of grass in city parks or barren desert in the interior are often used as soccer pitches for impromptu games. However, it is at professional matches that the sport turns into a religion and watching a game featuring one of the First Division clubs is a thrilling experience.

A colorful mural of the popular Boca Juniors football team

The first recorded soccer match *in Argentina was organized by the Buenos Aires Cricket Club in 1867 and played between two teams of British railroad workers, the White Caps and the Red Caps.*

The Alumni sports club team *from Buenos Aires's Belgrano district was one of the most important in the early 1900s. They won 10 of the 14 league champion-ships they contested.*

The Azteca Stadium in Mexico hosted the FIFA World Cup Final (1986) when Argentina won their second World Cup title.

FIRST DIVISION CLUBS

Organized by the Argentinian Football Association (AFA), the First Division is the top category of Argentinian soccer teams. It currently consists of 20 teams who play two single-round tournaments each year. The list shows the few clubs that have managed to stay in the First Division for decades.

River Plate's striker Gonzalo Higuain celebrating after scoring a goal in a First Division match

CLUB ATLETICO BOCA JUNIORS (Est.1905)
Stadium: La Bombonera
Capacity 60,000

CLUB ATLETICO RIVER PLATE (Est.1901)
Stadium: Monumetal
Capacity: 66,545

CLUB VÉLEZ SARSFIELD (Est.1910)
Stadium: José Amalfitani
Capacity: 49,540

CLUB SAN LORENZO DE ALMAGRO (Est.1908)
Stadium: Nuevo Gasómetro
Capacity: 43,500

CLUB ATLETICO INDEPENDIENTE (Est.1903)
Stadium: Libertadores de América
Capacity: 52,823

RACING CLUB (Est.1930)
Stadium: Presidente Perón
Capacity: 55,000

CLUB NEWELLS OLD BOYS (Est.1903)
Stadium: El Coloso del Parque
Capacity: 42,000

The offerings of soccer fans *decorate the front of the Suizo-Argentina private clinic in Buenos Aires, where the former Argentinian soccer star, Diego Maradona, was hospitalized in 2004. He remained in intensive care for several months as a result of a long period of drug and alcohol abuse which left him fighting for his life.*

WORLD CUP FACTS

The Argentinian national squad has won two World Cups – in 1978, when they hosted the event and beat Holland, and in 1986 against West Germany. Both victories have been plagued by controversy: in the former it has been claimed that the then military dictatorship paid for Argentina to win against Peru in the semi-finals; in the latter, Argentina beat England 2–1 in the quarter finals where the first goal was a handball by Diego Maradona. The second goal was a spectacular one-man display, also by Maradona, that shattered England's defence. The team was runners-up in the first tournament, held in 1930 in Uruguay, and in 1990 in Italy.

FIFA WORLD CUP FINAL (1986)

Argentina jumped to a 2–0 lead after 55 minutes, but West Germany scored two goals to equalize in the last 10 minutes. Then, with seven minutes remaining, Jorge Burruchaga scored a brilliant winning goal after receiving a pass from Maradona.

The Argentinian squad, *crowned with olive wreaths, celebrates with their gold medals at the 2004 Olympic Games in Athens, Greece. They defeated Paraguay 1–0 in the final match.*

SOCCER LEGENDS

Over the years, Argentina has produced a pantheon of great players that have outshone others with their skill, agility, and exquisite footwork. These include the footballer and coach Alfredo di Stefano, the striker Gabriel Batistuta, and the legendary Diego Maradona, who shares with Pele the title of the best football player in the world.

Alfredo di Stefano (b.1926), nicknamed Saeta Rubia (Blonde Arrow), was a player of immense stamina, versatility, and vision.

Mario Kempes (b.1954) played with a junior team at the age of seven and was known as El Matador (The Killer) at the height of his career.

Diego Maradona (b.1960) is one of the greatest footballers of all time, despite being embroiled in controversy on and off the pitch.

Oscar Ruggeri (b.1962), nicknamed El Cabezón (Big-headed One), was one of the most successful defenders to come out of Argentina.

Gabriel Batistuta (b.1969) is a prolific player who, at an international level, is Argentina's all-time highest goal scorer.

ARGENTINA THROUGH THE YEAR

Acountry that loves fun and celebrations, Argentina has a busy annual calendar, both for its cities and provinces. New Year's Eve is celebrated with fireworks and family reunions, after which many people begin their summer holidays on January 2. Some events are localized, and provincial towns and villages tend to uphold traditions with more enthusiasm than the cities of Buenos Aires,

Día de la Tradición in Buenos Aires

Córdoba, and Rosario. The colorful fiesta of Carnaval is an event of national importance in Gualeguaychú in the Entre Ríos province. The pre-Lent celebrations are still important to the villages of the Andean high plains, where they have been fused with pre-Columbian traditions. The capital loves its festivals, and art and culture extravaganzas are held all year.

Flowers in full bloom during spring in Patagonia

SPRING

In central Argentina, the temperate weather conditions of spring make this an excellent time to visit Córdoba, Buenos Aires, and Mendoza. Jacaranda and *ceibo* trees blossom in public parks and plazas, and flocks of migratory birds begin to arrive in the lagoons of the Pampas and the wetlands. Pre-summer storms are possible but not likely to last more than a day. Patagonia is warm and the weather is pleasant in the northern provinces by late spring (mid-October to November), making it the best time to visit Argentina.

SEPTEMBER

Festival Internacional de Buenos Aires *(early Sep)*, Buenos Aires. Taking place every two years, this event is the country's biggest arts festival, featuring prestigious theater, dance, and music acts from all over the world.
Eisteddfod *(early Sep)*, Gaiman. This ancient festival of Welsh culture features music, photography, literature, and art.
Fiesta Nacional del Inmigrante *(2nd week of Sep)*, Misiones. Dance, lively music, and exotic dishes pay homage to Argentina's welcoming of immigrants.

OCTOBER

La Virgen de Luján *(Oct 5)*, Luján. Faithful devotees walk 42 miles (68 km) from the city center to Luján's main

basilica to pay homage to the Virgin of Luján, patron saint of Argentina, Uruguay, and Paraguay.
Día de la Raza *(Mon nearest Oct 12)*, across Argentina. This festival officially celebrates the discovery of the Americas by Columbus, although, across the Andean Northwest, activists commemorate the many indigenous peoples massacred by the Spanish colonizers.
Festival Guitarras del Mundo *(mid-Oct)*, Buenos Aires. This is a lively two-week celebration of the guitar, with an emphasis on world folk traditions.
Casa Foa *(late Oct)*, Buenos Aires. This hugely popular design and architecture exposition is a platform for Argentinian designers, interior decorators, and landscape artists to showcase their work.

An indigenous music band performing on Día de la Raza

NOVEMBER

Día de Todos los Santos
(Nov 1), across the Andean
Northwest. People gather to
decorate cemeteries and
leave tokens at graves. In
some places traditional folk
rhythms are sung.

Día de la Tradición *(weekend
nearest Nov 12)*, across
Argentina. Gauchos in traditional attire lead horses decorated with silver-buckled
bridles in parades.

Abierto Argentino de Polo
(mid-Nov–mid-Dec), Buenos
Aires. This posh polo event
has gained popularity in
Argentina over the years.

SUMMER

With the whole country on
summer holiday, Argentina
celebrates the season with a
variety of music and tango
festivals. Buenos Aires plays
host to major music shows,
including the world's most
important tango festival.
Carnaval is not as big as in
Brazil, but is taken seriously
in Mesopotamia and the
Andean Northwest. Patagonia
is warmest in summer but
powerful winds roll across
the steppes. Many prefer to
head farther south to the temperate but relatively wind-
free climes of Tierra del
Fuego, departure point for
cruise tours to Antarctica.

DECEMBER

El Bolsón Jazz Festival *(early
Dec)*, El Bolsón. A festival
offering jazz shows in this
music-loving town.

Noche Buena *(Dec 24)*, across
Argentina. On Christmas Eve,
most of the restaurants and
hotels in cities and towns
organize theme parties at
colorfully decorated venues.

Navidad *(Dec 25)*, across
Argentina. On this day,
people go to church services
in the morning and celebrate
with a Christmas lunch. All
museums are closed and
many bars and restaurants
only open in the late afternoon or early evening.

Performers dressed in colorful costumes at Carnaval, Gualeguaychú

Festival Buen Día *(late Dec)*,
Buenos Aires. Dance, music,
and cocktails are the staples
of this celebration of youth
culture at the swanky barrio
of Palermo Viejo.

Fin de Año *(Dec 31)*, across
Argentina. The new year
holiday starts only at noon
so the morning is a regular
working day.

JANUARY

Año Nuevo *(Jan 1)*, across
Argentina. The new year in
the towns and cities of
Argentina is welcomed by
families and friends who
gather and set off fireworks.

Fiesta de la Cereza *(early Jan)*,
Santa Cruz. The main fruit-
growing farms in this fertile
corner of southern Patagonia
celebrate with music, dance,
and lots of healthy fruits.

Meat barbecued during the Año
Nuevo celebration

FEBRUARY

Carnaval *(early Feb)*, Buenos
Aires and Gualeguaychú. In
the town of Gualeguaychú in
the Entre Ríos province, the
locals bring color and
creative flair to street parades
during Carnival. In different
neighborhoods of Buenos
Aires, *murga* (bands of street
musicians) beat drums and
artistes dance to the music
in the streets and plazas.

Fiesta de la Pachamama
(Feb 6), Purmamarca. Folk
concerts are held on this
day along with ancient
rituals and mass feasts.
Indigenous and mestizo
groups pay tribute to the
important pre-Columbian
fertility goddess Pachamama
(Earth Mother).

Fiesta del Lupolo *(late Feb)*,
El Bolsón. The country's
main hop festival, this is
a lively beer-drinking party,
extremely popular with the
hippies and trekkers who
descend on this laid-back
town every summer.

Festival Buenos Aires Tango
(late Feb–early Mar), Buenos
Aires. The most important
festival of Argentina's celebrated export, the tango
festival attracts locals and
tourists alike. All kinds of
tango-themed events appeal
to skilled dancers as well as
visitors, from art and photography exhibitions and free
classes to live shows by
major tango stars.

Winner of the Wine Queen title at
Fiesta de la Vendimia

AUTUMN

Harvests are brought in
across the Pampas and fertile
highlands, and ripe grapes
are gathered in the wine-
producing provinces of
Mendoza, San Juan, La Rioja,
and Salta. The holiday season
is over, but most Argentinians
make a final trip to the
beaches of the Atlantic coast
and head for the tourist spots
in the north and south over
the Easter weekend.

MARCH

Fiesta de la Vendimia *(early
Mar)*, Mendoza. Kicking off
on the Sunday before the
festival proper, the city of
Mendoza hosts folk music
concerts, local produce fairs,
and all manner of grape-
themed events. On the
following Saturday evening,

Parque San Martín is the site
of a huge gala involving
celebrities and there is also
a local beauty competition
for the Wine Queen title.
Opera Season *(Mar–Dec)*,
Buenos Aires. The reopening
of the capital's magnificent
opera house, Teatro Colón,
is a major event for music-
lovers and draws many
famous singers and world-
class orchestras.
St. Patrick's Day *(Mar 17)*,
across Argentina. On this day
in Buenos Aires, locals get
together for an evening of
drinking and dancing,
especially at Irish-themed
bars such as the Shamrock
and Kilkenny.
Pascua *(Mar/Apr)*, across
Argentina. The celebration of
Easter Sunday, and its pre-
ludes of Jueves Santo and
Viernes Santo, sees masses
and solemn marches in many
towns and villages.

APRIL

Día de las Malvinas *(Apr 2)*,
across Argentina. Veterans all
over the country honor in
formal ceremonies their
comrades who fell in the
Malvinas War *(see p54)*.
Gala del Fin del Mundo *(late
Apr)*, Ushuaia. This music
festival offers a series of
classical concerts featuring
leading national and international performers.
Fería del Libro *(mid-Apr–
May)*, Buenos Aires. This
three-week book extrava-
ganza involves Argentinian
and international publishers
and guest writers. It is a
public as well as trade event.

Display of contemporary artwork
at ArteBA, Buenos Aires

MAY

Día del Trabajo *(May 1)*,
across Argentina. Marches
organized by trade unions
and protest groups on Labor
Day culminate with speeches
in plazas.
Fiesta del Algodón *(early
May)*, Chaco. Parades and
the crowning of the Cotton
Queen in the country's
cotton capital are the climax
of ten days of lively festivities.
ArteBA *(mid-May)*, Buenos
Aires. The city's biggest art
fair, featuring more than 70
national and international
galleries, as well as talks
by leading artists.
Día de la Revolución de Mayo
(May 25), Buenos Aires. Also
known as Día de la Patria, it
celebrates the May Revolution
of 1810 which ultimately led
to independence. In Buenos
Aires, grenadier guards
march down Avenida de
Mayo in the morning and
people stop at Café Tortoni
(see p68) for a coffee and
snack. In the evening,
a choir performs patriotic
songs at the city cathedral.

Buenos Aires military parade celebrates Día de la Revolución de Mayo

WINTER

Rain drenches the central provinces, and Patagonia turns bitterly cold. This is, however, the most sublime time to be south, as the Southern Right whales swim into Península Valdés and the breeding season begins. The ski season keeps Bariloche and Mendoza busy.

JUNE

Día de la Bandera *(3rd Mon)*, across Argentina. This day commemorates the death anniversary of General Manuel Belgrano, creator of the country's national flag. The white and sky-blue *bandera* (flag) is hoisted and the national anthem sung across the nation.

JULY

Día de la Independencia *(Jul 9)*, across Argentina. Less important than Día de la Revolución de Mayo, this is the day when flags are raised to honor the troops that ousted Spanish control.
Festival Nacional del Poncho *(late Jul)*, Catamarca. This colorful festival features exhibitions displaying beautiful handwoven ponchos, colorful decorated blankets and carpets, tapestries, and other regional textiles. Folk music concerts and lively dances are also held.

AUGUST

La Rural *(July–Aug)*, Buenos Aires. A huge agricultural fair, with prize bulls, cattle, sheep, and pigs displayed proudly by breeders from across the interior provinces. Gauchos put on shows and dazzle their audiences with daring equestrian stunts. Local food and organic produce stalls are also an important part of this lively event. Taking place over three weeks, the fair is attended by over 1.5 million people; avoid visiting the show over the weekend if possible.

People praying in church on Día de San Cayetano

Día de San Cayetano *(Aug 7)*, Buenos Aires. Praying and weeping believers gather at the church of St. Cayetano to ask for help from the patron saint of bread and work and to thank him for favors past. As St. Cayetano Day approaches, the streets fill up with tents around the San Cayetano church.
Fiesta Nacional de la Nieve *(mid-Aug)*, Bariloche. This snow festival kicks off with parades, ski races, and a torch-lit descent of Cerro Catedral. It includes the election of a National Snow Queen to herald the arrival of the season's snow.
World Tango Championship *(mid-Aug)*, Buenos Aires. This is an important annual gathering of skilled dancers, couples who don their best and compete at all levels. Free dance classes and concerts are part of the festivities.

PUBLIC HOLIDAYS

Año Nuevo (New Year's Day, Jan 1)
Jueves Santo (Maundy Thursday, Mar/Apr)
Viernes Santo (Good Friday, Mar/Apr)
Día de la Memoria (Memorial Day, Mar 24)
Día de las Malvinas (Malvinas War Veterans' Day, Mon nearest Apr 2)
Día del Trabajo (Labor Day, May 1)
Día de la Revolución de Mayo (May Revolution Day, May 25)
Día de la Bandera (Flag Day, 3rd Mon of Jun)
Día de la Independencia (Independence Day, Jul 9)
Día del Libertador General San Martín (General San Martín's Day, 3rd Mon of Aug)
Día de la Raza (Columbus Day, Mon nearest Oct 12)
Inmaculada Concepción de la Virgen María (Immaculate Conception Day, Dec 8)
Noche Buena (Christmas Eve, Dec 24)
Navidad (Christmas Day, Dec 25)
Fin de Año (Dec 31)

Día del Libertador General San Martín *(Aug 17)*, across Argentina. Flags are hoisted and hymns are sung to commemorate the anniversary of Independence hero José San Martín's death in France.

Couple participating in the World Tango Championship, Buenos Aires

The Climate of Argentina

Broadly, Argentina's climate can be divided into four types: arid, moderate, cold, and warm. The Andes, Antarctica, the Atlantic Ocean, and the sheer extent of the country also play a major role in determining the country's climate. In Buenos Aires, the *sudestada* (southeasterly winds) bring torrential rains while the *pampeano* weather system, influenced by the ocean, can bring electric storms from the western Pampas. The high plains of the Andean Northwest are warm during the day while Patagonia is subject to powerful winds that rise in the southwest and sweep across the plains unobstructed. The subpolar oceanic climate of Tierra del Fuego makes it windy and wet most of the year.

CLIMATE ZONES

- Arid Andean high plains: warm, dry, rainy in the north.
- Arid mountains: sunny, warm, wet summers, cold winters.
- Cold and wet: cold, snowy winters, windy spring.
- Tropical Serrano: long winters, windy, heavy storms.
- Subtropical: very hot, humid summers, mild winters.
- Mild semi-arid: mild summers, severe winters in parts.
- Temperate Serrano: hot summers, seasonal rainfall.
- Arid Patagonia: cool summers, cold winters, frequent storms.

Glaciar Perito Moreno in Parque Nacional Los Glaciares

ABRA PAMPA

°C/F

month	Apr	Jul	Oct	Jan
	19/66 02/36	15/59 -7/19	21/70 02/36	20/68 07/45
	12 hrs	13 hrs	11 hrs	11 hrs
	09 mm	00 mm	17 mm	80 mm

MENDOZA

°C/F

Month	Apr	Jul	Oct	Jan
	22/72 11/52	14/57 02/36	25/77 11/52	31/88 18/64
	11 hrs	10 hrs	13 hrs	14 hrs
	12 mm	07 mm	21 mm	30 mm

BARILOCHE

°C/F

Month	Apr	Jul	Oct	Jan
	13/55 02/36	05/41 01/34	13/55 02/36	21/70 08/46
	11 hrs	9 hrs	10 hrs	10 hrs
	61 mm	144 mm	41 mm	26 mm

Abra Pampa

Mendoza

Neuquén

Bariloche

Patagonia has sunny summers, with long days and cool nights.

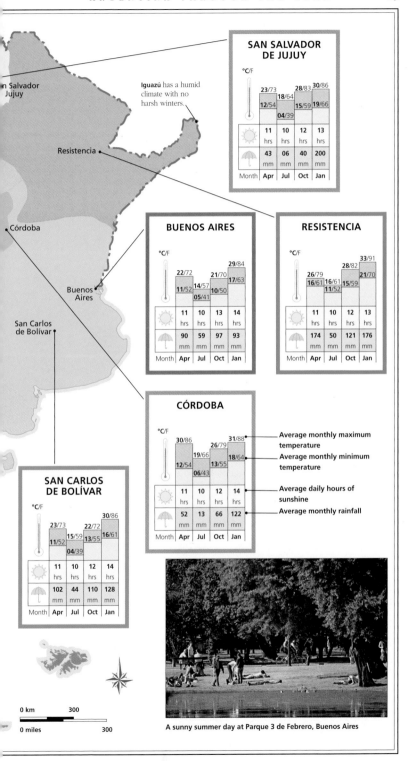

n Salvador
Jujuy

Iguazú has a humid
climate with no
harsh winters.

Resistencia

Córdoba

Buenos
Aires

San Carlos
de Bolívar

SAN SALVADOR DE JUJUY

°C/F				
	23/73	18/64	28/83	30/86
	12/54		15/59	19/66
		04/39		
☀	11 hrs	10 hrs	12 hrs	13 hrs
☂	43 mm	06 mm	40 mm	200 mm
Month	Apr	Jul	Oct	Jan

BUENOS AIRES

°C/F				
	22/72		21/70	29/84
	11/52	14/57	10/50	17/63
		05/41		
☀	11 hrs	10 hrs	13 hrs	14 hrs
☂	90 mm	59 mm	97 mm	93 mm
Month	Apr	Jul	Oct	Jan

RESISTENCIA

°C/F				
			28/82	33/91
	26/79	16/61	15/59	21/70
	16/61	11/52		
☀	11 hrs	10 hrs	12 hrs	13 hrs
☂	174 mm	50 mm	121 mm	176 mm
Month	Apr	Jul	Oct	Jan

CÓRDOBA

°C/F				
	30/86		26/79	31/88
	12/54	19/66	13/55	18/64
		06/43		
☀	11 hrs	10 hrs	12 hrs	14 hrs
☂	52 mm	13 mm	66 mm	122 mm
Month	Apr	Jul	Oct	Jan

Average monthly maximum temperature
Average monthly minimum temperature

Average daily hours of sunshine
Average monthly rainfall

SAN CARLOS DE BOLÍVAR

°C/F				
	23/73		22/72	30/86
	11/52	15/59	13/55	16/61
		04/39		
☀	11 hrs	10 hrs	12 hrs	14 hrs
☂	102 mm	44 mm	110 mm	128 mm
Month	Apr	Jul	Oct	Jan

0 km   300
0 miles   300

A sunny summer day at Parque 3 de Febrero, Buenos Aires

THE HISTORY OF ARGENTINA

A land of Native American civilizations for millennia, Argentina became a Spanish colonial backwater before transforming itself into one of the world's richest countries by the late 19th century. A study in paradox, it followed this by an era of populist politics, dictatorships, and fluctuating economic cycles. Never losing its vitality, today it is enjoying a robust recovery.

The vast area now known as Argentina was relatively sparsely populated until the period of European colonization in the 16th century. The most densely populated areas were the Mesopotamian northeast and Andean Northwest. In the former, the semi-nomadic Guaraní inhabited large villages, ruled over by male chiefs. They subsisted mainly on manioc, wild game, and maize. In the northwest, a number of distinct, sedentary cultures had evolved, each interlinked by trade. Collectively known as the Diaguita, these peoples were conquered and absorbed by the Inca Empire around 1480. Farther south, the Huarpe, who inhabited the Cuyo region, and the Mapuche, in northern Patagonia, had developed settled communities, subsisting on hunting, fishing, and the growing of crops such as corn and quinoa. Other groups were nomadic hunter-gatherers, including the Pampa and the Tehuelche, who roamed the central plains and Patagonian steppe respectively.

Group of Tehuelche people from Patagonia

SPANISH SETTLEMENT

Brief explorations into the region were made in the early 1500s by the Spanish and Portuguese, but the first serious attempt by Europeans at settling Argentina came in 1536. Spanish explorer Pedro de Mendoza sailed into the Río de la Plata estuary, founding the settlement of Nuestra Señora Santa María del Buen Aire on its southwestern bank. However, under attack from natives, Mendoza abandoned the region in 1537. Further efforts at settling the country emerged from the central Andes. Spanish conquistadors moved south from the defeated Inca Empire or east from the Chilean frontier, founding settlements such as Santiago del Estero in 1553 and Salta in 1582. By the 1600s, these focused on providing foodstuffs and livestock for the Spanish Viceroy in Lima.

Meanwhile, forced labor and the introduction of European diseases devastated indigenous populations, which dropped by over 90 percent in four generations.

TIMELINE

Detail of rock painting dating from 7000 BC

10,000 BC First human settlements appear in Argentina

AD 1520 Ferdinand Magellan makes landfall in Patagonia

AD 1480 Incan armies conquer northwest Argentina

15,000 BC	AD 1	AD 500	AD 1000	AD 1500

5000 BC First farming settlements appear

AD 1516 Spanish expedition lands in Río de la Plata estuary

AD 1536 Mendoza founds settlement on banks of Río de la Plata

◁ **An 18th-century artwork depicting European explorers consorting with indigenous tribes in Argentina**

16th-century engraving showing the nascent settlement of Buenos Aires on the banks of Río de la Plata

THE GROWTH OF BUENOS AIRES

In the late 16th century, Spain, threatened by Portuguese ambitions in the region, renewed efforts to settle eastern Argentina, and in 1580 an expeditionary force re-established the port of Buenos Aires. However, in an empire that coveted gold and silver, the new port offered neither and for decades it languished as a colonial backwater. Prosperity came in the 17th century with the smuggling of silver from Upper Peru and then the appearance of Argentina's first estancias (ranches) – the few cattle left behind by Mendoza's aborted expedition had multiplied into thousands on the fertile Pampas.

Apart from consolidating their empire, Spain's main aim was also to spread Roman Catholicism. Jesuits led the effort, founding several missions from 1610 onwards. Exempt from taxation, the missions developed lucrative plantations of yerba mate, used for infusions, and tobacco.

REFORM AND DISCONTENT

The War of the Spanish Succession (1702–1713) brought the Bourbon dynasty to the Spanish throne and also major changes in Crown policy. In 1768 Spain expelled the Jesuits from its colonies: their protection from taxation represented lost revenue. In 1776, it created the new Viceroyalty of Río de la Plata, declaring Buenos Aires capital of a territory encompassing Argentina, Uruguay, Paraguay, and Upper Peru. The effect was stunning: Buenos Aires's population boomed with immigrant merchants as it transformed itself into a dynamic commercial center. Interior cities expanded as the capital became an important market for their produce, shipping tobacco and yerba mate from the northeast, wine from the Cuyo region, and cotton from the northwest.

The commercial ascendancy of the new viceroyalty led to strict Crown enforcement of its monopoly over the trading system. This eventually created tensions between criollos, American-born Spanish who were mostly pro-free trade, and Spanish-born traditionalists, who defended Spain's monopoly. International events sharpened differences. Wars in North America and Europe saw Great Britain enforce blockades of the Atlantic, disrupting connections

TIMELINE

1553–82 Expeditions establish towns in the northwest and Cuyo area

1595 Sale of African slaves begins in Buenos Aires

1630–37 War between the Spanish and Diaguita Indians

| 1550 | 1590 | 1630 | 1670 |

1580 Spanish rebuild settlement of Buenos Aires

Jesuit seal

1610 First Jesuit missions established in the northeast

Ruins of the San Ignacio Miní mission

between metropole and colonies. With Spanish ships unable to reach the viceroyalty, illegal trade with non-Spanish merchants grew, prompting increasing calls from *criollos* for a loosening of Crown ties. At the same time, the defeat of invading British troops in 1806 and 1807 by Buenos Aires militia forces increased the capital's confidence in its ability to stand alone.

END OF COLONIAL RULE

The overthrow of Bourbon Spain by Napoleon's France in 1808 provoked a final collapse in Crown authority. In the 1810 Revolución de Mayo, criollos stripped the Spanish Viceroy of office; in 1816, after an armed struggle led by General José de San Martín, the United Provinces of the River Plate, Argentina's direct forerunner, declared independence. In their own push for separation, Upper Peru and Paraguay became independent rather than remain part of the former viceroyalty.

Despite independence, little political harmony existed among the new country's different provinces. Civil war broke out between Unitarists, urbanites who sought to maintain Buenos Aires's authority over the River Plate region, and Federalists, ruralists who desired a decentralized national government with greater provincial autonomy. War ravaged the country for two decades and led to the rise of *caudillos*, provincial strongmen who led militia forces into battle against the capital. In 1826, a pause in hostilities saw Unitarist Bernardino Rivadavia become the first president

Detail, Fortuny's *Congress of Tucumán, The Declaration of Independence of Argentina from Spain in 1816*

of an independent Argentina, but within a year fighting had recommenced. The struggle finally ended in 1835 with the surrender of all political power to Juan Manuel de Rosas.

THE ROSAS DICTATORSHIP

Federalist by convenience, Rosas had become governor of Buenos Aires in 1829. Sharing the Unitarists' belief in a strong central government, he transformed his Buenos Aires regime into a de facto national government with hegemonic power over the other provinces. Dissent was silenced by censorship and repression by the *mazorca*, Rosas's political police. By the end of his rule the country was an isolated and economically backward country. His brutality had, however, forged national unity – Unitarists and Federalists united to overthrow him in 1852 at Monte Caseros, which allowed for a period of reform and the creation of a functioning, unified state.

The 1852 *Batalla de Monte Caseros* by Penuti & Bernheim

Confederation of Argentina's shield

King Philip V, first ruler of the Bourbon dynasty	**1768** Spanish Crown orders expulsion of Jesuits	**1826** Rivadavia becomes first president of Argentina	
		1816 Congress of Tucumán declares Independence	

1710	**1750**	**1790**	**1830**
1713 War of Spanish Succession ends	**1752** Buenos Aires organizes militia to counter native population threat	**1776** Viceroyalty of the Río de la Plata established. Buenos Aires named capital	**1806–1807** Buenos Aires militia army twice defeats British invasion forces	**1816** San Martín defeats Spanish at Battle of Maipú	**1835–52** Rosas dictatorship

Battle of Tuyutí depicting the bloody Triple Alliance War in 1866, by 19th-century artist Cándido López

THE ARGENTINIAN BOOM

The decades that followed Rosas's overthrow saw the ratification of Argentina's federal constitution, which established a strong central government with autonomous provinces, and the creation of the Argentinian Republic, which came under the rule of a conservative oligarchy. The War of the Triple Alliance (1865–70) against Paraguay created a national army out of the provincial militias.

Along with political stability came expansionism. The government's Conquest of the Desert military campaign against the indigenous population annihilated resistance in the Pampas and Patagonia by 1880. Great tracts of land were opened up and foreign investors, responding to

A 19th-century painting showing the grand Teatro Colón in Buenos Aires

European demand, built numerous sheep ranches; wool exports increased tenfold between 1850 and 1880.

Post-1880, foreign investment, trade, and immigration exploded. Railroads built by the British linked rural areas to Buenos Aires and other port cities. Grain farming and ranching turned into fabulous successes, with Argentina becoming the world's primary cereal exporter and the second largest meat exporter. Prosperity sparked demographic growth: Argentina's population grew from about 2 million in 1869 to almost 8 million by 1914. Cities embodied the era's ambition. New metropolises sprang up and great public buildings and parks were built. The capital city became synonymous with sophistication: its newspapers gained international prestige; its theaters were vibrant and numerous; its new buildings, such as the Teatro Colón, were monuments to progress.

The boom, however, was fragile and interrupted by a severe financial crisis in 1890 that caused the collapse of the Argentinian currency. Progress also hid many problems: wealth was poorly distributed and interior provinces had become increasingly

TIMELINE

1865–70 War of the Triple Alliance pits Argentina, Brazil, and Uruguay against Paraguay

1878–79 Conquest of the Desert campaign ends indigenous resistance across the Pampas and Patagonia

1880 Buenos Aires becomes Federal Capital

1860	1870	1880	1890

1862 Bartolomé Mitre elected first president of the Argentinian Republic

Bartolomé Mitre

1877 First shipment of frozen beef from Argentina to Europe

1890 Financial crisis leads to the Revolution of 1890

distant from Buenos Aires and the Pampas, both economically and socially. Crowding in cities was a problem, and poor health and economic exploitation were common. Such disparities provoked uprisings and demands for greater political representation. In 1916, the newly formed Unión Cívica Radical (Radical Party) won power, marking the advent of popular politics after a century of elite rule.

Juan Perón in front of a portrait of José San Martín

plight, and their potential as a social and political force, went unrecognized until the emergence of an obscure army general, Juan Domingo Perón, who went on to become one of the most influential figures in Argentinian history.

THE RISE OF PERÓN

Juan Perón gained influence and power between 1943 and 1945 through his alliance with Argentinian labor unions. He became Vice President and Secretary of War in 1945; in the same year he was forced to resign by military opponents. Perón was arrested, but mass demonstrations organized by the trade union federation forced his release. A few days later, he married Eva Duarte. Coming from a poor rural family, she pursued a radio and film career in the capital before meeting the future president at a charity event. Together they changed the course of the country's politics for the next three decades to come.

POPULAR POLITICS AND MILITARISM

The rise of the Radicals coincided with World War I, a collapse in international grain prices, and recession. Strikes were called and social unrest continued into the 1920s. Inspired by totalitarian Europe, the armed forces began to view Argentina's democracy as flawed, and when the 1929 Wall Street crash unleashed a deeper depression, the military ousted the Radicals in 1930.

Argentina was returned to civilian rule in 1932, with the military backing a succession of conservative governments that became synonymous with fraud. Global recession, meanwhile, pushed unemployment in rural areas up to unprecedented levels, causing thousands of workers to migrate to the big cities. By the outbreak of World War II, Argentina had a new urban working class whose living conditions were desperate. Their

Military vanguards in the capital city during the 1930s coup

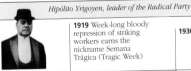

Hipólito Yrigoyen, leader of the Radical Party

1912 The Sáenz Peña Law introduces universal male suffrage	**1919** Week-long bloody repression of striking workers earns the nickname Semana Trágica (Tragic Week)	**1930** Argentina's first military coup	
			1943 Second military coup overthrows conservative regime
1910	**1920**	**1930**	**1940**
1916 Radical Party wins national elections		**1939–44** Argentina remains neutral for much of World War II	

The Peróns and Argentina

In 1946 the election of Juan Domingo Perón as president revolutionized Argentina. Via a populist movement that became known as Perónism, Perón empowered the urban poor and working-class masses by addressing their plight and offering them political participation. He and his charismatic wife Eva Perón, called Evita by supporters, became icons by lifting millions out of misery. In doing so they created a popular power base from which they transformed Argentina: building an authoritarian state able to intervene in all aspects of Argentinian life. The social elite branded the regime totalitarian and Perón a demagogue.

Eva Duarte with Juan Perón in 1945

Juan Perón's first presidential campaign *took place in 1946, after he served as Labor Minister in the military dictatorship of the early 1940s. Eva Duarte, affectionately called Evita (little Eva), a famous radio actress whose humble origins gained her popularity with the Argentinian people, played a key role in his victory.*

By becoming the champion *of the poorer classes or, as she called them, the* descamisados *(shirtless ones), and working to provide them with housing, food, and education via her social-welfare foundation, Evita transformed her celebrity status to adulated, saint-like savior.*

ADDRESSING THE CROWD AT PLAZA DE MAYO

Central to the Peróns' huge populist appeal was their ability to communicate with audiences. Enormous rallies – some numbering 350,000 – were held in Plaza de Mayo in Buenos Aires in which both Juan Perón and Evita would speak directly to the thronging crowds from the balcony of the presidential palace.

TIMELINE

Eva Perón in Madrid

1946 Perón elected president and launches 5-year economic plan

1947 Evita embarks on European Rainbow Tour; she wins Argentinian women the right to vote

1949 Perónists remove constitutional ban on presidential re-election

1946	1948	1950

Juan Perón taking the presidential oath

1948 Eva Perón Foundation established for the poor and homeless

Evita marking the fourth anniversary Perón's government.

Trade union support *formed the foundation of the Perónist movement. They became state controlled and answerable to Perón, whose setting of a minimum wage, salary increases, and better working conditions guaranteed their unconditional support.*

The first 5-year economic plan, *implemented by Perón in 1946, promoted domestic industrialization and the nationalization of existing industries under foreign control.*

Evita's death *from cancer in 1952 at the age of 33 was a severe blow to the Perónist cause. In an outpouring of national grief, her grand state funeral extended for over four days.*

Perón's regime unraveled *after 1952. The economy worsened, repression and censorship increased, and opposition parties and the Catholic church were attacked. In 1955 Perón gave a speech threatening civil war against his enemies. The military reacted by bombing Plaza de Mayo and forcing Perón into a 16-year exile.*

Plaque at Evita's grave in Recoleta Cemetery

951 Opposition newspaper *La Prensa* brought under Perónist control; Evita bids for position of Vice President

1954 Wave of strikes against government

1955 Juan Perón forced into exile in Paraguay

 1952

1954

1952 Perón wins re-election; inflation rises by 30 percent

1953 Perón launches second 5-year plan; repression of the rural classes, opposition parties, and Catholic church

Perón begins exile

UNDER PERÓN'S SHADOW

Post-1955, Argentina became polarized. The military exiled Perón and banned Perónism from the political process. Trade unions, however, remained loyal to the deposed president and worked towards making Argentina ungovernable in his absence. General strikes paralyzed the country. In 1971, with Argentina on the brink of anarchy, the military sanctioned the return of Perón.

Isabel Perón, Argentina's former Vice President

A SOCIETY AT WAR

Perón's third presidential term began in 1973 amidst spiralling guerrilla activity and a Perónist Party split between left- and right-wing factions. When he died a year later, a hard-right authoritarian regime led by his Vice President and third wife, Isabel Perón, succeeded him. The state-sponsored paramilitary force, Triple A, targeted left-wing subversives and, at the same time, the military engaged in open warfare with guerrillas. The economy went into freefall and inflation surpassed 1,000 percent.

Protest rally by women whose children disappeared during the armed forces' Dirty War in the 1970s

With Argentina in crisis, the military overthrew the government in 1976 and via the infamous Proceso de Reorganización Nacional, it unleashed upon Argentina a reign of brutality unprecedented in its history. Left-wing guerrilla forces were eliminated in the infamous Guerra Sucia (Dirty War), which exploded into a campaign of terror against the civilian population. Thousands of suspected enemies of the state "disappeared": they were arrested, taken to clandestine concentration camps, tortured, and killed. Thousands more were forced into exile. Practically all dissent was silenced. In 1981, the capital saw its first mass demonstrations since the coup. The regime's market economy had unravelled under high inflation and unemployment, and general strikes again paralyzed the country. As the dictatorship's authority crumbled, it made a desperate attempt to cling to power by appealing to national honor. In 1982 it launched an invasion of the Falkland Islands (Islas Malvinas), subject of a territorial dispute between the United Kingdom and Argentina since 1833. Britain counter-invaded and within 74 days its forces had overwhelmed their Argentinian counterparts. Its political standing shattered, the military returned Argentina to civilian rule.

DEMOCRACY AND DEFAULT

Following national elections the Radical Party were entrusted with the task of bringing reconciliation to a devastated country. However, unable

TIMELINE   *Pedro E. Aramburu*

1958 Argentina returns to civilian rule

1974 Perón dies. Succeeded by Isabel Perón

1973 Perón elected for a third presidential term

1976 Military Proceso de Reorganización Nacional begins

1984 Investigation into crimes committed during Dirty War leads to trial of junta leaders

1960	1965	1970	1975	1980	1985

1966 Military declares an end to all constitutional rule

1970 Left-wing guerrilla group kidnap and kill former president Pedro E. Aramburu

1977 Mothers of the "disappeared" start silent protest

1982 Invasion of Falkland Islands (Islas Malvinas) defeated

1987 Due Obedience Law blocks prosecution of lower-ranking officers accused of Dirty War crimes

An airlift taking place during the Falkland Islands (Islas Malvinas) war in 1982

to control a difficult economic situation, which spiralled into hyper-inflation, the Radicals were routed in the national elections of 1989. They handed over power to a reinvigorated Perónist Party, led by Carlos Menem. Menem implemented a neo-liberal program that emphasized massive privatization and pegged the peso to the dollar at one-to-one. The effect was striking; inflation dropped sharply, but local industry collapsed under foreign competition, provoking recession and record unemployment.

Argentinians turned to Fernando de la Rúa, head of the Radical-backed Alliance. He had promised to end both corruption and the continuing recession. The situation that confronted him, however, was dire. Heavy borrowing during the Menem years had left Argentina with a crippling foreign debt, and the new government was forced to adopt severe measures in order to stave off default. Still the recession deepened, leaving the poor destitute and the middle-class struggling. In December

2001, with rumors of default and devaluation at fever point, de la Rúa imposed emergency restrictions on cash withdrawals, preventing Argentinians from withdrawing their savings from banks. For many, it was the last straw. Thousands took to the streets, demanding the government's resignation. Looters stormed shops and full-scale riots prompted heavy-handed police repression. After two days of chaos had left 27 dead, de la Rúa resigned. There followed four presidents in 11 days, plus the largest debt default in history – US$150 billion. The final shock was a sharp devaluation of the peso in 2003, wiping millions from bank savings.

Post-2003 Argentina has rebounded. A surge in commodity prices prompted an export-driven economy that has grown at over 8 percent per year. Néstor Kirchner's repeals of the Due Obedience Law and of Menem's pardons of Dirty War leaders have won praise from human rights groups and led to new criminal trials. Although confidence in a better future remains fragile, Argentina's current political stability, growing tourism industry, and soaring agricultural exports bode well for the country.

Hundreds protest during the economic crisis in 2001, Buenos Aires

1999 Fernando de la Rúa elected president ahead of Perónist candidate

2002 Argentina records biggest debt default in history

2007 Cristina Fernandez wins presidential election

2009 Justicialist Party loses its majority in both houses of Congress

| 1990 | 1995 | 2000 | 2005 | 2010 | 2015 |

1994 Constitutional reform allows Menem to run for re-election and he wins second term

2003 Néstor Kirchner voted in as president

2001 Economic collapse leads to protests

2009 Government buys rights to televise soccer games in order to bail out First Division clubs that are crippled by heavy debt

Carlos Menem

BUENOS AIRES AREA BY AREA

BUENOS AIRES AT A GLANCE 58–59

PLAZA DE MAYO AND MICROCENTRO 60–75

SAN TELMO AND LA BOCA 76–85

PLAZA SAN MARTÍN AND RETIRO 86–93

RECOLETA 94–103

PALERMO AND BELGRANO 104–117

SHOPPING IN BUENOS AIRES 118–121

ENTERTAINMENT IN BUENOS AIRES 122–125

BUENOS AIRES STREET FINDER 126–131

Buenos Aires at a Glance

The largest city and port in Argentina, Buenos Aires covers an area of 78 sq miles (203 sq km), fanning out into the Pampas from its location on the western bank of Río de la Plata. The city proper is known as Capital Federal and is home to almost three million people. The capital falls into easily navigable areas – clustered around Plaza de Mayo are the central barrios of Retiro, San Telmo, and Recoleta. Towards the north are the parklands of Palermo, the old port of La Boca is to the south, while to the west start the grassy plains.

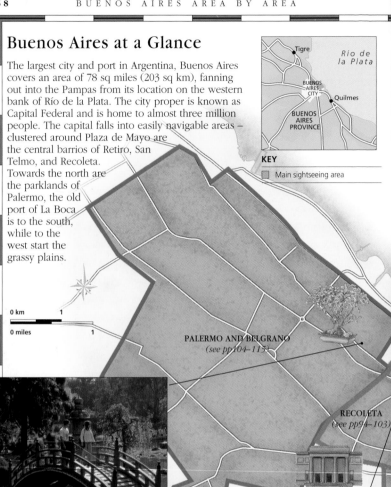

KEY

Main sightseeing area

PALERMO AND BELGRANO
(see pp104–113)

0 km 1
0 miles 1

RECOLETA
(see pp94–103)

Jardín Japonés (see pp106–7) *is located in the leafy barrio of Palermo. A quiet retreat from the bustling city, the immaculate gardens feature a large koi pond, a* yatsuhashi *(bridge of fortune),* taki *(waterfall), and a variety of flora indigenous to Japan.*

Museo Nacional de Bellas Artes (see p102) *is situated in the Recoleta barrio. In this museum, a large collection of Argentinian fine art sits alongside works by European artists such as Monet and Picasso.*

◁ **Pool and fountain in the center of Plaza del Congreso**

Galerías Pacífico (see p91) *is situated on the elegant Calle Florida and is one of the city's most fashionable shopping centers. This grand building is divided into four sectors and has a central cupola with a glass ceiling. Its most dramatic features are the murals added in 1945, painted by renowned Argentinian artists.*

Cabildo de Buenos Aires (see p65) *is a colonial-era civil edifice built in the 1500s. Its unadorned lines, colonnaded front, and shuttered façade stand in stark contrast to the more ornate buildings around Plaza de Mayo.*

AZA SAN
MARTÍN
D RETIRO
pp86–93)

PLAZA DE MAYO
AND MICROCENTRO
(see pp60–75)

SAN TELMO
AND LA BOCA
(see pp76–85)

Plaza Dorrego (see p78), *located in the colorful San Telmo barrio, is a lively community area. Lined by cafés and restaurants, the square plays host to street performers and live tango musicians and dancers who encourage audience participation. Over the weekends, the space is taken over by the antique market Feria de San Telmo.*

PLAZA DE MAYO AND MICROCENTRO

There has been a *plaza mayor* (town square) at this site since the city's second founding in 1580. During the early years of the Spanish conquest, it would have been both the main marketplace and the political and legislative center. Even now,

Statue on Plaza del Congreso

the Presidential Palace, national bank, and economic ministry line the plaza. When the city established itself as a maritime hub after Independence in 1816, Microcentro became the chief banking and trading district. The narrow crowded streets hark back to the days of Spanish colonization.

SIGHTS AT A GLANCE

Historical Sites, Streets, and Plazas
Avenida 9 de Julio y Obelisco **15**
Banco de la Nación **2**
Cabildo de Buenos Aires **4**
Café Tortoni **11**
Casa Rosada **1**
Correo Central **10**
La City **9**
Manzana de las Luces **8**
Palacio Barolo **13**
Palacio de Justicia **20**
Palacio de las Aguas Corrientes **22**
Plaza del Congreso **14**
Plaza Lavalle **19**
Puerto Madero **25**

Places of Worship
Catedral Metropolitana **3**
Iglesia del Santísimo Rosario y Convento de Santo Domingo **7**

Templo de la Congregación Israelita **17**

Theaters
Teatro Avenida **12**
Teatro Colón pp72–3 **16**
Teatro General San Martín **21**
Teatro Nacional Cervantes **18**

Parks
Reserva Ecológica Costanera Sur **24**

Museums
Museo de la Ciudad **5**
Museo de la Immigración **23**
Museo Etnográfico **6**

SEE ALSO
- ***Where to Stay*** pp274–5
- ***Where to Eat*** p292

GETTING AROUND
The ideal way to explore this compact area is on foot, although it is well-served by buses and has a dense network of Subte stations.

KEY

Street-by-Street map *pp62–3*

Subte station

Church

0 meters 700
0 yards 700

Map labels

Callao · CALLE PARAGUAY · AVE CÓRDOBA · CALLE VIAMONTE · CALLE TUCUMÁN · CALLE LAVALLE · Callao · Uruguay · CALLE RIOBAMBA · CTTE GRAL J D PERÓN · CALLE BARTOLOMÉ MITRE · Saenz Peña · Congreso · AVE DE MAYO · CALLE MORENO · CALLE VIRREY CEBALLOS · CALLE SAN JOSÉ · CALLE SALTA · CALLE VENEZUELA · CALLE MÉXICO · C COMB DE LOS POZOS · AVE ENTRE RÍOS · C COMB DE LOS POZOS · CALLE SARANDÍ · CALLE AYACUCHO · CALLE PARANÁ · CALLE TALCAHUANO · CALLE LIBERTAD · Tribunales · Pellegrini · 9 de Julio · CORRIENTES · D Norte · AVE R SÁENZ PEÑA · Lima · Mayo · Piedras · Catedral · Perú · Bolívar · Lavalle · CALLE TUCUMÁN · Florida · S MARTÍN · C 25 DE MAYO · L N Alem · Plaza de Mayo · PARQUE COLÓN · H YRIGOYEN · CALLE A ALSINA · AVE J A ROCA · Moreno · Belgrano · AVE BELGRANO · CALLE VENEZUELA · CALLE CHILE · AVE E MADERO · BV MACACHA GUEMES · AVE E MADERO · AVE PASEO COLÓN · AVE ING HUERGO · CALLE MANUELA GORRITI · Dique 4 · Dique 3 · CALLE JUANA MANSO · AVENIDA INT CARLOS NOEL · AVENIDA INT CARLOS NOI · CALLE DEALESSI · CALLE DEL CANAL · CALLE DE LOS ITALIANOS · CALLE DR T A RODRIGUEZ · AVE ANT ARGENTINA · Dársena Norte · Ante Puerto · RESERVA ECOLÓGICA COSTANERA SUR · Lago de las Gaviotas · Laguna de los Macaes

◁ Intricate carving on the pink-hued façade of Casa Rosada on Plaza de Mayo

Street-by-Street: Plaza de Mayo

The symbolic heart of Buenos Aires, Plaza de Mayo is a welcome open air space. During Spanish rule, this was an unpaved marketplace and meeting point for sailors, colonial officials, and traders. Today, the square is the city's commercial and administrative center, and has hosted political rallies and music concerts, and even witnessed aeriel bombardments. The plaza is dominated by the famous Casa Rosada; at its center is the Pirámide de Mayo, surrounded by towering palm trees. The plaza is flanked by other palatial buildings used mainly for administrative purposes. To the south begins the broad boulevard of Avenida de Mayo.

Ministerio de Economía
This ministry has played a special role in country's economic history

★ Casa Rosada
The Presidential Palace is called Casa Rosada for its bright façade, originally painted using a mixture of whitewash and oxblood ❶

Estatua de Garay

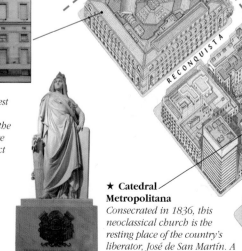

★ Banco de la Nación
Topped by a huge dome, the biggest in Latin America when the bank was completed in 1943, this was the first building in Argentina to have escalators. It was built by architect Alejandro Bustillo ❷

STAR SIGHTS
★ Casa Rosada
★ Banco de la Nación
★ Catedral Metropolitana

★ Catedral Metropolitana
Consecrated in 1836, this neoclassical church is the resting place of the country's liberator, José de San Martín. A wooden image of Santa María de la Rábida, the patron saint of the Americas, can be seen on the façade

Pirámide de Mayo
Although it has its origins in the first city plaza traced by founder Juan de Garay in 1580, the plaza takes its current name from the pyramid in the center which commemorates the Revolución de Mayo of 1810.

Palacio de Gobierno
The City Hall, the headquarters of the mayor of Buenos Aires, is a white neo-classical building located beside the Cabildo, from which the Spanish authorities ruled over Argentina.

Manzana de las Luces

Cabildo de Buenos Aires
Between 1748 and 1821, the city's affairs were managed here, the center of the intellectual debates that led to Argentinian Independence ❹

Legislatura de Buenos Aires
This 1930s building has an octagonal tower with five symbolic bells named La Pinta, La Argentina, La Niña, La Porteña, and La Santa María.

0 meters 100
0 yards 100

KEY

– – – Suggested route

The striking neoclassical façade of the Casa Rosada

Casa Rosada ❶

Balcarce 50. **City Map** 3 E5.
Tel (011) 4344-3802 (info); (011)
4344-3804 (tours). 🚌 24, 28, 29,
152. 🚇 Plaza de Mayo, Catedral.
🕐 10am–6pm Sat & Sun. 📷 🎫 ♿
www.museo.gov.ar

Famous as the building from
which Eva Perón addressed
her adoring supporters, the
Casa Rosada (Pink House)
has occupied a key role in
Argentinian history. Also
known as the Presidential
Palace, it was built between
1862 and 1885 on the site
of the Fuerte Viejo, the
city's main fort. The building
owes its distinctive pink hue
to the blending of lime

with ox blood, materials
commonly used in
construction at that time.

Over the years presidents,
elected and otherwise, as well
as soccer star Diego Maradona,
have used these famous balconies to stir national passions and to demonstrate
public support. The Casa
Rosada can be entered from
the south side, on Hipólito
Yrigoyen, via the **Museo de la
Casa Rosada**, which features
an interesting collection of
photographs and memorabilia
documenting the history of
the building and the country.
The museum has a 17,000-
volume library, an archive,
and a newspaper and magazine
collection. Visitors can also

stroll among the exposed
colonial catacombs of Fuerte
Viejo, which can be seen from
the pedestrian mall outside.

Banco de la Nación ❷

Avenida Rivadavia 325.
City Map 3 E5. *Tel* (011) 4347-
6000. 🚇 Plaza de Mayo, Catedral.
🚌 24, 28, 29, 74, 111, 140, 152.
🕐 currently closed to the public –
call ahead to check for details. ♿
**Museo Histórico y Numismático
del Banco de la Nación.**
Tel (011) 4347-6277.
🕐 10am–3pm Mon–Fri. ♿ 📷

Once the country's central
bank, the Banco de la Nación
is a grand example of the
characteristically fortress-like
edifices that house Buenos
Aires's older banks. Today,
it is the headquarters of the
country's largest high-street
bank, which is still managed
by the state, and is open to
clients and to the public.

Wide marble-floored
corridors and ornate decor
hark back to the 1940s and
50s, when the building was
erected and when Argentina
was enjoying a post-war
export boom. The bank's
famous architect, Alejandro
Bustillo, gave the city many
of its most prominent neoclassical buildings; these
include the elegant Museo
Nacional de Bellas Artes and
the Palais de Glace (see p102).
The Banco de la Nación also
houses **Museo Histórico y
Numismático del Banco de la**

PLAZA DE MAYO: A FLASHPOINT OF HISTORY

As the site of the main colonial fort, a battleground during
the English invasions, and a meeting place for pro-
Independence leaders, Buenos
Aires's most important plaza has
long been a stage for turbulent
events. The Peróns (see pp52–
53) were perhaps the most
adept users of Plaza de Mayo as
a popular gathering place: in
October 1945 a huge crowd led
by Evita gathered to call for the
release of her husband Juan
Perón from prison. During the
Dirty War of 1976–83 military
dictators made their pronounce-
ments from the plaza, and in 1982, President Leopoldo
Galtieri announced his decision to claim the Falkland
Islands (Islas Malvinas). In 2001, following the collapse of
the currency, the middle-classes joined unions and student
protesters at the plaza. Since the late 1970s, the Madres de
la Plaza de Mayo march there every Thursday to protest
the "disappearance" of their relatives during the Dirty War.

Mothers of the Disappeared
who gather in protest

The grand sweep of the Banco
de la Nación ceiling

The awe-inspiring Catedral Metropolitana, with its high ceiling and graceful arches

Nación on the first floor. It contains an excellent display on the Argentinian currency's turbulent history. The magnificent 164-ft (50-m) diameter dome on top of the building, only visible to passing helicopters, is the third largest in the world.

Catedral Metropolitana ❸

Avenida Rivadavia, cnr San Martín. **City Map** 3 E5. *Tel (011) 4331-2845.* 🚇 Plaza de Mayo, Catedral. 🚌 24, 29. 🕐 8am–7:30pm Mon–Fri, 8am–9:30pm Sat & Sun. 🕊 church services. 🕐 11:30am (part 1), 1:15pm (part 2), 3:30pm (full tour) Mon–Sat. 🕐 9am, 11am, 12:30 pm, & 6pm Mon–Fri; 11am & 6pm Sat; 11am, noon, 1pm, & 6pm Sun. 🚻 www.catedralbuenosaires.org.ar

The eighth Roman Catholic church to be built on this site, this Greco-Roman building is the seat of the diocese of Santísima Trinidad in Peru. Built between the 16th and 19th centuries, the Catedral Metropolitana has 12 columns on the façade symbolizing the Apostles, and above these a bas-relief showing Jacob meeting his son Joseph in Egypt. The somber baroque interior provides a cool escape from the busy and – in summer – sweltering plaza outside. The Venetian mosaic floors, silver-plated rococo altar, and a life-size Christ carved out of native *carob* wood are some of its outstanding features.

The mausoleum to the right of the nave contains the remains of Argentinian Independence hero, General José de San Martín (*see p49*).

Cabildo de Buenos Aires ❹

Volibar/Avenida de Mayo. **City Map** 3 E5. *Tel (011) 4342-6729.* 🚇 Plaza de Mayo, Catedral. 🚌 24, 28, 29. 🕐 10:30am–5pm Tue–Fri, 11:30am–6pm Sun. 🎟 🕐 3pm Fri, 12:30pm, & 3:30pm Sun. **Museo Histórico Nacional del Cabildo y de la Revolución de Mayo** *Tel (011) 4334-1782.* 🕐 same as the cabildo. 🎟

Built between 1725 and 1822, the Cabildo was the first building to be constructed completely from bricks. An elegant low-slung colonial-style building, it was the capital's hub of officialdom. Spain erected *cabildos* across its

empire, serving as town halls and administrative seats for the viceroys sent by the court in Madrid. It was chosen as an appropriate site for the first few meetings of the liberal intellectuals who would together form the first anti-Spanish junta in 1810.

Despite an attempt to remodel the building in a more Italianate style at the end of the 19th century, the plain, colonnaded front remains in a city where civic architecture is often devoted to neoclassical and Francophile pretensions.

The small on-site museum, **Museo Histórico Nacional del Cabildo y de la Revolución de Mayo**, contains the city's first printing presses, objects linked to the English invasions of 1806–7, and a silver and gold shield presented to Buenos Aires in 1807 from the Oruro government in Bolivia.

Colonial arches open into a cobbled courtyard, Cabildo de Buenos Aires

Museo de la Ciudad **5**

Defensa 219. **City Map** 3 E5.
Tel (011) 4343-2123. 🚇 Plaza de Mayo, Catedral. 🕐 11am–7pm Mon–Fri, 3–7pm Sun. 🎫 Wed free. **www**.museos.buenosaires.gov.ar/ciudad.htm

Located in the heart of the financial district, the Museo de la Ciudad is on the first floor of an elegantly adorned pharmaceutical building that was part of the Farmacia de la Estrella company, created in 1838 by Swiss immigrant Silvestre Demarchi. His sons moved it here in the 1890s. Regarded as one of the most important chemists in South America, it is still operating, selling a stock of traditional and homeopathic medicines on the ground floor.

The displays in the museum are rotated every few months and are dedicated to the everyday life of porteños, the people who live in Buenos Aires. They include aristocratic hats and combs used in the 19th century and *mate* gourds still used by all tea-sipping Argentinians. The much-prized art of *fileteado* is also well showcased. The building itself is of interest, as it is one of the few remaining townhouses from the period when wealthy Argentinians lived in the center – before

mass removal to Recoleta following the outbreak of yellow fever in 1871. One of the rooms is an excellent reconstruction of the living quarters of a typical patrician family of the period.

Museo Etnográfico **6**

Moreno 350. **City Map** 3 E5.
Tel (011) 4331-7788. 🚇 Catedral, Bolivar, Plaza de Mayo. 🕐 Feb–Dec: 1–7pm Tue–Fri, 3–7pm Sat & Sun. 🔵 Jan. 🎫 4pm Sat & Sun.

Founded by the scholar Juan B. Ambrosetti, this museum aims to document Argentina's vast indigenous culture. It houses a collection of ethnographic items ranging from masks and cooking implements used by the Araucana tribes that lived in the area before the arrival of Europeans, to accounts of Fuegian natives transplanted from their homes at the "end of the world" to East London. Exhibits include pelts from Bolivia, feathered headdresses from Chaco, and bark from Brazil. Also on display is jewelry and sculpture of the Mapuche – the only extant indigenous society in southern South America. Many of the Mapuche were uprooted from their Andean settlements in the late 19th century and relocated to the province of Buenos Aires.

Wooden Maori exhibit from New Zealand, Museo Etnográfico

Iglesia del Santisimo Rosario y Convento de Santo Domingo **7**

Defensa 422. **City Map** 1 E1.
Tel (011) 4331-1668. 🚇 Bolivar. 🕐 3–7pm Mon–Fri. ✝ 12:30pm Mon–Fri, 7pm Sat, & 11am Sun.

Work on this church began in the mid-18th century, and was completed 100 years later. It was built on land acquired by monks of the Dominican Order in 1601, soon after their arrival in Buenos Aires. The area stretched from Defensa down to the riverfront, present-day Paseo Colón, and was at first given over to vegetable allotments, livestock corrals, and a primitive chapel.

The church contains some interesting altars and artworks from the 17th and 19th centuries. People also come to the site to visit the mausoleum of Manuel Belgrano, designer of the Argentinian national flag. It is located on the east side near the entrance and is marked by an eternal flame. Post-Independence, the building was secularized and used as a museum and observatory. It was set ablaze by anticlerical Perónists in 1955 and later reconsecrated in 1967.

Manzana de las Luces **8**

Perú 272. **City Map** 3 E5.
Tel (011) 4342-9930. 🚇 Plaza de Mayo. 🕐 3pm Mon–Fri; 3pm, 4:30pm, & 6pm Sat & Sun. **www.**manzanadeluces.gov.ar **Iglesia de San Ignacio Tel** (011) 4331-2458. 🕐 11am–7pm daily. 🕐 3–6pm Sat & Sun. **Colegio Nacional de Buenos Aires Tel** (011) 4331-0733.

While the nickname "Block of Enlightment" was only coined in the 19th century, learning and liberty have been the guiding principles of this constellation of buildings for more than 400 years. The land was given to the Jesuits by the Spanish colonial authorities in 1616, who established a church and school. After

---

The Farmacia de la Estrella that houses the Museo de la Cuidad

For hotels and restaurants in this region see pp274–5 and p292

The hallowed gates of the Colegio Nacional de Buenos Aires

FILETEADO

Characterized by florid garlands and scrolls of bright colors, often including the sky-blue and white hues of the national flag, *fileteado* is a popular art form that is still seen on display in many storefront windows. The compositions sometimes include texts taken from local proverbs and sayings. Banned in the mid-1970s by the military government, who preferred straight lines and right angles – psychological and otherwise – it went underground and is now admired as a truly porteño art form.

A poster in *fileteado* style displaying ornamental scrollwork

being rigorously remodeled over the centuries, the church that stands today, **Iglesia de San Ignacio**, dates from 1734 and is the oldest in the city. There is also a cinema and a theater here.

Behind the church is the Procuravuria de las Misiones, where the Society of Jesus stored grain and tools for their missions in the northwest. When the Jesuits were expelled from Latin America in 1767, Vertíz, the viceroy of the day, had a school built on the site, the Real Colegio de San Carlos, which educated many of the key players in Argentinian Independence. In 1863 it was renamed as the more secular-sounding **Colegio Nacional de Buenos Aires**, and is still considered the city's most prestigious high school.

La City ⑨

City Map 3 E5. ⊜ *Catedral, Florida, Perú.* **Museo Mitre** San Martín 336. ◻ *noon–6pm Mon–Fri.* ▨ **Museo de la Policía** San Martín 353. ◻ *Feb–Dec: 2–6pm Tue–Fri.* ◉ *Jan.*

The Microcentro – a busy labyrinth of narrow lanes adjacent to Plaza de Mayo and populated by merchants and bankers – is nicknamed La City due to the British influence on Argentina's banking. In the 1980s, when inflation sky-rocketed, money changers plied their trade outside the banks, offering better rates to desperate citizens. With the collapse of the currency in

2001, the same streets were the target of protesters who marched banging on pots and pans. There are two small museums in the area – the **Museo Mitre** was the 19th-century residence of Bartolomé Mitre, one-time president and founder of the *La Nación* newspaper, while the **Museo de la Policía** covers the long history of crime and detection in Buenos Aires.

Correo Central ⑩

Sarmiento 151. **City Map** 3 E4. *Tel (011) 4891-9191.* ⊜ *Leandro N. Alem.* ◻ *9am–5pm Mon–Fri, 8am–1pm Sat.*

The Palacio de Correos y Telecomunicaciones is considered the most imposing of all Buenos Aires's buildings in the French beaux-arts style. The architect, Norbert Maillart, was a Frenchman, commissioned to build it by

President Miguel Juárez in 1888, although the building was only completed 40 years later. Occupying a single block, this elegant palace, now known simply as the Correo Central, symbolized both the increasing wealth of the country and its people, and the particularly important role of Buenos Aires as a port and hub of communications.

Sweeping mansard roofs, characterized by two slopes on each of the four sides, long vertical windows, and the south-facing façade, with its four pairs of columns, all echo the classic elements of the style, which became popular in the Americas after the 1893 World's Columbian Exhibition in Chicago. This was held to celebrate the 400th anniversary of Columbus's discovery of the New World. The old post office and the ground floor showcase artworks and stained-glass windows.

The elegant corridors of the Correo Central

Café Tortoni ⑪

Ave de Mayo 829. **City Map** 3 D5.
Tel (011) 4342-4328. 🚇 Piedras. ⏰
8:30am–10:30pm daily. 🚫 25 Dec
& 1 Jan. **Academia Nacional del
Tango** Avenida de Mayo 833. **Tel**
(011) 4345-6967. ⏰ 2:30–7:30pm
Mon–Fri. www.cafetortoni.com.ar

Opened in 1858, Café Tortoni
is named after a bohemian
drinking den on the famous
Boulevard des Italiens in Paris
and is probably the oldest
and grandest café in the city.
At the end of the 19th century, its basement was a popular meeting place for La Peña,
a group of local writers and
artists led by the painter
Benito Quinquela Martín.
Soon many of the city's greatest young talents, including
Jorge Luis Borges, Roberto
Arlt, and Alfonsina Storni, as
well as visitors such as
Federico García Lorca and
Luigi Pirandello, were seen
nursing a coffee at Tortoni.
A corner of the café, called
the Rincón de los Poetas
(Poet's Corner), harks back to
those days. Tango legend
Carlos Gardel also performed
here, and the café continues
to host tango and jazz concerts. Statesmen and visiting
dignitaries such as King Juan
Carlos of Spain and Hillary
Clinton have also stopped by.
The first floor is occupied
by the **Academia Nacional del
Tango**, which has a research
library for tango scholars.
There is also a schedule of
dance classes held here. The
classes cover all levels and
operate on a drop-in basis.

A quiet evening outside the brightly lit Teatro Avenida

The Academia is home to
a self-styled World Tango
Museum that opens daily.

Teatro Avenida ⑫

Avenida de Mayo 1222. **City Map** 3
D5. **Tel** (011) 4381-0662. 🚇 Lima.
⏰ 1–8pm daily.

If it were not for the preemin-
ence of the Teatro Colón (see
pp72–3) this beautiful theater,
reopened in 1994 after almost
being destroyed by a fire,
would get the attention it
deserves. Built along French
beaux-arts lines, with Italianate
elements, the theater has a
magnificent entrance.
The theater opened in
1908 with a play by Lope de
Vega. This initiated a steady
tradition of performing
Spanish zarzuela (Spanish
operetta) works, in keeping
with the Avenida de Mayo's
status as Buenos Aires's "most
Spanish" street – both in
terms of the architecture,
which copies that of the Old

World, and the number of
Spanish tapas bars and
restaurants that lie on or just
off the avenue. Among the
Teatro Avenida's many past
glories was a run of plays by
Federico García Lorca, who
lived at Avenida de Mayo
1152 between 1833 and 1934.

Palacio Barolo ⑬

Ave de Mayo 1370. **City Map** 3 D5.
Tel (011) 4383-1065. 🚇 Saenz Peña.
📷 4–6pm Mon & Thu. 🈲 ♿
www.pbarolo.com.ar/index.htm

Incorporating elements of
Dante's Divine Comedy, the
romantic, neo-Gothic Palacio
Barolo was built by architect
Mario Palanti. He was
commissioned by Luigi Barolo
– a great admirer of Dante
Alighieri – who arrived from
his native Italy in 1890 and
made money cultivating and
spinning cotton in the
northern province of Chaco.
In 1919, work began on
this grand 22-story building.
It is 328 ft (100 m) high,
reflecting the 100 cantos
of the Divine Comedy, while
nine literary citations carved
at the entrance hall echo
the nine infernal hierarchies.
The first 14 floors of the
Palacio are Purgatory, while
the heavens above are
crowned by a spectacular
domed lighthouse. The
number of offices on each
floor equals the stanzas that
the cantos contain. Some of
the details in the building are
still waiting to be decoded,
but this cryptic quality is perhaps what makes the edifice
a true homage to Dante.

A lively tango show at the landmark Café Tortoni

For hotels and restaurants in this region see pp274–5 and p292

Plaza del Congreso ⑭

Hipólito Yrigoyen. **City Map** 2 C5.
ⓔ Congreso. **Palacio del Congreso**
Tel (911) 4010-3000.
◻ 11am & 4pm Mon, Tue,
& Fri (guided tours only).
www.congreso.gov.ar

Argentina's government is modeled on the bicameral system of the US, and the domed Palacio del Congreso shares its architecture with the white Greco-Roman Congress structure in Washington, D.C. One of the last buildings of this type to be erected in Buenos Aires before the strong wave of fashionable Francophile architecture took over, the Congreso (as most porteños call the building) is a solid-looking granite-and-marble guardian of Plaza del Congreso to its east. Inaugurated in 1906 and designed by Vittorio Meano, who was also the architect of the Teatro Colón, the building is situated to face the **Casa Rosada** at the other end of the Avenida de Mayo, a symbolic reminder that power does not only belong to presidents but also to the people of the country.

Inside the Congreso is a library and several lavish salons, including the famous Salón Azúl (the Blue Room), with its colossal allegorical statues and an impressive 2,000-kg (4,400-lbs) bronze chandelier beneath the main cupola. The room has been used over the years for presidents lying in state.

Inside the Cámara del Senado (Senate) of the Palacio del Congreso

Out on the plaza, the exuberant centerpiece is the **Monumento a los Dos Congresos**, built to commemorate the first constitutional assembly of 1813 and the Congress of 1816. This imposing statue of the Republic waves a symbolic laurel branch and leans on a plough; below it are two female figures performing the patriotic duties of bearing the national arms and breaking the chains of enslavement.

On the smaller plaza to the east is the far calmer figure of Rodin's *Thinker*, one of the two copies in the Americas, who sits beneath the shade of the leafy jacaranda, *tipa*, and ceibo trees; close by is a statue of Mariano Moreno (1788–1811), a famous and revered Argentinian thinker, lawyer, and journalist, who was also one of the leading lights in the Revolución de Mayo of 1810 (see p49).

Surrounding the Plaza del Congreso is a scattering of interesting buildings, many of which evoke a more luxurious and wealthier past for porteños. One of the grandest, though gradually falling into disrepair, is the **Confitería Molino** (Windmill Café), named for the decorative windmill adorning its façade. Crowds of politicians used to drink their morning coffee here. The impressive **Edificio de la Inmobiliaria**, at the far eastern end of the plaza, adds an Italian and Oriental dash to the eclectic architecture of the barrio.

After the Plaza de Mayo, the Plaza del Congreso, apart from being a popular tourist spot, is one of the regular meeting places for protesters, student political parties, striking unions and, as the evidence suggests, innovative graffiti artists.

The imposing pillared façade and dome of the Palacio del Congreso

Avenida 9 de Julio and Obelisco ⑮

City Map 3 D4. ⊜ *Carlos Pellegrini, 9 de Julio.* 🚌 *39, 59, 67.*

This 460-ft (140-m) wide thoroughfare runs half a mile to the west of the Río de la Plata waterfront and has six lanes in each direction. It was blasted through the center of the city in the 1930s, creating a fitting backdrop for the towering 223-ft (68-m) **Obelisco** that stands at the intersection with Avenida Corrientes.

The magnificent Obelisco was designed by Argentinian architect Alberto Prebisch and was erected in 1936. Each of the monument's four faces illustrates an important event in Argentina's history: the first foundation of Buenos Aires in 1536; the second, more successful foundation in 1580; the creation of the federal capital in 1880; and the first hoisting of the national flag in San Nicolás church, which once stood at the same spot. The monument is one of the main icons of the city and a venue for various cultural activities. It also serves as a gathering spot for sports fans, who come here to celebrate when their favorite team wins.

Display of costumes at Museo del Instituto Nacional de Estudios de Teatro

Teatro Colón ⑯

See pp72–3.

Templo de la Congregación Israelita ⑰

Libertad 769. **City Map** 3 D4. **Tel** *(011) 4123-0102.* ⊜ *Tribunales.* 🚌 *29, 39, 109.* ☐ *3–5:30pm Tue and Thu.* **Services** *8am & 6:15pm Mon–Fri.* **Museo Judío de Buenos Aires Dr. Salvador Kibrick Tel** *same as the synagogue.* 🚫 🎫 *3:30pm Tue & Thu.*

The foundation stone for this beautiful synagogue was laid in 1897 by the Congregación Israelita de la Argentina

Old Torah at Museo Judío

(CIRA). This was a community organization created by a group of German, French, and British Jews in 1862. The imposing architecture of the building copies the Byzantine-influenced style of 19th-century German synagogues. It is still very much a working temple, and daily services as well as regular bar mitzvahs and marriage ceremonies are held here. The temple also houses, in its administrative office, **Museo Judío de Buenos Aires Dr. Salvador Kibrick**, which is named after the museum's founder. The displays tell the story of the arrival and settlement of Argentina's sizable Jewish community through paintings, religious art, and artifacts such as altar cloths, menorahs,

View of the magnificent altar of the Templo de la Congregación Israelita

manuscripts, and letters, including one sent by Albert Einstein in 1925 to the Argentinian Jews.

Teatro Nacional Cervantes ⑱

Libertad 815. **City Map** 3 D4. **Tel** *(011) 4815-8883.* ⊜ *Tribunales.* 🚌 *29, 39.* ☐ *Feb–Dec: 10am–8pm Wed–Sun.* ☐ *Jan.* 🎫 *2pm Tue (Spanish only).* **www**.teatro cervantes.gov.ar **Museo del Instituto Nacional de Estudios de Teatro Tel** *same as the theater.* ☐ *noon–6pm Mon–Fri.* 🎫 *same as the theater.* ☐

The only "national" theater to bear that name in the country, the Teatro Nacional Cervantes was once a grand structure. Heavy traffic and pollution has discolored the façade and given the ornate cornices and bas-reliefs an unsightly black sheen. Yet the building still manages to impress – it is built in the Spanish Habsburg Imperial style and takes a cue from the University in Alcalá de Henares in Madrid with its Plateresque elements (a 15th–16th century Spanish art form characterized by much ornamentation). The interior is decorated with materials imported from Spain, including mirrors from Seville, exquisite tapestries and drapes from Madrid, and tiles from Valencia and Tarragona.

The building was given to the city by Spanish actor María Guerrero and her husband Fernando Díaz de

Mendoza, who opened the theater in 1921 with a production of Lope de Vega's *La Dama Boba*. After a few years, mismanagement and poor box-office returns led to bankruptcy, and the building and business were taken over by the government.

In the early decades plays by great Spanish authors such as Calderón, Tirso de Molina, and Ventura de la Vega were the preferred repertoire, but nowadays the 1,700-seat theater is employed for anything from lively musicals aimed at school audiences to cutting-edge new dramas by emerging authors.

The theater also houses the **Museo del Instituto Nacional de Estudios de Teatro**, which provides a brief yet interesting account of thespian history in Argentina.

Plaza Lavalle ⓲

Bounded by Calles Tucuman & Viamonte. **City Map** 3 D4.
🚇 *Tribunales.* 🚌 *29, 39, 109.*

Honoring Juan Lavalle, who crossed the Andes with the hero of national liberation, José de San Martín, this green, leafy space is a welcome refuge from the surrounding traffic and scurrying young lawyers on their way between their offices and the nearby law courts.

The Palacio de Justicia, home to Argentina's legal system

In the 18th century, this area was still grassed over and was part of the suburbs of the original city; in 1822 the military used the site to build a weapons factory and as a barracks for their artillery.

In 1890, a group of 400 protesters took over the land to stage a demonstration against the presidency of Juarez Celman and during the ensuing battle with government forces, over 150 people were killed.

Around the present-day "plaza" – in fact, there are three other adjacent plazas – are a host of important buildings including the Teatro Colón and the Teatro Nacional Cervantes, as well as the oldest Jewish synagogue, the Templo Libertad, and the Palacio de Justicia, the seat of the Argentinian legal system.

Palacio de Justicia ⓴

Talcahuano 550. **City Map** 3 D4.
🚇 *Tribunales.* 🚌 *29, 39, 109.*

Built during the 1890s, the Greco-Roman Palacio was designed by Norbert Maillart, the architect behind Correo Central *(see p67)* and Colegio Nacional de Buenos Aires. It was inaugurated in 1942 and is home to the nation's scandal-ridden Supreme Court. The Palacio's main hall features *La Justicia*, a statue by the renowned sculptor Rogelio Yrurtia.

The court used to be open to the public but the frequency of marches and protests made the administration limit access around the perimeter of the building.

A winding path through the leafy environs of the peaceful Plaza Lavalle

Teatro Colón ⓰

Undoubtedly the most elegant edifice on the west side of Avenida 9 de Julio, Teatro Colón is the city's main lyric theater and a world-class center for classical music, ballet, and opera. Work began on the theater in 1880 and it opened its doors in 1908 with a performance of Italian composer Giuseppe Verdi's *Aida*. A succession of architects were involved in the Colón's evolution and they employed a pan-European approach to the building's architecture. Many great artistes, from Greek opera singer Maria Callas to German composer Richard Strauss, have performed here. The opulence of the building combined with fabulous performances makes this the capital's top cultural attraction.

View of the Teatro Colón entrance on Calle Cerrito

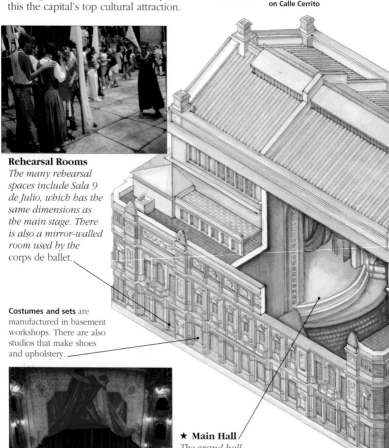

Rehearsal Rooms
The many rehearsal spaces include Sala 9 de Julio, which has the same dimensions as the main stage. There is also a mirror-walled room used by the corps de ballet.

Costumes and sets are manufactured in basement workshops. There are also studios that make shoes and upholstery.

★ Main Hall
The grand hall houses three floors of boxes that accommodate about 3,000 people. The acoustics, modeled after French and Italian opera houses, are world famous.

STAR SIGHTS

- ★ Main Hall
- ★ Soldi's Paintings
- ★ Façade on Libertad

Visiting Artistes

Over the years, notable artistes have performed here, including the Israeli-based pianist and conductor Daniel Barenboim, who visits his native Argentina to conduct the Teatro Colón's resident orchestra.

★ Soldi's Paintings

Argentinian painter Raúl Soldi was commissioned to paint the dome in the 1960s. It features a host of ethereal dancers, musicians, and opera singers.

The Staircase

The sweeping main staircase is made from white Carrara marble, with Portuguese marble banisters crowned by a pair of hand-carved lion heads.

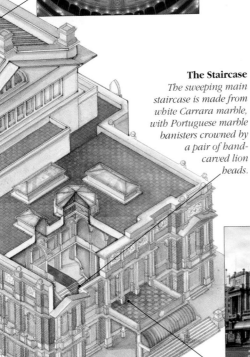

★ Façade on Libertad

Built in the French Renaissance style, this structure has Corinthian and Ionic capitals on the upper floors of the beautiful main entrance.

The Sala Martín Coronado auditorium at Teatro General San Martín

Teatro General San Martín ㉑

Avenida Corrientes 1530. **City Map** 2 C4. **Tel** (0800) 333-5254, (011) 4374-1385 (guided tours). 🚇 Uruguay. ⬜ box office: 10am–10pm daily. 📷 noon Tue–Fri. **www**.teatrosanmartin.com.ar **Centro Cultural San Martín Tel** (011) 4374-1251. ⬜ 7am–10pm.

Built in the 1950s, this state-sponsored arts complex uses reinforced concrete in the functional, box-like style popular at the time. It houses a 1,100-seat theater, two smaller theaters, a cinema, and a photograph gallery. World-class and top-notch local theater companies and major photographic exhibitions fill a busy schedule, while the cinema specializes in art-house retrospectives and screens daring, often obscure archival material. The huge lobby is often given over to free dance shows in the evenings and is a meeting place for students and art-lovers from all over the city.

Over the past few decades, Avenida Corrientes has lost many of its bookshops and is no longer quite the Broadway of Buenos Aires it used to be. This throws into sharper relief the importance of the Teatro San Martín as a well-funded, censor-free milieu for cutting-edge artists.

Two companies – the Contemporary Ballet and the Puppeteers Group – are based permanently at the theater. At the rear of the lobby it is possible to walk through to the **Centro Cultural San Martín**, which is, rather confusingly, a completely separate cultural center, with its own main entrance on Calle Sarmiento. This center is often used by emerging musical artists and aspiring photographers to showcase their talents to the mainstream.

Palacio de las Aguas Corrientes ㉒

Avenida Córdoba 1950. **City Map** 2 C4. 🚇 Callao, Facultad de Medicina. **Museo del Patrimonio Tel** (011) 6319-1104. ⬜ 9am–1pm Mon–Fri. 📷 11am Mon.

The Palacio de las Aguas Corrientes (Palace of Running Water), built between 1887 and 1895, is an ostentatious celebration of civic pride and eclectic vitality. Located down Avenida Córdoba, the Palacio is the road's most stunning building. Terra-cotta tiles were imported from Leeds in Britain, green slate from Sedan

The vivid façade of the striking Palacio de las Aguas Corrientes

in France, and marble from Azúl in the Buenos Aires province. Tall palm trees add to the tropical exuberance of the building, which is decorated with the shields of the various Argentinian provinces. The Palacio once housed the headquarters of Aguas Argentinas, the firm that evolved out of the old state-run water board during privatization under President Menem's government in the 1980s and 90s.

Housed within the building is the unusual **Museo del Patrimonio** that explains the history of water sanitation in Argentina and the world.

Sketch of ships arriving in Buenos Aires, Museo de la Inmigración

Museo de la Inmigración ㉓

Avenida Antártida Argentina 1355. **City Map** 3 E3. **Tel** (011) 4317-0285. 🚌 106, 101. ⬜ 10am–7pm Mon–Fri, 11am–6pm Sat & Sun. 📷 prior arrangement only (minimum of 10 people required).

This museum is housed in the former Hotel de Inmigrantes, and displays a collection of films, photographs, and other objects related to Argentina's immigrant history. In the last decades of the 19th century, the hotel was a boarding house where the newly arrived could relax, get a meal and medicines, and begin to make contacts to get work in the city. Located on the dockside, it was a welcome home away from home for the many economic and political refugees – mainly from southwestern Europe but also from the Levant, Russia, and Ukraine – who had neither family nor friends in the city. The hotel was funded by the state, and, as the key aim of Argentina's open-door policy was to populate the hinterland, men staying at the hotel were instructed in the use of agricultural machinery while women were offered classes in housekeeping. Many moved on to work in domestic service in the city's more wealthy households.

A family of black-necked swans, Reserva Ecológica Costanera Sur

Reserva Ecológica Costanera Sur 24

Avenida Tristán Achaval Rodríguez 1550. **City Map** 3 F4. *Tel (011) 4893-1588*. 99, 2. Apr–Oct: 8am–5:30pm Tue–Sun; Nov–Mar: 8am–7pm Tue–Sun. 10:30am & 3:30pm Sat & Sun (Spanish only).

In the 1970s, there was an attempt to reclaim the bog-lands of the riverside Costanera Sur using the Dutch polder system, which involves the draining and recovering of a water-covered area. When the development ran into difficulties, the land was colonized by tall pampas grass and four lakes were formed, creating an ideal wetland for the wading birds that migrate to the Pampas region each spring. Southern screamers, southern lapwings, coots, wattled jacanas, and flamingos are among the 200 species that can be spotted at the ecological preserve, formally recognized as such

in 1986. Well-marked footpaths wind through the leafy park, drawing joggers, trekkers, and cyclists. Apart from the daily ranger walks, guides lead groups on tours by moonlight every month.

Puerto Madero 25

East of Microcentro. **City Map** 3 F5. *Tel (011) 4515-4600*. 152, 111, 109. **www**.puertomadero.com **Buque Museo Fragata Presidente Sarmiento** www.ara.mil.ar **Coleccion de Arte Amalia Lacroze de Fortabat** www.coleccion fortabat.org.ar

Built as a result of a city competition held to design a new dock at Buenos Aires, Puerto Madero was used to store grain and other perish-ables during the exports boom of the late 19th century. However, the narrow wharves in this red-brick dockland proved unsuited to larger, more modern cargo ships, and

between 1911 and 1925 another port – Puerto Nuevo – was built a few miles north. For over 50 years Puerto Madero was left to decay, but in the early 1990s the area was rebuilt and nightclubs, a yacht club, restaurants, and a boutique hotel soon followed. In August 1998, Puerto Madero became Buenos Aires's 47th official barrio. It is unique as the only neighborhood where all streets are named after women.

Some porteños have criticized the gentrification of Puerto Madero as too elitist and lacking in cultural sites. Worth seeing, however, are Spanish architect Santiago Calatrava's Puente de la Mujer (Woman's Bridge), the **Coleccion de Arte Amalia Lacroze de Fortabat** featuring Argentinian art, and the *Presidente Sarmiento* ship built in Birkenhead – a British port town famous for its ship-building skills – which is now a floating maritime museum named **Buque Museo Fragata Presidente Sarmiento**.

The elegant Puente de la Mujer bridge at the Puerto Madero docks

SAN TELMO AND LA BOCA

The first European to arrive in what is now Buenos Aires, Pedro de Mendoza, made landfall in San Telmo in 1536, and between the 16th and mid-19th centuries this was the main residential district for colonial officials and their staff. La Boca, farther south, rose to prominence in the 19th century when Genoese settlers began to build their homes along the dockside. Now, the great majority of middle-class Argentinians choose to live in

Carving of a porteño woman, San Telmo

the smarter northern barrios of Recoleta, Palermo, and Belgrano. However, when asked where their city's soul resides, most porteños will admit that it is *el sur* (the south) of the city and when they want to revive the early days of Buenos Aires, they head to San Telmo and La Boca. The area is most famous for its colorful zinc shacks and its football team, Boca Juniors. Both San Telmo and La Boca lay claim to being the cradle of tango in the 1880s.

SIGHTS AT A GLANCE

Historical Sites, Streets, and Plazas

Calle Necochea ❿
Canto al Trabajo ❸
El Caminito ⓰
El Zanjón and Casa Mínima ❷
La Bombonera ⓯
La Vuelta de Rocha ⓬
Parque Lezama ❼
Plaza Dorrego ❶
Puente Nicolás Avellaneda ⓫
Teatro Catalinas Sur ❾

Places of Worship

Iglesia Ortodoxa Rusa ❻

Museums

Fundación Proa ⓮
Museo de Arte Moderno ❹
Museo de Bellas Artes de La Boca ⓭

Museo del Cine ❺
Museo Histórico Nacional ❽

SEE ALSO

• *Where to Stay* p275

• *Where to Eat* pp292–3

KEY

🚉 Railroad station

✚ Hospital

⛪ Church

0 meters   700
0 yards   700

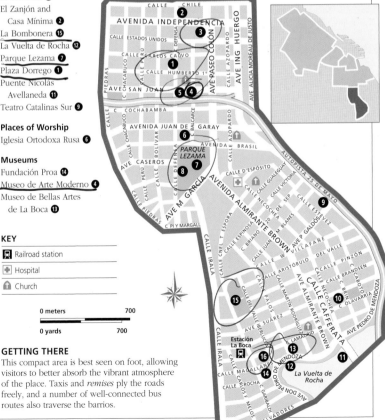

GETTING THERE

This compact area is best seen on foot, allowing visitors to better absorb the vibrant atmosphere of the place. Taxis and *remises* ply the roads freely, and a number of well-connected bus routes also traverse the barrios.

◁ **A colonial building with *fileteado* decoration, San Telmo**

The balcony terrace of a lively café overlooking Plaza Dorrego

Plaza Dorrego ❶

Corner Defensa and Humberto 1°.
City Map 1 E1. 🚌 24, 29, 126, 130, 152.

A lively and bustling area, Plaza Dorrego is popular with visitors wishing to take time out from walking around the city. It is an ideal place to while away time, lounging over a beer or coffee.

Located in the heart of the San Telmo barrio, this small cobblestoned plaza was formerly the station for carriages and carts passing through the city and is the oldest city square after Plaza de Mayo. Surrounded by beautiful two-storied buildings, many of which have been converted into bars, restaurants, and souvenir shops, it is a lively hub for locals and tourists alike. On weekdays, cafés set up tables in the plaza for people to drink and play cards or chess. On the weekends, the space is taken over by a popular antiques and bric-a-brac market, the **Feria de San Pedro Telmo** *(see p120)*, which claims to be the oldest in the city. It is ideal for browsing although sometimes it may get rather crowded.

The houses around Plaza Dorrego and on the neighboring streets were once the homes of patrician families, and many of the antiques on sale are the former fixtures and fittings of these now decaying properties. Bargains are few and far between but keep a look out for old vinyl records, antique *mates*, gramophone players, old ticket machines from the city's buses, the stylish fedorastyle *funyi* hats worn by male tango dancers, and examples of *fileteado*, the colorful indigenous porteño art form *(see p67)*.

Plaza Dorrego is also one of the few places in the city, weather permitting, to see informal open-air tango dancing in which tourists and locals participate.

Tango street performers

The area may sometimes feel like a tourist-trap, but it is popular with bohemian porteños and, out of season, has a genuinely romantic air.

El Zanjón and Casa Mínima ❷

Defensa 755. **City Map** 1 E1.
Tel (011) 4361-3002. 🚌 24, 29, 130, 152. ⬚ only guided tours.
🅿️ 🎫 *El Zanjón: 11am–3pm (hourly) Mon–Fri, 2–6pm (hourly) Sun; Casa Mínima: 10:30am & 3pm Mon–Fri (call in advance).*
www.elzanjon.com.ar

El Zanjón is a restored residence where the living conditions of urban Argentinians can be traced for over three centuries. It is an eclectic mix of an 1830s façade, 18th-century fixtures and fittings, and even older inner walls. In colonial times, a rivulet known as El Zanjón de Granados flowed through this spot and was used to remove sewage. French tiles, African pipes, English china, and other objects have all been found on the site, indicating the cosmopolitan traffic that passed through here.

A two-minute walk away, on Pasaje San Lorenzo, is **Casa Mínima** (Minimal House), an example of the only truly indigenous architectural style to come out of Buenos Aires, the *casa chorizo* (sausage house). These are long, thin dwellings with a narrow frontage and a corridor that stretches about half a block deep. The Casa Mínima was built in the 1880s by freed slaves on a tiny parcel of land granted to them by a benevolent master.

The narrow frontage of the Casa Mínima

The impressive Canto al Trabajo sculpture

Canto al Trabajo ❸

Paseo Colon 800. **City Map** 1 E1.
🚌 24, 29, 126, 130, 152.

Unveiled in 1927, this spectacular bronze sculpture by the famous Argentinian sculptor, Rogelio Yrurtia, was originally located in Plaza Dorrego. It depicts 14 muscular laborers towing a colossal boulder in true Sisyphean style. The sculpture is an allegory of working-class hardship and the dignity of women. The Spanish name means "Ode to Work." Much loved by porteños, the sculpture nonetheless attracted the city's many graffiti artists and in 1998 an iron fence was erected around the plinth in an attempt to keep them out.

Museo de Arte Moderno ❹

Avenida San Juan 350. **City Map** 1
E2. **Tel** (011) 4361-1121. 🚌 29, 64,
86, 130, 152. ◯ Mar–Jan: 10am–
8pm Tue–Fri, 11am–8pm Sat & Sun.
◉ Feb. 🎫 🎫 5pm Tue, Wed, Fri, &
Sun (Spanish only). **www**.museos.
buenosaires.gov.ar/mam.htm

Housed in a recycled tobacco depot and opened in 1956, the Museo de Arte Moderno features a façade of bright red English bricks and a door made of wood and iron. It has no permanent collection but rotates a number of exhibitions through the year.

The displays have contained minor works by Renoir and Monet, an assortment of pieces by Matisse, Dali, Miró, and Mondrian, and important pieces by leading Argentinian artists Xul Solar and Berni. The works of Leon Ferrari

and Kenneth Kemble, both contemporary Argentinian conceptual artists, are also exhibited. Of particular interest are the panoramas by the engraver Pompeyo Audivert and beautiful murals by the Galician-born Luis Seoane. The museum is also used as a venue for avant-garde music shows and screens international films in collaboration with Museo del Cine.

Museo del Cine Pablo Cristian Ducrós Hicken ❺

Defensa 1220. **City Map** 1 E2.
Tel (011) 4361-2462. 🚌 29, 64, 86,
130, 152. ◯ 10am–7pm Tue–Fri,
11:30am–6:30pm Sat & Sun. ♿
🚭 **www**.museodelcine.gov.ar

Named for the film historian who founded the institute in 1971, this museum has exhibition rooms filled with posters, old film reels, projectors, and costumes. The collection includes over 2,500 posters that are vivid evocations of the 1930s, 40s, and 50s, the golden era of cinema in the city, and when tango movies were all the rage. There are also posters and stills from the age of silent films and from the 1970s onward, when political dissent began to figure in the discourse of some left-leaning directors. The Museo del Cine is also considered an important educational and archival center and has a well-stocked library on Argentinian cinema.

A promotional poster displayed at the Museo del Cine

FINDING A MILONGA

The word *milonga* is possibly of African origin, and while alluding to a type of lively tango beat and a country guitar-based folk genre, it also refers to a salon night in a tango club. Unlike formal shows and classes, *milongas* are aimed at those who have a basic knowledge of tango steps. The basic rules are that men invite women to dance for three musical tracks after which the partners rest; nobody talks during the dance; and only those who know how to tango get up. Although live orchestras are rare these days, there are good *milongas* all over the city. The ideal place to start in San Telmo is the Centro Cultural Torquato Tasso which hosts *milongas* over the weekend. The Club Gricel and La Viruta are other well-known salons, where classes are combined with the main event.

Tango classes for beginners at Club Gricel

The striking sky-blue onion domes of the Iglesia Ortodoxa Rusa

Iglesia Ortodoxa Rusa **6**

Brasil 315. **City Map** 1 E2. *Tel* (011) 4361-4274. 🚌 10 & 29. ◯ varies according to church itinerary. ✚ 5pm & 8pm Sat, 10am & 11:30am Sun.

Work on the Iglesia Ortodoxa Rusa began in 1901, with a ceremony attended by Argentina's president, Julio A. Roca, and it was completed in 1904. Topped by five onion domes, the church was built using raw materials imported from St. Petersburg in Russia and, even after its completion, Tsar Nicholas II continued to send artworks and other valuables to decorate the interior. As well as a variety of Byzantine works and icons, a painting of the last Russian tsar, by Argentinian artist Carlos Ganzalez Galeano, can also be viewed inside.

The number of domes represents Jesus and the four apostles who were the authors of the four gospels. The sky-blue color and star motifs of the domes are intended to emulate the sky. The chains that hang between them, while unnecessary in Buenos Aires's temperate climate, are employed in Russia to stabilize the cupolas in the event of strong gales.

Parque Lezama **7**

Corner Brasil and Defensa. **City Map** 1 E2. 🚌 10, 24, 29, 39, 64, 130, 152. ◯ Daily.

Many historians claim that this peaceful park is the likely site where Pedro de Mendoza made landfall in Buenos Aires in 1536 while sailing up Río de la Plata. A monument in the corner of the park at Brasil and Defensa records this event as the "first foundation of Buenos Aires," though Mendoza failed to actually establish a city. Between the 17th and 19th centuries, the land belonged to a number of families, some with British connections. In the 1860s the famed landscape architect José Gregorio Lezama had a private park and botanical gardens laid out here, and many of the soaring *tipa* and palm trees date from this period. In 1894 his estate sold the land to the municipal authorities, and, three years later, the Lezama mansion became the Museo Histórico

Nacional. Unlike Parque 3 de Febrero *(see p106)*, which is a magnet for tourists, local and international, Parque Lezama is a quiet community area, well used by San Telmo residents. On the weekends especially, elderly porteños can be spotted here playing chess, while families picnic and youngsters play, cycle, and skate around.

Opposite the park, on the corner of Brasil and Almirante Brown, is the famous **Mural Escenográfico Parque Lezama**. In the popular tradition of artists such as Antonio Berni, Quinquela Martín, and Florencio Molina Campos, it celebrates iconic characters of the traditional barrio – the tango dancer, the football player, the barrio cop, and the nosy neighbor. Among the well-known faces here are crooner Carlos Gardel, soccer legend Diego Maradona, and button-accordion virtuoso Aníbal Troilo.

Parque Lezama is often the venue for small concerts hosted by local bands as well as a weekend crafts fair organized by artisans, which stretches north along Calle Defensa to Avenida San Juan.

A stroll through the Sunday crafts fair at Parque Lezama

Bells on display at the Museo Histórico Nacional

Museo Histórico Nacional ❽

Defensa 1600. **City Map** 1 E2. **Tel** (011) 4307-1182. 🚌 10, 24, 29, 39, 64, 130, 152. ⬤ Feb–Dec: 11am–5pm Tue & Fri, 3–6pm Sat, 2–6pm Sun. ⬤ Jan. 🖼

Originally called Museo Histórico de la Capital, Museo Histórico Nacional was created by mayor Francisco Seeber in 1889. It is housed in an elegant Italianate mansion, formerly the home of the wealthy Lezama family. The displays present a concise history of Argentina from the 16th through to the 19th century. There are 30 rooms that trace, through relics and paintings, the dramas of the Jesuit missions and the battles between the Spanish and indigenous tribes, and between royalists and republicans. Finally, the turbulent 19th century is documented – this was the period when rival factions fought over the newly independent nation. Donations from living relatives of important figures from the Revolución de Mayo and the Wars of Argentinian Independence (see p49) make up most of the museum's excellent collection.

One of the more interesting exhibits is a series of paintings produced by Argentinian painter and soldier Cándido López (see p30) portraying moving scenes from the war against Paraguay in the 1870s, in which he also fought. Oddly enough, little else is covered here, and there is nothing to

illustrate the reign of the Peróns, the social and economic horrors of the 1970s, or the more recent financial disasters that threw the country into disarray.

Teatro Catalinas Sur ❾

Avenida Benito Perez Galdós 93. **City Map** 1 F3. **Tel** (011) 4300-5707. 🚌 10, 24, 29, 64. **www**.catalinasur.com.ar

Formed in 1982 by artistes from the neighborhood of La Boca, Teatro Catalinas Sur is now open to everyone. This actors' cooperative has a well-known theater troupe which uses a comic, carnivalesque approach to present an irreverent, alternative view of Argentinian history.

The elements of la murga (a local street dance with roots in Buenos Aires's African community) are coupled with iconic Argentinian figures, including the Peróns, Diego Maradona and other football stars, church leaders, and even Buenos Aires waiters. These elements are thrown into the dramaturgical melting pot to create works that are witty and wild but which also function as serious historical commentaries.

Some shows are performed outdoors, using the amphitheater at Parque Lezama, but the company's headquarters remains at this converted warehouse, where most of their plays are performed.

Calle Necochea ❿

La Boca. **City Map** 1 F3. 🚌 10, 24, 29, 64.

It is still possible to catch vestiges of La Boca's disreputable dockside vibe on this street, mainly evident in the garish façades and faded signs on the shop fronts. Many of these used to be brothels and dimly lit bars where sailors and newly arrived settlers could play a few rounds of cards, have a drink, squabble, and also try out some tango steps. Even until the mid-1990s, many of the cantinas – low-budget bars for working men and women – still had an "outlaw" quality, but gentrification and the widespread fascination with chic, branded entertainment has led to Calle Necochea's decline. It is still an ideal place, however, for crisp, freshly baked pizza and reasonably priced beer.

Raucous live performance at the Teatro Catalinas Sur

Houses painted in vibrant colors along El Caminito, La Boca ▷

View of boats docked at La Vuelta de Rocha

Puente Transbordador Nicolás Avellaneda ⑪

Ave Pedro de Mendoza, cnr Almirante Brown. **City Map** 1 F4. 🚌 29, 33.

The Puente Transbordador Nicolás Avellaneda is named for the president who governed Argentina between 1874 and 1880. Porteños famously refer to it as "the bridge in La Boca's" and it appears in numerous tango-themed films as an evocative icon of the city. Opened in 1914 by the Ferrocarriles del Sur railroad company, it stands as a reminder of the country's prosperous grain-rich era.

This "transporter bridge" looks as sturdy as when it first opened, but it has in fact not been used since 1940. Gondolas were once suspended from the bridge and towed across the Riachuelo, taking people and goods over the river to the southern suburbs. This function is now fulfilled by the adjacent iron bridge, which, confusingly, bears the same name.

La Vuelta de Rocha ⑫

Doctor del Valle Iberlucea y Avenida Don Pedro de Mendoza. **City Map** 1 F4. 🚌 29, 33, 152, 159.

It is popularly said that to truly understand tango you need to loiter awhile at this street on the elbow of the

Riachuelo River. La Vuelta de Rocha (The Corner) is a grubby yet picturesque sub-barrio of La Boca that claims to be the cradle of the dance that seduced *fin de siecle* Paris. It also lays claim to an interesting history. Given to the merchant Antonio Rocha in 1635, La Vuelta became a makeshift port. It was here that Admiral Guillermo Brown assembled a small but determined navy to fight in the Independence Wars. Later it was the disembarkation point for thousands of Genoese immigrants and the berth of *Vapor de la Carrera*, a steamship that once sailed daily to Montevideo and now houses a quaint restaurant and a colorful artisan fair. La Vuelta's steamships and sailors are long gone but the spirit of adventure still lingers.

Display of wares at the crafts market at La Vuelta de Rocha

Museo de Bellas Artes de La Boca Benito Quinquela Martín ⑬

Ave Pedro de Mendoza 1835. **City Map** 1 F4. *Tel* (011) 4301-1080. 🚌 29, 33, 152. ◻ 10am–5:30pm Tue–Fri, 11am–5:30pm Sat & Sun. 📷 by prior arrangement. ♿ 🚫

The building that houses the Museo de Bellas Artes dates back to 1933, when famous Argentinian artist Benito Quinquela Martín (1890–1977) donated a plot of land to the nation. He stipulated that a primary school, a gallery, and a workshop be built on the site. The museum assumed its current form in 1968 when Martín donated 50 of his watercolors and 27 of his oil paintings to be hung there. The works of other prominent Argentinian artists are also displayed, as well as various objects related to the port's history. Several of the terraces in the house hold works by well-known Argentinian sculptors including Rogelio Irurtia and Correa Morales.

The artist Benito Quinquela Martín

While many Argentinian artists have been associated with La Boca, which is still a hugely popular bohemian area, the name and reputation of Benito Quinquela Martín towers above them all. His watercolors depict everyday life as it once was on and by the river, and the close relationship between the artist, his work, and his environment is vividly evident in the La Boca that he portrayed.

Fundación Proa ⑭

Ave Pedro de Mendoza 1929. **City Map** 1 F4. *Tel* (011) 4303-0909. 🚌 29, 33, 152, 159, 168. ◻ 11am–7pm Tue–Sun. 🚫 📷 by prior arrangement. ♿ 🚫 🖥 🌐 www.proa.org

Opened in 1996, the Fundación Proa is housed in an elegant Italianate building that dates back to the end of the 19th century. Within the traditional exterior there are three modern floors and a roof terrace, allowing for an extensive and varied year-round program of exhibitions that include painting, sculpture, and photography. Various video installations, concerts, and conferences are also included in the eclectic itinerary.

Exhibit at Museo de la Pasion Boquense

Six temporary exhibitions are held each year. The primary focus is on 20th-century Latin American art, though not exclusively or dogmatically so. In past years, for example, the museum has exhibited many exciting works ranging from Mexican archaeological finds to contemporary Italian abstract paintings.

Refurbished in 2007, the Fundación Proa now has more spacious exhibition areas and improved facilities. Already considered one of the best art museums in Buenos Aires, this stylish and brilliantly curated gallery is a treasure trove for the culturally minded tourist.

La Bombonera ⑮

Brandsen 805. **City Map** 1 E3.
Tel (011) 4309-4700. 🚌 29, 33, 152, 159, 168. ⬤ 11am–5pm daily.
🚫 restricted on match days. ♿ 🖥
🎦 **Museo de la Pasion Boquense**
Tel (011) 4362-1100. ⬤ 10am–6pm daily. 📷 🎥 call to verify.
www.museoboquense.com

Oddly named La Bombonera (The Chocolate Box), in reference to its particularly compact structure, this football stadium was built in 1940 and remodeled in the 1990s by the club's president, Mauricio Macri. It has seen many exciting matches and been packed with similarly passionate audiences. When empty, however, it has an eerie stillness and solemnity like a battlefield devoid of its two armies. Visiting the on-site museum, the **Museo de la Pasion Boquense**, is infinitely

less exciting than going to a match, and football fans, convinced the game has sold its soul, should avert their eyes from all the overpriced memorabilia. It does, however, have flashy audio and visual gizmos and statistic-heavy display boards, celebrating Boca Juniors' many trophies and showing a reverence for their former players that borders on idolatry. A modern addition to the museum is *El Diez*, a statue of Diego Maradona.

El Caminito ⑯

Del Valle Iberlucea 1300.
City Map 1 F4. 🚌 29, 33, 152, 159.

Recognized as Argentina's only open-air museum, El Caminito (Little Lane) is a short pedestrianized street jutting out west from La Vuelta de Rocha. Its name is taken from a tango song reminiscent of a melancholic Shakespearean reflection on the ravages of time, written in 1926 by locals Peñaloza and Filiberto. Although the street is overcrowded with vendors and pamphleteering restaurant staff, its charms have not been entirely obliterated by commercialization. What

Empty stands that fill to capacity for matches at La Bombonera

draws the multitude of photographers and makes El Caminito a staple of glossy coffee-table books are the houses which flank the street and whose corrugated zinc walls and roofs are painted in vivid colors. There is a predominance of blues and yellows, which are the colors of the Boca Juniors football team. This polychromatic practice was devised by 19th- and early 20th-century Genoese immigrants, who scrounged pots of paint from wherever they could to brighten up their otherwise dismal, and usually over-crowded, slum dwellings. Now the street brims with displays of artworks, handi-crafts, and sculptures.

One of the colorful buildings flanking El Caminito

PLAZA SAN MARTÍN AND RETIRO

I t is hard to imagine that this commuter-filled area was once a "retreat" for 17th-century monks. Later, slave markets and military barracks were established here, and huge armies were readied for the Independence Wars in the early 19th century. The proximity of railway

Monument of José de San Martín

stations and passenger and cargo ports made Retiro a natural hub of commerce. Fortunately, Plaza San Martín provides a shaded refuge in the heart of the hustle and bustle. The plaza is lined with the twin splendors of *ombú* trees and the marble homage to San Martín by renowned French sculptor, Louis Joseph Daumas.

SIGHTS AT A GLANCE

Historical Sites, Buildings, and Plazas
Círculo Militar ❸
Edificio Kavanagh ❻
Estación Retiro ❽
Galerías Pacífico ❺
Monumento a los
   Caídos en Malvinas ❶
Palacio Haedo ❹

Palacio San Martín ❷
Plaza Embajada de Israel ❿
Torre de los Ingleses ❼

Museums and Galleries
Museo de la Shoá ⓫
Museo Municipal de Arte
   Hispanoamericano IFB ❾

GETTING AROUND
The main railroad station here is Estación Retiro, while the Subte stations are Retiro, San Martín, and Catalinas. The area is easy to explore on foot, although most of the sites are also accessible by bus.

KEY

   Street-by-Street map *pp88–9*

Ⓢ Subte station

🚉 Railroad station

⛪ Church

SEE ALSO

• *Where to Stay* p276

• *Where to Eat* p293

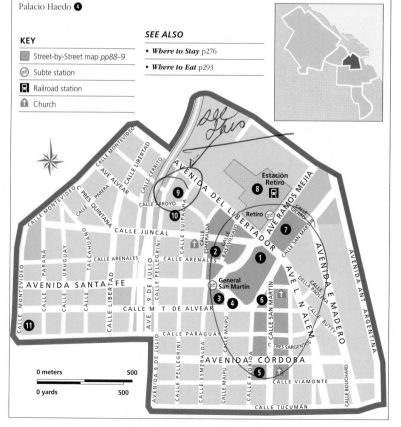

Street-by-Street: Plaza San Martín

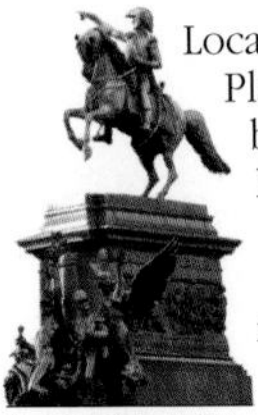

Statue of Jose San Martín in the plaza

Located in the distinguished Retiro barrio, Plaza San Martín is known for its beautiful buildings, which owe a clear debt to French and Italian architecture. Lining the plaza are the famous Círculo Militar, Palacio Haedo, and Palacio San Martín, remnants of the city's prosperous belle époque era in the late 19th and early 20th centuries. The area is a commercial hub and offers some of the capital's best shopping. With its grassy lawns and tree-lined avenues, the plaza is a popular outdoor leisure spot with porteños.

★ Galerías Pacífico
Built in the 1890s, this grand shopping mall is famous for its chic shops and frescoes by leading Argentinian artists ❺

Centro Naval
This beaux-arts beauty, built in 1914, was meant to reflect the nobility of the naval profession. The wonderfully ornate and striking doors are noteworthy.

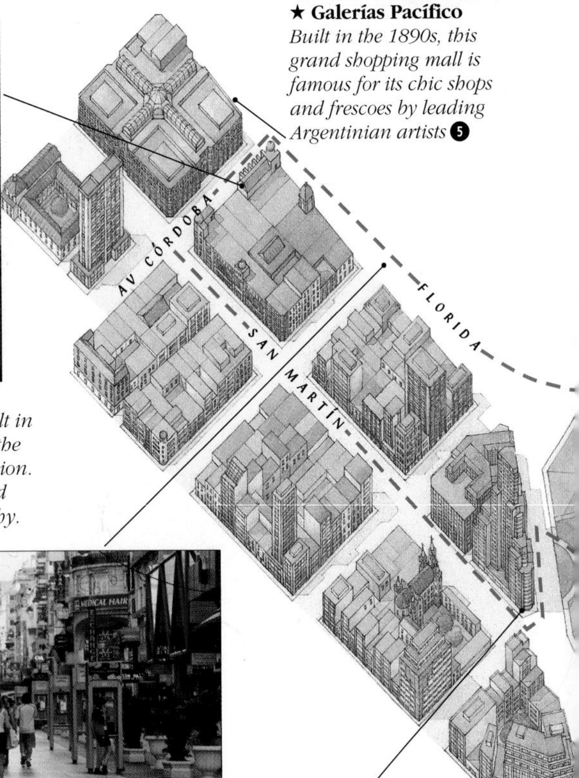

Calle Florida
The city's most famous street, Calle Florida is celebrated by poets, tango singers, and shoppers alike. It is home to the Jockey Club and the elegant Confitería Richmond.

STAR SIGHTS

★ Galerías Pacífico

★ Edificio Kavanagh

★ Palacio San Martín

★ Edificio Kavanagh
Known as a modernist masterpiece, this residential tower block was built in the 1930s. Standing at 395 ft (120 m), it was for a time the tallest building in South America ❻

Círculo Militar
Built between 1902 and 1914 as the mansion of the aristocratic Paz family, this marble edifice, modeled on palaces in France's Loire Valley, is now owned by the society of retired military officers who bought this grand building in 1938 ❸

Palacio Haedo
Once the residence of the elite Haedo family, this neo-Gothic palace is now used as the headquarters of the National Parks administration ❹

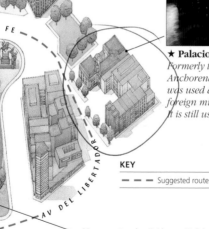

AV SANTA FE

★ Palacio San Martín
Formerly the palatial home of the wealthy Anchorena family, this opulent structure was used as the headquarters for the foreign ministry between 1936 and 1989. It is still used for ceremonial purposes ❷

AV DEL LIBERTADOR

KEY

– – – Suggested route

Monumento a los Caídos en Malvinas is a somber black wall unveiled in 1990. It honors the 649 soldiers who died in the 1982 Falklands conflict ❶

Estación
Retiro

Torre de los Ingleses
This handsome redbrick Palladian clock tower was presented to Buenos Aires by the city's English expatriate community in 1916 ❼

| 0 meters | 100 |
| 0 yards | 100 |

Monumento a los Caídos en Malvinas for soldiers lost in the Falklands War

Monumento a los Caídos en Malvinas ❶

Plaza San Martín. **City Map** 3 E3. 🚇 Retiro. 🚌 130, 152, 93.

Located at the foot of the grassy slope that leads up to the busy Plaza San Martín, Monumento a los Caídos en Malvinas is a cenotaph made up of 25 somber black marble plaques. Inscribed on them are the names of the 649 Argentinian soldiers, seamen, and airmen who lost their lives in the 1982 conflict (*see p54*). A symbolical eternal flame burns over a map of the South Atlantic islands. Every morning the Argentinian flag is raised, and flies high through the day next to the monument. Soldiers in uniform, from the three branches of the military, perform the changing of the guard every two hours until 6pm.

Palacio San Martín ❷

Arenales 761. **City Map** 3 E3. **Tel** (011) 4819-8092. 🚇 Retiro, San Martín. 🚌 61, 93, 99, 130, 152. 📷 11am Thu, 3pm, 4pm, 5pm Fri.

Formerly known as the Anchorena Palace, Palacio San Martín was built by architect Alejandro Christophersen at the request of Mercedes Castellanos de Anchorena and her sons, once one of the richest landowning families in the city. Built between 1905 and 1909 in beaux-arts style, the palace is considered one of Argentina's finest historical monuments. It is located opposite Parque San Martín and made up of three linked houses set around a garden. Architectural features include an imposing gated entrance, fine ironwork, and the ornamental Salón Dorado, modeled on the Hall of Mirrors of the Palace of Versailles. The palace was acquired by the Ministry of Foreign Affairs in 1936. They used it for their headquarters until the offices moved to a building across the road on Calle Esmeralda. The Palacio San Martín is presently used mainly for ceremonies and social events, but it opens for guided tours.

The building also houses a good collection of pre-Hispanic American art and, in the garden, a piece of the broken Berlin Wall, gifted by German president Roman Herzog in 1999.

Exquisite stained glass at Palacio San Martín

Círculo Militar ❸

Ave Santa Fe 750. **City Map** 3 D3. **Tel** (011) 4311-1071. 🚇 Retiro, San Martín. 🚌 61, 93, 99, 130, 152. 📷 11am & 3pm Tue & Fri, 11am & 4pm Wed–Thu, 11am Sat. ♿ 🅿 www.circulomilitar.org **Museo de Armas de la Nación** ◻ 1–7pm Mon–Fri.

Formally named Palacio Paz and Palacio Retiro, the Círculo Militar is situated on the southwestern side of Plaza San Martín. Covering a plot of over 2.3 sq miles (6 sq km), the structure was built by French architect Louis-Marie Henri Sortais and commissioned by José Camilo Paz, founder of *La Prensa* newspaper. The elaborate building, which boasts several splendid ballrooms, took 12 years to complete and was not inaugurated until 1914, two years after Paz died. The Hall of Honor, covered in gilded bronze and marble, is now used for conferences. The main façade, on Avenida Santa Fé, was inspired by the Chateau de Chantilly in France. Since 1938, one wing of the palace has been occupied by an officer's club – the Círculo Militar – and another houses the **Museo de Armas de la Nación**, which has an excellent collection of over 2,000 exhibits relating to the military, including weapons and uniforms, some of which date back to the 12th century.

The extravagant entrance of the Círculo Militar

The interior of Galerías Pacífico topped by beautiful frescoes on its dome

Palacio Haedo ❹

Ave Santa Fe 690. **City Map** 3 E4.
Tel (011) 4311-0303. Retiro, San
Martín. 61, 93, 99, 130, 152.
9am–7pm Mon–Fri.

Built in 1880, this neo-Gothic
building was once the grand
residence of the Haedos.
They were one of the handful
of porteño families who
amassed great wealth in the
late 19th century, owing to
the boom in meat exports.

The building has since
passed through various
hands, but the current occu-
pants, the Asociación de
Parques Nacionales, have
been in residence since 1942.
The ground floor is open to
visitors, where leaflets on
Argentina's national parks
are handed out. The building
also houses the Biblioteca
Francisco P. Moreno.

Galerías Pacífico ❺

Florida 753. **City Map** 3 E4.
Tel (011) 5555-5110. Florida.
6, 93, 130, 152. 10am–
10pm Mon–Sat, noon–10pm Sun.
11:30am & 4:30pm Mon–Sat,
1pm & 4:30pm Sun.
www.galeriaspacifico.com.ar
Centro Cultural Borges 10am–
9pm Mon–Sat, noon–9pm Sun.
www.ccborges.org.ar

Located on Florida, one
of the city's busiest pedestrianized shopping streets,

Galerías Pacífico *(see p120)* is
a handsome shopping mall.
Built in 1889 by architects
Francisco Seeber and Emilio
Bunge as a one-stop empo-
rium for the city's elite, it was
reputedly inspired by the
famous Paris department store
Le Bon Marché. The building
was later taken over by state
railroad offices and became
known as Edificio Pacífico,
after the railroad line that ran
through Argentina to Chile
and the Pacific Coast. In 1945,
the structure was substantially
remodeled and a series of
striking frescoes by
Argentinian muralists Berni,
Castagnino, Colmeiro, and
Urruchúa were added to the
central cupola.

It wasn't until the early
1990s that the structure
was given an elegant
makeover for its
current function as
an upmarket shopping
mall and home of the
Centro Cultural Borges
arts center. Named
after the country's
most famous
literary icon,
this active
institute holds
international
painting and
photographic
exhibitions,
along with art
auctions and
experimental
dance and
music shows.

Edificio Kavanagh ❻

Florida 1065. **City Map** 3 E3.
San Martín, Retiro. 93 & 152.

This national landmark,
394 ft (120 m) tall, was South
America's tallest building
when it was completed in
1935, as well as the highest
reinforced concrete building
in the world. Edificio
Kavanagh was financed by
the Irish heiress Corina
Kavanagh, who was from a
wealthy ranching family, and
who reputedly used up her
entire inheritance in construc-
ting the edifice. The imposing
tower features symmet-
rical setbacks and
gradual surface
reductions, and the
style was hailed as
one of the world's
best examples of
the marriage
between Art Deco,
modernism, and
rationalism. With
integrated air
conditioning
and advanced
plumbing, the
105 apart-
ments in this
tower repre-
sented the
height of
technology
and func-
tionality in
their day.

**A view of the monolithic Edificio
Kavanagh from Plaza San Martín**

Torre de los Ingleses ❼

Plaza Fuerza Aérea Argentina.
City Map 3 E3. 🚇 *Retiro.* 🚌 *130, 93, 109, 140, 28, 106, 129, 152.*
⬜ *noon–7pm Wed–Sat.*

Presented to the nation as part of the centennial celebrations of the Revolución de Mayo in 1810 *(see p49)* by the Anglo-Argentinian community, Torre de los Ingleses (Tower of the English) was not inaugurated until 1916. Although the official name was changed to Torre Monumental in the wake of the 1982 conflict *(see p54)*, the local residents still know the tower by its original name.

The clock tower was British-designed and nearly all the building material was brought over from England. Built in Palladian style, the tower has ornate reliefs of the British and Argentinian coats of arms above its main entrance. Ascending the tower, the clock's pendulum stands at 128 ft (39 m) and has five bronze bells. Similar to the clock in Westminster Abbey in London, the tower clock also chimes on the quarter-hour. On the tip of the clock tower is the weathercock, which is in the form of an Elizabethan sailing ship. The balcony offers splendid views of the surrounding area, including the park in which the clock tower stands. The building has been renovated and is now used as a tourist office providing information on the museums in Buenos Aires. The gazebo, however, is closed to the public for safety reasons.

Grand main hall of Retiro Mitre on Avenida Ramos Mejía

Estación Retiro ❽

Ave Ramos Mejía 1550. **City Map** 3 E3. **Tel** (011) 4310-0700. 🚇 *Retiro.* 🚌 *130, 106, 129, 93.*

Standing beside each other on Avenida Ramos Mejía, three busy railway terminals, Retiro Mitre, Retiro Belgrano, and Retiro San Martín make up the Estación Retiro complex. Of the three, the British-designed Retiro Mitre is the biggest and most architecturally significant. At the time of its construction, it was one of the largest stations in the world. It opened in 1915 and is reminiscent of grand old European stations with a French-style cupola and an English framework. A plaque on the steel structure reads Francis Morton & Co. Ltd., Liverpool. The central hall is an impressive space and contains a distinctive light-green circular ticket area. Retiro station used to be the main terminal for services to Córdoba

and the Andean Northwest between the 1900s and the late 1940s when Perón nationalized the British-run rail system at great cost to the state.

Now, a large map near the entrance of the station shows Argentina's once extensive but now much-depleted rail network. The station serves as a terminal for short-distance trains from Buenos Aires province, including the popular line to the delta town of Tigre *(see pp116–17)*. Next to the Retiro station is the city's large and bustling main bus terminal.

Museo Municipal de Arte Hispanoamericano Isaac Fernández Blanco ❾

Suipacha 1422. **City Map** 3 D3. **Tel** (011) 4327-0272. 🚇 *Retiro, General San Martín.* 🚌 *59, 61, 93.* ⬜ *2–7pm Tue–Sun.* 📷 🎫 *3pm Sat (in Spanish).*

Located in a gorgeous 1922 baroque mansion known as Palacio Noel after its architect Martín Noel, this museum houses a significant collection of Spanish American art, silverware, furniture, and religious artifacts dating from the colonial period to the era of independence. The museum first opened to the public in 1910 in the home of Isaac Fernández Blanco, a wealthy aristocrat. Opened with Blanco's personal collection of art and artifacts, it was the first such private museum in Argentina. When Fernández Blanco and his family moved out in 1921, he gave over his mansion completely to the museum, and donated it to the city. Until his death in 1928, he continued to buy and donate objects to the collection. In 1947, the

Jesuit statue exhibit

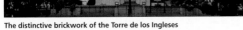

The distinctive brickwork of the Torre de los Ingleses

Museo Municipal de Arte Hispanoamericano Isaac Fernández Blanco

Museo de la Shoá ⓫

Montevideo 919. **City Map** 2 C4.
Tel (011) 4811-3588. 🚌 59.
⬜ 11am–7pm Mon–Thu, 10am–
4pm Fri. ⬛ Sat, Sun. 🎦 🎦 only
Spanish. **www**.fmh.org.ar

Set up by the local Fundación
Memoria del Holocausto in
1999, the Museo de la Shoá
is dedicated to preserving the
memory of people who died
in the Holocaust. It traces the
background of the Holocaust
from pre-war Jewish life in
Europe and the rise of Nazi
power, to the Resistance, the
Final Solution, and the survivors' search for a home in the
aftermath. Along with the
accounts of these tragic events
unfolding in Europe, the exhibition also explores the difficult lives of Jewish families in
Argentina, and the
country's social and
political responses
to them. The exhi-
bition includes a
section on the Nazi
war criminals who
were in hiding in
Argentina. The
explanatory texts
are in Spanish but
the exhibition,
including strong
visual elements,
allow the visitor to follow the
stories and incidents through
an abundant collection of
photographs and an array of
historical texts, maps, and
other related objects. The
museum also has a clear and
strong educational agenda
on the topics of racism, anti-
Semitism, and xenophobia.

museum's collection was
moved to its current location
in the Palacio Noel, merging
with the Museo Colonial
that was already based in
the Palacio.

The museum also acquired
items from a third municipal
museum to add to its exhibits.
The original collection has
been expanded over the years
with a variety of purchases
and donations, with the most
significant by Celina González
Garaño, who donated around
750 items in 1963. The most
outstanding items in the
museum, include more than
100 beautiful antique dolls.
The vast collection of
colonial-era silverware is
thought to be the most
significant of its kind in the
world. There is also Luso-
Brazilian furniture, porcelain,
decorative arts, pretty costumes, and elegant tapestries.
The mansion itself is a joy
to explore, especially the
tranquil Andalusian-style
patio which is decorated
with ivy and shaded by
centenarian trees.

Plaza Embajada de Israel ⓾

Calle Arroyo, corner Suipacha.
City Map 3 D3. 🚇 Retiro. 🚌 59.

Not much remains on the site
of Plaza Embajada de Israel
after a truck, driven by a
suicide bomber, smashed into
the Israeli embassy. The blast
killed 29 people and
wounded hundreds more
on March 17, 1992 *(see p25)*.
A nearby church and school
were also destroyed
in the tragic inci-
dent. A memorial
plaza has been set
up near the site –
it comprises seven
benches and 22
trees planted in
rows of two, each
standing for the
memory of the
victims of the blast.
Informative plaques
explain the details
of the horrific event and list
the names of the victims in
both Hebrew and Spanish.

A scarred and ruined
embassy wall has been left as
it was after the explosion and
it stands in stark contrast to
the ornate museums around it.
At night, the embassy wall is
beautifully lit up.

**Eichmann exhibit,
Museo de la Shoá**

Photos of Jewish victims of the Holocaust, Museo de la Shoá

RECOLETA

Only a street away from the traffic hubs and port depots of Retiro, Recoleta is altogether another world. This area was adopted by upper-class porteños after yellow fever broke out in San Telmo in 1871. Since then it has blossomed into a model of bourgeois refinement with old masters at the Museo Nacional de Bellas Artes and book signings at Centro Cultural Recoleta.

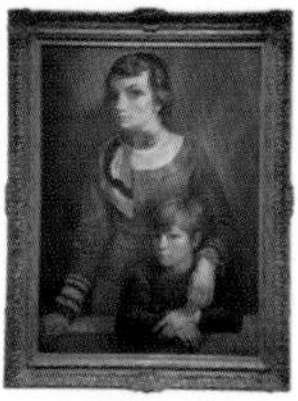

A painting by Lino Spilimbergo, Museo Nacional de Bellas Artes

Visitors can roam the labyrinth of Cementerio de la Recoleta or watch canines being pampered by hired walkers in the parks. In recent years, a hippy market has established itself in the area and attracts visitors from less wealthy districts, but for all its new found democratic appeal, Recoleta shimmers with old-style glamor and appeals as much for its inaccessible wealth as its accessible pleasures.

SIGHTS AT A GLANCE

Historical Sites and Buildings

Alvear Palace Hotel 5
Biblioteca Nacional 8
Café La Biela 4
Cementerio de la Recoleta (pp100–1) 3
Centro Cultural Recoleta 2
Iglesia de Nuestra Señora del Pilar 1
Palais de Glace 6

Museums and Galleries

Museo Casa de Ricardo Rojas 9
Museo Nacional de Bellas Artes 7
Museo Xul Solar 10

GETTING AROUND

Most sights are fairly well-concentrated and can easily be explored by foot. The two museums farther away, including Museo Xul Solar, are best reached by bus or Subte stations Pueyrredón and Agüero, which are close by.

KEY

Street-by-street map *pp96–7*
Subte station
Church

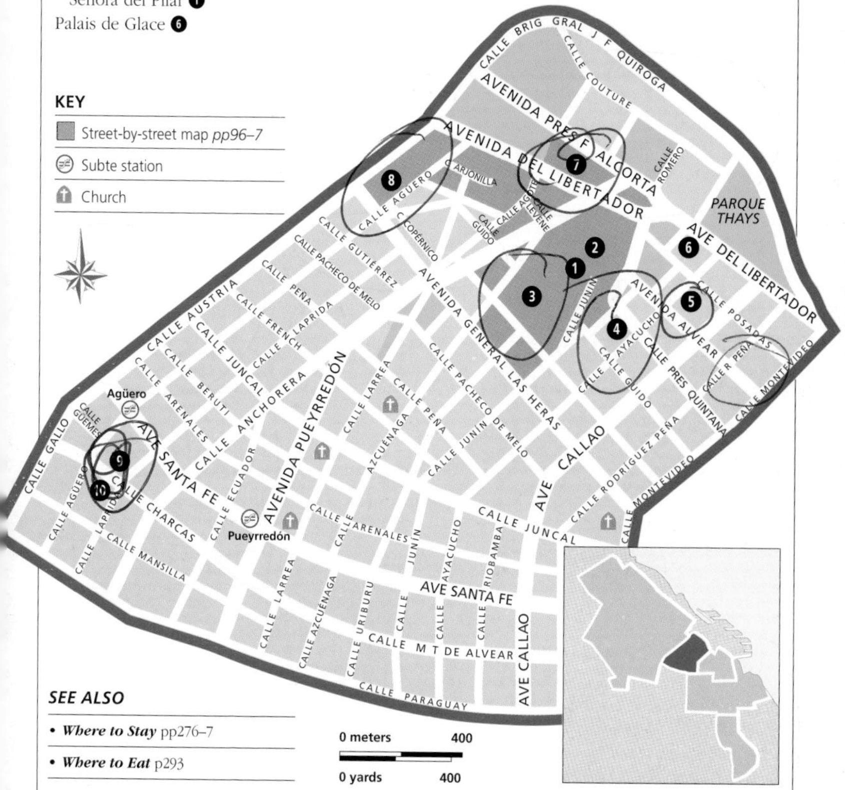

SEE ALSO

• ***Where to Stay*** pp276–7

• ***Where to Eat*** p293

◁ One of the many grand tombs at Cementerio de la Recoleta

Street-by-Street: Recoleta

Recoleta stretches from downtown Buenos Aires
to Calle Austria, but its heart is to be found in the
cluster of leafy plazas and public buildings that
surround the barrio's famous cemetery. The area
has grand apartment buildings built in the early
1900s and boasts of Café La Biela, one of the
smartest and most famous *confiterías* in town.
Also located here is the national fine arts museum,
a lively cultural center, a five-star hotel, and a
beautiful old church. The capital's early 20th-
century Francophile aspirations are evident in the
barrio's architecture and in the name of the best-
known green space in the area – Plaza Francia.

★ Cementerio de la Recoleta
*This labyrinthine necropolis is
the resting place of many presidents, military heroes, and well-
known patrician families* ❸

Iglesia de Nuestra Señora del Pilar
*Consecrated in 1732, this Spanish-style
church houses a superlative baroque altar
featuring a wrought-silver frontal* ❶

**Centro Cultural
Recoleta**
*This sprawling
complex, also known
as Centro Cultural
de Buenos Aires,
is dedicated to
promoting contem-
porary Argentinian
music, theater,
and film* ❷

Café
La Biela

Alvear
Palace
Hotel

Palais de Glace
*Opened by the aristocrat Baron de
Marchi in the 1920s, the one-time ice
rink and ballroom is now an excellent
arts-focused exhibition center. Legend
has it that tango star Carlos Gardel
was shot here by a jealous rival* ❻

Biblioteca Nacional
Designed by three prominent local architects, the Biblioteca Nacional took almost 30 years to complete. When it finally opened in 1992, it was hailed as a brutalist masterpiece. The Peróns' house used to stand at this spot ⓼

0 meters 100

0 yards 100

Plaza Francia
Surrounded by a French-style residential area, this dramatic monument to Liberty was presented to the nation by France in 1910.

★ Museo Nacional de Bellas Artes
Formerly a water-pumping station, this neoclassical building houses Argentina's most important collection of art. As well as a strong permanent display, there are many temporary exhibitions ⓻

KEY

--- Suggested route

STAR SIGHTS

★ Cementerio de la Recoleta

★ Museo Nacional de Bellas Artes

Plaza Intendente Alvear
Named for the mayor who gave the capital a major overhaul a century ago, this sloped plaza is now the site of one of the most popular weekend arts and handicraft markets.

The exquisite baroque altar at the Iglesia de Nuestra Señora del Pilar

Iglesia de Nuestra Señora del Pilar ❶

Junín 1904. **City Map** 2 C2.
Tel (011) 4803-6793. 🚌 10, 17, 60, 92, 110. ⏱ varies. ✝ 7:50am, 11am, & 7:30pm Mon–Fri; 8:30am, 11am & 7pm Sat; 8:30am, 10am, 11am, noon, 7pm, 8pm, & 9pm Sun.
www.basilicadelpilar.org.ar

Donated to the monks of Recoleta in 1716 by Zaragoza-born entrepreneur Don Juan de Narbona, this church takes its name from Zaragoza's patron saint, Señora del Pilar (Virgin of Pilar). Jesuit architect Andrés Blanqui built it along the lines of a classic Spanish church of the period. Refinements, including an exterior clock made in Britain and *pas-de-Calais* ceramic tiles, were added later.

The exterior murals are inspired by the work of Spanish painter Fernando Brambilia, an 18th-century specialist in perspective. They show a panoramic view of the river and recount the history of the church as well as the area. Inside is a beautiful baroque altar, featuring Inca motifs, which was brought along the Camino Real mule-train route from Peru. The church is often open between services, and visitors can wander down into the crypt and see a small but interesting collection of religious art contained in one of the adjoining cloisters.

Centro Cultural Recoleta ❷

Junín 1930. **City Map** 2 C2.
Tel (011) 4803-1040. 🚌 10, 17, 60, 92, 110. ⏱ 2–9pm Tue–Fri, 10am–9pm Sat & Sun. ♿ 🎫 **www**.centroculturalrecoleta.org

This complex of buildings dates from the 17th century and is one of the oldest in the city. The plot was donated to the monks of Recoleta in 1716 and Jesuit architects Juan Krauss and Juan Wolf drew up the plans. Andrés Blanqui is thought to have worked on the façade and interiors of the on-site monastery. During the 19th century the building served as an art school founded by liberation hero General Manuel Belgrano, and also as a refuge for the local homeless.

The Recoleta barrio became popular with the middle-classes in the 1870s. During this time, the first mayor of Buenos Aires, Torcuato de Alvear, began a campaign to Europeanize and embellish the city and this prime chunk of real estate was reclaimed

Centro Cultural Recoleta, venue of exciting artistic experimentation

for the barrio. Architect Juan Buschiazzo was responsible for the refurbishment, adding the pavilions, elegant Italianate terraces, and a chapel, which is now an auditorium. After a brief period as a home for the elderly, the complex was remodeled in 1980 and became the Centro Cultural Recoleta (CCR).

The barrio may be ultrabourgeois, but there is nothing conservative about the schedule of art events that take place at this sprawling cultural center. About 20 galleries are used for stimulating visual arts exhibitions, various theatrical works, and film projections. A number of small dance and theater companies use the CCR as a rehearsal space.

Cementerio de la Recoleta ❸

See pp100–1.

Café La Biela ❹

Avenida Quintana 596. **City Map** 2 C2. **Tel** (011) 4804-0449. 🚌 59, 60, 101, 102, 110. ⏱ 7–3am daily. ♿ **www**.labiela.com/eng/menu.htm

If it lacks the atmosphere and artistic ghosts of the grand Café Tortoni (*see p68*), La Biela still has a certain old-world appeal. The terrace could be housed in the streets of Rome or Paris, except perhaps for the tentacle-like branches of the ancient gum tree that cast a cool, leafy

A contemporary installation at the Centro Cultural Recoleta

For hotels and restaurants in this region see pp276–7 and p293

THE DOGS OF RECOLETA

It is common for wealthy Recoleta families, living in an apartment without the required open space, to hire a *paseadores* (a professional dog-walker). Since it became fashionable during the 1970s to own a pure-breed mutt – huskies, chows, and rare breeds are particularly desirable – wealthier porteño families have paid a young, usually male, person to walk their dog. There is great demand for the service, and every employee will happily walk between ten and 25 dogs, looking rather like a maypole at the center of dancing, dueling, and occasionally knotting, ribbons. Recoleta's wide, green spaces and Palermo's lovely Parque 3 de Febrero are the preferred rest stops, as they are located close to the dogs' palatial homes and are ideal for a run in the open. Unfortunately, there is little control of dog dirt and since the scoops are shunned by walkers and well-to-do owners alike, visitors should check carefully before sitting and spreading their picnic on the grass.

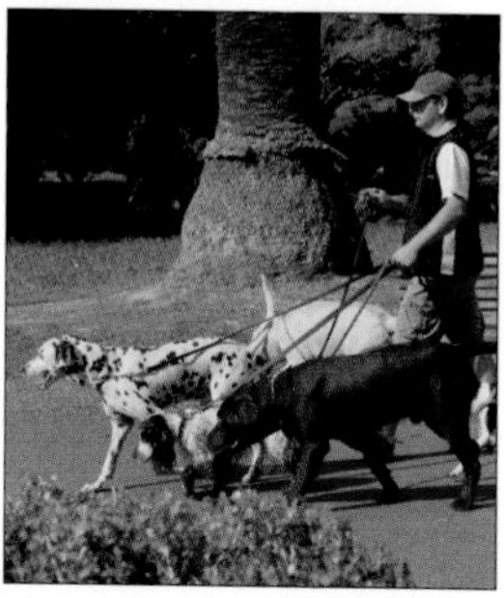

A busy afternoon for a local walker

shade. Super-efficient waiters come and go, carrying weighty silver trays of *masitas* (fine pastries) and perfectly machined cups of espresso. There has been a café on this corner since the early 1850s but La Biela became what it is today during the 1950s when racing-car drivers met here for their post-race drinks. Monochrome photographs hanging on the inside walls hark back to this period. Nowadays it is a favorite for people-watchers, wealthy tourists, and artists who moved into Recoleta before estate prices sky-rocketed.

Alvear Palace Hotel [5]

Avenida Alvear 1891. **City Map** 3 D2. ***Tel*** *(011) 4808-2100.* 🚌 *67, 93, 130.* ♿ 🖥 🛍 **www**.alvearpalace.com

Built in 1923, the Alvear is considered by many to be Buenos Aires's only truly grand hotel *(see p276).* Occupying a city block where the British Embassy used to stand, the grand 16-floor building (five of them are subterranean) is a monument to Francophilia both inside and out. It is a lasting emblem of the city's aspiration to be seen as the "Paris of South America." This luxury hotel has modernized its facilities by adding a spa and keeping its restaurants at the cutting edge of culinary fashion. Fortunately this has been done without losing any of its romance or sacrificing the impeccable personal service that the richest and most powerful visitors to the city expect. Over the years, these guests have included Spanish kings, Japanese emperors, American presidents, as well as just about every journalist and media boss from all around the world.

The bars and restaurants are popular and open to the public. The most pleasant is the lovely glass-roofed L'Orangerie, where guests can indulge in a lavish breakfast spread out beneath the streaming rays of the morning sun. Also highly rated is the La Bourgogne restaurant.

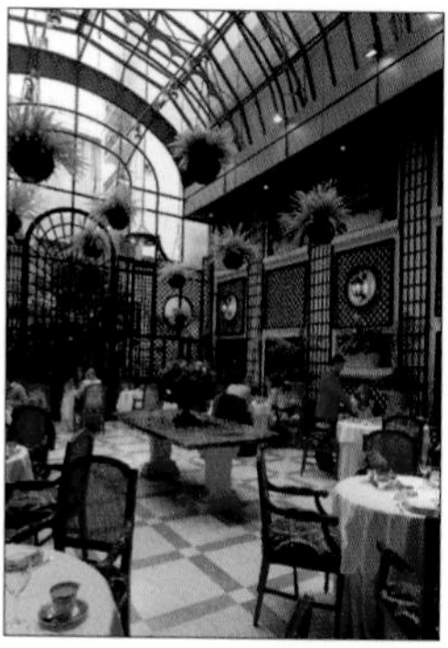

The glass-roofed L'Orangerie restaurant, Alvear Palace Hotel

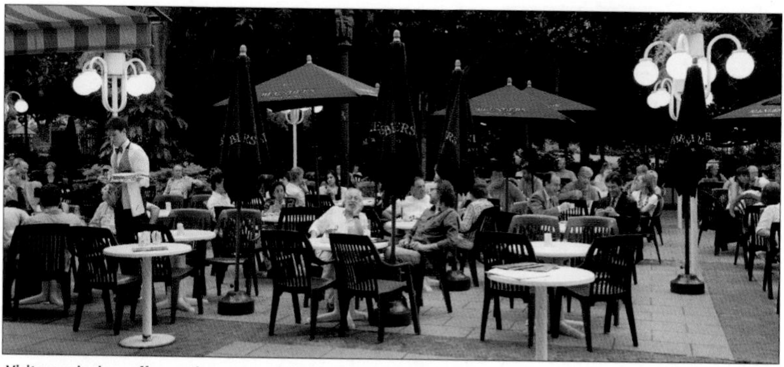

Visitors enjoying coffee on the terrace of the bustling Café La Biela

Cementerio de la Recoleta ③

One of the world's great necropolises, Cementerio de Recoleta occupies an area of 14 acres (5.5 ha), easily the size of an entire city block. Argentina's first president Bernadino Rivadavia commissioned French architect Próspero Catelin to design the cemetery, which opened in 1822. It boasts wide leafy avenues, narrow, marble-walled streets, smart, polished façades, and small, dark alleys. There are more than 6,400 tombs and mausoleums in the cemetery, 70 of which are recognized as National Historic Monuments. The architecture is eclectic, ranging from bombastic Greco-Roman mini-palaces to wedding-cake style experiments in Romanticism to earthy-looking piles of stones.

One of the central tree-lined avenues of the cemetery

Narrow Lanes
These are laid out in a grid fashion, replicating the city beyond, and turning the quiet necropolis into a marble labyrinth – cold, impenetrable, and slightly eerie.

Tomb of Sáenz Peña, a former president.

VICENTE LÓPEZ STREET

José Hernández's Tomb
Author of the national poetry epic, Martín Fierro, Hernandez is one of several writers to have a tomb among the rich and powerful. He is laid to rest in an elegant white mausoleum.

Tomb of Bartolomé Mitre, a former president and the founder of *La Nación*.

JUNÍN STREET

★ Eva Perón's Tomb
A simple black stone affair, the tomb attracts a large number of pilgrims and tourists, all of whom pause to read a plaque with an extract from her famous "I will be millions" speech.

STAR SIGHTS

★ Eva Perón's Tomb

★ The Paz Family Tomb

The many grand tomb structures forming a miniature cityscape

VISITORS' CHECKLIST

Avenida Quintana & Junín 1760.
City Map 2 C2. 🚌 17, 61,62,
67, 92, 93, & 110. 🛈 cnr Ave
Quintana and Junín 1760, (011)
4803-1594. 🕐 8am–5:45pm
daily. 📷 11am Tue & Thu.

KEY

– – – Suggested route

Julio Argentino Roca's Tomb
*A general in the army during the
1870s, Roca led the Conquest of the
Desert campaign (see p50). He was
president of the Argentinian republic
from 1880 to 1886 and 1898 to 1904.*

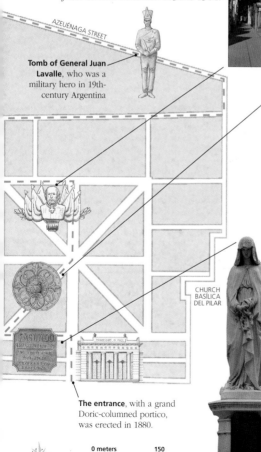

AZEUÉNAGA STREET

**Tomb of General Juan
Lavalle**, who was a
military hero in 19th-
century Argentina

CHURCH
BASÍLICA
DEL PILAR

★ **The Paz Family Tomb**
*José C. Paz was a diplomat,
Congressman, and the founder
of* La Prensa *newspaper. The
family tomb is a grand edifice
carved in white stone.*

Facundo Quiroga's Tomb
*Nicknamed "Tiger of the
Plains," the assassinated
gaucho caudillo (see p185)
has a tomb adorned by a
dolorosa (weeping Virgin)
carved by Milanese sculptor
Antonio Tantardini.*

The entrance, with a grand
Doric-columned portico,
was erected in 1880.

0 meters 150

0 yards 150

Palais de Glace ❻

Posadas 1725. **City Map** 3 D2.
Tel (011) 4804-1163. 🚌 17, 61, 62,
67, 92, 124, 130. ⏱ 2–8pm
Tue–Sun. 🎫 4pm & 6pm Sat & Sun.
🖥 www.palaisdeglace.org

Officially known as the
National Palace of the Arts,
the Palais de Glace (Palace
of Ice) was inaugurated in
1910. It was initially designed
to hold an ice-skating rink,
modeled closely on Paris's
own Palais de Glace.

The ice rink idea did not
prove popular and in 1915
the palace became a tango
ballroom and during the
1920s, it was the city's key
party venue. In 1931, the
building was donated to the
Fine Arts Institute and became
an art gallery. From 1954 to
1960 it was used as a television studio for the channel
Canal Siete. The palace was
later converted back into an
art gallery and declared a
National Monument in 2004.

The Palais de Glace, with
its crowned columns and
vaulted dome, can be enjoyed
as one of the finest examples
of Parisian-style architecture
in the city. It is also an important exhibition space for
national and international
shows which include photography, paintings, and sculpture. The palace hosts the
annual Antiques Fair organized
by the Association of Friends
of the National Museum of
Decorative Arts. It is still held
in high regard for its historic
contribution to tango.

The severe neoclassical façade of Museo Nacional de Bellas Artes

Museo Nacional de Bellas Artes ❼

Avenida del Libertador 1473.
City Map 2 C2. **Tel** (011) 4803-
0802. 🚌 67, 93, 130. ⏱ 12:30–
7:30pm Tue–Fri, 9:30am–7:30pm
Sat, Sun, & public holidays. 🎫 5 &
6pm daily (Spanish only). 🖥 📷
www.mnba.org.ar

In 1932, Argentina's National
Fine Arts Museum moved to
occupy one of the city's major
waterworks facilities, where it
has remained ever since. The
interior was completely
remodeled under the super-
vision of Alejandro Bustillo,
one of the country's greatest
architects. The neoclassical
façade has changed little
since the original facility
opened in 1870. Apart from
some subsequent expansion
and renovation work, the
museum, with its spacious
and well-lit salons, remains
much as it was when President
Justo cut the ribbon in 1933.

Currently the museum
comprises 34 exhibition
rooms divided over three
sprawling floors. There are
more than 12,000 works in
the permanent collection,
although only 700 can be
displayed at any one time.
The specialist art library, also
open to the public, contains
more than 150,000 volumes.

The collection housed in
the Museo Nacional de Bellas
Artes is one of the most out-
standing in South America.
On display are works by
many of the canonical figures
in art history, including Goya,
Rubens, Rembrandt, El Greco,
Rodin, Klee, Renoir, Degas,
Picasso, and Toulouse-Lautrec.
The exhibits also include

some of the most famous
names in Argentinian art,
including Antonio Berni,
Xul Solar, Leon Ferrari, Raquel
Forner, Prilidiano Pueyrredón,
Fernando Fader, and Antonio
Seguí, represented by some
of their best-known and most
influential works. The influences of European art are
vividly apparent in the
Argentinian works, but the
divergences the artists make
to illustrate the local view-
point are interesting. For
example, a painter like Berni
used the techniques of social
realism to specifically portray
his own unique criollo (mixed
race) environment.

The museum is gradually
shaking off its reputation
as a cautious, hidebound
institution. In 2004 it opened
its first branch in the
Patagonian city of Neuquén,
and in 2005 it added a permanent display of pre-Columbian
art. Audio tours and a well-
stocked bookshop have
helped make it an excellent
modern museum.

The elegant space of the Palais de
Glace now used for art exhibitions

Retrato de Manuelita Rosas (1840)
by Prilidiano Pueyrredón

Biblioteca Nacional ❽

Agüero 2502. **City Map** 2 B2.
Tel (011) 4808-6000. 🚌 60, 95, 130.
ℹ️ photo ID required for entry. ⬜
Feb–Dec: 9am–9pm Mon–Fri, noon–
7pm Sat & Sun. ⬤ Jan. 🗓 3pm Mon,
Tue, & Thu. ♿ 📧 www.bn.gov.ar

One of the largest libraries in the Americas, Argentina's Biblioteca Nacional houses a vast collection exceeding two million volumes. Books, journals, and important historical manuscripts are stored in its huge underground vaults. These include a first edition of *Don Quixote*, the personal literary collection of General Belgrano, and a 1455 Gutenberg Bible. The library's most treasured possessions are books that were printed before 1501. Among these pieces are works by Saint Augustine, Dante, and Cicero.

The building itself is none too glamorous; built on the site of the palace where the Peróns lived, it is a T-shaped slab of poured concrete that flaunts its functionality in classic brutalist style. Architecturally very popular when conceived in the 1960s, the look was slightly dated by the time it finally opened to the public in 1992. The position of library director has been held by novelist Jose Marmol, historian Paul Groussac, and most famously, author Jorge Luis Borges, all of whom went blind during their terms.

Museo Casa de Ricardo Rojas ❾

Charcas 2837. **City Map** 2 B3.
Tel (011) 4824-4039. 🚇 Agüero.
🚌 39, 68, 152. ⬜ 9am–7pm
Mon–Fri. 🗓 3pm daily. ♿

This beautiful dwelling, set rather incongruously amid the residential high-rises of Barrio Norte, was the home of the notable writer and pedagog Ricardo Rojas from 1929 until

The personal library of Ricardo Rojas decorated with Inca symbols

his death in 1957. The house was donated to the country by his widow and opened as a museum in 1958. Rojas remained fascinated by the relationship between pre-Columbian and colonial America, which he conceived as a dialog as well as a clash of cultures. Built with a mix of Spanish and Inca styles, the house was designed to embody this doctrine. This is particularly evident in the patio and cloisters, where the columns are decorated with various traditional Inca symbols. The façade mimics Casa Histórica in Tucumán city. Rojas's furnishings and household objects have also been well preserved, along with his personal library, which comprises more than 20,000 volumes. The museum

Literary icon Jorge Luis Borges

is a fascinating window not only into the mind, but also into the lifestyle of a brilliant writer-scholar.

Museo Xul Solar ❿

Laprida 1212. **City Map** 2 A3.
Tel (011) 4824-3302. 🚇 Agüero.
🚌 39, 68, 152. ⬜ noon–8pm
Tue–Fri, noon–7pm Sat. 🏷 🗓 4pm
Tue–Thu, 3:30pm Sat (prior arrangement for English). ♿ 🚫 📷
www.xulsolar.org.ar

Once the residence of the 19th-century porteño artist Xul Solar, this 20th-century townhouse has been converted into the excellent Museo Xul Solar. Described by Jorge Luis Borges as "one of the most singular events of our time," Xul Solar was an eccentric visionary. On display at the museum are his otherwordly paintings, done mainly in watercolor and tempera. His art seems to be a blend of ideas drawn from various sources such as Hieronymous Bosch, William Blake, and Jules Verne, while at the same time being entirely original. The cryptic landscapes he depicts are inhabited by angels, demons, and jesters, flying reptiles and machines, ladders that lead nowhere, and Sphinxes restyled as cave paintings. Solar takes the viewer through a very bizarre looking-glass world.

Apart from these paintings, the museum contains a range of equally bizarre objects from Solar's collection. These include quasi-scientific instruments, masks, and sculptures.

Display of Xul Solar's eccentric artwork at the Museo Xul Solar

PALERMO AND BELGRANO

The sprawling barrios of Palermo and Belgrano boast open spaces filled by parks, a racecourse, and the city zoo. Palermo grew in the late 19th century during the presidency of Sarmiento, who was responsible for the building of Jardín Botánico and Parque 3 de Febrero. Belgrano was named after Manuel Belgrano, a military leader who designed the country's national flag. These barrios are considered superior by most Argentinians for their many urban conveniences and museums, which include MALBA. Their parks are loved by porteños, who come en masse at weekends to walk, jog, or share a round of *mate* on the lawns.

***Eternal Spring* at Museo Arte**

SIGHTS AT A GLANCE

Historical Sites, Buildings, and Plazas

Belgrano 17
Campo Argentino de Polo 11
Cementerio de la Chacarita 18
Centro Cultural Islámico Rey Fahd 12
Escuela de Mecánica de la Armada 14
Hipódromo Argentino de Palermo 10
La Rural 13
Las Cañitas 15
Plaza Serrano 19

Parks and Gardens

Jardín Botánico 5
Jardín Japonés 3
Jardín Zoológico 4
Parque 3 de Febrero 1

Museums and Galleries

Museo Argentino de Ciencias Naturales 20
Museo de Arte Latinoamericano de Buenos Aires (MALBA) pp110–11 7
Museo de Arte Popular 8
Museo de Artes Plásticas 2
Museo Evita 6
Museo Nacional de Arte Decorativo 9
Museo Nacional del Hombre 16

KEY

- Subte station
- Railroad station
- Hospital
- Church

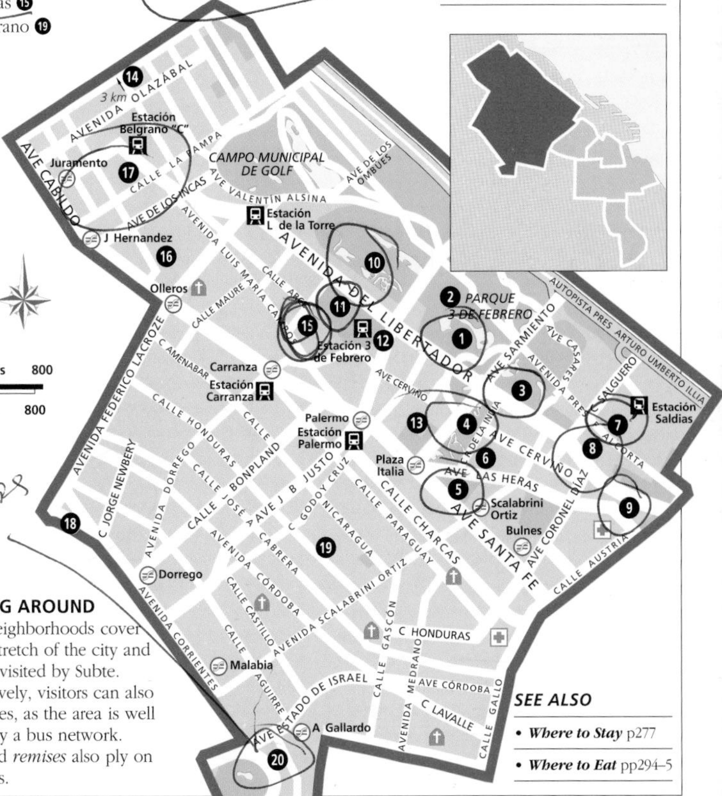

GETTING AROUND

These neighborhoods cover a large stretch of the city and are best visited by Subte. Alternatively, visitors can also take buses, as the area is well served by a bus network. Taxis and *remises* also ply on the roads.

SEE ALSO

- ***Where to Stay*** p277
- ***Where to Eat*** pp294–5

◁ **Jacaranda in bloom, Parque 3 de Febrero**

Contemporary art displays at the Museo de Artes Plásticas Eduardo Sívori

The museum covers a huge range of styles and media, including the academic naturalism of Sívori and the Impressionist landscapes of Ramón Silva and Walter de Navazio. Works displayed span the postimpressionist and Cubist periods, all the way to Surrealism, Pop Art, and Hyperrealism. The museum moved to its current picturesque home, not far from the Rosedal at Parque 3 de Febrero, in 1995, and now has a small shop, sculpture garden, and café.

Parque 3 de Febrero ❶

Avenida Adolfo Berro. **City Map** 5 E2 🚇 *Palermo, Lisando de la Torre.* 🚇 *Palermo, Plaza Italia.* 🚌 *10, 34, 36, 37, 67, 130.*

The capital's largest and most popular park, Parque 3 de Febrero is also known as the Bosques de Palermo (Palermo Woods). In the 19th century, the land was owned by Argentinian dictator Juan Manuel de Rosas. Following his defeat by General Urquiza in the Battle of Caseros on February 3, 1852, all his land was confiscated and earmarked for public use. In 1874, the site was converted into a park styled after Paris's Bois de Boulogne and London's Hyde Park and named Parque 3 de Febrero, after the Battle of Caseros. French landscape architect Charles Thays was responsible for the design of the park, as well as that of the nearby Jardín Botánico. It was inaugurated in 1875 by President Nicolás Avellaneda.

Apart from beautifully tended lawns, the park contains a variety of attractions that include a spherical planetarium and the Velódromo Municipal, which was opened in 1951 for the Pan-American Games. Most popular is the Rosedal, a rose garden designed by landscape architect Benito Carrasco, which features about 12,000 rose bushes, a boating lake with pedalos and rowing boats, a wooden bridge, and pergola. The space also has a Poet's Garden, with busts of famous poets, among them Jorge Luis Borges, Federico García Lorca, and Shakespeare.

Among the monuments in the park are the Monumento a los Españoles, erected as part of the centenary celebrations of the Revolución de Mayo in 1810 (*see p49*); Auguste Rodin's monument to Sarmiento; and a monument to General Urquiza. Over the weekends the sprawling park gets plenty of joggers, family picnickers, walkers, and bicyclists.

Bonsai plant at Jardín Japonés

Museo de Artes Plásticas Eduardo Sívori ❷

Avenida Infanta Isabel 555. **City Map** 5 E2. **Tel** *(011) 4774-9452.* 🚌 *10, 34, 36, 37, 67, 130.* ⏰ *noon–8pm Tue–Fri, 10am–8pm Sat & Sun.* ♿ 🅿 🛈 **www**.museo sivori.org.ar

The Museo de Artes Plásticas Eduardo Sívori houses a diverse and significant collection of over 4,000 pieces of art, among them drawings, paintings, sculptures, and tapestries, dating from the 19th century to the present day. The museum was founded in 1938 as the Museo Municipal de Bellas Artes, Artes Aplicadas y Anexo de Artes Comparadas, but was later renamed for the famous Buenos Aires artist Eduardo Sívori (1847–1918).

Jardín Japonés ❸

Avenida Casares and Avenida Berro. **City Map** 5 F3. **Tel** *(011) 4804-4922.* 🚌 *10, 34, 36.* ⏰ *10am–6pm daily.* ♿ 🅿 🛈 *3pm Sat (Spanish only).* 🍴 ♿ **www**.jardinjapones.com.ar

These peaceful and carefully maintained gardens were created in 1967 as a gift to the city by its sizeable Japanese community. They feature clear manmade lakes and islands. These are crisscrossed by pretty red wooden bridges, such as the curved Puente de la Buena Ventura, leading to the Isla de los Dioses (Island of the Gods). A wealth of flora flourishes here, much of which was imported from Japan, including sakura, ginkgo, and black pines. There are also giant koi carp

Koi Pond, one of the manmade lakes at the Jardín Japonés

in the lake, and ducks roaming the gardens. The pagoda houses a tearoom and a Japanese restaurant, and hosts many exhibitions and events. Within the park is the Campana de la Paz, the bell that is sounded every year to celebrate World Peace Day on September 21.

Jardín Zoológico ❹

Avenida Sarmiento and Avenida Las Heras. **City Map** 5 E3. *Tel (011) 4011-9900.* 🚇 *Palermo.* 🚌 *Plaza Italia.* 🚌 *15, 36, 37, 60, 152.* ⭕ *10am–6pm Tue–Sun.* 🎟 *free for children under 12.* ♿ **www.**zoobuenosaires.com.ar

Located at this site since 1888, this handsome city zoo started out with a total collection of 650 animals and 53 different species. Today, over 2,500

One of the elegant greenhouses at the Jardín Botánico

species, including 49 reptiles, 89 mammals, and 175 birds, inhabit the 44-acre (18-ha) site. The zoo's first director, Eduardo Ladislao Holmberg, played an important role in the design of the park, deciding to house the animals in buildings that reflect their country of origin. This makes for an interesting array of architectural styles, including a reproduction of an Indian temple, a French palace, and a Templo de Vesta with 16 Corinthian columns, as well as a range of sculptures and statues. Among the popular

Elephants at the Jardín Zoológico

attractions today are a reptilium, an aquarium, and a re-creation of a subtropical jungle. The areas are well labeled and the zoo has a strong conservation agenda.

Jardín Botánico ❺

Santa Fe 3951. **City Map** 5 E4. *Tel (011) 4831-4527.* 🚇 *Palermo.* 🚌 *Plaza Italia.* 🚌 *15, 36, 37, 60, 152.* ⭕ *9am–6pm daily.* 📷 *10:30am & 3pm Sat & Sun; 9pm on last Fri of the month.*

The city's elegant Botanical Gardens, opened in 1898, were designed by famous French landscape architect Charles Thays. He lived in a Tudor-style house in the gardens from 1892 to 1898 while he was the director of parks and public walkways. His house now contains a botanical library. The 17-acre (7-ha) site boasts over 5,500 species of plants from Argentina and around the world, and are organized by family, origin, and use.

Of the gardens' five greenhouses, the first and most significant was brought over from France from the 1900 Paris Exhibition. Built out of iron and glass in Art Nouveau style, the structure measures 3,000 sq ft (280 sq m), and houses tropical and subtropical species. In addition to its floral riches, the Jardín Botánico has a wealth of public art, including impressive sculptures, busts, and monuments. The park is also home to hundreds of feral cats.

JUAN MANUEL DE ROSAS (1793–1877)

This infamous figure rose to prominence as a leader of the patriotic gaucho armies who fought against the European expeditionary forces, following Argentinian Independence. In 1829, Rosas became governor of Buenos Aires and instigated campaigns to massacre the indigenous peoples of the southern Pampas. Rosas portrayed himself as a man of the people, but with his private paramilitary army, *la mazorca*, he perpetrated countless outrages in Argentina and launched invasions of Uruguay and Paraguay. In 1851, he became supreme ruler of the newly created Argentinian Confederation which plunged into civil war as powerful adversaries rose up against the *rosista* faithful (whose sympathies lay with Rosas). Rosas was toppled in 1852 and forced into exile, living out the rest of his days as a farmer in Southampton, England. There is not a single street or plaza in Buenos Aires honoring his name, but Rosas is still an icon for many ultra-conservatives.

Dictator Juan Manuel de Rosas, who ruled with an iron fist

The beautiful 20th-century building that houses Museo Evita

Museo Evita ❻

Lafinur 2988, Palermo. **City Map** 5 E3. **Tel** (011) 4807-0306. 🚇 Plaza Italia. 🚌 39, 59, 93. 🕐 Dec–Mar: 11am–7pm Tue–Sun; Apr–Nov: 1pm–7pm Tue–Sun. 📷 🎦 on request. 🚻 limited. 🖥 www.evitaperon.org

The museum dedicated to Eva Perón is housed in an early 20th-century mansion that once belonged to the aristocratic Carabaza family. The building was converted into a shelter for the homeless in 1948, when it was bought by the Eva Perón Social Aid Foundation. After the fall of the Perón government, it was used for administrative purposes until mid-2002. Opened later that year, the museum is run by the Instituto Nacional Eva Perón which aims to preserve the legacy of her life and work for the people of Argentina.

The displays trace Eva Perón's life and passions faithfully, while some of the exhibits include items which belonged to the families who once took shelter in the house. However, the most impressive exhibits are Evita's posters, famous photographs, jewelry, and her Dior dresses. One of the most memorable images shows Evita saluting the "shirtless ones" from the balcony of Casa Rosada *(see p64)*. There is also an image of Evita, scrubbed and spotless, amid a crew of grubby miners. Other rare exhibits include magazine articles dating from when she was a radio star in the 1930s.

Museo de Arte Latinoamericano de Buenos Aires (MALBA) ❼

See pp110–11.

Museo de Arte Popular José Hernández ❽

Ave del Libertador 2373, Palermo. **City Map** 5 F3. **Tel** (011) 4803-2384. 🚌 37, 59, 60. 🕐 1–7pm Wed–Fri, 10am–8pm Sat, Sun, and pub hols. 🚫 1 Jan, 1 May, Good Friday, & Dec 25. 📷 🎦 by reservation only. 🖥 www.mujose.org.ar

Named for José Hernández, the author of *Martín Fierro*, Argentina's first and only national epic, this slightly untidy museum has one of the finest collections of Argentinian popular art,

Wide wooden doors at Museo de Arte Popular José Hernández

including traditional, urban, indigenous, and rural variants. The museum is a salutary reminder that to understand Argentina and its history, it is necessary to be aware of the importance of its rural heritage and customs.

Housed in an early 20th-century building that was once a hotel, the museum comprises over 8,000 traditional and handmade objects of staggering diversity, showcasing the techniques and materials of both the country's indigenous population and the early colonial settlers.

Among the exhibits are beautifully wrought silverware, masks, musical instruments, and rudimentary weaponry. The pretty patio garden is a great place for a packed lunch.

Interior of Museo de Arte Popular José Hernández

Museo Nacional de Arte Decorativo ❾

Avenida del Libertador 1902, Recoleta. **City Map** 2 B2. **Tel** (011) 4802-6606. 🚌 59, 60, 67, 93. 🕐 11am–7pm Tue–Sun. 🚫 last week Dec & first week Jan. 📷 Tue free. 🎦 4:30pm Tue–Sat, 2:30pm Tue–Sun (in English). 🚻 by arrangement. 🍴 🖥 🖥 www.mnad.org

Once home to the wealthy art lover and Chilean diplomat Errázuriz-Alvear, this early 20th-century French-style mansion was declared a listed national monument in 1998. It houses Argentina's only major decorative arts museum, with a collection of over 4,000

French-style ornate façade of Museo Nacional de Arte Decorativo

objects, ranging from Roman sculptures to contemporary silverware. The bulk of the pieces are of either Oriental or European origin and date from the 16th to the 20th century. Many were donated by Buenos Aires's richest and most celebrated families, including the Errázuriz-Alvears. Among the well-known names whose works are on display are those of Edouard Manet and Auguste Rodin, represented by a portrait and several small sculptures respectively. Temporary exhibitions usually focus on contemporary artisan-type work from Argentina's interior provinces. Although the museum has a varied collection, many prefer just to walk around the beautiful mansion.

Garden sculpture at Museo de Arte Decorativo

Hipódromo Argentino de Palermo ⑩

Avenida del Libertador 4104, Palermo. **City Map** 5 D2. **Tel** (011) 4778-2800. 🚇 Ministro Carranza. 🚌 130, 160, 166. ⬜ varies. ♿ 🍴 📷 🛍 **www.**palermo.com.ar

When Buenos Aires's Hipódromo Argentino de Palermo opened its doors in 1876, it had a capacity of only 2,000 people. Today, that has grown to about 100,000. Although its early years were considered its golden days,

major races still pull in a large crowd from across the country. Thought to be one of the best racecourses in the world, the Hipódromo has three tracks, of which two are used for training while the main track is used for competitions. On average, there are ten meetings per month, usually on Mondays, Saturdays, and Sundays. Races start every half hour. The Hipódromo also hosts what is easily the biggest date on the Argentinian turf calendar, the Gran Premio Nacional in November, which draws massive crowds. The other prominent race, held annually, is the Gran de las Americas. For the best betting, punters should visit the basement of the neoclassical Tribuna Oficial, where over 4,000 slot machines are kept. The belle époque architecture of the grandstand and manicured gardens adds an elegant touch to this popular sports ground.

Campo Argentino de Polo de Palermo ⑪

Avenida del Libertador 4300, Palermo. **City Map** 5 D2. **Tel** (011) 4777-6444. 🚇 Ministro Carranza. 🚌 130, 160, 166. 🚫 ♿ 📷 **www.**aapolo.com

Opened in 1928, Campo Argentino de Polo de Palermo is the country's major stadium and one of the best places to see international polo stars, including Adolfo Cambiaso, one of Argentina's top polo players. Also known as Catedral del Polo, the stadium has a capacity of 45,000 spectators and is used for many other purposes, including concerts.

Polo is played in Buenos Aires from September through to November (*see pp36–7*). The Abierto Argentino de Palermo (Argentinian Open) is contested at the end of the season. After the game, everyone enjoys the tradition of stomping down the divots on the pitch at half time.

A polo match in progress at the Campo Argentino de Polo de Palermo

Museo de Arte Latinamericano de Buenos Aires (MALBA) ❼

Opened in 2001 to house the art collection of Argentinian millionaire and philanthropist Eduardo F. Costantini, Museo de Arte Latinoamericano de Buenos Aires (MALBA) is probably the best privately administered art gallery in Argentina. The building is a striking example of contemporary architecture, which cleverly combines earth-colored, stone-clad trapezoid shapes. It houses over 200 works of 20th-century Latin American art, including pieces by Frida Kahlo and Fernando Botero alongside Argentinian masters Antonio Berni, Jorge de la Vega, and Leon Ferrari.

The strikingly contemporary cuboid form of MALBA

★ Manifestación (1934)
Argentinian painter Antonio Berni is best known for his slightly grotesque portraits of the urban working classes, as shown in this painting of a protest march.

Temporary exhibition space is used to showcase contemporary art, including the work of fashion designers such as Martín Churba.

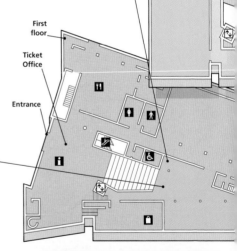

First floor

Ticket Office

Entrance

Atrium
One of the most distinctive features of the museum, the glass walls of the MALBA atrium are specially built to allow natural light to flood the exhibition space.

Siete últimas canciones (1986)
The most successful of the younger generation of Argentinian artists is Guillermo Kuitca, whose abstract works are influenced by design forms in the mass media, cartography, and the theater.

For hotels and restaurants in this region see p277 and pp294–5

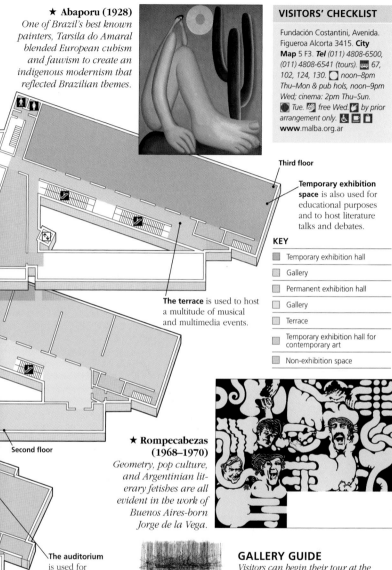

★ **Abaporu (1928)**
One of Brazil's best known painters, Tarsila do Amaral blended European cubism and fauvism to create an indigenous modernism that reflected Brazilian themes.

VISITORS' CHECKLIST

Fundación Costantini, Avenida. Figueroa Alcorta 3415. **City Map** 5 F3. *Tel* (011) 4808-6500, (011) 4808-6541 (tours). 67, 102, 124, 130. noon–8pm Thu–Mon & pub hols, noon–9pm Wed; cinema: 2pm Thu–Sun. Tue. free Wed. by prior arrangement only. **www**.malba.org.ar

Third floor

Temporary exhibition space is also used for educational purposes and to host literature talks and debates.

KEY

	Temporary exhibition hall
	Gallery
	Permanent exhibition hall
	Gallery
	Terrace
	Temporary exhibition hall for contemporary art
	Non-exhibition space

The terrace is used to host a multitude of musical and multimedia events.

Second floor

★ **Rompecabezas (1968–1970)**
Geometry, pop culture, and Argentinian literary fetishes are all evident in the work of Buenos Aires-born Jorge de la Vega.

The auditorium is used for special events and film projections.

STAR EXHIBITS

★ Manifestación (1934)

★ Abaporu (1928)

★ Rompecabezas (1968–1970)

GALLERY GUIDE

Visitors can begin their tour at the contemporary art exhibition space on the ground floor. The first floor, however, is the heart of the museum, with over 270 painting displays dating from the 1900s. The third floor is devoted to temporary exhibitions and it has a terrace for outdoor events.

Sin título (1979)

Leon Ferrari is one of Argentina's best-known conceptual artists; his striking sculptures use wood, plaster, and ceramics and often employ newspaper clippings and texts.

The towering minarets of the Centro Cultural Islámico Rey Fahd

Centro Cultural Islámico Rey Fahd ⑫

Avenida Intendente Bullrich 55. **City Map** 5 D2. **Tel** (011) 4899-1144. 🚌 15, 36, 37, 60. ⬤ 9am–6pm Mon–Fri. 🕌 noon Tue & Thu. ♿ www.ccislamicoreyfahd.org.ar

Inaugurated in 2000, this cultural center and imposing, modern Gulf-style mosque were designed by Saudi architect Zuhair Faiz on land donated by the former Argentinian president Carlos Menem. The 10-acre (4-ha) site contains King Fahd Mosque with a 160-ft (50-m) high blue and white dome and two minarets.

The mosque is the largest in South America, with a colossal prayer room that accommodates over 1,000 worshipers. It houses schools that conduct Islam and Arabic classes, and has a library and conference and sports facilities. The center's pleasant gardens and water fountains provide a cool retreat from the busy city.

La Rural ⑬

Avenida Santa Fe 4201. **City Map** 5 E3. **Tel** (011) 4777-5500. 🚌 15, 36, 37, 60. ⬤ only for events.

Named after the most important agricultural event in the Argentinian calendar since the late 19th century, this showground and exhibition space is used as an exporting platform and is a cultural, entrepreneurial, and social center located in the heart of Buenos Aires.

La Rural is a two-week-long agricultural fair that takes place annually in August. It attracts thousands of spectators who come to see a large number of animals, most of which are cattle. Breeders travel from all over Argentina to showcase their livestock.

The showground itself was built by the Sociedad Rural Argentina in the 1870s, and it now also has a modern exhibition hall, which is used for other events and shows.

Escuela de Mecánica de la Armada (ESMA) ⑭

Avenida del Libertador 8209. 🚊 Estación Rivadavia. 🚌 29, 60, 130, 160.

For most Argentinians the acronym "ESMA," short for Escuela de Mecánica de la Armada (The Naval Mechanics School), has a grim resonance. A facility of the Argentinian Navy, it was used as an illegal detention center during the dictatorial rule of the National Reorganization Process which lasted from 1976 to 1983 (see p54). It was here that some of the worst atrocities were committed during the country's military rule. Political prisoners, many of whom were simply teachers or lawyers with

A busy day at the La Rural agricultural fair

left-wing leanings, were brought here, commonly in unmarked Ford Falcons, tortured and, usually, killed. It is estimated that around 5,000 people were interned at ESMA during the so-called "Dirty War." Most shocking of all were the cases of pregnant women who were detained here, allowed to give birth, then killed so that their children could be given up for adoption to "friends" of the junta.

As part of Argentina's ongoing struggle to come to terms with this dark era, the government has committed itself to the construction of a "Space for Memory and the Promotion and Defence of Human Rights," which will be housed within these grounds.

Las Cañitas ⑮

Calle Baez, Arévalo. **City Map** 5 D2.
🚌 *15, 29, 60, 64, 118.*

Named after the sugarcane that used to grow here when the land was part of General Rosas's (*see p107*) sprawling private estate, Las Cañitas is a fashionable and pricey residential barrio. Although wedged between bustling Belgrano and several lively avenues including Báez and Arévalo, the streets here are relatively sedate and dead

One of the many excellent restaurants in the posh Las Cañitas suburb

ends keep traffic levels down. During the mid-1990s, ultrahip restaurants such as Soul Café and Novecento (*see p295*) began to appear in the area, setting in motion a spate of exclusive gastronomic openings. Soon they were followed by bars, boutiques, and apartment blocks. Las Cañitas became established as the social hub for the well-heeled and its model of development was copied by Palermo Soho and later, San Telmo. The Cañitas Creativa street market on Fridays and Saturdays is an attempt to bring culture and craft to the neighborhood, but the accent in the area is mainly on cool clothes and consumerism.

Museo Nacional del Hombre ⑯

3 de Febrero 1370/8. **City Map** 4 B1. **Tel** *(011) 4784-9971.* 🚌 *60.*
🕐 *11am–7pm Mon–Fri.* 🚫 🎫 *for groups only.* **www**.*inapl.gov.ar*

A small, well-maintained museum, the Museo Nacional del Hombre is part of the Instituto Nacional de Antropología y Pensamiento Latinoamericano, which is dedicated to research in the areas of social anthropology and folklore. The building houses exhibits relating to the prehistory and contemporary status of indigenous South American and Argentinian groups. These peoples include the Mapuche, Tehuelche, Diaguita, and numerous others of the

Chané mask, Museo Nacional del Hombre

Tierra del Fuego region, many of whom were wiped out by European colonizers. Among the 5,000 exhibits, some of which are reproductions, are traditional crafts, textiles, musical instruments, masks, and costumes. Noteworthy are the Mapuche silver jewelry and Chané masks, which are made of the native *palo borracho* tree. The museum shop has a small but excellent crafts selection.

VILLA FREUD

An oft-repeated claim is that Buenos Aires has more shrinks per capita than any other city on earth. Psychoanalysis first became a prominent feature of intellectual life in the 1920s and among the many European immigrants were a large number of avant-garde philosophers, academics, and psychia-

Sigmund Freud, Austrian neurologist and psychiatrist

trists. By the early 1970s, psychoanalysis had established itself as a popular university field. In recent decades, television shows portray visits to a *psicólogos* (psychiatrist) to be as ordinary an experience in the daily life of middle-class porteños as going to a tennis lesson or meeting for a family barbecue. As the area of Palermo around Plaza Güemes is typically middle-class and full of psychoanalysts and psychiatrists, it has become known as Villa Freud.

grano ⓱

Northwest of Palermo. 🚶 138, 942.
🚇 Juramento, Belgrano C, Belgrano
R. 🚌 60, 65, 114, 118, 152.
🛒 Sat & Sun.

Named after Manuel
Belgrano, the Independence
hero who designed the
national flag, Belgrano was
the capital of the Argentinian
Republic for a few weeks in
1880. When the authorities in
the capital found themselves
at odds with the provincial
government, it was chosen
as a neutral seat of power.

These days, the only
evidence of this former glory
is the town hall, now the
Sarmiento Historical Museum,
and the church of **La
Inmaculada Concepción**,
known to the locals as
La Redonda because of
its circular walls. The
barrio has a good
range of bars, restau-
rants, and retail outlets
and Buenos Aires's
only Chinatown is also
located here. Belgrano
proper is a typical
middle-class area, but
heading towards
Belgrano Residencial
beyond Avenida
Cramer, the high-rise
apartment blocks
suddenly give way to
cobblestoned streets, private
houses, and grand mansions.
An English parish church still
stands on Cramer, and many
houses ape the mock-Tudor
style found in England.

Chessboard-tiled dining room at Museo de Arte Español Enrique Larreta

🏛 Museo de Arte Español Enrique Larreta

Avenida Juramento 2291. **Tel** (011)
4783-2640. 🚇 Juramento. 🚌 60,
65, 114, 118. 🕒 3–8pm Wed–Mon.
🎫 Thu free. 🎨 5pm Mon–Fri, 4 &
6pm Sat & Sun. ♿ limited. 📷
www.museos.buenosaires.gov.ar/
larreta.htm

San Martín de
Tours at Museo
de Arte Español

Located in the heart of
Belgrano, this small
museum is housed in
the former residence
of writer Enrique
Larreta (1874–1961).
He was an important
figure in Argentinian
modernism and was
nominated for the
Nobel Prize in 1941.
The house has light-
soaked indoor patios
and an ornamental
garden surrounded by
Andalusian fruit trees.
The displays include paintings
from the Renaissance and
baroque eras, wooden furniture, sculptures, and
weaponry collected over
several trips Larreta made

to Spain to do research for
his 1908 historical novel, *The
Glory of Don Ramiro*. There
are also several portraits of
Larreta himself for which he
sat in Paris in 1912. The
collection in the museum was
substantially augmented in
1997 with 30 paintings and
objects from the Museo de
Arte Hispanoamericano Isaac
Fernández Blanco, including
valuable works by Sánchez
Coello and Pantoja de la Cruz.

🏛 Museo Casa de Yrurtia

O'Higgins 2390. **Tel** (011) 4781-
0385. 🚇 Juramento. 🚌 60, 65.
🕒 1–7pm Tue–Fri, 3–7pm Sun. 🎫
Thu free. 🎨 5pm Sun. ♿ 🚫 📷
Celebrated sculptor Rogelio
Yrurtia and his wife, the
painter Correa Morales,
bequeathed their stylish
neocolonial house to the
nation in 1942. It opened as a
museum in 1949. All the
pieces exhibited are from the
couple's personal collection
and testify to their eclectic
tastes. There are sculptures,
mostly figurative works in
bronze or plaster, and among
the paintings are still lifes,
landscapes, and portraits by
Correa Morales alongside
those of other Argentinian
painters such as Martin
Malharro, Benito Quinquela
Martín, and Octavio Pinto.
Standing out amongst the
pieces is *Rue Cortot*, an early
Picasso. There is also an
interesting collection of Asian
domestic porcelain items, and
textiles and woven carpets
from Mexico and Bolivia. The
furniture is a mix of Victorian
English and Second Empire
French. The garden is lined
with plane trees, a Canary
Island palm, and grapevines.

The neocolonial façade of Museo Casa de Yrutia

Cementerio de la Chacarita ⑱

Guzmán and Jorge Newbery.
City Map 4 A4. **Tel** (011) 4553-9338. 🚇 Federico Lacroze. 🚌 39, 45, 71, 93. ⏰ 7am–6pm daily.
📷 3pm, 2nd & 4th Sat. ♿

Buenos Aires's largest cemetery, though not its most famous or aristocratic, was inaugurated in the wake of the yellow fever epidemic, which swept the city in 1871. The plague was so severe it was reported that 576 bodies were buried at Cementerio de la Chacarita during a single day. Since then the necropolis has expanded to 234 acres (95 ha) and is now one of the largest in the world. The cemetery dominates the neighborhood of Chacarita, indeed it is almost a barrio in its own right, having numbered streets and convenient car access. Burials of well-known personalities often draw the media and large crowds to the cemetery. It is the final resting place of many famous Argentinians, though no longer of Juan Perón, who used to be buried here, but whose remains were moved to a family mausoleum in 2006.

The Dinosaur Room at Museo Argentino de Ciencias Naturales

Plaza Serrano ⑲

Honduras & Borges. **City Map** 5 D4.
🚌 15, 39, 110, 141, 168.

Officially named Plaza Cortázar, Plaza Serrano is the focal point of the fashionable area known as Palermo Viejo or, as of more recently, Palermo Soho. Characterized by early 20th-century Spanish-style architecture, this area was once a residential barrio. It is now packed with alternative bars and restaurants serving global cuisine. In the 1990s artists and designers moved into the area to take advantage of low rents, a trend that created a flourishing alternative scene after the economic collapse in 2001. Located to its north is the area known as Palermo Hollywood, which is now an upmarket eating district.

Museo Argentino de Ciencias Naturales Bernardino Rivadavia ⑳

Ave Angel Gallardo 490. **Tel** (011) 4982-1154. 🚇 Angel Gallardo. 🚌 65, 97, 105, 112, 124. ⏰ 2–7pm daily. 📷 only in summer. ♿ 🛗 🎁 **www**.macn.secyt.gov.ar

One of the oldest in the country, this museum dates back to 1823 and is the brain-child of Argentina's first president, Bernardino Rivadavia. In 1937, it moved to its current venue, an Italianate building specifically designed and built to house the museum, unusual in a city where most museums were incorporated into various existing structures.

There are over 15 large exhibition spaces, each devoted either to a class of fauna or flora or to a habitat. Fish, mammals, invertebrates, and plant life are all covered, and the squawks and whistles of Argentinian birdlife can be heard in the impressive Sounds of Nature salon.

The star attraction of the venue is the Dinosaur Room, with its reconstructed skeletons, mostly made using bones unearthed in the Patagonian region, where the museum's team of paleontologists continue to carry out research.

The tomb of tango singer Carlos Gardel, at Cementerio de la Chacarita

Farther Afield

Located around the capital are a number of interesting towns and suburbs that offer a variety of activities. Gaucho traditions thrive at the Feria de Mataderos, a weekly crafts and bric-a-brac market in the colorful barrio of Mataderos. Beyond this is the riverside town of Tigre, whose Paraná Delta is a hugely popular attraction. The jungle-clad delta houses a complex river-system teeming with flora and birdlife. Río de la Plata can easily be crossed by ferry to explore Argentina's Isla Martín García or the UNESCO World Heritage Site of Colonia del Sacramento in Uruguay.

Leather belts sold at the popular artisanal Feria de Mataderos

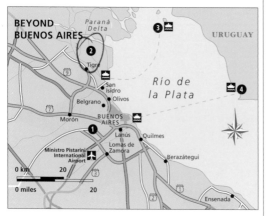

BEYOND BUENOS AIRES

KEY

▨	Buenos Aires city center
▢	Built-up area
✈	International airport
⛴	Ferry port
═══	Expressway
═══	Major road
══	Minor road

Feria de Mataderos ❶

Road Map C3. Lisandro de la Torre y Avenida de los Corrales, Barrio de Mataderos. **Tel** (011) 4342-9246 (Mon–Sat); (011) 4687-5602 (Sun). 55, 92, 97, 126, & 155. ⬜ Jan–Mar: 6pm–1am Sat; Apr–Dec: 11am–9pm Sun. **www**.feriademataderos.com.ar

Buenos Aires's weekly Feria de Mataderos is a day-long artisans' fair, street party, and gaucho hoedown combined into one. The idea behind the event is to showcase local arts

SIGHTS AT A GLANCE

Colonia del Sacramento ❹
Feria de Mataderos ❶
Isla Martín García ❸
Tigre & the Delta ❷

and crafts from the country's interior provinces. There is a wide array of items to pick up, including handcrafted *mate* gourds from Misiones and ponchos from Catamarca. Visitors can also sample traditional regional delicacies such as *locro* (stew), *tamales* (steam-cooked dough), and empanadas (stuffed pastry).

Skillful gaucho equestrian feats are performed and a variety of folk music is played, including the lively *chamamé*, an accordion-based folkloric style from the Litoral region. Audience participation is actively encouraged. The Feria de Mataderos attracts a few folk musicians of international renown, such as Victor Heredia and Chango Spasiuk.

Tigre and the Delta ❷

Road Map C3. 17 miles (27 km) N of Buenos Aires. 🏠 301,000. 🚌 60. ⬜ daily. **www**.tigre.gov.ar

Founded in 1820, Tigre was named for the jaguars hunted in the area by the first European settlers. Its location at the neck of the Paraná Delta made it an important port city, and for decades its quaysides were piled with timber and fruit shipped in from upriver farms and from the islands of the delta itself.

Tigre's port, Puerto de Frutos, holds a daily craft fair which draws thousands of tourists and locals. The city also has quiet, leafy, cobble-stoned streets flanked by elegant neocolonial mansions.

Ferry used to transport visitors in Tigre

The most impressive of them is the imposing Club de la Marina, built in 1876.

Charming though Tigre is, its main appeal is as a jumping-off point for river trips into the Paraná Delta, a diluvial natural labyrinth comprising over 6,500 miles (10,500 km) of canals, rivers, and marshes, as well as countless islands. Many of these river islands are home to small and self-sufficient communities; others are privately owned and built over with smart and exclusive weekend residences, restaurants, watersport centers, and lodgings. The islands can easily be reached by river bus from the Estación Fluvial in Tigre or by chartered rides on one of the many boats moored in Puerto de Frutos.

Jacaranda blossoms covering a path at Isla Martín García

Isla Martín García ❸

Road Map D3. Río de la Plata. 🏯 150. 🚢 from Tigre, daily.

Although comprising a small area of land, Isla Martín García has been fought over by Spain, Brazil, Portugal, Uruguay, Britain, and France; it was finally conquered by the Argentinian Navy in 1886. The island's fortifications were used as prisons and many A-list political detainees did stretches here, including Presidents Hipólito Yrigoyen and Marcelo T. de Alvear. A thorough account of Isla Martín García's long and violent history is related through the displays in the small **Museo Histórico**, located near the center of the island,

close to the old lighthouse. One of the conditions of the 1973 Argentina-Uruguay treaty, which ended the sovereignty squabble, was that the island be converted into a nature preserve. Now, Isla Martín García has a strong reputation among ornithologists and visitors come for the flora and fauna as much as for the fortifications. There are over 200 species of birds found here including parrots, woodpeckers, white herons, falcon-like *chimangos*, and snail kites.

Colonia del Sacramento ❹

Road Map D3. 🏯 22,000. 🚢 from Puerto Madero.

Founded by the Portuguese in 1680, Colonia del Sacramento is a sleepy coastal Uruguayan town whose Barrio Histórico has been preserved intact since the colonial era. In recognition of this, and to guard against intrusive development, the district was declared a UNESCO World Heritage Site in 1996.

After a century-long fight, the town was ceded by its founders to the Spanish in the late 1770s, who held it until the Independence wars. Portuguese and Spanish influences resulted in the cobblestoned streets, leafy plazas, elegant churches, and stucco-façaded mansions that abound in Barrio Histórico.

Around its fig- and palm tree-lined central square, Plaza Mayor, are a number of museums and historical

The serene interior of the Iglesia Matriz, Colonia del Sacramento

buildings. These include the **Museo Portugués**, with excellent samples of maps on the Portuguese voyages of discovery, and the **Museo Municipal**, which houses an array of indigenous artifacts. To the east of the plaza is the Iglesia Matriz, Uruguay's oldest church, with religious artworks that date back over two centuries. Leading off from the square is Calle de los Suspiros (Street of Sighs), one of the region's most photographed lanes, paved with rough cobblestones and flanked by colonial houses.

Visitors can end their day with a stroll on the beach watching the sunset after a meal at one of the town's excellent restaurants.

Museo Portugués
Casa Historica, Calle de San Pedro, in front of Plaza Mayor.
⏰ 11:15am–4:45pm daily. 📷

Museo Municipal
Calle del Comercio, in front of Plaza Mayor. ⏰ 11:15am–4:45pm daily. 📷

One of the picturesque cobblestoned streets in Colonia del Sacramento

SHOPPING IN BUENOS AIRES

uenos Aires has more upscale malls and smart fashion boutiques than any other city in Latin America. The many great bargains on offer here make the capital a shopper's delight. Leather bags and jackets, silverware, and antiques are the classic purchases for visitors, while handicrafts from across Argentina are available at specialist stores and markets, such as the popular Feria Plaza Francia

Antique piece, Feria de San Pedro Telmo

and Feria de San Pedro Telmo. Even non-fashionistas should take a stroll round Palermo Viejo to see the amazing range of homespun designs and fabrics on show. Buenos Aires is home to thousands of small retailers, ranging from textile outlets in the bustling neighborhoods to stylish delis and wine stores selling boutique products and offering a personalized shopping experience.

CRAFTS AND GIFTS

Although the best traditional handicrafts are found in Argentina's interior provinces, where they are locally made, it is definitely worth exploring the craft shops in Buenos Aires. Most souvenir shops cluster around the downtown area, on and off the famous shopping street, Calle Florida. **Kelly's** stocks a wide range of pottery, weavings, *mate* gourds, and all manner of ornaments featuring the Argentinian national colors. **Tierra Adentro** is a smart store for high-end collectibles and native musical instruments. There are beautiful ponchos for sale at **Del Monte** and **Arte Étnico Argentino**, both in Palermo Viejo. For quirky gifts, visit **Calma Chicha**. As well as cowhide cushions, rugs, and leather bags, the shop also specializes in traditional Argentinian crafts with a modern twist.

An array of items at Feria de San Pedro Telmo, San Telmo barrio

Tango-themed souvenirs are very popular. Tango memorabilia is stocked at **Zival's**, an emporium on the corner of Callao and Corrientes. There is a well-established industry in kitsch artwork, and, increasingly, tango fashion. For a range of interesting collectibles, including wonderful old posters, T-shirts, and ancient musical scores, visit the **Club de Tango**.

For visitors wishing to purchase original jewelry, there are ornate contemporary silver creations at **María Medici** and more ethnic necklaces and earrings at **Plata Nativa**.

ART AND ANTIQUES

There are more than 20 small commercial galleries in the downtown area of Buenos Aires. These include well-established showcases such as the **Ruth Benzacar** gallery

and **Fundación Federico Klemm**, and those such as **Galería Rubbers** and **Daniel Abate**, which concentrate on emerging Argentinian painters and sculptors. Located in Palermo is **Elsi del Rio**, another gallery with an eye for promising young artists.

Calle Defensa in San Telmo has a string of antique stores, stocking anything from early 20th-century gramophones to 18th-century statues and original wooden trunks used by early European immigrants. **Feria de Pulgas** is a dusty flea market in Palermo Viejo that sells clocks, glass soda bottles, ceramic vases, paintings, and even old cars and wooden beds. **Gil Antigüedades** stocks lovely silver-plated *mate* gourds and Victorian clothing, while **HB Antigüedades**, located in an old mansion, displays an array of interesting items that some shoppers may find gaudy.

Leather jackets, bags, and ponchos at a gaucho shop

FASHION

Palermo Viejo is the epicenter of Argentina's haute couture industry, while Recoleta remains the barrio for more traditional fashions. Some designers, such as Martin Churba of **Tramando, Martin Churba**, have already made it big on catwalks in Milan and New York; others, such as mid-range designers **Ona Sáez** and **Juana de Arco**, are well-liked by porteños for their chic and urban designs. Popular fashions tend to follow European trends fairly closely, so big malls stock Armani, Burberry, Louis Vuitton, and other well-known international designers.

For menswear, check out the creations of **Hermanos Estebecorena**, while for cool porteño trends, visit **Félix**. Located close by, on Calles Murillo and Scalabrini Ortíz, are several excellent leather shops offering their wares at near-wholesale prices. There are many shops that specialize in children's clothes in the capital, and there are even boutiques that sell haute couture for babies only a couple of months old. **Owoko** in Palermo Viejo is a bright and bubbly emporium, selling pyjamas, dresses, T-shirts, and trendy trousers. A free kids' storybook is given away with every purchase. Another popular clothes shop here is **Cheeky**, which has seasonal collections and purveys a more classic, stylish line in urban gear for young people.

LINGERIE AND SWIMWEAR

There are numerous high street stores in Buenos Aires known for selling good-quality lingerie. Even small neighborhood underwear shops dress their windows in lace and satin finery. The biggest name in the country is **Caro Cuore**, which sells lingerie for women at fairly reasonable prices. The brand has branches in the malls and is stocked by all general retailers.

For something more exotic and daring, try **Amor Latino, Lingerie & Corseterie**, which experiments with fluff and lace on the garments, or **Zoel**, specializing in the porteña penchant for multicolored thongs and miniscule straps.

For sporty swimwear, there are dozens of excellent sports gear shops located all over the capital, including a branch of **Speedo**. The local fashion retailer, **Salsipuedes**, stocks its own swimming trunks and Al Ver Veras bikinis.

NEWSPAPERS, BOOKS, AND MUSIC

As in all Argentinian cities, the *kiosko* (newspaper stand) is a popular sight in Buenos Aires. The capital of Latin America's most literate country has a diverse and generally

The Ateneo Grand Splendid bookshop

high-quality press. There are tango *kioskos* in Corrientes, ones that sell law-related books and magazines in the Tribunales area, and posh stands at the airport selling coffee-table books and the latest novels. Newspapers, magazines, and literature can all be obtained at the *kioskos* in Recoleta and Mircrocentro.

The English-language *Buenos Aires Herald* is sold in many of the centrally located stands. For a wide range of English-language books, visit **Ateneo Grand Splendid** on Avenida Santa Fe and also its branches along Calle Florida. Another good choice is **KEL Ediciones** branch, which is also very popular with English students and teachers.

More sought out by tourists are coffee-table picture books and fancy editions of famous Argentinian classics, such as Borges's poems and short stories and *Martín Fierro* by José Hernández. These are available at branches of **Boutique del Libro** and **Cúspide**. The former has an outlet in Palermo Viejo and the latter has a branch in the Recoleta Village mall.

Zival's is well known for tango books and also offers an excellent and extensive range of Argentinian tango, folk, jazz, and rock CDs. Branches of **Musimundo**, found throughout the city, are often cheaper for best-selling CDs.

A shop selling a wide range of leather goods, Recoleta

WINE AND FOOD

The boom in delis and wine stores is relatively new, pushed on by the increasing number of wealthy tourists in the city looking for good wines and local products. Travelers not bound for the Mendoza region should definitely explore the wine shops in the capital. For personal service, which includes wine tastings, go to **Ligier**. They also help with organizing overseas shipping. **Winery** is a smart wine super-market with a range of stock from all regions, while **La Finca** is more focused on less well-known boutique vintages from Mendoza.

There are *panaderías* (bakeries) throughout the city, and most high streets have *dietéticas* (health stores) stocking vitamins, whole-grain biscuits, diet products, and snacks. *Confiterías* (large cafés) sell fresh pastries and sandwiches. To try the city's best *medialunas* (sweet croissants), visit **Dos Escudos**.

Al Queso Queso and **La Casa del Queso** stock mild, milky cheeses and cured meats from the provinces as well as olives, antipasto, breads, and other bites. **La Fondue: Gourmet Food Shop** also stocks cheeses and other gourmet treats. To try *alfajor*, the local cookies, visit **Havanna**, which has outlets all across the city.

Stall in popular flea market, Feria de San Pedro Telmo, San Telmo

MARKETS

The best handicraft markets in Argentina are found in the towns and cities of the interior, especially those where indigenous and mestizo cultures continue to thrive. For those who are limited to buying in the capital, the **Feria Plaza Francia** is good for bags, *mate* gear, and jewelry.

The larger **Feria de San Pedro Telmo**, on Plaza Dorrego, stocks tango souvenirs, old vinyl, and low-grade antiques. The Feria de Pulgas is a great place for a rummage: this huge shed is full of rusty old lamps, brass beds, books, and scratched records. Ideal bargains are available for those furnishing houses or aiming at a retro look for a bar or restaurant.

Out on the western edge of the capital is the Feria de Mataderos *(see p116)*. At this bustling gaucho-themed flea market, look out for works by Florencio Molina Campos, the country's best-known cartoonist. His excellent sketches for the calendars of the Compañia Argentina de Alpargatas are now considered collector's items all over the world.

SHOPPING MALLS

Buenos Aires's oldest shopping center, **Patio Bullrich** opened in 1988 and stocks exclusive designer wear including Dior, Versace, and Ralph Lauren, as well as beautiful Argentinian couture creations. The grand Galerías Pacífico *(see p91)* was renovated in the late 1990s, and is now a multi-tiered emporium of high-street fashion chain outlets, shoe shops, and gift and knickknack *kioskos*.

Alto Palermo and the larger, more handsome **Abasto** are good for perfumes and health shops. They also house popular local chains such as **Chocolate** and **María Vázquez**. **Unicenter** is a classic US-style mall, with huge electrical and white goods stores. *Galerías* (small malls) offer less expensive clothes and ornaments, and **Galería Bond Street** off Santa Fe stocks "goth" and alternative fashionwear.

The spacious and elegant interior of the Patio Bullrich shopping mall

DIRECTORY

CRAFTS AND GIFTS

Arte Étnico Argentino
El Salvador 4656.
City Map 5 D4.
Tel (011) 4832-0516.

Calma Chicha
Honduras 4925.
City Map 5 D4.
Tel (011) 4831-1818.

Club de Tango
Parana 123, 5th Floor.
City Map 2 C3.
Tel (011) 4372-7251.

Del Monte
Uriarte 1440.
City Map 4 C4.

Kelly's
Paraguay 431.
City Map 3 E4.

María Medici
Niceto Vega 4619.
City Map 4 C4.
Tel (011) 4773-2283.

Plata Nativa
Galería Del Sol, Florida
860. **City Map** 3 E4.
Tel (011) 4312-1398.

Tierra Adentro
Arroyo 882.
City Map 3 D3.
Tel (011) 4832-2592.

Zival's
Ave Callao 395. **City Map**
2 C4. *Tel (011) 5128-
7505.* www.zivals.com

ART AND ANTIQUES

Daniel Abate
Pasaje Bollini 2170.
City Map 2 C2.
Tel (011) 4804-8247.

Elsi del Rio
Arévalo 1748.
City Map 4 C3.
Tel (011) 4899-0171.

Feria de Pulgas
Niceto Vega & Dorrego,
Palermo Viejo.
City Map 5 D4.

Fundación Federico Klemm
Marcelo T. de Alvear 626.
City Map 3 E4.
Tel (011) 4312-4443.

Galería Rubbers
Alvear 1595. **City Map** 3
D3. *Tel (011) 4816-1864.*

Gil Antigüedades
Humberto Primo 412.
City Map 1 E2.

HB Antigüedades
Defensa 1016.
City Map 1 E1.
Tel (011) 4361-3325.

Ruth Benzacar
Florida 1000. **City Map** 3
E4. *Tel (011) 4313-8480.*
www.ruthbenzacar.com

FASHION

Cheeky
Abasto, Ave Corrientes
3247. *Tel (011) 4959-
3549.* **City Map** 2 A4.

Félix
Gurruchaga 1670.
City Map 5 D4.
Tel (011) 4832-2994.

Hermanos Estebecorena
El Salvador 5960.
City Map 4 C3.

Juana de Arco
El Salvador 4762.
City Map 5 D4.

Ona Sáez
Ave Santa Fe 1651.
City Map 1 C3.

Owoko
El Salvador 4694.
City Map 5 D4.
Tel (011) 4831-1259.

Tramando, Martin Churba
Rodriguez Peña 1973.
City Map 3 D3.
Tel (011) 4811-0465.

LINGERIE AND SWIMWEAR

Amor Latino, Lingerie & Corseterie
El Salvador 4813.
City Map 5 D4.

Caro Cuore
Galerías Pacifico local
235. **City Map** 3 E4.

Salsipuedes
Honduras 4814.
City Map 5 D4.

Speedo
Abasto, Ave Corrientes
3247. **City Map** 2 A4.
Tel (011) 4959-3463.

Zoel
Paseo Alcorta shopping
mall. **City Map** 2 B1.

NEWSPAPERS, BOOKS AND MUSIC

Ateneo Grand Splendid
Avenida Santa Fe 1860.
City Map 2 C3.

Boutique del Libro
Thames 1762, Palermo
Viejo. **City Map** 5 D4.

Buenos Aires Herald
www.buenosaires
herald.com

Cúspide
Village Recoleta.
City Map 2 C3.
Tel (011) 4807-5716.
www.cuspide.com

KEL Ediciones
Marcelo T de Alvear
1369. **City Map** 3 D3.
Tel (011) 4814-0143.
www.kel-ediciones.com

Musimundo
Ave Santa Fe 1844.
City Map 2 C3.
Tel (011) 4814-0370.
www.musimundo.com.ar

WINES AND FOOD

Al Queso Queso
Uruguay 1276.
City Map 3 D3.
Tel (011) 4811-7113.
www.alquesoqueso.com

Dos Escudos
Montevideo 1690.
City Map 3 D3.
Tel (011) 4812-2517.

Havanna
Florida 159.
City Map 3 E5.
www.havanna.com.ar

La Casa del Queso
Ave Corrientes 3587.
City Map 2 A4.
Tel (011) 4862-4794.

La Finca
Costa Rica 4615, Palermo
Viejo. **City Map** 5 D4.

La Fondue: Gourmet Food Shop
Salguero 3069.
City Map 5 F3.
Tel (011) 4806-8958.

Ligier
Ave Santa Fe 800.
City Map 3 E3.
Tel (011) 4515-0126.
www.ligier.com.ar

Winery
Ave Corrientes 302.
City Map 3 E4.
Tel (011) 4394-2200.
www.winery.com.ar

MARKETS

Feria de San Pedro Telmo
Plaza Dorrego, San Telmo.
City Map 1 E1.

Feria Plaza Francia
Plaza Francia, Recoleta.
City Map 2 C2.

SHOPPING MALLS

Abasto
Ave Corrientes 3247.
City Map 2 A4.
Tel (011) 4959-3400.
www.abasto-shopping.
com.ar

Alto Palermo
Ave Santa Fe 3253.
City Map 2 A2.
Tel (011) 5777-8000.
www.altopalermo.com.ar

Chocolate
Alto Palermo Shopping
Mall. **City Map** 2 A2.
Tel (011) 5777-8072.

Galería Bond Street
Ave Santa Fe 1670.
City Map 2 C3.

María Vázquez
Alto Palermo Shopping
Mall. **City Map** 2 A2.
Tel (011) 4815-6333.

Patio Bullrich
Ave del Libertador 750.
City Map 3 D3.
Tel (011) 4814-7400.

Unicenter
Paraná 3745, Martínez.
City Map 2 C3.
www.unicenter.com.ar

ENTERTAINMENT IN BUENOS AIRES

One of the great capitals for arts and leisure, Buenos Aires impresses visitors from across the world with its cultural variety. Porteños have an insatiable appetite for theater, sports, music, and just about any event that brings people together. On a Sunday, strolling around Parque 3 de Febrero, visitors can watch an impromptu football match and spot people picnicking under the trees

Singer at San Telmo

or drinking *mate*. Visitors can see gauchos competing in equestrian events at Feria de Mataderos, or watch a soccer match at one of the capital's numerous stadiums. The cultural calendar through the year *(see pp40–43)* includes the annual Feria del Libro in April, and February's International Tango Festival which gives everyone an opportunity to test their feet with a few steps of the national dance.

Music poster for a Beatles tribute show on Avenida Corrientes

ENTERTAINMENT GUIDES AND TICKETS

There are myriad sources of entertainment information available in the capital. The well-known London listings magazine **Time Out** has a franchise in Buenos Aires that publishes a visitors' guide twice a year. Every Friday, the *Buenos Aires Herald (see p119)* contains a listings guide called **getOut!**, covering both English and Spanish language film and theater, exhibitions, and other entertainment events. Both the major national newspapers, **Clarín** and **La Nación**, also publish comprehensive entertainment guides on Fridays. For tango fans, the specialist listings magazine **El Tangauta** is available at *kioskos* in the downtown area and covers tango events across the city.

Tickets for a range of entertainment events can be bought at **Ticketmaster and Ticketek**. For cheap seats at

theaters and shows, there are several branches of **Cartelera Baires** ticket outlets on Calle Lavalle in the city center. For a major sporting event or football match, it is advisable to talk to a hotel concierge or contact the local ground agent. **Curiocity** and **Tangol** are both highly recommended local agents who sort out everything from transport to seats, and even ensure security.

MUSIC AND DANCE

A handful of venues provide stages for major national and international shows for folk rock, UK and US rock stars, and offbeat composers. **Teatro Opera** and **Gran Rex** are good venues for rock, classical, and world music, while **ND Ateneo** and **La Trastienda** are more intimate venues for tango, folk, jazz, and fusion. **Luna Park**, a former boxing arena, is an important venue for *cumbia*, salsa, and other Latin music performances, and

shows by international bands. **Notorious**, a smart CD store with a café and restaurant, is a great venue for edgy jazz and virtuoso rock-crossover gigs. **Estadio Obras** in the Nuñez district is *de rigueur* for alternative rock and independent bands, and other entertainers such as Roxy Music and Kraftwerk who played there in the late 1990s.

Belgrano's **Monumental Stadium** is the main venue for huge crowd-pullers such as U2 and the Rolling Stones, and Argentinian mass-market performers such as Bersuit Vergarabat, Los Piojos, and Soda Stereo. La Boca's La Bombonera *(see p85)*, and various other large football grounds have hosted international performers such as the Bee Gees, Peter Gabriel, and Mercedes Sosa. Tickets are not available at the stadiums as they are merely venues and do not manage the promotional aspects of concerts.

A jazz concert at the popular restaurant Notorious

A tango show in progress in a theater in Buenos Aires

TANGO SHOWS AND CLASSES

The range of tango on show is infinite. For high-quality glitzy shows, head to **La Esquina de Carlos Gardel** or **Piazzolla Tango** in the Abasto neighborhood. **Señor Tango** has been around for years but is a rather corporate affair. **Bar Sur** is a smaller venue and is an ideal place to listen to the singers up close.

Milongas (see p79) offer a far more authentic tango experience. The **Centro Cultural Torquato Tasso** and **Club Gricel** host events that welcome both diehard dancers and curious visitors. The **Confitería Ideal** is a good place for an atmospheric and aesthetic music and dance experience. This old café holds tango classes for beginners in the afternoon. On Tuesdays and Fridays, there are *milongas* from 11pm with a live band playing under dim lights, and just a handful of couples on a dance floor swirling with tobacco smoke.

Most *milonga* nights are preceded by a tango class. Local agents such as Tangol or Curiocity arrange tango tours for visitors.

BARS AND CLUBS

Buenos Aires's bars and clubs are an ideal place to while away time, or to meet interesting people from the city. Most of them are open until the early hours which leaves a lot of time to explore the city's many night-out options. **Dadá** and **La Cigale** are some well-known places with a vibrant bar scene. Calle Báez in Las Cañitas is mainly known as a popular hangout to check out TV celebrities and football stars. For expatriates, **Kilkenny** and **The Shamrock** are more than convivial. If you want to play the porteño part to perfection, go to Café Tortoni (see p68) or Confitería Ideal to try local whiskies or liqueurs such as Legui or Cynar. To enjoy a drink with Argentinian folk, a good option is to head for Plazoleta Cortazar in Palermo Viejo and cruise down to Avenida Honduras or Borges. Also an excellent place to sip coffee and cognac in the city is Café La Biela (see pp98–9) in Recoleta. Some of the coolest nightclubs include **Niceto Vega Club** and **Mint** for the stylish crowd, and **El Living**, which draws a more mixed clientele. Visit **Metropolis** to see authentic *cumbia* (see p26). Fans of Brazilian samba and dancing can head for **Maluco Beleza** in the Tribunales barrio.

CLASSICAL MUSIC AND THEATER

Many of the venues listed for music and dance are also sometimes the venues for classical composers and theater groups. Other venues with a classical repertory include Teatro Colón (see pp72–3), Teatro Avenida (see p68), **Auditorio San Rafael** in Nuñez, and the **Catedral de San Isidro**, which is located in San Isidro.

Theater in Buenos Aires is classified as "Corrientes" and "off-Corrientes." The former is lined with huge theaters offering amateur revues that usually feature small-time celebrities. For a more artistic experience, Teatro General San Martín (see p74) or Teatro Nacional Cervantes (see pp70–71) are good places to stop by. Off-Corrientes venues such as **Espacio Callejón** or **Grupo de Teatro Catalinas Sur** in La Boca also offer a stimulating night out. The latter has been putting on fabulous performances for over 20 years by mixing various European art forms such as opera and *zarzuela*. The biennial **Festival Internacional de Buenos Aires**, held for a fortnight in September, includes a range of national and international theater, dance, and musical performances.

Outside Grupo de Teatro Catalinas Sur

Match between Boca Juniors and River Plate at La Bombonera

SPECTATOR SPORTS

Major sporting events such as rugby internationals and high-profile race days attract large crowds, while a football international or a *clásico* (a derby match between two historic rivals) draws multitudes. Any game between leading football teams is unforgettable, while a *superclásico*, a match between Boca Juniors and River Plate, is a clash of national importance. River Plate's Monumental Stadium is big but not very atmospheric, while La Boca's La Bombonera is usually filled with a passionate audience. Other major matches are held at the **Vélez Sarsfield** and **Ferrocarril Oeste**. Marred by violence off the pitch, football matches should ideally be attended in the company of locals who are familiar with security arrangements.

Major horse races at Hipódromo Argentino de Palermo *(see p109)* and **Hipódromo de San Isidro** attract large crowds, as do games at Campo Argentino Polo de Palermo *(see p109)*.

Another popular sport is tennis. Tickets for the Davis Cup and Copa Telmex, and other matches featuring national heroes such as David Nalbandian, Gaston Gaudio, and Guillermo Coria are much sought after. Visitors can buy tickets only at **Asociación Argentina de Tenis**.

Rugby Union is popular in Argentina, especially in Buenos Aires and Tucumán, and there are several clubs in the northern suburbs of the capital. The competitions are held mainly in Buenos Aires and in Punta del Este. The official website of **Unión Argentina de Rugby** has a schedule of national and international tournaments.

PLAYING SPORTS

Porteños are usually active people and most use their local park or the huge green swathe of parks and plazas between Museo de Bellas Artes and Parque 3 de Febrero for jogging or cycling.

There are gyms all over Buenos Aires; many of the smartest are in five-star hotels and it is easy to get a day pass there. To take a swim, some clubs such as the **Club de Amigos** issue day passes. Many branches of the **Megatlon Gym** chain in Buenos Aires also have pools. Anyone keen to warm up their equestrian talents, or planning a visit to an estancia or a cross-country trek, can take a class at **Club Alemán** or **Club Hípico**, both in Palermo. For visitors who prefer an adventurous holiday, the **Renosto Nautica y Deportes** club in San Fernando in Greater Buenos Aires organizes waterskiing and wakeboarding.

ENTERTAINMENT FOR CHILDREN

The people of Buenos Aires adore children and they are welcomed everywhere. The *heladerías* (ice-cream parlors) in the city are sure to keep children smiling. There is often a circus passing through the capital, and mimes and jugglers, found everywhere in the city, will also keep children occupied. Buenos Aires is proud of its clowns and puppeteers, and to see a free show visit **La Calle de los Titeres** in the Constitución barrio. However, it is advisable to check if the show is aimed only at Spanish-speaking audiences.

Several major venues are designed for children, including the **Museo de los Niños** in the Abasto shopping mall. The museum takes children on tours, introducing them to career options ranging from medicine, construction industries, and fast food. Also popular is the main city zoo, the Jardín Zoológico *(see p107)* which has 89-odd species of mammals. The **Parque de la Costa**, an out-of-town amusement park, can be reached by train through the northern suburbs. Another park located outside the capital is the wildlife park, **Parque Temaikén**.

Cyclists at Parque 3 de Febrero in Palermo

DIRECTORY

ENTERTAINMENT GUIDES AND TICKETS

Cartelera Baires
Ave Corrientes 1382.
City Map 3 D4.
Tel (011) 4372-5058.
www.cartelerabaires.com

Clarín
www.clarin.com.ar

Curiocity
Juncal 2021, Piso 4.
Tel (011) 4803-1113.
www.curiocitytravel.com

El Tangauta
www.eltanguata.com

getOut!
www.getout.com.ar

La Nación
www.lanacion.com.ar

Tangol
Tel (011) 4312-7276.
www.tangol.com

Ticketek
Tel (011) 5237-7200.
www.ticketek.com.ar

Ticketmaster
Tel (011) 4321-9700.

Time Out
www.timeout.com.ar

MUSIC AND DANCE

Estadio Obras
Ave del Libertador 7395.
Tel (011) 4702-3223.

Gran Rex
Ave Corrientes 857.
City Map 3 D4.
Tel (011) 4322-8000.

La Trastienda
Balcarce 460.
City Map 1 E1.
Tel (011) 4342-7650.
www.latrastienda.com

Luna Park
Bouchard 465.
City Map 3 E4.
Tel (011) 5279-5279.
www.lunapark.com.ar

Monumental Stadium
Ave Figueroa Alcorta 7997.
Tel (011) 4789-1200.

ND Ateneo
Paraguay 918. **City Map** 3 D4. **Tel** (011) 4328-2888.

Notorious
Avenida Callao 966.
City Map 2 C4.
Tel (011) 4815-8473.
www.notorious.com.ar

Teatro Opera
Ave Corrientes 860.
City Map 3 D4.
Tel (011) 4326-1335.

TANGO SHOWS AND CLASSES

Bar Sur
Estados Unidos 299.
City Map 1 E1.
Tel (011) 4362-6086.

Centro Cultural Torquato Tasso
Defensa 1575.
City Map 1 E2. **Tel** (011) 4307-6506. www.torquatotasso.com.ar

Club Gricel
La Rioja 1180.
Tel (011) 4957-7157.

Confitería Ideal
Suipacha 384.
City Map 3 D4.
Tel (011) 5265-8069.

La Esquina de Carlos Gardel
Carlos Gardel 3200,
Barrio del Abasto.
Tel (011) 4867-6363.
www.esquinacarlos
gardel.com.ar

Piazzolla Tango
Guemes Gallery, Florida 165 / San Martín 170.
Tel (011) 4344-8200.
www.piazzollatango.com

Señor Tango
Vieytes 1655.
Tel (011) 4303-0231.
www.senortango.com.ar

BARS AND CLUBS

Dadá
San Martín 941.
City Map 3 E4.
Tel (011) 4314-4787.

El Living
Marcelo T de Alvear 1540.
Tel (011) 4811-4730.
www.living.com.ar

Kilkenny
Marcelo T de Alvear 399.
City Map 3 E4.
Tel (011) 4312-7291.

La Cigale
25 de Mayo 722.
City Map 3 E4.
Tel (011) 4312-8275.

Maluco Beleza
Sarmiento 1728.
City Map 2 C4.
Tel (011) 4372-1737.

Metropolis
Ave Santa Fe 4389.
City Map 5 D3.

Mint
Avenida Costanera Rafael Obligado.
Tel (011) 4771-5870.

Niceto Vega Club
www.nicetoclub.com

The Shamrock
Rodriguez Pena 1220.
City Map 2 C4.
Tel (011) 4812-3584.

CLASSICAL MUSIC AND THEATER

Auditorio San Rafael
Ramallo 2606, Nuñez.
www.fundacion
sanrafael.com.ar

Catedral de San Isidro
Ave del Libertador 16199.
Tel (011) 4743-0291.

Espacio Callejón
Humahuaca 3759.
Tel (011) 4862-1167.

Festival Internacional de Buenos Aires
www.festivaldeteatroba.
com

Grupo de Teatro Catalinas Sur
Benito Perez Galdós 93.
City Map 1 F3.
www.catalinasur.com.ar

SPECTATOR SPORTS

Asociación Argentina de Tenis
www.aat.com.ar

Ferrocarril Oeste
www.ferrocarriloeste.
com.ar

Hipódromo de San Isidro
www.hipodromosan
isidro.com

Unión Argentina de Rugby
www.uar.com.ar

Vélez Sarsfield
Avenida Juan B. Justo 9200.
Tel (011) 4642-0643.
www.velezsarsfield.
com.ar

PLAYING SPORTS

Club Alemán
Avenida Dorrego 4045.
City Map 5 E1.
Tel (011) 4778-7060.
www.clubaleman.
com.ar

Club de Amigos
Avenida Figueroa Alcorta 3885.
City Map 5 F2.
Tel (011) 4801-1213.
www.clubdeamigos.
org.ar

Club Hípico
Avenida Figueroa Alcorta 4800.
City Map 5 F2.
Tel (011) 4778-1982.

Megatlon Gym
www.megatlon.com

Renosto Nautica y Deportes
Avenida del Libertador 2136, San Fernando.
City Map 2 B2.
Tel (011) 4725-0260.

ENTERTAINMENT FOR CHILDREN

La Calle de los Titeres
Avenida Caseros 1750.

Museo de los Niños
Avenida Corrientes 3247.
Tel (011) 4861-2325.
www.museoabasto.org.
ar/home.php

Parque de la Costa
Vivanco 1509.
Tel (011) 4002-6000.
www.parquedelacosta.
com

Parque Temaikén
Ruta Provincial 25,
Vivonce 1509, Escobar.
Tel (03488) 436-900.
www.temaiken.com.ar

BUENOS AIRES
STREET FINDER

The map given below shows the different areas of Buenos Aires covered by the street finder maps – Plaza de Mayo and Microcentro, San Telmo and La Boca, Plaza San Martín and Retiro, Recoleta, and Palermo and Belgrano. The map references given in the text for places of interest, hotels, restaurants, entertainment venues, and shops refer to these maps. Map references are also given for hotels *(see pp274–7)* and restaurants *(see pp292–305)*. The first figure in the map reference indicates which Street Finder map to turn to, and the letter and number which follow refer to the grid reference on that map.

A visitor in Buenos Aires

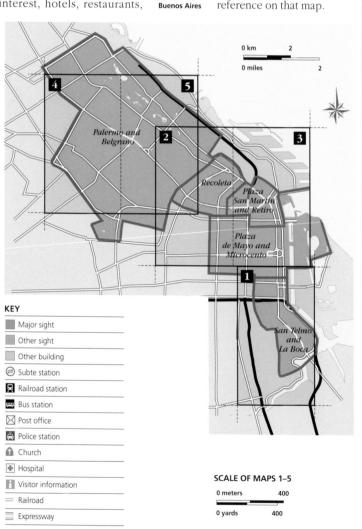

0 km   2
0 miles   2

4 **5**

Palermo and Belgrano

2 **3**

Recoleta

Plaza San Martín and Retiro

Plaza de Mayo and Microcento

1

San Telmo and La Boca

KEY

▪	Major sight
▪	Other sight
▪	Other building
Ⓢ	Subte station
🚆	Railroad station
🚌	Bus station
⊠	Post office
🚔	Police station
⛪	Church
✚	Hospital
ℹ	Visitor information
=	Railroad
=	Expressway

SCALE OF MAPS 1–5

0 meters   400
0 yards   400

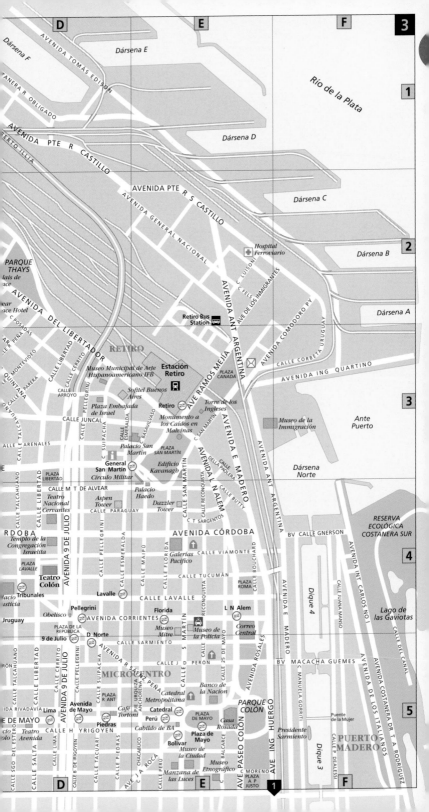

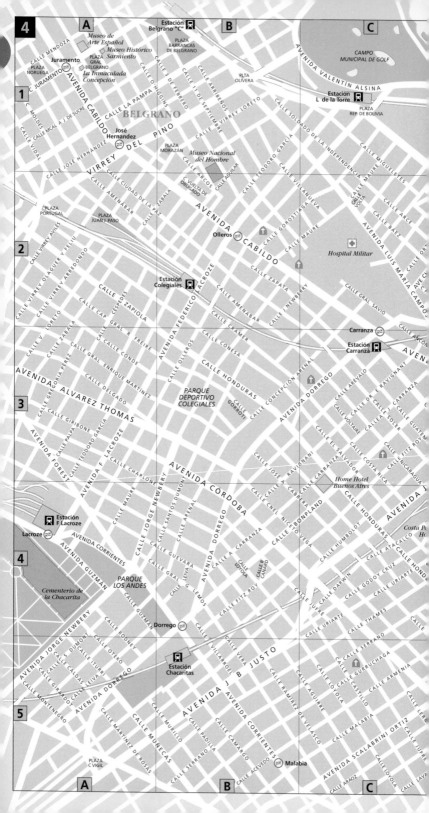

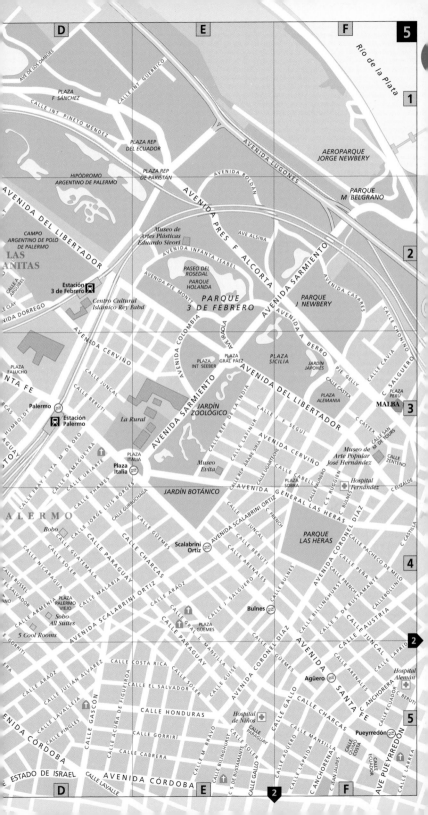

ARGENTINA REGION BY REGION

ARGENTINA AT A GLANCE 134–5

THE PAMPAS 136–155

ARGENTINIAN MESOPOTAMIA 156–175

CÓRDOBA AND THE ANDEAN
NORTHWEST 176–201

CUYO AND THE WINE COUNTRY 202–219

PATAGONIA 220–255

TIERRA DEL FUEGO AND
ANTARCTICA 256–267

Argentina at a Glance

By virtue of its sheer size, Argentina has an array of varied and magnificent landforms. The central Pampas is characterized by vast, flat, and fertile grassland, while to the west lie the rugged, snowcapped Andes. The north of Argentina has spectacular waterfalls and subtropical forests, while the south of the country is riddled with rivers, lakes, glaciers, and mountains. Wildlife is plentiful and adventure activities abound, ranging from whale-watching and trekking to white-water rafting and off-road driving. Buenos Aires, Córdoba, Rosario, and Mendoza provide urban counterpoints to Argentina's lonely, wild expanses, offering excellent museums, restaurants, hotels, and shopping opportunities.

CÓRDOBA AND
THE ANDEAN
NORTHWEST
(see pp176–20)

La Rioj

CUYO AND THE
WINE COUNTRY
(see pp202–219)

Sa
Ra

Neuqué

PATAGONI
(see pp220–2)

The bodegas *of the Mendoza region grow Torrontés grapes, which produce the characteristic Argentinian white wine, considered among the best in the world. Home to over 1,000 vineyards, Mendoza has a sunny and mild climate through the year.*

| 0 km | 250 |
| 0 miles | 250 |

Cueva de las Manos
(see p243) *is a UNESCO World Heritage Site in Parque Nacional Francisco P. Moreno. The caves have more than 2,000 magnificent stenciled handprints on the walls made by adults and children, dating back around 9,500 years.*

Parque Nacional Los Glaciares (see pp250–51) *is located in the Santa Cruz province. A UNESCO World Heritage Site, the park is divided into two parts – the northern sector consists of Glaciar and Lago Viedma, while the southern sector has the major Glaciars Perito Moreno, Upsala, and Spegazzini.*

◁ Panoramic view of the multicolored rock strata of Quebrada Humahuaca, Córdoba province

ARGENTINIAN
MESOPOTAMIA
(see pp156–175)

Corrientes · Posadas

Parque Nacional Iguazú (see pp172–5), *a UNESCO World Heritage Site, has spectacular waterfalls along the Iguazú River surrounded by subtropical rainforest. The star attraction is the 2,300-ft (700-m) high Garganta del Diablo waterfall.*

Córdoba

Rosario

Buenos Aires
La Plata

THE PAMPAS
(see pp136–155)

Santa Rosa

Mar del Plata

Bahía Blanca

Salta (see pp194–5), *located at the foothills of the Andes mountains, is the charming capital city of the eponymous province. Considered Argentina's most beautiful city, it is famous for its old-style Spanish colonial architecture and stunning scenery.*

Catedral de la Inmaculada Concepción, *located in the city of La Plata (see pp140–43) in the Buenos Aires province, is the largest church in Argentina. It is heavily influenced by European Gothic and has a characteristic red-brick façade.*

Comodoro Rivadavia

Elephant seal and penguin colonies *dot the icy barrenness of the Tierra del Fuego landscape. This stretch of land is famous for its spectacular scenery, wildlife, and ancient glaciers.*

TIERRA DEL
FUEGO AND
ANTARCTICA
(see pp256–267)

THE PAMPAS

S *olitary ombú trees, stunning birdlife, and grand estancias are the most visible sights on the rolling grasslands that extend from the Atlantic coast and Río de la Plata in all directions. Settled in the 18th century, the Pampas is the economic heartland of this cattle-raising, farming nation, and the iconic gaucho who oversees this domain remains a heroic archetype for many Argentinians.*

The original inhabitants of the Pampas were the Querandi, who lived a semi-sedentary lifestyle on the fertile plains. During the 18th century, the Spanish colonial authorities established a frontier across the region. As the natives were forced out, ranches were established and by the mid-19th century, wealthy families had divided up most of the land. In the chain of towns around the capital – San Miguel del Monte, Mercedes, and San Antonio de Areco – are some of the most famous estancias in the country. The introduction of new cattle breeds and, later, refrigeration and fencing, led to economic booms in the late 19th century and in the 1930s and 40s. The fencing did, however, spell an end for the free-roaming habits of the gauchos.

In the 20th century, the Atlantic coast became a place of rest and recreation for wealthy porteños, leading to the rapid growth of coastal towns. These beach resorts, now popular with locals and visitors alike, generate a large amount of revenue for the tourism sector, although the Pampas is the most productive in terms of agriculture and industry.

In summer, backpackers and adventurous souls head for the ancient mountain ranges to the south of the province, whose slopes provide an opportunity for many outdoor activities such as mountain biking, rock climbing, and trekking. An array of gaucho activities await visitors who opt to stay at one of the many working estancias scattered in the Pampas, while exclusive tourist ranches offer luxury accommodation.

A row of fishing boats docked at the Mar del Plata port

◁ Female gaucho herding cattle on the Pampas plains

Exploring the Pampas

The unrelenting plains of the Pampas region offer plenty of opportunity for horseback riding and gaucho activities at the many estancias. Away from the empty spaces, La Plata is a vibrant university city, San Antonio de Areco is a charming colonial town, and Luján houses the country's most important Catholic shrine, La Virgen de Luján. The most popular beach resorts are Mar del Plata, Villa Gesell, Miramar, and Pinamar. Heading south, the land begins to roll and, eventually, rise to the green and dramatic mountains of the Sierra de la Ventana and Tandil, which afford an array of outdoor adventure sports.

Stained-glass detail, Catedral de la Inmaculada Concepción, La Plata

SIGHTS AT A GLANCE

Towns and Cities
Bahía Blanca ⓯
Balcarce ⓾
Chapadmalal ➐
La Plata pp140–43 ➊
Luján ➋
San Antonio de Areco ➌
Santa Rosa ⓰
Tandil ⓫

Resorts
Mar del Plata ➍
Miramar ➑
Necochea ➒
Pinamar ➏
Villa Gesell ➎

Estancias
Estancia Cerro de la Cruz ⓮

Parks and Areas of Natural Beauty
Parque Nacional Lihué Calel ⓱
Parque Provincial Ernesto Tornquist ⓭
Sierra de la Ventana ⓬

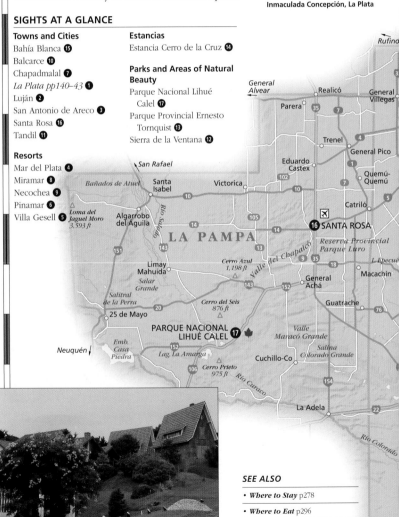

Charming houses near the beach, Pinamar

SEE ALSO

• *Where to Stay* p278

• *Where to Eat* p296

For additional map symbols *see back flap*

GETTING AROUND

The region can be best explored by car or bus. Ruta Provincial 11 links Buenos Aires to La Plata and also offers great views of the Atlantic coast. Ruta Nacional 2 goes to Mar del Plata, while Ruta Nacional 3 is good for Sierra de la Ventana. Several highways head west across the Pampas towards Mendoza and Neuquén. Travelers need a sturdy car to explore the unmetalled backroads of the Pampas. There are flights between Buenos Aires and Mar del Plata, Bahía Blanca, and Santa Rosa.

View of the slopes of Sierra de la Ventana

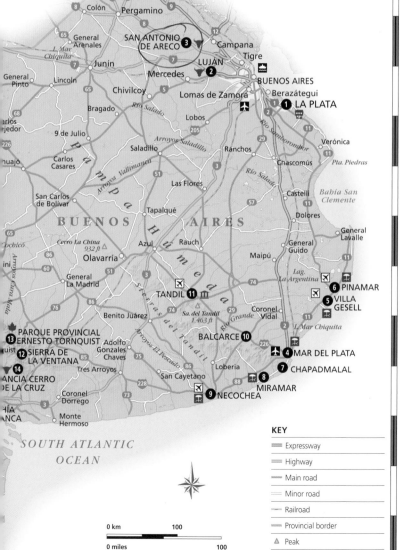

KEY

▬▬	Expressway
▬▬	Highway
▬▬	Main road
▭▭	Minor road
┈┈	Railroad
▬▬	Provincial border
△	Peak

0 km   100

0 miles   100

La Plata ❶

Founded in 1882, the well-organized city of La Plata is the seat of government for Buenos Aires province. Built in under two decades, it is the country's first entirely planned city, earning it the nickname Ciudad Milagro (Miracle City). La Plata boasts several spectacular buildings, world-class museums, and two top-league football teams. The city center, planned in detail by French architect Pierre Benoit, consists of 23 plazas connected by broad Parisian-style boulevards lined with trees and impressive public buildings. The city has a rich and vibrant cultural life, mainly due to the three major universities that attract students from all over Argentina.

Statue at Plaza Mariano Moreno

View of the sparkling white neoclassical Palacio de la Legislatura

🚏 Plaza Mariano Moreno
Bounded by Calles 12, 14, 54, & 50.
Catedral de la Inmaculada Concepción Tel *(0221) 424-0112.* ◯ *8am–noon, 2–9pm daily.* ✔ ♿
Palacio Municipal Tel *(0221) 427-1535.* ◯ *9am–5pm Mon–Fri.* ✔ 🖥

Covering four blocks and located towards the southern side of the city, Plaza Mariano Moreno is a popular public space. It was here that La Plata's foundation stones were laid in 1882, along with a time capsule containing documents that record the event.

The square is lined with remarkable buildings, and foremost among these is the **Catedral de la Inmaculada Concepción**. Located on the southern edge of the plaza, it was inspired by the great Gothic cathedrals of Amiens and Cologne. The cathedral, with its unmistakable reddish brick façade and soaring 370-ft (112-m) high twin towers, is deservedly La Plata's most famous landmark. The cornerstone was laid in 1884, and the church was inaugurated in

1932 to mark La Plata's 50th anniversary. It is the largest structure built in this style in the Americas, with a surface area of 75,350 sq ft (7,000 sq m) and a capacity of 14,000.

Facing the cathedral at the northern end of the square is **Palacio Municipal**. Built in the 1880s in German Renaissance style, the ivory-white complex covers over

The red-brick façade of Catedral de la Inmaculada Concepción

150,700 sq ft (14,000 sq m), including the gardens. The star attraction is the Salón Dorado (Gold Room) on the first floor, reached via a marble staircase. The floor is made from Slavonic oak and the outstanding bronze chandeliers have 78 lamps apiece. Temporary art exhibitions as well as various civic functions are held here.

🎭 Teatro Argentino
Avenida 51, between Calles 9 & 10.
Tel *(0221) 429-1700.* ◯ *10am–8pm Tue–Sun.* ✔ ♿ ⌀ 🖥 🛗
www.teatroargentino.ic.gba.gov.ar

Built in 1890, Teatro Argentino is considered the second greatest opera venue in the country after Teatro Colón *(see pp72–3).* It became a reputed stage for singers from both home and abroad during the "golden age" of theater in the 1930s and 40s. The curtain fell in 1977 after the building was razed by a fire. It was finally reopened in 2000 with an excellent production of Puccini's *Tosca*.

There are now two auditoria: one dedicated to the classical composer Alberto Ginastera, with a capacity of 2,200, and the other, with space for 300 spectators, is named after tango maestro Astor Piazzolla, and devoted to chamber music recitals.

🏛 Palacio de la Legislatura
Plaza San Martín. **Tel** *(0221) 422-0112.* ◯ *10am–6pm daily.* 📷 ♿ 🖥

Built in the 1880s, the neoclassical Palacio de la Legislatura has three principal points of entry, comprising porticoes held up by four Ionic columns and crowned with sculptural groups. Both the sculptural elements and the reliefs on the façade are allegorical representations of various events from Argentina's history, including the abolition of slavery, the May Revolution, and the Declaration of Independence.

The ceiling of the grand Representative's Chamber was decorated by the well-known Argentinian painter Grazziano Mendilaharzu. It depicts a blazing sun, echoing the design of the national flag.

Casa de Gobierno nestled within its leafy garden environs

VISITORS' CHECKLIST

Road Map C3. 35 miles (55 km) SW of Buenos Aires.
👥 *580,000.* [i] *Calle 5, 1728; (0221) 425-2195.* 🚆 🚌

🏛 Pasaje Dardo Rocha

Plaza San Martín, Calle 50 between Aves 6 & 7. ***Tel*** *(0221) 425-1990.*
🕐 *8am–10pm daily.* ♿ 🍴 🖥 🛍

Now an excellent cultural center, Pasaje Dardo Rocha was once La Plata's railroad station until it was destroyed by fire in 1887, five years after opening. It then endured decades as a makeshift base for various organizations including the postal service, the regional archives, and even several radio stations. In 1994, the building assumed its current and hopefully permanent role as the best multifunction cultural center in the city. Within the elegant three-story Italianate façade and French-style slated roof there is a small arts cinema and the grand Museo de Arte Contemporáneo Latinoamericano, with its excellent displays. It also has several art galleries that cluster around a beautifully lit, columned central hall.

🏛 Casa de Gobierno

Plaza San Martín, Calle 6 between Aves 51 & 53. ***Tel*** *(0221) 429-4185.*
🕐 *8am–10pm daily.* 👣 ♿ 🚫📷

Located at the northern end of Plaza San Martín, Casa de Gobierno is a Flemish Renaissance-style building, with an impressive mansard roof and dome. It was designed by Belgian architect Julio Doral and construction began in 1882. Among its famous features are the marble staircases, the Salón Dorado (Gold Room), and the sylvan Palm Patio.

🏛 Museo de La Plata

See pp142–3.

🌳 Paseo del Bosque

Avenida 1 & Plaza Rivadavia.
🕐 *daily.*

La Plata's largest municipal park, Paseo del Bosque is an open space covering just over 150 acres (60 ha). Its leafy environs house an old-fashioned zoo with many animals including rhinos and Patagonian foxes as well as a botanical garden with examples of Argentina's most emblematic trees, including the *ombú* and the *ceibo*. There is an astronomical observatory that opens mainly in winter to the public. The artificial lake offers rowing boat and pedalo options, while to its west is the open-air theater, Teatro Martín Fierro, with various good productions on offer.

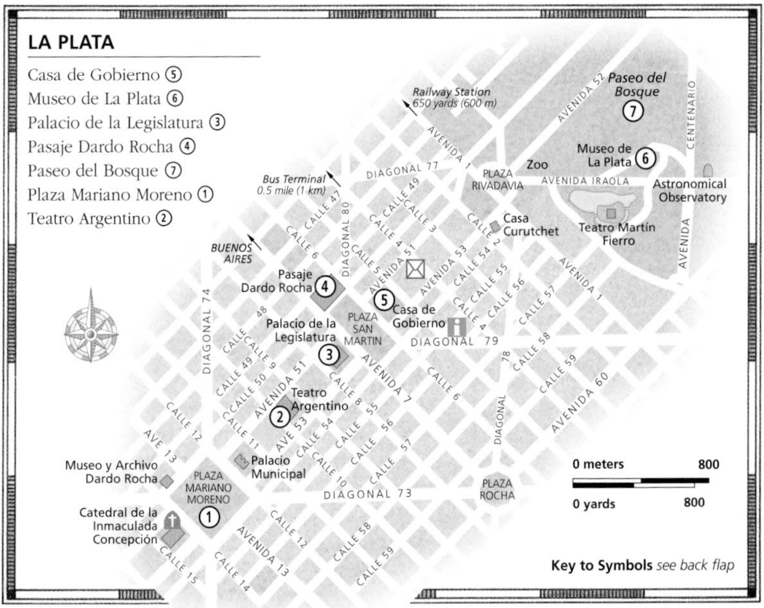
LA PLATA
Casa de Gobierno 5
Museo de La Plata 6
Palacio de la Legislatura 3
Pasaje Dardo Rocha 4
Paseo del Bosque 7
Plaza Mariano Moreno 1
Teatro Argentino 2
Railway Station 650 yards (600 m)
Bus Terminal 0.5 mile (1 km)
BUENOS AIRES
Paseo del Bosque
Museo de La Plata
Zoo
PLAZA RIVADAVIA
AVENIDA IRAOLA
Astronomical Observatory
Casa Curutchet
Teatro Martín Fierro
Pasaje Dardo Rocha
Casa de Gobierno
Palacio de la Legislatura
PLAZA SAN MARTIN
DIAGONAL 79
DIAGONAL 77
DIAGONAL 80
DIAGONAL 74
DIAGONAL 73
DIAGONAL 78
CENTENARIO
Teatro Argentino
Palacio Municipal
Museo y Archivo Dardo Rocha
PLAZA MARIANO MORENO
Catedral de la Inmaculada Concepción
PLAZA ROCHA
AVENIDA 1
AVENIDA 7
AVENIDA 13
AVENIDA 51
AVENIDA 53
AVENIDA 52
AVENIDA 60
0 meters 800
0 yards 800
Key to Symbols see back flap

La Plata: Museo de La Plata

The first purpose-built museum in Latin America, opened in 1888, Museo de La Plata is an important showcase of findings as well as an academic hub. Argentina has been the location of many dramatic dinosaur finds, and the museum boasts the original skeleton of a herbivorous *Titanosaurus* and extensive collections of the extinct giant megafauna of the Cenozoic period. Geological and archaeological exhibits, including fantastic animalistic stone sculptures from the Condorhuasi culture of Catamarca, as well as old oil paintings of the huge beasts that used to roam the Pampas, complete the collection.

A saber-toothed tiger statue at the entrance to the museum

Ethnography Gallery
On display are examples of textiles, weapons, cooking implements, jewelry, and other items used by the country's many indigenous groups. Some were collected by the museum's founder Francisco P. Moreno.

Second floor

Entomology Gallery
The entomology room is filled with various species of beetles, vividly colored butterflies such as the Papilio thoas thoantides (above), *and larvae and pupae at every stage of their development.*

Ticket office

Entrance

★ Jawbones of the Blue Whale
Marine life is a significant part of the zoology display and the gigantic jawbones of the blue whale are a highlight. Also of note are the bird samples collected by naturalist William Henry Hudson in the 19th century.

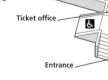

STAR FEATURES

★ Jawbones of the Blue Whale

★ La Ciénaga Ceramics

★ Paleontology Gallery

For hotels and restaurants in this region see p278 and p296

Circular Entrance Hall

Visitors are welcomed by the sight of a beautiful domed hall, usually flooded with sunlight. The walls are decorated with paintings of the country's native animals.

VISITORS' CHECKLIST

Paseo del Bosque s/n. *Tel* (0221) 425-7744. ◯ 10am–6pm Tue–Sun, 10am–10pm Sat. ◯ Jan 1, May 1, Dec 24, 25, & 31. 🖼 🎫 9am–2pm Mon–Fri. ♿ 🛍 www.fcnym.unlp.edu.ar/museo

★ La Ciénaga Ceramics

With an extensive and excellent collection, this section showcases the exquisite gray-black ceramics made by the La Ciénaga populations of Catamarca between the 2nd and 5th centuries AD.

Latin American Archaeology preserves the ancient cultures of Peru and Bolivia.

KEY

▢	Biological Anthropology
▢	Ethnography
▢	Latin American Archaeology
▢	Northwest Argentinian Archaeology
▢	Zoology
▢	Entomology
▢	Temporary exhibitions
▢	Egypt Room
▢	Time and Matter
▢	Paleontology
▢	The Earth
▢	Non-exhibition space

The Time and Matter section aims to archive geological time.

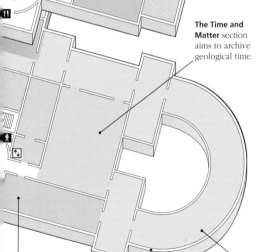

The Earth section offers an interactive approach to the cosmos.

First floor

GALLERY GUIDE

To the right of the entrance hall is the paleontological collection while the opposite side of the ground floor has zoological and entomological exhibits. The upper floor introduces man's role in the world. Some rooms and exhibits may be temporarily closed due to renovation work.

★ Paleontology Gallery

This section documents the country's many fossil findings including the Neuquensaurus, which appeared in Argentina 71 million years ago.

The stunning Basílica Nuestra Señora de Luján

Luján ❷

Road Map C3. 45 miles (70 km) W of Buenos Aires. 🚶 94,000. 🚉 🚌 www.lujanargentina.com

Known as La Capital de la Fe (Capital of the Faith), Luján owes its existence to a "miracle." In 1630 a terra-cotta statuette of the Virgin Mary was being transported from Brazil to Peru by ox cart. At the spot where Luján's cathedral now stands, the cart got stuck. Taken as a divine hint that the statue was destined to travel no farther, a chapel was built to house the relic.

Presently, Luján attracts an estimated six million pilgrims a year and thousands of people make the trip from Buenos Aires on foot. There are also excellent restaurants and cafés around the town's central square.

🛈 Basílica Nuestra Señora de Luján

San Martín 51. **Tel** (02323) 420-058. 🕙 7am–8pm daily. 📷 10am–5pm Mon–Fri, 10am–6pm Sat & Sun. ♿ ✝ 8–11am, 5pm & 7pm daily. www.basilicadelujan.org.ar
With its 350-ft (106-m) high twin spires towering majestically over the Pampas,

Luján's neo-Gothic cathedral, and the famous relic it protects, is easily the town's biggest draw. Starting out as a small chapel, it was built up between 1887 and 1932, and has ethereal stone details and a circular stained-glass window depicting the Virgin Mary. Surrounding this window are statues of the 12 apostles and the four evangelists. The cathedral can be entered through one of the three huge bronze doors; the terracotta statue of the Virgin Mary is stored behind the altar in the Camarín de la Vírgen.

🏛 Complejo Museográfico Enrique Udaondo

Lezica 917. **Tel** (02323) 420-245. 🕙 noon–6pm Wed–Fri, 10:15am–6pm Sat, Sun, & public hols. 📷 🎥 noon–6pm Wed–Fri. 🅿️
There are four museums housed within this complex, which is made up of the former *cabildo* (town hall) and Casa del Virrey (Viceroy's Residence). The principal collection is at the *cabildo*, which was once a prison; famous past inmates here include General Bartolomé Mitre (*see p50*).

The collection exhibits items related to the area's history, including a range of colonial silverware. The Gaucho Museum has exhibits illuminating the history of the gaucho while the Transport Museum displays the country's first steam locomotive and the first Argentinian hydroplane to cross the Atlantic. The pavilion nearby has a collection of documents and mementos relating to Argentina's presidents.

🍴 Estancia Los Talas

12 miles (20 km) E of Luján. **Tel** (02323) 494-995. 🅿️
More than just another attractive ranch, Los Talas is part of Argentinian history. Built in 1824, it was confiscated by General Manuel de Rosas (*see p107*) in 1840 and returned to the original owners 12 years later, after Rosas's defeat at the Battle of Caseros. Rosas didn't stay at the ranch, but billeted some of his troops there and let his horses graze on the pastures. Now a hotel, the sprawling estancia still retains furnishings and uniforms that date from this volatile epoch. Most extraordinary is its library, one of the most important in the country, comprising over 40,000 volumes. It includes handwritten books from the 13th century, a number of editions printed before 1800, and priceless archives of the works of some of Argentina's most famous influential thinkers.

Velocipedo display, Transport Museum

The lush environs of Complejo Museográfico Enrique Udaondo

Pulpería La Blanqueada at Museo Gauchesco Ricardo Güiraldes

San Antonio de Areco ❸

Road Map C3. 70 miles (115 km) NW of Buenos Aires. 🏛 20,000. 🚌 🐎 Dia de la Tradicion (weekend nearest to Nov 12). **www**.sanantonio-deareco.com

For a town increasingly promoted as a tourist destination, San Antonio de Areco has retained almost all of its charm and authenticity. Colonial houses line the leafy roads and working cowboys wear traditional *bombachas* (baggy trousers) and neckerchiefs. Set next to a lovely coastline, the town also has excellent restaurants and is close to some of Argentina's most exclusive estancias.

San Antonio de Areco owes much of its fame to the writer Ricardo Güiraldes (*see p31*). His 1926 masterpiece, *Don Segundo Sombra*, is set in the area and its eponymous gaucho protagonist is famous in Argentinian literature. Güiraldes's family ranch, La Porteña, is nearby.

Pleasantly quiet for most of the year, the town comes alive in November for the Día de la Tradición, a boisterous festival of country dancing and equestrian stunts celebrating gaucho traditions.

🏛 Museo Gauchesco Ricardo Güiraldes

Caminar Güiraldes s/n°. **Tel** (02326) 455-839. ◯ 11am–5pm Wed–Mon. 🎟 📷 3:30pm Mon–Fri, 12:30pm & 3:30pm Sat, Sun. ♿ Accessed by crossing a bridge over Río Areco at the northern edge of the town, this

museum complex, which opened in 1938, comprises several open-air and enclosed exhibition spaces. One of the best known is the Pulpería La Blanqueada, a tavern that featured in Güiraldes's *Don Segundo Sombra*. The museum is mostly dedicated to the author, though it also exhibits paintings by several Argentinian and Uruguayan artists. The building itself, with its colonial tiles, trellis windows, and patios bowered with palm trees, is a pleasant place to visit.

🏛 Taller y Museo de Platería Criolla y Civil

Lavalle 387. **Tel** (02326) 454-219. ◯ 10am–12:30pm, 3:30–6pm daily. 🎟 📷 🚫 📷 José Draghi is a local silversmith with an international reputation. His workshop and museum are housed in a 19th-century neoclassical Italianate mansion. The pieces that Draghi and his team

Silver stirrups, Taller y Museo de Platería Criolla y Civil

Silversmiths working at the Taller y Museo de Platería Criolla y Civil

manufacture adhere closely to traditional methods and classic designs of gaucho silverware, but also incorporate subtle modern twists. Visitors can watch the making of a range of items including spurs, belt buckles, belts, and stirrups. The in-house museum has two exhibition areas devoted to visual art either inspired by, or directly related to, gaucho themes. Over 180 pieces are on display at any time. Guides explain the history of gaucho silverware and the accessories that a cowboy wears.

🍷 Estancia El Ombú

5 miles (8 km) NW of San Antonio de Areco. **Tel** (02326) 492-080. 🎟 ♿ **www**.estanciaelombu.com The *ombú* tree used to be known as the "lighthouse of the Pampas," because it was often the only shade gauchos could find when crossing endless grasslands. It is a fitting name for a welcoming estancia that offers guests homemade food, guided horse rides, and even a round of golf. The beautiful main house was built in 1880 for General Ricchieri, whose Italian heritage helped determine the style of the pink-colored, vine-clad palazzo. The park is stunning, dotted with century-old oak trees, araucarias, eucalypti, and, of course, *ombús*. The ranch also has a collection of old weaponry.

🍷 Estancia La Bamba

8 miles (13 km) NW of San Antonio de Areco. **Tel** (02326) 456-293. 🎟 ♿ **www**.la-bamba.com.ar Owned by the Aldao family for several generations, La Bamba is perfect for a taste of traditional gaucho life. Sepia-soaked family photographs line the walls and the rooms are filled with antique French furnishings. There is a reconstructed *pulpería* (small grocery store), and estancia activities such as horse riding are available. La Bamba is also famous for being the backdrop for the legendary Argentinian movie, *Camila* (1984).

View of gauchos herding cattle on the sweeping Pampas plains ▷

Mar del Plata ❹

Road Map C3. 250 miles (400 km)
S of Buenos Aires. 🚶 🚂 🚌

Founded in 1874, Mar del
Plata is Argentina's seventh
largest city and its most popular seaside resort. Originally
an important port, the city
developed as a tourist destination in the early 20th century, attracting rich porteños
from Buenos Aires.

During the 1930s and 40s,
many of the resort's luxury
residences were built in
pintoresco style, which drew
on European influences
ranging from Swiss chalets to
mock-Tudor cottages. Most of
these houses, however, were
demolished in the 1960s to
make room for today's generic
condos and skyscrapers.

Mar del Plata has long
ceased to be a getaway solely
for the wealthy. With the 2002
devaluation of the Argentinian
peso making international
trips prohibitively expensive
for middle-class families,
there has been a resurgence
in the resort's popularity.
During the peak season in
January and February, the
town's population swells to
over 3 million, ensuring that
its 11 miles (17 km) of
beaches are always crowded.

Much of Buenos Aires's
entertainment, fashion, and
sporting industry moves to
Mar del Plata in summer,
bringing with them a lively
cultural scene. The city's international film festival is held
in the off-season in March.

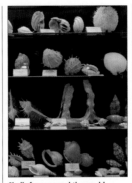

**Shells from around the world
displayed in Museo del Mar**

🏛 Museo del Mar

Avenida Colón 1114. **Tel** *(0223)*
451-9779. ☐ *Jan–Feb: 10am–11pm
daily; Mar–Dec: varies.* 📷
📹 *6–11pm.* ♿ 🚻 🏪
A shrine to keen collector
Benjamin Sisterna, Museo del
Mar is built around
his collection of sea-
shells. Sisterna spent
most of his adult life
scouring the world's
beaches for rare
samples, managing to
pack over 30,000
into his knapsack
over the course of
26 trips. The shells
are now part of this museum's
permanent collection. It is
divided into different sections,
some of which are dedicated
to types of marine ecosys-
tems, and others to geo-
graphical locations. The shells
are displayed in glass cabinets
with informative explanatory
labels. The museum also
includes an aquarium with

**A butterfly display,
Museo de Ciencias
Naturales**

various marine specimens
from Mar del Plata's waters,
as well as displays of
contemporary art and
cultural objects.

🏛 Museo Municipal de Ciencias Naturales Lorenzo Scaglia

Avenida Libertad 3099. **Tel** *(0223)*
473-8791. ☐ *Jan–Feb: 6–11pm;
Mar–Dec: varies.* 📷 🚻 🏪
www.grupopaleo.com.ar/
museoscaglia
Originally founded in 1938,
this excellent museum houses
the extensive fossil collection
of Don Lorenzo Scaglia, who
moved to Argentina from Italy
in 1877 and settled in Buenos
Aires. The museum moved to
its current location in 1967.
As well as exhibiting fossils
from all over the world, the
museum has a number of
well-organized exhibition
spaces devoted to
different disciplines
within the natural
sciences, including
geology, paleon-
tology, ornithology,
and taxidermy. There
is a vast collection
of stuffed birds,
including *chimangos*
and *ñandúes*. The
museum also has a salt and
freshwater aquarium, where
visitors will find small sharks,
piranhas, and some of
Argentina's most common
freshwater species such as
pacú and dorados. A trip to
the museum can be followed
by a meal at one of the fine
seafood restaurants clustered
around the port area.

A sunny day at the busy seaside resort of Mar del Plata

For hotels and restaurants in this region see p278 and p296

The exterior of Museo Municipal de Arte Juan Carlos Castagnino

🏛 Museo Municipal de Arte Juan Carlos Castagnino

Colón 1189. **Tel** (0223) 451–3553. ☐ Jan–Feb: 5–10pm Wed–Fri; Mar–Dec: varies. 🎫 ☑ ☐ ☐

Built in 1909, this museum is housed in a striking mock-Anglo-Norman-style mansion of turrets and timbers. Its collection of 450 paintings is dominated by the works of local artist Juan Carlos Castagnino (1908–1972). Depicting his hometown in a style that was influenced by European expressionism, while being essentially figurative, Castagnino also produced etchings based on Goya's celebrated "Horrors of War" series. He achieved great fame with his detailed illustrations for a 1962 edition of *Martín Fierro*.

Castagnino's self-portrait

The building is noted for its elegant Art Nouveau interior, designed by the famous Belgian decorator Gustavo Serrurier-Bovy. It is a work of art in its own right, packed with playful and extravagant details such as carvings of the five flying ducks over the fireplace. Much of Bovy's work was destroyed during World War II and this museum's collection is one of the few remaining examples of his creations. The furniture in the building is considered some of the finest in the world. Temporary exhibitions, which focus both on local and national artists, are held here all year round.

🎭 Centro Cultural Villa Victoria

Matheu 1851. **Tel** (0223) 492-0569. ☐ Jan–Feb: 1–10pm Wed–Mon; Mar–Dec: varies. 🎫 ☑ ☐ ☐

A fine writer, intellectual and critic, Victoria Ocampo influenced most of Argentina's modern literary greats. She was known as an excellent hostess and the soirées she organized at her villa were famous. She is mentioned in Graham Greene's dedication to his well-known novel *The Honorary Consul*. Built by her father as a present to her aunt, the beautiful house was inherited by Ocampo in the 1930s. The writer lived here intermittently until her death in 1979. She bequeathed the building to UNESCO in 1973, although it reverted to municipal control in 1981 when it came to be known as the Centro Cultural Villa Victoria.

Surrounded by a sprawling park, the center is well maintained. The building is of architectural interest, constructed from Norwegian wood specially shipped to Buenos Aires in 1911. The wood was then transported by train to Mar del Plata. The big house has 11 bedrooms but only one of the rooms contains the original antique furnishings. The center now holds a large number of diverse exhibitions, events, and conferences throughout the year.

Fishing trawlers at the harbor in Banquina de Pescadores

🎭 Banquina de Pescadores

South of city center, past Plaza Grande.

This working fisherman's wharf teems with activity, brightly painted fishing boats, and the unmistakable smell of fish. The best time to go to Banquina de Pescadores is when the fishermen return at dusk, bringing with them packed crates of bass, squid, and many other seafood delicacies. The dock also has a colony of male sea lions, who have made the port their home and clamor for scraps from the fishermen. Their numbers vary according to the season and as they are not shy of humans, visitors can get near enough to observe them at close quarters. The port is also known for its excellent seafood restaurants, many of which are dotted around the wharf.

The famous literary retreat Centro Cultural Villa Victoria, Mar del Plata

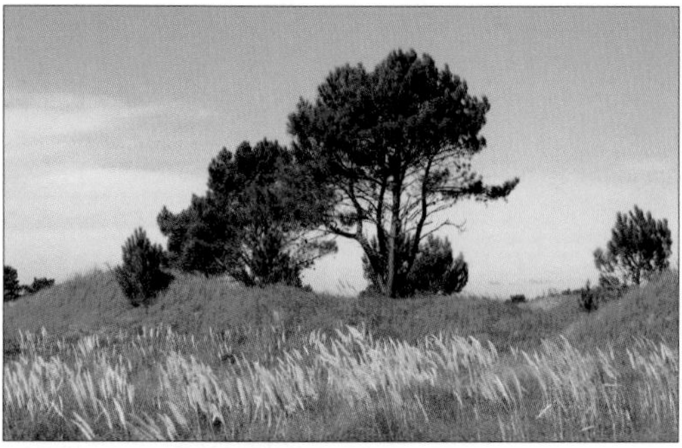

Sand dunes and pine trees behind the beach in Pinamar

Villa Gesell 5

Road Map D3. 62 miles (100 km) NE of Mar del Plata. 👥 *26,000.* ✈ 🚌 [i] *Ave 3, (02255) 478-042.* 🎭 *Patron Saint (Jul), Beer Festival (Aug).* **www.** welcomeargentina.com/villagesell

The beach resort of Gesell was only a dream when Don Carlos Idaho Gesell bought 7 sq miles (18 sq km) of sand dunes on the Atlantic coast in 1931. Here, he built a house for his family, now the Gesell Museum, and protected the dunes by planting several Australian acacia trees. By the 1950s, it had become a fledgling tourist resort, although the town was only officially founded in 1968.

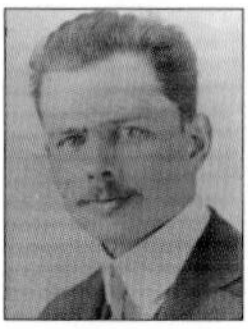

Portrait of Don Carlos Gesell

Now Villa Gesell is filled with lively restaurants, bars, and nightclubs. There is a wide range of hotels, from bed-and-breakfasts to inns and *hospedajes* (lodges). Gesell is popular with youngsters as there are plenty of beach activities such as quad biking and surfing.

Environs

Just 6 miles (10 km) south of Gesell is **Faro Querandi**, a lighthouse built in 1922. At a height of 180 ft (55 m), with a total of 276 steps, this tower is still in service. About 17 miles (27 km) south, **Parque Natural Pinar del Norte** has ancient woodlands and a dune preserve. The striking expanse of slopes with its complex ecosystem supports diverse grasses and mammals.

Pinamar 6

Road Map D3. 12 miles (20 km) N of Villa Gesell. 👥 *22,000.* 🚆 ✈ 🚌 [i] *Bunge 654, (02254) 491-680.* **www.** welcomeargentina.com/pinamar

The resort town of Pinamar is surrounded by fragrant copses of pines planted during the 1940s and 50s. Founded in 1944 by Munich-born architect Jorge Bunge, Pinamar was built with a clear vision of urban development. The commercial center has a good handicrafts market.

In the late 1980s, wealthy porteños wanted a smarter resort than Pinamar and so Cariló was founded 4 miles (6 km) away, a pretty village of wooden houses and beachside bungalows.

Chapadmalal 7

Road Map C3. 14 miles (23 km) S of Mar del Plata. 👥 *2000.* 🚌

An indigenous name meaning "between streams," Chapadmalal is one of the greenest resorts on the Atlantic coast. At the end of the 19th century, the town was known mainly for a ranch owned by founder and first president of the then recently created Nueva Sociedad Rural Argentina, José T. Martínez de Hoz. When he died in 1888, the ranch was divided between his two sons, one of whom built the Estancia Santa Isabel. There are a few hotels, most of which were built when Chapadmalal hosted some events in the 1955 Pan-American Games. Golf and windsurfing are popular activities here.

🐂 **Estancia Santa Isabel**
www.santa-isabel.com.ar

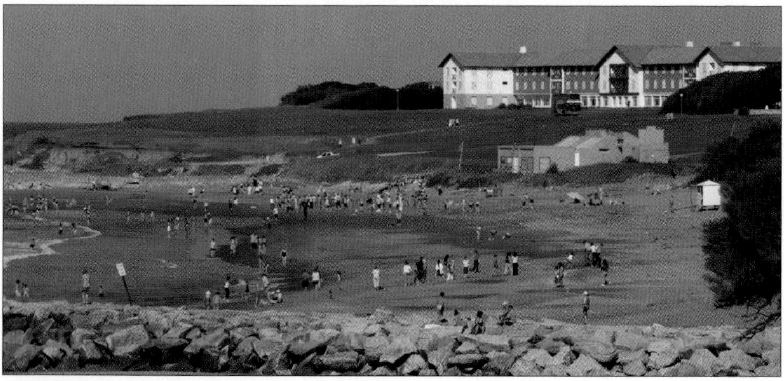

One of the greener beach resorts in Argentina, Chapadmalal

For hotels and restaurants in this region see p278 and p296

Rows of tents lining Miramar beach on a sunny day

Miramar ❽

Road Map C3. 25 miles (40 km) S of Mar del Plata. 🚃 🚆 ℹ️ *Ave Costanera & Calle 21, (02291) 420-190.* **www**.miramar.gov.ar

Well known as a resort for families and children, Miramar is known as Ciudad de los Niños y de las Bicicletas (City of Children and Bicycles). Popular during the 1980s, it is now somewhat faded and lacks the smart restaurants, trendy bars, pretty houses, and hotels of the resorts to the north. A small surfing community sets up shop every summer to make use of Miramar's extremely powerful wave breaks.

High-rise buildings overshadow the main promenade but a short walk away is the **Vivero Dunícola Florentino Ameghino**, a group of forested dunes. Here, there is a barbecue area, a small nature museum, a children's playground, and the Bosque Energético (Energy Wood), where an unusual variety of conifers and pines grow.

Necochea ❾

Road Map C3. 60 miles (97 km) SW of Miramar. ✈️ 🚃 🚆 ℹ️ *cnr Ave 79 and Ave 2, (02262) 425-983.* **www**.necochea.gov.ar

Residents of towns deep inside the southern Buenos Aires province and northern Patagonia often choose to visit Necochea over Mar del Plata. The waters are cool here, but summer daytime temperatures soar as high as 33° C (91° F). The resort's

wide strip of dunes is calmer and more picturesque than the high-rise beachside developments that plague the busier resorts to the north. Half a dozen beaches, pretty woods, a lake, an amphitheater in the **Parque Miguel Lillo**, fossils at Punta Caballido, and the thriving fishing harbor provide entertainment for families. There is ample opportunity for hiking, cycling, dune trips, and rafting on Río Quequén. Windsurfers, jet-skiiers, and sailors enjoy the gusting sea breezes off Necochea. Popular among divers is Punta Negra, just 3 miles (5 km) from the center. A little farther up the coast is Cueva del Tigre, famous for its fishing spots.

A small Danish community and a significant Basque community thrive in the town. Some Basque restaurants here specialize in local seafood.

Sunlit forest in Parque Miguel Lillo, Necochea

Balcarce ❿

Road Map C3. 32 miles (52 km) NW of Mar del Plata. 🏃 *42,000.* 🚃 ℹ️ *Calle 17, (02266) 425-758.* 🎪 *National Potato Fiesta (Mar).*

Most Argentinians associate the name of Balcarce with cars, potatoes, and small traditional cookies called *alfajor*. The land around the town is especially good for growing potatoes, grains, and aromatic grasses for the many cattle-rearing farms. This low-key resort town is popular with Buenos Aires families.

The town is famous as being the birthplace of Juan Manuel Fangio, and the **Museo del Automovilismo Juan Manuel Fangio** is a popular tourist site. Along with soccer star Maradona and tennis player Guillermo Vilas, Fangio remains a legendary sportsman. He was a record-making Formula 1 driver during the 1950s, the first decade of Formula 1 racing. He won the world championship five times, the same as Michael Schumacher, until the latter took his sixth title in 2003. The museum is housed in a century-old building, filled with Fangio memorabilia and a collection of old cars. The most impressive exhibit is located on the top floor – the original Mercedes-Benz Silver Arrow that Fangio drove to victory in 1954.

Also worth visiting in Balcarce are the town hall and cemetery entrance, both of which were designed by architect Francisco Salamone in Art Deco style. The town is also the arena for the annual National Potato Fiesta. Cerro El Triunfo (Triumph Hill), located a mile (2 km) away, is good for walkers and trial motorcyclists.

Juan Manuel Fangio on one of his races

🏛 **Museo del Automovilismo Juan Manuel Fangio**
Corner of Dardo Rocha and Mitre. **Tel** (02266) 425–540. 🕙 10am–7pm daily. 🅿️ ♿ 🖥 🚻
www.museofangio.com

Horse riding on a sunny evening in the open countryside outside Tandil city

Tandil ⓫

Road Map C3. 100 miles (160 km) S of Buenos Aires. 🏔 *110,000.* 🚌 ℹ *Ave Espora 1120, (02293) 432-073.* **www**.tandil.gov.ar

The attractive town of Tandil nestles among Sistema de Tandilia. These are gently undulating granite hills that rise to about 1,800 ft (550 m) above sea level. The town offers weekend breaks to porteños who want a getaway to the hills but cannot travel as far as the Andes. Tandil is extremely popular during Easter, the time when the Stations of the Cross procession takes place. The walk ends at Monte Calvario, a hillock topped by a large cross east of the town.

The cobblestoned town center, Plaza Independencia, has been the focal point of

Giant crucifix at the top of Monte Calvario, east of Tandil

life in Tandil ever since the Fuerte Independencia (Fort of Independence) was built on the site in 1823. It was razed 50 years later to make way for the town's expansion. The nearby neo-Gothic **Templo de la Inmaculada Concepción**, built in 1878, incorporates stones from the fort.

Tandil's **Museo de Bellas Artes**, located south of the plaza, boasts works by local artists as well as a handful of minor pieces by acknowledged Argentinian masters such as Berni and Quinquela Martín. North of Plaza Independencia is another interesting site, the **Museo Tradicionalista**, which has exhibits of photographs and art collected by local families. There is also a good replica of a *pulpería*, a saloon-cum-general store, around which gaucho life revolved.

Tandil has good restaurants and bars along with a lively nightlife. It is also famous for its cured meats and cheeses. Visitors should head southwest out of town to explore the nearby hills. Cerro El Centinela is the most popular climb, while the higher Sierra Las Animas is more difficult. Horse riding and mountain biking are popular activities.

🏛 **Museo de Bellas Artes**
Chacabuco 367. **Tel** (02293) 432-067. ⏰ 8:30am–12:30pm, 5–9pm Tue–Fri. 🔒 Jan. **www**.tandil.gov.ar

🏛 **Museo Tradicionalista**
4 de Abril 851. **Tel** (02293) 435-573. ⏰ 4–8pm Tue–Sun. 📷

Sierra de la Ventana ⓬

Road Map C3. 20 miles (30 km) NW of Sierra de la Ventana village. 🚌 ℹ *Avedel Golf s/n°, Sierra de la Ventana; (0291) 491-5303.* 🅰

The Pampas region is mostly undulating, but the Sierra de la Ventana rises to more than 3,900 ft (1,200 m) above sea level. The range is named after the *ventana* (window), a rock formation on the tallest of its peaks, Cerro de la Ventana. This summit is situated within Parque Provincial Ernesto Tornquist. The range is more rugged than Sistema de Tandilia and is a popular spot for outdoor adventure, drawing hikers, climbers, cyclists, horseback riders, as well as casual weekenders. The area is also popular with nature-lovers as it supports a large variety of

The "window" formation at the summit of Cerro de la Ventana

For hotels and restaurants in this region see p278 and p296

wildlife which includes foxes, pumas, guanaco, armadillos, and the copper iguana.

There are three small villages from which to access the range: Tornquist, Villa Ventana, and Sierra de la Ventana. They are all quiet, laid-back places, but the last has a greater range of services for tourists as well as a choice of several small hotels.

Parque Provincial Ernesto Tornquist ⓭

Road Map C3. 14 miles (22 km) NW of Sierra de la Ventana town. **Tel** *(0291) 491-0039.* 🚍 🗐 *Jan–Feb: 8am–5:30pm daily; Mar–Dec: 9am–5pm daily.*

Covering an area of 26 sq miles (68 sq km), this park offers some of the area's best climbing. It has wrought-iron gates at the entrance, beyond which is a small visitors' center providing useful information on the local ecosystem via audiovisual aids. It houses displays of the area's flora and fauna and a 3D topographical map.

Within the park limits is the 3,700-ft (1,130-m) Cerro de la Ventana, with a well-marked trail leading to the summit. There are also the moderately difficult Cerro Blanco and Claro Oscuro circuits, which offer spectacular views of the area. Numerous short strolls can also be made to waterfalls, the most popular of which is the Garganta del Diablo. The weather can turn unpredictable above 3,300 ft (1,000 m) and it would be best to hire a local guide on the harder treks.

An interesting site within the park is the **Reserva Natural Integral**. This is a strictly controlled area where herds of wild horses can be seen. There are also a number of caves, one of which has ancient paintings on its walls. Birds of prey and common carrion eaters such as *chimangos* and *carranchas* can be seen circling on thermals above the range.

The quiet Estancia Cerro de la Cruz surounded by greenery

Estancia Cerro de la Cruz ⓮

Road Map C3. 2 miles (3 km) E of Sierra de la Ventana village. 🚍 🗐 🖰 **www**.estanciacerrodelacruz. com

Designed by renowned architect Alejandro Bustillo, this English-style wood-and-stone house is one of the grander estancias in southern Buenos Aires province. The estancia was acquired in 1935 by Argentinian engineer Eduardo Ayerza, who started the first breeding ranch specializing in Polled Hereford cattle in Argentina. During its heyday, the ranch had a separate butler's residence, dormitories for employees, huge barns, and nine silos (warehouses) for storing grains and cereal. Black and white photographs on the inside walls of the main house record these times.

Now open as a five-room hotel, it is popular with nature tourists, golfers, and wealthy hunters who come to this region of Argentina for hunting expeditions.

THE MOUNTAINS OF THE PAMPAS

Long before the cataclysms that brought about the Andes chain, violent geological movements beneath the Pampas forced the land upwards to 1,659–3,600 ft (500–1,100 m) above sea level. The two main ranges are Sierra de la Ventana and Sistema de Tandilia. The former is formed mainly from sedimentary rock dating from the Paleozoic period (570–250 million years ago), and its cool blues and greys make for a striking contrast with the Pampas spread below. The jagged ridges and high peaks mean trekking can be challenging. Sistema de Tandilia is older, with formations dating back to the Precambrian period (4,600–575 million years ago), and has smooth curves, ideal for light treks. Rheas, *chimango* hawks, armadillos, and European hares are common sights on these highlands.

View of the Sierra de la Ventana rising from the Pampas plains

Barber shop kept intact inside Museo del Puerto, Bahía Blanca

Bahía Blanca **⑮**

Road Map C3. 235 miles (380 km) SW of Tandil. ⛿ 260,000. ✈ 🚌 ℹ Alsina 65 (0291) 459-4000. 🎭 Fiesta de San Silverio (Jun). **www**.bahiablanca.gov.ar

Known as the Liverpool of Argentina, Bahía Blanca has a history, like the famous English city, that is inseparable from the sea. In 1828, a fortress was established here, principally as a maritime base for defending the southern coast against Brazilian invaders. In 1884, railroads were laid by British firms and Bahía enjoyed a commercial and cultural dynamism that made it unique on this otherwise remote strip of Atlantic coast. Around the same time, 12 miles (20 km) southeast of the city, Puerto Belgrano was created and today it is the country's largest naval base.

By the end of the 19th century, apart from being a powerful railroad and naval base, Bahía Blanca was booming due to grain and meat exports. When Argentina needed a major cargo port to service the farms of southern Buenos Aires, an Anglo-Argentinian engineer named Don Guillermo White built wharves here which, even today, remain the busiest outside Buenos Aires.

The modern city is no tourist hotspot, but Avenida Alem, with its assortment of European architectural styles and Plaza Rivadavia, makes

for a pleasant stroll. Located southwest of the plaza, the Barrio Inglés, with its red-brick semi-detached houses built for railroad workers, reminds visitors of the railroad boom of the 1880s. The main attraction in the city is **Museo del Puerto**, housed in an old customs building, dedicated to the history and evolution of the port. The main exhibition is made up of *tableaux vivant*, mannequins of sailors, dockworkers, barmen, and shopkeepers, who represent "local lifestyles." The museum's archive contains photographs, documents, and recorded oral histories. The entire port quarter is worth visiting on Sundays, when

Old steering wheel at Museo del Puerto

traditional *cantinas* serve steaks and pastas.

Every June, *bahienses*, as the locals are known, pay homage to the Italian saint San Silverio, the patron saint of fishermen.

> 🏛 **Museo del Puerto**
> Guillermo Torres 4180. **Tel** (0291) 457-3006. ⊙ 9am–1pm Mon–Fri.
> 🍴 **www**.bahiablanca.gov.ar

Santa Rosa **⑯**

Road Map C3. 75 miles (120 km) NW of Bahía Blanca. ⛿ 100,000. ✈ 🚌 ℹ Ave Luro 400, (02954) 425-060.

Founded in 1892 shortly after Argentinian forces had vanquished the native Mapuche settlements, the city of Santa Rosa was originally little more than a handful of estancias, granted to officers who had taken part in the Conquista del Desierto campaign *(see p50)*. Today, this friendly city has grown into an important transport hub and has two main urban centers. The relatively newer Centro Cívico is where the government offices and the bus terminal are located. The more interesting area is around Plaza San Martín, where there is a quasi-modernist cathedral, several cafés, and **Museo Provincial de Historia Natural**. The museum's collection of indigenous artifacts is limited,

The Centro Cívico building at Santa Rosa

but there are fine examples of Patagonian fauna and some dinosaur fossils, that were discovered when the town center was redeveloped in 1994. Santa Rosa is also the base from which to explore the impressive Parque Nacional Lihué Calel.

Environs
Around 23 miles (35 km) south of Santa Rosa is **Reserva Provincial Parque Luro**. A former estate, the land was once owned by Pedro Luro, a relative of General Roca and son of one of the creators of the resort of Mar del Plata *(see pp148–9)*. The area was taken over by the provincial authorities in 1996. Luro had built a French-style château here called El Castillo, and imported deer from Europe so he could go hunting in grand old European aristocratic style.

Today, the preserve is home to many native animals such as pumas, armadillos, red foxes, wild cats, guanacos, ferrets, and *ñandús*. It also has exotic species including red deer and wild boars. Guided tours, on foot or on horseback, take visitors around the beautiful château, through thick forests of native trees, and up onto the dunes that surround the green park.

Guanacos roaming freely in Parque Nacional Lihué Calel

Crested Caracara at Lihué Calel

unusual mix of vegetation supporting both ferns and spiked cacti. The most commonly found is the Traitor plant, which is a densely spiked cactus. The park has over 150 bird species while its pride is the reclusive puma which is rarely seen. Gray foxes roam freely, especially near campsites, and wild mountain cats, herds of *ñandús*, guanacos, wild boar, and armadillos can easily be spotted. Venomous snakes such as *yarará* and coral snakes are

also found and it is advisable for visitors to stay away from thick bushes or unexplored paths. Spring is the best time to visit the park; walkers and cyclists can go on self-guided trips to see indigenous cave paintings by the region's first inhabitants or venture on a tougher scramble to the top of the highest peak, the 1,902-ft (580-m) Cerro de la Sociedad Científica. The campsite here is free and has showers and barbecues. There is also a service station that houses a slightly old motel, which has some basic facilities.

Parque Nacional Lihué Calel ⓱

Road Map B3. 140 miles (225 km) SW of Santa Rosa. *Tel (02952) 436-595.* 🚌 ⭘ *daily.* ⛺

Created in 1977, Parque Nacional Lihué Calel covers about 39 sq miles (100 sq km). Meaning "hills of life" in the native Mapuche language, the slopes at Lihué Calel are relatively fertile in comparison to the surrounding plains. This is because the sierras were formed by intense volcanic activity nearly 200 million years ago and retain water provided by scarce rains. The park has an

---

THE NATIVE FRONTIER
Spanish viceroys in pre-independent Argentina were more concerned with protecting the Buenos Aires port and the trade routes to the north than with indigenous populations. Shortly after Independence in 1816, however, the leaders of the newly formed Argentinian Republic turned their attention to the Pampas and Patagonia. The first to wage a military campaign against the indigenous population, in order to acquire their land, was Juan Manuel Rosas *(see p49)* in

southern Argentina in the 1830s. In the 1870s, General Roca, later president, led the Conquista del Desierto *(see p50)*. His campaign moved south beyond Río Negro, vanquishing the Mapuche and Tehuelche and rounding up survivors who were relocated to central Buenos Aires province. A turning point was the surrender in 1885 of Valentín Sayhueque, an important *cacique* (pre-Columbian tribal chief) and head of the Manzaneros. Today, the Mapuche live in the provinces of Buenos Aires, La Pampa, Neuquén, Río Negro, and Chubut.

General Roca who led the Conquista del Desierto

ARGENTINIAN MESOPOTAMIA

*A*rgentina's subtropical northeast, Mesopotamia has a landscape dominated by the mighty Ríos Paraná and Uruguay, giving it a name that means, in Greek, "the land between rivers." This region is noted for its high level of rainfall, which gives rise to lush forests teeming with wildlife and tropical flora, huge embalsados (floating islands), and acres of glistening wetlands.

The region's original inhabitants were the Guaraní who, by the 16th century, were living mainly in small agricultural communities. Jesuit missionaries arrived in the 1550s, aiming to evangelize the Guaraní and protect them from Spanish colonial exploitation by building the first of many missions in 1609. In the 19th century, Mesopotamia served as the battleground for the post-Independence civil war between Unitarios and Federales.

By the 20th century, ranching and grain agriculture were bringing in new income but at the cost of the environment, prompting the creation of several national parks to counter deforestation. Today, Mesopotamia's economy remains dependent on farming and forestry, although tourism, driven by natural wonders such as Iguazú Falls and Esteros del Iberá, is also an important source of income.

The region is a nature lover's paradise, with miles of *yatay* palm forests, wooded marshes, and subtropical jungles. Several national parks serve to protect the area's abundant flora and fauna and offer visitors an opportunity for various outdoor activites ranging from boating and wildlife-watching to camping and trekking. In contrast to the verdant wilderness are the bustling urban centers with their well-preserved colonial buildings and busy calendar of lively folk music festivals and carnival celebrations.

Marsh deer, a common sight in the breathtaking natural preserve Esteros del Iberá

◁ Paul the Apostle carved in stone at the ruins of San Ignacio Miní, Misiones

Exploring Argentinian Mesopotamia

Stunning natural highlights and historical architecture are the main tourist attractions of the region. Palm-fringed beaches edge the islands and banks of Ríos Paraná and Uruguay. Some of the best beaches can be found at Rosario, Colón, and Gualeguaychú. The region's biggest city, Rosario, brims with museums, galleries, and monumental architecture. Santa Fe and Corrientes have beautifully preserved colonial streets, and San Ignacio Miní houses 300-year-old Jesuit ruins. Off-the-beaten-track destinations include Yapeyú, the birthplace of General San Martín, and Mercedes, gateway to the vast Esteros del Iberá.

SIGHTS AT A GLANCE

Towns and Cities
Colón **7**
Corrientes **12**
Gualeguaychú **5**
Mercedes **10**
Paraná **3**
Resistencia **13**
Rosario pp160–61 **1**
Santa Fe **4**
Yapeyú **9**

Historical Buildings
Palacio San José **6**
San Ignacio Miní **16**

National Parks and Preserves
Esteros del Iberá pp166–7 **11**
Parque Nacional Chaco **14**
Parque Nacional El Palmar **8**
Parque Nacional Iguazú pp172–5 **17**
Parque Nacional Pre-Delta **2**
Parque Nacional Río Pilcomayo **15**

SEE ALSO

• **Where to Stay** p279
• **Where to Eat** p297

Cathedral on Plaza Primero de Mayo, Paraná

For additional map symbols *see back flap*

General Enrique Mosconi
Tartagal
Ingr. Guillermo N. Juárez
Complejo Hidrico R. Teuco-Lag. Yema
Laguna Yerma
FORMO
Río
Gran Chaco
CHACO
Río Guay
Castelli
Tres Isletas
Salta
Preside Roqu
Campo Largo Sáenz F
Las Breñas
General Pinedo
Villa Berthet
Villa Angela
Santa Sylvania
SANTA F
Añatuya
Tostado
Vera
Ceres
San Cristóbal
San Javi
San Justo
Helvecia
Rafaela
Córdoba
SANTA FE PAR
Diamante
PARQU NACION PRE-DE
Córdoba
San Lorenzo
ROSAR
Río Cuarto
San Nicolás de Los Arroyos
Melincué
Venado Tuerto
Lag. La Picasa
Rufino Junín

GETTING AROUND

The area's main airports are at Rosario, Corrientes, Resistencia, and Puerto Iguazú. There are regular flights that connect Paraná and Resistencia to Buenos Aires. A reliable option is long-distance buses that link the main towns and cities. Motorists following the course of Río Paraná via Ruta Provincial 11 and Ruta Nacional 12 should note that main river crossings are via the Rosario-Victoria and Corrientes-Resistencia road bridges, and the Sante Fe-Paraná subfluvial tunnel.

An effigy at the Carnaval celebrated in Gualeguaychú, Entre Ríos

Río Pilcomayo
Río Porteño

15 Laguna Blanca

PARQUE NACIONAL RÍO PILCOMAYO

Asunción

Río Riacho Pilagá

Pirané

Río Paraguay

Formosa

San Francisco de Laishi

14 PARQUE NACIONAL CHACO

Puerto Iguazú

17 PARQUE NACIONAL IGUAZÚ

El Dorado

Montecarlo

Bernardo de Irigoyen

San Pedro

SAN IGNACIO MINÍ   **MISIONES**

RESISTENCIA

13 12

CORRIENTES

Itatí Río Paraná

Yacyretá Dam Posadas

Berón de Estrada

16

Campo Grande

13 El Soberbio

adai

Empedrado

Ituzaingo

San Miguel

Oberá

San Javier

Río Uruguay

Saladas

Río Esteros del Sta. Lucía

11

San Roque

ESTEROS DEL IBERÁ

L. del Iberá

CORRIENTES

Santo Tomé

nquista

MERCEDES

10

La Cruz

Alvear

squina Sauce

Curuzú Cuatia

9 YAPEYÚ

Paso de Los Libres

Río Guayguiraró

Río Macreyá

Monte Caseros

San José de Feliciano

ENTRE RÍOS

Federal

Emb. Salto Grande

Concordia

18 8 PARQUE NACIONAL EL PALMAR

PALACIO SAN JOSÉ

6

7 COLÓN

Concepción del Uruguay

16

5

GUALEGUAYCHÚ

Médanos

Río Uruguay

0 km   100

0 miles   100

KEY

▬▬	Expressway
▬▬	Highway
▬▬	Main road
═══	Minor road
┄┄	Railroad
▬▬	International border
▬▬	Provincial border

View of a beautiful sunset over the Río Paraná, Corrientes

Rosario ❶

Located on the west bank of Río Paraná, Rosario is an industrial powerhouse that enjoys a vibrant cultural scene. This port city first underwent explosive growth at the end of the 19th century, when its surrounding pampas became one of the world's largest grain-producing regions and its port engaged in foreign trade for the first time. Many of the city's impressive constructions date from that period and reflect its Francophile influences. Today, with its architectural heritage, theaters, and museums, Rosario is one of the country's most lively urban destinations.

Monumento Nacional a la Bandera

The majestic Puente Rosario-Victoria bridge over Río Parana

🍴 La Costanera

Avenida Belgrano. **Museo de Arte Contemporáneo Rosario (MACRO)** Ave Estanislao López 2250. **Tel** (0341) 480-4981. ☐ Jan–Feb: 4–10pm; Mar–Dec: 2–8pm. 🟢 Wed. 🎟 🎥 Spanish only. 👤 📷

Stretching over 6 miles (10 km), Rosario's *costanera* (coast) offers spectacular views of Río Paraná. At its southern end is the pretty **Parque Urquiza** while a short walk to the north are old grain silos (warehouses). Housed within a brightly painted silo, **Museo de Arte Contemporáneo Rosario (MACRO)**, is an outstanding example of the area's vibrant cultural life.

Along the riverfront's northern section are the river beaches of La Florida and Rambla Catalunya. A short stroll north are Costa Alta, a waterfront promenade, and the **Puente Rosario-Victoria**, a suspension bridge linking Rosario with the neighboring province of Entre Ríos.

🏛 Monumento Nacional a la Bandera

Avenida Santa Fe 581. **www.** monumentoalabandera.gov.ar

Rosario's Monumento Nacional a la Bandera commemorates the inaugural hoisting of the Argentinian flag by military hero General Manuel Belgrano on a nearby island in 1812. The work of architect Angel Guido, it is made from unpolished marble. The tower is flanked by patriotic sculptures and bas-reliefs depicting the country's diverse geography. General Belgrano's remains lie in a crypt at the base of the tower, from where a lift climbs towards its summit offering panoramic vistas of city and river. Guido's design is completed by the **Patio Cívico** (civic courtyard) and the neoclassical Propileo (vestibule). On the Avenida Santa Fe side of the vestibule is **Galería de Honor a las Banderas**, a museum that honors the national flags of the Americas.

🏛 Plaza 25 de Mayo

Ave Córdoba and Buenos Aires.

The city's historical heart, Plaza 25 de Mayo is a pleasantly shaded plaza. At its eastern end stands the Italianate **Basílica Catedral Santuario Nuestra Señora del Rosario**, built in the 19th century. In its crypt is a shrine housing an image of the Virgin Mary brought from Spain in 1773. On the Avenida Santa Fe side of the plaza is the elegant **Museo de Arte Decorativo Firma y Odilo Estévez**. Other interesting buildings include **Edifício Bola de Nieve**, the city's tallest structure when built in 1907, and Palacio del Correo. **Pasaje Juramento**, flanked by running water and sculptures by Salta-born artist Lola Mora, links the plaza to the Monumental Nacional.

🏛 Che Guevara Museum

Plaza de la Cooperacion.

Dedicated to the Cuban revolutionary hero, Ernesto Che Guevara, this museum brings to notice his birthplace – Rosario. Most of the 1,400 items were donated by family and friends of Che, including Alberto Granados, whose journey with Che across Latin America was immortalized in the 2004 movie, *The Motorcycle Diaries*. Exhibits include Che's combat uniforms, which he wore during the Cuban Revolution. The apartment building where he spent his early infancy stands two blocks away at Urquiza and Entre Ríos but is inaccessible to the public.

Entrance to Che Guevara's first home in Rosario

For hotels and restaurants in this region see p279 and p297

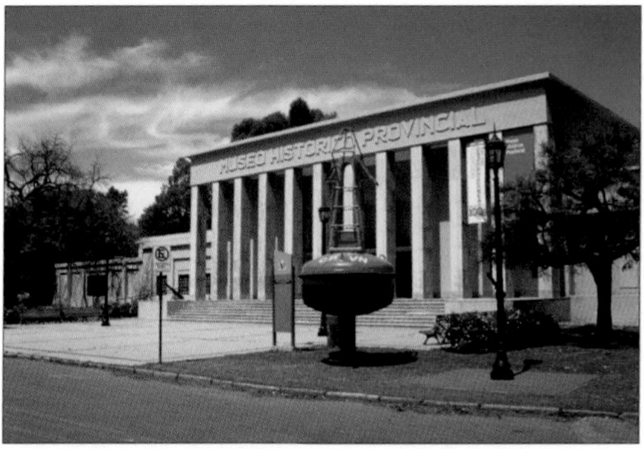

Museo Histórico Provincial Julio Marc in Parque de la Independencia

VISITORS' CHECKLIST

Road Map C2. 186 miles (290 km) from Buenos Aires. 👥 *1,200,000.* ✈ 🚌 ℹ *Ave Belgrano y Buenos Aires, (0341) 480-2230.* 🛒 *Sat, Sun.* 🎉 *La Semana de la Bandera (Jun), Fiesta Nacional de Colectividades (Nov).* **www**.rosario.gov.ar

Parque de la Independencia

Bounded by Pellegrini, 27 de Febrero, Moreno y Lagos. ♿ 🍴 ☕

🛍 **Museo Municipal de la Ciudad** Boulevard Oroño 2300. ***Tel*** *(0341) 480-8665.* ⏰ *9am–6pm Mon–Fri, 2pm–8pm Sat, Sun.* 🎫 *Spanish only.* ♿ ☕ 🛍

Opened in 1902, the grand Parque de la Independencia is Rosario's largest and most beautiful green space. Within walking distance of the city center, it is packed during weekends with picnicking families, rollerskaters, and local artisans. Its many attractions include an ornamental rose garden, a lake, football stadium, and two museums. **Museo Municipal de la Ciudad** has interesting exhibits on the city's social and political history and the nearby **Museo Histórico Provincial Julio Marc**, houses excellent historical displays from pre-Columbian times onwards.

Museo Municipal de Bellas Artes Juan B. Castagnino

Avenida Pelligrini 2202. ***Tel*** *(0341) 480-2542.* ⏰ *varies (call in advance).* 💲 *contributions welcome.* 🎫 *varies (call in advance).* ♿ 🛍 **www**.museocastagnino.org.ar

Inaugurated in 1937, this exceptional museum was the culmination of an initiative by *Rosarino* progressives to transform their city into a cultural capital and banish the city's reputation as the "Chicago Argentino," earned for its port industry, mafia activity, and numerous red light areas.

Spanning two floors, the museum houses mainly modern Argentinian art from the 19th century to the present day. There are works by great Argentinian artists such as Benito Quinquella Martín and *Rosarino* artist Antonio Berni. European art from the 17th century onwards is also displayed. The museum's main attraction lies in the curators' decision to eschew any kind of thematic or chronological organization and place contemporary pieces alongside more traditional works in a dynamic and unpredictable mixture of forms.

ROSARIO

Key to Symbols *see back flap*

Che Guevara Museum 4
La Costanera 1
Monumento Nacional a la Bandera 2
Museo Municipal de Bellas Artes Juan B. Costagnino 6
Parque de la Independencia 5
Plaza 25 de Mayo 3

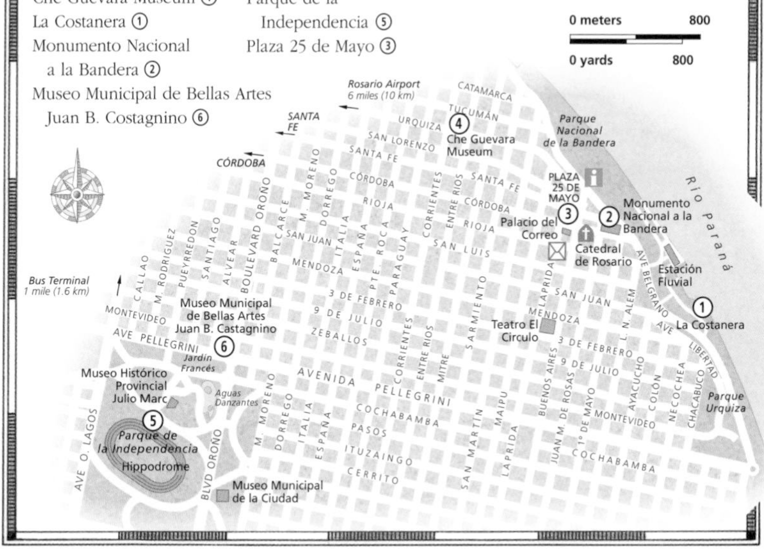

Parque Nacional Pre-Delta ❷

Road Map C2. 62 miles (100 km)
N of Rosario. 🛈 *25 de Mayo 389,*
Diamante; (0343) 498-3535.
⭕ *daily.* Ⓐ

Created in 1992, Parque
Nacional Pre-Delta protects
10 sq miles (26 sq km) of
subtropical wetlands. The
landscape is a mosaic of
marshland, floating islands,
lakes, and drainage channels.
The islands, edged by lush
forests, are marked at their
centers by deep, almost
permanently inundated
depressions. These form
lagoons that harbor the park's
main botanical feature, the
irupé, the giant Victoria water
lily, which sits on the
water's surface like a
floating bowl.

Myriad bird
species, including the
ringed kingfisher, which
is the park's symbol,
and numerous large
wading birds are easily
sighted. Other animals
include the semi-
aquatic capybara,
coipu, and a popu-
lation of broad-nosed caiman.
As only a fraction of the park
is accessible by foot, there are
boat excursions that embark
from the park's entry point at
La Jaula. The longest one
navigates the narrow water
channels to **Isla Las Mangas**,
where there is a hiking trail
that leads to **Laguna Los
Baños**. This lake is often
covered with *irupés*.

Colorful ringed kingfisher

View of a water channel, Parque
Nacional Pre-Delta

Paraná ❸

Road Map C2. 84 miles (136 km) N
of Rosario. 🚉 *238,000.* ✈ ▭
🛈 *Ave Buenos Aires 132, (0343)*
423-0183. 🎭 *Festival Provincial del*
Mate (Feb). **www**.parana.gov.ar

A historic destination,
Paraná is home to fine
19th-century architecture
and long stretches of river
beaches. It was declared
capital of the Argentinian
Confederation in 1854,
and on its main square,
Plaza Primero de Mayo,
stands the old **Antiguo
Senado de la
Confederación**, the
nation's then seat of government. Ornamented by classic
Italianate fountains and *yatay*
palms, the plaza is fronted by
Palacio Municipal, **Escuela
Normal Paraná**, and the neo-
Renaissance façade of the
Catedral Municipal. Three
blocks west of the plaza is the
excellent **Museo y Mercado
Provincial de Artesanías**,
which displays and sells

native crafts. North of the
plaza, **Parque Urquiza**,
Paraná's public park, descends
the bank of Río Paraná
towards palm-fringed beaches.
Boats to the facing islands
depart regularly from the
river's waterfront.

🏛 **Museo y Mercado
Provincial de Artesanías**
Urquiza 1239. **Tel** *(0343) 420-8891.*
⭕ *varies (call in advance).* 🚫 *Mon.*

Santa Fe ❹

Road Map C2. 104 miles (167 km)
N of Rosario. 🚉 *370,000.* ✈ ▭
🛈 *Blvd Galvez & Piedro Vittori,*
(0342) 457-1881. **www**.welcome
argentina.com/santfe/

Steeped in history, Santa Fe
also has a spectacular architectural heritage. Its most
important buildings cluster
around Plaza 25 de Mayo.
The whitewashed façade of
the Jesuit-built **Iglesia Nuestra
Señora de los Milagros** con-
ceals a lavish interior that
contains a painting of the
Immaculate Virgin from 1634
by Cavaillé-Coll. Dominating
the square's southern end, the
beautiful **Casa de Gobierno**
was built on the site of the
colonial *cabildo* where the
Argentinian Constitution was
signed in 1853.

South of the square is
**Iglesia y Convento de San
Francisco**, built between 1662
and 1695, with a beautifully
conserved interior. A stroll
away from the church is
**Museo Histórico Provincial
Brigadier General Estanislao
López**, which functions within
a colonial house. Its variety
of exhibits includes antique,
ornate *mate* gourds and
unique displays on the 19th-
century struggle between
Unitarios and the Urquiza-
led Federalists.

⛪ **Iglesia y Convento de San
Francisco**
Amenábar 2257. ⭕ *7am–5pm*
daily.

🏛 **Museo Histórico Provincial
Brigadier General Estanislao
López**
San Martín 12490. **Tel** *(0342) 457-*
3529. ⭕ *Tue–Sun.* 🎟 🚫 *Tue–Fri.*
www.museohistorico-sfe.gov.ar

The elegant façade of Catedral Municipal, Paraná

The Paraná River System

The great Río Paraná is the longest river in Argentina and the second longest in all of South America. This mighty waterway flows 2,479 miles (3,990 km) from its source in tropical Brazil to its mouth at the temperate Atlantic, draining an area of more than 380,000 sq miles (100,000 sq km). On its course through Argentina, it forms a natural border with Paraguay before snaking southwest, marking the western limit of Argentina's island-like Mesopotamia region. In its far south, the river forms the Paraná Delta, a floodplain and great labyrinth of drainage channels, wetlands, and river islands. A subtropical microhabitat at the heart of a temperate zone, the jungle-like delta forms a dramatic contrast with the arable pampas that surround it.

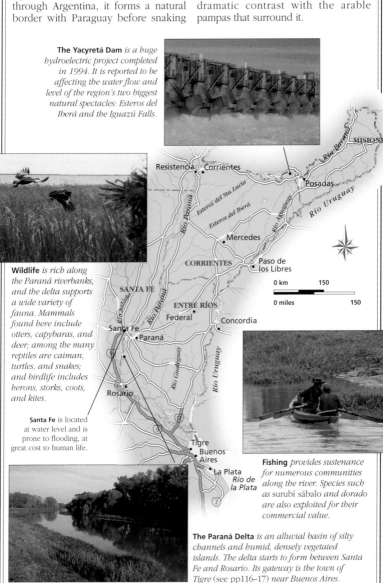

The Yacyretá Dam *is a huge hydroelectric project completed in 1994. It is reported to be affecting the water flow and level of the region's two biggest natural spectacles: Esteros del Iberá and the Iguazú Falls.*

Wildlife *is rich along the Paraná riverbanks, and the delta supports a wide variety of fauna. Mammals found here include otters, capybaras, and deer; among the many reptiles are caiman, turtles, and snakes; and birdlife includes herons, storks, coots, and kites.*

Santa Fe is located at water level and is prone to flooding, at great cost to human life.

Resistencia · Corrientes

Posadas

MISIONES

Río Paraná

Esteros del Sta. Lucía

Esteros del Iberá

Río Miriñay

Río Uruguay

Mercedes

CORRIENTES

Paso de los Libres

SANTA FE

ENTRE RÍOS

Río Salado

Río Paraná

Federal

Santa Fe · Paraná

Concordia

Río Gualeguay

Río Uruguay

Rosario

Tigre · Buenos Aires

La Plata

Río de la Plata

0 km 150

0 miles 150

Fishing *provides sustenance for numerous communities along the river. Species such as surubí sábalo and dorado are also exploited for their commercial value.*

The Paraná Delta *is an alluvial basin of silty channels and humid, densely vegetated islands. The delta starts to form between Santa Fe and Rosario. Its gateway is the town of Tigre (see pp116–17) near Buenos Aires.*

Gualeguaychú ❺

Road Map C2. 140 miles (226 km)
SE of Paraná. 🏠 100,000. 🚌
ℹ️ *Plazoleta de los Artesanos, Paseo del Puerto; (03446) 423-668.* 🚆 *Sat.*
🎭 *Carnaval (Jan & Feb).*
www.gualeguaychu.gov.ar

Derived from the Guaraní phrase for "river of the large jaguar," Gualeguaychú sits on the bank of its namesake river, a tributary of Río Uruguay. It is most famous for its Carnaval, when thousands of revelers descend on this small town to enjoy the country's biggest and most extravagant summer celebration. Festivities center around the **Corsódromo**, an open parade ground overlooking Gualeguaychú's old railroad line and train station.

Outside of Carnaval, the town attracts visitors for its river beaches, which stretch over 12 miles (20 km). **Parque Urquiza**, across the river, has some of the most popular beaches. Also noteworthy is the town's colonial architecture; two immaculately restored early-1800s abodes, **Azotea de Lapalma** and **Solar de los Haedo**, are open to the public as museums. **Instituto Magnasco**, Gualeguaychú's main cultural space, houses many local artworks and historical artifacts.

🏛 **Azotea de Lapalma**
San Luis y Jujuy. *Tel (03446) 437-028.* ⏱ *varies (call in advance).*
🌙 *Sun, Mon, & Tue.* 📷 🎫 *by prior arrangement (Spanish only).*

🏛 **Solar de los Haedo**
San José y Rivadavia. 🌙 *Sun, Mon, & Tue.* 📷 🎫 *by prior arrangement (Spanish only).*

The grand reception hall at General Urquiza's Palacio San José

Palacio San José ❻

Road Map C2. 68 miles (110 km)
N of Gualeguaychú. *Tel (03442) 432-620.* 🚍 *from Concepción del Uruguay.* ⏱ *8am–6:30pm Mon–Fri, 9am–6pm Sat & Sun.* 📷 🎫 *Spanish only.* **www**.palaciosanjose.com.ar

Built between 1848 and 1860, this Italianate palace was an architectural statement of power and influence for regional *caudillo* and Federalist leader, General Justo José Urquiza (1801–70). Declared a national monument, the palace sits in forested countryside and is recognizable by the tall watchtowers that stand at either end of its pink, arcaded façade. Surrounded by magnificent ornamental gardens, the palace is built around two inner courtyards. Rooms include the richly decorated Sala de los Espejos, where the General entertained guests,

Bust of General Justo Urquiza

and the Sala de Tragedia, Urquiza's bedroom, where he was assassinated in 1870. Outbuildings include a private chapel, notable for its frescoes and ornate altar. Also set within the gardens is a large artificial lake.

Colón ❼

Road Map C2. 180 miles (290 km)
SE of Paraná. 🏠 22,000. 🚌 ℹ️ *Ave Costanera y Gouchón, (03447) 421-996.* 🎭 *Fiesta Nacional de Artesanías (Feb).* **www**.colon.gov.ar

A picturesque settlement on the western bank of Río Uruguay, the little town of Colón is the perfect venue for a relaxing break. Its riverside setting facilitates a variety of activities, including swimming, boating, and lounging in the thermal waters of its public spa.

Its balustraded riverfront stretches 6 miles (10 km) and overlooks, at its northern and southern reaches, long sections of sandy, palm-fringed beaches. Boats to the facing river islands depart regularly from the waterfront. The town's oldest buildings are found clustered around the port area. Here, **Estación Fluvial**, Colón's railroad station, is an elegant, Italianate construction encircled by tall *yatay* palms. Several more historical buildings front Plaza San Martín and the main Avenida 12 de Abríl. On the avenue, **Teatro Centenario** is a well-restored theater, dating back to 1925.

A relaxing day at the beach on the banks of Río Uruguay

Towering *yatay* palm protected at Parque Nacional El Palmar

Parque Nacional El Palmar ❽

Road Map C2. 31 miles (50 km) N of Colón. ⚑ *Ruta Nacional 14, Ubajay (03447) 493-053.* ☐ *daily.* 🖼 🍴 🔲 🔼 ⚠

Covering an area of 33 sq miles (85 sq km), Parque Nacional El Palmar was created in 1965 to conserve the *yatay* palm, which once covered most of the Entre Ríos and Corrientes provinces. These tall, slender trees were in danger of extinction from mass clearing for farming and forestry in the early 20th century. The park also protects large swathes of marshland and gallery forest.

The park is home to myriad fauna, including reptiles such as the *tegu* lizard and the ostrich-like *ñandú*. The wetlands and gallery forests are a refuge for herons, king-fishers, caracaras, and wood-peckers, while otters and capybaras inhabit the park's riverbanks. Hiking trails criss-cross the park, which is also traversable by car.

Yapeyú ❾

Road Map D2. 245 miles (395 km) SE of Corrientes. 🏠 *3,000.* 🚌 ⚑ *Sargento Cabrán y Gregoria Matorra (03772) 493-198.*

Founded as a base in 1626 by Jesuits seeking to evangelize the indigenous Guaraní, Yapeyú is better known to Argentinians as the birthplace of revered Independence hero General José de San Martín (*see p49*). At the eastern edge of the main Plaza San Martín is **Templete Sanmartiano**, which preserves the ruins of the small military fort where the liberator spent his childhood. To the south of the plaza is **Museo de Cultura Jesuítica Guillermo Furlong**, which sits atop the Jesuit mission's red sand-stone foundations. It houses Jesuit arti-facts and wooden panels detailing the history of the region. At the southern end of town is **Museo Sanmartiano**, displaying weaponry that belonged to the San Martíns.

Wooden horse display, Museo Jesuítica

🏛 **Museo de Cultura Jesuítica Guillermo Furlong**
Sargento Cabrán. **Tel** (03772) 493-320. ☐ *8am–noon & 4–7pm Tue–Sun.*

🏛 **Museo Sanmartiano**
Ave Libertador s/n. **Tel** (03772) 493-011. ☐ *7am–11pm daily.* 🖼

Mercedes ❿

Road Map C2. 167 miles (270 km) SE of Corrientes. 🏠 *35,000.* 🚌 ⚑ *Acceso Oeste, (03773) 402-575.* 🎊 *Fiesta del Chamamé (Nov).*

Viewed as a gateway to the stunning Esteros del Iberá (*see pp166–7*), Mercedes is a sleepy town with lovely 19th-century streets and distinc-tive adobe buildings. The town's single museum is housed within the **Casa Municipal de Cultura**. Exhibits here include bayoneted rifles recovered from 19th-century civil war battle-grounds. Mercedes has several shops, such as **Manos Corrientes**, that sell exquisite gaucho ware. A 6-mile (9-km) drive west of town is the roadside shrine to local popular figure, Gauchito Gil.

🏛 **Casa Municipal de Cultura**
Parque Mitre. ☐ *Dec–Mar: 4pm–8pm daily; Apr–Nov: 8am–12pm, 2pm–6pm daily.*

THE LEGEND OF GAUCHITO GIL

Popular saint Gauchito Gil was a deserter from a 19th-century provincial war. On escaping to the mountains, he became a Robin Hood-type figure who stole from rich landowners to give to the poor. His legend was sealed on his capture, where at his hanging he is said to have whispered to his executioner, "When you go home you will find your son dying. Pray for my intercession, for the blood of an innocent can perform miracles." The hangman returned home to find his son in agony. After the child's recovery he erected a cross hung with a red ribbon in honor of Gauchito. Today, this site is a ribbon-festooned, candle-adorned shrine covered with messages beseeching the intercession of Gauchito. Such is Argentina's reverence for this popular saint, who is not recognized by the Vatican, that each January on the anniversary of Gil's hanging, up to 100,000 pilgrims visit the shrine.

Gaucho Antonio Gil's shrine where pilgrims tie red ribbons

Esteros del Iberá ⓫

Covering over 5,200 sq miles (13,700 sq km), the stunning Iberá wetlands are a biologically diverse wilderness of water, marshland, and islands. The reserve derives its name from the Guaraní for "shining waters," hinting at the clear-water lagoons that occupy 25 percent of its surface area. Water from these lagoons seeps into a network of narrow channels, each flanked by marshland and *embalsados* (floating islands). Guides steer boats along the channels, allowing visitors to observe a subtropical wildlife that includes over 350 bird species and numerous reptiles and mammals.

A flowering bromeliad

Visitors on a walkway accompanied by a guide

Caiman
Two species of caiman inhabit the preserve, the black caiman (above), and the smaller broad-nosed caiman. They can be found lounging on the banks of embalsados.

Capybara
Weighing about 155 lb (70 kg), capybaras are the world's largest rodents. Ubiquitous within the preserve, they live in large groups on the banks of lagoons.

Marshlands at the edge of lagoons are the habitat of reclusive mammals such as the marsh deer.

Mburucuyá · Eros de Santa Lucia · San Migu

Bella Vista ← · Santa Rosa · (118)

Concepción

Eros del Batel

C O R R I E N T E S

Río Corrientes · Laguna Trin · Lagur Fernán

(123)

Mercedes

Curuzú Cuatiá

(13) · (40)

Black Howler Monkey
Usually seen only through binoculars, these noisy primates inhabit the canopy of the preserve's forests. Their "howl" is more like a deafening roar, and can be heard from quite a distance away.

STAR SIGHTS

★ Laguna Iberá

★ Colonia Carlos Pellegrini

★ **Laguna Iberá**
The preserve's most visited lake is easily accessible by trips on boats and horseback and nocturnal safaris. These explore its marshland, floating islands, and water channels, as well as the abundant wildlife they harbor.

VISITORS' CHECKLIST

Road Map D2. 75 miles (120 km) NW of Mercedes. ✈ chartered flights only. 🚌 from Mercedes. ℹ boats arranged at Colonia Carlos Pellegrini. 🕐 7:30am–6pm daily. 📷 ♿ 🍴 🛖 **Note:** the best time to visit is in winter (Jun–Jul).

KEY

═══ Main road

── Minor road

-- Park boundary

🛥 Boat service

⛺ Campsite

ℹ Visitor information

★ **Colonia Carlos Pellegrini**
This charming and quiet village of sandy streets, artisans' shops, and adobe buildings fronts the banks of Laguna Iberá and is where most lodging options can be found. Boat and horse-riding excursions head daily from here into the wetlands.

THE BIRDS OF ESTEROS DEL IBERÁ

A haven for over 350 bird species, the preserve is an ornithological paradise. Among the most brightly colored are the scarlet-headed blackbird, yellow-billed cardinal, and vermilion flycatcher. Tall wading birds include numerous species of heron, stork, and limpkin. Biggest of all is the jabiru stork, the tallest stork in the Americas. Birds of prey include the ground-dwelling crested caracara. The savanna hawk is commonly seen gliding over the preserve's savanna, home also to the greater rhea.

A couple of nesting jabiru storks

Estancia Rincón del Socorro
One of several upscale estancias in or bordering the preserve, Rincón del Socorro (see p314) is a beautifully restored tourist ranch owned by conservationist and former North Face clothing magnate Douglas Tompkins.

Corrientes ⓬

Road Map C1. 168 miles (270 km) NW of Mercedes. 🏙 350,000. ✈ 🚌 🚆 ℹ *9 de Julio & Ave Costenera (03783) 474-829.* 🚢 *Sat & Sun.* 🎭 *Carnaval (Jan).* www.welcome argentina.com/corrientes

With a history stretching back to 1558, Corrientes was founded on the eastern bank of Río Paraná as a staging post between Asunción, Paraguay, and Buenos Aires. It was a major battleground in the 19th century in the struggle between Unitarios and Federalists, and also from 1865 to 1870, during the War of Triple Alliance against Paraguay (*see p50*).

Today Corrientes possesses an extraordinary wealth of colonial and 19th-century architecture. Its well-conserved historical center lies roughly between streets 9 de Julio, Buenos Aires, Mendoza, and Avenida Costanera. Housed in a lovely colonial-era building, **Museo de Artesanía Tradicional Folklórica** exhibits native crafts. A plethora of 19th-century buildings includes **Casa de Gobierno**, whose pink exterior is an eclectic mix of architectural styles. Three blocks north, Avenida Costanera is a river-side promenade which offers great views of Río Paraná.

🏛 **Museo de Artesanía Tradicional Folklórica**
F.J. de la Quintana 905. **Tel** *(03783) 475-945.* ◯ *varies (call in advance).* 🔘 *Sat.* 🕐 *Spanish only.* 🔳

Shady promenade of Avenida Costanera in Corrientes

The green wetland at the Parque Nacional Chaco

Resistencia ⓭

Road Map C1. 12 miles (19 km) W of Corrientes. 🏙 350,000. ✈ 🚌 ℹ *Julio Roca 20, Plaza 25 de Mayo, (03722) 458-289.* 🚢 *Fri & Sun.* 🎭 *Bienal Internacional de Escultura (Jul).* www.resistencia.gov.ar

Known as Ciudad de las Esculturas (City of Sculptures), the lovely town of Resistencia has more than 400 sculptures that adorn its streets and parks. The city is also known for its Bienal Internacional de Escultura, a festival in which inter-national sculptors transform the city's main Plaza 25 de Mayo into an open-air art studio and work-shop. Among Resistencia's main attractions are its museums. **Museo del Hombre Chaqueño Ertivio Acosta** houses artifacts belonging to the native Wichí, Toba, and Mocovi communities. **El Fogón de los Arrieros** is a museum and art gallery; its eclectic displays include a painting by well-known artist, Raúl Soldi, and boxing gloves that belonged to former world champion Carlos Monzón.

🏛 **Museo del Hombre Chaqueño Ertivio Acosta**
J.B. Justo 274. **Tel** *(03722) 453-005.* ◯ *varies (call in advance).* 🈯

🏛 **El Fogón de los Arrieros**
Brown 350. **Tel** *(03722) 426-418.* ◯ *8am–noon, 9–11pm Mon–Fri, 8am–12pm Sat.* 🈯

Wooden wheel at El Fogón de los Arrieros

Parque Nacional Chaco ⓮

Road Map C1. 69 miles (112 km) E of Resistencia. 🚌 ℹ *Captán Solari, (03727) 496-166.* ◯ *daily.* 🈯 🅿

Created in 1954, Parque Nacional Chaco is a protected area of exceptional biodiver-sity. Covering 58 sq miles (150 sq km), it conserves residual forests of the *quebracho* tree, a species that once covered the entire western part of Chaco. The *quebracho,* which produces large tannin yields and durable hardwood, had declined due to farming and forestry. The park also protects swamp, palm savanna, and gallery forest. These diverse habitats provide refuge for an extraordinary array of wildlife that includes an estimated 341 bird species. The most easily spotted are wading birds such as jacanas, herons, and jabiru storks. Mammals are more difficult to observe. Raucous howler monkeys, which are heard rather than seen, inhabit the forest canopy, while other large reclusive species include the giant anteater, maned wolf, and puma. Following rainfall, the paw marks of big predators can be spotted on trails. Reptiles include the com-monly sighted broad-nosed caiman. Bird-watching and hiking are the main activities on offer here. A variety of trails start from the park's reception area. The 3-mile (5-km) trek to the **Carpincho** and **Yacaré** lagoons provides excellent bird-watching opportunities. A single road, often impassable during the wet season (November–March), provides vehicle access through to the *quebracho* forests.

Parque Nacional Río Pilcomayo ⑮

Road Map C1. 224 miles (360 km) N of Resistencia. 🚌 *Resistencia to Laguna Blanca via Formosa.* 🛈 *Ave. Pueyrredón & RN86, Laguna Blanca; (03718) 470-045.* ⭘ *daily.* 🅰

Bounded to its north by Río Pilcomayo, Argentina's river border with Paraguay, this 185-sq-mile (490-sq-km) park shares much of the flora and fauna found in Parque Nacional Chaco. However, it contains more, and larger, bodies of water. The park's main highlights are the beautiful **Laguna Blanca** and the **Esteros Poi**, both of which are reachable by foot and vehicle trails.

The park's biggest lake, Laguna Blanca, is edged by forests alive with noisy howler monkeys, toco toucans, and pretty ringed kingfishers. The park has a myriad of other animals, including elusive mammals such as the maned wolf, which is also the park's symbol, and the graceful ocelot. The lake is a popular bathing spot, despite the presence at its shoreline of broad-nosed caiman and capybara, neither of which bite. It is advisable, however, to swim with shoes on. Visitors are also advised not to feed the fish.

Located to the west of the lake, the Esteros Poi marshland is inhabited by easily sighted wading birds such as herons, jabiru storks, and jacanas.

Apart from Resistencia, the nearest major town to Parque Nacional Río Pilcomayo is Formosa, 112 miles (180 km)

Elusive maned wolf found in the Parque Nacional Río Pilcomayo

north in the Formosa province. Taxis and *remises* (licensed mini-cabs) run regularly from Formosa to the park entrance. The towns of Laguna Naick-Neck and Laguna Blanca sit near its southern limit. The latter is linked to Formosa by bus and has better tourist facilities. The small town is also the location for the park's administrative headquarters.

Ringed kingfisher at Laguna Blanca

San Ignacio Miní ⑯

Road Map D1. 230 miles (370 km) E of Corrientes. 🚶 *6,200.* 🚌 *from Corrientes.* 🛈 *Avenida Sarmiento, Acceso a San Ignacio.* **www**.misiones-jesuiticas.com.ar

A UNESCO World Heritage Site, the Jesuit ruins at San Ignacio Miní are the most stunning and extensive of the six ruins that remain from the

Jesuit-Guaraní missions founded in the region in the 17th century.

The entrance of the site, the **Centro de Interpretación**, has themed rooms which depict the story of the mission from its founding to its eventual decline following the Jesuits' expulsion from the New World in 1767 by the Spanish colonial authorities. It also has a few exhibits that touch on Guaraní life. A short grassy path leads to the ruins among which lies a large and still clearly recognizable central plaza. Dominating the plaza is the mission's imposing red-sandstone church designed by Italian architect Juan Brasanelli in a sophisticated style known as Guaraní baroque. Its lavishly gilded interior no longer exists and the roof has long since crumbled away but its magnificent portal, adorned with bas-reliefs sculpted by skilled Guaraní artists, stands as a testament to the building's original splendor. In a second square adjacent to the church are the Jesuit priests' quarters, together with the remains of a cemetery, libraries, dining-rooms, and a kitchen.

The ancient ruins occupy nearly six blocks of the village of San Ignacio, which has a wide range of accommodation and restaurant options. There are also sound and light shows that recount the area's rich history.

🏛 **Centro de Interpretación**
Alberdi s/n. **Tel** (03752) 470-186.
⭘ *7am–7pm daily.* 📷

The Jesuit ruins of San Ignacio Miní, founded in the 17th century

A panoramic view of the magnificent horseshoe-shaped Iguazú Falls ▷

Parque Nacional Iguazú ⑰

Colorful butterfly found at the park

A UNESCO World Heritage Site, the subtropical rainforest of Parque Nacional Iguazú provides the setting for one of the world's great natural wonders, the mighty Iguazú Falls. Iguazú derives its name from the Guaraní word for "big water," a fitting description for a series of cataracts that stretches 2 miles (3 km) and comprises over 250 individual waterfalls. Once a source of legend for the Guaraní people, the falls retain an awe-inspiring, primordial beauty for visitors. Most arrive on day trips from nearby Puerto Iguazú, exploring the park via a network of catwalks and trails.

Visitors taking a walk along the Circuito Inferior

★ Garganta del Diablo

At 262 ft (80 m) high, Garganta del Diablo (Devil's Throat) is the biggest and most spectacular of the cataracts. Catwalks cross extremely close to its waters.

```
0 meters        50
0 yards         50
```

MAP OF IGUAZÚ FALLS

Estación Garganta del Diablo

KEY

— Road

--- Trail

— Railroad

-·- International border

ℹ Area de Recepción

Puerto Canoas Restaurant

Río Iguazú superior

BRAZIL

Isla San Martín

Circuito Superior

Circuito Inferior

ARGENTINA

Tropical das Cataratas Hotel

Río Iguazú inferior

Sendero Macuco

Viejo Hotel Cataratas

Area de Recepción

General Service Area

Amphitheater

Sheraton International Hotel

Train Station

```
0 meters        100
0 yards         100
```

Tropical das Cataratas offers luxury accommodation as well as awe-inspiring views of the falls.

Tren Ecológico de la Selva
This train leaves from the Area de Recepción, stopping at Estación Cataratas for Circuito Superior and Circuito Inferior before heading to Estación Garganta del Diablo.

★ **Salto San Martín**
The second largest after Garganta del Diablo, this magnificent waterfall is best viewed from Isla San Martín.

Isla San Martín

Circuito Superior

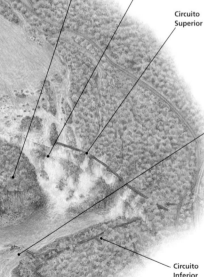

Powerboat trips
Inflatable boats depart from Circuito Inferior, taking visitors on exciting rides to the foot of Salto San Martín.

Circuito Inferior

Sendero Macuco

★ **Wildlife**
Refuge to over 430 bird species and 70 types of mammals, the Paranaense rainforest abounds with colorful animal life.

Exploring Parque Nacional Iguazú

Although exploring the breathtaking Parque Nacional Iguazú involves traversing dense rainforest, the task is made easier by an eco-train that runs the length of its crowning feature, the magnificent Iguazú Falls, and by a network of walkways that lead both along the top and to the base of the tumbling cataracts. Other trails head away from the water into the jungle, where tropical birds and capuchin monkeys can be observed. For thrill-seekers, excursions include powerboat trips to the foot of the falls, a salutary and soaking reminder of the awesome power and inventiveness of nature.

The foaming Salto Bossetti seen from Circuito Superior

KEY

- ▬ Major road
- ═ Minor road
- ▬ ▬ International border
- - - - Park boundary

Key to Symbols *see back flap*

Circuito Superior and Circuito Inferior

🚉 *from Estación Cataratas.*
✔ *arranged at park entrance.*
♿ *Circuito Superior only.*

An hour-long trail that runs along the upper lip of the falls, Circuito Superior (Upper Circuit) affords spectacular views of the waterfalls framed by verdant jungle, tumbling into a swirling abyss of bubbling white water. Dazzling rainbows, formed in the spray thrown up by the crashing water, arch across the river and the falls.

Circuito Inferior (Lower Circuit) is also an hour-long walk, and includes steep stairs. It crosses the dripping rainforest to the foot of several cataracts, allowing visitors to observe the forest and falls from much closer quarters. Boats depart from a jetty on the Circuito Inferior for **Isla San Martín**, a rocky, forested island that offers stunning views of the falls, all the way to Garganta del Diablo (Devil's Throat).

Area de Recepción

165 ft (50 m) from park entrance.
Tel (03757) 491-444. ◯ 8am–7pm daily. ▫

All visits to Parque Nacional Iguazú start at the Area de Recepción. Here, the Centro de Interpretación Yvirá Retá has displays on the park's abundant flora and fauna as well as the human history of the greater Atlantic rainforest which the park helps to protect. It also has exhibits showing the devastating effects of farming and logging on the forest.

From the Area de Recepción, the falls are approached via the **Tren Ecológico de la Selva**, a propane-powered eco-train, or via the **Sendero Verde** (Green Trail), an easy 20-minute walk through tropical forest filled with birdlife. Both routes lead to the **Estación Cataratas** train station, from which point it is a short stroll to the Circuito Superior and Circuito Inferior trails and the thunderous roar and spray of the cataracts.

Wildlife displays within the Centro de Interpretación

Garganta del Diablo

🖼 📷 *arranged at park entrance.* ♿
The biggest and most
jaw-dropping of all the falls,
the Garganta del Diablo
waterfall is reachable only by
taking the eco-train to its final
destination, **Estación Garganta
del Diablo**. From the station, a
1.4-mile (2.2-km) walkway
cuts across the Upper Río
Iguazú and jungle river
islands before approaching
almost to the lip of the 260-ft
(80-m) high horseshoe-
shaped cataract. The walk
takes about 2 hours and it
is advisable to wear water-
proof clothing and bring
plastic bags to protect
cameras from the vapor that
rises from the waterfall.

An awe-inspiring view of the spectacular Garganta del Diablo

Sendero Macuco

📷 *arranged at park entrance.*
Compared to the busy
Circuito Superior and Circuito
Inferior trails, Sendero
Macuco (Macuco Trail) is a
quieter, less trodden track.
It leads away from the waterfalls into the surrounding
jungle of tall *lapacho* and
palo rosa trees, where several
species of fauna, including
myriad birds and butterflies,
coatimundis and capuchin
monkeys can be observed.
The 2-hour-long trail ends at
a small rock pool located at
the base of the beautiful **Salto
Arrechea** waterfall. The pool
is a good place for swimming.

Boat Excursions

Tel (03757) 421-600. 📷 *arranged at
Area de Recepción.* **Jungle Explorer**
www.iguazujunglexplorer.com
There are several options for
boat excursions within the
park. **Aventura Naútica** is a
12-minute powerboat trip
along the Lower Iguazú River
to the base of the 230-ft (70-
m) high Salto San Martín
waterfall. The hour-long **Gran
Aventura** leads to the same
destination, after an open-
truck drive via the Sendero
Yacaratia jungle track, and a
4-mile (6-km) powerboat ride,
which includes a mile (2 km)
of rapids. Departing from the
Estación Garganta del Diablo,
the **Paseo Ecológico** is a
gentle boat journey that glides
alongside the gallery forests

of the Upper Iguazú River.
Tour operator **Jungle Explorer**
runs each of these excursions.

Brazilian Side

⏱ *Dec–Mar: 9am–6pm daily; Apr–
Nov: 9am–5pm daily.* 📷 🖼 🚻
Offering panoramic vistas of
the Garganta del Diablo, the
Brazilian side of the falls is a
short distance away. A trip
can include a visit to Parque
dos Aves Foz Tropicana,
which has rare bird species.
For a longer stay on the
Brazilian side, the city of **Foz
do Iguaçu** has numerous hotel
options. Brazilian immigration
rules require some national-
ities, including citizens of the
United States, Canada, Japan,
and Australia, to obtain a visa
prior to travel.

THE WILDLIFE OF PARQUE NACIONAL IGUAZÚ

A haven for some 430 bird and over 70 mammal species,
Parque Nacional Iguazú boasts extraordinary bio-
diversity. Though much of its fauna, including the giant
anteater, the pig-like tapir, and the powerful jaguar, is
reclusive, a diverse range of wildlife can be spotted
along the trails. Most visible are coatimundis, raccoon-
like creatures that approach visitors for food. The jungle
canopy is home to chattering capuchin monkeys, who
descend to the forest floor to forage and can be
observed from the Macuco Trail. Kaleidoscopically-
colored butterflies abound: the beautiful heliconius, its
jet-black wings emblazoned with yellow and red flashes,
is ubiquitous. Reptiles include caiman and the often
sighted iguana. Birdlife is also abundant. Great dusky
swifts nest on rock faces behind the falls and dart in and
out of the vapor kicked up by the tumbling water.
Predatory kites can be seen gliding high in the sky and
jungle trails are enlivened by exotically plumaged
toucans (best observed early in the morning), parrots,
trogons, caciques, and other tropical birds. Wading birds
fish in streams and at the top of the falls.

Capuchin monkey, usually found in the
canopy of the park's forests

Coatimundi, one of the most commonly
spotted mammals in the park

CÓRDOBA AND THE ANDEAN NORTHWEST

Varied and distinctive, the landscape of this region is marked by deep canyons stratified into all the colors of the rainbow, huge salt lakes shimmering with pink flamingos, and prairies baked by the intense heat of the subtropical sun. With a tangible pre-Columbian and colonial past, the Northwest boasts well-preserved landmarks set amid spectacular desert and mountain scenery.

The pre-conquest settlers of this region were the Aymara, Quechua, Comechingones, and Sanavirones. With the arrival of the Spanish conquistadors in the 1500s, some tribes were displaced and many rendered extinct. The Jesuit priests, who followed the colonizers in the 16th century, played a leading role in the development of the towns of Santiago del Estero, Tucumán, Córdoba, Salta, and Jujuy as major administrative, cultural, and religious centers.

Today, the region is still thrillingly Andean; the influence of the Aymara- and Quechua-speaking people from Jujuy – their folk music, beautiful textiles, and cuisine – extends down into the more mestizo societies of Tucumán and Salta. The land and its guardian Pachamama (Earth Mother) are also central to the local mindset. Agriculture and livestock provide most of the area's income, coupled with a growing tourism industry.

Much of the region's beauty can be experienced on road journeys through the Cafayate and Humahuaca *quebradas* (ravines).

Most cities have a well-preserved Jesuit heritage with colonial churches, convents, and civic edifices that give them an old-world feel. The south of the province is considered by many to be Argentina's second wine region, after Mendoza, and a source of delicious semi-sweet Torrontés wines as well as some exceptional red varietals produced by local boutique wineries.

Finca La Rosa, converted from a bodega into a wine-themed hotel and spa, Cafayate

◁ Spectacular view of a towering rock face in Parque Nacional Talampaya, La Rioja

Exploring Córdoba and the Andean Northwest

The region's eponymous capital Córdoba is a popular university town, characterized by beautiful old colonial buildings. Beyond the city, heading west, the roads invariably zigzag into the Andean foothills and on to the high passes of the Argentina-Chile border. To the east lie the grassy plains of Santiago del Estero and to the north, the scrublands of Jujuy and the tropical jungle in Salta. The scenery while traveling to quiet villages such as San Salvador de Jujuy, Cafayate, and Cachi is breathtaking, especially against the spectacular backdrop of the canyons of the Quebrada de Humahuaca.

SIGHTS AT A GLANCE

Towns and Cities

Alta Gracia ❷
Cachi ❷⓪
Cafayate ❶❼
Córdoba pp180–81 ❶
Cosquín ❺
Jesús María ❼
La Cumbre ❻
La Rioja ❾
Molinos ❶❾
Salta pp192–5 ❷❷
San Fernando del
  Valle de Catamarca ❶❶
San Miguel de Tucumán ❶❹
Santiago del Estero ❶❷
Tafí del Valle ❶❺
Termas de
  Río Hondo ❶❸
Villa General
  Belgrano ❸
Yavi ❷❺

National Parks

Monumento Natural Laguna
  de los Pozuelos ❷❹
Parque Nacional Calilegua ❷❻
Parque Nacional El Rey ❷❼
Parque Nacional
  Los Cardones ❷❶
Parque Nacional Quebrada
  del Condorito ❹
Parque Nacional
  Talampaya ❶⓪

Sites of Interest

Quebrada de
  Cafayate ❶❽
Quebrada de
  Humahuaca pp196–
  200 ❷❸
Quilmes ❶❻
Santa Catalina pp186–7 ❽

MONUMENTO
NATURAL LAGUNA ❷❹
DE LOS POZUELOS

Cerro Pantzos
17,152 ft
Abra
Pampa

JUJUY

QUEBRADA DE
HUMAHUACA

San Salva
de Ju
SAL

PARQUE NACIONAL
LOS CARDONES ❷❶
CACHI ❷⓪
❶❾ MOLIN

Volcán Antofalla
20,013 ft

QUEBRADA DE
CAFAYATE ❶❽

Antofagasta
de la Sierra

CAFAYATE ❶❼

QUILMES ❶❻

Paso de San
Francisco
15,775 ft

TAFÍ DEL
VALLE ❶❺
TUCUM
Monteros

CATAMARCA

Cerro Palca
17,263 ft

Aguilares

Mte.Pissis
22,578 ft

Belén

Cerro Bonete
22,175 ft

Tinogasta

Saujil

La Me

46

SAN FERNANDO
DEL VALLE DE ❶❶
CATAMARCA

Villa San José
de Vinchina

Famatina

Ancasti

Villa Castelli

75

Villa Unión

LA RIOJA ❾

40

LA RIOJA

76

Patquia

PARQUE NACIONAL ❶⓪
TALAMPAYA

Chamical

Olta

38

Malanzán

Chepes

PARQUE NACIO
QUEBRA
DEL CONDO

A view of Cerro de los Siete Colores (Hill of Seven Colors), Purmamarca

Museo Histórico Provincial Marqués de Sobremonte, Córdoba

GETTING AROUND
The area's main airports, San Miguel de Tucumán and Salta, have regular flights that connect the cities to Buenos Aires. Better options, however, are long-distance buses or hiring a car to explore the Andean Northwest region. Ruta Nacional 9, the old Camino Real, connects Córdoba to Quebrada de Humahuaca, while Ruta Provincial 40 winds near Quebrada de Cafayate. It is advisable to drive with particular care as the roads can be rough in the Andean foothills.

KEY

▬▬	Expressway
▬▬	Highway
—	Main road
▭▭	Minor road
˗•˗	Railroad
▬▬	International border
▬▬	Provincial border
△	Peak

0 km   100

0 miles   100

SEE ALSO
• *Where to Stay* p280
• *Where to Eat* p298

Rows of handicraft stalls at Tilcara, Quebrada de Humahuaca

Córdoba ❶

Set in a wide valley in the central sierras, Argentina's second city is a bustling modern metropolis and university town. Founded in 1573, the city boasts some of the country's most impressive colonial architecture, including the "Jesuit Block," all of which has been carefully preserved. With a population that is predominantly of Italian descent, Córdoba is reputed for its warm hospitality and strong civic pride. An important commercial and industrial center, Córdoba's proximity to the mountains makes for a pleasant stopover between Buenos Aires and the Andean Northwest.

Equestrian statue of José San Martín in Plaza San Martín

🏛 Plaza San Martín

Cnr Buenos Aires & San Jerónimo. **Cabildo** ⬜ 8am–8pm daily. **Tel** (0351) 4341-200. **Iglesia Catedral Tel** (0351) 422-3446. ⬜ 9am–12:30pm & 4:30–8pm daily.
Since its founding, this single block has been the focal point of Córdoba city. Adorned with Italianate cast-iron fountains, acacias, palm trees, and native *palo borracho* and *lapacho* trees, it is a subtropical refuge from the city. The plaza features a monument to liberation hero José San Martín. Loved by the locals, it is a popular venue for strolls.

The **Cabildo**, formerly the colonial headquarters, sits on the western side of the plaza. The original building was erected here at the end of the 16th century, functioning at various times as prison, law courts, and police station, as well as provincial parliament. The present building dates from the 1780s; elegant arches decorate the white façade, while antique lamps hang over the vaulted colonnade supported by slender pillars.

The nearby **Iglesia Catedral** was built in 1782 and is the country's oldest cathedral. Part-baroque, part-neoclassical, the church has towers are notable for the angelic trumpet-players wearing the exotic garb of the Guaraní craftsmen who sculpted them. Inside, rococo features and a floor of Valencian tiles enliven the somber atmosphere. A finely wrought silver tabernacle is housed in a side-chapel to the left of the 19th-century main altar.

Also overlooking the square are the Banco Nación; the remains of the colonial mansion of the city's first bishop, Manuel Mercadillo; and Museo Gregorio Funes, which houses a collection of Catholic artifacts and regularly holds art exhibitions.

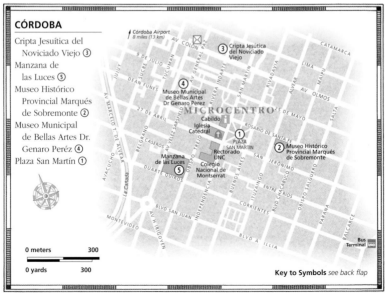

CÓRDOBA

Cripta Jesuítica del Noviciado Viejo ③
Manzana de las Luces ⑤
Museo Histórico Provincial Marqués de Sobremonte ②
Museo Municipal de Bellas Artes Dr. Genaro Peréz ④
Plaza San Martín ①

0 meters   300
0 yards   300

Key to Symbols see back flap

🏛 Museo Histórico Provincial Marqués de Sobremonte

Rosario de Santa Fe 218. *Tel (0351) 433-1664.* 🕐 *10am–3pm Tue–Fri, 9am–2pm Sat.*

The superb 18th-century building that houses this museum was once the city's largest colonial residence, home of the Governor-General of Córdoba, Marqués de Sobremonte, between 1784 and 1798. He was largely responsible for modernizing the city's sanitation.

While only a few of the items on display in the museum belonged to the Marqués, most are from the same period. These include some wonderful paintings in the style of the Peruvian Cusco School, some of which have been restored and seem to glow ethereally in the light. The cedarwood altarpiece in the Capilla Azul (Blue Chapel) and the religious paintings in the adjoining room compete for attention with various secular displays of pharmaceutical products, musical instruments, and home furnishings.

⛪ Cripta Jesuítica del Noviciado Viejo

Corner, Rivera Indarte and Avenida Colón.
🕐 *9:30am–3pm Mon–Fri.*
Unearthed in 1989, this underground site was a Jesuit novitiate in the 1600s and 1700s, until the Society of Jesus was expelled from Argentina in 1773. The remnants of the original brickwork can be seen in fragments on the walls. The three original naves carved into the rock are used to house cultural exhibitions and conferences. Good acoustics also enable theatrical performances here.

🏛 Museo Municipal de Bellas Artes Dr. Genaro Pérez

Avenida General Paz 33. *Tel (0351) 434-1646.* 🕐 *10am–8pm Tue–Sun.*
www.agora.com.ar/museogp
Dedicated to Argentinian works of the 18th and 19th centuries, this municipal art gallery is located in a lovely 19th-century mansion built

The stylish exterior of Museo Municipal de Bellas Artes

in the French style by its patrician owner, Dr. Tomás Garzón. Many of the paintings hail from the local Cordobesa School, whose leading practitioner was Genaro Pérez (1807–54). Many of the works are influenced by the French Impressionists, with a focus on the landscapes of the sierras and portraits of local politicians and aristocrats. There is also a collection of artworks from the 1880s and the 1920s, the former characterized by social realism, and the latter by European Cubism and Surrealism.

Antique guitar at Museo Histórico

⛪ Manzana de las Luces

Obispo Trejo 242. *Tel (0351) 433-2075.* **Iglesia de la Compañía**
🕐 *8am–1pm & 5–8pm Tue–Sun.*
🛈 *noon & 8pm.*
Granted by the colonial rulers to the Jesuits in 1583, Manzana de las Luces (Block of Enlightenment) is also called Manzana de los Jesuitas (Jesuit Block). From here the Society of Jesus oversaw their mission to evangelize the natives across central and northwestern Argentina, as well as the administration of their farming and agricultural interests. This complex, along with five Jesuit estancias located in the province, was recognized by UNESCO as a World Heritage Site in 2000.

Iglesia de la Compañía
was built in 1640 and is the country's oldest surviving Jesuit temple. The interior and

exterior are simple, almost rustic in their lack of adornment, while the nave has panels depicting the trials of the Jesuits. The most striking elements of the church are the Cusco altarpiece and the elaborate pulpit. A doorway marked Puerta del Cielo (Gateway to Heaven) provides access to the Capilla Doméstica. This small space is a model of artisanal church decoration, featuring bamboo and raw-hide panels painted using vegetable pigments.

South of the church is the **Rectorado de la Universidad Nacional de Córdoba (UNC)**. Dating from 1621, this is Argentina's oldest university. Shaded patios, bougainvillea, and well-stocked libraries make this a pleasant place of study. The **Colegio Nacional de Monserrat** located nearby is another Jesuit edifice. An earlier school, located outside the city, was founded in 1687, but was transferred to the present site in 1782, after the Jesuit priests had been expelled. An all-male school until 1998, it still enjoys a reputation as an elite center of learning. The neocolonial shell is embellished with majolica tiling, ornate doorways, and window grills.

The grand Cusco altarpiece at Iglesia de la Compañía

The altar and pews of Iglesia Parroquial Nuestra Señora de la Merced

Alta Gracia ❷

Road Map B2. 25 miles (40 km) SW of Córdoba. 🏘 43,000. 🚌 🛈 (0810) 555-2582. www.altagracia.gov.ar

In the prosperous agricultural belt of the Calmuchita Valley is the small, historic town of Alta Gracia. It was founded by the Jesuits on land granted to them in the 17th century by the colonial government. The Jesuits built a large ranch, part of a network of similar sites developed to help fund the Universidad Nacional de Córdoba, one of Latin America's oldest universities. The Alta Gracia estancia, which fell into disuse after the Jesuits' expulsion in 1773, was named a UNESCO World Heritage Site in 2000. It is now the **Museo Histórico Casa del Virrey Liniers**.

Alta Gracia came into prominence in the 1920s and 30s when it attracted wealthy Argentinians in search of fresh air and second homes. The most famous of these were the families of Ernesto Che Guevara and Spanish composer Manuel de Falla.

To the north of the city is the Tajamar, an artificial lake built by the Jesuits in 1653 and probably the first of its kind in the Americas. Located here is the town's clock tower, built in 1938 to commemorate Alta Gracia's 350th anniversary.

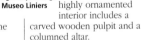
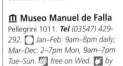

Religious painting, Museo Liniers

🔒 Iglesia Parroquial Nuestra Señora de la Merced

Plaza Manuel Solares. **Tel** (03547) 421-203. 🕐 9am–noon & 3:30–6pm daily. 🛈 Jan–Feb: 8pm Mon–Sat, 10am Sun; Mar–Dec: 6pm Mon–Sat, 10am & 6pm Sun.

Designed by Andrés Blanqui, also responsible for many other Jesuit ecclesiastical buildings, this church is one of Argentina's best extant examples of the late Italian baroque style. Its curved outer walls were designed to resemble a cross. The highly ornamented interior includes a carved wooden pulpit and a columned altar.

🏛 Museo Manuel de Falla

Pellegrini 1011. **Tel** (03547) 429-292. 🕐 Jan–Feb: 9am–8pm daily; Mar–Dec: 2–7pm Mon, 9am–7pm Tue–Sun. 📷 free on Wed. 📷 by prior arrangement.

Fleeing the Franco regime in 1939, Manuel de Falla, one of Spain's greatest modern composers, lived in Argentina until his death in 1946. From 1942 onwards he lived in Alta Gracia in a small house which has been converted into this excellent museum.

The Museo Manuel de Falla re-creates the composer's life, showcasing his music and various musical influences with exhibits that include his library, his piano, and his personal letters. Although Manuel de Falla chose to live in Alta Gracia because of its reputation for fresh mountain air, one of the displays is the machine used to roll his cigarettes. Piano and chamber music recitals are occasionally held in the concert hall in the garden.

🏛 Museo del Che Guevara

Avellaneda 501. **Tel** (03547) 428-579. 🕐 Jan–Feb: 9am–8pm daily; Mar–Dec: 2–7pm Mon, 9am–7pm Tue–Sun. 📷 free on Wed. 📷 by prior arrangement. 🚶 limited. www.altagracia.gov.ar/museos/che

Known as Villa Beatriz, this pretty mock-Tudor house was one of several dwellings occupied by the Guevara family during the 1930s. In 2001, it was reopened as a museum, or more as a shrine, dedicated to the revolutionary Che Guevara.

Although they do not provide an in-depth analysis of his life and ideals, the displays feature an interesting collection of family photos, Cuban banknotes, school report cards, letters from Che to his favorite aunt, and editions of books by authors favored by the adolescent Guevara, including Freud, Baudelaire, Pablo Neruda, and Jules Verne.

Home of Spanish composer Manuel de Falla, which is now a museum

Villa General Belgrano ❸

Road Map B2. 55 miles (89km)
SW of Córdoba. 🏠 *5,000.* 🚌
🎷 *Oktoberfest Beer Festival (Oct).*
www.elsitiodelavilla.com

Founded in the 1930s, Villa General Belgrano is one of Argentina's top holiday resorts. A significant percentage of the population is descended from the surviving crew of the *Admiral Graf Spee*, the German pocket battleship scuttled off the Uruguayan coast in 1939. A monument to the crew stands in Plazoleta Graf Spee.

The town's main thoroughfare, Avenida Julio Roca, is lined with beer cellars and souvenir shops, the former purveying excellent and authentic German food and drink; the latter, an assortment of tourist merchandise. With its chocolate shops, Lutheran chapels, and strains of oom-pah music, Villa Belgrano still preserves a vibrant Germanic atmosphere, especially when it explodes into life in October with the increasingly popular annual beer festival.

Parque Nacional Quebrada del Condorito ❹

Road Map B2. 53 miles (85 km)
SW of Córdoba. 🚌 ℹ️ *Fundación Cóndor, (03541) 433-371.* ⏰ *9am–6pm daily.* 🎫 *by prior arrangement.*
🏕 Ⓐ *by prior arrangement.*
www.parquesnacionales.gov.ar

Covering an area of 16 sq miles (41 sq km), Parque Nacional Quebrada del Condorito is one of the few places in the world where condors can be seen in their natural habitat. The park surrounds a deep, misty gorge that cuts through the hills of the Pampa de Achala. The ravines form an ideal breeding ground for condors, and adult birds with wing spans of over 10 ft (3 m) can be seen

A pleasant mid-summer view of the meandering Río Cosquín

circling majestically overhead. Numerous trails, some arduous and slippery, wind down the steep canyon and alongside the river at the bottom. There is a wide variety of flora and fauna that can be found along the way, including giant ferns and rare white gentians, wild cats, foxes, indigenous rodents, and several types of snake, none of which are venomous.

The majestic condor

Cosquín ❺

Road Map B2. 40 miles (63 km)
NW of Córdoba. 🏠 *17,000.* 🚌
ℹ️ *Ave San Martín, (03541) 454-644.* 🎷 *Festival Nacional de Folklore (Jan).* **www**.cosquinturismo.com.ar

Dating back to colonial times, Cosquín is one of the oldest settlements in the region. This bustling town is built on

the banks of the river of the same name and in the shadow of the 4,150-ft (1,260-m) El Pan de Azúcar. The summit of this sugar-loaf mountain affords great views of the sierras. It can be reached by *aerosilla* (chairlift) from the well-signposted lower station located at the foot of the hill.

Cosquín's fame rests on its unofficial status as Argentina's folklore capital. The Festival Nacional de Folklore, held annually in January in Plaza Próspero Molina, draws many folk and classical musicians, and dance troupes and fans from around Argentina and beyond.

The town's best year-round visitor attraction is Museo Camín Cosquín, on the RN38, which displays local archeological and paleontological finds, including fossils, semi-precious stones, jewelry, and ceramics crafted by the area's pre-Hispanic inhabitants.

The revolutionary Che as a young man

THE BOYHOOD OF ERNESTO GUEVARA

It was because four-year-old Ernesto Guevara suffered from asthma that his family left behind the muggy climate of Rosario for the drier air of Alta Gracia in 1932. Although he never shook off the asthma, his childhood was both happy and active and he excelled at sports. The young Ernesto's mind was no less agile. He competed in local chess tournaments from a young age and plundered his father's library for literary treasures ranging from Jack London to Sigmund Freud. For the adult Che, life would only become richer. He left Córdoba to study medicine at the University of Buenos Aires in 1947, before embarking on the first of his well-chronicled cross-country journeys in 1949. His radicalism dates from here; the restlessness and travel-hunger of a boy who read London and Verne long before he touched Marx and Trotsky was already present.

The faded exterior of the once-exclusive Hotel Edén at La Falda

La Cumbre ⑥

Road Map B2. 59 miles (95 km) N of Córdoba. 🏠 7,000. 🚌 ℹ️ Ave Caraffa 300, (03548) 452-966. www.alacumbre.com

The name La Cumbre (The Summit) was given to this town because it was the last and highest stop on the old British-built railroad line that began from Córdoba city. The trains stopped chuffing up the hill a long time ago, but La Cumbre's timbered mock-Tudor cottages, lovely manicured lawns, and the famous golf club still testify to the long-standing Anglo-Saxon presence. La Cumbre is a laid-back town known for its trout fishing spots and horse-riding. It has also become synonymous with adventure sports such as hang gliding and paragliding. Competitions are held here annually in March. Some of the best views of the surrounding Punilla Valley can be had from the climb up to the Cristo Redentor statue on Cerro Viarapa.

Environs
Just 8 miles (13 km) south of La Cumbre, **La Falda** is a larger town and another good base for outdoor pursuits. Visitors can tour the interiors of the town's once exclusive Hotel Edén that closed in the 1960s; in its heyday, it welcomed royalty, presidents, and a former patents clerk named Albert Einstein.

Jesús María ⑦

Road Map C2. 32 miles (51 km) N of Córdoba. 🏠 21,000. 🚌 ℹ️ Ave San Martín. 🎭 Fiesta Nacional de Doma y Folklore (Jan).

Founded in the 16th century, the sleepy market town of Jesús María was once an important link in the chain of agricultural estancias built by the Jesuits to feed and fund the University of Córdoba. Most of the town's historical buildings date from the mid-1700s. In 1946 the old church, convent, *bodega,* and residences were converted into **Museo Jesuítico Nacional de Jesús María**. The museum contains an excellent collection of archaeological finds and sacred relics as well as works by local artists. The famous Jesuit winery can also be visited. It was here, so the story goes, that the first colonial wine served to the Spanish royal family was produced.

In January the town's population temporarily swells to over 200,000 when it plays host to one of Argentina's most popular gaucho and folk festivals, the Fiesta Nacional de Doma y Folklore. Lasting ten days, this fiesta combines extremely daring feats of horsemanship with improvised folk singing that doubles as a commentary on the rodeo action.

🏛 **Museo Jesuítico Nacional de Jesús María**
Pedro de Oñate s/n. **Tel** (03525) 420-126. ⏰ 8am–7pm Tue–Fri, 10am–noon & 2–6pm Sat & Sun. 📷 🎥 on request.

The Museo Jesuítico Nacional de Jesús María

Santa Catalina ⑧

See pp186–7.

A gaucho textile display at Museo Folklórico in La Rioja

La Rioja ⑨

Road Map B2. 290 miles (467 km) NW of Córdoba. 🏠 150,000. ✈️ 🚌 ℹ️ Avenida Pelagio B Luna 345, (03822) 426-345. www.municipio larioja.gov.ar

Located at the foot of the granite Velasco Sierras, La Rioja is the capital city of the namesake province. Founded in 1591 by Juan Ramírez de Velasco, it has been struck regularly by major earthquakes over the intervening centuries, the most destructive of which was in 1894. The city was an unremarkable agricultural outpost until the 1970s, when industrialization sparked a population surge. Although a pleasant city to visit most of the year, it is uncomfortable during the summer months when temperatures regularly exceed 40° C (104° F). The best time to visit is in spring, when the climate is relatively cool and the parched air is perfumed by the multitude of blossoms of the jacaranda and orange trees. Due to these blooms, La Rioja has often been referred to as La Cuidad de los Naranjos (the City of Oranges).

Stunning red cliffs at Parque Nacional Talampaya, weathered by centuries of wind and rain

Around Plaza 25 de Mayo, the city's main square, is the neo-colonial government building, Casa de Gobierno, and to the south, **Catedral San Nicolás de Bari**, which contains a 17th-century image of the saint, carved from walnut wood. **Iglesia Santo Domingo**, one block east of the plaza, dates from 1623 and is said to be the oldest building in Argentina. Its highlights include the carob-wood doors, carved by indigenous artisans in the 17th century. Located west of the plaza, **Museo Folklórico** is a superbly organized reconstruction of a Victorian Riojano dwelling, packed with hand-carved furnishings and gaucho gear. It also has a display on local myths and legends.

⌂ Iglesia Santo Domingo
B Luna and Lamadrid.
○ 9am–8pm daily. ✦ &

⌂ Museo Folklórico
Pelagio B Luna 811. **Tel** (03822) 428-500. ○ 9am–1pm, 4–8pm Tue–Fri, 9am–1pm Sat & Sun. ✦ 9am–1pm Sat & Sun. & ⊡ ⊡

Parque Nacional Talampaya ➓

Road Map B2. 135 miles (216 km) SW of La Rioja. **Tel** (03825) 470-356. ⊞ ○ May–Sep: 8:30am–5:30pm daily; Oct–Apr: 8am–6pm daily. ✦ ✦ ⚠ www.talampaya.com

Designated a national park by President Menem in 1997, Parque Nacional Talampaya is also a UNESCO World Heritage Site. Its name comes from the indigenous words *ktala* (the local *tala* bush), and *ampaya* (dry riverbed). The park covers an area of 97 sq miles (251 sq km) and contains some of Argentina's most amazing natural

features, including sheer sandstone cliffs that soar up to 590 ft (180 m) from the plain. Millions of years of torrential rain and dry, gritty winds have sculpted the cliffs into fantastic shapes, their anthropomorphic qualities earning them imaginative nicknames such as The Monk and The Three Kings. Apart from the rock forma-tions, guides can also point visitors towards pre-Columbian glyphs scratched into the cliff faces and patches of rare flora. Condors and eagles glide majestically overhead. Apart from the wind and the occasional bird cry, the predominant sound is one of silence.

An equestrian statue of San Martín at La Rioja's Plaza 25 de Mayo

THE LEGEND OF FACUNDO QUIROGA

One of the most famed and feared of Argentina's early 19th-century gaucho chieftains, Juan Facundo Quiroga (1790–1835) was born into a poor family of cattle breeders. He was nicknamed "the tiger of the plains" by his friends and enemies alike. Quiroga fought briefly in the

19th-century lithograph of Quiroga greeted by supporters

revolutionary wars before rising quickly to the head of the Andean provincial armies. When his *de facto* military rule came under threat from the Centralist forces of President Rivadavia, who had established a "Unitarian" constitution in 1826, Quiroga led his Federalist army through a series of victories and defeats until finally beating the Centralist army in Salta. In 1934, while en route to Buenos Aires after a mission in the northern provinces, he was ambushed and murdered by gunmen. Facundo's lasting fame owes as much to his biographer, writer and statesman Domingo Sarmiento, as to his own infamous achievements.

Santa Catalina ⑧

A UNESCO World Heritage Site, this Jesuit estancia was founded in 1622. It became an important agricultural and sheepfarming establishment, yet its most important function was as the provider of thousands of mules for cargo trains traveling along the Camino Real between Buenos Aires and Alto Perú (now Bolivia). The extensive site contained workshops, a smithy, a carpentry, two flour mills, and a reservoir; there were also residences for priests, native laborers, and slaves. Its soaring main church is one of the best examples of colonial baroque in the country. While it is now administered by the state in accordance with a presidential decree, Santa Catalina remains the private property of the Díaz family.

Remnants of a broken Jesuit bell

Corridor characterized by plain brick walls and curved ceiling

Rear Courtyard
The rear patio is surrounded by workshops and possibly residences for laborers, though slaves were housed in a building apart from the main complex.

STAR FEATURES

★ Central Courtyard

★ Altar

★ Church Façade

★ **Central Courtyard**
The grandest of the three main patios, this is enclosed by a vaulted gallery and has a central fountain. Cloisters and workshops occupy the rooms along the sides.

★ Altar
Above the main wooden altar stands a gilded retablo (altarpiece) housing an image of Saint Catherine (Santa Catalina). Other wooden statues include one of the Señor de la Humilidad y la Paciencia, and another of the crucified Christ.

VISITORS' CHECKLIST

Road Map C2. 13 miles (20 km) N of Jesús María.
Tel (03525) 421-600.
Jan–Feb: 10am–1pm & 3–5pm Tue–Sun; Mar–Dec: 10am–1pm & 2–6pm Tue–Sun.
Apr–Sep: 10am–1pm Tue–Sun; Oct–Mar: 10am–1pm & 3–7pm Tue–Sun.

The cemetery is where priests and workers were buried, some of whom had spent their entire life at the estancia.

Front Courtyard
A quiet and plain patio, the front courtyard would have been used by the Jesuit priests to receive deliveries from the neighboring towns as well as for non-ecclesiastical gatherings.

★ Church Façade
The high and elegant white façade has two towers and curved pediments framing the doorway, typical of the baroque school of architecture.

Statue of Virgen del Valle, Catedral de Nuestra Señora del Valle

San Fernando del Valle de Catamarca ⓫

Road Map B2. 96 miles (154 km) NE of La Rioja. 141,000. ✈ República 446, (03833) 437-229. National Poncho Festival (Jul). www.turismocatamarca.gov.ar

Founded in 1683, San Fernando del Valle de Catamarca, usually called just Catamarca by the Argentinians, is the capital of the San Fernando province. It is a quiet town that has a number of sights worth seeing, although it is advisable to keep away during the area's hot summer months.

The city's nucleus is its main square, Plaza 25 de Mayo, designed by French landscaper Charles Thays. The palm, orange, and *palo borracho* trees provide welcome shade from the blistering afternoon sun. On the western side of the square is the 19th-century neoclassical **Catedral de Nuestra Señora del Valle**. Under its brick-red terracotta façade, it houses, in an elaborate antechamber, one of the country's most venerated religious relics: the diamond-crowned statue of the Virgen del Valle. She is said to have "appeared" to locals in the 19th century, and her graven image now attracts thousands of pilgrims on the saint's feast day in December.

Catamarca's lively annual National Poncho Festival, held traditionally in July, also draws a large number of people, including the cream of folkloric talent from all across the country. The city also serves as an ideal base for those who wish to explore the province's rugged and lovely unspoilt backcountry.

> 🏛 **Catedral de Nuestra Señora del Valle**
> Plaza 25 de Mayo. ○ 7am–noon, 5–8pm daily.

Santiago del Estero ⓬

Road Map C1. 130 miles (210 km) NE of Catamarca. 245,000. ✈ Libertad, 417 (0385) 4213-253.

Founded in 1553, Santiago del Estero is Argentina's oldest city. It was once full of attractive colonial architecture, most of which has been damaged by natural causes or razed to make way for new buildings.

There are, however, a few sites worth visiting, including the neoclassical **Catedral**, built in 1867 on the site of the former 16th-century structure. It contains a variety of ancient relics of saints. The **Provincial History Museum**, set in a grand 18th-century town house, is also a fascinating place to explore.

Santiago del Estero has a strong musical tradition. It was the birthplace of the *chacarera*, one of Argentina's most exuberant folkloric styles, which developed in the mid-19th century *(see*

pp28–9). Another folk rhythm and dance here is the *zamba*, and there are regular concerts by top-notch performers coming from across Argentina.

The neoclassical exterior of the Catedral, Santiago del Estero

Termas de Río Hondo ⓭

Road Map B1. 40 miles (65 km) NW of Santiago del Estero. 27,000. ✈ Caseros 132, (03858) 421-721. www.lastermasde riohondo.gov.ar

Located on the banks of Río Dulce (Sweet River), Termas de Río Hondo is South America's biggest spa town, packed in the high season with visitors "taking the cure." The spring waters are rich in minerals and known for their healing properties. They gush out of every hotel tap and fill several public baths across town. The waters are said to be particularly effective against rheumatism and hypertension.

A pool filled with spring water in a spa hotel, Termas de Río Hondo

The Hall of Independence at the Casa Histórica de la Independencia

San Miguel de Tucumán ⑭

Road Map B1. 98 miles (158 km) NW of Santiago del Estero. 🏔 *530,000.* 🛬 🚌 🎇 *Ave de Setiembre 484, (0381) 430-3644.*

The biggest and economically most important town in northwest Argentina, San Miguel de Tucumán is located in the Rió Salí Valley, to the east of the towering Sierra de Aconquija. Usually known simply as Tucumán, the town is a hectic, relatively thriving metropolis, with a youthful population and vibrant nightlife. The city has played a key role in Argentinian history – it was here, on July 9, 1816, that Argentina declared her independence from the Spanish crown. The room in which the fateful démarche was delivered can be visited at the **Casa Histórica de la Independencia**. The house, with a series of creeper-draped patios and whitewashed colonnades, was originally built in the late 1700s, but was razed to the ground in the late 19th century. It was replaced by a replica in the 1940s. A sound-and-light show in the garden re-enacts the story of how independence was declared.

Plaza Independencia is the focal point of San Miguel de Tucumán, with native trees, a large pool, fountains, and a statue representing Liberty. Located nearby is **Museo Folklórico**, housing a wide collection of *mate* ware, textiles, and traditional musical instruments.

🏛 **Casa Histórica de la Independencia**
Congreso 141. **Tel** *(0381) 431-0826.* ◷ *10am–6pm Mon–Fri, 1pm–7pm Sat, Sun & public hols.* 🎇
www.casaindependencia.com.ar

Tafí del Valle ⑮

Road Map B1. 66 miles (107 km) W of Tucumán. 🏔 *4,500.* 🚌 🎇 *Tafí del Valle, (03867) 421-009.* **www**.tafidelvalle.com

Peruvian pelican, Casa Histórica de la Independencia

A popular weekend getaway during the blistering summer months, Tafí del Valle is a small town. It is located significantly higher than Tucumán, making it cooler with average summer temperatures of 12° C (54° F). The road taking travelers up from the sticky lowlands winds through forests and lemon orchards, and up into the pleasant highlands. Sunny

but bearable weather is guaranteed all year round, making Tafí del Valle an ideal base for hiking, fishing, and horse-riding trips. Trails snake their way up the surrounding peaks, which include Cerro El Matadero and Cerro Pabellón, both topping 10,000 ft (3,000 m).

The town has a number of hotels, restaurants, and adventure tourism agencies around the central plaza.

Quilmes ⑯

Road Map B1. 110 miles (177 km) NW of Tucumán. 🚌 ◷ *8:30am–dusk daily.* 🎇 🎇 🎇 *limited.* 🌿

One of the most important and best preserved archaeological sites in Argentina, the Quilmes ruins are the last vestiges of a city founded by the pre-Incan tribe of the same name in the 9th century AD. It was originally intended to be a bulwark against the advancing Inca incursions. The population peaked here in the 17th century, at close to 6,000. The settlement had by then held out for around 150 years against attacks by the better armed Spanish conquerors.

The ruins have been expertly excavated and preserved – stone walls, terraces, and even entire buildings can be seen, and the effect of walking through them is haunting. The excellent on-site museum displays tools and weaponry excavated in the area. The Hotel Ruinas de Quilmes is located at the foot of the ruins.

The excavated Quilmes ruins dating back to the 9th century AD

Cafayate

Road Map B1. 140 miles (225 km)
NW of Tucumán. 🏛 *12,000.* 🚌
ℹ *Ave San Martín (03868) 422-442.*
🎭 *Folk Festival (Mar).* **www.**
welcomeargentina.com/cafayate

Considered one of the prettiest towns in Argentina, Cafayate is a natural stopover for anyone touring the Valles Calchaquíes or traveling between Quilmes, Tucumán, and Salta. Cafayate was settled at the beginning of the 18th century by Franciscan missionaries. They made use of the two rivers passing through, Río Chuschas and Río Loro Huasi, to create indigenous farming reserves. Cafayate was officially founded in 1840, and soon after, a number of *bodegas* were established on the slopes that rise gradually around the edges of town.

With the tranquil ambience of a village, Cafayate today has restaurants, museums, and a few colonial mansions. Southwest of the main plaza is **Museo de Arqueología Calchaquí**, whose ceramic and urn displays tell the story of the area's native inhabitants. The nearby **Museo de la Vid y del Vino** displays a variety of wine-related relics.

The vineyards of Cafayate are exceptional, the grandest being Finca La Rosa. Now the **Patios de Cafayate Hotel and Spa**, La Rosa was established in 1892. Surrounded by vineyards and geraniums and rose bushes, this sprawling colonial-style ranch is a

The huge monolith El Obelisco at Quebrada de Cafayate

classic Argentinian aristocratic estancia. It also has a wine-themed spa and a stylish swimming pool.

🏛 **Museo de Arqueología Calchaquí**
Colón 200. ⏱ *10am–10pm daily.*

🏛 **Museo de la Vid y del Vino**
RN 40. ⏱ *8am–9pm daily.* 📷

🛏 **Patios de Cafayate Hotel and Spa**
RN 40 & RN 68, Salta. **Tel** *(03868) 421-747.* **www**.starwoodhotels.com

Quebrada de Cafayate ⑱

Road Map B1. 12 mile (20 km)
N of Cafayate. 🚌

The Quebrada de Humahuaca *(see pp196–200)* wears the UNESCO World Heritage Site title but for many travelers in northwestern Argentina, the red-rock ravine of Cafayate is just as memorable. The towering walls of the ravine are an explosion of scarlet and crimson, rust, and vermilion. Río Conchas flows through the valley floor, but only a narrow strip of land is fertile.

Wind and storm showers over the years have led to erosion, leaving behind surreal rock formations. Some outstanding ones have been given nicknames, such as the gigantic Los Médanos (The Dunes) and El Obelisco. A huge ravine on the east side is known as La Garganta del Diablo (The Devil's Throat), while a solitary rock is named El Sapo (The Toad).

An excellent paved road, the Ruta Nacional 68, runs through this north–south ravine, connecting Cafayate with Salta. Along the route, locals sell handicrafts, such as ceramics, as well as snacks.

Molinos ⑲

Road Map B1. 155 miles (250 km)
N of Cafayate. 🏛 *4,000.* 🚌
🎭 *Virgin of the Candelaria (Feb).*

Founded in the mid-17th century, Molinos (Mills) was a feudal estate producing cornflour, wheatflour, alfalfa peppers, and wine until Argentinian Independence in 1816. Most visitors only pass through this remote hamlet on a drive through the Valles Calchaquíes. However, the town's colonial, 18th-century **Iglesia San Pedro Nolasco de Molinos** is well worth a visit. A small preserve nearby gives protection to native *vicuña*.

The dramatic landscape of cactus-clad slopes around the town is ideal for riding and trekking. Around 6 miles

Fermentation tanks in one of Cafayate's many *bodegas*

A Spanish-style parish church built in the 1600s, Molinos

(10 km) away from town is the Estancia Colomé, a huge vineyard and agricultural estate owned by Swiss businessman, Douglas Hess. It has an art gallery, a smart restaurant, a good library, and an open-air pool with sweeping views of the surrounding beautiful mountains.

Cachi ⑳

Road Map B1. 85 miles (136 km) N of Cafayate. 🏠 4,000. 🚌 ℹ Ave Guemes & Benjamin Solillas, (0800) 444-0317. 🎭 Fiesta de San José (Mar).

Founded in the 18th century, Cachi is a quiet village with a rustic atmosphere, retaining only a few original adobe properties from that period. This picturesque village, known for its pretty plaza lined with palms and orange trees, is located at the foot of the towering, snowcapped Nevado del Cachi which stands at 20,932 ft (6,380 m). The small **Museo Arqueológico Pío Pablo Díaz** to the east of the plaza has displays of items used by the original inhabitants of Valles Calchaquíes. Also worth a visit is the extensively restored **Iglesia San José**, located north of the main plaza, with a classic white façade, wooden floor, and remarkable cactus-wood altar. Small shops around the town center sell local crafts that include ceramics and ponchos with lovely designs.

At 7,480 ft (2,280 m) above sea level, Cachi's microclimate is pleasant for most of the year. The rainfall it receives keeps the maize terraces, vineyards, and plantations of peppers and legumes looking green and healthy. A scenic drive to the nearby hamlet of Cachi Adentro offers lovely views of lush farmlands interspersed with carpets of red pepper fields drying in the sun.

🏛 **Museo Arqueológico Pío Pablo Díaz**
⏰ 8:30am–6pm Mon–Sat, 8:30–2:30pm Sun. **Tel** (03868) 491-080.

The 16-ft (5-m) tall *cardones* at the Parque Nacional Los Cardones

Parque Nacional Los Cardones ㉑

Road Map B1. 16 miles (25 km) N of Cafayate. 🚌 ℹ Ave San Martin s/n°, (03868) 496-005. ⏰ daily. www.parquesnacionales.gov.ar

Created in 1996, the 158-acre (64-ha) Parque Nacional Los Cardones protects the *cardón* cacti that cover this dusty valley, as well as other species of flora that are suited to the arid climate. The preserve was established to protect the *cardones* that were widely being used for firewood or to

Wooden shovel, Museo Arqueológico

make furniture. Although some of the gigantic cacti can reach heights of 16 ft (5 m), these plants grow only a few millimeters every year. They are found between 8,858 ft (2,700 m) and 18,044 ft (5,500 m) above sea level.

Rare bird species such as the endemic Steinbach's canastero and the little-known Zimmer's tapaculo can be spotted throughout the park, along with condors, falcons, and numerous species of tyrant and finch. Parque Nacional Los Cardones is also an important paleontological site, containing traces of dinosaur footprints dating from more than 70 million years ago.

THE WINES OF SALTA

There has been wine-making in the scattered oases of the province of Salta since the days of the Spanish Conquest. In the 17th century, winemakers in the area supplied priests and monks, who needed wine for mass. Today, there are *terroirs* at a variety of altitudes, ranging from 5,577 ft (1,700 m) in Cafayate and 6,561 ft (2,000 m) in Yacochuya Comarca de la Viña to 7,874 ft (2,400 m) in Colomé. Benefitting from long hours of sunshine and fast-flowing streams fed by rains that wash off the high peaks to the west, the vineyards of Salta are some of the most visually striking in the world. Cabernet Sauvignons and Malbecs prosper here, as do Chardonnay and Chenin. A small number of vineyards are also succeeding with Tannat, a grape that is more often associated with Uruguay.

The most famous varietal from Salta is the aromatic Torrontés white, a wine that has fallen out of favor in Europe but thrives in this region. Its success has made the wine Argentina's most popular after Malbec.

Grapes ready to be picked at a *bodega*

Street-by-Street: Salta ⍟

Many of Salta's well-preserved colonial gems are centered around Plaza 9 de Julio and a short stroll takes visitors down streets lined with churches and civic buildings, as well as handsome 18th- and 19th-century townhouses. When the town was founded in 1582, the plaza was sited here to provide an outpost with strategic views over the surrounding plain. Natural moats, long since covered over in the *microcentro*, were another factor that made the city an attractive settlement. The main cathedral, *cabildo*, and the city's cultural center are all on the plaza, and the most striking church, Iglesia San Francisco, is two blocks west.

★ Iglesia Catedral
This neoclassical cathedral dates from 1882, the third centenary of the city.

Museo de Arqueología de Alta Montaña de Salta
An ancient mummy discovered in the Andes, a ceramics collection, and carnaval masks are the highlights of this museum dedicated to pre-Columbian cultures of the Northwest.

Casa de Gobierno
Now a cultural center that goes by the grand name of Casa Cultural América, this striking building, built in 1913 along Francophile lines, was once the former headquarters of the provincial government.

Cabildo de Salta, built in the 17th century, is a beautifully restored whitewashed structure, which houses an eclectic collection of religious art and archaeological finds.

STAR SIGHTS

★ Iglesia Catedral

★ Iglesia San Francisco

★ Plaza 9 de Julio

For hotels and restaurants in this region see p280 and p298

★ **Iglesia y Convento San Francisco**

Salta's most iconic church, built between the mid-18th and mid-19th centuries, is a grandiose exercise in exuberant Italianate neoclassicism. It houses images of Señora de las Nieves (Our Lady of the Snow) and San Pedro de Alcántara, attributed to Spanish sculptor and architect Alonso Cano.

0 meters   50

0 yards   50

KEY

– – – Suggested route

Convento de San Bernardo

CÓRDOBA

JULIO CASEROS

BUENOS AIRES

GENERAL ALVARADO

Museo Casa Uriburu
One of the finest neocolonial edifices in Salta, this late 18th-century house boasts period furnishings formerly used by the powerful Uriburu family.

El Solar del Convento, once a Jesuit convent, is now a restaurant serving regional specialties *(see p298)*.

★ **Plaza 9 de Julio**
Bordered by elegant recovas (arcades), this plaza is Salta's social hub and a great spot for people-watching over coffee.

Exploring Salta

Founded in 1582, Salta is derived from the Diaguita word *sagta*, which means "beautiful." With its dramatic Andean backdrop, its array of well-preserved colonial and neocolonial buildings, and its thriving cultural and gastronomic scene, it is a city that lives up to its name. As well as being the ideal base from which to explore its namesake province, Salta provides a range of interesting things to see and experience.

Antique chair, Museo Histórico del Norte

A large number of the city's most beautiful and historically important buildings are clustered around Plaza 9 de Julio. Salta has excellent restaurants and lively *peñas* (folk music venues) where many regional delicacies can be sampled, such as the delicious *empanadas salteñas* and *locro* stew.

A cluster of sidewalk cafés lining the streets of Salta

🏛 Plaza 9 de Julio

Bounded by Calles Caseros, Espana, Alberdi, & Zuviera.

One of the most attractive and best-maintained town squares in the country, Plaza 9 de Julio is Salta's center and the most logical place from which to start exploring the city. The middle section of the square comprises plenty of greenery in the form of palm and *tipa* trees, as well as fountains, benches, and a lovely 19th-century bandstand. It is bordered on all sides by elegant *recovas*, perfect for sipping a coffee and watching the city's ebb and flow.

The northern end of the plaza is dominated by the cream-colored **Iglesia Catedral**. Originally a neo-Gothic structure, it was built by Italian architects in 1882 to mark the city's third centenary, and later remodeled in the neoclassical style. Some eye-catching frescoes adorn the interior walls.

🏛 Cabildo de Salta

Caseros 549. *Tel* (0387) 421-5340. ⏰ 9am–6pm Tue–Fri. 🎫🎟 3pm. ♿ 🖥 📷 www.museonor.gov.ar/cabildo **Museo Histórico del Norte** *Tel* same as the cabildo. ⏰ Feb–Dec: 9:30am–1:30pm & 3:30–8:30pm Tue–Sat, 9:30am–1:30pm Sun; Jan: 9:30am–1:30pm Tue–Sun.

Flanking the entire southern end of Plaza 9 de Julio, the white-façaded Cabildo de Salta was originally built in the early 17th century and is the oldest surviving colonial structure in the city. The *cabildo* was extensively, and rather clumsily, reconfigured in 1780, resulting in two rows of arches that do not line up. Inside the *cabildo* is the **Museo Histórico del Norte**, which exhibits various artifacts from the pre-Columbian, colonial, and 19th-century epochs, including coins, archaeological finds, architectural blueprints, and colonial furniture. Noteworthy is the superb 18th-century wooden pulpit depicting Saints Augustine, Jerome, Ambrose, and Aquinas. Temporary exhibitions are held regularly and showcase the work of contemporary artists from the region. Workshops and activities for children also take place here.

🏛 Museo de Arqueología de Alta Montaña de Salta

Mitre 77. *Tel* (0387) 437-0499. ⏰ 9am–1pm & 4–9pm Tue–Sun & public hols. 🎫 free Wed. 🎟 prior arrangement only. ♿ 🖥 📷 www.maam.org.ar

Dedicated to cultures and peoples found in high-altitude locations, this is one of the best museums of its kind in the country. It was set up by the provincial government in order to exhibit the Llullaillaco Children. These three Inca infants were found in 1999, preserved in ice near the peak of Mount Llullaillaco, the highest peak in the Salta province. They were buried in the 1400s just prior to the Spanish conquest and a natural process of mummification left them perfectly preserved. The permanent collection includes over 150

The elegant arches and shaded courtyard of Cabildo de Salta

For hotels and restaurants in this region see p280 and p298

The striking Iglesia y Convento San Francisco

several centuries, the overall effect is a pleasing one of harmony and balance, of Latino exuberance tempered by Latinist rigor.

🔒 Iglesia y Convento San Bernardo

Calle Caseros 73. *Tel (0387) 431-0092.* ○ *9–11:30am & 4–6pm daily.* ⚡ 🔒 *7:45am Mon–Sat, 8am & 10:30am Sun.*

The oldest surviving ecclesiastical complex in Salta, Iglesia y Convento San Bernardo is considered one of the most beautiful religious buildings in the country. This convent is still a Carmelite nunnery and thus closed to the public, except for occasional matins. It was originally intended to be a hospital dedicated to Saint Andrew. The earliest parts of the building date from the late 16th century. In 1846, both the patron saint and the function were switched and it became a monastery.

Carved rococo door at the Iglesia y Convento San Bernardo

Several earthquakes and the late 19th-century enthusiasm for "improvement" meant that the structure has been much altered over the centuries. However, the dark, intricate rococo doors that are still in place were carved from walnut wood by indigenous craftsmen in 1762 and installed in 1845.

The site is still evocative: the building is set against the foothills of the Andean mountains, with simple lime-washed walls bathed in soft light falling from lamps in wrought-iron fittings.

artifacts that were buried with the children, originally intended to accompany them into the next world, but are now on display to the public.

Temporary exhibitions at the museum illuminate other aspects of indigenous culture, with a particular focus on pre-Hispanic textiles and tapestries – objects of primary importance in a culture that never developed alphabetical writing. Other activities at the museum include workshops on archaeology, multimedia storytelling sessions for children, and lively classes on Andean dance.

🔒 Iglesia y Convento San Francisco

Calle Córdoba 15. *Tel (0387) 431-0830.* ○ *8am–noon & 5–9pm Mon–Sat.* 📷 ⚡ 🔒 *9am & 8pm Mon–Sat, 9am, 11:30am, & 8pm Sun.*

Probably Salta's best-known landmark, this spectacular church endures as one of the finest examples of both neoclassical and colonial architecture in the country. The main building and convent date from the mid-18th century, while the façade, with its Latin inscriptions and eclectic symbols, and the atrium are the work of Italian architect Luigi Giorgi and were completed in 1870. A statue of Saint Francis, his habit flowing and his arms folded within it, stands in the courtyard, while the slender tower dominates the city's skyline. Miraculously, for a building completed piecemeal over

Salta's Tren de las Nubes passing over Polvorilla bridge

TRAIN TO THE CLOUDS

Designed by US engineer Richard Fontaine Maury, this famous route connects north Argentina with the mining regions of Chile. Although the line was inaugurated in 1948, the train assumed its current, purely touristic, function in the 1970s. The train leaves once a week from General Belgrano station in Salta, taking passengers on a 280-mile (450-km), 15-hour round trip that includes 29 bridges, 13 viaducts, and countless breathtaking vistas and heart-stopping moments. Salta's Tren de las Nubes (Train to the Clouds) is not a metaphorical conceit – it is entirely descriptive. The highest and last of the viaducts, La Polvorilla, launches into thin air at 13,850 ft (4,220 m) above sea level and takes the train above as well as through the cloud line, giving passengers the impression of being on some kind of otherworldly, celestial express.

Quebrada de Humahuaca ㉓

The magnificent Quebrada de Humahuaca is a
geological marvel, a canyon steeped in Argentinian
history. As the road rises beyond Purmamarca, the
technicolor strata of the walls of the Río Grande Valley
are revealed. At dawn and sunset, shades of rose,
emerald, violet, and every hue of yellow and brown
can be seen glowing on the rocky surface. Adding
human warmth to this beautiful landscape are a
cluster of towns that hold fiercely to native traditions.
The indigenous communities pay homage to the
Pachamama of their ancestors and every festival
is celebrated with a colorful carnival parade and
wonderful folk concerts.

Shops selling traditional clothes
and crafts, Tilcara

★ **Tilcara**
*The liveliest of the quebrada
towns, Tilcara is the site of an
important pucará (pre-
Columbian fortification) that
was discovered in 1903 and
reconstructed in the 1950s.*

Maimará is a charming village
nestling next to a hill known
as Painter's Palette.

Posta de Hornillos
*The restored site was
once the residence of
General Belgrano
during the inde-
pendence struggle.*

El Aguilar

J U J U Y

Huacalera

Tilcara

Maimará

Purmamarca

Tumbaya

Río Grande

Quebrada

Volcán

52

9

León

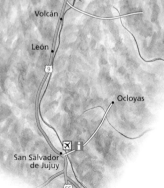

Ocloyas

San Salvador
de Jujuy

Salta

66

★ **Purmamarca**
*Apart from the multihued rock strata
on Cerro de los Siete Colores (Hill of
Seven Colors), this town is also famous
for its artisanal markets.*

La Quiaca

bra Pampa

Potrero

Pueblo
Viejo

Tres Cruces

Iruya

Iturbe

Humahuaca

ia

0 km   20

0 miles   20

KEY

— Expressway

— Highway

— Minor road

☒ Domestic airport

ℹ Visitor information

Iruya

This well-preserved hamlet with cobblestoned streets has a timeless feel and is an excellent base for taking walks into the beautiful surrounding countryside.

★ Humahuaca

With adobe houses and whitewashed walls, Humahuaca is the most populated settlement in the valley. Well worth visiting are the Iglesia de la Candelaria, the cabildo, *and the excellent handicraft stores.*

Uquia

This quiet village is noted for its Cusco School paintings of arcabuceros – *angels armed with Spanish weapons – on display in its 17th-century church, Iglesia de San Francisco de Paula.*

STAR SIGHTS

★ Tilcara

★ Purmamarca

★ Humahuaca

Exploring Quebrada de Humahuaca

The easiest way to explore the stunning *quebrada* landscape is to drive along Ruta Nacional 9, which runs from the picture postcard village of Purmamarca to the junction for the idyllic hamlet of Iruya. The road up is flanked by the towering walls of the massive multi-colored gorge and the drive is especially beautiful in the mornings and evenings when the western side is soaked by sunrise and the eastern wall is hit by sunset, bringing out the flaming orange and vermilion of the mountains. To see man-made wonders along this ancient route – whitewashed colonial chapels, lush fields of quinoa, and alpaca farms – take detours to the villages of Tilcara, Uquia, Maimará, and Humahuaca.

Cerro de los Siete Colores under a blue sky in Purmamarca

San Salvador de Jujuy

75 miles (121 km) N of Salta.
🏠 240,000. ✈ 🚌 ℹ *Gorriti 295, (0388) 422-1326.* **www**.turismo. jujuy.gov.ar **Museo Histórico Provincial Juan Lavalle** *Lavalle 256.* **Tel** *(0388) 422-1355.* ◯ *8am–8pm Mon–Fri, 9am–1pm & 4–8pm Sat & Sun.* 💾 📷 *10am, 11:30 am, 5pm, & 6:30pm.* 📷

The capital of Jujuy province, San Salvador de Jujuy is the highest provincial capital in the country. Located 4,166 ft (1,270 m) above sea level, and flanked by Ríos Grande and Xibi Xibi, the city enjoys a temperate climate. Founded in 1563, Jujuy was destroyed and rebuilt several times due to wars and earthquakes. The city's history can best be traced through its churches that are scattered around the central Plaza General Belgrano.

To the west stands the **Catedral**, which was built in 1606. Among its treasures is the baroque pulpit, designed by local artisans in the 18th century. Its carvings, which depict Biblical subjects such

as Jacob's ladder, are richly detailed and show both the skill of the craftsmen and the enduring eloquence of religious art.

Two blocks west of the plaza is the neocolonial **Iglesia San Francisco**, which was built between 1925 and 1927. It is best known for its Spanish baroque pulpit, which was carved by 18th-century Bolivian craftsmen.

Grand interior of the Iglesia San Francisco in San Salvador

South of the main plaza is **Museo Histórico Provincial Juan Lavalle**, which houses colonial paintings and artifacts. Its claim to fame, however, is its reputation as a crime scene. General Juan Lavalle was assassinated here during Argentina's civil wars in the 1840s. The hole through which the lethal bullet passed is still visible. Three blocks west of the museum is the 18th-century **Capilla de Santa Bárbara**, with an outstanding collection of religious paintings.

Quiet for most of the year, Jujuy offers little apart from leisurely strolls through its cobblestoned streets. It is an excellent base from which to explore the province's remote areas including the two cloud forest national parks, Calilegua *(see p201)* and the less accessible Barítu.

Purmamarca

40 miles (65 km) NW of Jujuy.
🏠 *2,100.*

The picturesque village of Purmamarca nestles at the bottom of the gorge of the same name. It owes its fame to the hill that overlooks it, **Cerro de los Siete Colores** (Hill of Seven Colors). The contrasting shades of the rock's strata range from grimy orange to psychedelic purple and are at their glittering best just after sunrise. A sign-posted route takes visitors to a viewing point just outside the village.

Posta de Hornillos

45 miles (73 km) NW of Jujuy.
◯ *9am–6pm daily.*

Built in 1772, this wonderfully evocative adobe-walled building was once a stop-off point on the route that connected the colonial vice-royalties of Upper Peru (now Bolivia) and Río de la Plata. In 1979, it was converted into a museum and its 19 rooms display old furniture, weapons of war, costumes, and historical documents from the 18th and 19th centuries. Its other claim to fame is that General Belgrano rested here after defeating the Spanish in the battles of Tucumán and Salta in 1813.

A view of tombs and crosses set against the breathtaking backdrop of the *quebrada*, Maimará

Maimará

47 miles (76 km) N of San Salvador de Jujuy. 2,000.

Overlooked by the beautiful multicolored rock formations of the *quebrada*, the village of Maimará is best known for its man-made stoneworks. The extraordinarily diverse range of tombs and crosses found in its cemetery form a chaotic hillside necropolis. The different colored tombs are littered with bright bouquets of paper flowers.

Tilcara

52 miles (84 km) NW of Jujuy. 5,640. Belgrano 590, (0388) 495-5720. Fiesta de la Pachamama (Aug). **Museo Arqueológico Doctor Eduardo Casanova** Belgrano 445, Plaza Alvarez Prado. *Tel (0388) 495-5006.* varies (call in advance). **Museo Irureta de Bellas Artes** Corner, Belgrano & Bolívar. *Tel (0388) 495-5124.* varies (call in advance).

Dominated by the dramatic mountains that surround it, Tilcara is a tiny village with a pleasant, easy-going air. It is quiet for most of the year, although it attracts a large number of visitors when the annual Pachamama festival is celebrated. For centuries, the town has been a hub of crafts-men and artists and many galleries and workshops remain today.

Housed in a lovely colonial building, **Museo Arqueológico Doctor Eduardo Casanova** has a collection of pre-Columbian artifacts from across Latin America including ceramics, menhirs, and even a mummy. There are over 5,000 pieces in the permanent collection and two salons hold temporary exhibitions all year.

In Museo Ernesto Soto Avendaño, the rooms are dedicated to the sculptor who created Monumento a la Independencia de Humahuaca.

The small **Museo Irureta de Bellas Artes** displays over 100 engravings, paintings, and sculptures by modern Argentinian artists. Works of Hugo Irureta, the sculptor who founded the museum, are also displayed. Located close by is Museo José Antonio Terry, whose exhibition space is dedicated to the painter who was born

Sculpture at Museo Arqueológico Doctor Eduardo Casanova

in Buenos Aires, but spent most of his working life in Tilcara. Here he produced oil paintings depicting land-scapes and local personalities.

Tilcara's most popular attrac-tion is an open-air Inca "museum," the Pucará de Tilcara. This hilltop fortress, situated half a mile (1 km) away from town, predates the arrival of the Incas by up to five centuries. It was first excavated in 1903 and has been res-tored and preserved since the 1950s under the auspices of the University of Buenos Aires. The old fortress, which includes a botanical garden of native flora, mostly cacti, affords wonderful views of the *quebrada*.

Uquia

62 miles (100 km) N of San Salvador de Jujuy. 315. **Iglesia de San Franscico de Paula** 10am–noon & 2–4pm daily.

Set against a backdrop of red-rock mountains and lush *quebracho* trees, Uquia is a picturesque village centered around a delightful square and a pretty church. The 17th-century **Iglesia de San Franscico de Paula** and its tower are painted in spotless white with bright green doors.The church is famous for its unusual paintings of "warring angels" from Collao in Bolivia.

The whitewashed façade of Museo Ernesto Soto Avedaño, Tilcara

A view of picturesque Humahuaca nestled in the Andean hills

Humahuaca

78 miles (125 km) N of Jujuy.
🏔 12,000. 🚌 **Iglesia de la
Candelaria y San Antonio** Buenos
Aires 383. ⬜ 9:30am–noon & 4–
7pm Mon–Fri.

Founded in 1591, Humahuaca
is the largest town between
San Salvador de Jujuy and
the Bolivian border. It has a
picturesque town center, and
its narrow, roughly-paved
streets and rustic adobe
houses are classically Andean.

The town's star attraction is
**Iglesia de la Candelaria y San
Antonio**, also a National
Historical Monument. This
striking white church was
built by the Jesuits toward the
end of the 17th century, and
has undergone extensive
restoration after it was largely
destroyed by an earthquake
in 1873. The interior is richly
ornamented, with two rococo
altarpieces depicting various
Biblical events. Other artworks in the church include
the series called *The Twelve
Prophets*, completed in 1764
by well-known Cusco School
artist Marcos Sapaca.

The handicraft shops in
town, well-stocked with
souvenirs, and the tiny folk
music venues are highly
popular with tourists.
Humahuaca is also a good
base from which to explore
the haunting landscapes of
Puna Jujeña, an area of wild
highland, lagoons filled with
pink flamingos, and tiny
mud-brick hamlets.

Iruya

44 miles (70 km) N of Humahuaca.
🏔 1,200. 🚌

Overlooking the river of the
same name, Iruya is a
beautiful Andean hamlet
located 9,120 ft (2,780 m)
above sea level. Time seems
to pass slowly here, and the
fortified walls, cobblestoned
streets, and whitewashed
adobe dwellings are much
as they have always been.

The village's focal point is
its church, the colonial **Iglesia
de Nuestra Señora del Rosario
y San Roque**. Here, on the
first Sunday of October, the
feast of Our Lady of the
Rosary is held, a surreal
procession of masked figures
that blends elements from
Easter festivals and pre-
conquest animistic rituals.

View of Iglesia de Nuestra Señora
del Rosario y San Roque

Monumento Natural Laguna de los Pozuelos ㉔

Road Map B1. 30 miles (48km) NW
of Iruya. **Tel** (03887) 91-048. 🚌
ℹ Macedonia Gras 141, Abrapampa.
⬜ daily. 🅰 by prior arrangement.

Situated in a natural basin
between Sierra de Cochinoca
and Sierra de Rinconada, this
remote wildlife preserve rises
11,810 ft (3,600 m) above sea
level. Spread over an area
of 58 sq miles (153 sq km),
the park is one of the most
important wetlands in
South America.

Although it has shrunk in
recent years after a few dry
summers, the park's lagoon
still takes up about half the
total area. It is the habitat
of large flocks of Andean
flamingos and numerous
other species of wildfowl
including teals, avocets, and
ducks. Shy *ñandús* (lesser
rheas) can also be spotted
scuttling away for cover.
The best way to observe
these birds at close quarters
is by walking through the
park from its entrance rather
than driving. The park can be
accessed at any time but it is
advisable to drop in at the
guardería (ranger station),
which is located on the south
side of the lake, for a chat
with the knowledgeable and
welcoming *guardaparques*
(park rangers).

Yavi ㉕

Road Map B1. 195 miles (314 km)
N of Jujuy. 🏔 300. 🚌

Another sleepy high-plains
hamlet of sloping cobble-
stoned streets and adobe
houses, Yavi also seems to
have given modernity the slip.
The village dates from the late
17th century when nobleman
Juan Fernández Campero, the
first Marqués del Valle del
Toxo in Spain, married into
the area's landholding family.
In 1708, Spain's King Phillip V
named him Marqués of Tojo,
a unique honor in colonial
Argentina. The well-preserved
18th-century family home,

Sweeping view of towering peaks covered in verdant *yunga* forest, Parque Nacional Calilegua

Casa del Marqués Campero, still stands and is now an interesting museum exhibiting some of the ruling dynasty's memorabilia. Standing next to it is a 17th-century church, **Iglesia de Nuestra Señora del Rosario y San Francisco**. Behind its whitewashed façade are the region's best preserved colonial interiors, complete with a wonderfully ornate baroque pulpit. The interior would be even more impressive had not some of the church's treasures been looted during the border disputes with Chile in the late 1970s. The windows are perhaps the most unusual feature, as their panes are made of wafer-thin onyx, casting a surreal, yellow-orange glow over the nave.

The 18th-century Casa del Marqués Campero, now a museum

Parque Nacional Calilegua ㉖

Road Map B1. 75 miles (120 km) NE of Jujuy. **Tel** (03886) 422-046. 🚌 ⬜ 9am–6pm daily. ⬜ ⬜

Comprising over 290 sq miles (763 sq km) of subtropical *yunga* forests, lakes, and rivers, Parque Nacional Calilegua is the largest of the national parks in northwest Argentina. Thanks to its easy accessibility, it is also the most visited. The park served as the setting for Gerald Durrell's popular 1960s book *The Whispering Land*. Parque Nacional Calilegua is easy to navigate with many trails that weave through dense and tangled cloud forest, often leading above the tree line and to the drier prairies of the high *puna*. As well as diverse flora, which changes according to the altitude and humidity, brown eagles, condors, and northern *huemul* deer can also be seen. Jaguars and pumas roam the forests, though both species have a well-founded fear of humans. Mornings and evenings are the best times to see these animals. Visitors can hire guides and also find useful maps and information at the park's entrance.

Parque Nacional El Rey ㉗

Road Map C1. 155 miles (250 km) SE of Jujuy. **Tel** (03487) 4312-683. 🚌 ⬜ 9am–dusk Mon–Sat. ⬜

Created in 1948, Parque Nacional El Rey is one of three cloud forest parks in northwest Argentina, the others being Calilegua and Baritú to the north. It rises to an average of 2,950 ft (900 m) above sea level and the peaks are usually enveloped in thick cloud, keeping most of the plant life lush and green even in the drier months. Previously a private estate, the park now protects 155 sq miles (408 sq km) of *yunga* forests. Strikingly diverse in both flora and fauna, El Rey is home to a number of endangered mammals including jaguars and pumas.

Toucan in Parque Nacional El Rey

The avian population, totalling over 150 species, is more visible and includes the emblematic giant toucan and several species of parrot and eagle. Numerous footpaths and one major vehicle trail snake around the park from the visitor center. The best trail for bird-watchers is the 8-mile (13-km) Senda Pozo Verde, which climbs through the bird-filled forest to a small beautiful lake.

CUYO AND THE WINE COUNTRY

K nown as the wine cellar of Argentina, Cuyo is noted for a landscape dominated by plains covered with acres of lush vineyards. To the west of the province are the towering Andes, which give way to the fertile wine-producing valleys. Heading east, the landscape changes dramatically to one of sand dunes and rocky desert formations shaped by the region's dry and dusty Zonda wind.

The original inhabitants of the Cuyo region were the Huarpe people, colonized by Chile's Captain-General Garcia de Mendoza in the late 1500s. Although Cuyo was administratively under Chile and was a flourishing region, it was isolated from Santiago de Chile by the snows of the Andes for months on end. This encouraged a self-sufficiency that survived even after the area became part of independent Argentina.

The region is a vital energy storehouse as most of the country's petroleum and natural gas reserves are found here. Its main economic activity, however, is agriculture, most notably viticulture. Meltwater from the snowcapped Andean peaks flows into canals that irrigate the region's many vineyards. Mendoza alone contributes 70 percent of Argentina's wine production, and the world-class Malbec is the region's specialty. Cuyo's wines in turn are driving its tourism sector, which also offers a wide array of outdoor activities that attract locals and visitors from around the world. These range from mountain-climbing and white-water rafting in summer to skiing at Las Leñas in winter. The region's cities have good museums, sprawling parks, and verdant plazas, as well as quality restaurants and accommodation options. Growing areas of interest, however, lie in the fossil-rich deserts and dramatic canyon country of Ischigualasto and Las Quijadas, both emblematic of Argentina's impressive achievements in paleontology.

Rows of wooden wine barrels in the cellar of Zapata Agrelo winery, Luján de Cuyo

◁ View of the magnificent El Hongo balancing rocks at Parque Provincial Ischigualasto, San Juan

Exploring Cuyo and the Wine Country

Cuyo is a year-round destination and the city of
Mendoza is the best base from which to explore the
region due to its easy access to wineries and proximity
to sights such as Parque Provincial Aconcagua.
Highlights to the north and east, such as the dramatic
Parque Provincial Ischigualasto and Parque Nacional
Sierra de las Quijadas, and sights in and around
Malargüe are about a day's drive away. Many activities,
such as hiking and climbing, take place at Aconcagua,
along with rafting and kayaking on Río Mendoza
arranged by tour operators from Mendoza. Skiing is also
popular at Los Penitentes and Las Leñas. Wineries are
open to visitors most of the year.

Round concretions found at Parque Provincial Ischigualasto

SIGHTS AT A GLANCE

Towns and Cities

Malargüe ⑮
Mendoza pp206–9 ❶
Pismanta ⑨
San Agustín del
  Valle Fértil ⑪
San José de Jáchal ⑧
San Juan ⑦
San Luis ⑬
San Rafael ⑭
Uspallata ❸

Tours

*Mendoza Winery Tour
  pp210–11* ❷

National and Provincial Parks

Parque Nacional
  Sierra de las Quijadas ⑫
Parque Provincial
  Aconcagua ⑥
Parque Provincial
  Ischigualasto ⑩

Ski Resorts

Las Leñas ⑯
Los Penitentes ❹

Sites of Interest

Cristo Redentor ❺

For additional map symbols *see back flap*

GETTING AROUND

Cuyo has a good network of highways, and while they are mostly paved, drivers should be careful on the two-lane roads as they can be dangerous, especially around blind curves. A rental car is ideal for visiting scattered sights within a compact area such as Mendoza and its vicinity. Hiring a car and driver for the day, however, can be cheaper and more convenient, especially for visiting wineries. Buses are reliable for intercity travel as they are frequent and comfortable.

Old bottling machines in Bodega La Rural

SEE ALSO

• *See Where to Stay* pp281–2

• *See Where to Eat* pp299–300

PARQUE PROVINCIAL ISCHIGUALASTO **10**

SAN AGUSTÍN DEL VALLE FÉRTIL **11**

Río Bermejo

Parque Provincial le Fértil

510

Mte. Corralitos
10,374 ft

del ador aucete 141

Cordoba

Pampa de las Salinas

dia Agua

Río San Juan

142

PARQUE NACIONAL SIERRA DE LAS QUIJADAS **12**

Pampa del Salado

n Martín

Santa Rosa

La Paz

153

Comandante Salas

NDOZA

Almirante La Lata

146

Río Diamante

SAN RAFAEL

General Alvear

143

ro Peceño 48 ft

ro Nevado 500 ft

Río Atuel

Pampa de la Varita

Neuquén

Quines

Villa General Roca

147

146

La Toma

SAN LUIS **13**

20

79

Córdoba

Córdoba

20

Rosa del Conlara

1

Concarán

2

El Morro
5,377 ft

Río Cuarto

8

Villa Mercedes

Travesía Puntana

Varela

148

Junín

SAN LUÍS

Navia

Junín

188

Canalejas

Río Salado

55

KEY

▬	Expressway
▬	Highway
▬	Major road
▬	Minor road
▬	Railroad
▬	International border
▬	Provincial border
△	Peak

0 km   100

0 miles   100

View of Laguna de Horcones, Aconcagua

Mendoza [1]

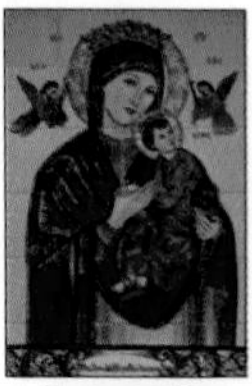

A tiled panel in a church in Chacras de Coria

Lying at the base of the eastern Andes, Mendoza was devastated by the 1861 earthquake. Extensively rebuilt, it now has lush landscaped plazas decorated with striking tilework, murals, statuary, and fountains. The heart of the country's wine industry, the city is an ideal base from which to explore many excellent *bodegas* (wineries) that dot the area. It draws a large number of foreign tourists through the year, especially during the city's wine harvest festival in March. Even during the winter months, Mendoza gets visitors who enjoy the clear, mild days and go skiing in the nearby Andes.

🏛 Plaza Independencia

Espejo, Chile, Rivadavia & Patricias Mendocinas. 🚌 🛍 *Sat & Sun.*

Museo Municipal Arte Moderno ***Tel*** *(0261) 425-7279.* ⏰ *9am–8pm Mon–Sat, 4–9pm Sun & pub hols.* 📷 🎟 ♿ 🖥 🛍

Occupying the city's geographical center, Plaza Independencia is Mendoza's modern hub. Shaded by sycamores and acacias, it hosts a weekend crafts fair and live concerts. It is also the site of Teatro Quintanilla, a live theater venue, the subterranean **Museo Municipal de Arte Moderno**, and the prestigious 1920s Plaza Hotel, which has been refurbished by the Hyatt chain *(see p282)*.

🏛 Plaza España

Ave España and Montevideo. 🚌 ♿

Built by traditional artisans from Spain in the 1940s, Plaza España is the most colorful and visually dramatic of all Mendoza's plazas. It has lacquered tile murals and geometric Moorish designs on its fountains and benches. The murals reflect themes from Argentinian and Spanish literature and history, including the famous *Don Quixote*, the gaucho classic *Martín Fierro*, Columbus's voyage, and the Spanish missionaries of Argentina.

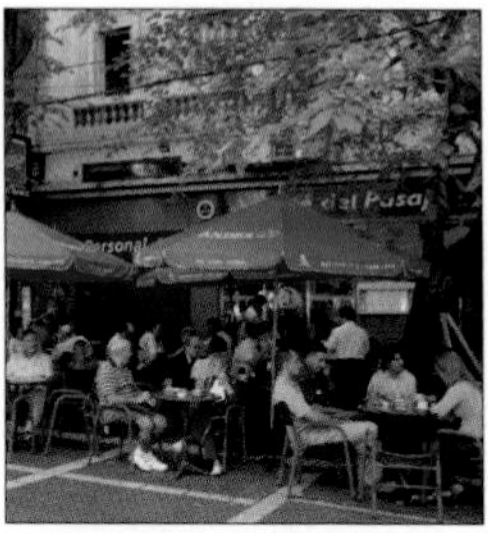

A bustling sidewalk café in Mendoza city

🏛 Plaza Italia

Montevideo and 25 de Mayo. 🚌

Densely planted with palms and conifers around a central fountain and studded with statuary on Roman themes, Plaza Italia, once called Plaza Lima, honors Mendoza's Italian immigrants and their heritage. Argentinian sculptor Luis Perlotti created the Etruscan-style wolf that symbolizes the founding of Rome. Even the grapes that produce Mendoza's wines get their symbolic tribute here.

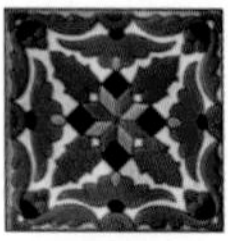

Spanish-style tiled murals at Plaza España

🏛 Plaza Chile

Gutiérrez and 25 de Mayo. 🚌

Shaded by a large *aguaribay* tree, Plaza Chile is centered around a monument dedicated to the friendship

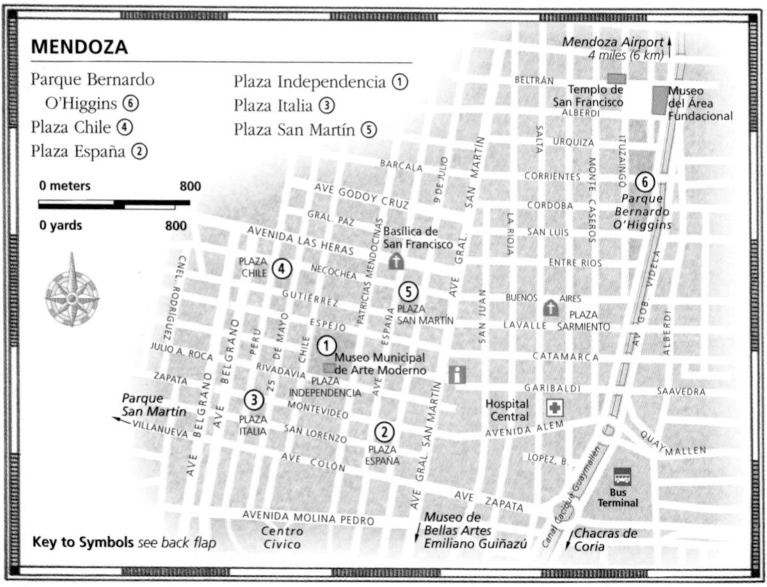
MENDOZA
Parque Bernardo O'Higgins 6
Plaza Chile 4
Plaza España 2
Plaza Independencia 1
Plaza Italia 3
Plaza San Martín 5
0 meters 800
0 yards 800
Mendoza Airport 4 miles (6 km)
Templo de San Francisco
Museo del Área Fundacional
Parque Bernardo O'Higgins
Basílica de San Francisco
PLAZA CHILE
PLAZA SAN MARTÍN
PLAZA SARMIENTO
Museo Municipal de Arte Moderno
PLAZA INDEPENDENCIA
PLAZA ITALIA
PLAZA ESPAÑA
Parque San Martín
Hospital Central
Bus Terminal
Centro Cívico
Museo de Bellas Artes Emiliano Guiñazú
Chacras de Coria
BELTRÁN
ALBERDI
URQUIZA
CORRIENTES
CÓRDOBA
SAN LUIS
ENTRE RÍOS
BUENOS AIRES
LAVALLE
CATAMARCA
GARIBALDI
AVENIDA ALEM
LÓPEZ, B.
SAAVEDRA
QUAYMALLEN
AVE ZAPATA
AVENIDA MOLINA PEDRO
AVE COLÓN
SAN LORENZO
MONTEVIDEO
RIVADAVIA
ESPEJO
GUTIÉRREZ
NECOCHEA
AVENIDA LAS HERAS
GRAL. PAZ
AVE GODOY CRUZ
BARCALA
JULIO A. ROCA
ZAPATA
VILLANUEVA
CNEL RODRÍGUEZ
BELGRANO
AVE BELGRANO
PERÚ
25 DE MAYO
CHILE
AVE ESPAÑA
PATRICIAS MENDOCINAS
9 DE JULIO
SAN MARTÍN
AVE GRAL. SAN MARTÍN
SAN JUAN
LA RIOJA
SALTA
MONTE CASEROS
ITUZAINGÓ
AV GOB. VIDELA
Canal Cacique Guaymallén
Key to Symbols see back flap

between Argentina and Chile. Created by Chilean sculptor Lorenzo Domínguez, it shows Argentinian Independence hero, José de San Martín, and Chile's liberator, Bernardo O'Higgins, together. The plaza gained its name in recognition of Chile's assistance after the 1861 earthquake. Mendoza welcomes Chileans to celebrate their mid-September Independence days here.

🏛 Plaza San Martín
Ave España and Gutiérrez.

🏛 ♿ Basilica de San Francisco
Ave España and Necochea.
◯ 6–8pm Tue–Sat.

Before crossing the Andes to Chile, Independence hero José de San Martín spent extended periods in Mendoza. This plaza, earlier known as Plaza Cobo, commemorates that fact with an equestrian statue, a replica of one that stands in Buenos Aires's namesake plaza. Across the street, the neoclassical **Basílica de San Francisco** contains the image of Nuestra Señora del Carmen de Cuyo, the patron saint of San Martín's Army of the Andes. There is also a mausoleum with the remains of his family. Despite the devastating earthquakes of 1861 and 1927, the basilica still stands immaculate.

♣ Parque Bernardo O'Higgins
Ituzaingó and Buenos Aires. 🚌 ♿
Museo del Área Fundacional
Alberdi 571. **Tel** (0261) 425-6927.
◯ 9am–7pm Tue–Sat, 3–7pm Sun.
📷 🎥 ♿ 🖼 🏛

At the eastern edge of downtown Mendoza, Parque Bernardo O'Higgins is a greenbelt that stretches north for several blocks to the city's original site, where **Museo del Área Fundacional** covers the excavated foundations of the colonial *cabildo* (town hall). The museum is also notable for its indigenous Huarpe artifacts, an impressive set of historical dioramas, and a collection of historical photographs. In addition to the museum, the park also has an aquarium. Nearby are the crumbling ruins of the 18th-century **Templo de San Francisco**, nearly leveled in

The Museo del Área Fundacional in Parque Bernardo O'Higgins

the 1861 earthquake that spurred the city's relocation to the southwest.

♣ Parque San Martín
Ave Emilio Civit and Avenida Boulogne Sur Mer. 🚌

In the 19th century, French architect Charles Thays left a legacy of magnificently landscaped public parks and private properties throughout the country. None, however, surpasses Mendoza's Parque San Martín, crowned by **Cerro de la Gloria**. Atop

The ornate gates at Parque San Martín

its summit, Uruguayan sculptor Juan M. Ferrari's Monumento al Ejercito Libertador pays homage to San Martín's Army of the Andes.

The iron-filigree gates at the park's main entrance lead to a diverse woodland, punctuated by a rose garden, horse track, zoo, and museums. Other sights include a Greek-style

VISITORS' CHECKLIST

Road Map B2. 1095 miles (1760 km) W of Buenos Aires.
🏙 110,000. ✈ 🚌
ℹ San Martin 1143, (0291) 420-2800. 🎉 Fiesta Nacional de la Vendimia (Mar).
www.turismo.mendoza.gov.ar

theater, which is the main venue for the fall wine festival, and the **Estadio Islas Malvinas**, which hosted the 1978 World Cup matches.

🏛 Chacras de Coria
Ave Emilio Civit and Boulogne Sur Mer. 🚌 ♿ Sat & Sun. **Museo Provincial de Bellas Artes Emiliano Guiñazú** San Martín 3651, Mayor Drummond, Luján de Cuyo. **Tel** (0261) 496-0224.
◯ varies (call in advance).

Only 15 minutes away from downtown Mendoza, the leafy suburb of Chacras de Coria was once the capital's kitchen garden and orchard. Many of its dirt roads still survive, but over the years it has morphed into a gourmet ghetto of fancy restaurants and wine bars. The central Plaza Geronimo Espejo is the site of an art and antiques fair every Sunday. Chacras is also home to the **Museo Provincial de Bellas Artes Emiliano Guiñazú**, a fine arts museum in an erstwhile summer residence surrounded by gardens.

View from Cerro de la Gloria in Parque San Martín

The Wines of Mendoza

The province of Mendoza is the locus of Argentina's wine industry and produces more than 80 percent of the country's wine. In colonial times, Mendoza's first vines arrived from neighboring Chile and spread along the Andean front range. From the late 19th century, European, especially Italian, immigration spurred production for Argentina's growing urban market, in what is now the world's fifth-biggest wine producer. From the 1970s, Argentina began to produce fine wines for export. Since then, burgeoning foreign investment has accelerated the process. Dozens of *bodegas* are open for tours, tasting, and dining. Several wineries have their own guesthouses as well.

Neatly arranged wooden casks at Bodega La Rural

THE GRAPE GROWING PROCESS

The production of Mendoza's wine is aided by the area's altitude and climate, which is temperate and semi-arid, offering plenty of sunlight and little rainfall. However, the height of the Andes can cause climatic features, such as the withering Zonda wind, to be more destructive than on the plains.

High altitudes receive increased ultraviolet light, improving grape color by enhancing tannins and pigments; the altitude also concentrates grape sugars, making the wine complex and intense.

Irrigation *takes place through an elaborate system of dams and canals that are fed by the region's many rivers, including Río Mendoza. These rivers carry the melting snows of the Andes mountain range.*

Vineyards remain healthy and free from fungal diseases due to the high altitudes that ensure good air circulation.

GOOD PRODUCERS AND VINTAGES

- Luigi Bosca – *Luigi Bosca Malbec Reserva 2002, Luigi Bosca Syrah Reserva 2001*
- Bodega Terrazaz de los Andes – *Malbec 2005*
- Bodega Caro Amancaya – *Malbec and Cabernet Sauvignon 2005*
- Bodega Catena Zapata – *Malbec 1999*
- Rutini – *Rutini Cabernet Malbec 2004*
- Alta Vista – *Alta Vista Malbec Mendoza Premium 2004*

Hail nets *are common over Mendoza vineyards. Due to the heat and high altitude, electrical storms are frequent in summer and can bring destructive hail at any time. Many growers reduce their risk with scattered vineyards, but some take the additional, but labor-intensive, precaution of protective netting for their grapes.*

THE MAKING OF MENDOZA WINE

Mendoza wineries produce countless varietals and blends, including international standards such as Cabernet Sauvignon, Pinot Noir, and Chardonnay. Their signature wines are the deep red Malbec and the dry white Torrontés.

Torrontés, *probably a cross between an American and eastern Mediterranean grape, is Argentina's characteristic white grape, and produces a dry but fruity wine.*

Malbec grapes *were once abundant in southeast France but responded better to Argentina's arid west. The bluish-black, thin-skinned, and soft-pulp grape reaches its highest development in Maipú in Mendoza.*

Newly harvested grapes *first undergo a sorting process and are crushed lightly to bring them in contact with selected yeasts. Fermentation then happens in temperature-controlled stainless steel tanks.*

Wine *is among the country's premier exports and has recently doubled in volume and quality. Malbec is the most popular and recognized varietal, alongside others such as Syrah, Merlot, and Chardonnay.*

FIESTA NACIONAL DE LA VENDIMIA

This wine harvest festival is Mendoza's single biggest event, with nearly 50,000 tourists crowding the city. It takes place on the first full weekend of March. The festival begins with the Blessing of the Fruits ceremony and ends with fireworks at the Teatro Griego.

The harvest festival, *uninterrupted since 1936, begins with the grape gathering in January and February. It culminates in March when people line the streets to watch the Harvest Queen parade.*

Teatro Griego *in Mendoza's Parque San Martín is the venue for the Harvest Queen competition. The complex holds about 22,000 people and thousands more view the events from the surrounding hills.*

Mendoza Winery Tour ❷

Although much of the Mendoza wine route is suburban, southern Luján's sycamore-studded landscape opens onto vast vineyards with Andean panoramas, while the snow-covered Cordón del Plata provides a spectacular backdrop to the poplar-lined roads of Uco Valley. Some *bodegas* are intimate boutiques while others are massive, isolated monuments. Some have long local histories, others house art galleries and excellent gourmet restaurants. Nearly all, however, have opened their doors for tours and tasting.

Carving on wine casket

Bodega Salentein ⑩
Set in the heights of Tunuyán, Bodega Salentein is famous for its architecture, wines, restaurant *(see p300)*, accommodations, and fine art space.

Cavas Wine Lodge ⑨
Set amongst its own modestly sized vineyards, Cavas Wine Lodge offers premium accommodations *(see p282)*, and has its own outdoor swimming pool, a restaurant, and a book-lined living room. It also hosts occasional cultural events.

KEY

▬ Tour route

═ Major road

═ Minor road

✦

0 km   5

0 miles   5

TUPUNGATO

AGR

Chandon ⑦
Located on Luján's outskirts, Chandon is one of the first foreign vintners to operate in Argentina. This French-operated *bodega* has produced sparkling wines and others since 1959.

Catena Zapata ⑧
Rising high above the lush vineyard, Catena Zapata's Mayan pyramid structure makes it Mendoza's most attention-grabbing winery. The varietals and blends are also just as remarkable.

Escorihuela ①
Mendoza's most central winery, Bodegas Escorihuela is home to celebrity chef Francis Mallman's excellent restaurant 1884 *(see p299)*.

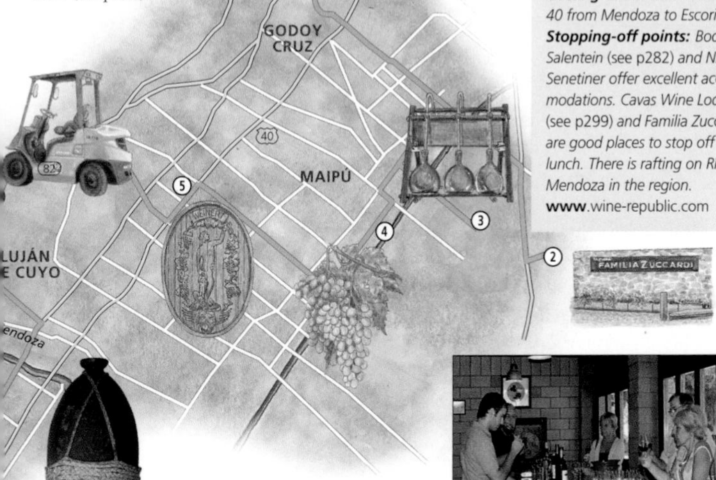

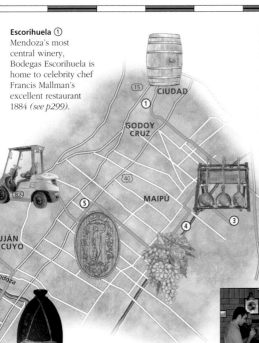

TIPS FOR VISITORS

Starting point: *Escorihuela, 3 miles (4 km) S of Mendoza.*
Length: *80 miles (130 km). The tour needs at least two days and it is best to hire a car and driver.*
Getting there: *Ruta Nacional 40 from Mendoza to Escorihuela.*
Stopping-off points: *Bodega Salentein (see p282) and Nieto Senetiner offer excellent accommodations. Cavas Wine Lodge (see p299) and Familia Zuccardi are good places to stop off for lunch. There is rafting on Río Mendoza in the region.*
www.wine-republic.com

Bodega La Rural ③
In addition to a diversity of vintages, Bodega La Rural in Maipú has Argentina's finest wine museum, with displays of machinery, presses, and artifacts that contributed to the Mendoza wine industry.

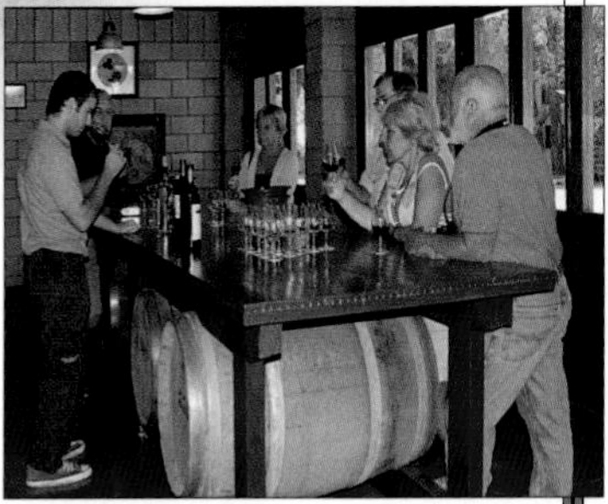

Familia Zuccardi ②
Located on the outskirts of Maipú, Familia Zuccardi hosts a wine tasting fair in November. This gathering is the biggest event at any Mendoza winery.

López ④
Since its creation in the late 19th century, this modernized *bodega* is still managed by the third and fourth generation of the founding López family. It produces some less common vintages such as Pinot Noir and Semillón.

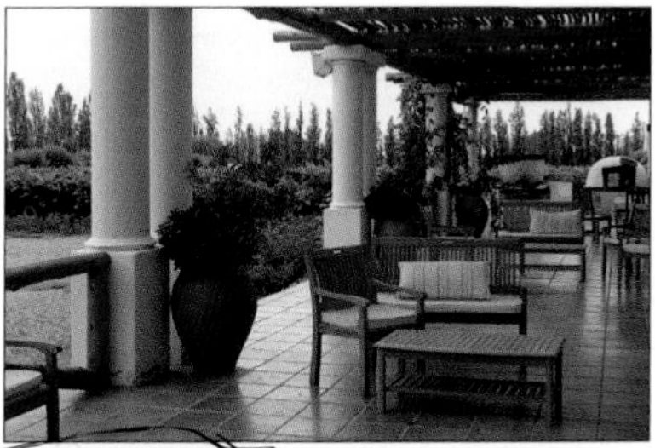

Nieto Senetiner ⑥
Situated within secluded, manicured grounds in Luján, the stylish conglomerate-owned Nieto Senetiner, complete with guesthouse, more closely resembles a boutique winery.

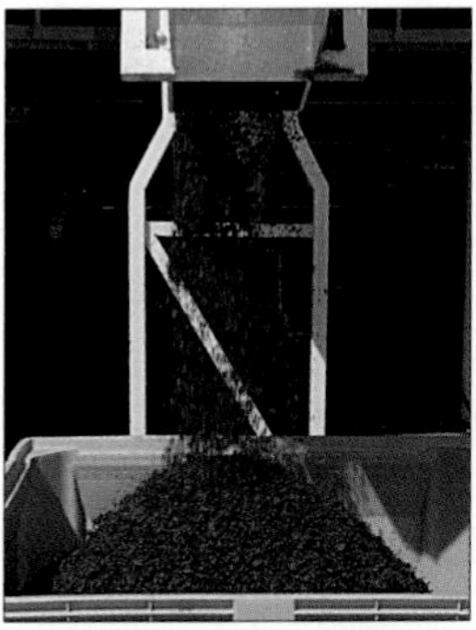

Bodega y Cavas de Weinert ⑤
Founded in 1975 and located in Luján de Cuyo, the unique Cavas de Weinert arranges tours exploring the restored historic cellars filled with huge oak casks.

Uspallata ❸

Road Map B2. 89 miles (140 km)
N of Mendoza. 🏔 3,284. 🚌
ℹ *junction of Ruta Nacional 7 and
Ruta Provincial 39, (02624) 420-410.*

At the headwaters of Río
Mendoza, Uspallata, the
biggest settlement between
Gran Mendoza and the
border, occupies a scenic
valley. Its resemblance to
Central Asian highlands is so
striking that the location was
chosen for the 1997 movie
Seven Years In Tibet, starring
actor Brad Pitt.

While Uspallata has only a
few sights to explore, several
rafting and kayaking com-
panies offer trips on the sedi-
ment-clogged Río Mendoza
(see p312). Though it lacks
difficult rapids, it gets big
waves during the spring
runoff, which is the best time
for a good kayaking and
rafting experience.

Environs
The surrounding countryside
along Ruta Provincial 52 and
other nearby roads has a
cluster of interesting historic
sights. About 1.2 miles (2 km)
west of Uspallata, stand the
Bóvedas Históricas Uspallata,
whitewashed domed kilns
that date from the 17th century. They were used for
metallurgy even in pre-
Columbian times. A short distance to the northeast, there
are several beautiful pre-
Columbian petroglyphs and a
shrine to the Mapuche "saint"
Ceferino Namuncurá *(see p25)*
at the lava outcrop of **Cerro
Tunduqueral**. Another route to
Mendoza continues via a
zigzag road past the hot

A Los Penitentes ski resort in summer

springs of **Villavicencio**, which
have been closed for many
years because of a legal
dispute. This route was the
same taken by Independence
hero José de San Martín's
Army of the Andes and also
Charles Darwin a couple of
decades later. To the north,
along Ruta Provincial 39
toward Calingasta, the
**Comunidad Huarpe
Guaytamari** is an
indigenous outpost
with a llama farm and
handicrafts market.

Los Penitentes ❹

Road Map B2. 40 miles (65
km) W of Uspallata. 🚌 🍴
📷 🅿 ♿ www.mendoza
ski.com

From Uspallata,
rugged roads to the
west give way to spectacular
scenery all the way to Los
Penitentes. At 8,464 ft (2,580 m)
above sea level, Los
Penitentes is the best skiing
option for Mendoza-based
visitors. Better known as Villa
Los Penitentes, the village is

filled with several
brightly painted ski
resorts. Set against
the backdrop of the
Andes mountain
range are 26 snow-
dust tracks, ideal
for both profes-
sional and amateur
skiers. The town
is also a base for
Aconcagua-bound
hikers and climbers.
Modern ski-lifts
run at weekends
during selected
months for visitors
to enjoy the fabulous valley
and mountain views.

Cristo Redentor ❺

Road Map B2. Ruta Nacional 7,
near Las Cuevas. 🚌 📷 🅿
📷 www.cristoredentorchiar.
galeon.com

Cristo Redentor
statue on the
Chile border

After Argentina and
Chile resolved one of
their countless border
differences in 1902, the
two countries, under
the auspices of British
King Edward VII, signed
a pact to determine
the Andean boundary
between them. As part
of the pact, they
installed a 26-ft (8-m)
statue of Christ,
13,779 ft (4,200 m)
above sea level. The
statue was made by
Uruguayan sculptor Mateo
Alonso using metal from
cannons and other weapons.
The road to the saddle where
the statue stands is a vertiginous zigzag that yields spectacular panoramas of the Río
Mendoza Valley.

For many years, the old
route to Cristo used to be the
main international highway.
It has since been superseded
by a tunnel, but tour buses
and private cars still transport
visitors to the statue.

However, the road is open
only between January and
March; the rest of the year
it is closed due to heavy
snowfall. When the road is
open, most tours go up to the
17,817-ft (5,430-m) high **Cerro
Tolosa**, where climbers train
to scale Aconcagua.

Domed kilns used to smelt metal, Bóvedas Históricas Uspallata

Spectacular backdrop of Laguna de Horcones, Parque Provincial Aconcagua

Parque Provincial Aconcagua ❻

Road Map B2. 115 miles (185 km) W of Mendoza. 🚌 ⓘ *Ranger station, Horcones; (0261) 156-210-118.* 📷 **Permits** *Mendoza, (0261) 4252-090.* ◯ *8am–6pm daily (for entry).* 🅿 ♿ 🅰 www.aconcagua. mendoza.gov.ar

One of the country's most well-known parks, Parque Provincial Aconcagua contains one of the world's highest summits. At 22,841 ft (6,962-m), **Cerro Aconcagua** has been the goal of many novice mountaineers as, unlike Mount Everest and other famous peaks, it enjoys easy access and requires no technical climbing skills. By the traditional northwest route, the "Roof of the Americas" is relatively a low-difficulty

climb. This does not mean that it is easy; prospective summiteers must be in good physical condition to deal with oxygen deficits, not to mention extreme weather conditions. On other, more technical routes, the issue is even more clear-cut: more than 100 climbers have died on Aconcagua and a professional guide is imperative for non-mountaineers.

Fortunately, Aconcagua has more to offer than just its summit. From its visitor center, only 2 miles (4 km) north of the highway, day-trippers can take a short hike to **Laguna de Horcones** (Horcones Lake) for spectacular views. Another option is to go ahead to Confluencia, an intermediate camp for trekking to **Plaza Francia** and to **Plaza de Mulas**. In three days, backpackers can reach Plaza Francia, the

14,763-ft (4,500-m) base camp for Pared Sur, Aconcagua's difficult south face. In a week, they can reach and return from Plaza de Mulas, where most mountaineers start their final climb to the summit. Here, backpackers should be prepared for summer gridlock and competition for campsites. It is mandatory for hikers to have permits for every walk beyond Horcones and to have an ascent permit to continue beyond Plaza de Mulas. The **Glaciar Polaco** route, about 9 miles (15 km) east of Los Penitentes, is longer and slightly less difficult than the south face.

Unlike many national parks, Aconcagua has relatively little to offer other than its spectacular scenery. This is one of the Andes's most barren sectors, with little vegetation and few mammals. Some visitors may spot the Andean condor, which came close to extinction due to hunting, circling on the thermals.

About 4 miles (7 km) west of Los Penitentes is **Puente del Inca** which takes its name from a natural bridge over Río Mendoza. The site, however, is currently closed to visitors as a fissure has made it potentially dangerous. Puente del Inca is home to the **Cementerio de los Andinistas**, an Aconcagua climbers' cemetery. The area has street stalls from where visitors can pick up souvenirs.

🏚 **Puente del Inca**
Ruta Nacional 7, Km 175. 🍴
♿ 🅰

Natural rock formation at Puente del Inca

Bodega Cheval des Andes against the snowy Andes mountains, Luján de Cuyo ▷

The sunlit patio of Casa Natal de Sarmiento in San Juan

San Juan **❼**

Road Map B2. 102 miles (165 km)
N of Mendoza. 🏠 115,566. ✈ 🚌
ℹ Sarmiento 24 Sur, (0264) 4210-
004. **www**.welcomeargentina.com/
sanjuan

The modern city of San Juan
is nestled in the valley of Río
San Juan. The city has played a
key role in Argentinian history
as the birthplace of the cosmopolitan author, diplomat,
educator, and former president,
Domingo F. Sarmiento. It is
also the place where populist
Juan Domingo Perón entered
the public eye during the relief
efforts of Argentina's worst
ever earthquake in 1944. With
hardly a building more than a
century old, San Juan is a
young and modern city. Its
wine industry and the beautiful
Casa Natal de Sarmiento are
the town's main tourist
attractions. Declared a
national monument in 1911,
Casa Natal de Sarmiento is a
typical colonial house with
spacious sunlit interiors built
around a large patio with
plenty of trees. Damaged in
the violent earthquake on
January 15, 1944, it has been
restored several times.

🏛 **Casa Natal de Sarmiento**
Sarmiento 21 Sur. **Tel** (0264)
422-4603. ◻ 8:30am–1:30pm
Mon–Sun, 5–9:30pm Tue–Fri
& Sun. 🎫 **www**.casanatal-
sarmiento.gov.ar

San José de Jáchal **❽**

Road Map B2. 96 miles (155 km)
N of San Juan. 🏠 10,901. 🚌
ℹ San Juan s/n; (02647) 420-003,
ext. 311. 🎎 Fiesta de la Tradición
(Nov). **www**.jachal.gov.ar

A gaucho town, Jáchal is
known for handwoven blan-
kets and ponchos but it is
more famous as a base for
exploring the surrounding
villages, the high Andes, and
white-water rafting in the
town's river. The major attraction is the 19th-century **Iglesia
San José**, a national historical
monument that houses Cristo
Negro, a unique image of the
crucified Christ.

Environs
About 14 miles (23 km) east
of Jáchal, Huaco is the site of
the adobe tomb of gauchesco
poet, Buenaventura Luna.
To the west, Ruta Nacional
150 leads over the Cuesta del
Viento to the hamlet of
Rodeo, the starting point for
rafting down Río Jáchal.

🔒 **Iglesia San José**
San Juan. ◻ daily.

A thermal bath under an open sky
in Pismanta

Pismanta **❾**

Road Map B2. 116 miles (187 km)
NW of San Juan, Ruta Nacional 150.
🚌 from San Juan to Jáchal.
www.hoteltermaspismanta.com.ar

From Jáchal, Ruta Nacional
150 leads southwest to the
modest hot-spring oasis of
Pismanta, where the hotel has
a good restaurant and enormous hot baths that are also

THE DIFUNTA CORREA
About 37 miles (60 km) east of San Juan's provincial
capital is the popular Difunta Correa shrine at Vallecito
village. According to one of the legends, Deolinda Correa,
a young widow, died of thirst while following her conscript
husband during the 19th-century civil wars. Her baby,
however, survived at her breast. Despite doubts that she
ever existed, this "miracle" made her a popular "saint."
Today, at Easter and other times, the sprawling shrine
attracts thousands of pilgrims, who leave tokens of grati-
tude – ranging from models of modest houses to antique
automobiles in mint condition – for various favors granted.

Miniature roadside shrines to the Difunta Correa

La Esfinge (The Sphinx) rock formation at Parque Provincial Ischigualasto

open to non-guests. The highway continues to the 15,680-ft (4,780-m) **Paso de Agua Negra**, the highest pass between Argentina and Chile. Open from December to March, it is one of the best places to see the *penitentes*, conical snow formations resembling hooded monks.

Parque Provincial Ischigualasto ⓾

Road Map B2. 202 miles (325 km) NE of San Juan. 🚌 *from San Juan.* 🛈 *25 de Mayo y Las Heras, San Juan; (02646) 491-100.* ⬜ *museum & park: Apr–Sep: 9am–4pm; Oct–Mar: 8am–5pm.* 🎟️ *inclusive of museum price.* 🎟️ ♿ 🏪 🖥️ 🛍️

Less colorful than the red sandstone canyons of Sierra de las Quijadas *(see p218)* and the desert parks of the Andean Northwest, the Triassic sediments and volcanic ash of Ischigualasto have brought about some of the top dinosaur discoveries of recent decades. In a country where paleontologists have not received the widespread recognition they deserve, the park, also known as the Valley of the Moon, is slowly changing the situation. With impressive exhibits and informative tours, it has now become an imperative stop-off for both specialists and visitors in general.

Since its designation as a UNESCO World Heritage Site, together with Parque Nacional Talampaya *(see p185)* across the provincial border in La Rioja, the park has opened a branch of the Universidad Nacional de San Juan's

Museo de Historia Natural. Housed in a high-ceilinged warehouse adapted as a museum, its lifesize models of *Eoraptor lunensis*, *Herrerasaurus ischigualastensis*, and other dinosaurs that roamed the earth up to 228 million years ago are the starting point for informative backcountry tours. University students explain in Spanish the process of reconstructing the skeletons before leading 2-hour vehicle excursions past unique landforms such as La Esfinge (The Sphinx) and El Hongo (The Mushroom).

Due to the terrible summer heat, most animals are nocturnal but visitors may be able to spot the Patagonian hares, rheas, red foxes, armadillos, pumas, and the rarely spotted condors. The main plant varieties found are four kinds of cactus, native *brea* trees, and *jarilla* shrubs.

Visitors touring the backcountry must either have their own vehicles or arrive with a private operator from San Agustín del Valle Fértil. Rare wet weather can make the road for the 24-mile

Dinosaur display at the museum in Parque Provincial Ischigualasto

(40-km) circuit inaccessible. Most of these tours visit the park in the morning and Talampaya in the afternoon before heading back to San Agustín.

In addition to the vehicle tour, visitors can also take a 3-hour hike to the 5,734-ft (1,748-m) summit of the barrow-like **Cerro Morado** for panoramic views of Ischigualasto and north to Talampaya. Best done in the morning, the hike necessitates hiring a guide at the park ranger station at the entrance.

Pre-Columbian petroglyphs at Piedra Pintada

San Agustín del Valle Fértil ⓫

Road Map B2. 250 km (400 miles) NE from San Juan. 🚌 *3,889.* 🚌 🛈 *General Acha s/n, (02646) 420-104.* 🎏 *Founding of San Agustín (Apr).*

Unlike the blazing deserts to its north and south, the cozy oasis of San Agustín del Valle Fértil (Fertile Valley) enjoys a verdant woodland setting at the base of Sierra de la Huerta. The place is filled with wide maize fields, a pasture for goats, and olive groves. Improved highways and visitor services have made it the best place for travelers to arrange tours to Ischigualasto in San Juan and Talampaya across the provincial border in La Rioja.

San Agustín has a cluster of archaeological sites nearby, including pre-Columbian petroglyphs at **Piedra Pintada**, just across Río Seco. Another highlight of the town is **Parque Provincial Valle Fértil**, a large roadless area in the enticing mountains to the west and southwest.

Parque Nacional Sierra de las Quijadas ⑫

Road Map B2. 104 miles (167 km) SE of San Juan. ▥ *from San Juan & San Luis.* ℹ️ *San Luis, (02652) 445-141; ranger station at park entrance.* ◯ *8am–9pm daily.* 🎫 ✔ *only Spanish.* ▢ ⚠ www.parques nacionales.gov.ar

The enormous orange-red sandstone canyons of Parque Nacional Sierra de las Quijadas get far fewer visitors than their spectacular scenery merits. A treasurehouse for paleontologists, this impressive network of canyons is part of a northern paleontological circuit that includes San Juan's Ischigualasto *(see p217)* and La Rioja's Talampaya *(see p185)*.

About 120 million years ago, in the Cretaceous period, *pterosaurs* (flying reptiles) roamed the area freely. A half-hour hike from the park's entrance leads to the **Loma del Pterodaustro**, a fossil-field of dinosaur remains.

A gravel road leading up a narrow sedimentary canyon emerges onto the spectacular panoramas of the **Potrero de la Aguada**, which is located about 5 miles (8 km) from the park entrance. This is a veritable maze of small canyons leading to a dry lake bed. Much photographed, the majestic Aguada is best enjoyed during sunset when it takes on a fiery orange color. Guided descents into the canyons take about 3 or 4 hours. For less ambitious hikers, there is a relatively easy nature trail that skirts the canyon rim while passing cacti, aloes, and shrubs. A more ambitious hike follows the canyon rim south for about half an hour, and has better views from higher cliffs.

In addition to its natural appeal, Las Quijadas also has numerous archaeological sites. Between the park entrance and Aguada, the recently excavated **Hornillos Huarpes**, ovens where the park's pre-Columbian peoples fired their ceramics, is a sight of interest.

Moorish-style Iglesia de Santo Domingo

San Luis ⑬

Road Map B2. 174 miles (280 km) E of Mendoza. 🏠 *152,198.* ✈ ▥ ℹ️ *Avenida Illia and Junin, (02652) 423-957.* www.sanluis.gov.ar

Calling itself the Gateway to Cuyo, San Luis is a tidy provincial capital whose colonial grid contains attractive public spaces such as **Plaza Pringles**. This is the center of the city, dominated by the neoclassical **Iglesia Catedral** with its twin bell towers and elaborately sculpted pediment. To the northwest is Avenida Illia, a restaurant and bar district. Four blocks south, also impressively landscaped, is **Plaza Independencia**, the city's other central square and home to **Palacio de Gobierno**, the provincial government house. Opposite the plaza is **Iglesia de Santo Domingo**, a 17th-century church built in Moorish style.

Environs
Only 12 miles (20 km) northeast of San Luis is the hill station of **Potrero de los Funes**, where the capital's residents take a break with watersports or horse-riding in the nearly roadless Sierra de San Luis.

🏛 **Iglesia Catedral**
Pringles and Rivadavia. *Tel (0264) 424-414.* ◯ *daily.*

View of the red rocks of the Potrero de la Aguada, Parque Nacional Sierra de las Quijadas

For hotels and restaurants in this region see pp281–2 and pp299–300

San Rafael ⓮

Road Map B3. 143 miles (230 km)
S of Mendoza. 🏛 110,000. 🚌
ℹ *Avenida Hipólito Yrigoyen 741,
(02627) 437-859.* **www**.sanrafael.
gov.ar

A tidy mid-size city, San
Rafael is known for the many
sights that surround it. Located
where Ríos Diamante and
Atuel emerge from the Andean
foothills, San Rafael has gradually enveloped many of the
sprawling vineyards and prosperous wineries that once
grew around it. It may lack
the provincial capital's
fashionable boutique opera-
tions, but growers such as
Bodega Valentín Bianchi
and Suter, both highly
respected names in the
wine industry, are
located here.

In addition to irrigating
the vineyards, Río Atuel
is a starter river for rafters
while the wilder Río
Diamante offers some
of the most exciting
white-water rafting
in the country.

*A fine wine
from Bodega
Valentín Bianchi*

🏛 Bodega Valentín Bianchi
Ruta Nacional 143, Las Paredes,
San Rafael. **Tel** *(02627) 435-600.*
⏲ *9am–12:30pm & 2–5:15pm
Mon–Sat.* 📷
www.vbianchi.com

Malargüe ⓯

Road Map B3. 115 miles (186 km) S
of San Rafael. 🏛 17,710 🚌
ℹ *Ruta Nacional 40 and Pasaje
La Orteguina, (02627) 470-027.*
📷 *Fiesta Nacional de Chivo (Jan),
Día de Malargüe (Nov).* **www**.
malargue.gov.ar

A laid-back town, Malargüe
has one of the most spectacular landscapes in Argentina.
The town is perhaps best
known for its lively week-
long Fiesta Nacional del
Chivo (National Goat
Festival). One of the sights
that the city offers is **Museo
Regional Malargüe**. Housed
in a colonial building, the
museum has a varied collection that includes clay pipes
required for religious ceremonies, jewelry, a mummified

Display of rural life in the Museo Regional Malargüe

corpse, and even dinosaur
remains. The small city is also
the base for exploring provincial preserves with
caves, bird-rich wetlands,
and volcanic cones.

Environs
A wealth of little-visited
nature preserves sur-
round Malargüe, the most
popular of them being
**Reserva Natural Laguna
de Llancanelo**. Located 13
miles (20 km) south of
the city, this is a
sprawling 155-sq
mile (400-sq mile)
wetland with flocks
of migratory birds. **Reserva
Natural La Payunia** is a 1,700-
sq mile (4,400-sq km) volcanic preserve with at least
10,000 guanacos and other
species of wildlife. **Reserva
Natural Caverna de las Brujas**
is a series of stunning lime-
stone underground caves that
are open to the public.

🏛 Museo Regional Malargüe
Avenida San Martin s/n. **Tel** *(02627)
470-154.* ⏲ *9am–1pm & 4–7pm,
Tue–Sun.* ♿ 📷

Las Leñas ⓰

Road Map B3. 43 miles (70 km)
NW of Malargüe. **Tel** *(02627)
471-100.* 🚌 🍴 📷
www.laslenas.com

Located in the Andes,
northwest of Malargüe, Las
Leñas has abundant snow and
the best infrastructure of any
Argentinian ski resort north of
Bariloche *(see p238)*. Some
consider it the best in the
country. Open from mid-June
to early October, it enjoys a
longer season than Los
Penitentes, the province's
other popular ski center.

The resort has the capacity
to house almost 3,000 skiers
in hotels and apartments, and
the base clientele at Las
Leñas are mainly porteños
and foreigners on week-long
packages. Still, Las Leñas
offers half-price lift tickets
to day-trippers who lodge
in nearby Malargüe.

Winter is high season
here, but Las Leñas remains
open over summer for
mountain bikers, hikers,
and other recreationists.

View of a snowcapped mountain at Las Leñas ski resort in summer

PATAGONIA

A vast wilderness of glistening lakes, vertiginous peaks, sweeping glaciers, empty, barren plains, and rugged coastline, Patagonia was first roamed by dinosaurs, and later was long the preserve of indigenous groups. The region is perhaps best known, though, for its pioneer era, when visionaries and adventurers came ashore in search of a better life at the bottom of the world.

Two main indigenous groups originally inhabited Patagonia – the Mapuche and Tehuelche. Portuguese explorer Ferdinand Magellan was the first European to discover the region in 1520. Adventurers, merchants, and pirates followed in his wake, although no permanent colony was established until the late 18th century.

After gaining its independence, Argentina made concerted efforts to settle Patagonia. In 1865, Welsh pioneers landed at Puerto Madryn. In the same decade, the Argentinian government launched military campaigns against the Mapuche and Tehuelche, putting an end to all indigenous resistance in the region. Towns such as Junín de los Andes and Bariloche were founded in the Mapuche heartland and populated by European immigrants. Railroads, ports, and new settlements were built to serve the burgeoning wool industry. Today, oil, gas, and fishing have usurped wool as Patagonia's major source of income and a blossoming tourist industry has added further prosperity to the region.

Visitors can enjoy a wide range of outdoor activities, including horse-riding, trekking, fly-fishing, boating and rafting, and wildlife watching, all the while admiring Patagonia's spectacular scenery. Its cities and towns remain busy centers of culture and entertainment, offering excellent museums and restaurants. Some, like Trelew and Gaiman, are still quintessentially Welsh, complete with chapels, teashops, and Welsh-style houses. In essence, the region has changed little from its pioneer past and remains a beautiful, remote, and sparsely populated wilderness.

A colony of sea lions basking on a gravel beach in Península Valdés

◁ The icy peak of Cerro Torre, Parque Nacional Los Glaciares

Exploring Patagonia

Dotted with lakes and overlooked by the Andes, the Lake District is Patagonia's most popular destination. Its biggest town, Bariloche, receives many visitors but there are quieter alternatives such as San Martín de los Andes, El Bolsón, and Villa La Angostura. In the deep south of Patagonia is Glaciar Perito Moreno, which is in the same national park as Argentina's trekking capital, El Chaltén, and Mount Fitz Roy. The Atlantic coast has great opportunities for spotting marine fauna, especially at the Peninsula Valdés nature preserve. Inland is the remote Patagonian steppe with Cueva de las Manos and century-old estancias.

KEY

- Highway
- Main road
- Minor road
- International border
- Provincial border
- △ Peak

SEE ALSO

- ***Where to Stay*** pp283–6
- ***Where to Eat*** pp301–2

***Guanacos* grazing on a mountain slope**

GETTING AROUND

The best way to get around Patagonia is by air or long-distance bus. Bariloche and El Calafate have international airports and many smaller destinations are served by domestic flights. Bus services linking towns and cities in the region are reliable, though some remote sights can be reached only by car or via organized excursion. Motorists should note that many roads are unpaved and gas stations scarce. This is especially the case on Ruta Nacional 40.

SIGHTS AT A GLANCE

Towns and Cities

Aluminé [22]
Bajo Caracoles [38]
Bariloche [26]
Camarones [8]
Carmen de Patagones [1]
Comodoro Rivadavia [9]
El Bolsón [28]
El Calafate [48]
El Chaltén [46]
El Maitén [29]
Esquel [31]
Gaiman [6]
Gobernador Gregores [41]
Hipólito Yrigoyen [40]
Junín de los Andes [23]
Los Antiguos [35]
Neuquén [18]
Perito Moreno [34]
Puerto Deseado [11]
Puerto Madryn [3]
Puerto San Julián [13]
Río Gallegos [15]
Río Turbio [49]
San Martín de los Andes [24]
Trelew [5]
Tres Lagos [43]
Trevelín [32]
Viedma [2]
Villa El Chocón [20]

National and Provincial Parks

Bosque Petrificado José Ormachea [10]
Monumento Natural Bosques Petrificados [12]
Parque Nacional Laguna Blanca [21]
Parque Nacional Lanín p237 [25]
Parque Nacional Los Alerces [33]
Parque Nacional Los Glaciares pp250–55 [45]
Parque Nacional Monte León [14]
Parque Nacional Nahuel Huapi pp238–9 [27]
Parque Nacional Perito Moreno [39]
Reserva Provincial Cabo Vírgenes [17]
Reserva Provincial Península Valdés pp226–7 [4]
Reserva Provincial Punta Tombo [7]

Estancias

Estancia Monte Dinero [16]
Estancia Telken [36]

Sites of Interest

Centro Paleontológico Lago Barreales [19]
Cueva de las Manos [37]
Lago Cardiel [42]
Lago del Desierto [47]
Lago San Martín [44]
Museo Leleque [30]

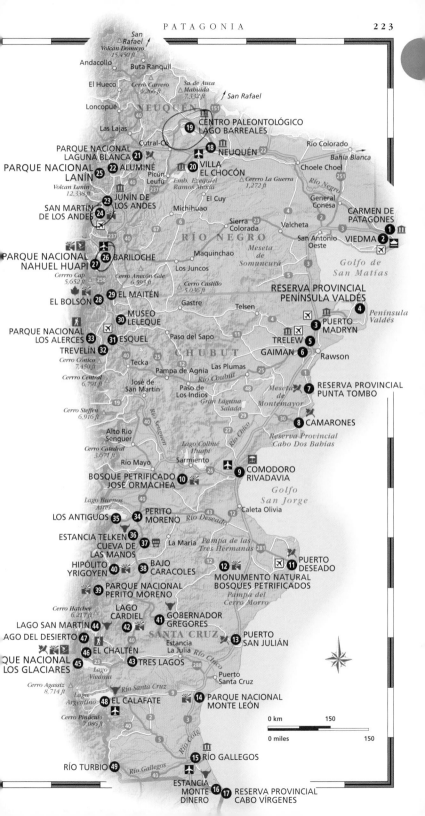

A view from Viedma across Río Negro of Iglesia Parroquial Nuestra Señora del Carmen

Carmen de Patagones ❶

Road Map C4. 569 miles (915 km) S of Buenos Aires. 👥 *20,000.* 🚐
🚌 ▮ *Bynon 186, (02920) 461-777.*
🎪 *Fiesta de 7 de Marzo (Mar).*

Both the northern gateway to Patagonia and a historical jewel, the small town of Carmen de Patagones was founded as a fort settlement in 1779. The first settlers arrived from Spain a year later and were forced to dig caves into the banks of Río Negro for shelter, the remains of which can still be seen.

To explore the town's history, visitors should head to the jumble of streets between Plaza 7 de Marzo and the port area. On the waterfront, housed in a building dating from 1799, is **Museo Histórico Regional Emma Nozzi**. It has displays on 19th-century Carmen de Patagones; one of the old settlers' caves can be accessed via the museum's patio.

On the plaza is **Iglesia Parroquial Nuestra Señora del Carmen**. Two Brazilian flags hang on either side of its altar, captured in 1827 after the defeat of a Brazilian invasion force. On the same block, although slightly obscured, is the **Torre del Fuerte** watchtower, the single surviving remnant of the town's original military fort. Several mud-brick abodes from the early 1800s, located south of the tower, are open to visits, including **Rancho Rial**, while **Casa de la**

Cultura is one block east of the tower. Most famous, though, is **La Carlota**, an 1820s house accessed via guided tour from the Museo Histórico.

🏛 **Museo Histórico Regional Emma Nozzi**
Ave J.J. Biedma 64. **Tel** (02920) 462-729. 🕐 *varies (call in advance).*

Viedma ❷

Road Map C4. 1 mile (2 km) S of Carmen de Patagones. 👥 *60,000.*
✈ 🚌 🚐 ▮ *Ave Francisco de Viedma 51, (02920) 427-332.*
🎪 *Fiesta de 7 de Marzo (Mar).*

Located across Río Negro from Carmen de Patagones, Viedma is a small town that offers good traveler services. It also boasts what is considered to be Patagonia's most aesthetically inspired

museum, **Museo Salesiano Cardenal Cagliero**. It is housed within the **Manzana Histórica**, a historical city block that was once the head-quarters of the Salesian mission that was established in 1880. The museum preserves some splendid architectural details and displays various religious artifacts. Also worth visiting is **Museo Antropológico Gobernador Eugenio Tello** at Plaza San Martín, which has displays on the area's pre-Columbian civilizations.

🏛 **Museo Salesiano Cardenal Cagliero**
Avenida Rivadavia 34. 🕐 *varies.*

🏛 **Museo Antropológico Gobernador Eugenio Tello**
Avenida San Martín 263. **Tel** (02920) 425-900. 🕐 *varies (call in advance).*

THE WELSH IN PATAGONIA

A Welsh farmhouse in Gaiman

The Welsh presence in Patagonia dates from 1865, when 153 pioneers set sail for a land they saw as free of English domination. They made landfall two months later, founding Puerto Madryn on the Argentinian coast, before settling 60 miles (100 km) to the south in the more fertile Chubut Valley. It is this region that constitutes the heart of Welsh Patagonia. Here, Welsh chapels dot the landscape, teahouses are run by the pioneers' descendents, and, in Gaiman especially, the Welsh language is widely spoken. The year's biggest celebration is the Eisteddfod *(see p40)*, a Welsh music and poetry festival that dates from medieval times.

Puerto Madryn ❸

Road Map B4. 227 miles (365 km)
SW of Viedma. 🏚 80,000. ✈ 🚌
ℹ Ave Roca 223, (02965) 456-067.
www.madryn.gov.ar/turismo

On the shores of Golfo
Nuevo, Puerto Madryn has a
historical background that
dates from 1865, when the
first group of Welsh pioneers
landed on its shores. It is the
gateway to one of the world's
greatest marine spectacles at
Reserva Provincial Península
Valdés, and is known for its
sandy beaches, relaxed pace,
and good seafood restaurants.
   The town's excellent
**Museo de Ciencias Naturales y
Oceanografía** provides information on the thriving ocean
life nearby, while the outstanding **EcoCentro** aims to
promote an understanding of
threatened marine species.
   Located close by, Playa El
Doradillo is a protected beach
and breeding area for the
Southern Right whale, while
Punta Loma is home to a
year-round sea lion colony.

🏛 **Museo de Ciencias
Naturales y Oceanografía**
Domecq García & José Menéndez.
Tel (02965) 451-139. ◯ varies (call
in advance). 🖼

🏛 **EcoCentro**
Julio Verne 3784. **Tel** (02965) 457-
470. ◯ varies (call in advance).
www.ecocentro.org.ar

Reserva Provincial Península Valdés ❹

See pp226–7.

Prehistoric plants at Museo
Paleontológico Egidio Feruglio

Trelew ❺

Road Map B4. 40 miles (65 km) S
of Puerto Madryn. 🏚 120,000. ✈
🚌 ℹ Pellegrini 780, (02965) 431-
519. **www**.trelewpatagonia.gov.ar

A small, attractive town,
Trelew is an ideal base from
which to explore the Welsh
villages of the Chubut Valley.
Its name in Welsh means
"village of Lewis."
Much of its
original Welsh
character has
changed, and
most visitors stop
by instead for the
town's **Museo
Paleontológico
Egidio Feruglio**,
Argentina's premier
paleontological museum. The
museum has extensive fossil
collections that date back 540
million years. The star exhibits, however, are the life-
sized dinosaur skeletons and
the dinosaur eggs. For an

echo of Trelew's pioneer past,
visit the historically themed
**Museo Regional Pueblo de
Luis**, housed within the city's
old railroad station, and the
settlers' graves at **Capilla
Moriah's** cemetery, which
include that of Lewis Jones,
the town's founder.

🏛 **Museo Paleontológico
Egidio Feruglio**
Avenida Fontana 140. **Tel** (02965)
432-100. ◯ varies (call in advance).
🖼 🖥 **www**.mef.org.ar

🏛 **Museo Regional Pueblo
de Luis**
Avenida 9 de Julio & Fontana.
Tel (02965) 424-062. ◯ 8am–8pm
Mon–Fri, 2–8pm Sat & Sun. 🖼

Gaiman ❻

Road Map B4. 11 miles (18 km)
W of Trelew. 🏚 6,000. 🚌
ℹ Belgrano, between Rivadavia &
28 de Julio; (02965) 491-571.

Founded in 1874, Gaiman
is the most quintessentially
Welsh of all the
villages of the
Chubut Valley. Best
known for its tea-
houses, Gaiman is
also rich in history.
The small **Museo
Histórico Regional**,
housed in the old
railroad station, has
excellent exhibits on Gaiman's
pioneer past. Situated within
a few blocks of the town's
flower-filled Plaza Roca are
Primera Casa, Gaiman's first-
built house, and **Capilla Vieja**,
its oldest chapel, both of
which date from the pioneer
era. The most authentic of
Gaiman's teahouses, **Ty
Gwyn**, **Ty Nain**, and **Plas y
Coed**, are also located close
to Plaza Roca.
   Also near the plaza is
Parque El Desafío, an interesting site filled with Joaquín
Alonso's works. The "Dali
of recycling," Alonso has
molded thousands of cans,
bottles, and household appliances into works of art that
include re-creations of the Taj
Mahal and Picasso's paintings.

Sign outside a Welsh
teahouse in Gaiman

🏛 **Museo Histórico Regional**
28 de Julio 705. ◯ 3–7pm
Tue–Sun. 🖼

A summer day at the beach in Puerto Madryn

Reserva Provincial Península Valdés

A UNESCO World Heritage Site, Península Valdés is one of the world's great nature preserves. Its rugged 310-mile (500-km) coastline is a haven for an astonishing, and easily observable, array of marine fauna that includes Southern Right whales, killer whales, elephant seals, sea lions, Magellanic penguins, and millions of marine birds. Its interior is an arid wilderness, the eastern extension of the Patagonian steppe, populated by dry-land fauna including guanacos and the ostrich-like rhea. It is marked at its center by two large salt lakes. Day-long safaris depart from Puerto Madryn, though many visitors seek longer stays at one of the peninsula's estancias.

Visitors' Center
This is where visits to the peninsula begin. The center houses a small museum that provides a useful introduction to the reserve's stunning array of flora and fauna.

Puerto Pirámides
The peninsula's only village, Puerto Pirámides has a smattering of hotels and restaurants. It is one of the best places in the world to watch whales.

Sea lions and elephant seals inhabit the peninsula's coast through the year.

Golfo San Jo
Isla de los Pájaros
Viedma
Istmo *Ameghino*
Pue Pirán
Golfo Nuevo
Puerto Madryn

KEY

=== Main road
=== Minor road
🛈 Visitor information
✕ Domestic airport
⛴ Ferry service

STAR SIGHTS

★ Golfo Nuevo

★ Punta Norte

★ Punta Delgada

★ Golfo Nuevo
The Southern Right whales visit the Golfo Nuevo between June and December each year to breed and bear young. Whale-watching excursions start from Puerto Pirámides and visitors can get extremely close to the whales.

Orca attacking a sea lion
pup in shallow surf

FEEDING FRENZY

Península Valdés is believed to be the only place in the world where orca (killer whales) engage in the spectacle of intentional beach stranding. The orca uses the tide and storms the beach head on, deliberately running itself aground to catch its prey, usually a sea lion pup or an adult penguin. When subsequent waves lift the orca back into the ocean it shares its prey with the rest of its pod. This phenomenon takes place at Caleta Valdés and, more often, at Punta Norte.

VISITORS' CHECKLIST

Road Map C4. 35 miles (56 km) NE of Puerto Madryn. ✈ *Puerto Madryn.* 🚌 *from Puerto Madryn.* 🚌 *from Puerto Pirámides (Sep–Nov).* ℹ **Puerto Madryn** *Ave Roca 223, (02965) 453-504;* **Istmo Ameghino** *Centro de Interpretación;* **Puerto Pirámides** *(02965) 495-048.* 📷 🎫 🍴 **Faro Punta Delgada** *Tel (02965) 458-444.* **www**.puntadelgada.com

★ Punta Norte
This is a breeding spot for elephant seals and sea lions and the favorite hunting ground of killer whales. The place also has a marine museum.

Punta
Norte

erto
ván

El Gran
Salitral

Caleta
Valdés

Salina
Chica

Salina
Grande

Punta
Delgada

Caleta Valdés
Magellanic penguins and elephant seals share the beach at this sheltered lagoon. It is also visited by killer whales that storm the beach and prey on these animals.

Salina Grande is one of two inland salt lakes that lie in a basin, which, at 138 ft (42 m) below sea level, is the fourth deepest depression on the planet.

0 km   10

0 miles   10

★ Punta Delgada
An easily observed colony of elephant seals inhabits the beach at the base of this blustery cliff. At the cliff top is luxury estancia Faro Punta Delgada, site of a century-old lighthouse.

Reserva Provincial Punta Tombo ❼

Road Map B4. 66 miles (107 km) S of Trelew. ⏰ Sep–Apr: 8am–8pm daily. 🚗 ℹ️ *Ruta Provincial 1 S of Trelew, (02965) 15 565–222.* 📷 📶
www.welcomeargentina.com

A narrow, stony peninsula that juts out abruptly into the Atlantic Ocean, Punta Tombo's claim to fame is that it harbors South America's largest colony of Magellanic penguins. From September to April, over 650,000 of these black and white birds use the peninsula to incubate their eggs and prepare their offspring for migration. They nest in scrapes underneath the bushes and both male and female penguins take turns to guard their nests, protecting eggs from avian predators. These predators include the giant petrel as well as various species of gull, skua, and cormorant.

These humble penguins are not as glamorous as their larger cousins, the king and emperor penguins. While they can be observed from extremely close quarters, visitors need to be careful not to touch them. An ideal time to visit is between November and January when there are plenty of chicks. Apart from these penguins, several marine birds can also be spotted.

The nearby countryside is a great place to see land fauna, including Patagonian hares, guanacos, and greater rheas. Easy day trips run daily from Trelew and Puerto Madryn to the preserve.

Camarones ❽

Road Map B5. 156 miles (252 km) S of Trelew. 🏠 *1,100.* ℹ️ *Thomas Espora y San Martin, (0297) 496-3040.* 🎉 *Fiesta Nacional del Salmón (Feb).*

Literally translating into "shrimps," Camarones is a small, picturesque fishing village of one-story buildings and dusty streets. Located on the shores of an eponymous bay, this village is the main point of access to **Reserva Provincial Cabo dos Bahías**.
Museo Histórico de Camarones, with historical displays on the village's pioneer past, is its one cultural point of reference. A second museum is being planned to honor former Argentinian president Juan Domingo Perón *(see pp52–3)*, who spent much of his childhood here.

A Magellanic penguin

Environs
About 19 miles (30 km) southeast of the town is Reserva Provincial Cabo dos Bahías, which protects a 12,000-strong colony of Magellanic penguins. Visitors can also observe the sea lion colony on Isla Moreno.

🏛 **Museo Histórico de Camarones**
Estrada & Belgrano. ⏰ *4–8pm daily.* 📷 🎫 *Spanish only.*

Comodoro Rivadavia along the majestic Golfo San Jorge

Comodoro Rivadavia ❾

Road Map B5. 229 miles (370 km) S of Trelew. 🏠 *250,000.* ✈️ 🚌 ℹ️ *Rivadavia 430, (0297) 446-2376.* www.welcomeargentina.com

Argentina's oil capital and one of the biggest cities on its Atlantic coast, Comodoro Rivadavia is located on the shores of the majestic **Golfo San Jorge** and is overlooked by **Cerro Chenque**. Also the leader in renewable energy, the city is home to Latin America's biggest wind farm.

Drilling rigs and storage tanks can still be seen in the city, where oil was first struck in 1907. The site can be visited at **Museo Nacional del Petróleo**, where exhibits trace the evolution of Argentina's oil industry. The city's railroad history is traced at **Museo Ferroportuario**. The short taxi ride to Cerro Chenque ends with breathtaking vistas of Golfo San Jorge, the city, and the beaches at the upscale resort of **Rada Tilly**.

Environs
The eerily silent wind farm, **El Parque Eólico Antonio Morán**, is 7 miles (12 km) outside Rada Tilly.

🏛 **Museo Nacional del Petróleo**
Carlos Calvo & San Lorenzo, Barrio General Moscón, Km3. **Tel** *(0297) 455-9558.* ⏰ *varies (call in advance).* 📷 🎫 *Spanish only.*

🏛 **Museo Ferroportuario**
Ave Rivadavia & 9 de Julio. **Tel** *(0297) 447-3330.* ⏰ *varies (call in advance).*

Guanacos in the Reserva Provincial Punta Tombo

Bosque Petrificado José Ormachea ❿

Road Map B5. 109 miles (175 km)
W of Comodoro Rivadavia. ◯ Oct–
Mar: 8am–9pm daily; Apr–Sep: 9am–
6:30pm daily. 🚌 to Sarmiento, then
taxi. 🖼 🛈 Ave San Martín,
Sarmiento, (0297) 489-8282.

An otherworldly spectacle,
this petrified forest has its
origins in the Cretaceous
period, 65 million years ago.
Although far smaller and
more recently formed than
the Monumento Natural
Bosques Petrificados, it is
more easily accessible. Many
tour operators in Comodoro
Rivadavia run daily excursions
to the forest.

**Southern elephant seals on Isla
Pingüino near Puerto Deseado**

Puerto Deseado ⓫

Road Map B5. 177 miles (286 km) S
of Comodoro Rivadavia. 🏘 15,000.
✕ 🚌 🛈 San Martín 1225, (0297)
487-0220. 🎭 Fiesta del Marinero
(Jan). **www**.welcomeargentina.com

Located on the sheltered
estuary of Río Deseado, the
little port town of Puerto
Deseado is one of Patagonia's
best-kept secrets. It owes its
name to English privateer
Thomas Cavendish, who
sailed into the estuary in 1586,
naming its natural harbor after
his flagship, the *Desire*.
**Reserva Natural Ría del
Deseado** protects the estuary's
marine fauna. Boat excursions
head into the preserve, which
is a breeding ground for the
graceful Commerson's dolphin
and haven to many marine-
bird species. Trips include
visits to the cliffside nesting
sites of red-legged and rock
cormorants, and to **Isla de los
Pájaros**, home to a colony of
Magellanic penguins. On the
way to the preserve, boats

Fossilized remains at the Monumento Natural Bosques Petrificados

pass the spot where the British
warship HMS *Swift* was shipwrecked in 1770. The wreck
was only discovered in 1982.
Rescued items, including bells
and Wedgewood china, are
displayed at **Museo Municipal
Mario Brozoski**.
The town is Patagonia's
busiest fishing port today, but
in the past it depended on the
shipping of wool and meat
transported via rail from the
interior. The former railroad
station now houses **Museo de
la Estación Ferrocarril**. At the
center of the town stands a
passenger wagon built in
1898, which was used to transport federal police during the
Santa Cruz rebellion in 1921.

Environs
Around 16 miles (25 km)
south of town, **Isla Pingüino**
protects a small breeding
colony of southern elephant
seals and Patagonia's only
nesting colony of the rockhopper penguin.

🏛 **Museo Municipal Mario
Brozoski**
Belgrano y Colón. **Tel** (0297) 487-
1358. ◯ varies (call in advance).

Monumento Natural Bosques Petrificados ⓬

Road Map B5. 159 miles (256 km)
W of Puerto Deseado. 🚌 to Puerto
Deseado, then taxi. ◯ 8am–6pm
daily. 🖼 from Puerto Deseado.

Covering an area of 58 sq
miles (150 sq km), the haunting Monumento Natural
Bosques Petrificados is
Patagonia's largest petrified
forest. The park has its origins
in the Jurassic period, 150
million years ago, when the
Andes did not exist and humid
winds blew in nonstop from
the Pacific Ocean, causing
incessant rain and encour-
aging the growth of tropical
forests. When the Andes
formed, volcanic activity
buried these forests under volcanic ash. Fossilized trees are
scattered across the landscape,
rooted to the spot where they
were petrified. Colossal in
size, the biggest measure up
to 115 ft (35 m) in height and
10 ft (3 m) in diameter. Tour
operators run excursions from
Puerto Deseado.

The fishing fleet on the Río Deseado in Puerto Deseado

Commerson's dolphins can be spotted easily in the bay of San Julián

Puerto San Julián ⑬

Road Map B5. 238 miles (383 km)
S of Puerto Deseado. 🏠 10,000.
🚌 ⓘ Ave San Martín, between
Rivadavia & Moreno, (02962) 452-
009. **www**.sanjulian.gov.ar

Claiming to be the birthplace
of Patagonia, Puerto San
Julián was the site of the
first European settlement in
Argentina, founded by
Portuguese explorer
Ferdinand Magellan in 1520.
Francis Drake soon
followed suit, dropping
anchor in its shingle-
banked bay in 1578.
Despite numerous
attempts at colonization,
a permanent settlement
was not established until
the early 1880s, with
the arrival of British
sheep farmers from
the Falkland Islands
(Islas Malvinas).
    The highlights in the city
include **Museo Rosa Novak**,
which has displays on early
sheep-farming pioneers, and
Monumento Primera Misa,
where the country's first
mass was held the day after
Magellan's landfall. Located
nearby, **Museo Muestra
Arqueología** has exhibits
on the region's indigenous
cultures. However, the star
attraction are the lively pods
of Commerson's dolphins in
San Julián's bay. Also in the
bay are **Isla Cormorán** and **Isla
Justicia**, whose shores are
home to large colonies of
Magellanic penguins.

Environs
Unspoilt beaches and some
historical sites dot the beautiful coastal Avenida Hernán de
Magallanes, which stretches
north from San Julián. The
stretch is a 34-mile (55-km)
drive on the coastal circuit
along the San Julián bay
offering spectacular views.

🏛 **Museo Muestra
Arqueología**
Ave Costanera 900. 🕐 varies.
⏺ mid-Mar–mid-Dec: Sat–Sun.

Parque Nacional
Monte León ⑭

Road Map B6. 28 miles (45 km) SE
of Puerto Santa Cruz. 🚌 to Luis
Piedra Buena, then taxi. ⓘ 9 de
Julio and Belgrano, Puerto Santa
Cruz. 🕐 Nov–Apr: daily. 🍴 Ⓐ

Cormorants on
Monte León cliffs

Apart from being
Argentina's newest
national park, this is also
the only one situated
along the country's
Atlantic coast.
Parque Nacional Monte León
was created in 2004 to protect
25 miles (40 km) of coastline
and 183 sq miles (474 sq
kms) of Patagonian steppe. Its
virgin coastline, dotted with

La Olla in Parque Nacional Monte León

islands, reefs, coves, cliffs,
and caverns, is its biggest
attraction. The park provides
refuge to marine fauna that
includes sea lion and penguin
colonies, pods of the graceful
black and white Commerson's
dolphin, over 130 species of
birds, and three types of
cormorant. The park's coast is
also a station for cetaceans
such as the Austral Frank
whale. Highlights within the
park include **Monte León
Island**, a marine bird nesting
site, and **La Olla**, a natural
rock formation consisting of a
circular cavity supported by a
98-ft (30-m) high natural arch.
    A short distance inside the
park entrance, Hosteria Monte
León, part of the estancia of
the same name, offers grand
upscale lodging.

▼ **Hosteria Monte León**
Ruta Nacional 3, Km 2385.
Tel (011) 4621-4780.

Río Gallegos ⑮

Road Map B6. 215 miles (347 km)
S of PuertoSan Julián. 🏠 86,000.
✈ 🚌 ⓘ Ave San Martín & Roca,
(02966) 438-725. **www**.riogallegos.
gov.ar

An important port city, Río
Gallegos is also the capital
of Santa Cruz province. The
first people to settle here
were British sheep farmers
from the Falkland Islands
(Islas Malvinas) in the 1880s.
    In 1885, Río Gallegos
became the port from
which local wool
produce was exported.
Nicknamed "white gold,"
wool sustained the local
economy until the 20th
century, when the ship-
ping of coal from Río
Turbio (see p247) brought
about new prosperity.
Today, it is this "black
gold" and gas that
provide Río Gallegos
with most of its income.
    Much of the city's
architecture dates from
the 1930s, especially
along its main street,
Avenida San Martín.
However, some out-
standing examples of
pioneer-era construction

Pioneer-era building from the 1890s, now housing Museo de los Pioneros, Río Gallegos

can still be seen. Built by Salesian missionaries in 1899, the corrugated-tin and wood structure of **Catedral Nuestra Señora de Luján** is characteristic of that period, as is the 1890s building that houses **Museo de los Pioneros**. This museum narrates the story of the early sheep settlers. The nearby **Museo Ferroviario Roberto Gailán** is housed in an old railroad depot and run by workers laid off after the closure of the old Río Turbio-Río Gallegos train line. Restored 50-year-old steam engines that once worked the line are on display in the forecourt.

🏠 Catedral Nuestra Señora de Luján
Ave San Martín 739. ⬜ 9am–6pm Mon–Fri.

🏛 Museo de los Pioneros
Elcano & Juan Bautista Alberdi. **Tel** (02966) 437-763. ⬜ 10am–7:30pm daily. 🎧 Spanish only.

🏛 Museo Ferroviario Roberto Galián
Mendoza 75. **Tel** (02966) 426-766. ⬜ 10am–7pm daily. 🎧 Spanish only.

Estancia Monte Dinero **⑯**

Road Map B6. 75 miles (120 km) S of Rio Gallegos. 🚌 **Tel** (02966) 426-900. ⬜ Oct–Apr.

Founded in 1880 by a pioneering Patagonian family, the Fentons, this beautiful ranch is a working sheep farm. Guests stay in the main house, while activities include sheep-shearing and herding demonstrations as well as trekking, bird-watching, and horse-riding.

One trail leads to Monte Dinero, a hill with breathtaking vistas of the Magellan Strait and Tierra del Fuego. Excursions from the estancia run into Reserva Provincial Cabo Vírgenes, which is only 9 miles (15 km) away.

Reserva Provincial Cabo Vírgenes **⑰**

Road Map B6. 82 miles (133 km) S of Rio Gallegos. 🚌 🎧 🛈 Ave San Martín & Roca, (02966) 438-725. **Reserva** ⬜ 9am–4pm daily. 🎧

Located at the far southern tip of the Argentinian mainland, at the entrance to the Strait of Magellan, Reserva Provincial Cabo Vírgenes protects the second biggest colony of Magellanic penguins in South America after Reserva Provincial Punta Tombo (see p228). Over 100,000 penguins use the cape as a nesting ground from September to April. Visitors can observe these charismatic birds from close quarters along a 1-mile (2-km) long nature trail.

In the northeastern corner of the preserve is the **Faro de Cabo Vírgenes** lighthouse, built by the Argentinian Navy in 1904. Its 400-watt bulb throws a beam at least 25 miles (40 km) into the sea. Visitors can climb the 91 steps to the top for splendid vistas of the strait. A short stroll away is the lovely **Al Fin y al Cabo** teahouse, owned by the Estancia Monte Dinero. Daily excursions to the preserve are arranged by tour operators from Río Gallegos.

The lighthouse built by the Argentinian Navy at Cabo Vírgenes

The Paleontology of Patagonia

Spectacular fossil finds in Patagonia since the 1980s have led scientists to hail the region as the paleontological promised land. Discoveries include some of the biggest dinosaurs to have roamed the planet, and other prehistoric beasts such as huge terror birds and ocean-dwelling crocodiles. These finds, viewed alongside Patagonia's petrified forests, have enabled experts to depict what prehistoric Patagonia looked like: a tropical jungle roamed by gargantuan beasts. The finds also provide an exciting dimension to traveling in Patagonia. With paleontological tourism taking off, most fossil parks, fossilized forest areas, and dig sites now welcome visitors.

One of the many fossilized trees in Patagonia's petrified forests

Argentinosaurus huinculensis *is the biggest dinosaur discovered to date. This colossal herbivore lived 90 million years ago, measured 125 ft (38 m) in length, and weighed a massive 112 tons (102 tonnes).*

Rodolfo Coria led the field study of both the *Argentinosaurus* and *Giganotosaurus.*

THE BIG FINDS

Big fossil finds in Patagonia in the last two decades have included the discovery of several new prehistoric species and the world's biggest dinosaur nesting ground. These great finds have forced scientists to rewrite theory on the size, behavior, and evolution of prehistoric life.

The biggest finds are unearthed from rock dating from the Cretaceous period 65 to 144 million years ago.

Giganotosaurus carolinii *was one of the world's biggest carnivores, 45 ft (14 m) long and weighing 10 tons (9 tonnes). Its skull was a frightening 6 ft (1.8 m) long, easily the size of a bathtub. The creature hunted* Argentinosaurus *in packs.*

Dakosaurus andiniensis *was nicknamed Godzilla for its dinosaur-like snout. This marine crocodile ruled the oceans 140 million years ago. Its discovery site in Patagonia was once a deep bay in the Pacific Ocean.*

THE FOSSIL FINDERS

Patagonia's biggest finds were first spotted by laypersons. Rancher Guillermo Heredia found *Argentinosaurus* on his farm in northwest Patagonia; car mechanic Ruben Carolini unearthed *Giganotosaurus;* and the bones of *Dakosaurus* were found by visitors in northwest Patagonia in 2005.

The first dinosaur eggs *were excavated from the world's largest dinosaur nesting ground in 1997 by scientists in Patagonia. Another discovery was by a family in Lamarque in Patagonia.*

PATAGONIA'S FOSSIL SITES

1   Auca Mahuevo
2   Bosque Petrificado José Ormachea *(see p229)*
3   Bryn Gwyn
4   Lago Barreales *(see p234)*
5   Monumento Natural Bosques Petrificados *(see p229)*
6   Plaza Huincul
7   Villa El Chocón *(see p237)*

Raúl Vacca of Museo Paleontógico Egidio Feruglio (MEF) in Trelew is a world expert in the preparing and mounting of fossilized skeletons.

Digging tools and excavation brushes are used to separate the fossil from its entombing sediments, and then to clean it.

IMPORTANT EVENTS

1989: *Argentinosaurus*, the world's biggest dinosaur, discovered near Plaza Huincul.
1995: The huge carnivore *Giganotosaurus* unearthed in Villa El Chocón.
1997: Dinosaur embryos with skin tissue intact discovered at Auca Mahuevo.
1999: MEF museum opens in Trelew, showcasing major fossil finds *(see p225)*.
2000: Field work begins at Lago Barreales, Argentina's largest fossil site.
2005: Discovery of *Dakosaurus*, giant marine crocodile.
2006: World's largest-known terror bird, *Phorusrhacid*, uncovered in Patagonia.

HOW THEY LOOKED

Argentinosaurus had massive limbs and a very long neck and tail. *Giganotosaurus* was an agile predator with short arms and powerful legs. *Dakosaurus andiniensis* had fins and a fish-like tail.

The ocean-dwelling *Dakosaurus andiniensis*

The herbivore *Argentinosaurus huinculensis*

The carnivore *Giganotosaurus carolinii*

A *Titanosaurus* embryo seen with the surrounding rock

Contemporary Argentinian paintings at Museo Nacional de Bellas Artes

Neuquén ⓲

Road Map B4. 345 miles (557 km)
NW of Viedma. ♦ 300,000. ✈
▭ from Viedma. ℹ Félix San Martín
182, (0299) 442-4089. ⌂ Sat & Sun.
☼ Aniversario de la Ciudad Neuquén
(Sep), Feria Artesanos (Nov).
www.neuquentur.gov.ar

Patagonia's commercial
hub, Neuquén is the capital
of the province of the
same name. It was a
center for the region's
wool and leather indus-
try, and its location at
the confluence of Ríos
Limay and Neuquén
made it an important
agricultural center in
the otherwise arid
province. The arrival
of the railroad in the
early 1900s further benefitted
the town and the discovery of
oil in the region in the 1960s
and the development of a
hydroelectric industry in the
1990s led to rapid growth.

A popular stopover for
those visiting the dinosaur
destinations Villa El Chocón
and Plaza Huincul, Neuquén
is a conurbation of low-rise
buildings that can be divided
into two distinct sectors: *el
alto* (uptown) and *el bajo*
(downtown). The tree-shaded
Parque Central divides these
two areas and is where most
of Neuquén's cultural sights
are found.

North of the park is **Museo
Nacional de Bellas Artes
(MNBA)**, housed in a
minimalist-style building and
inaugurated in 2004. Its permanent collection features
European art from the
Renaissance to the 19th century, along with works from
all over Argentina. Running
along the length of the park,

but now largely in disuse,
is the city's railroad line.
Housed in the line's old
accommodation building is
Museo Paraje Confluencia,
with displays on the history
of Neuquén. In the renovated
cargo warehouse nearby is
the Sala de Arte Emilio
Saraco, with temporary
exhibitions by
Argentinian artists.

Environs
About 31 miles (50 km)
north of the town, in
San Patricio del Chañar,
are several vineyards
that have raised the
profile of Patagonian
wine-making.
Bodega del Fin del
Mundo runs guided
tours daily.

Sculpture by Alfredo
Bigatti, MNBA

🏛 **Museo Nacional de Bellas
Artes (MNBA)**
Mitre & Santa Cruz, Parque Central.
Tel (0299) 443-6268. ⌂ Dec–
Mar: 9am–9pm Tue–Fri, 6–10pm
Sat–Sun; Apr–Nov: 9am–8pm
Tue–Fri, 4–8pm Sat–Sun. 🎦 6pm
Tue–Sun (Spanish only).

🏛 **Museo Paraje Confluencia**
Independencia & Córdoba.
Tel (0299) 155-553-082. ⌂ Dec–
Mar: 8am–9pm daily; Apr–Nov:
8am–8pm daily.

Centro Paleontológico Lago Barreales ⓳

Road Map B3. 40 miles (65 km)
N of Neuquén. ▭ to Añelo, then
taxi. ⌂ Mon–Sun. 🎦 prior
arrangement only. www.
proyectodino.com.ar

Situated on the northern
shore of Lago Barreales,
Centro Paleontológico Lago
Barreales is the largest
paleontological excavation
site in Argentina. It is also the
only one of its kind in South
America open to visitors all
year round. Born out of an
initial excavation in 2001, the
site has a remote location
which makes it difficult to get
to, but those that make the
effort are well rewarded.

The activities at the site
range from a short yet informative guided tour to a two-
day stay at the center during
which visitors work alongside
helpful site technicians and
paleontologists in the extrac-
tion, preparation, and restoration of dinosaur fossils.

The accommodation offered
is rustic, but personalized
service is emphasized with
only four visitors permitted
to stay at any one time.

Archaeological discoveries
at the site, which so far
number over a staggering
1,000 vertebral fossils and
more than 300 plant fossils,
have been the subject of
worldwide attention since the
dig began in 2001. Previously
undiscovered dinosaurs
include *Futalognkosaurus
dukei*, a colossal 118-ft (36-m)
long herbivore, and
Unenlagia paynemili, thought

Replica dinosaur skeletons on display at Museo Municipal Cármen Funes

to be an important link in the evolution of dinosaurs to birds. The fossilized remains of these and other finds are on display at the center.

Environs
Around 62 miles (100 km) southwest of Centro Paleontológico is Plaza Huincul, excavation site of *Argentinosaurus huinculensis* (*see pp232–3*), the largest dinosaur to have ever been discovered in the world. Visitors can see its huge fossilized skeleton at the town's **Museo Municipal Cármen Funes**.

🏛 **Museo Municipal Cármen Funes**
Avenida Córdoba 55. *Tel* (0299) 496-5486. ◯ *varies (call in advance).* 🖼 📷 ⓹

A dramatic roadside sign outside the small town of Villa El Chocón

Villa El Chocón ⑳

Road Map B4. 50 miles (80 km) SW of Neuquén. 🏘 *1,500.* 🚌 *from Neuquén.* ℹ (0299) 4901-242. www.interpatagonia.com/elchocon

The small settlement of Villa El Chocón was purpose-built in 1967 to provide housing to the workers of the nearby hydroelectric dam. It remained entirely anonymous until 1993 when local car mechanic and amateur paleontologist Ruben Carolini unearthed the virtually complete skeleton of the largest carnivorous dinosaur ever known to have walked the planet. The 100-million-year-old fossilized skeleton of the enormous 10.5 ton (9.5 tonne), 46-ft (14m) long *Giganotosaurus carolinii* (*see pp232–3*) is the star display at the town's **Museo Municipal Ernesto Bachmann**, along with myriad other fossils unearthed in the area. **Museo de Sitio** is

A dinosaur skeleton at Museo Municipal Ernesto Bachmann

situated 2 miles (3 km) south of the town's center, where on the shore of an artificial lake the large footprints of the herbivorous dinosaur Iguanodon lay preserved. More such footprints can be observed 4 miles (7 km) north of Villa El Chocón at Cañadon Escondido.

🏛 **Museo Municipal Ernesto Bachmann**
Accesso Centro Commercial. *Tel* (0299) 4901-230. ◯ *Dec–Mar: 8am–9pm daily; Apr–Nov: 9am–7pm Mon–Fri, 9am–8pm Sat & Sun.* 🖼 *under 6 free.* 📷 *Spanish only.* ⓹

🏛 **Museo de Sitio**
Ruta Nacional 237. ◯ *9am– 6:30pm daily.* 📷

Parque Nacional Laguna Blanca ㉑

Road Map B4. 93 miles (150 km) W of Neuquén. 🚌 ℹ *Ejército Argentino 217, Zapala, Neuquén; (02942) 431-982.* ⚠

Covering 44 sq miles (113 sq km), this national park is a haven for keen ornithologists.

It was created in 1940 to provide a protective habitat for the area's large population of black-necked swans, which today number over 2,000. Located in the western reaches of Neuquén province and surrounded by volcanic desert, this scenically stunning park also provides refuge to over 200 other bird species, including large colonies of wading and aquatic birds such as grebes, sandpipers, coots, ducks, and flamingos. These can be sighted in their thousands along the nature trail that hugs the western shore of the park's largest body of water, the **Laguna Blanca**. They can be observed at close quarters particularly during the southern hemisphere's spring season, when the elaborate courtship rituals take place. The best time to visit the lagoon is in the morning as it is far less windy.

Linked by the same trail, **Laguna Verde**, another large lake within the national park, is also populated by large colonies of colorful flamingos and is an important stopover site for migrating shorebirds. Swans are present all year round but birdlife is best observed between November and March.

Activities within the park include trout fishing but only by permit, which can be bought at the visitors' center. Camping is possible on the western shore of Laguna Blanca, although daily buses run to and from the park from the nearby town of Zapala.

A flock of flamingos at Parque Nacional Laguna Blanca

Sculpture of Jesus and his Disciples along Via Christi, Junín de los Andes

Aluminé ②

Road Map B4. 176 miles (284 km) W of Neuquén. 🏔 1,300. 🚌 from Neuquén. 🛈 Centro de Informes, Cristian Joubert 321, (02942) 496-001. **www**.welcomeargentina.com/alumine

Situated within the Mapuche heartland, the pleasant settlement of Aluminé was founded as a military fortification in 1884. This was during the Conquista del Desierto *(see p50)*, the bloody campaign against the indigenous tribes. The fort no longer exists and Aluminé is today a sleepy Andean town, a rafting and fishing destination ringed by rugged hills. Rafting enthusiasts are drawn by the rapids of Río Aluminé; anglers by the trout- and perch-rich waters of Ríos Quillén and Pulmarí. The town is an ideal base for trips into the northern section of Parque Nacional Lanín.

Junín de los Andes ②

Road Map B4. 242 miles (390 km) SW of Neuquén. 🏔 5,000. 🚌 from Neuquén. 🛈 Padre Milanesio 590, (02972) 491-160. 🎉 Semana de la Artesania (Jul); National Trout Festival (Dec). **www**.junindelos andes.gov.ar

The region's oldest settlement, Junín de los Andes was founded in 1883 as an army outpost during the offensive against the Mapuche. Several expressions of this tribal culture are still found on the streets around the *araucaria*-shaded Plaza San Martín.

Museo Mapuche is a good starting point, with Mapuche

artifacts dating as far back as 12,000 years ago. The nearby **Iglesia Nuestra Señora de las Nieves** is an aesthetic blend of indigenous and Roman Catholic symbolism. Its stained-glass windows and main crucifix, portraying a resurrected Christ in Mapuche dress, are standout features. On a hillside overlooking the town there is the **Via Christi**, a 1-mile (2-km) walk comprising statues depicting the life of Christ, each handcrafted in the image of the Mapuche. The town is one of the gateways to Parque Nacional Lanín and visitors heading there should go first to **Delegación Parque Nacional Lanín**. Junín de los Andes is also Patagonia's fishing mecca, skirted by rivers rich in trout.

Fly-fishing sign near Junín

🏛 **Museo Mapuche**
Ginés Ponte & Don Bosco. ⏱ varies.

Delegación Parque Nacional Lanín
Padre Milanesio 550.
Tel (02972) 492-748. ⏱ varies (call in advance).

San Martín de los Andes ②

Road Map B4. 118 miles (190 km) S of Aluminé. 🏔 30,000. ✈ 🚌 from Neuquén. 🛈 Ave San Martín and Juan Manuel de Rosas, (02972) 425-500. 🎉 Fiesta Nacional de Montañés (Aug).

Idyllically situated on the eastern lip of Lago Lácar, San Martín de los Andes is arguably Patagonia's loveliest town. Despite increased tourist interest and a construction boom, strict planning laws have ensured that it retains much of its original charm. At the center of town, **Museo Primeros Pobladores** has ethnographic exhibits on the region's colonization by Europeans. Several short treks lead into Parque Nacional Lanín nearby. Visitors wanting longer excursions into the park should head first to the **Intendencia Parque Nacional Lanín** for information.

Environs
Just 12 miles (19 km) from town is the Chapelco Ski Resort *(see p311)*, with 20 slopes of varying difficulty and a world-class snowboarding park. The maximum drop is 2,394 ft (730 m).

🏛 **Museo Primeros Pobladores**
Juan Manuel de Rosas 700.
Tel (02972) 428-676. ⏱ 10am–7pm Mon–Fri, 2–7pm Sat & Sun.

Intendencia Parque Nacional Lanín
Perito Moreno & Elordi. **Tel** (02972) 427-233. ⏱ 8am–3pm Mon–Fri.

Boats for hire along the shore of Lago Lácar, San Martín de los Andes

For hotels and restaurants in this region see pp283–6 and pp301–2

Parque Nacional Lanín ㉕

Covering an area of 1,465 sq miles (3,795 sq km), this jewel of a national park was formed in 1937 and protects glacial lakes, volcanic summits, and lush forests. It is divided into north, central, and southern sections, each with its own gateway town, and each accessible by gravel road. Both roads and hiking trails traverse the park, skirting beautiful lakes and crossing various species of native forest. Over 200 animal species find refuge here, from the introduced wild boar to the native *pudú*, the world's smallest deer. Excellent campsites abound in the area as well.

VISITORS' CHECKLIST

Road Map B4. 14 miles (22 km) SW of Aluminé. ▦ from Junín and San Martín de los Andes. ℹ *Intendencia Perito Moreno & Elordi, San Martín de los Andes;* (02972) 427-233. ▦ ✔ ⚠ www.patagonia-argentina.com

Araucaria forests flourish here. The tree is sacred to the Mapuche, who eat its fruit and use its resin for medicine.

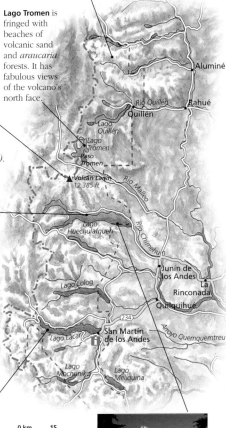

Lago Tromen is fringed with beaches of volcanic sand and *araucaria* forests. It has fabulous views of the volcano's north face.

★ **Volcán Lanín**
A star attraction, Volcán Lanín is the park's highest peak at 12,385 ft (3,776 m). The 3-day trek that leads to its crater is physically extremely demanding.

Fly-fishing
The fly-fishing season runs from November to April. Angling hotspots include Lagos Huechulafquen and Tromen and Ríos Malleo, Quillén, and Chimehuin.

Lago Lácar is the most accessible of Lanín's lakes. It is worth exploring its southern shore, especially the beaches Quila Quina and Catritre, and the trek to Lago Escondido.

0 km 15
0 miles 15

KEY

═══	Main road
═══	Minor road
- -	Park boundary
▬ · ▬	International boundary
▲	Peak
ℹ	Visitor information

Lago Huechulafquen
The park's biggest lake offers boat trips across its sparkling waters with spectacular views of Volcán Lanín's southern face.

Bariloche ❷❻

Road Map B4. 124 miles (200 km) S of San Martín de los Andes. 120,000. *Centro Cívico, (02944) 423-022.* La Fiesta de la Nieve (mid-Aug). **www**.bariloche.com.ar

Situated on the southeastern shore of Lago Nahuel Huapi, Bariloche attracts visitors all year due to its location within Parque Nacional Nahuel Huapi and its proximity to Villa Cerro Catedral. Founded in 1902, Bariloche was first populated by colonies of Swiss, Italians, and Germans. These communities left their imprint on the city's cultural landscape, not least by giving rise to Bariloche's reputation as Argentina's chocolate capital.

At the heart of the city, facing the lake, is the Centro Cívico, housing **Museo de la Patagonia Francisco P. Moreno**. This museum features exhibits on the region's flora, fauna, and indigenous cultures. Also located in the Centro Cívico is the tourist information office which offers advice on traveling to nearby spots within the national park. The easiest hiking route from town is the Circuito Chico which skirts the beaches Playa Bonita and Serena. Those planning longer trips into the park should begin their trip at the park's Intendencia, a block away.

🏛 **Museo de la Patagonia Francisco P. Moreno**
Centro Cívico. **Tel** (02944) 422-309. varies. under 10 free.

Municipal building and clocktower in Centro Cívico, Bariloche

Parque Nacional Nahuel Huapi ❷❼

Created in 1934 from land donated by naturalist and explorer Francisco P. Moreno, Parque Nacional Nahuel Huapi is Argentina's oldest national park. It is also its most visited, with over half a million people per year drawn by pristine landscapes and a range of outdoor activities that include trekking, skiing, fly-fishing, and rafting. At the heart of the park lies the huge and beautiful Lago Nahuel Huapi. Bariloche, on its southeastern shore, is Patagonia's largest tourist center; Villa La Angostura and Villa Traful, farther north, are quieter, less-visited alternatives.

★ **Villa La Angostura**
Gateway to Parque Nacional Los Arrayanes within Parque Nacional Nahuel Huapi, Villa La Angostura is known for its boutique hotels and fine restaurants.

Parque Nacional Los Arrayanes
Covering the Quetrihué peninsula, this park protects ancient myrtle woods. Hiking trails cross to the forests at the peninsula's southern tip. Boat trips also run from Villa La Angostura.

Rio Manso boasts class II–IV rapids and is a favorite with white-water rafting enthusiasts.

CHILE

Villa La Angostura
Osorno
Parque Nacional Los Arrayanes
Puerto Blest
Cerro Tronador 11,400 ft
Lago Roca
Lago Martin

STAR SIGHTS

★ Villa La Angostura

★ Llao Llao

0 km   10

0 miles   10

KEY

▬▬ Highway

══ Minor road

- - Park boundary

-■- International border

- - Provincial boundary

▲ Peak

✈ International airport

Ⓐ Campsite

ℹ Visitor information

Isla Victoria
This is a forested island famous for its 2,000-year-old rock paintings.

VISITORS' CHECKLIST

Road Map B4. 95 miles (153 km) SW of Bariloche.
✈ *Bariloche.* ▦ *from Bariloche.*
ℹ *San Martin 24, Bariloche, (02944) 423-111.* 🎿 💺 🚻 🍴
Ⓐ **www**.parquesnacionales. gov.ar ***Note:*** *the best time to go is from December to March; skiing is late June to August; trekking is from December to March. Snow is common between May and September.*

Lago Falkner

Caleufú

Lago Traful Ⓐ

Villa Traful

Neuquén

237

Valle Encantado

NEUQUÉN

231

★ Llao Llao Hotel and Resort
Open since 1938, this hotel (see p310) features a golf course, private beach, and fantastic views of three lakes. Its restaurant is open to non-guests.

Nahuel Huapi

...ia

...o Nahuel Huapi

Villa Cerro Catedral
Patagonia's premier ski destination, this resort owes its name to the peak of Cerro Catedral. Other activities are hiking and paragliding.

...opez

San Carlos de Bariloche

Villa Cerro Catedral

Bariloche ✈

▲ Cerro Catedral 7,835 ft

258

RÍO NEGRO

Ⓐ *Lago Mascardi*

Villa Mascardi

CRUCE DE LAGOS
Of all the routes that cross the Andes between Patagonian Argentina and Chile, the Cruce de Lagos is the most spectacular. The crossing is by land and boat, begins in Bariloche and finishes in Puerto Varas in Chile, traversing two national parks along the way. Passengers travel through forests thick with *alerce, lenga,* and cypress trees, and cross four separate lakes, including the emerald-green Lago Todos los Santos in Chile. Four volcanoes, including Chile's Volcán Osorno and the mighty 11,400-ft (3,478-m) Cerro Tronador in Argentina, can be seen at close range. Both one- and two-day tickets are available for the crossings; the latter allows time to soak in the scenery.

Picturesque cruise between Patagonian Argentina and Chile

...ago Steffen

El Bolsón

Landscape just south of the sleepy town of El Bolsón, Patagonia

El Bolsón ㉘

Road Map B4. 75 miles (120 km)
S of Bariloche. 🏠 20,000. 🚌
ℹ️ *Avenida San Martín y Gral,
(02944) 492-604.* 🛒 *Tue, Thu,
& Sat.* 🎭 *La Fiesta Nacional del
Lúpulo (Feb).* **www**.elbolson.com

Gaining its reputation as a
hippy retreat in the 1970s, El
Bolsón is a laid-back
town, where a
relaxed atmosphere
lingers to this day.
Buskers, backpackers,
and street vendors
all converge in this
town during the
summer, joined by an
increasing number of
families seeking a
quieter alternative to
Bariloche in the north.

Spinning tops at
Feria Artesanal

   Although tourism is growing
in El Bolsón, the local
economy has traditionally
relied on forestry and hops
grown on small farms called
chacras. These *chacras* also
produce excellent organic
honey and soft fruits and can
be visited through the year.
Good beers made from local
harvests can be sampled at
the well-known brewery
nearby, **Cervecería El Bolsón**.
The town's popular market
place, **Feria Artesanal**, sells
an assortment of woolen and
leather products, jewelry,
and ceramics, all made by
local craftspeople.
   Offering great walks and
views is the nearby **Cerro
Piltriquitrón**. Towering over
El Bolsón, this summit, at a

height of 7,415 ft (2,260 m),
is the highest in the area. It
offers great opportunities for
adventure sport. **Mirador
Plataforma** is a lookout point
offering vistas of the Andean
mountains and Lago Puelo. A
further 40-minute walk away
is the **Bosque Tallado**, a carved
forest comprising sculptures
worked from the trunks of
trees burned by a
forest fire in the early
1980s. A 3-hour trek
leads hikers to the
mountain's summit.

Environs
Around 10 miles (16
km) from El Bolsón,
**Parque Nacional Lago
Puelo** was created to
protect trees such as
the hazel and the *ulmo*,
native to Chile. The short
Bosque de las Sombras nature
trail is popular, while rafting,
horse-riding, and fly-fishing
are also possible in the park.

🏞️ **Parque Nacional Lago
Puelo**
ℹ️ *Oficina de Informes, (02944)
499-232.* 📷 🔺

El Maitén ㉙

Road Map B4. 43 miles (70 km) N
of El Bolson. 🏠 5,000. 🚌 ℹ️ *Ave
Rivadavia & Ave San Martín, (02945)
495-016.* 🎭 *Fiesta Nacional del Tren a
Vapor (Feb).* **www**.elmaiten.com.ar

An old railroad town, El
Maitén is where the work-
shops for the **La Trochita**

(Little Gauge) steam trains are
located. First built in the early
1940s and still operable today,
these workshops can be visited on the old station grounds,
where a small, efficient work-
force hand-manufactures
locomotive parts from old
machinery to rebuild coaches.
La Trochita is believed to be
the world's oldest functioning
steam train. It was built in
1922 to transport local wool
and timber production. Also
on the station grounds is
Museo Ferroviario, a small
museum dedicated to the
town's railroad heritage.
La Trochita departs from
El Maitén six times a week
in summer.

🏛️ **Museo Ferroviario**
Estación El Maitén. **Tel** (02945) 495-
190. ◯ *Dec–Mar: 8am–8pm daily;
Apr–Nov: 9am–5pm daily.*
📷 📹 *on request.*

**La Trochita steam train halted at El
Maitén station**

Museo Leleque ㉚

Road Map B4. 25 miles (40 km) S of El Maitén. **Tel** (02945) 455-151. ◻ Thu–Tue. ◯ May, Jun, & Sep 🖼 ◻

A rustic estancia converted into a museum, Museo Leleque holds a 14,000-strong collection of artifacts narrating Patagonia's history. Displays are divided between four rooms and follow a historical itinerary, beginning with the arrival of the first indigenous populations in Patagonia 13,000 years ago and continuing up to the present day. Among the fascinating exhibits is a contract for the acquisition of horses signed by Santiago Ryan, a pseudonym used by outlaw Butch Cassidy.

A partially woven Tehuelche rug exhibit at Museo Leleque

Esquel ㉛

Road Map B4. 112 miles (180 km) S of El Bolsón. 🏘 35,000. ✈ 🚌 ℹ Ave Alvear & Sarmiento, (029) 4545-1927. 🎿 La Fiesta del Esqui (Sep). **www**.esquel.gov.ar

With its beautiful valley setting and snowcapped Andean backdrop, Esquel is a welcome change from the surrounding arid steppe. A laid-back town with a handful of tourist sites, it is the ideal base from which to visit nearby attractions such as Parque Nacional Los Alerces and the popular **La Hoya** ski resort. With 24 pistes of varying difficulty, this family-oriented ski resort keeps Esquel open to tourism in the winter months. The town's biggest draw, La Trochita, departs from Esquel's well preserved railroad station.

BUTCH CASSIDY AND THE SUNDANCE KID

In 1901 the SS *Soldier Prince* set sail from New York for Argentina. On board were James Ryan and Harry Place – better known as Butch Cassidy and the Sundance Kid – America's most notorious bank robbers and members of the feared Wild Bunch. Fleeing the law, the two Americans, together with Sundance's girlfriend, Etta Place, had decided to head to remote Patagonia. In the village of Cholila, near Esquel, where Butch and Sundance eventually settled, locals still talk of the gringo gunslingers, while the house they built and lived in for six years can be visited on the edge of town.

The cabin built by Butch Cassidy & the Sundance Kid

Trevelin ㉜

Road Map B4. 14 miles (24 km) S of Esquel. 🏘 10,000. 🚌 ℹ Plaza, (02945) 480-091. **www**.patagonia-argentina.com

A short drive from Esquel is the Welsh village of Trevelin. Though officially founded in 1918, it had been a settlement since the 1880s, when pioneers made the journey from their settlements near the Atlantic Coast. Here, they built the mills that gave the town its name. Housed within one of the flourmills is **Museo Regional Trevelin**, displaying Welsh artifacts. Capilla Bethel is the town's small Welsh chapel. A short trip from Trevelin are the **Nant y Fall** waterfalls – seven separate falls that drop majestically from heights of up to 197 ft (60 m).

🏛 **Museo Regional Trevelin**
Calle Viejo Molino. ◻ varies. 🖼 📷 on request.

Parque Nacional Los Alerces ㉝

Road Map B4. 28 miles (45 km) W of Esquel. ℹ Villa Futalaufquen, Ruta Provincial 71; (02945) 471-015. ◻ daily. 🖼 ♦ ⛺

Covering 1,015 sq miles (2,630 sq km) and considered to be the most pristine of northern Patagonia's parks, Parque Nacional Los Alerces was created to protect the *alerce* tree, a beautiful, towering species that can exceed 197 ft (60 m) in height and live for 4,000 years.

Though numerous hiking trails crisscross the park, the only way to access its *alerce* woods is via the **Circuito Lacustre**, a boat and trekking excursion that traverses majestic lake and glacier scenery. The excursion's highlight is its end point, the striking Millennium tree, a 2,600-year-old *alerce*.

A beautiful lake located in Parque Nacional Los Alerces

One of the quiet streets running through Perito Moreno

Perito Moreno [34]

Road Map B5. 334 miles (538km) S of Esquel. 👥 *4,500.* 🚌 ℹ *Ave San Martín & Gendarmería Nacional, (02963) 432-732.* 🎉 *Festival Cueva de las Manos (Feb).*

Named for the Argentinian naturalist and explorer, Francisco Moreno, and not to be confused with Glaciar Perito Moreno *(see p254)* or Parque Nacional Perito Moreno *(see p244)*, this town is a popular stopover for those traveling along Ruta Nacional 40. The most populous town in this area of the Santa Cruz province, it is an ideal base from which to explore the World Heritage Site of **Cueva de las Manos** as well as Parque Nacional Perito Moreno to the south. Most will find this town a sprawling and somewhat nondescript settlement, where little goes on. Life revolves around the main avenue, Avenida San Martín, which is ideal for evening walks. The avenue is given dashes of color by the politically motivated graffiti.

Los Antiguos [35]

Road Map B5. 35 miles (56km) W of Perito Moreno. 👥 *4,000.* 🚌 ℹ *Ave 9 de Julio 446, (02963) 491-261.* 🎉 *Fiesta Nacional de la Cereza (Jan).* **www**.losantiguos.gov.ar

With its benign microclimate and idyllic location on the shore of **Lago Buenos Aires**, this little town derives its name from the Tehuelche *I Keu Kenk*, meaning "place of my ancestors."

Los Antiguos was built on a site used millennia ago by the Tehuelche as a place of retirement. The archaeological richness of the area is such that ancient burial mounds are still being discovered. The town is now known as Argentina's cherry capital, although its *chacras* also produce other high-quality jams and liqueurs. Family-run **Chacra Don Neno**, at the center of town, is among the best of these farms. The town's other highlight is Lago Buenos Aires, the second biggest freshwater lake in South America, on the border between Argentina and Chile. Its pristine trout- and salmon-rich waters attract anglers.

Estancia Telken [36]

Road Map B5. 16 miles (25 km) S of Perito Moreno. ***Tel*** *(02963) 432-079, (011) 4325-3098 (reservations).* ◻ *Oct–Apr.*

An authentic sheep-rearing farm, Estancia Telken has been in the hands of the same landowning family, of Scottish descent, since 1915. The estancia's sprawling tree-lined grounds cover 80 sq miles (207 sq km) and spread majestically across the Patagonian steppe towards the Lago Buenos Aires plateau.

Treks and horse-riding are arranged at the estancia. The trails around the area include sights such as millennia-old rock carvings, while for the nature enthusiasts, guanaco, lesser rhea, and numerous species of birds can be observed. It also provides an excellent base from which to explore Cueva de las Manos and Lago Buenos Aires.

A view of the majestic Andes across a sparkling river and a shelter belt of poplar trees, Los Antiguos

The ancient stencilled handprints at Cueva de las Manos

Cueva de las Manos ㊲

Road Map B5. Ruta Provincial 97, 100 miles (161 km) S of Perito Moreno. ☐ 9am–7pm daily. 🖼 🎫 🛈

Hidden deep within the Río Pinturas Canyon, inside the borders of breathtaking Parque Nacional Perito Moreno, Cueva de las Manos (Cave of Hands) is Argentina's finest example of prehistoric cave art. Declared a UNESCO World Heritage Site in 1999, it has dumbfounded experts since its discovery in 1881 and still hosts ongoing archaeological work.

The main cave measures 79 ft (24 m) in depth, with an entrance 49 ft (15 m) wide and an initial height of 33 ft (10 m). The ground inside the cave, however, has an upward slope and soon the height is reduced to no more than 7 ft (2 m).

A visit to the cave, where the rock paintings date from as far back as 9,500 years ago, is a moving experience. Vivid, kaleidoscopic, stencilled hand negatives, left by children and adults, are spread throughout the 1,968-ft (600-m) long trail. Numbering more than 2,000, they are thought to be evidence of the artists' belief in the permanent contact between man and mother earth. The paint used in the negatives would have been mixed orally, using mineral pigments found at the site combined with anything

from water to saliva and even urine. Once in liquid form the paint would be spat out over the hand on the wall.

The hunters' intimate relationship with nature is depicted in the early paintings; the hunting scenes are of great anecdotal value, showing guanacos being chased across the canyon, surrounded, and then killed with long spears and stones. The sense of movement is striking, with both the energetic hunter and prey depicted in dynamic form. Other paintings illustrate

the link between the hunters' earthly world and its spirit equivalent. Paintings from 7,000 years ago show hundreds of heavily pregnant guanacos standing still. These are interpreted to be some kind of painted prayer, beseeching the return of the animals during a period of drought, which had seen them migrate to better pastures.

Stylized forms mark the cave's most recent art, dating from 1,500 to 4,000 years ago. Biomorphic motifs of frogs, lizards, hawks, and pumas, and geometrical shapes such as concentric circles, zigzag lines, and combined triangles adorn the cave walls. These abstract forms continue to confound experts.

Archaeological work at Cueva de las Manos is ongoing, so visitors get a chance to marvel at the rock art by guided tour only. Tour groups leave the visitor center several times daily. Tour agencies in Perito Moreno run excursions to the cave; visitors can also seek lodging with Estancia Telken or Estancia Los Toldos (see pp314–15), both of which are conveniently located nearby.

ARGENTINA'S LONELIEST ROAD

No road in Argentina inspires solitude and introspection quite like Ruta Nacional 40. Never winding and seemingly never ending, Ruta Nacional 40 runs the entire length of Argentina, but finds its true heart in the wilderness of Patagonia; and nowhere more so than in the 390-mile (628-km) stretch of nothingness that lies between Perito Moreno and El Calafate. Here, Ruta Nacional 40 becomes a rocky, gravel artery, surrounded by a featureless landscape of scrub grass and broad horizons. A howling wind is the traveler's only accompaniment; encounters are few and far between, this being a region of isolated, century-old sheep estancias and forgotten villages. Left behind by time, they evoke the spirit of a Patagonia of old.

An empty, lonely stretch along Ruta Nacional 40

The only hotel in the village, Hotel Bajo Caracoles

Bajo Caracoles ③⑧

Road Map B5. 80 miles (130 km) S
of Perito Moreno. 🚶 100. 🚌

For motorists driving south
on Ruta Nacional 40 from
Perito Moreno, Bajo Caracoles
is the first stopover point.
Surrounded by the vast
Patagonian steppe, it is a
remote settlement of about
15 families. The town has the
only gas station on the
national highway between
Perito Moreno and Tres
Lagos, a stretch of over 310
miles (500 km). The village is
home to a small hotel that
contains its sole restaurant
and phone booth.

Parque Nacional Perito Moreno ③⑨

Road Map B5. 102 miles (165 km)
SW of Bajo Caracoles. 🚌 🖪 *Ave
San Martin 882, Gobernador
Gregores; (02962) 491-477.* 🅰

Due to its remote location
and extreme climactic conditions, Parque Nacional Perito
Moreno remains Patagonia's
wildest and best-preserved
national park. Visitors able to
traverse its borders will find
landscapes of pristine beauty
abundant in wildlife.
  Covering 490 sq miles
(1,268 sq km), the park
encompasses two separate
ecological regions. The
Patagonian steppe covers its
eastern section, forming an
elevated plain of scrub and
grassland at 2,950 ft (900 m)
above sea level. In the park's
western section this scrub is
replaced by thick swathes of
lenga forest, which rise to an

altitude of 3,936 ft (1,200 m),
and have as their backdrop
the snowy peaks of the beautiful Andean cordillera.
  The opportunities for
nature-spotting are varied and
many. Well-marked trails
cross breathtaking scenery
that features eight beautiful
lakes. Elegant fine-boned
guanaco abound along their
shores, and some 160 bird
species are found in the park.
  Visitors should expect
extreme weather conditions.
In winter temperatures drop
to a chilling -25° C (-13° F),
and it can snow even in
summer. The best times to
visit are in the southern
hemisphere's late spring
and early autumn. Luxury

accommodation in and
around the park are Estancia
La Oriental and Estancia
Menelik *(see pp314–15).*

Hipólito Yrigoyen ④⓪

Road Map B5. 122 miles (197 km)
S of Perito Moreno. 🚶 250. 🚌

Off Patagonia's more beaten
track but beautifully situated,
Hipólito Yrigoyen is a small
settlement on the shore of
Lago Posadas, at the foot
of the southern Andes. It is
still usually known by its old
name, Posadas, taken from
the lake. People who visit the
town do so for three main
reasons – fishing, hiking, and
mountain climbing. The lake
is a popular spot among
anglers and the catch includes
smelt, perch, and salmon.

Environs
Around 2 miles (3 km) south
of Hipólito Yrigoyen is the
Cerro de Los Indios archaeological site with 3,000-year-
old rock paintings. The area's
star attraction is **Cerro San
Lorenzo**. At 12,155 ft (3,702
m), it is one of the highest
peaks in southern Patagonia.

Breathtaking view of Lago Posadas with the Andes in the distance

A herd of guanaco wandering on the vast Patagonian steppe near Tres Lagos

Gobernador Gregores ④

Road Map B5. 218 miles (352km) S of Perito Moreno. 👥 *3,500.* 🚌
ℹ️ *Ave San Martín & Ruperto Barrenchea, (02962) 491-192.*

Situated in the middle of the windy Patagonian steppe, deep in sheep territory, Gobernador Gregores is characteristic of the many isolated settlements that dot the southern stretch of Ruta Nacional 40. A farming town that was once an important stopover for landowners transporting wool from the Andes to the ports on the Atlantic coast, its chief attractions today are the working estancias that dot the surrounding landscape.

As well as farming sheep, these beautiful ranches provide visitors isolation and relaxation, together with activities such as horse riding, birdwatching, and fishing. Estancia La Angostura, in the same family since 1878, and Estancia Río Capitán *(see pp314–5)* are two of the most recommended. Motorists driving along Ruta Nacional 40 should note that the town, situated 45 miles (72 km) off the national highway, provides basic accommodations and also has the only gas station between Bajo Caracoles to the north and Tres Lagos to the south, a stretch of over 248 miles (400 km).

Lago Cardiel ④

Road Map B5. 43 miles (70 km) W of Gobernador Gregores. 🚌
ℹ️ *Ave San Martín & Ruperto Barrenchea, Gobernador Gregores; (02962) 491-192.*

The clear turquoise waters of Lago Cardiel are easy to spot for those traveling along Ruta Nacional 40. The lake is overlooked by the dramatic peak of **Mount El Puntudo**, and stands out from the surrounding steppe, providing welcome relief for eyes grown accustomed to scrub grass and flat plains. The colorful colonies of black-necked swans and pink flamingos that inhabit the lake's shores can also be seen from the roadside.

Brimming with rainbow trout and salmon, the lake's principal recreational activity is angling. The nearby estancias can make arrangements for excursions.

Tres Lagos ④

Road Map B6. 108 miles (174km) S of Gobernador Gregores. 👥 *200.* 🚌 🅰️

The tiny settlement of Tres Lagos owes its name to its proximity to the lakes **Viedma**, **San Martín**, and **Tar**. The town was originally founded to serve the sheep ranches that could be found around the three lakes. Wool from the estancias would be brought to Tres Lagos where it was loaded onto wagons for the two-month long journey to the port at Puerto Santa Cruz on the Atlantic coast. More prosaically, this remote settlement today serves mainly the motorists traveling along Ruta Nacional 40, its gas station being the only one on the long, empty stretch of highway between Bajo Caracoles and El Calafate *(see p247)*. It also has a free municipal campsite.

Flamingos over the turquoise waters of Lago Cardiel

Lago San Martín

Road Map B5. 138 miles (222 km) N of Tres Lagos. 🚶 *500.* 🚌 *from El Chaltén.* ℹ️ *Ave Güemes 21, El Chaltén; (02962) 493-270.*

Straddling the border between Argentina and Chile, where it is known as Lago O'Higgins, this lake derives its two names from the popular Independence heroes of the two countries, who united forces in the early 19th century to defeat Spain. Lago San Martín marks the starting point of the Austral, Argentina's Deep South, and its surrounding landscape is one of dramatic Andean peaks and glacial lakes.

Though remote, the lake has two lovely estancias located on its shores, Estancia La Maipú and Estancia El Cóndor *(see pp314–15).* Both offer treks, horse rides, and bird-watching tours into the surrounding forests. Trails, along which Andean condors are seen, lead to a number of lookout points that offer breathtaking views of the lake and the Andes. Excursions to the lake are run by tour agencies in El Chaltén. However, the lake is rendered inaccessible at times due to unpredictable weather that makes navigation difficult.

Hikers on their way to Mount Fitz Roy, El Chaltén

Parque Nacional Los Glaciares 45

See pp250–55.

El Chaltén 46

Road Map A5. 81 miles (130 km) W of Tres Lagos. 🚶 *500.* 🚌 ℹ️ *Ave Güemes 21, (02962) 493-011.* 🎉 *Fiesta Nacional del Trekking.*

With its wind-pummeled gravel streets and rugged Andean setting, El Chaltén gives every impression of being an old frontier settlement rather than the country's newest town. It was created in 1985 as a geopolitical maneuvre in a long-running border dispute between Argentina and Chile.

First populated by border guards and government employees, El Chaltén has since blossomed into Argentina's foremost trekking destination. Situated within Parque Nacional Los Glaciares, it is an ideal base from which to explore the northern section of the park. In summer, its 500 permanent residents are joined by almost 60,000 hikers and climbers drawn by the trails that lead to the base of the highest summit, Mount Fitz Roy, in the Fitz Roy massif. The base offers an opportunity to go ice-trekking on the Viedma and Torre glaciers.

The best time to visit is autumn as well as October and November when the town is less crowded.

Lago del Desierto 47

Road Map A5. 23 miles (37 km) N of El Chaltén. 📅 *Dec–Mar daily.* 🚌 ℹ️ *(02962) 493–011.*

A long-hidden jewel, Lago del Desierto (Lake of the Desert) was unveiled to tourists in 1995, when Argentina's border dispute with Chile came to an end and sovereignty over the lake's shores was finally ruled in its favor.

Tours lasting a full day pass through the forests of the Río de las Vueltas valley before arriving at the lake's southern shore. From there a number

View of Río de las Vueltas making its way through forests

of treks are possible, the low-difficulty hike to **Glaciar Huemul** being highly recommended. The trail passes through dense forests of *lenga* and *ñire* before reaching the glacier and the emerald-green lagoon that sits at its base. From the lake's southern bank, visitors can also go to **Punta Norte** on its northern bank, which offers fabulous views of the lake and the north face of awe-inspiring Mount Fitz Roy.

From Punta Norte, tourists can trek to the Chilean border post on the coast of Lago San Martín. Boats depart from the border post, crossing the lake to the Chilean town of Villa O'Higgins.

El Calafate ④⑧

Road Map B6. 137 miles (220 km) S of El Chaltén. 🏔 *17,000*. ✈ 🚌 *from El Chaltén.* 🚏 *Terminal de Omnibus, Ave Julio A Roca 1004; (02902) 491-090.* 🎭 *Fiesta de Bautismo del Lago Argentino.* **www**.turismo.elcalafate.gov.ar

Located on the shore of Lago Argentino, El Calafate is the area's biggest tourist center. The town is the perfect base from which to explore the southern section of Parque Nacional Los Glaciares, including its biggest attraction, the magnificent Glaciar Perito Moreno.

A bustling tourist center with smart shops, restaurants, and a relatively benign micro-climate, El Calafate comes as a welcome relief to visitors arriving from the barren Patagonian steppe to the north. The city's main cultural point of reference is the interesting **Museo Regional Municipal El Calafate**, which recounts the area's history from the point of arrival of its first indigenous groups. **Centro de Interpretación Histórica Calafate**, a private museum run by a group of local academics, also traces local history. Its photographic and pictorial displays explain the region's human and environmental past. A short walk away is **Reserva Municipal Laguna Nimez**, a nature

Brightly colored shops at the main shopping center, El Calafate

preserve on the shore of Lago Argentino that protects about 100 species of birds.

Environs
Several ranches near town offer comfortable accommodation. Guests can take part in ranch activities at Estancia Alice *(see pp314–15)*. Hostería Alta Vista, a ranch built in the late 19th century, is located on the grounds of Estancia La Anita. Excursions across the estancia include views of Glaciar Perito Moreno.

🏛 **Museo Regional Municipal El Calafate**
Ave del Libertador 575.
Tel *(02902) 491-924.* ⏰ *8am–7pm Mon–Fri.* ♿

🏛 **Centro de Interpretación Histórica Calafate**
Almirante G. Brown & Guido Bonarelli. **Tel** *(02902) 492-799.* ⏰ *Dec–Mar: 10am–8pm daily; Apr–Nov: 11am–6pm daily.* 🖼
📷 🏠

Estancia Alice, a working sheep ranch, near the town of El Calafate

Río Turbio ④⑨

Road Map B6. 160 miles (257km) S of El Calafate. 🚌 *from El Calafate, Río Gallegos.* 🚏 *Plazoleta Agustín del Castillo, (02902) 421-950.*

Situated in a remote corner of Patagonia, 4 miles (6 km) from the border with Chile, the gritty mining town of Río Turbio was known mainly for one thing – coal. Due to Argentina's ongoing mining industry depression, the coal mines lie abandoned at the edge of town, a short distance from the Villa Dorotea border patrol. A small section, where miners give demonstrations of their work, can be visited by guided tour, arranged at the tourist information office in town. The town's other highlight is its narrow-gauge railroad line, laid in the early 1950s to transport Río Turbio's coal to Río Gallegos on the Atlantic coast. The ageing locomotives that work the line are a throwback in time. Once the most southerly line in the world, the railroad ceded this distinction after the construction of the new railroad line in Ushuaia in 1994. Turbio's other draw is its attractive wooded hillsides 2.5 miles (4 km) south of the town. This is where the **Valdelén** winter-sports complex is located. This ski center has gentle slopes which are ideal for beginners.

View of the walkway that runs close to the astonishing Glaciar Perito Moreno ▷

Parque Nacional Los Glaciares ㊹

A UNESCO World Heritage Site, Parque Nacional Los Glaciares derives its name from the 47 major glaciers and numerous smaller ones that lie within its boundaries. In its northern sector is Argentina's trekking capital, El Chaltén, gateway to the magnificent Mount Fitz Roy; in its southern zone lies the awe-inspiring Glaciar Perito Moreno. Trips combining both sections of the park are increasingly popular, although the southern zone remains more accessible; its dazzling glaciers and lakes are just a day trip away from the town of El Calafate.

LOCATOR MAP

☐ Area illustrated

– – International border

★ **Mount Fitz Roy**
The towering granite needles of Mount Fitz Roy dominate the park's northern region. Trails run from El Chaltén to the foot of Mount Fitz Roy and Cerro Torre, the two highest peaks in the massif.

Glaciar Agassiz, with few tourists and no walkways, is the antithesis of Glaciar Perito Moreno.

Glacier Onelli is one of three glaciers that converge on iceberg-choked Laguna Onelli.

★ **Glaciar Upsala**
The giant Upsala descends into the northern arm of Lago Argentino. Boat excursions cruise past its front wall after winding their way across the iceberg-studded lake, all the while under the gaze of snowy mountains.

Glaciar Spegazzini
Visited on excursions to Glaciar Upsala, Glaciar Spegazzini boasts the biggest snout in the national park, rising to a height of 443 ft (135 m) in parts.

STAR SIGHTS

★ Mount Fitz Roy

★ Glaciar Upsala

★ Glaciar Perito Moreno

ICE CALVING

The periodic rupture and collapse of Glaciar Perito Moreno's 197-ft (60-m) front wall provides a great spectacle. This extraordinary phenomenon is caused when the glacier advances close to Península Magellanes, damming the Brazo Rico (Rico Arm) of Lago

The spectacular ice calving on the Glaciar Perito Moreno

Argentino. With no outflow, the lake's water rises until the pressure of its weight forces the dam to burst and, in a cataclysmic explosion of ice and water, causes the glacier's front wall to come crashing down. Visitors in 2007 were the last lucky witnesses of this event.

VISITORS' CHECKLIST

Road Map A6. 50 miles (80 km) W of El Calafate. ✈ *El Calafate.* 🚌 *from El Calafate, El Chaltén.* 🛈 **El Calafate** *Ave del Libertador 1302, (02902) 491-005;* **El Chaltén** *Ruta Provincial 23, (02962) 493-004.* 🏕🅿🅷 📷🅰 www.losglaciares. com. **Fitz Roy Expediciones** *El Chaltén, (02962) 493-017.* **Serac Ski and Andinismo** *El Chaltén, (02962) 493-066.*

0 km 15
0 miles 15

KEY

═ Main road
═ Minor road
‐ ‐ Trail
‐ ‐ Park boundary
▲ Peak
⛴ Boat service
🛈 Visitor information
🅰 Campsite

EXPLORING THE PARK

Once inside the park, Puerto Punta Bandera in the southern sector is the departure point for lake excursions on Lago Argentino and to see Glaciar Perito Moreno. In the park's northern section, several trails of varying levels of difficulty begin at the national park office at El Chaltén, and organized excursions go to remote sections of the park.

Lago Argentino
Fed by the glacial meltwater of several rivers, Lago Argentino is the country's biggest lake. Cruises take visitors around its drifting icebergs before approaching the front walls of glaciers.

★ Glaciar Perito Moreno
The park's single greatest attraction, Glaciar Perito Moreno is visited every year by thousands hoping to witness the astonishing spectacle of the collapse of the glacier's front wall.

Exploring the Northern Sector

The northern sector of Parque Nacional Los Glaciares is dominated by the awe-inspiring peaks of Mount Fitz Roy. Since the 1930s, climbers have attempted to conquer the 11,168-ft (3,402-m) Mount Fitz Roy and the 10,280-ft (3,133-m) Cerro Torre. They are considered two of the world's most technically challenging mountains as their summits are formed by "mushrooms" of snow and ice that are in constant danger of collapse. More recently, avid hikers have also flocked to the area, converting the tiny settlement of El Chaltén into Argentina's trekking mecca.

Campsite on a sunny hillside

Centro de Visitantes Guardaparque Pedro Fonzo

Ave San Martín. **Tel** *(02962) 493-004.* ◯ *Dec–Mar: 9am-6pm daily; Mar–Dec: 9am-4pm Mon–Fri.*
Visitors planning to go for treks in the national park should first register at this office. It is conveniently located at the entrance to El Chaltén. The staff are friendly, helpful, and able to give advice on difficult trails and expected weather conditions. Climbing permits can also be purchased here.

🏚 Sendero Laguna Torre

This low-difficulty, 6-mile (10-km) hike can be done in one day from El Chaltén. Hikers should note that the return journey takes about 7 hours. The trail follows the Río Fitz Roy valley and climbs through lush *lenga* and *ñire* forests, finally ending at Laguna Torre, a hidden emerald lake that sits at the foot of the magnificent Cerro Torre. Breathtaking views from the lake encompass the mountain, its sister peaks, Egger at 9,514 ft (2,897 m) and Standhart at 9,186 ft (2,798 m), and the sweeping **Glaciar Torre**.

Ice-trekking excursions on Glaciar Torre can be arranged in El Chaltén. Hikers can choose between the single- and two-day options; the latter involves a night's stay at the basic yet comfortable Thorwood base camp, with basic facilities, close to the beautiful Laguna Torre.

🏚 Sendero Laguna de los Tres

Laguna de los Tres is a glacial tarn that sits at the base of Mount Fitz Roy. The trail to its shores is arguably the most scenic in the park. The outward trek from El Chaltén takes around 5 hours, making a return hike just about possible in a day. Otherwise, it is best to plan for two days and set up camp.

The trail's first section, an easy 3.5-hour hike to **Río Blanco**, traverses a landscape of ancient woodland, marshy wetlands, and crystal-clear lagoons. Visitors must note that camping here is permitted only for climbers who have made arrangements at the park office. Midway to Río Blanco, and a 10-minute detour from the main trail, is **Laguna Capri**, a secluded lake with fantastic vistas of the Fitz Roy range. Basic campsites for visitors are located here and at **Campo Poincenot**, 2 miles (3 km) away.

Río Blanco marks the trail's final section to Laguna de los Tres, named in honor of the trio of French climbers, René Ferlet, Guido Magnone, and Lionel Terray, who became the first to scale Mount Fitz Roy in 1952. A medium-level trek, it ascends an incline that gets progressively steeper, rising 1,312 ft (400 m) in a mile (2 km). Views from the lake are magnificent, with towering Mount Fitz Roy rising above the lake and the **Glaciar de los Tres** spilling downwards towards its far shore.

The spectacular Laguna de los Tres at the foot of Mount Fitz Roy

For hotels and restaurants in this region see pp283–6 and pp301–2

🦅 Sendero Piedra del Fraile

Hikers wishing to further explore the national park should make the trek to Piedra del Fraile, a base camp located at the northern edge of the massif. A 4-hour trail to the camp starts at Campo Poincenot and follows the Río Blanco and Río Eléctrico valleys. The trail skirts **Glaciar Piedras Blancas** and passes through quiet *lenga* forests. The latter half of the trail offers great views of Mount Fitz Roy's north face. On reaching Piedra del Fraile there is a private camping ground with hot water and cabins. Trails from Piedra del Fraile lead up to the **Southern Patagonian Ice Field**. Week-long expeditions to the ice fields, suitable only for experienced snow- and ice-trekkers, can be organized with tour operators in El Chaltén.

View of Glaciar Viedma rising from the waters of Lago Viedma

🦅 Glaciar Viedma

Covering a vast area of 378 sq miles (978 sq km), this immense river of ice is the biggest glacier in South America. Boat excursions to its 131-ft (40-m) high face leave from **Puerto Bahía Túnel** on Lago Viedma's northern shore. Most trips range from 2 to 6 hours in length. The longer excursions are the most spectacular, allowing visitors to disembark and see the magnificent glacier close-up. There are also undemanding hikes that can be arranged to the beautiful glacial caves or a 1.5-hour trek across the glacier's icy surface. Professional guides provide equipment, including crampons. The guides are all knowledgeable and speak both Spanish and English. Many tour operators run excursions to the glacier from El Chaltén.

KEY

=== Minor road

-- Trail

Boat service

Visitor information

Campsite

THE CERRO TORRE CONTROVERSY

It was hailed as the greatest mountaineering feat of all time but many doubt that it actually happened. On January 28, 1959, Italian climber Cesare Maestri, together with Austrian Toni Egger, set out to scale the unconquered Cerro Torre, then considered the world's toughest peak. Six days later, Maestri alone reached the base. He said that both Egger and he had made it to the summit but the Austrian had been killed by an avalanche on their descent. The pair's camera was also lost in the accident. One of the greatest climbers of his day, Maestri demanded to be taken on his word. Investigations found no trace of the pair's equipment beyond the lower reaches. Embittered, Maestri's response to his critics was to make two more attempts to climb the summit, but in vain. Now in his seventies, he still holds that he and Egger were the first to conquer Cerro Torre.

The Italian mountaineer Cesare Maestri

Exploring the Southern Sector

The southern sector of Parque Nacional Los Glaciares is characterized by the magnificent glaciers that spill downward from the Southern Patagonian Ice Field, the great frozen plateau of ice that sits atop the southern Andes. These glaciers are remnants of the Ice Age, when they stretched far beyond their current boundaries, reaching the Patagonian steppe and gouging deep U-shaped valleys as they advanced. On the glaciers' retreat at the end of the Pleistocene era 10,000 years ago, these huge troughs were filled with meltwater, forming the region's great lakes.

Glaciar Perito Moreno

53 miles (85 km) W of El Calafate. *from El Calafate.* *from Península Magellanes.* *Ave Libertador 1302, (02902) 491-005.*

Glaciar Perito Moreno is a spectacular sight at 19 miles (31 km) in length and 2.5 miles (4 km) in width. Its ice flows down from the cordillera into the milky, mineral-rich waters of **Lago Argentino**, Argentina's largest lake.

The most popular way to observe the glacier is from the catwalks on **Península Magellanes**, 492 ft (150 m) across Lago Argentino from the glacier's face. Descending the catwalks is an auditory and visual experience heightened each time a huge chunk of ice breaks off the glacier's face and tumbles into the **Canal de los Témpanos** (Iceberg Channel) in a process known as calving.

Boat excursions start from docks **Muelle Bajo de las Sombras** and **Muelle Perito Moreno**, ferrying visitors to the glacier's front wall.

Glaciar Upsala

75 miles (120 km) NW of El Calafate. *from Puerto Punta Bandera.* *Fernandez Campbell, Avenida Libertador 867, (02902) 491-155.* **www.patagonia-argentina.com**

Although less accessible than Glaciar Perito Moreno, this glacier is far bigger, stretching to a mammoth 31 miles (50 km) in length and covering a surface area of 230 sq miles (595 sq km). Once the biggest glacier in South America, it is now fast disappearing at a rate of 656 ft (200 m) per year and has lost its title to Glaciar Viedma. Scientists attribute this to global warming.

Full-day catamaran excursions to Glaciar Upsala depart daily from **Puerto Punta Bandera**. The outward journey sails the **Brazo Upsala** (Upsala Arm) of Lago Argentino, threading its way through a mass of huge blue icebergs towards the glacier's face. Tour operators also take visitors to Glaciars **Onelli**, **Agassiz**, and **Spegazzini** before returning to dock.

Lago Roca

34 miles (55 km) SW of El Calafate. *from El Calafate.* **Estancia Nibepo Aike www.**nibepoaike.com.ar

A hidden gem, Lago Roca is a turquoise lake fringed with forests and overlooked by snowy peaks. It offers excellent camping and trekking opportunities. For hikers, the highlight is the 3-hour, medium-level trail to the 4,220-ft (1,286-m) summit of **Cerro Cristal**; from the top there are tremendous views of Glaciar Perito Moreno, Lago Argentino, and the Torres del Paine mountain range in Chile.

Near Lago Roca is **Estancia Nibepo Aike**, which was founded by Croatian pioneers at the beginning of the 20th century. It is a working farm with plenty of ranch activities.

Hostería Helsingfors

112 miles (180 km) N of El Calafate. *Tel (011) 4315-1222.* Nov–Mar. **www.helsingfors.com.ar**

Located on the beautiful southwestern shore of Lago Viedma is Hostería Helsingfors. Founded in 1917 by Finnish pioneer Alfred Ranstrom, the ranch was named for his country's capital Helsingfors (Helsinki in Swedish).

At the estancia, guests can choose from eight beautifully fitted rooms and enjoy a range of excursions that include boat trips across the lake to Glaciar Viedma and treks into the surrounding spectacular mountains.

The turquoise Lago Roca overlooked by forests and snowy peaks

For hotels and restaurants in this region see pp283–6 and pp301–2

Flora of Parque Nacional Los Glaciares

Although over half its surface area is cloaked in ice, Parque Nacional Los Glaciares, with three distinct habitats within its borders, also shelters a rich diversity of flora. In its eastern section, the Patagonian steppe is given dashes of color by the flowers of *calafate* and *mata guanaco* shrubs. Heading west the steppe gives way to a transition forest of *ñire* trees and colorful species such as the *Zapatito de la Virgen* flower. In the park's far west

Berries near Glaciar Perito Moreno

this transition zone meets the great Magellanic forest, a humid area that is home to the region's greatest concentration of plant life. Receiving an annual rainfall of 31–79 inches (80–200 cm), this forest is thick with *lenga* trees and, during the southern hemisphere's spring season, dappled with flowers, including five species of orchid. Different species of flora can be sighted along trails that flank glaciers and Mount Fitz Roy.

THE MAGELLANIC FOREST
This forest of southern beech grows upwards from the edges of glaciers and lakes, ascending the slopes of surrounding mountains to an altitude of 3,280 ft (1,000 m). Dominant *lenga* and smaller *coihue* trees are its signature species.

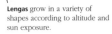

Lengas grow in a variety of shapes according to altitude and sun exposure.

Zapatito de la Virgens *are bell-shaped flowers that decorate trails around Mount Fitz Roy and Cerro Torre.*

Calafates *dot the steppe, with yellow flowers and sweet blueberries. According to myth, whoever eats a calafate berry will return to Patagonia.*

Chilcos *are delicate, intensely-colored flowers that flourish in the shady, damp undergrowth of the Magellanic forest.*

Notro *shrubs thrive in the humid Magellanic forest, blooming red flowers in spring. They are easily sighted on trails.*

White dog orchids *are one of the five species of orchid that adorn the forest floor during springtime.*

TIERRA DEL FUEGO AND ANTARCTICA

The remote archipelago of Tierra del Fuego really does feel like el fin del mundo – the end of the world – where the great Andean mountain range finally meets the sea. Only the continent of Antarctica lies beyond, and the area serves as the main jumping-off point for intrepid travelers eager to glimpse this sparkling, shifting mass of blue and white ice, the world's last great wilderness.

Tierra del Fuego is separated from the rest of South America by the Strait of Magellan. The archipelago consists of a main island, Isla Grande, and a group of smaller islands. Its land mass is divided equally between Argentina and Chile, the border between the two countries running from the Strait in the north to Canal Beagle in the south.

The Strait is named for Portuguese explorer Ferdinand Magellan, who became the first European to discover the archipelago in 1520. He called it Tierra del Fuego (Land of Fire) for the numerous fires he witnessed along its coastline, warning signals from one indigenous tribe to another that something unusual had arrived.

The Selknam, Kaweskar, Manekenk, and Yámana tribes would later draw the attention of English naturalist Charles Darwin, before Anglican missionaries became the first outsiders to settle the region in 1871, near the present-day city of Ushuaia. Sheep farmers followed, together with further missionaries in the form of the Salesians of Don Bosco, who established their mission near what is now Río Grande, the region's biggest city.

Antarctica, the world's coldest and driest continent, sits 620 miles (1,000 km) across the Drake Passage from Ushuaia. For centuries a source of mystery – the ancient Greeks thought it a populated and fertile land, only blocked by monsters – the continent was not discovered until the 1820s. Today, Antarctica is experiencing a tourist boom with up to 30,000 visitors drawn each year to its silent world of icebergs and glaciers, a haven for an astonishing array of marine fauna.

Cormorants crowding the rocks on an island in Canal Beagle, near Ushuaia

◁ Church of the Misión Salesiana, founders of the city of Río Grande

Exploring Tierra del Fuego and Antarctica

Ushuaia is the region's biggest tourist draw, home to some outstanding museums and a gateway to the natural spectacles of Canal Beagle and Parque Nacional Tierra del Fuego, and the ski resort of Cerro Castor. North of Ushuaia, Río Grande is a popular angling destination and site of an historic Salesian mission. In the summer, Ushuaia is the departure point for 10- to 21-day Antarctic cruises to the South Shetland Islands and the Antarctic Peninsula. Longer routes take in the Falkland Islands and South Georgia.

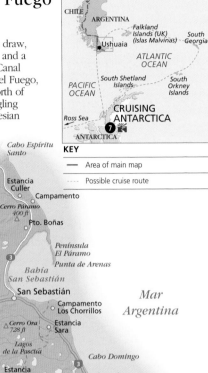

CHILE
ARGENTINA
Falkland Islands (UK) (Islas Malvinas)
South Georgia
Ushuaia
ATLANTIC OCEAN
PACIFIC OCEAN
South Shetland Islands
South Orkney Islands
Ross Sea
CRUISING ANTARCTICA
⑦
ANTARCTICA

KEY

— Area of main map

---- Possible cruise route

SEE ALSO

• **Where to Stay** p287

• **Where to Eat** p303

KEY

▬▬ Highway

— Minor road

-- Track

▬▬ International border

△ Peak

Tourists in a Zodiac landing craft view an iceberg in waters off Antarctica

---

Cabo Espíritu Santo

Estancia Culler
Campamento

Cerro Páramo 400 ft
Pto. Boñas

Península El Páramo
Punta de Arenas

Bahía San Sebastián

Punta Arenas

San Sebastián

Campamento Los Chorrillos

Cerro Ora 728 ft
Estancia Sara

Lagos de la Pascua

Cabo Domingo

Estancia Salvador

Estancia San Julio
Estancia María Behety

Estancia Violeta

Misión Salesiana de la Candelaria

CHILE

Río Moneta

RÍO GRANDE ⑥
Cabo Peñas

Río Grande
Estancia Aurelia

Estancia José Menéndez

TIERRA DEL FUEGO

Estancia La Rosita

Estancia El Rodeo

Estancia Viamonte

Estancia Marina

Pto. Río Apen

Estancia La Porteña

Cabo Santa Inés

Estancia Inés

Estancia Los Cerros
Estancia La Criolla

Estanc Rolito

Pto. La Cumbre

Lago Chepelmuth

Estancia Carmen
Lago Yehuin

Estancia María Cristina

Estancia Ushuaia
Tolhuin

Lago **Fagnano**

PARQUE NACIONAL TIERRA DEL FUEGO

Estancia La Porfiada

⑤
Cerro Martial 3,182 ft
USHUAIA ①

③ CERRO CASTOR

Cerro Cornú 4,888 ft

Cerro Quintar 3,772 ft

Sierra Lucas Bridg

Monte Olivia 4,356 ft
Faro Les Éclaireurs
Las Islas de los Lobos

ESTANCIA HARBERTON

④

Puerto Almanza
Isla Martillo

Estar Mo

CANAL BEAG ②

Mar Argentina

For additional map symbols see back flap

Modern residences fringing the shoreline of the sheltered bay of Ushuaia

SIGHTS AT A GLANCE

Towns and Cities
Río Grande ❻
Ushuaia ❶

National Parks and Areas of Natural Beauty
Canal Beagle ❷
Cruising Antarctica pp264–7 ❼
Parque Nacional Tierra del Fuego ❺

Historic Site
Estancia Harberton ❹

Ski Resort
Cerro Castor ❸

GETTING AROUND
The best way to get around Tierra del Fuego is by air or long-distance bus. Both Ushuaia and Río Grande have international airports; regular bus services run between the two cities (journey time 8 hours) and link both cities to the Argentinian mainland. Journeys to the mainland from the archipelago cross the Argentina-Chile border and foreign passports will be stamped at the border control. Medium-sized icebreakers and ice-proof cruise ships depart from Ushuaia for Antarctica, each with Zodiac landing craft for onshore excursions. Icebreakers also carry on-board helicopters.

0 km   30

0 miles   30

Estancia
María Luisa

Bahía
Thetis

Cabo
San Vicente

Cabo
San Diego

Isla de los Estados

Cabo
San Juan

△ *Monte Bahía*
2,368 ft

Lago Luz

*Bahía
Buen
Suceso*

Península Mitre

Monte Spegazzini
2,431 ft

*Bahía
Blossom*

Estancia
Bahía Aguirre ○

Monte Atocha
3,366 ft

*Estrecho
de le Maire*

*Bahía
Canepa*

*Bahía
Aguirre*

*Cabo Buen
Suceso*

Bahía Sloggett

Ushuaia ❶

Road Map B6. 🏠 60,000. ✈️
🚌 from Río Grande or El Calafate.
ℹ️ Avenida San Martín 674, (02901)
424-550. 🎵 Festival Música Clásica
de Ushuaia (Apr). **www**.e-ushuaia.
com

Situated at the bottom tip of
Isla Grande, Ushuaia is best
reached by air. Coming in to
land over the icy peaks of
Cerro Martial and Monte
Olivia, and the frigid waters of
Canal Beagle, only heightens
one's sense of arrival at the
end of the world.

The city began as a penal
colony in 1884, part of an
Argentinian government plan
to populate their half of the
archipelago as a means of
reaffirming sovereignty. The
colony foundered but the
convicts remained, transferred
to the infamous Ushuaia
prison, which, from 1902 to
1947, housed the country's
most notorious criminals.

Visitors can explore the old
prison at the fascinating
Museo Marítimo de Ushuaia.
Guided tours take in the prison's cramped cells and
recount the crimes of its most
notorious convicts. A separate
section is devoted to Ushuaia's
maritime history, with displays
covering 500 years of navigation. Also good are **Museo del
Fin del Mundo** and **Museo
Yámana**: the former houses

historical and zoological displays, its star exhibit the
rescued figurehead of the
Duchess of Albany, an English
vessel shipwrecked off the
coast in 1883; the latter traces
the history of the region's
indigenous people.

High above Ushuaia, the
beautiful **Glaciar Martial** offers
panoramic views of the city
and Canal Beagle. To reach it,
take the chairlift from **Centro
Recreativo Glaciar Martial**,
before trekking the final
stretch to its base.

🏛 Museo Marítimo de Ushuaia
Yaganes & Gobernador Paz.
Tel (02901) 437-481.
🕙 mid-Dec–mid-Mar: 9am–8pm
daily; mid-Mar–mid-Dec: 10am–8pm
daily. 🖼 📷 mid-Dec–mid-Mar:
10am daily. ♿ 🖥 📷
www.museomaritimo.com

🏛 Museo del Fin del Mundo
Avenida Maipú 175.
Tel (02901) 421-863.
🕙 mid-Dec–mid-Mar: 9am–8pm
daily; mid-Mar–mid-Dec: noon–7pm
Mon–Sat. 🖼 📷 in Spanish only.
♿ 📷

🏛 Museo Yámana
Rivadavia 56. **Tel** (02901) 422-874.
🕙 mid-Dec–mid-Mar: 10am–8pm
daily; mid-Mar–mid-Dec: noon–7pm
daily. 🖼 📷

Centro Recreativo Glaciar Martial
Avenida Luis Fernando Martial.
🕙 10:30am–5:30pm daily. 🖼 🖥
Note: no buses to the chairlift, best
to hire a taxi and walk back down.

Jagged peaks near Ushuaia, seen
from across Canal Beagle

Canal Beagle ❷

Road Map B6. 🚤 Muelle Turístico,
Ushuaia; (02901) 437-666.

Several agencies run tours
by catamaran along the icy
waters of Canal Beagle
(Beagle Channel). Tickets
can be bought at Ushuaia's
Tourist Pier from where
excursions depart. The short-
est of these head for the **Faro
Les Eclaireurs** lighthouse,
before returning via Las Islas
de los Lobos, home to a sea
lion colony, and Las Islas de
los Pájaros with its bird colony. Longer excursions head
out to the 19th-century
Estancia Harberton, still managed by the descendants of
an Anglican missionary who
named the estancia for his
wife's birthplace in England.

Cerro Castor ❸

Road Map B6. Ruta Nacional 3, Km
26.5, 16 miles (26 km) E of Ushuaia.
Tel (02901) 499-302. 🚌 from
Ushuaia. 🕙 mid-June–mid Oct.
🖼 🍴 🖥 📷 ⛷
www.cerrocastor.com

The world's southernmost
ski resort, Cerro Castor boasts
19 slopes with a maximum
drop of 2,532 ft (772 m), the
majority appropriate for
beginner and intermediate
skiers. There is good off-piste
skiing, plus a snowboarding
park and, at the resort's base,
a cross-country skiing circuit
that has a good claim to being
the most scenic in Argentina,
passing through forests thick
with *lenga* beech trees.

The former Government House, Ushuaia

For hotels and restaurants in this region see p287 and p303

Estancia Harberton ❹

Road Map B6. 53 miles (85 km)
E of Ushuaia. *Tel* (02901) 422-742.
☐ *mid-Oct–mid-Apr: 10am–7pm
daily.*

The oldest estancia in Tierra del Fuego, Estancia Harberton was built in 1886 for Anglican missionary Thomas Bridges in return for his pioneering work among the region's native people, which included compiling the first English-Yámana dictionary. His son Lucas continued the literary tradition, writing *The Uttermost Part of the Earth*, an account of a young boy growing up amongst the Yámana.

The family estancia is now run by their descendants and can be reached by road or boat excursion along Canal Beagle. Guided tours take in its extensive gardens, wool shed, boathouse, carpenter shops, and family cemetery. Visitors can also make the boat trip to **Isla Martillo** (or Yecapasela), a nature preserve with colonies of Magellanic and gentoo penguins.

Parque Nacional Tierra del Fuego ❺

Road Map B6. 🚂 *from Ushuaia.*
🛈 *Ruta Nacional 3, Km 3047;
Avenida San Martín 1395, Ushuaia,
(02901) 421-315.* ☐ *24 hours daily.*
📷 ⚠ **Tren del Fin del Mundo**
station off Ruta Nacional 3, 5 miles
(8 km) W of Ushuaia. *Tel* (02901)
431-600. **www**.trendelfindelmundo.
com.ar

Stretching north from Canal Beagle and across Lago Fagnano, this beautiful park was founded to protect 266 sq miles (689 sq km) of *lenga*, *ñire*, and *coihue* woods. The park encompasses lakes, mountains, glaciated valleys, and a pristine sea coast, which form a protective haven for more than 100 bird and mammal species. Numerous trails run through the park; short treks include forest and shoreline walks. Of the more demanding hikes, the trek to **Pampa Alta** offers outstanding

A view along the Río Oyando, Parque Nacional Tierra del Fuego

vistas of the channel. Access to the national park is via road or the **Tren del Fin del Mundo**, a narrow-gauge tourist train that follows the line of the old "Convict Train" used to ferry prisoners into the forest for hard labor.

Río Grande ❻

Road Map B6. 137 miles (220 km)
NE of Ushuaia. 👥 *80,000.* ✈
🚌 *from Ushuaia or Río Gallegos.*
🛈 *Rosales 350, (02964) 431-324.*
www.interpatagonia.com/
riogrande

The largest settlement on Tierra del Fuego, Río Grande is known mainly as a fishing destination due to its proximity to the trout-rich waters of Río Menéndez. Its history dates back to 1893 when the first Salesian missionaries, led by a Monseñor Fagnano, arrived to evangelize the Selknam. Now an agricultural college, the Misión Salesiana can still be visited, where the excellent **Museo Regional Monseñor Fagnano** traces its history and that of the people it aimed to convert.

In town, **Museo de la Ciudad Virginia Choquintel** has displays on the city's past.

Environs
Along the coast from Río Grande is **Estancia Viamonte**, a jewel of a sheep estancia founded in 1902 by the sons of Thomas Bridges, and today run by their descendants. Visitors are sometimes even allowed to stay in Lucas Bridges's bedroom. Named for the founder of the Misión Salesiana, **Lago Fagnano** is the largest lake on Tierra del Fuego and an excellent spot for trout fishing. The tiny village of Tolhuin sits on the lakeshore and is a tranquil base for exploring the area.

🏛 **Museo Regional Monseñor Fagnano**
Misión Salesiana, Ruta Nacional 3,
Km 2800. *Tel* (02964) 421-642.
☐ *mid-Dec–mid-Mar: 10am–7pm
Tue–Sun; mid-Mar–mid-Dec: 9am–
12:30pm & 3–7pm Mon–Fri (8pm
Sat–Sun).* 📷 🎥 *on request.*
www.misionrg.com.ar

🏛 **Museo de la Ciudad Virginia Choquintel**
Alberdi 555. *Tel* (02964) 430-647.
☐ *9am–5pm Mon–Fri, 3–7pm Sat.*
📷 *on request.* ♿

Cruising Antarctica ●
The Subantarctic Islands

Ice-strengthened cruise ships depart from Ushuaia for the vast, white expanse of the Antarctic continent. There are myriad routes to choose from but popular ports of call include the Antarctic Peninsula and the South Shetland Islands and, on longer cruises, the rugged island chains of Subantarctica. Trips explore a breathtaking, silent world of gigantic icebergs, tumbling glaciers, dazzling ice shelves, and marine wildlife that includes numerous species of whales and dolphins, seals and penguins, and millions of marine birds. A human history is palpable too, in the haunting form of abandoned whaling stations and gravesites bearing the names of Heroic Age explorers.

Brightly painted houses around Christ Church cathedral, Stanley

The Falkland Islands (Islas Malvinas)
310 miles (500 km) NE of Ushuaia.
👥 2,913. ✈ weekly flights via Punta Arenas, Chile, and monthly via Río Gallegos. 🚢 from Ushuaia.
ℹ Jetty Visitor Center, (00500) 22215. www.visitorfalklands.com

Surrounded by the cold South Atlantic Ocean and shrouded in controversy throughout their modern history, the Falkland Islands (Islas Malvinas) are a popular stop-off on longer Antarctic cruises. An archipelago consisting of two main islands, East and West Falkland, and several hundred smaller ones, the Falklands attract thousands of visitors each year with marine wildlife that is as prolific as it is spectacular, with over 60 breeding bird species and numerous marine mammals. Easily approached, this fauna is observed in its greatest numbers on small offshore islands such as **West Point Island**, **New Island**, and **Carcass Island**, all essential stops on Subantarctic itineraries. Star attractions include five kinds of penguin,

the rare rockhopper penguin included, and the world's largest breeding populations of black-browed albatross. Offshore, elephant seals, sea lions, fur seals, dolphins, and killer whales roam the waters.

All cruises to the Falklands include a stop at the capital, **Stanley**. Built on a north-facing slope to catch the sun throughout the year and lined with rows of colorful cottages and well-kept gardens, Stanley, with a population of some 2,000, is much more reminiscent of an English village than a capital city. Tours should start at the Jetty Visitor Center by the passenger dock before taking in the main sights, which include the **Falkland Islands Museum**, with displays on the islands' natural and human history; the cathedral and 1982 War Memorial; and Government House, which dates from 1845. The Maritime History Trail tours Stanley Harbor, once an important port of call for vessels crossing Cape Horn and today dotted with hulking shipwrecks. At low tide visitors can explore a number of ships and dive to see others.

Outside Stanley, short excursions include visits to **Gypsy Cove** and **Volunteer Point**, home to large penguin colonies, and to Goose Green, site of fierce fighting in the 1982 Falklands War.

🏛 **Falkland Islands Museum**
Holdfast Road, Stanley. **Tel** (00500) 27428. ⬤ 9:30am–4pm Mon–Fri, 2–4pm Sat–Sun. 🎫 🖼 ♿ 🛍

PLANNING A CRUISE

Cruises (11–13 days) to the Antarctic Peninsula always include the South Shetland Islands. Longer trips (18–20 days) include South Georgia and the Falkland Islands.
Ship types vary, but all are ice-strengthened. Remote Weddell Sea and Ross Sea areas are accessed by icebreaker ships.
Best time to travel is in summer from November to March: days are longer and warmer, and the wildlife more abundant.
See also pp312–13.

THE FALKLAND ISLANDS (ISLAS MALVINAS)

SOUTH ATLANTIC OCEAN

Carcass Island
Gladstone Bay
West Point Island
Roy Cove
New Island
Chartres
West Falkland
Fox Bay East
Port San Carlos
Port Louis
Salvador
Volunteer Point
San Carlos
Gypsy Cove
STANLEY
Port Howard
East Falkland
Goose Green
Mount Pleasant
North Arm
Lively Island
Speedwell Island

0 km   50
0 miles   50

Key to Symbols see back flap

KEY

═══ Main road

– – Track

A blue-colored pinnacle iceberg near Coronation Island, South Orkneys

South Georgia

860 miles (1,385 km) E of the Falkland Islands. **www**.sgisland.org
South Georgia Museum
http://sgmuseum.gs

A dramatic island of soaring, ice-clad mountains and huge glaciers, South Georgia is a haven for an astonishing concentration of marine fauna. The best and most visited wildlife sites are on its more hospitable northern coast, where **Salisbury Plain** and the **Bay of Isles** are home to large rookeries of king penguins, and **Albatross Islet**, a nesting colony of the rare, semi-mythical wandering albatross. Cruise stops also explore the human history of South Georgia, which was a magnet to thousands of seal hunters and whalers in the late 19th and early 20th centuries, though today the island has no permanent population. At **Grytviken** visitors can explore the eerie remnants of an abandoned whaling station, complete with the rusting hulks of several ships slowly sinking into the harbor. Within its grounds are the **South Georgia Museum**, which houses displays on the island's human and natural history, a small restored church, and an old whalers' cemetery. The cemetery includes the gravesite of British explorer Ernest Shackleton, who made the first crossing of South Georgia on the final leg of his rescue of the crew of the stricken *Endurance* (see p267).

South Orkney Islands

574 miles (924 km) SW of South Georgia.

En route from South Georgia to the Antarctic, but much less visited than the other Subantarctic Islands, are the remote South Orkney Islands. Linked to the Antarctic Peninsula by a massive range of submarine mountains, the South Orkneys comprise two large and several smaller islands, each covered in snow and ice and punctuated by barren mountains. Zodiac landings take place on the biggest island in the chain, **Coronation Island**, where Shingle Cove is refuge to a rookery of Adelie penguins and a breeding colony of Weddell seals. Conditions permitting, visits also explore **Laurie Island**, site of an Argentinian meteorological station that has been in operation since 1904.

Macaroni penguins congregating on the shoreline, South Georgia

ANTARCTIC WILDLIFE

The wildlife of the Subantarctic Islands and Antarctica is every bit as breathtaking as the region's stunning landscapes. Biggest of all is the blue whale, the world's largest animal, which visits Antarctica during the summer to feed on abundant krill. Humpback, minke, sei, fin, and orca whales can also be sighted together with several species of dolphin. Onshore, penguins are the greatest attraction: eight different species form breeding colonies, from smaller chinstrap and punk-like macaroni penguins to colorful king and emperor penguins. Seals, including huge elephant seals, crabeater, Weddell, leopard, and fur seals, slumber on ice floes and beaches. On cliff sides, an incredible array of marine birds, from petrels, shags, terns, and skuas to rare species of albatross, gather in nesting colonies. Like most Antarctic fauna, they are best observed in summer, February especially.

Cruising Antarctica
The Antarctic Peninsula

The biggest thrill of any Antarctic cruise is setting foot on the frozen continent itself. The simplest and most popular way of doing so is on routes that explore the Antarctic Peninsula, the northern tip of the Antarctic continent, and the South Shetland Islands, an archipelago of over twenty islands that lies to its north. Onshore excursions to both peninsula and islands enter a magical, blue-white world of hypnotic scale and beauty, in which glaciers, peaks, and abundant marine wildlife vie for attention with gigantic icebergs and haunting historical sites.

LOCATOR

— Area of main map

Paradise Bay *is one of the peninsula's most magical spots, with a backdrop of ice-blue water, glacier-covered islands, and huge floating icebergs. Its waters are visited by humpback and minke whales. Elephant, crabeater, and Weddell seals doze on ice floes.*

Port Lockroy is home to an historic research station and the world's most southerly post office, complete with souvenir shop and museum.

The Lemaire Channel *is Antarctica's most picturesque channel, earning it the nickname "Kodak Gap". Its immense scenery includes sheer-sided, precipitous peaks that rise over 3,000 ft (1,000 m) from the water's edge, hanging glaciers, and deep-blue icebergs of all shapes and sizes.*

Neko Harbor faces a magnificent glacier that calves regularly; the loud crack and boom of tumbling ice can be heard from the beach.

The Ross Sea region can be accessed on extended icebreaker cruises. Helicopter excursions fly over Mount Erebus volcano and the Dry Valleys, one of the world's most extreme deserts.

To Ross Sea

Whale spotting *is best in the Antarctic summer, February especially. Easily observed species include humpback and minke whales. Endangered sei and fin whales can also be sighted.*

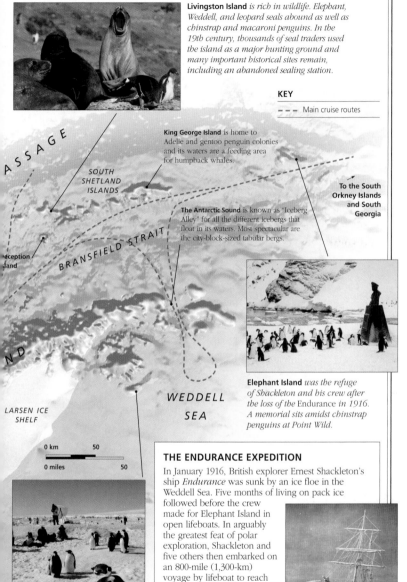

Livingston Island *is rich in wildlife. Elephant, Weddell, and leopard seals abound as well as chinstrap and macaroni penguins. In the 19th century, thousands of seal traders used the island as a major hunting ground and many important historical sites remain, including an abandoned sealing station.*

KEY

--- Main cruise routes

SOUTH SHETLAND ISLANDS

King George Island is home to Adelie and gentoo penguin colonies and its waters are a feeding area for humpback whales.

To the South Orkney Islands and South Georgia

The Antarctic Sound is known as "Iceberg Alley" for all the different icebergs that float in its waters. Most spectacular are the city-block-sized tabular bergs.

A S S A G E

BRANSFIELD STRAIT

eception
land

LARSEN ICE SHELF

WEDDELL SEA

0 km   50

0 miles   50

Elephant Island *was the refuge of Shackleton and his crew after the loss of the* Endurance *in 1916. A memorial sits amidst chinstrap penguins at Point Wild.*

THE ENDURANCE EXPEDITION

In January 1916, British explorer Ernest Shackleton's ship *Endurance* was sunk by an ice floe in the Weddell Sea. Five months of living on pack ice followed before the crew made for Elephant Island in open lifeboats. In arguably the greatest feat of polar exploration, Shackleton and five others then embarked on an 800-mile (1,300-km) voyage by lifeboat to reach the whaling station on South Georgia. Landing on an un-inhabited side of the island, they hiked 36 hours over mountains, glaciers, and cliffs before reaching their goal. Three failed rescue attempts followed before Shackleton finally reached his near-starving men on Elephant Island in August 1916.

Snow Hill Island *is off-the-beaten-track Antarctica. Refuge to a nesting colony of emperor penguins, it is accessed on icebreaker cruise ships that scythe through the pack ice of the Weddell Sea.*

The Endurance **trapped in ice before sinking**

TRAVELERS'
NEEDS

WHERE TO STAY 270–287

WHERE TO EAT 288–303

SHOPPING IN ARGENTINA 304–307

ENTERTAINMENT IN ARGENTINA 308–309

OUTDOOR ACTIVITIES AND SPECIALIZED
HOLIDAYS 310–315

WHERE TO STAY

Tourism is booming across Argentina and there is an abundance of accommodation options to satisfy every taste and budget. At the top end of the range are five-star deluxe hotels, which provide exclusive service and first-class amenities. A quintessentially Argentinian experience, luxury estancias in the country's rural interiors combine bucolic relaxation and breathtaking vistas. International and domestic chain hotels are well represented in urban and tourist destinations, together with a burgeoning boutique hotel scene that offers a more personable and aesthetically-driven alternative. Visitors traveling to national parks can stay at well-equipped campsites, while economical hotel options include modern hostels, cabin complexes, and budget hotels.

Sign outside a guesthouse, Gaiman

The peaceful Hotel El Manantial del Silencio, Purmamarca

GRADINGS

Hotels are graded from one to five stars, although Argentina's classification system differs from the international star system and is often not the best guide to quality, with the exception of five-star hotels. A common anomaly involves a hotel receiving a lower rating than it deserves, often because the local tourist office has not yet upgraded it, or because hotels themselves have opted to stay in a lower category in order to avoid higher taxes. Cabin complexes and *hosterías* (small hotels) are awarded a separate grading of between one and three stars.

PRICING AND BOOKING

Pricing depends greatly on location – hotel rates in Buenos Aires and popular tourist destinations such as

Patagonia's Lake District are higher than those in other parts of the country. At the top end are five-star deluxe hotels, which typically charge US$300 or more per night. These are followed in order of cost by five-star and boutique hotels, four- and three-star hotels, and cabin complexes. At the low end of the price range, hostels and campsites are often better value alternatives to budget hotels.

Exclusive fishing and hunting lodges charge up to US$750 per night. Facilities and services provided include access to the best game areas and helicopter or light aeroplane transport. Outside of this category, most estancias, including working ones in Patagonia and guest ranches in the Buenos Aires province, charge between US$100 and US$200 per night.

Rates vary greatly between low (April to November) and peak season (December to March), when prices rise

considerably, especially at Atlantic beach resorts and in Patagonia's Lake District. Conversely, they tend to drop in Buenos Aires as business travel slows and porteños leave the city for their summer vacations.

Some hotels, since the devaluation of the Argentinian peso in 2002, have operated a dual pricing policy for Argentinian residents and foreign tourists. Foreigners pay more and are charged in US dollars. This is particularly common in Patagonia.

TAXES

Hotels in Argentina charge 21 percent in *Impuesto de Valor Agregado* or IVA (Value-Added Tax or VAT). This tax should be included in the quoted rate, but it is worth checking when booking in order to avoid any unwelcome surprises when checking out. All hotel rates quoted on pages 274–287 include IVA.

The stylish tango-themed Mansión Dandi Royal, San Telmo (see p275)

◁ Vibrantly colored store exterior in the La Boca barrio, Buenos Aires

The lobby of the luxurious Alvear Palace Hotel, Recoleta *(see p276)*

LUXURY HOTELS

Ranging from the palatial and regal to the chic and post-modern, Argentina's luxury hotels are comparable to the best and the most exclusive anywhere in the world. Besides prime locations, they offer spacious, beautifully furnished suites and rooms, first-rate services, and a wide range of amenities. These usually include state-of-the-art conference facilities, spas, swimming pools, modern fitness centers, spacious, well-maintained gardens, boutique shops, and excellent multi-cuisine restaurants.

Depending on location, luxury hotels may also provide access to a marina, golf course or a private beach. It is advisable to make reservations well in advance, especially during Argentina's peak season.

CHAIN HOTELS

There are various Argentinian chain hotels at the mid- and upper ranges of the market, as well as the usual big international names. Local operator **Dazzler Hoteles** has several hotels in the capital and one in Bariloche. **Design Suites**, emphasizing stylish and comtemporary designs, has hotels in El Calafate, Salta, and Ushuaia, as well as Buenos Aires and Bariloche. International chains such as **Starwood**, **Hilton**, **Hyatt**, and **Sofitel** are also well represented in the country.

BOUTIQUE HOTELS

Boutique hotels are becoming increasingly common in design-conscious Argentina. Buenos Aires leads this trend, especially its fashionable Palermo Viejo district, where numerous boutique establishments have opened since 2002, mostly in converted belle-époque houses. These include the lovely 1555 Malabia House *(see p277)*, **Krista Hotel**, and BoBo *(see p277)*. Historical San Telmo, in the city's south, has followed suit: choices here include a 15-room, tango-themed renovated mansion, Mansión Dandi Royal *(see p275)*. Boutique hotels can now also be found in several destinations across Argentina, including major tourist centers such as Salta, Mendoza, and Patagonia's Lake District, where innovative design concepts often fit seamlessly with their surroundings.

"Chain" boutique hotels have also entered the market. The **Esplendor** chain, run by Argentina's Fen Group, has exclusive boutique hotels in Buenos Aires and El Calafate, and is among the most upscale in the country.

HOSTERÍAS

Hosterías are sometimes known as *posadas* and usually house between three and 15 rooms. Room rates vary, depending on the degree of comfort and style provided. At the top end, deluxe *hosterías* offer exclusive luxury and charge accordingly;

lower down the scale, one- to three-star *hosterías* often provide much more welcoming, comfortable alternatives to equivalently priced hotels.

Double room at Che Lulu Trendy Hotel, Palermo *(see p277)*

BUDGET ACCOMMODATION

One- and two-star hotels are usually centrally located within towns and cities. Most include breakfast in their rate and access is either to a *baño compartido* (shared bathroom) or *baño privado* (private bathroom). Many have rooms with ceiling fans and cable TV. Bed linen is provided but guests may have to use their own towels.

Hospedajes and *pensiones* also provide cheap accommodation. The former is a large family home with a few extra bedrooms to spare, while the latter is also a family house offering short-term stays shared between visitors and permanent lodgers.

The Hostería Ave Maria at Tandil in the Pampas region

ESTANCIAS

Estancias can be found all across the Argentinian interior. An increasing number have opened their doors to tourism since the peso's devaluation in 2002. Visitors now have the luxury of choosing from a wide and varied range of options, with architectural styles that include everything from Italianate mansions to adobe haciendas and century-old prefabricated buildings.

There are primarily two types of accommodations available – working and guest estancias. Working estancias remain primarily dedicated to cattle or sheep farming and offer a more authentic ranch experience. Guests take part in farm activities and evening meals are enjoyed together with the owners. Patagonia and Tierra del Fuego have the largest numbers of such ranches. Guest estancias, on the other hand, are dedicated solely to tourism. There are several of these in the Buenos Aires province as well as in the Andean Northwest and Argentinian Mesopotamia. At both types of ranches visitors can enjoy a host of activities that range from horse-riding and fishing to bird-watching, trekking, and biking *(see pp314–15)*.

The spa at Cavas Wine Lodge, Mendoza *(see p282)*

Many estancias have offices in Buenos Aires, where English-speaking staff take bookings and answer queries. The NGO **Estancias de Santa Cruz** handles reservations and enquiries on behalf of many ranches in the Patagonia and Tierra del Fuego regions. **Red Argentina de Turismo Rural** works with estancias in the Buenos Aires province, the Andean Northwest, and Argentinian Mesopotamia. **Estancias Argentinas** also represents estancias in the Buenos Aires province and has a few affiliates in Córdoba and Argentinian Mesopotamia. Specialist travel agencies can also organize estancia stays; **Lan & Kramer Travel Services** is one of the most reputable. Alternatively, visitors can also contact the ranches directly.

BODEGAS

Catering to the luxury travel market, several *bodegas* (wineries) in Argentina's wine-growing regions offer exclusive lodging. Most are located in Mendoza, although some *bodegas* in Salta also feature wine lodges. All boast extraordinary settings and stunning mountain views, and offer insights into the world of viticulture *(see pp208–11)*.

Guests can take part in many activities from wine tastings and vineyard visits to the annual harvest. A growing trend is the incorporation of a wine spa, where treatments are based on grapes and other wine products.

SELF-CATERING AND CABIN COMPLEXES

There are several options for self-catering accommodation. Most cities have apart-hotels, which have standard hotel features, but also larger rooms with a kitchenette and small eating area. In the south of Argentina, *cabañas* (cabin complexes) are extremely common, especially in the Patagonian Lake District. The cabins typically consist of a master bedroom, kitchen, lounge, and spare bedrooms. Most are designed in the style of Alpine log cabins, idylli-cally situated within shaded woods or on river-banks, and well-equipped with phone and cable television. The cabin complexes are ideal for families and anyone wishing to avoid more nondescript, but equivalently priced, three-star hotels.

Living room at Estancia La Bamba in San Antonio de Areco *(see p145)*

RENTED APARTMENTS

For longer stays in Buenos Aires, several agencies specialize in short- and long-term rented apartments for foreign visitors. These apartments are fully furnished with modern appliances. Rents are relatively high, often three times that of an unfurnished apartment, but easily facilitated and with none of the red tape that often precludes renting the latter. **Buenos Aires Travel Rent** and **Buenos Aires Stay** are two well-established rental agencies with over 100 apartments to offer.

YOUTH HOSTELS

Argentina is served by an extensive network of youth hostels such as **Che Lagarto**. Most cities have at least one establishment recognized by Hostelling International (HI), where both rooms and single-sex dorm accommodations are available. Student travel agency, **Asatej**, is the representative of HI in Argentina and makes hostel reservations throughout the country. Enquiries can be made at tourist information offices.

NATIONAL PARKS AND CAMPSITES

There are three types of campsites within Argentina's national parks. The best-

Campsite in Parque Nacional Los Glaciares, Patagonia *(see pp250–55)*

equipped are *camping organizados*, usually located near park entrances. These have hot showers, cooking facilities, laundry services, and supply stores. *Camping agrestes*, located deeper within the parks, are limited to cooking facilities, water supplies, and toilets. The basic *acampe libre* are for hikers exploring remote areas. All three are marked on park maps and on hiking trails. *Refugios* are basic wooden cabins situated on mountain trails within national parks and are used by trekkers or climbers on overnight ascents.

DISABLED TRAVELERS

Few hotels in Argentina have special facilities for disabled travelers. Those that do are mostly in the five-star category and are indicated with

the appropriate symbol in the hotels listings *(see pp274–87)*. In many cases, however, hotels without special facilities will do all they can to accommodate people in wheelchairs by giving them easily accessible, ground-floor rooms (when available), and help with stairs and entering and leaving lifts.

TIPPING

Tipping in Argentina is in proportion with most other parts of the world. Hotel porters who help with bags on arrival are usually given a *propina* (tip) of between US\$1 and US\$2. For waiting staff in hotels it is customary to leave about 10 to 15 percent of the total value of the bill. On checking out it is a good idea to leave a small tip for the cleaning help.

DIRECTORY

CHAIN HOTELS

Dazzler Hoteles
Tel *(011) 5217-5700.*
www.fenhoteles.com

Design Suites
Tel *(011) 5199-7465.*
www.designsuites.com

Hilton
Tel *(011) 4891-0000.*
www.hilton.com

Hyatt
Tel *(011) 5171-1234.*
www.hyatt.com

Sofitel
Tel *(011) 4131-0000.*
www.sofitel.com

Starwood
www.starwoodhotels.
com

BOUTIQUE HOTELS

Esplendor
www.esplendorhoteles.
com

Krista Hotel
Bonpland 1665, Palermo.
City Map 4 C3.
www.kristahotel.com.ar

ESTANCIAS

Estancias Argentinas
Ave Diagonal Pte 616.
Tel *(011) 4343-2366.*

Estancias de Santa Cruz
Maipú 864 3°, Buenos Aires. *Tel* *(011) 5237-4043 (reservations).*
www.estanciasdesanta
cruz.com

Lan & Kramer Travel Services
Florida 868 1°, Capital Federal, Buenos Aires.
Tel *(011) 4312-2355.*

Red Argentina de Turismo Rural
Florida 460, Sede de la Sociedad Rural, Buenos Aires. *Tel* *(011) 4328-0499.* **www**.ratur
estancias.com.ar

RENTED APARTMENTS

Buenos Aires Stay
Tel *(011) 4803-5184.*
www.bastay.com

Buenos Aires Travel Rent
www.buenosaires-
travelrent.com

YOUTH HOSTELS

Asatej
Tel *(011) 4114-7611.*
www.asatej.com

Che Lagarto
Tel *(011) 4343-4845.*
www.chelagarto.com

Choosing a Hotel

The hotels in this guide have been chosen for their excellent facilities and locations. The list covers a range of price categories from budget to exclusive accommodations. Visitors must note that hotel rates vary, being at a premium during the high tourist season in January and February. For map references, see pp126–31.

PRICE CATEGORIES
The price ranges are for a standard double room per night, including taxes, service charges, and breakfast.
$ under $50
$$ $51–$100
$$$ $101–$150
$$$$ $151–$200
$$$$$ over $200

BUENOS AIRES

PLAZA DE MAYO AND MICROCENTRO Gran Hotel Hispano $
Avenida de Mayo 861 *Tel* (011) 4345-2020 *Fax* (011) 4331-5266 *Rooms* 60
Map 3 E5

Stepping inside the old wood-and-glass door of the Gran Hispano takes visitors back to the way hotels were in the capital 50 years ago. Service is personal and rooms are clean and comfortable. Visitors must ask for a room off the street if they want peace and quiet. There is a bar and a coffee shop. **www.hhispano.com.ar**

PLAZA DE MAYO AND MICROCENTRO 725 Buenos Aires $$
Ave Roque Saenz Peña 725 *Tel* (011) 4131-8000 *Fax* (011) 4131-8028 *Rooms* 192
Map 3 E5

Designed by Alejandro Bustillo, this French-influenced neoclassical building has been revamped to appeal to the corporate traveler. It boasts a central location and high-speed Wi-Fi access throughout. The Centrino restaurant serves good Argentinian food and the breakfast buffet is excellent. **www.725buenosaireshotel.com**

PLAZA DE MAYO AND MICROCENTRO Hostería Posta Carretas $$
Esmeralda 726 *Tel* (011) 4322-8567 *Fax* (011) 4394-8372 *Rooms* 90
Map 3 D4

The hotel's name alludes to the old wagon stops that once crisscrossed the country, and the rustic theme – wooden doors, fireplace, lodge-style decor – is rare and refreshing in this urban-obsessed city. The beamed-ceiling restaurant serves Argentinian and Continental dishes, and there is also a cozy bar. **www.postacarretas.com.ar**

PLAZA DE MAYO AND MICROCENTRO La Cayetana Historic House $$
Mexico 1330 *Tel* (011) 4383-2230 *Rooms* 11
Map 3 D5

In a setting of soulless high-rises, this hotel is a refuge from modern Buenos Aires. Set in a beautifully restored 1820s house, the hotel offers rooms that are all designed differently, with names such as *federal*, *caudillo*, and *patriota*, evoking the turbulent days of the civil wars in the 19th century. Buffet breakfast. **www.lacayetanahotel.com.ar**

PLAZA DE MAYO AND MICROCENTRO V&S $$
Viamonte 887 *Tel* (011) 4322-0994 *Fax* (011) 4327-5131 *Rooms* 13
Map 3 E4

Brightly decorated rooms and all the services backpackers need – laundry, Internet, library, kitchen, communal terrace – make this a popular budget choice with young explorers. Accommodation options range from shared dorms to single and double rooms with en suite bathrooms. **www.hostelclub.com**

PLAZA DE MAYO AND MICROCENTRO Broadway Hotel & Suites $$$
Avenida Corrientes 1173 *Tel* (011) 4378-9300 *Fax* (011) 4378-9259 *Rooms* 110
Map 3 D4

Located in the heart of the financial district, this hotel has comfortable rooms and spacious suites which have adopted American film icons as their theme. The suites have sitting rooms, kitchenettes, compact bedrooms, and baths with whirlpool tubs. Facilities include a gym, sauna, and meeting space. **www.broadway-suites.com.ar**

PLAZA DE MAYO AND MICROCENTRO Castelar Hotel & Spa $$$
Avenida de Mayo 1152 *Tel* (011) 4383-5000 *Fax* (011) 4383-8388 *Rooms* 151
Map 3 D5

A classic in the city's political hub, the Castelar is a good-value, traditional, mid-range hotel with lovely views of the bustling Avenida de Mayo from many of its rooms. It has an excellent martini bar and an elegant Turkish spa, along with attentive staff. **www.castelarhotel.com.ar**

PLAZA DE MAYO AND MICROCENTRO Claridge Hotel $$$
Tucumán 535 *Tel* (011) 4314-7700 *Fax* (011) 4314-8022 *Rooms* 152
Map 3 E4

The white portico, high-backed chairs, and mashed potatoes on the menu remind visitors that this is an outpost of Old England. The Claridge Hotel is still a place where foreigners as well as locals like to enjoy afternoon tea or an early gin. Rooms are bright and inviting. **www.claridge.com.ar**

PLAZA DE MAYO AND MICROCENTRO Esplendor de Buenos Aires $$$
San Martín 780 *Tel* (011) 5217-5710 *Fax* (011) 4526-8800 *Rooms* 49
Map 3 E4

Opened as the Phoenix Hotel in the 1900s, this hotel would have been one of the first sights that immigrants saw when getting off the boats at the end of the street. It is much improved after extensive renovation. Rooms are stylishly designed, with abstract paintings and large, comfortable beds. **www.esplendorbuenosaires.com**

Key to Symbols *see back cover flap*

PLAZA DE MAYO AND MICROCENTRO NH Jousten

Avenida Corrientes 280 **Tel** *(011) 4321-6750* **Fax** *(011) 4321-6775* **Rooms** *84*

The best boutique hotel in the downtown area, the Jousten combines cool, minimalist service and an excellent in-house Spanish restaurant. The buffet breakfast is huge, and here on business, the place is casual enough for a drink or a social meeting. **www.nh-h**

PLAZA DE MAYO AND MICROCENTRO Dazzler Tower

San Martín 920 **Tel** *(011) 5217-5799* **Rooms** *88*

Coolly understated decor and helpful staff have made this hotel a popular choice with tourists as well as business visitors. Broadband access is available in all the bedrooms, and holistic massages are offered to help visitors relax after corporate meetings or sightseeing. **www.dazzlertower.com**

PLAZA DE MAYO AND MICROCENTRO Intercontinental $$$$

Moreno 809 **Tel** *(011) 4340-7100* **Fax** *(011) 4340-7199* **Rooms** *309*   **Map** *3 D5*

This 17-story tower has top-notch rooms with high-speed Internet access, minibars, safes, coffeemakers, desks, and king or double beds. Luxurious marble baths are fitted in the en suite bathrooms. Service here is another strength and the staff have good local knowledge. **www.intercontinental.com**

PLAZA DE MAYO AND MICROCENTRO Faena Hotel + Universe $$$$$

Martha Salotti 445, Dique 2, Madero Este **Tel** *(011) 4010-9000* **Rooms** *110*   **Map** *1 F1*

Rooms are simply yet tastefully furnished Art Deco-style, with mirror-paneled cupboards and velvety carpets. Faena offers access to a luxury spa, a small concert venue, an elegant bistro, and a lovely outdoor pool. The library lounge has a roaring fire going in the winter and live music in the evenings. **www.faenahotelanduniverse.com**

PLAZA DE MAYO AND MICROCENTRO Hilton Buenos Aires $$$$$

Avenida Macacha Guemes 351, Dique 3 **Tel** *(011) 4891-0000* **Fax** *(011) 4891-0001* **Rooms** *417*   **Map** *3 F5*

Even when it is buzzing with corporate guests the huge glass and chrome lobby of the Hilton feels spacious. The amenities are deluxe, bedrooms are large, and the pool is possibly the best in town. An unbeatable location to explore Reserva Ecológica Costenera Sur and the Puerto Madero area *(see p75)*. **www.hilton.com**

PLAZA DE MAYO AND MICROCENTRO Hotel Madero $$$$$

Rosario Vera Peñalosa 360, Dique 2, Madero Este **Tel** *(011) 5776-7777* **Rooms** *193*   **Map** *1 E1*

Hotel Madero is chic and understated, with a spacious and serene terrace and a fantastic cocktail bar. This is one of the city's quietest corners, which is ideal for discerning business travelers or families looking for a relaxing stay. **www.hotelmadero.com**

PLAZA DE MAYO AND MICROCENTRO Panamericano $$$$$

Carlos Pellegrini 551 **Tel** *(011) 4348-5000* **Fax** *(011) 4348-5250* **Rooms** *376*   **Map** *3 D4*

This twin-tower establishment has a gym, squash court, massage rooms, juice bar, beauty salon, and a 1,000-seater conference center. There is an English-style pub, a Japanese restaurant that offers good sushi and stunning views, and Tomo I *(see p292)*, which serves excellent international cuisine. **www.panamericanobuenosaires.com**

PLAZA DE MAYO AND MICROCENTRO Sheraton Buenos Hotel $$$$$

San Martín 1225 **Tel** *(011) 4318-9000* **Fax** *(011) 4322-9703* **Rooms** *742*   **Map** *3 E3*

Located in the heart of the city, the Sheraton is a luxury hotel with two pools, tennis courts, and a well-equipped gym. The guest rooms are spacious and tastefully decorated in relaxing pastel colors. The views of the city and Río de la Plata from the top floor are spectacular. **www.sheraton.com**

PLAZA DE MAYO AND MICROCENTRO Sofitel Buenos Aires $$$$$

Arroyo 841 **Tel** *(011) 4131-0000* **Fax** *(011) 4131-0001* **Rooms** *144*   **Map** *3 D3*

Housed in a landmark 1930s building, the Sofitel has grand and luxurious rooms. The bar off the main lounge is crammed with books and dark little corners for lounging. The French and Mediterranean restaurant, Le Sud, has won many followers around town. **www.sofitelbuenosaires.com.ar**

SAN TELMO AND LA BOCA Posada Historica Gotan $

Sanchez de Loria 1618, Boedo **Tel** *(011) 4912-3807* **Rooms** *9*

A lovely tango-themed hotel, the Posada Historica Gotan is located on a street famed for its associations with the dance. All the rooms are clean and well-decorated along contemporary lines, with views across a pretty shaded passageway to the hotel's Italianate patio. **www.posadagotan.com**

SAN TELMO AND LA BOCA Cocker Hotel $$

Avenida Juan de Garay **Tel** *(011) 4362-8451* **Rooms** *5*   **Map** *1 E2*

A beautifully converted San Telmo townhouse, this hotel is named after its owners' pet spaniel. Elegantly decorated with antiques bought at local stores, the rooms are an ideal balance of old-school grandeur and new boutique style. This hotel is a popular choice with San Telmo's gay tourist crowd. **www.thecocker.com**

SAN TELMO AND LA BOCA Mansión Dandi Royal $$

Piedras 922 **Tel** *(011) 4361-3537* **Fax** *(011) 4307-7623* **Rooms** *30*   **Map** *1 D1*

Murals, paintings, and the soundtrack in the lobby are all in line with this self-styled "tango hotel." It offers classes in the adjoining salon and special dance packages for tangophiles. In keeping with the golden age theme, rooms are lavishly appointed with elaborate bedspreads and grand wooden furniture. **www.dandiroyal.com.ar**

...MARTÍN AND RETIRO Aspen Towers

🎁 🍴 🎬 🗐 📶 W $$

...7 Tel (011) 4313-1919 Fax (011) 4313-2662 Rooms 75   **Map** 3 D4

...a major refurbishment in 2006, the services and guest rooms in this long-established hotel have vastly improved. ...ole floors, cool sofas, and mirrored walls are the new look in the luxurious lobby. The in-house restaurant specializes ...n Japanese food and serves a superior breakfast. **www.aspentowers.com.ar**

PLAZA SAN MARTÍN AND RETIRO Lancaster

🎁 🍴 🎬 🗐 🕭 W $$

Avenida Córdoba 405 Tel (011) 4311-3021 Fax (011) 4311-3021 Rooms 105   **Map** 3 E4

A 1940s hotel which boasts inviting public areas and friendly staff. The lobby lounge has velour sofas, a reading area, and an English-style wood-paneled drawing room. A pub-style restaurant offers traditional food while another in-house dining area, Catalina, serves tasty regional dishes. **www.lancasterhotel-page.com.ar**

PLAZA SAN MARTÍN AND RETIRO Milhouse

🗐 🕭 W $$

Hipólito Yrigoyen 959 Tel (011) 4345-9604 Fax (011) 4343-5038   **Map** 3 D5

One of the liveliest, friendliest hostels in town, the Milhouse was constructed at the end of the 19th century using the best building materials from Europe. With a well-equipped laundry room, an in-bound travel agency, and inexpensive dorm rooms, this hotel is ideal for long-term visitors. **www.milhousehostel.com**

PLAZA SAN MARTÍN AND RETIRO Marriott Plaza

🅿 🎁 🍴 🎬 🗐 🕭 W $$$$$

Florida 1005 Tel (011) 4318-3069 Fax (011) 4318-3000 Rooms 320   **Map** 3 E4

A stunning beaux-arts building on Plaza San Martín, this is one of the capital's few grand old hotels. Built in 1909, the Plaza, as it is commonly known, has long been a favorite bedsit of presidents and celebrities. European antiques, leather chairs, and Francophile fittings are backed up with hi-tech amenities. **www.marriottplaza.com.ar**

RECOLETA Art Hotel

🗐 W $$

Azcuenaga 1268 Tel (011) 4821-4744 Rooms 36   **Map** 2 B3

An art gallery, whose exhibits change every month, occupies the entire ground floor of this chic hotel. The rooms all have comfortable beds and the service is efficient and personalized. Although there is no restaurant, a well-stocked bar remains open every afternoon through to late evening. Tango lessons and Jacuzzi available. **www.arthotel.com.ar**

RECOLETA Design Suites & Towers

🅿 🎁 🎬 🗐 🕭 W $$

Marcelo T. de Alvear 1683 Tel (011) 4814-8700 Fax (011) 4814-8700 Rooms 58   **Map** 2 C3

The etched-glass doors of this hotel open onto a chrome lobby with glazed concrete floors and halogen lighting. Public areas and guest rooms are decked out with open closets, white walls, and the latest fixtures from France, Italy, and Tribeca. The room price includes a pass to one of the city's finest health centers. **www.designsuites.com**

RECOLETA Park Châteaux Kempinski

🅿 🎁 🎬 🗐 $$$

Talcahuano 1253 Tel (011) 6777-0400 Fax (011) 6777-0430 Rooms 66   **Map** 3 D5

A highly desirable residence for anyone who wants to be around the Recoleta area, the Park Châteaux Kempinski is tasteful and an unusual blend of baroque and boutique. The service, dining, and guest rooms are faultless, although the public areas may be regarded by some as gaudy. **www.kempinski.com**

RECOLETA Melia Recoleta Plaza

🅿 🎁 🍴 🎬 🗐 🕭 W $$$$

Posadas 1557–59 Tel (011) 5353-4000 Fax (011) 4891-3812 Rooms 57   **Map** 3 D2

A stylish property in Recoleta, the Melia offers excellent personalized service. The guest rooms are well-appointed and attractive. Added-value services include Internet access in the rooms, public areas with speedy Wi-Fi, an excellent buffet breakfast, and access to the gym and spa. **www.meliabuenosaires.solmelia.com**

RECOLETA Alvear Palace Hotel

🅿 🎁 🍴 🎬 🗐 🕭 W $$$$$

Avenida Alvear 1891 Tel (011) 4808-2100 Fax (011) 4804-0034 Rooms 210   **Map** 3 D2

The Alvear Palace (*see p99*) is widely regarded as the best hotel in Buenos Aires. The rooms are opulent and the suites are decorated with antique French furniture and original oil paintings. Food at the L'Orangerie breakfast room or in the French bistro, La Bourgogne, is top-notch. **www.alvearpalace.com**

RECOLETA Caesar Park

🅿 🎁 🍴 🎬 🗐 🕭 W $$$$$

Posadas 1232 Tel (011) 4819-1100 Fax (0800) 0022-3727 Rooms 173   **Map** 3 D3

Slightly cheaper than upmarket competitors, this 18-story hotel located opposite the chic Patio Bullrich mall is ideal for both business and pleasure. Rooms are fitted with expensive pastel fabrics and the decor is subtle and traditional. The in-house Argentinian restaurant, Agraz, is one of the city's best. **www.caesar-park.com**

RECOLETA Four Seasons Hotel

🅿 🎁 🍴 🎬 🗐 🕭 W $$$$$

Posadas 1086 Tel (011) 4321-1200 Fax (011) 4321-1201 Rooms 165   **Map** 3 D3

Opulent and exclusive, the Four Seasons draws rock stars and visiting actors. The lobby bar is well-stocked with champagne, the outdoor pool is Roma-themed, the spa is decorated with Inca motifs, and the in-house restaurant, Galani, serves some of the best Italian food in town. **www.fourseasons.com**

RECOLETA Loi Suites

🅿 🎁 🍴 🎬 🗐 W $$$$$

Vicente Lopez 1955 Tel (011) 5777-8950 Fax (011) 5777-8999 Rooms 112   **Map** 2 C3

A sophisticated hotel with rooms offering views of the Recoleta cemetery (*see pp100–101*). The low-ceilinged lobby has recessed lighting, potted plants, and subtle marble and floral accents. Rooms are crisply contemporary, with gray or buff carpeting, ebony appointments, and sleek Japanese-inspired platform beds. **www.loisuites.com.ar**

Key to Price Guide *see p274* **Key to Symbols** *see back cover flap*

RECOLETA Palacio Duhau Park Hyatt [P] 🍴 🏊 🏋 ▤ ♿ [W] $$$$$

Avenida Alvear 1661 **Tel** *(011) 5171-1234* **Fax** *(011) 5171-1235* **Rooms** *165* **Map** *3 D3*

This luxury hotel is located in the fashionable Recoleta shopping and residential district. Interiors in the public areas are fresh and modern, the spa and gym are among the best in town, and the rooms have high ceilings and polished hardwood floors. An extensive art collection is used to decorate the long corridors. **www.hyatt.com**

PALERMO AND BELGRANO Che Lulu Trendy Hotel 🌳 ▤ [W] $

Pasaje Emilio Zola 5185 **Tel** *(011) 4772-0289* **Rooms** *8* **Map** *5 D4*

Plants and paintings by local artists make this guest house a bright, fun place and its location is both tranquil and ideal for accessing tourist sites in Palermo. Guests can meet in the lounge and relax watching television after a long day of sightseeing. Apartment rentals also available. **www.luluguesthouse.com**

PALERMO AND BELGRANO Posada Palermo 🌳 ▤ ♿ [W] $$

Salguero 1655 **Tel** *(011) 4826-8792* **Rooms** *4* **Map** *5 E4*

Set in a *casa chorizo*, a sausage-shaped house that is Buenos Aires's only original architectural style *(see pp34–5)*, Posada Palermo has warmly decorated rooms done up in rustic orange, red, and purple. All have en suite bathrooms with Wi-Fi access. The common areas are scattered with sofas and bric-a-brac. **www.posadapalermo.com.ar**

PALERMO AND BELGRANO 248 Finisterra 🏊 ▤ [W] $$$

Baez 248 **Tel** *(011) 4773-0901* **Rooms** *11* **Map** *4 C2*

Located in the heart of fashionable Las Cañitas, this stylish boutique hotel is a converted two-story family home built in the 1950s. It has communal areas soaked in natural light, ideal for enjoying a glass of wine or champagne. Decorated in warm pastel colors, guest rooms are simple without being minimalist. **www.248finisterra.com**

PALERMO AND BELGRANO 5 Cool Rooms ▤ ♿ [W] $$$

Honduras 4742 **Tel** *(011) 5235-5555* **Rooms** *17* **Map** *5 D4*

Bare pine floors, stainless steel furnishings, and gravel and bamboo give this minimalist hotel a quiet, Zen-like quality. Three of the rooms have balconies, and all guests have access to 24-hour Wi-Fi. The place has a serene atmosphere and the staff are warm and friendly. **www.fivebuenosaires.com**

PALERMO AND BELGRANO BoBo [P] 🍴 ▤ ♿ [W] $$$

Guatemala 4882 **Tel** *(011) 4774-0505* **Rooms** *7* **Map** *5 D4*

A sophisticated hotel aiming at the young urban traveler, BoBo is very much a part of the hip Palermo bar and dining scene. Each of its rooms is designed with a theme in mind: pop, classic, techno, minimalist, rationalistic, Art Deco, and traditional Argentinian. **www.bobohotel.com**

PALERMO AND BELGRANO Home Hotel Buenos Aires 🍴 🏊 ▤ ♿ [W] $$$

Honduras 5860 **Tel** *(011) 4778-1008* **Fax** *(011) 4779-1006* **Rooms** *17* **Map** *4 C3*

Since opening in 2005, this boutique property has won a number of accolades in designer magazines and become a favorite with both local celebrities and visiting rock stars. All the rooms overlook either the garden, the tree-lined street, or the interior patio. **www.homebuenosaires.com**

PALERMO AND BELGRANO Soho All Suites ▤ ♿ [W] $$$

Honduras 4762 **Tel** *(011) 4832-3000* **Fax** *(011) 4832-3000* **Rooms** *21* **Map** *5 D4*

The accent here is on tasteful boutique and the comfortable suites are painted in a combination of calming pastels and dramatic reds. Along with the well-trained and friendly staff come a range of first-class services such as laptop and mobile phone rental. The hotel's location is excellent for exploring Palermo. **www.sohoallsuites.com**

PALERMO AND BELGRANO 1555 Malabia House ▤ ♿ [W] $$$$

Malabia 1555 **Tel** *(011) 4833-2410* **Fax** *(011) 4832-3345* **Rooms** *15* **Map** *4 C4*

Owned by an interior designer, this former convent has been turned into a stylish boutique hotel. All rooms have queen-size beds and guests have access to small courtyard gardens illuminated by natural light. Note that there is no restaurant, although great eating options are available at nearby Palermo Viejo. **www.malabiahouse.com.ar**

PALERMO AND BELGRANO Costa Petit Hotel 🏊 ▤ [W] $$$$

Costa Rica 5141 **Tel** *(011) 4776-8296* **Fax** *(011) 4776-8294* **Rooms** *4* **Map** *4 C4*

The Costa attempts to recreate the luxurious atmosphere of an old-fashioned family house. It has a tasteful array of bookcases, lush sofas, and handmade furniture. Guest rooms boast circular wall mirrors, large beds, marble baths, and balconies looking out onto the attractive courtyard. **www.costapetithotel.com**

FARTHER AFIELD Casona la Ruchi 🌳 [P] 🏊 $$

Lavalle 557, Tigre **Tel** *(011) 4749-2499* **Rooms** *5* **Road Map** *C3*

An 1891 mock-Tudor mansion built right by the river, Casona la Ruchi offers traditional and comfortable rooms, although visitors have to share the bathrooms. Staying here is rather like living in an old country estancia with rustic Argentinian furnishings – wrought-iron beds and big wooden chairs. **www.casonalaruchi.com.ar**

FARTHER AFIELD Plaza Mayor [P] ▤ [W] $$

Calle del Comercio 111, Colonia del Sacramento, Uruguay **Tel** *(0598) 5227-524* **Rooms** *15* **Road Map** *C3*

Located a boat trip across Río de la Plata in Uruguay, the friendly Plaza Mayor is set in a cozy, colonial-style stone mansion. The rooms are all clean and comfortable and some of the nicest feature crisp all-white linen, comfortable furniture, and smart fittings with exposed stone walls. **www.colonianet.com/plazamayor**

THE PAMPAS

BAHIA BLANCA Hotel Austral

P ⋔ ⊞ ▤ W $$

Avenida Colon 159 **Tel** *(0291) 456-1700* **Rooms** *88*   **Road Map** *C3*

One of the smartest properties in town, this modern hotel is popular mostly with conference organizers and corporate travelers. The spacious lobby, however, doesn't feel officious and the staff are extremely helpful and efficient. The guest rooms are airy and comfortable. **www.hoteles-austral.com.ar**

LA PLATA San Marco Hotel

P ▾ ▤ & W $$

Calle 54 n° 523 **Tel** *(0221) 422-9322* **Rooms** *50*   **Road Map** *C3*

Although this nondescript tower does not look anything special, the lobby service is polite and efficient and the rooms are clean and well-lit, with en suite bathrooms. Some have sweeping views of the city. The hotel also offers gym facilities. **www.sanmarcohotel.com.ar**

MAR DEL PLATA Hotel Amsterdam

P ▤ W $$

Boulevard Maritimo Patricio Peralta Ramos 4799 **Tel** *(0223) 451-5137* **Rooms** *29*   **Road Map** *C3*

Built as a family home in the 1920s, the Amsterdam is one of Mar del Plata's more intimate hotels. The luxury suites are spacious and clean, and there is a sea view from almost every room. Conveniently located for Playa Chica, the landmark Torreón del Monje, and the city golf club. **www.hotelamsterdam.com.ar**

MAR DEL PLATA Sheraton

P ⋔ ≋ ▾ ▤ & W $$

Alem 4221 **Tel** *(011) 414-0000* **Rooms** *191*   **Road Map** *C3*

A modern, mid-rise tower which enjoys great views over the golf club and the beaches of Playa Grande. The rooms are decorated in muted tones, with white bedding and comfortable chairs and sofas. Ten conference rooms means the place draws a substantial number of business visitors. **www.sheratonmardelplata.com.ar**

MIRAMAR Refugio de Mar

P ≋ ▾ & W $$

Avenida 9 n° 749 **Tel** *(02291) 434-115* **Rooms** *22*   **Road Map** *C3*

Perfect to get into Argentina's Atlantic coast beach vibe, these smart, clean cabins are just five blocks from the town center and come with Wi-Fi, maid service, and fridges. Up to six people can sleep in a single cabin, so the deal also works out to be quite economical. **www.refugiodemarmiramar.com.ar**

NECOCHEA Hostería del Bosque

P ⋔ ▤ W $

Calle 89, 350 **Tel** *(02262) 420-002* **Rooms** *12*   **Road Map** *C3*

A pretty French-Basque mansion which has been cleverly reimagined as a comfortable guesthouse. Hostería del Bosque is located in a quiet residential area and has a small garden filled with tumbling bougainvillea and potted plants. Rooms are old-fashioned and romantic, with lots of natural light. Room service available 24 hours. **www.hosteria-delbosque.com.ar**

PINAMAR Hotel Las Calas

P ⋔ ▾ ▤ W $$$

Bunge 560 **Tel** *(02254) 405-999* **Rooms** *16*   **Road Map** *D3*

This lodge-style boutique hotel has simply decorated, spacious rooms with gleaming wooden floors. Dining is in a small bar, which serves an excellent breakfast with bread made on site every morning. The restaurant offers cured meats, wines, freshly baked pizzas, and also special seasonal meals. **www.lascalashotel.com.ar**

SANTA ROSA Hotel Calfucura

P ⋔ ≋ ▤ W $

San Martín 695 **Tel** *(02954) 433-303* **Fax** *(02954) 423-612* **Rooms** *96*   **Road Map** *C3*

Although more than 40 years old, this high-rise hotel still looks smart and gleaming. The rooms are spacious and done up in interesting contemporary designs that make use of traditional Argentinian motifs. There is a decent restaurant and the higher floors afford panoramic views of the city and beyond. **www.hotelcalfucura.com**

TANDIL Lo de Olga Gandolfi

▤ $

Chacabuco 977 **Tel** *(02293) 440-258* **Rooms** *10*   **Road Map** *C3*

This lovely town house, built in 1918, has been fully refurbished and given a bright, vibrant paint job without sacrificing any of its character. Rooms are a little on the small side but they are spotlessly clean and there is an airy common living room with views over the garden. An outdoor barbecue is available for guest use. **www.lodeolgagandolfi.com.ar**

VILLA GESELL Hotel Bahia

P ⋔ ≋ ▾ ▤ & W $$

Avenida 1, n° 855 **Tel** *(02255) 462-960* **Fax** *(02255) 462-838* **Rooms** *32*   **Road Map** *D3*

Although the hotel is housed in a rather unattractive concrete tower, the rooms, painted in lovely pastel shades, offer spectacular views of the sea. They are also equipped with a fridge, television, hair dryer, and all other amenities. There is a small but pleasant spa, a gym, and a highly rated restaurant. **http://hotelbahiavg.com.ar**

VILLA VENTANA Hotel Atero

P ⋔ ▤ $

Cnr Avenida San Martín and Guemes **Tel** *(0291) 491-5002* **Rooms** *12*   **Road Map** *C3*

A small, peaceful three-star hotel that probably offers the most comfortable beds in town. The rooms are simply furnished and have basic amenities that include cable television. Service is friendly, attentive, and courteous. The restaurant serves excellent food and is a huge draw for non-residents as well.

Key to Price Guide *see p274* **Key to Symbols** *see back cover flap*

ARGENTINIAN MESOPOTAMIA

COLÓN Hotel Costarenas ⏹⏹⏹⏹⏹⏹⏹ $$

Avenida Quirós & 12 de Abril **Tel** *(03447) 425-050* **Rooms** *77*   **Road Map** *C2*

A modern spa-hotel, Costarenas is located on the coastal avenue overlooking Río Uruguay. Rooms come with king- or queen-sized beds, and amenities include a state-of-the-art spa and two lounge areas, one with great views of the river and its islands. Rooms with a beach view are worth the extra dollars. **www.hotelcostarenas.com.ar**

CORRIENTES Hotel Turismo ⏹⏹⏹⏹⏹ $

Entre Ríos 650 **Tel** *(03783) 433-174* **Rooms** *43*   **Road Map** *C1*

Built in the Spanish hacienda style, fronting Río Paraná, the Turismo is a delightful retreat. Its cool interior consists of polished wood, chandeliers, spiral staircases, and wide corridors. There is a huge outdoor pool and the atmospheric restaurant is among Corrientes's best. Rooms are great value for money.

ESTEROS DEL IBERÁ Irupé Lodge ⏹⏹⏹⏹⏹ $$

Calle 1 & Ruta Provincial 40, Colonia Carlos Pellegrini **Tel** *(03752) 438-312* **Rooms** *7*   **Road Map** *D2*

Located in Colonia Carlos Pellegrini and constructed on wooden poles on the shores of Laguna Iberá, this lovely lodge has rooms in pastel colors and a large garden with tropical birds. The owners, a Swiss-Argentinian couple, arrange transfers from Mercedes as well as Cessna flights from Iguazú. **www.irupelodge.com.ar**

GUALEGUAYCHÚ Hotel Aguay ⏹⏹⏹⏹⏹⏹⏹⏹ $$

Avenida Costanera 130 **Tel** *(03446) 422-099* **Rooms** *30*   **Road Map** *C2*

Gualeguaychú's top-rated hotel, the friendly Aguay emphasizes river views – 20 of its rooms and the rooftop pool, breakfast bar, and terrace all overlook the adjacent river. Artwork abounds as the owner's mother is a painter; other touches include motion-sensitive lighting on corridors. **www.hotelaguay.com.ar**

PARANÁ Gran Hotel Paraná ⏹⏹⏹⏹⏹⏹⏹ $$

Urquiza 976 **Tel** *(0343) 422-3900* **Fax** *(0343) 422-3979* **Rooms** *120*   **Road Map** *C2*

The Gran Hotel Paraná is ideally located – fronting Paraná's main square and within easy reach of its museums. Rooms come in three price categories, guaranteeing options for both the budget and business traveler. Service is excellent and there is a small spa and gym to relax and work out in. **www.hotelesparana.com.ar**

PUERTO IGUAZÚ Hostería Los Helechos ⏹⏹⏹⏹⏹⏹ $$

Paulino Amarante 76 **Tel** *(03757) 420-338* **Rooms** *60*   **Road Map** *D1*

This charming hideaway has plenty to offer the budget tourist, from a central location and lovely flower-filled garden with a pool to a restaurant that dishes up homemade regional specialities. The decor may be a little dated for some, but all rooms are clean and generously proportioned. **www.hosterialoshelechos.com.ar**

PUERTO IGUAZÚ Hotel Esturión ⏹⏹⏹⏹⏹ $$$

Avenida Tres Fronteras 650 **Tel** *(03757) 421-468* **Fax** *(03757) 420-100* **Rooms** *128*   **Road Map** *D1*

The Esturión's best feature is its fabulous river and rainforest vistas, seen from both the spacious suites and lounge areas. There is also a sloping garden with tropical flora, a large pool, and lovely interior design touches, such as native-bamboo mirror frames and Guaraní-inspired paintings in each of the rooms. **www.hotelesturion.com**

PUERTO IGUAZÚ Hotel Saint George ⏹⏹⏹⏹⏹⏹⏹⏹ $$$

Avenida Córdoba 148 **Tel** *(03757) 420-633* **Fax** *(03757) 420-633* **Rooms** *100*   **Road Map** *D1*

Located at the center of town, the Saint George's signature feature is its outdoor pool, set within a colorful tropical garden and flanked by an outdoor gym and sauna as well as a bar. Spread over five floors, the rooms are simply furnished but comfortable, and overlook either the street or garden. **www.hotelsaintgeorge.com**

ROSARIO Hotel Majestic ⏹⏹⏹⏹⏹ $$

San Lorenzo 980 **Tel** *(0341) 440-5872* **Fax** *(0341) 448-2922* **Rooms** *50*   **Road Map** *C2*

Aptly named, the Majestic is a grand French-style building that dates from 1908. Occupying half a city block, it boasts a delightful façade, lined with lacy iron balconies and topped by an elegant cupola. The renovated, re-equipped interior is very modern and has good-sized, well-priced rooms. **www.hotelmajestic.com.ar**

ROSARIO Ros Tower Hotel ⏹⏹⏹⏹⏹⏹⏹ $$$$

Mitre 299 **Tel** *(0341) 529-9000* **Rooms** *139*   **Road Map** *C2*

The Ros Tower is Rosario's first five-star hotel. Rooms are contemporary, stylish, and excellently equipped. Amenities are fantastic and best of all is the 16th-floor spa, with deck and outdoor heated pool, both of which offer panoramic views of the city, the river, and the Paraná Delta. **www.rostowerhotel.com.ar**

SAN IGNACIO MINÍ Hotel Portal del Sol ⏹⏹⏹⏹⏹ $

Rivadavia 1105 **Tel** *(03752) 470-005* **Rooms** *13*   **Road Map** *D1*

This hotel is a short stroll to the Jesuit ruins. There are ten private rooms, all with television, powerful showers, and firm mattresses, and three dormitories, each sleeping up to six persons. Staff are very helpful and can advise on bus times to Puerto Iguazú. **www.lacarpaazul.com**

CÓRDOBA AND THE ANDEAN NORTHWEST

CAFAYATE Vieja Posada [P] $

Diego de Almagro 87 ***Tel*** *(03868) 422-251* ***Rooms*** *6* ***Road Map*** *B1*

Beautiful, airy Italianate neocolonial *posada* with leafy public areas and elegantly furnished bedrooms. The hotel is just two blocks away from Cafayate's main plaza, and the staff are very helpful when it comes to organizing wine tours or other more active excursions. **www.viejaposada.com.ar**

CÓRDOBA Tango Hostel 🍴 [W] $$

Fructuosa Rivera 70 ***Tel*** *(54351) 425-6023* ***Rooms*** *6* ***Road Map*** *C2*

Simple but spotless hostel with young, enthusiastic managers and a range of rooms, some en suite and others with shared bathrooms. There is also a one-bedroom apartment available for short- and long-term stays. Spanish lessons are on offer and the restaurant has an "any time" breakfast menu, as well as vegetarian food. **www.latitudsurtrek.com.ar**

CÓRDOBA Estancia La Paz [P] ≋ ▤ ♿ [W] $$$

Ruta E66, Km 14, Ascochinga ***Tel*** *(03525) 492-073* ***Fax*** *(03525) 492-073* ***Rooms*** *21* ***Road Map*** *C2*

Once President Julio A. Roca's grand estate, this luxurious estancia-hotel is ideally located for exploring the sierras and Jesuit estancias. Apart from having a pool and solarium on site, the estancia also organizes treks, horse-riding, bird-watching, and fishing trips. There are also a polo and golf course. **www.estancialapaz.com**

CÓRDOBA Dos Lunas 🍴 [W] $$$$

Alto Ongamira, Todos Los Santos ***Tel*** *(011) 156-219-5390* ***Rooms*** *5* ***Road Map*** *C2*

A beautiful, remote country estate high up in the hills, this house is designer rustic, full of gorgeous old furniture, ponchos hanging on the wall, and exquisite antiques. The owners cook wonderful country dishes and give tips on a range of walks in the surrounding region. **www.doslunas.com.ar**

HUMAHUACA Hostal Azúl [P] 🍴 ♿ $

Barrio milagrosa s/n ***Tel*** *(03887) 421-596* ***Rooms*** *8* ***Road Map*** *B1*

Located slightly out of town, Hostal Azúl is set against an awe-inspiring backdrop of rocky mountains. Brightly colored rugs give a splash of colour to this simple and friendly little hotel which has wooden furniture and an array of interesting bric-a-brac. **hostalazul@arnet.com.ar**

MOLINOS Hostal de Molinos 🍴 ≋ $$

Ossa de Montiel ***Tel*** *(03868) 494-002* ***Road Map*** *B1*

A sprawling 18th-century estate, Molinos keeps intact the old Spanish tradition of austere interiors and little decoration. The rooms feature wrought-iron beds handsomely dressed with handwoven blankets. The service is personal and efficient. Molinos is the perfect base for organizing horseback treks. **www.hostalelmolino.net**

PURMAMARCA El Manantial del Silencio [P] 🍴 ≋ [W] $$

Ruta Nacional n° 52, Km 3.5 ***Tel*** *(0388) 490-8080* ***Fax*** *(0388) 490-8081* ***Rooms*** *19* ***Road Map*** *B1*

A former monastery, this hotel has rooms that are minimally yet tastefully decorated. A well-trained chef cooks Andean dishes in the smart restaurant. This place is a favorite with business people from Jujuy, celebrities from Buenos Aires and the US, and even some European royals. **www.hotelmanantial.com.ar**

SALTA Solar de la Plaza [P] 🍴 ≋ 🍸 ▤ ♿ [W] $$$

JM Leguizamon 669 ***Tel*** *(0387) 431-5111* ***Fax*** *(0387) 431-5111* ***Rooms*** *30* ***Road Map*** *B1*

The Solar de la Plaza prides itself on combining personalized, boutique service with an old-style setting. The rooms are decorated with regional handicrafts made from iron, alpaca, and wood, while the restaurant is one of the best in town, offering new takes on Andean recipes. **www.solardelaplaza.com.ar**

TAFI DEL VALLE Hostería Lunahuana [P] 🍴 [W] $

Gobernador Critto 540 ***Tel*** *(03867) 421-330* ***Fax*** *(03867) 421-360* ***Rooms*** *32* ***Road Map*** *B1*

A low-slung colonial-style hotel with well-decorated rooms that are all spacious and painted a simple white. They also have lovely textiles on the walls and antique furnishings. The hotel's restaurant specializes in regional food, such as empanadas, *humitas*, and *tamales*. **www.lunahuana.com.ar**

TILCARA Posada de Luz [P] ≋ ▤ ♿ [W] $

Amrosetti, cnr Alverro ***Tel*** *(0388) 495-5017* ***Rooms*** *6* ***Road Map*** *B1*

A genius for color and design is evident in all the rooms of this delightful hotel – warm, natural pastel hues make the bedrooms and spacious public areas restful. There are large gardens, and cane matting provides shady walkways on the patios. The staff can organize musical evenings and llama rides for guests. **www.posadadeluz.com.ar**

TILCARA Rincon de Fuego [P] 🍴 ▤ ♿ [W] $$

Ambrosetti 445 ***Tel*** *(0388) 495-5130* ***Rooms*** *6* ***Road Map*** *B1*

A stunning boutique hotel that pays homage to life in Quebrada de Humahuaca *(see pp196–200)*. It takes the best from pre-Columbian house designs and Hispanic architecture, and has cane ornaments and rough stone walls. The exceptional restaurant serves vegetables grown in its own organic patch. **www.rincondefuego.com**

Key to Price Guide *see p274* **Key to Symbols** *see back cover flap*

CUYO AND THE WINE COUNTRY

LOS PENITENTES Hotel Ayelen

P ⅠⅠ ⓦ ⓢⓢ

Ruta Nacional 7, Km 165 **Tel** *(0261) 427-1283* **Fax** *(0261) 427-1123* **Rooms** *48* **Road Map** *B2*

A rugged mountain hotel, Ayelen is located near the Penitentes ski area a short distance east of Parque Provincial Aconcagua. Rooms are spacious but plain; the windows are small to conserve heat in winter and hence the views and natural light are limited. In summer, the hotel offers a shuttle service to the park entrance. **www.ayelen.net**

MALARGÜE Hostel Internacional Malargüe

P ⅠⅠ ⓦ ⓢ

Finca 65, Colonia Pehuenche **Tel** *(02627) 470-391* **Rooms** *9* **Road Map** *B3*

A semi-rural hostel with extensive grounds, it has easy access to the elite ski resort of Las Leñas (*see p219*). The dormitories are basic yet comfortable and have private baths and floor heating. The place offers home-made meals, a bar, kitchen access, and rental bikes. The service is friendly and informal. **www.hostelmalargue.net**

MENDOZA Hostel Independencia

▤ ⓦ ⓢ

Mitre 1237 **Tel** *(0261) 423-1806* **Rooms** *8* **Road Map** *B2*

Just steps from the central Plaza Independencia, this immaculately renovated century-old house has crowded dormitory accommodations but more comfortable private rooms. Amenities include a wine bar, barbecue area, and kitchen privileges. Operators arrange vineyard visits and other excursions. **www.hostelindependencia.com.ar**

MENDOZA Hotel Milena

P ▤ ⓢ

Pasaje Babilonia 17 **Tel** *(0261) 420-2490* **Fax** *(0261) 420-2490* **Rooms** *20* **Road Map** *B2*

Modern and central, this cozy hotel's cul-de-sac location ensures quiet despite its proximity to a number of busy roads. The tidy utilitarian rooms are on the small side but are well maintained. Although it lacks a restaurant, the place has a cafeteria and bar, with 24-hour room service. **www.milenahotel.com.ar**

MENDOZA Hotel Puerta del Sol

▤ ♿ ⓦ ⓢ

Garibaldi 82 **Tel** *(0261) 420-4820* **Fax** *(0261) 420-4820* **Rooms** *75* **Road Map** *B2*

A modest but modern downtown hotel, this is just minutes from the Sarmiento pedestrian mall and Plaza Independencia. The rooms have standard amenities and are bright, cheerful, and immaculate. Although the hotel is located near two busy avenues, the huge trees outside it dilute the noise. **www.hotelpuertadelsol.com.ar**

MENDOZA Hotel Balbi

P ⚊ Ⅶ ▤ ♿ ⓦ ⓢⓢ

Avenida Las Heras 340 **Tel** *(0261) 423-3500* **Fax** *(0261) 438-0626* **Rooms** *108* **Road Map** *B2*

A classic high-rise hotel, this place originally opened for the busy wine harvest festival. Rooms and common areas both eschew contemporary design, and furnishings fall short of contemporary style, but everything is well maintained. It has its own gallery, focusing on regional artists, and a chamber music salon. **www.hotelbalbi.com.ar**

MENDOZA Hotel Carollo

P ⚊ ▤ ♿ ⓦ ⓢⓢ

25 de Mayo 1184 **Tel** *(0261) 423-5666* **Fax** *(0261) 423-5666* **Rooms** *50* **Road Map** *B2*

A well-managed business-oriented hotel on a tree-lined street, Carollo is close to restaurants and bars. The carpeted rooms are above average in size, with standard furniture for its price range, while common areas are equally conventional. Centrally controlled air-conditioning requires a call to the front desk. **www.hotelcarollo.com**

MENDOZA Parador del Angel

P ⚊ ▤ ♿ ⓦ ⓢⓢ

Newbery 5418 **Tel** *(0261) 496-2201* **Rooms** *8* **Road Map** *B2*

Set in a century-old adobe building, this bed-and-breakfast place has lush, spacious gardens, and is located in the heart of Mendoza's "gourmet ghetto." The rooms are decorated in rustic style with local artworks and crafts items collected from the owners' travels in northwestern Argentina, Europe, and Asia. **www.paradordelangel.com.ar**

MENDOZA Plaza Italia

▤ ⓦ ⓢⓢ

Montevideo 685 **Tel** *(0261) 423-4219* **Rooms** *4* **Road Map** *B2*

Cozy and quiet but relatively formal, this family-run place has four upstairs bedrooms with antique furniture and contemporary baths. Common areas include the breakfast room and patio. It is centrally located across from Plaza Italia and has easy access to quality restaurants and entertainment. **www.plazaitalia.net**

MENDOZA Hotel Huentala

P ⅠⅠ ⚊ Ⅶ ▤ ♿ ⓦ ⓢⓢⓢ

Primitivo de la Reta 1007 **Tel** *(0261) 420-0766* **Fax** *(0261) 420-0766* **Rooms** *81* **Road Map** *B2*

Centrally located, this hotel has been renovated as a boutique affiliate of the Sheraton chain. The rates are reasonable, but the upgrade has not completely overshadowed its conventional Francophile pretensions in the furnishings and common areas. The subterranean wine bar, however, shows some originality. **www.huentala.com**

MENDOZA Finca Adalgisa

P ⅠⅠ ⚊ ▤ ♿ ⓦ ⓢⓢⓢⓢ

Pueyrredón 2222 **Tel** *(0261) 496-0713* **Fax** *(0261) 496-0713* **Rooms** *11* **Road Map** *B2*

A comfortable semi-suburban hotel, with its own small vineyard, winery, and an excellent tapas restaurant. The renovated adobe house has three rooms, while a newer building in a similar style has larger rooms and suites, some with terraces and views of the pool, vineyard, and surrounding landscape. **www.fincaadalgisa.com.ar**

MENDOZA Cavas Wine Lodge

P ⑪ ♨ ☰ ☰ ⎙ Ⓦ $$$$$

Costaflores s/n **Tel** *(0261) 410-6927* **Rooms** *14*   **Road Map** *B2*

Surrounded by vineyards and views of the Andes, this luxurious new spa hotel is close to Mendoza city. Rooms are free-standing adobes with plunge pools and rooftop terraces, scattered among the vines for maximum privacy. The restaurant *(see p299)*, spa, and other common areas occupy a separate structure. **www.cavaswinelodge.com**

MENDOZA Hotel Termas Cacheuta

P ⑪ ♨ ☰ ⎙ Ⓦ $$$$$

Ruta Provincial 82, Km 38 **Tel** *(02624) 490-152* **Rooms** *16*   **Road Map** *B2*

A traditional spa hotel set among the foothills northwest of Mendoza city, this replaces earlier hotels destroyed by floods. A hydroelectric dam protects the current place, which has modern conveniences on sprawling, finely landscaped grounds, with palms and pepper trees. The rates include full board. **www.termascacheuta.com**

MENDOZA Park Hyatt Hotel

P ⑪ ♨ ☰ ☰ ⎙ Ⓦ $$$$$

Chile 1124 **Tel** *(0261) 441-1234* **Fax** *(0261) 441-1235* **Rooms** *186*   **Road Map** *B2*

Only the neocolonial façade of the original Plaza Hotel remains and this modern luxury hotel, built in its place, makes a modest imprint on the cityscape. Sizeable rooms are contemporary in design; some have lovely city and Andean views. A soaring atrium lobby makes brilliant use of natural light. **www.mendoza.park.hyatt.com**

SAN AGUSTÍN DEL VALLE FÉRTIL Hostería Valle Fértil

P ⑪ ♨ ☰ ☰ ⎙ $$

Rivadavia 1510 **Tel** *(02646) 420-015* **Rooms** *38*   **Road Map** *B2*

A modest hilltop resort hotel set in extensive grounds within a scenic village with access to the wild backcountry of Sierras Pampeanas. The plain rooms have kitchen and barbecue facilities. The hotel makes a good base for excursions to Ischigualasto *(see p217)* and Talampaya *(see p185)*. **www.alkazarhotel.com/vallefertil**

SAN JUAN Hostel Argentina

☲ ⑪ ☰ ⎙ Ⓦ $

Avenida Cordoba 317 **Tel** *(0264) 420-1835* **Rooms** *7*   **Road Map** *B2*

Along with dorm accommodation and attractive common areas, this spacious old hotel also has private rooms and secluded garden apartments. Although the meals are unremarkable, the restaurant has a good stock of underrated local wines. The friendly staff helps arrange excursions. **www.sanjuanhostel.com**

SAN JUAN Hotel Alkázar

P ⑪ ♨ ☰ ☰ ⎙ Ⓦ $$

Laprida 82 Este **Tel** *(0264) 421-4965* **Fax** *(0264) 421-4977* **Rooms** *104*   **Road Map** *B2*

Popular with business travelers, this modern high-rise hotel is located in downtown San Juan. Except for the spacious suites, the rooms are smaller than one might expect in a place with a four- or five-star rating. The efficient staff is experienced in dealing with international clientele. **www.alkazarhotel.com.ar**

SAN JUAN Hotel Termas de Pismanta

P ⑪ ♨ ☰ ☰ ⎙ $$

Ruta Nacional 150 **Tel** *(02647) 497-091* **Fax** *(02647) 497-092* **Rooms** *34*   **Road Map** *B2*

Although well past its prime, this hot springs hotel, primarily visited by retired Argentinians, retains a certain 1950s charm. Inexpensive thermal baths are complemented by diverse spa services, and a moderately priced decent restaurant. The staff are efficient and friendly. **www.hotelpismanta.com.ar**

SAN LUIS Hotel Aiello

P ⑪ ♨ ☰ ☰ $$

Avenida Presidente Illia 431 **Tel** *(02652) 425-609* **Fax** *(02652) 425-694* **Rooms** *61*   **Road Map** *B2*

An architecturally undistinguished mid-range hotel, Aiello has ample rooms and comfortable, conventional furniture. The relatively small windows, however, allow limited natural light. The busy yet quiet location is an easy walk from San Luis's restaurant and pub district. Computer room available for guest use. **www.hotelaiello.com.ar**

SAN RAFAEL Hotel Jardín

☲ P ⑪ ☰ ⎙ Ⓦ $

Avenida Hipólito Yrigoyen 283 **Tel** *(02627) 434-621* **Fax** *(02627) 434-621* **Rooms** *27*   **Road Map** *B3*

Despite the kitschy pseudo-colonial exterior, this is a well-managed and comfortable hotel. The downstairs rooms, however, are fairly dark. Although it faces a busy avenue, the hotel has a large peaceful patio to relax in. The breakfast is forgettable, but low rates make it an excellent value meal. **www.hoteljardinhotel.com**

SAN RAFAEL Tower Inn & Suites

P ⑪ ♨ ☰ ☰ ⎙ Ⓦ $$

Avenida Hipólito Yrigoyen 774 **Tel** *(02627) 427-190* **Fax** *(02627) 436-947* **Rooms** *96*   **Road Map** *B3*

The tallest hotel in Mendoza province, this provides the city's only full-service accommodations. Frequented by business travelers, this modern building took 35 years to complete after construction commenced in 1966. In addition to standard amenities, it has a casino and a spa with sauna. **www.towersanrafael.com**

TUNUYÁN Bodega Salentein

P ⑪ ☰ ☰ Ⓦ $$$$$

Emilio Civit 778 **Tel** *(0261) 441-1000* **Fax** *(0261) 423-8565* **Rooms** *8*   **Road Map** *B3*

A secluded guesthouse located on the grounds of its namesake winery *(see pp210–11)*, Salentein offers spectacular Andean views, hiking, horse-riding, and its own trout-stocked pond. Guests can tour and taste at the subterranean winery, which has its own ground-level art gallery and restaurant *(see p300)*. **www.salenteintourism.com**

USPALLATA Gran Hotel Uspallata

☰ ⎙ Ⓦ $$

Ruta Nacional 7, Km 1149 **Tel** *(0261) 420-4820* **Fax** *(0261) 420-4820* **Rooms** *74*   **Road Map** *B2*

A handsome renovated structure, Hotel Uspallata has comfortable no-frills rooms, but the sprawling grounds, with rows of towering poplars, are the star in a scenic area where *Seven Years in Tibet* was filmed. The hotel's most unusual feature is a four-lane bowling alley. **www.granhoteluspallata.com.ar**

Key to Price Guide *see p274* **Key to Symbols** *see back cover flap*

PATAGONIA

ALUMINÉ Hotel Pehuenia 🌳 [P] 🍴 ♿ [W] $

Ruta Provincial 23 & Capitán Crouzeilles **Tel** *(02942) 496-340* **Rooms** *42* **Road Map** *B4*

All rooms at the charming and rustic Pehuenia have Andean vistas, though a few extra dollars means river views too. Amenities and services include a large communal lounge, quiet reading room, and, for anglers, fly shop and fishing guides. The staff also arrange rafting, horse-riding, and trekking trips. **www.hotelpehuenia.com.ar**

BARILOCHE Hotel Quillén [P] [W] $

Avenida San Martín 415 **Tel** *(02944) 422-669* **Fax** *(02944) 422-669* **Rooms** *28* **Road Map** *B4*

Located in the city center, the Quillén (Strawberry Fields) is the pick of Bariloche's budget hotels. On its fourth floor there is a small spa, with staff at hand to give therapeutic massages, while a third of the rooms have uninterrupted lake views. The hotel has English-speaking staff. **www.hotelquillen.com.ar**

BARILOCHE Hostería Costas del Nahuel [P] 🏊 [W] $$

Avenida Bustillo 937 **Tel** *(02944) 439-919* **Rooms** *15* **Road Map** *B4*

An excellent value inn, this *hostería* is located on the shore of the lake, and a brief walk from Centro Cívico. All rooms are en suite; there is a communal lounge and an outdoor pool close to the lake. The poolside terrace is perfect for breakfasts and barbecues. The helpful staff can arrange excursions and car rental. **www.costasdelnahuel.com.ar**

BARILOCHE Hotel Tres Reyes [P] [W] $$$

Avenida 12 de Octubre 135 **Tel** *(02944) 426-121* **Fax** *(02944) 424-230* **Rooms** *53* **Road Map** *B4*

On Bariloche's coastal avenue, one block from the main drag, this pleasant mid-range choice has light, large, and comfortable rooms, some with beautiful lake views. Furnishings and decor are somewhat dated, but there is a quiet private garden at the back of the hotel as well as an inviting lounge area. **www.hoteltresreyes.com**

BARILOCHE Design Suites Bariloche [P] 🍴 🏊 🍸 ♿ [W] $$$$

Avenida Bustillo, Km 2.5 **Tel** *(02944) 457-000* **Fax** *(02944) 457-000* **Rooms** *54* **Road Map** *B4*

Built in a strikingly contemporary design, Design Suites faces the lake and has spacious, stylish standard rooms with mountain views and suites with lounge Jacuzzis and extraordinary lake vistas. Facilities include indoor and outdoor pools. A shuttle service runs downtown and to ski slopes in the winter. **www.designsuites.com**

BARILOCHE Kenton Palace [P] 🍴 🍸 ▤ ♿ [W] $$$$$

Morales 338 **Tel** *(02944) 456-654* **Rooms** *72* **Road Map** *B4*

Well located one block from Bariloche's Centro Cívico and about two from Lago Nahuel Haupi, this glossy hotel has bright, spacious double rooms. Most of them have great lake views and all are decorated in relaxing creamy tones. The excellent amenities include a spa and a restaurant serving regional cuisine. **www.kentonpalace.com.ar**

BARILOCHE Villa Huinid Resort & Spa [P] 🍴 🏊 🍸 [W] $$$$$

Avenida Bustillo, Km 2.6 **Tel** *(02944) 523-523* **Fax** *(02944) 523-523* **Rooms** *73* **Road Map** *B4*

A few minutes from downtown Bariloche, Villa Huinid is idyllically located overlooking Lago Nahuel Huapi. Each of its rooms is light, modern, and tastefully decorated. Facilities include an indoor pool, children's playroom, and spa. Guests can also rent one of 12 mountain-style cottages. **www.villahuinid.com.ar**

COMODORO RIVADAVIA Austral Plaza Hotel [P] 🍴 🏊 🍸 ▤ ♿ [W] $$

Moreno 725 **Tel** *(0297) 447-2200* **Rooms** *164* **Road Map** *B5*

Popular with business travelers and tourists, the Austral has generously sized, thickly carpeted, and excellently equipped double rooms. Elegant suites come with sea views, Jacuzzi, and superior hardwood furnishings. There is also a first-rate restaurant and a brand new pool and spa. **www.australhotel.com.ar**

COMODORO RIVADAVIA Comodoro Hotel ▤ [W] $$

9 de Julio 770 **Tel** *(0297) 447-2300* **Fax** *(0297) 447-3363* **Rooms** *105* **Road Map** *B5*

The Comodoro was the hotel of choice for visiting oil executives when it first opened in 1976. Today, it is a little frayed around the edges but is still a good medium-budget choice, with simply furnished but spacious and clean rooms spread over eight floors. It also has a convenient downtown location. **www.comodoro-hotel.com.ar**

EL BOLSÓN La Posada de Hamelín 🌳 [P] $

Int. Granollers 2179 **Tel** *(02944) 492-030* **Rooms** *4* **Road Map** *B4*

For a fairytale trip to El Bolsón, book a stay at this enchanting *posada*. Everything is warm and welcoming, from the ivy-clad exterior to the wooden furnishings and charming rooms, each distinct in decor, each with its own private bathroom. Home-made breakfasts are delicious; the owners are very hospitable. **www.posadadehamelin.com.ar**

EL BOLSÓN Hotel Amancay [P] 🍴 ♿ $$

Avenida San Martín 3207 **Tel** *(02944) 492-222* **Rooms** *16* **Road Map** *B4*

This rustic hotel is located two blocks from the town center and boasts a spectacular backdrop formed by the Andes mountain range. The atmosphere is tranquil and the hotel cozy and inviting. There is a full restaurant and bar, and breakfast is prepared with home-baked goods. Room service available. **www.hotelamancaybolson.com.ar**

EL CALAFATE Hostería Los Nires
P W $

9 de Julio 281 **Tel** *(02902) 493-642* **Rooms** *7*   **Road Map** *B6*

Three blocks from the main avenue, the quiet, cabin-like Los Nires has simple, warm rooms, five of which are doubles. All are carpeted – important in the winter months – and come with tasteful wood furnishings. Perhaps the best feature is the lounge area with a roaring open fireplace and snug sofas.

EL CALAFATE Hostería Schilling
    $$

Gob. Paradelo 141 **Tel** *(02902) 491-453* **Fax** *(02902) 491-453* **Rooms** *21*   **Road Map** *B6*

A little jewel of an inn, this *hostería* has stacks of character. Standard doubles are a throwback to the 1970s with faded, flowery wallpaper; superior rooms cost more but are modern. Communal spaces include a garden and patio shaded by tall pine trees, and a comfortable lounge and television area. **www.hosteriaschilling.com.ar**

EL CALAFATE Los Canelos
P $$$

Pto. San Julián 149 **Tel** *(02902) 493-890* **Rooms** *10*   **Road Map** *B6*

One of several hotels to open on the picturesque Altos de Calafate hillside at the edge of town, this stands out for its attractive Alpine design and warm, rustic interior. Visitors can choose from ten small but snug rooms, six with vistas of Lago Argentino, and also enjoy the flower-filled, landscaped garden. **www.loscanelos.com**

EL CALAFATE Design Suites
P $$$$$

Calle 94 No 190, Playa Lago Argentino **Tel** *(02902) 494-525* **Rooms** *60*   **Road Map** *B6*

Located on a peninsula fronting Lago Argentino, Design Suites combines fabulous location with striking design. Rooms come with steppe view or, for a few dollars more, stunning floor-to-ceiling lake vistas. Amenities include a heated pool, a spa, and art gallery. Shuttles make the 10-minute trip to town. **www.designsuites.com**

EL CALAFATE Posada Los Alamos
P $$$$$

Ing. Hector Mario Guatti 1350 **Tel** *(02902) 491-144* **Rooms** *144*   **Road Map** *B6*

This exclusive hideaway at the heart of El Calafate is just two blocks from the town's main avenue. It has tennis courts, a spa, and even a three-hole golf course with a lake challenge. Very family friendly with baby-sitting service and children's pool. Rooms are light, airy, and supremely comfortable. **www.posadalosalamos.com**

EL CHALTÉN Nothofagus B&B
    $$

Hensen esq Riquelme **Tel** *(02962) 493-087* **Rooms** *7*   **Road Map** *A5*

A small place with a warm, homely feel, Nothofagus has blue clapboard walls and timber roofing. Of the seven rooms, six are doubles, three with private bathrooms. The staff provides a laundry service and can prepare tasty, filling lunchboxes for day treks into Parque Nacional Los Glaciares.

EL CHALTÉN Hostería El Puma
P $$$

Lionel Terray 212 **Tel** *(02962) 493-095* **Fax** *(02962) 493-017* **Rooms** *12*   **Road Map** *A5*

Owned by a local mountaineer, this charming, upscale inn has tastefully decorated rooms, all rustically calming with bare-brick walls, wooden beams, stripped floorboards, and valley views. Communal areas include an atmospheric lounge with open fireplace and a first-rate restaurant. **www.hosteriaelpuma.com.ar**

EL CHALTÉN Posada Lunajuim
P $$$

Trevisán 45 **Tel** *(02962) 493-047* **Fax** *(02962) 493-047* **Rooms** *20*   **Road Map** *A5*

An attractive mountain inn, this has a boutique feel, with distinct and well-designed rooms. Visitors should ask for one of four rooms with views of Mount Fitz Roy, or for a more spacious room in the hotel's newer wing. Other features include a lounge area with a well-stocked library and a decent restaurant. **www.posadalunajuim.com.ar**

EL CHALTÉN Los Cerros
P $$$$$

San Martín s/n **Tel** *(02962) 493-182* **Rooms** *44*   **Road Map** *A5*

Standard doubles at this impressive, and very exclusive, mountain lodge come with king-sized beds, hydromassage baths, and wide views of the Río de las Vueltas valley. The service is excellent and there is a gourmet restaurant with yet more fantastic vistas, as well as a spa and a full outdoor excursion program. **www.loscerrosdelchalten.com**

ESQUEL Hotel Sol del Sur
P $$

9 de Julio 1094 **Tel** *(02945) 452-189* **Fax** *(02945) 452-427* **Rooms** *53*   **Road Map** *B4*

Central and modern, the Sol del Sur makes up in amenities what it lacks in character. Its in-house agency arranges fishing and skiing trips and there is a well-stocked ski shop. Rooms are good value but the best feature is the breakfast bar with panoramic views of the city and mountains. **www.hsoldelsur.com**

ESQUEL Cumbres Blancas
P $$$

Avenida Ameghino 1683 **Tel** *(02945) 455-100* **Rooms** *20*   **Road Map** *B4*

With hillside views, Cumbres Blancas (Snowy Summits) is a lovely *hostería* with warmly decorated, elegantly furnished rooms. Amenities include a restaurant specializing in regional cuisine and a large private garden with a small lake, putting green, and its own colony of wild rabbits. **www.cumbresblancas.com.ar**

GAIMAN Hostería Gwesty Tywi
P $

M D Jones 342 **Tel** *(02965) 491-292* **Rooms** *6*   **Road Map** *B4*

A block and a half from Gaiman's main street, this warm, family-run inn has comfortable rooms and lots of communal space that includes a lounge area, a pleasant, flower-filled garden, and a sun terrace with tables for alfresco drinks. The friendly staff can arrange excursions and transfers. **gwestywi@yahoo.com.ar**

GAIMAN Hostería Ty Gwyn
P ⅋ ▤   Ⓢ
9 de Julio 111 **Tel** *(02965) 491-009* **Rooms** *4*   **Road Map** B4

Housed within the teahouse of the same name, this lovely little place is owned by Welsh-speaking descendants of Gaiman's first settlers. There are two double and two single rooms; all open onto a balcony with views of Río Chubut. Delicious home-made breakfasts are served in the teahouse. **www.tygwyn.com.ar**

JUNÍN DE LOS ANDES Hostería Chimehuin
P ♿   Ⓢ
Coronel Suarez & 25 de Mayo **Tel** *(02972) 491-132* **Fax** *(02972) 492-503* **Rooms** *23*   **Road Map** B4

The Chimehuin consists of four separate whitewashed buildings, the oldest of which is 60 years old. Amazingly, given its economical rates, the inn overlooks a running stream and private islet, accessible only to guests. A small number of balconied rooms have views of both features. **www.interpatagonia.com/hosteriachimehuin**

LOS ANTIGUOS Hostería Antigua Patagonia
P ⅋ 📺 ▤   Ⓢ
Ruta Provincial 43, Acceso Este **Tel** *(02963) 491-038* **Rooms** *16*   **Road Map** B5

Located close to the center of Los Antiguos, this hotel fronts the shore of Lago Buenos Aires. Rooms come with views of both lake and snowcapped cordillera and include standard facilities such as central heating, television, and private bathrooms. The staff can arrange fishing, horse-riding, and trekking trips. **www.antiguapatagonia.com.ar**

NEUQUÉN Hotel Suizo
P ▤ ♿ W   ⓈⓈ
Carlos H. Rodriguez 167 **Tel** *(0299) 442-2602* **Rooms** *50*   **Road Map** B4

Warm, family-run, and centrally located, the Suizo is really two hotels in one, with rooms spread over old and new sections of the same house. The latter are marginally more expensive although they are all bright, spacious, and well-appointed, and come with broadband and Wi-Fi facilities. **www.hotelsuizo.com.ar**

NEUQUÉN Hotel del Comahue
P ⅋ ♨ 📺 ▤ W   ⓈⓈⓈ
Avenida Argentina 377 **Tel** *(0299) 443-2040* **Fax** *(0299) 447-3331* **Rooms** *99*   **Road Map** B4

Used mostly by visiting business executives, the Comahue is Neuquén's premier hotel and boasts an outdoor pool, gourmet restaurant, stylish wine bar, and well-equipped gym. Modern rooms and suites receive lots of natural light and are spotlessly clean. The service is consummately professional. **www.hoteldelcomahue.com**

PENINSULA VALDÉS Hostería The Paradise
P ⅋ ▤ ♿ W   ⓈⓈⓈⓈ
2° bajada al mar, Puerto Pirámides **Tel** *(02965) 495-003* **Fax** *(02965) 495-030* **Rooms** *12*   **Road Map** C4

Located in the peninsula's only village, this romantic little hideaway sits just yards from rugged beach, sandy cliffs, and stunning marine fauna. Rooms are rustically cool with bare-brick walls, tiled floors, and lovely views. The staff can arrange marine safaris, horse-riding, diving, and sand-boarding excursions. **www.hosteriaparadise.com.ar**

PERITO MORENO Hotel Belgrano
P ⅋   Ⓢ
Avenida San Martín 1001 **Tel** *(02963) 432-019* **Rooms** *25*   **Road Map** B5

Popular with backpackers, Hotel Belgrano has basic but comfortable single and double rooms as well as dormitories. The owners can advise on bus timetables and visits to Cueva de las Manos. Bruce Chatwin, the British author who wrote *In Patagonia*, stayed here while journeying across the region. **www.hotelbelgrano.com**

PUERTO DESEADO Hotel Los Acantilados
P ⅋ ▤ ♿ W   Ⓢ
España 1611 **Tel** *(0297) 487-2167* **Rooms** *40*   **Road Map** B5

Perched on a cliff above the port area, Los Acantilados offers Puerto Deseado's best accommodation. More than half the rooms come with wide vistas of Río Deseado. The spacious suites have nice touches such as power showers and full-length dress mirrors. **www.pdeseado.com.ar/acantour**

PUERTO MADRYN Hostería Hipocampo
▤ P   Ⓢ
Vesta 33 & Boulevard Alte. Guillermo Brown **Tel** *(02965) 473-605* **Rooms** *10*   **Road Map** B4

A small gem of an inn, Hipocampo is situated on a corner of the coastal avenue, a short walk from downtown Puerto Madryn. The reception area has a lovely, pebbled marine garden; three rooms have vistas of Golfo Nuevo in which whales can be seen between June and October. **www.hosteriahipocampo.com**

PUERTO MADRYN Hotel Bahía Nueva
P ♿ W   ⓈⓈ
Avenida Roca 67 **Tel** *(02965) 451-677* **Rooms** *40*   **Road Map** B4

A traditionally styled lobby, with tall bookcases, open fireplace, and big sofas sets an inviting tone for this mid-range hotel. Standard doubles are well-equipped and presentable, if a little small; for a little extra visitors can choose one of four spacious suites with ocean views. Tasty home-made breakfasts are a plus. **www.bahianueva.com.ar**

PUERTO MADRYN Yene Hue Hotel & Spa
P ⅋ ♨ 📺 ▤ ♿ W   ⓈⓈⓈⓈ
Avenida Roca 33 **Tel** *(02965) 471-496* **Rooms** *64*   **Road Map** B4

The Yene Hue is a superbly equipped hotel with heated outdoor pool, modern gym, and a spa with masseurs on hand to remove the knots that traveling has put in. Spacious, thickly carpeted rooms come with ocean or city views, plus a balcony depending on the price category. **www.australiset.com.ar**

PUERTO MADRYN Hotel Territorio
P ⅋ 📺 ▤ ♿ W   ⓈⓈⓈⓈ
Boulevard Alte. Guillermo Brown 3251 **Tel** *(02965) 470-050* **Fax** *(02965) 471-524* **Rooms** *36*   **Road Map** B4

The Territorio has raised the standard of hotel design in Patagonia. Stylishly modern, it pays homage to the town's past with a stone and aluminium façade that is symbolic of the city's pioneer-era homes. Inside, beautifully appointed rooms boast ocean vistas, as do the lounge and dining areas. **www.hotelterritorio.com.ar**

PUERTO SAN JULIÁN Hotel Ocean 💳 [P] $

Avenida San Martín 959 **Tel** *(02962) 452-350* **Rooms** *13* **Road Map** *B5*

On San Julián's main avenue, Hotel Ocean is a good budget to mid-range option. Rooms are brightly painted and come with private bathrooms, television, and firm beds. The staff are helpful and very friendly, although the building itself may seem somewhat unattractive as it was originally home to a hospital clinic. **hocean959@yahoo.com.ar**

RÍO GALLEGOS Hotel Comercio [P] ♿ [W] $$

Avenida Roca 1302 **Tel** *(02966) 420-209* **Rooms** *53* **Road Map** *B6*

The paint may be peeling from its façade but the Comercio is still an excellent hotel. Grand columns and concertina-doored lifts remain from its glorious past, but extensive refurbishment of its interior has added more modern flourishes, and the rooms are some of the best in town. **www.hotelcomercio.informacionrgl.com.ar**

SAN MARTÍN DE LOS ANDES Le Village [P] ☰ ♿ [W] $$

General Roca 816 **Tel** *(02972) 427-698* **Fax** *(02972) 427-020* **Rooms** *23* **Road Map** *B4*

Located in the center of town, this Swiss-inspired building impresses with its warm lobby and open fireplace, timber beams, and *lenga* wood furnishings. This rustic decor is repeated throughout the hotel. Along with rooms, guests can rent one of five well-equipped six-person cabins. **www.hotellevillage.com.ar**

SAN MARTÍN DE LOS ANDES Cerro Abanico 💳 [P] 🍴 ≋ $$$

Ruta 7 Lagos, Km 4.5 **Tel** *(02792) 423-723* **Rooms** *8* **Road Map** *B4*

A boutique hotel, this place has a privileged location within Parque Nacional Lanín *(see p237)*. Rooms are stylishly minimalist, with distinctive color schemes. The ones on the second floor offer better views of Lago Lácar. The terrace and large, sloping garden also enjoy great vistas. There is also an apartment available for up to five people.

SAN MARTÍN DE LOS ANDES Le Chatelet [P] 🍴 ≋ 🍸 ♿ [W] $$$$

General Villegas 650 **Tel** *(02972) 428-294* **Rooms** *31* **Road Map** *B4*

Perhaps the most impressive of San Martín's many Alpine-inspired hotels, Le Chatelet has light, airy rooms ornamented with Mapuche weavings and *lenga*-wood carvings. Amenities include a spa, with beauty and massage treatments, kids' playroom, and outdoor pool. The staff can arrange excursions. **www.hotellechatelet.com.ar**

SAN MARTÍN DE LOS ANDES Ten Rivers & Ten Lakes Lodge [P] 🍴 $$$$

Circuito Arrayan, Km 4 **Tel** *(011) 5917-7710* **Fax** *(011) 4962-8995* **Rooms** *4* **Road Map** *B4*

A beautiful, secluded mountain lodge, this place sits halfway up Cerro Arrayán, a short drive from town. There are four suites, each of which opens onto a private veranda with incredible vistas of Lago Lácar and the snow-topped Andes. Adjacent to the lodge is the century-old Arrayán teahouse. **www.tenriverstenlakes.com**

TRELEW Hotel Touring Club [P] [W] $

Avenida Fontana 240 **Tel** *(02965) 425-790* **Fax** *(02965) 425-790* **Rooms** *30* **Road Map** *B4*

Butch Cassidy and the Sundance Kid, several Argentinian presidents, and author Antoine de Saint-Exupéry all stayed at the Touring Club in its early 20th-century heyday. Now a little faded, it is nonetheless a splendid budget choice, with a grand staircase, atmospheric bar, and bright double rooms. **www.touringpatagonia.com.ar**

TRELEW Hotel Rayentray 🍴 [W] $$

San Martín 101 **Tel** *(02965) 434-702* **Fax** *(02965) 435-559* **Rooms** *110* **Road Map** *B4*

Trelew's best-equipped hotel, the centrally located Rayentray has spacious, well-appointed rooms as well as a heated pool, spa, and restaurant that serves international cuisine. Staff can arrange excursions to Punta Tombo *(see p228)* and Península Valdés *(see pp226–7)*, as well as free airport transfers. **www.cadenarayentray.com.ar**

VIEDMA Hotel Austral [P] 🍴 ☰ ♿ [W] $

25 de Mayo & Avenida Villarino **Tel** *(02920) 422-615* **Rooms** *100* **Road Map** *C4*

The choice of former President Raul Alfonsín when he visited, the Austral is the most modern of Viedma's hotels and is the only one that overlooks the city's best feature, Río Negro. Generously sized rooms come with views of the river, as do the comfortable lounge and dining areas. **www.hoteles-austral.com.ar**

VILLA EL CHOCÓN La Posada del Dinosaurio [P] 🍴 ☰ [W] $

Costa del Lago, Barrio 1 **Tel** *(0299) 490-1200* **Fax** *(0299) 490-1201* **Rooms** *8* **Road Map** *B4*

The most outstanding feature of this guest house is its stunning location on the shores of the Ezequiel Ramos Mexía lake. Modern rooms come with balconies overlooking the jade-colored water, as does the spacious lounge area. Its restaurant is the best in town, serving trout and pasta specialities. **www.posadadinosaurio.com.ar**

VILLA LA ANGOSTURA Hostería Posta de los Colonos [P] [W] $$

Los Notros 19 **Tel** *(02944) 494-390* **Rooms** *20* **Road Map** *B4*

A rustically styled lobby sets the tone for this friendly, family-run hotel, situated at the heart of Villa La Angostura's small town center. Rooms are a little on the small side, but nonetheless snug, homely, and cabin-like, with low timber-beamed ceilings. Visitors should ask for one with vistas of Cerro Bayo. **www.postaloscolonos.com.ar**

VILLA LA ANGOSTURA Hostería La Escondida [P] 🍴 ≋ 🍸 [W] $$$$

Avenida Arrayanes 7014 **Tel** *(02944) 475-313* **Rooms** *14* **Road Map** *B4*

A lovely boutique hotel with a secluded location on the shores of Lago Nahuel Huapi, La Escondida has beautifully appointed rooms with stunning lake views. Amenities include a small spa, an outdoor heated pool close to the lake, and a gourmet restaurant, splendidly housed in a century-old cottage. **www.hosterialaescondida.com.ar**

Key to Price Guide *see p274* **Key to Symbols** *see back cover flap*

TIERRA DEL FUEGO AND ANTARTICA

LAGO FAGNANO Hostería Kaikén

P ⑪ 🗏 🔥 W $$

Ruta Nacional 3, Km 2942 **Tel** *(02901) 492-372* **Fax** *(02901) 492-372* **Rooms** *20* **Road Map** *B6*

Sitting on the forested shores of Lago Fagnano, this appealing inn is located close to Tolhuin village. The rooms are modestly furnished and come with lake views. The staff can arrange transfers to and from airports in Ushuaia and Río Grande, as well as boat, horse-riding, and bird-watching excursions. **www.hosteriakaiken.com.ar**

RÍO GRANDE Hotel Federico Ibarra

P ⑪ 🗏 W $

Rosales 357 **Tel** *(02964) 430-071* **Rooms** *35* **Road Map** *B6*

Ideally situated on the main plaza, the Ibarra is Río Grande's single three-star hotel. Rooms are fairly modern, if a little bare, and all have cable television and private bathrooms. Visitors should choose one with a view of the square or a quieter room towards the back of the hotel. **www.federicoibarrahotel.com.ar**

RÍO GRANDE Hotel Villa

P ⑪ 🗏 W $

Avenida José de San Martín 281 **Tel** *(02964) 424-998* **Rooms** *10* **Road Map** *B6*

A good budget choice, this downtown hotel is centrally located, if slightly frayed at the edges. Rooms come reasonably sized, with cable television and private bathrooms, and there is broadband Internet access in the lobby. There is also a well-equipped apartment for guests willing to pay extra. **hotelvilla@live.com**

RÍO GRANDE Hostería Posada de los Sauces

P ⑪ 🗏 🔥 W $$

Elcano 839 **Tel** *(02964) 430-868* **Rooms** *23* **Road Map** *B6*

A charming *posada*, this place is a more pleasant alternative to Río Grande's many nondescript hotels. One block from the ocean and three from the city center, it has homely rooms, a recommendable restaurant, and a snug, atmospheric bar that comes with timber ceilings and an open fireplace. **www.posadadelossauces.com.ar**

USHUAIA Hostería Pioneros del Sur

🔥 W $$

Avenida Maipú 1453 **Tel** *(02901) 433-911* **Rooms** *6* **Road Map** *B6*

Located on the coastal avenue opposite the bay, the good-value Pioneros del Sur has brightly painted double rooms, each with hydromassage baths to unwind in after a hard day's trekking within Parque Nacional Tierra del Fuego *(see p261)*. The communal lounge has cable television and views of Ushuaia Bay. **www.pionerosdelsur.com.ar**

USHUAIA Hotel Cap Polonio

⑪ W $$

Avenida San Martín 746 **Tel** *(02901) 422-140* **Fax** *(02901) 422-131* **Rooms** *30* **Road Map** *B6*

Named for the first tourist boat to arrive in the bay in 1923, the Cap Polonio is a family-orientated hotel in the city's main area. Rooms are functional but lacking in charm and intimacy: more welcoming is the friendly staff, who help organize excursions. Amenities include a children's playroom. **www.hotelcappolonio.com.ar**

USHUAIA Hotel Tierra del Fuego

⑪ 🔥 W $$

Gobernador Deloqui 198 **Tel** *(02901) 424-901* **Fax** *(02901) 424-902* **Rooms** *43* **Road Map** *B6*

This downtown hotel emphasizes tranquillity with salmon-pink and beige tones predominating along with lots of native wood – a soothing combination after a long day outdoors. Around half of the rooms have bay views and all are very spacious and well equipped. **www.tierradelfuegohotel.com**

USHUAIA Hotel Los Naranjos

⑪ ⑪ 🔥 W $$$

Avenida San Martín 1446 **Tel** *(02901) 435-862* **Fax** *(02901) 435-873* **Rooms** *27* **Road Map** *B6*

It's difficult to miss the honeycomb façade of this smart hotel on Ushuaia's main avenue. It's just as difficult to deny the hotel's attractiveness: from the mustard and orange hues of its interior to its generously proportioned rooms. Most have vistas of Canal Beagle and the rest offer views of the Andes. **www.losnaranjosushuaia.com**

USHUAIA Hotel del Glaciar

P ⑪ 🔥 W $$$$

Avenida Luis Fernando Martial 2355 **Tel** *(02901) 430-640* **Fax** *(02901) 430-636* **Rooms** *124* **Road Map** *B6*

Located close to the city center, this elegant option overlooks Glaciar Martial. Rooms come with vistas of the bay or glacier and are well-designed and have comfortable king-sized double beds. The hotel has lounge areas decorated in Patagonian-ranch style and a gourmet restaurant. **www.hoteldelglaciar.com**

USHUAIA Los Acebos Ushuaia Hotel

P ⑪ 🔥 W $$$$

Avenida Luis Fernando Martial 1911 **Tel** *(02901) 424-234* **Rooms** *62* **Road Map** *B6*

Perched on a forested hilltop, adjacent to sister hotel Las Hayas, the more modern, and economical, Los Acebos boasts comparable views of the bay and Canal Beagle. Warm, comfortable rooms come in muted tones and are thickly carpeted and generously sized. The staff are pleasant and professional. **www.losacebos.com.ar**

USHUAIA Las Hayas Resort Hotel

P ⑪ 🏊 ⑪ 🔥 W $$$$$

Avenida Luis Fernando Martial 1650 **Tel** *(02901) 430-710* **Fax** *(02901) 430-719* **Rooms** *90* **Road Map** *B6*

Built in the style of a French château, overlooking Ushuaia from a hilltop location, the sumptuous Las Hayas has regally decorated, beautifully equipped rooms, and first-class facilities. Rooms come with bay or mountain views, while amenities include a spa, squash court, and an excellent restaurant *(see p303)*. **www.lashayashotel.com**

WHERE TO EAT

The people of Argentina are as passionate about good food and drink as they are about life, music, and tango. Their culinary tastes have evolved over the years and now incorporate a variety of world cuisines. The definitive dining experience, however, is still to be found at a neighborhood *parrilla* (steakhouse). Roadside *parrillas* are

Bar sign at a museum

located all across Argentina, offering a country-style family barbecue experience. Here, meat is propped up on stakes, roasted around a fire, and served alfresco. In this diverse country, it is possible to catch a quick bite at a chain burger or pizza outlet and still find places to enjoy the wide variety of ethnic cuisines of the Old World.

An established and popular *parrilla* serving grilled meats

PARRILLAS

Sprinkled throughout the country, *parrillas* (steakhouses) are the most popular eating places in Argentina. Typically, a visit starts off with a plate of bites, often tasty mini empanadas (stuffed pastry) and a glass of red wine, before moving on to *chorizo* (flavorful sausage), a portion of provolone cheese, and assorted offal. The main meal follows, almost always a grilled steak, accompanied by a side order of salad.

Parrillas often do grilled salmon, and some offer vegetarian alternatives. Desserts are fruit, ice cream, or perhaps a crème caramel. The main point of eating at a *parrilla* is to stretch out the eating experience and chat a lot between courses. If a *parrilla* is packed, it probably means it is really good, and the bustle and the banter is all part of the general bonhomie that makes this Argentinian institution so special.

BARS AND CONFITERÍAS

After the *parrilla*, the other institution that every barrio must have is a bar. In Argentina, this means a "café-bar" and it is a good place for meeting friends and chatting with family members. As well as coffee and juices, most café-bars serve toasted sandwiches, *medialunas* (sweet croissants), and liquor.

For a more substantial salad or steak sandwich, visitors should go to a *confitería* – a larger café with more tables, longer menus, and sadly, often less atmosphere. During the last decade, these classic ancient bars and *confiterías* have been joined by a wave of dimly lit cocktail and wine bars, and although ideal for a night out, they tend to target a younger crowd of drinkers.

CHAIN RESTAURANTS

During the 1990s, American and European trends began to wear away at Argentina's rather grand old dining traditions. Although failing to completely win over the Argentinian youth, chain burger outlets and pizzerias grew in popularity. There was a boom in what is known as the *tenedor libre* (free fork). These "all-you-can-eat" restaurants offer a fixed price menu and tend to be locally owned chains that follow a basic

formula. Most of the dishes are spread out in a self-service buffet. Some of the smarter local chains also offer grilled meat, pastas, and even Chinese food. Like the global franchises, these local chain restaurants lack atmosphere, but they are cheap and offer great vegetarian options as the food is on show and can be checked for meat.

EATING HOURS

In Argentina, eating between 9 and 10pm is normal and between 10pm and midnight is completely acceptable. Most restaurants close very late while *confiterías* and cafés are open from dawn to dusk, often for 24 hours.

Lunch and breakfast are served at the usual times. Many people grab breakfast en route to work, while lunch in the office areas brings out thousands of staff between 1 and 3pm.

A bustling local restaurant, Buenos Aires

A cluster of busy pavement cafés on a pedestrianized street in Sarmiento, Mendoza

PRICES AND PAYING

At *tenedor libre* (all-you-can eat buffet) restaurants and at many small eateries serving fixed menus, prices are generally lower than in smarter eating places. Prices on menus do not usually show the obligatory 21 percent IVA (*Impuesto al Valor Agregado*, the Argentinian equivalent of VAT or Value-Added Tax). In addition, some of the more upscale restaurants in Buenos Aires and other tourist areas charge a *cubierto* (cover charge) of $2–$3 per person. Service charge is almost never included in the bill, and a typical tip would be 10 to 12 percent of the bill, left on the table or handed to the waiter.

Credit cards can be used in most restaurants, with Visa and MasterCard being the most popular, but in far-flung provinces or villages off the beaten track, it is important to have some cash on hand. Traveler's checks may be accepted in big hotels or restaurants.

WHEELCHAIR ACCESS

In big cities, upmarket restaurants will have ramps or designed access to suit all diners. Elsewhere, however, hardly any eateries make special provision for wheelchair users. That said, Argentinian waiting staff are generally helpful and will do everything short of knocking down a wall to open a door and make a diner feel welcome. In the capital, restaurants in newly developed areas such as Puerto Madero *(see p75)* are adapted for wheelchair users.

CHILDREN

Argentinians, as a rule, adore children and, much to the chagrin of couples and peace-loving singles, restaurants will happily accommodate families with two or three noisy infants. Big *parrillas* and upscale restaurants will have high chairs, but there is rarely room for maneuvering prams. Child portions are usually available, but visitors can ask for a spare plate and dish out a portion from their meal.

FOOD HYGIENE

In well-visited areas of Argentina, food hygiene and health standards are generally good. Visitors should drink

A chef cooking fresh *paella* at a street fair, Buenos Aires

purified water, bottled carbonated water, or *gaseosas* (soft drinks) if they are wary of the water. Bottled water is available in *kioskos*, hotels, bars, and service stations. Avoid salads and uncooked vegetables in the smaller towns and villages in the subtropical regions and in villages that are less visited. Shellfish and seafood on the coast are generally fresh and well-washed, but treat open-air markets and roadside vendors with caution.

VEGETARIANS

Vegetarian restaurants are not common in Argentina and it is important to insist *No como carne* (I do not eat meat). Vegetables are grown across the country, so most restaurants will have fresh squash, salad, potatoes, and other roots. Fruit is abundant and cheap. *Tenedor libre* restaurants often offer a range of salads and vegetarian dishes in their buffets, which means diners can see clearly what they are getting.

SMOKING

A non-smoking law for all restaurants and bars in the country came into place in 2006. However, in 2008, the law was amended to allow restaurants in Buenos Aires to establish smoking sections. All other provinces continue to operate a blanket non-smoking rule in all public bars and eateries.

The Flavors of Argentina

Argentinians really do eat the best and biggest steaks on the planet, and the *asado* (open-air barbecue) is an important community ritual as well as a delicious meal. Other meats, especially lamb and pork, are also integral to the national diet, sometimes described as *cocina criolla* (Creole cuisine). Fish is less popular, despite the extensive coastline and large hake and squid reserves of the south Atlantic. A few vestiges of the pre-Columbian kitchen have survived, and corn (maize) remains an important ingredient in the kitchens of the Andean Northwest.

Freshly picked corn

Rounding up a herd of cattle on an estancia

CENTRAL ARGENTINA AND THE PAMPAS

The cattle-grazing heartland is around Buenos Aires, and some of the best beef is sold to smart *parrillas* in the capital. As well as prime cuts of beef, most *parrillas* offer spicy pork and blood sausages and a range of *achuras* (offal) such as sweetbreads, kidneys, and tripe. An *asado* has the same fare, cooked outdoors over a wood fire and often served on a *brasero* (coal-heated platter). *Provoleta* (grilled provolone cheese) is also served, and accompaniments include a *criolla* salad of lettuce, onions, tomato, and piquant *chimichurri* (sauce of red peppers, herbs, and garlic). In winter, the favorite traditional dish is a warming stew called *locro*.

THE NORTHWEST

The cuisine of the Andean Northwest often features grilled goat's meat and, in specialty restaurants, the meat of the llama. There is superb trout in the rivers of the Córdoba sierras, and the German colonists brought a taste for cured meats with them – often washed down with beer from a local microbrewery. Traveling

Beefsteaks — Provoleta cheese — Chimichurri sauce — Morcilla (blood sausage) — Sausages — Criolla salad — Salami, cheese, and olives

Some of the elements of a typical Argentinian *asado*

EVERYDAY EATING IN ARGENTINA

Street food and finger food are very popular in Argentina – two iconic snacks are *choripán* (pork sausage sandwich) and empanadas, which can be baked or fried and stuffed with anything from ground beef to corn to plums and Roquefort. Café society is important in the cities, with coffee accompanied by delicate sandwiches *de miga* (slices of ham and cheese on ultra-thin bread), and sweet pastries. All towns have cooks of Italian descent, and pizzas (often served with a slice of *fainá*) are excellent. Almost everywhere visitors will see locals tucking in to basic pasta dishes, *milanesas* (veal and chicken cutlet), grilled hake, *criolla* salads, empanadas, and barbecued meat. These are the staples of everyday Argentinian eating, and they are usually delicious.

Oregano, basil and garlic

Pizza con fainá *is a cheese-laden pizza accompanied by slices of* garbanzo *(chick-pea) pancake called* fainá.

Preparing an *asado* for hardworking and hungry gauchos

PATAGONIA AND TIERRA DEL FUEGO

Many specialties of the south, such as fine lamb, were introduced by colonists. Cured meats are popular and, in most Andean regions, platters of venison and wild boar are typical appetizers. The huge coast is the source of culinary riches such as *centolla* (spider crab), hake and shrimp dishes, and paellas. In Chubut, the Welsh community serves scones and *torta galesa* (fruit cake) in colorful teahouses.

farther north, visitors are more likely to be offered pre-Columbian staples such as tamales (corn wraps, stuffed with ground meat and onion) and *humitas* (steamed corn wraps sometimes containing cheese). Quinoa is starting to appear on menus promoting regional cuisine. Desserts often feature local conserves, made from *cayote* (sweet pumpkin) and *tuna* (prickly pear), perhaps served with goat's cheese or a mild cow's milk cheese.

THE NORTHEAST

This is the region for grilled fish such as *pejerrey*, dorado, and *surubí*. The meat of the caiman and capybara, the latter considered an acquired taste, are served in some rural eateries. The subtropical climate promotes an abundance of fruits, and fruit-based sauces accompany meat and fish dishes. *Mandioca* (cassava) is used instead of wheat for empanadas, and rice, grown across the wetlands, is often served in place of potatoes.

Fresh trout caught in the clear waters of the Córdoba sierras

ON THE MENU

Alfajor Cookie sandwich filled with *dulce de leche*, a toffee-flavored milk jelly.

Empanadas Semi-circular stuffed pastries.

Matambre Pork flank or skirt steak, usually grilled.

Medialuna Sweet croissant served in many cafés.

Milanesa con papas fritas Veal or chicken schnitzel with French fried potatoes.

Ñoquis Potato dumplings traditionally eaten on the 29th of the month.

Pulpo a la Gallega Octopus in oil with hot red pepper and coarse salt, usually served with potatoes in the Galician style.

Ubre Cow's udder – only to be found on the most gaucho-friendly menus.

Cazuela de Mariscos, *a dish of Spanish origin, is made with mussels and clams, baked in herb tomato sauce.*

Locro, *a stew of beans, pork, potato, corn, and squash, is traditionally eaten on May 25 – Independence Day.*

Flan *is a light crème caramel dessert to which Argentinians often add whipped cream or dulce de leche.*

Choosing a Restaurant

The restaurants in this guide have been selected for their atmosphere, location, facilities, and value. Reservations are advisable, especially in the cities. All restaurants are non-smoking, apart from in Buenos Aires where smoking is allowed within a specified area. Entries are arranged alphabetically within price categories by area.

PRICE CATEGORIES
The price ranges are for a meal for one, including tax and service charges and a half bottle of house wine.

$ under $7
$$ $8–$15
$$$ $16–$25
$$$$ $26–$35
$$$$$ over $35

BUENOS AIRES

PLAZA DE MAYO AND MICROCENTRO Status [V] $$
Virrey Cebellos 178, Congresso ***Tel*** *(011) 4382-8531* **Map** *2 C5*

A simple dining room, this restaurant is one of the best in town for authentic Peruvian cuisine. The food is tasty and reasonably priced. The specialties here include *ceviche* (marinated seafood salad), *papa a la huancaína* (potatoes in cheesy sauce), and *sancochos* (stews).

PLAZA DE MAYO AND MICROCENTRO Cantina Pierino [V] $$$
Lavalle 3499 ***Tel*** *(011) 4864-5715* **Map** *2 A4*

Run by the original owner's grandson, this restaurant was once a favorite of tango legends such as Astor Piazzolla and Anibal Troilo. Serving authentic Italian food that is good value for money, Cantina Pierino offers home-made pastas, *milanesas* (veal cutlets), baked aubergine, and other popular dishes.

PLAZA DE MAYO AND MICROCENTRO Restó $$$$$
Montevideo 838 ***Tel*** *(011) 4816-6711* **Map** *2 C4*

Argentinian chef Guido Dassi cooks delicious fish, beef, and chicken dishes. The menu changes seasonally and diners must remember to make reservations on Thursday and Friday nights. The wine list is carefully selected and customers also have the option to bring their own drinks ($13 corkage). Closed Sat & Sun.

PLAZA DE MAYO AND MICROCENTRO Tomo I [V] $$$$$
Hotel Panamericano, Carlos Pellegrini 521 ***Tel*** *(011) 4326-6695* **Map** *3 D4*

One of Buenos Aires's best restaurants, this sophisticated temple of haute cuisine is located in the Panamericano *(see p275)* and owned by the Concaro sisters. All dishes are lovingly prepared and the pastas come particularly recommended. Their wine list is high-end and exclusive. Although rather expensive, Tomo I is definitely worth a try.

SAN TELMO AND LA BOCA El Desnivel $$
Defensa 855 ***Tel*** *(011) 4300-9081* **Map** *1 E1*

One of San Telmo's best *parrillas* and extremely popular with visitors, El Desnivel is a classic neighborhood steakhouse. Most of the dishes on the menu are inexpensive, service is friendly, and waiters are quick with the orders. As it is usually crowded at the weekend, it is advisable to go early or book in advance.

SAN TELMO AND LA BOCA Il Matterello $$
Martin Rodriguez 517 ***Tel*** *(011) 4307-0529* **Map** *1 E3*

One of the few classic Italian eateries, this restaurant is located near La Boca's warehouses and port offices. Pastas are perfectly *al dente* and sauces are simple but tasty. The menu includes lasagna, ravioli, tagliatelle, and pasta dishes, and desserts such as tiramisu and *postre de la nonna* (grandma's sweet).

SAN TELMO AND LA BOCA Miramar $$
Avenida San Juan 1999 ***Tel*** *(011) 4304-4261* **Map** *1 E1*

Spanish omelet, *rabo de buey* (oxtail dish), and other Spanish standards are the trademarks of the Miramar restaurant. Their wine store has a good selection. A light lunch option of Spanish tortilla, shrimps, or their frog legs Provençal is fabulous.

SAN TELMO AND LA BOCA Comedor Nikkai [V] $$$
Avenida Independencia 732, cnr Piedras ***Tel*** *(011) 4300-5848* **Map** *1 D1*

Official eatery of the local Japanese community, Comedor Nikkai serves some of the best sushi in Buenos Aires. Apart from sushi, the place is well known for its fish, seaweed, and Japanese tempura and yakitori dishes, and quality is always assured. Located in a vibrant area, Nikkai is an atmospheric place to dine.

SAN TELMO AND LA BOCA La Brigada $$$
Estados Unidos 465 ***Tel*** *(011) 4361-4685* **Map** *1 E1*

A cut above San Telmo's other steakhouses, La Brigada prides itself on old-fashioned, formal service and excellent *achuras* (offal) such as *chorizo* (spicy sausages), *morcilla* (blood sausage), and crispy *chinchulines de chivito* (knots of intestine) as well as big steaks. The Don Pedro (ice cream, walnuts, and whiskey) is a must for dessert.

SAN TELMO AND LA BOCA L'Embruix
Chile 812 esq Piedras **Tel** *(011) 4342-5687*

Map *1 D1*

Chef Karina Navarro and her husband brought their successful restaurant, L'Embruix, from Barcelona to Buenos Aires. Dishes inspired by the flavors of Catalonia and the Mediterranean, including *fideuà* (noodle paella) and *canalones Catalanes* (ground beef or chicken cannelloni in a creamy sauce), are served in their sleek dining room. Closed Sun.

PLAZA SAN MARTÍN AND RETIRO El Establo
Paraguay 489, Retiro **Tel** *(011) 4311-1639*

Map *3 E4*

This well-decorated restaurant is tourist-friendly and very popular with airline staff. The waiters can speak some English. It is a classic *parrilla* and serves huge, inexpensive steaks. There are some classic dishes on the menu such as Serrano ham, tortilla, and a wide range of pizzas, salads, and pastas.

PLAZA SAN MARTÍN AND RETIRO Filo
San Martín 975, Retiro **Tel** *(011) 4311-0312*

Map *3 E4*

An authentic Italian joint, Filo serves over 100 delectable flat-base pizzas. The place also has a fabulous selection of meat dishes and Italian gnocchi, risottos, as well as fresh pasta dishes. It is also a great place to just go for a cocktail, although it can be crowded from Thursday through Saturday. There is a DJ Mon–Sat.

PLAZA SAN MARTÍN AND RETIRO Empire Thai
Tres Sargentos 427 **Tel** *(011) 4312-5706*

Map *3 E4*

With well-designed interiors, Empire Thai serves delicious Thai food. They can do a perfect green curry on demand, although most of the dishes on the menu are either chilli-free or less spicy to suit diners. Coconut and fruits are used to keep dishes sweet, and the satays are delicious.

RECOLETA El Cuartito
Talcahuano 937 **Tel** *(011) 4816-1758*

Map *3 D4*

An old-fashioned restaurant, this pizzeria is an ideal place for a great night out. Its pizza toppings are standard – from the usual ham and tomato to tomato and garlic, provolone, or onion-based *fugazettas* – but El Cuartito uses good mozzarella. The restaurant offers hearty portions at a reasonable price.

RECOLETA Bi Won
Junin 548, Once **Tel** *(011) 4372-1146*

Map *2 C4*

In the heart of Koreanovich – as former Jewish barrio Once is often called – Bi Won serves red hot *kimchi* (the Korean national dish of marinated, fermented vegetables), spinach, and other Korean standards. Meat dishes are prepared on the table and meals come as ten-plate buffets with eight tasty side dishes.

RECOLETA Cumaná
Rodriguez Peña 1149 **Tel** *(011) 4813-9207*

Map *2 C3*

A country-kitchen, Cumaná is a great place to try *locro*, the national stew made with beans, pork, chicken, vegetables, and red peppers. A mud oven is used to prepare many of the dishes and the mouth-watering aromas come rushing into the restaurant every time the kitchen door is opened.

RECOLETA Piola
Libertad 1078 **Tel** *(011) 4812-0690*

Map *3 D3*

This swanky pizzeria attracts the hip crowd in the capital. Opened in the early 1990s, Piola is part of a chain started in Italy. The Napolitana (cheese, beef, tomatoes, garlic) is a specialty but there are also 50 other toppings to choose from. They also serve pasta and a variety of salads.

RECOLETA Rodi Bar
Vicente Lopez 1900 **Tel** *(011) 4801-5230*

Map *2 C4*

Just a brief walk away from Cementerio Recoleta *(see pp100–1)*, Rodi Bar is a relaxed venue serving breakfast, lunch, and dinner. Sample Argentinian provincial masterpieces such as lentil stew, *mondongo* (tripe), or hake in seafood sauce. The waiters also recommend exploring Spanish imports such as *pulpo a la gallega* (octopus in tomato and pepper sauce).

RECOLETA Gran Bar Danzon
Libertad 1161 **Tel** *(011) 4811-1108*

Map *3 D3*

A great bar with a wine list of over 400 vintages, Danzon has a soothing ambience for a perfect evening. The restaurant pioneered good wines in the late 1990s and serves whites by the glass. The food is mainly Latin American with Patagonian lamb and a variety of duck dishes as highlights.

RECOLETA Lola
Roberto M Ortiz 1805 **Tel** *(011) 4804-5959*

Map *2 C2*

Elegantly decorated with beautiful art on the walls, including cartoons by well-known Uruguayan cartoonist Hermengildo Sabat, Lola is a classic for a great night out. It has a European-style menu, one of the best in town. The *milanesas*, steaks, salmon served in champagne sauce, and braised duck are good, as is the *ravioli de centolla* (king crab ravioli).

RECOLETA Oviedo
Beruti 2602 **Tel** *(011) 4822-5415*

Map *2 B3*

One of the city's top Spanish restaurants, Oviedo offers all the great Atlantic fish – sole, hake, bass – as well as beef, pork, and lamb dishes. They also serve excellent imported hams and cheese. Their wine list is considered one of the best in Buenos Aires.

PALERMO AND BELGRANO Bio   🖼 Ⅴ $$

Humboldt 2199, Palermo **Tel** *(011) 4774-3880*   **Map** *4 C3*

A vegetarian restaurant, this place serves excellent dishes to tempt even non-vegetarians. The menu offers seasonally available vegetable dishes and organic, locally-sourced stews, gazpacho (a chilled soup made with chopped tomatoes, cucumber, onion, red pepper, and herbs), smoothies, and great salads.

PALERMO AND BELGRANO Cielito Lindo   🖼 🍷 $$

El Salvador 4999, Palermo **Tel** *(011) 4832-8054*   **Map** *4 C4*

A *cantina*-style Mexican restaurant, Cielito Lindo serves refreshing margaritas as well as scrumptious enchiladas. The outdoor seating area is a good place to enjoy dinner on a pleasant evening. The place is usually crowded at weekends with lengthy queues outside the restaurant. It is advisable to arrive early.

PALERMO AND BELGRANO El Preferido de Palermo   🧍 ♿ Ⅴ $$

Guatemala 4801 **Tel** *(011) 4774-6585*   **Map** *4 C3*

One of the few old-style saloons left in Buenos Aires, this corner restaurant seems to be straight out of a story by Jorge Luis Borges. In operation since 1952, El Preferido de Palermo is located in the same block where the famous writer grew up. The food is decent Spanish cuisine – try especially the paella and noodle-based *fideua*.

PALERMO AND BELGRANO Kansas   ♿ 🖼 Ⅴ 🍷 $$

Avenida del Libertador 4625 **Tel** *(011) 4776-4100*   **Map** *5 D2*

With neon lighting and modern architecture, American-style Kansas is the place to have a quality burger, a rack of beef and pork ribs, or a vast Texan-sized steak. The restaurant is big and always busy, and it is advisable to arrive early as they do not take reservations.

PALERMO AND BELGRANO Krishna Veggie Lunch   🧍 🖼 Ⅴ $$

Malabia 1833 **Tel** *(011) 4833-4618*   **Map** *5 D4*

Offering Indian food, Krishna Veggie Lunch is the perfect place for those who are tired of eating meat. Choose the spicy *pakoras* (batter-fried mix of onions and other vegetables), *bhajis*, vegetable *thalis* and masala *raita* (yoghurt mix) for an authentic meal. The rooms are aptly decorated with idols and posters of Indian gods and goddesses.

PALERMO AND BELGRANO La Cupertina   Ⅴ $$

Cabrera 5296 **Tel** *(011) 4777-3711*   **Map** *4 C4*

La Cupertina's decor is fairly standard for a corner restaurant, but their cheese and onion or meat empanadas (stuffed turnovers), lentil stew with chocolate, and sandwiches are well worth trying. Meals are best digested with red wine spiked with a shot of soda. The flan is recommended for dessert.

PALERMO AND BELGRANO Me Leva Brasil   📖 🖼 $$

Costa Rica 4488 **Tel** *(011) 4832-4290*   **Map** *5 D4*

A place to relax and enjoy a *caipirinha* (rum and lime cocktail), this restaurant serves authentic Brazilian rice-and-bean-based dishes. The delicious *empadinhas* (shrimp pies) and *rissoles* (croquettes) are tempting and the seafood banquets are delicious. On some nights, visitors might be lucky enough to see or participate in a samba show.

PALERMO AND BELGRANO Miranda   🖼 🍷 $$

Costa Rica 5602 **Tel** *(011) 4771-4255*   **Map** *4 C3*

Over the last few years *parrillas* have become quite trendy and Miranda is where many porteños come to feast on *lomo* (pork tenderloin), *chorizo* (spicy sausage), and other classics. The steaks are tender and well-prepared, although the prices are slightly on the steeper side for a neighborhood grill.

PALERMO AND BELGRANO Bar Uriarte   🖼 🍷 $$$

Uriarte 1572 **Tel** *(011) 4834-6004*   **Map** *4 C4*

Bar Uriarte is a beautifully designed restaurant with an open kitchen. Most of the cuisine on offer is inspired by fresh Mediterranean cooking. A good option is to start with the *polenta blanca dorado con espinacas* (grilled polenta with spinach) or the parmesan-crusted baked scallops, and continue with the home-made pastas, or crisp wood-fired pizzas.

PALERMO AND BELGRANO Dominga   🖼 Ⅴ 🍷 $$$

Honduras 5618 **Tel** *(011) 4771-4443*   **Map** *4 C4*

A quiet retreat with its own sunlit patio, Dominga is part sushi bar and part bistro. The main menu includes risotto cakes, fresh fish dishes, and an occasional Thai curry. They also serve delicious semolina gnocchi, and tasty starters such as couscous salad and tabbouleh. Closed on Sundays.

PALERMO AND BELGRANO La Cabrera   🖼 🍷 $$$

Cabrera 5099 **Tel** *(011) 4831-7002*   **Map** *4 C4*

Housed in a building that used to be a general store, La Cabrera is now the area's trendiest steakhouse. The friendly waiters serve large portions of beef, and the *morcilla* (blood sausage) accompanied with roasted almonds is recommended. The restaurant also has another branch, La Cabrera Norte, located a block away.

PALERMO AND BELGRANO La Casa Polaca   ♿ 🖼 $$$

Jorge Luis Borges 2076, Palermo Viejo **Tel** *(011) 4899-0514*   **Map** *5 D4*

Almost all Buenos Aires's immigrant communities have a place to meet and soak up Old World stories. La Casa Polaca is for the Polish social scene, where diners can feast on goulash, rollmops (rolled pickled herring fillet), steak and chips from the Pampas, and the standard Argentinian *locro* (stew). They also stock authentic vodkas.

Key to Price Guide *see p292* **Key to Symbols** *see back cover flap*

PALERMO AND BELGRANO María Magdalena Restó
🏠 V 🍷 $$$

Humboldt 1551, Palermo **Tel** *(011) 4772-2008* **Map** 5 D2

This former butcher's shop in Palermo Hollywood has found new life as the María Magdalena Restó. Inventive dishes such as *ciervo envuelto en crepine de cordero* (venison cooked in savory juices), and various versions of *bondiola de cerdo* (port shoulder), duck, salmon, and trout are on the menu. The atmosphere is warm and service attentive. Closed Sun.

PALERMO AND BELGRANO Novecento
🛗 🎵 🏠 🍷 $$$

Báez 199, Las Cañitas **Tel** *(011) 4778-1900* **Map** 4 C2

With branches in New York, Punta del Este, and Miami, this modern Argentinian cuisine franchise has won over expatriates and tourists as well as Las Cañitas regulars. The peppered steak is delicious and the *provoleta ahumada* (grilled smoked provolone) comes with just the right kind of crunchy edges.

PALERMO AND BELGRANO Romeo y Julieta RestoBar
🛗 🏠 V 🍷 $$$

Gorriti 5675, Palermo **Tel** *(011) 4771-3213* **Map** 5 D5

Situated in the trendy Palermo Hollywood district, this restaurant serves good Mediterranean cuisine. Dishes include *bondiola braseada en cerveza negra* (stout-braised pork shoulder) and *ravioles de cordero* (lamb-stuffed ravioli). The dining room is black and white with artwork displayed throughout for a touch of color. Closed Sun.

PALERMO AND BELGRANO Social Paraiso
🏠 V 🍷 $$$

Honduras 5182 **Tel** *(011) 4831-4556* **Map** 4 C4

Chef-owner Feerico Simoes was raised on Syrian-Lebanese cuisine, and now serves scintillating eastern Mediterranean delights that are unique in Buenos Aires. Brazilian passion fruit mousse and Szechuan pepper ice cream suggest that there are no bounds to his multinational menu or his creative zeal.

PALERMO AND BELGRANO Green Bamboo
🛗 🏠 🍷 $$$$

Costa Rica 5802 **Tel** *(011) 4775-7050* **Map** 4 C3

Conveniently located on a street corner in the heart of Palermo, Green Bamboo is a tastefully decorated Vietnamese restaurant. One of the pioneers of ethnic food at the end of the 1990s, they offer a range of light Southeast Asian dishes. Their long cocktail list offers some of the best drinks in Palermo.

PALERMO AND BELGRANO Guido
🎵 🏠 V 🍷 $$$$

Blvd. Cervino 3943 **Tel** *(011) 4802-1262* **Map** 5 E3

A bustling neighborhood restaurant, colorfully decorated Lucky Luciano is owned by two Italian brothers. The restaurant offers pastas with buffalo, lamb, pork, or fresh fish, doused in rich tomato- or cream-based sauces. Their excellent wine list complements the tasty meals.

PALERMO AND BELGRANO Mykonos
🎵 🛗 🎿 V 🍷 $$$$

Olleros 1752, Belgrano **Tel** *(011) 4779-9000* **Map** 4 C1

Mykonos transports you from the streets of Buenos Aires to the Greek Islands with its classic Greek cuisine that includes favorites such as *spanakopita* (spinach pie), moussaka, and baklava. Festive patrons order a shot of ouzo and join in with the traditional dancing – some even breaking a plate or two – that takes place nightly during dinner. Closed Sun.

PALERMO AND BELGRANO Olsen
🏠 V 🍷 $$$$

Gorriti 5870 **Tel** *(011) 4776-7677* **Map** 4 B3

Swiss-managed, Scandinavian-themed, and with an Argentinian chef, Olsen is very much a potpourri of the porteño variety. Visitors should try long-forgotten yet timeless dishes such as *bondiola de cerdo con conseva de frutos rojos* (pork shoulder with berry sauce). The vodka menu is the longest in town, and the cocktail waiters can rustle up great smoothies.

PALERMO AND BELGRANO Maat Club Privado Gourmet
🛗 🎵 🏠 V 🍷 $$$$$

Sucre 2168, Belgrano **Tel** *(011) 4896-1818* **Map** 4 A1

With its stately British decor in one of the grand old homes of Belgrano, the Maat Club is an elegant choice for sophisticated diners. The menu changes seasonally and includes culinary delights featuring variations on shellfish, pasta, red meat, and wild game. Highly recommended but formal dress and advance reservation required. Closed Sun.

PALERMO AND BELGRANO Pura Tierra
🏠 V 🍷 $$$$$

3 de Febrero 1167, Belgrano **Tel** *(011) 4899-2007* **Map** 4 B2

The cuisine in this upscale Belgrano restaurant is classic Argentinian with a contemporary twist. Traditional dishes, such as rabbit coated with mustard and almonds, are beautifully presented. The *mollejas dorades en miel de caña y limón conserva* (sautéed sweetbreads with sugar cane honey and preserved lemons) is a house specialty. Closed Sun.

PALERMO AND BELGRANO Sucre
V 🍷 $$$$$

Sucre 676 **Tel** *(011) 4782-9082* **Map** 4 C4

A temple of modern Argentinian cuisine, Sucre is the place to come to explore everything that the provinces produce, from Andean maize wraps to Patagonian lamb to rib-eye steak to spider crab, though all presented and prepared with a modern twist.

FARTHER AFIELD II Novo María de Luján
🛗 🏠 V 🍷 $$$

Paseo Victorica 611, Tigre **Tel** *(011) 4731-9613* **Road Map** C3

This warm eatery in Tigre is a friendly country-style restaurant. Apart from serving large portions of salad and meat, the place experiments with spider crab, a specialty from Ushuaia. The *minuta* (short-order) menu has a delicious range of *milanesas* (veal cutlets). All the meat served is tender and sinew-free.

THE PAMPAS

BAHIA BLANCA Bizkaia
Soler 769 **Tel** *(0291) 452-0191*   **Road Map** *C3*

Colorfully decorated and well located, Bizkaia has strong Basque connections. A wide variety of exquisite fish dishes are on offer for the main course. The place is also well known for its tapas and starters. All the desserts are worth a try.

LA PLATA Don Quijote
Plaza Paso 146 **Tel** *(0221) 483-3653*   **Road Map** *C3*

Delicious food and welcoming staff make this classic neighborhood restaurant well known and loved. Great pastas and excellent grilled meats are served and the place is also known for its seafood. Most of the dishes on the menu are reasonably priced.

MAR DEL PLATA Chichillo
Avenida Martinez de Hoz, corner 12 de Octubre **Tel** *(0223) 489-6317*   **Road Map** *C3*

A casual seafood place in the old port, Chichillo is very popular among Argentinian holidaymakers. The main highlights are the fried squid rings and the baby squid and hake dishes. There are two floors in Chichillo – downstairs offers canteen-style self-service, while the seating upstairs is attended by waiters.

MAR DEL PLATA Viento en Popa
Avenida Martinez de Hoz 257 **Tel** *(0223) 489-220*   **Road Map** *C3*

This popular restaurant offers outstanding seafood dishes, which include mussels, shrimps, and octopus served in simple preparations – a hint of garlic, a touch of mayonnaise – so the freshness of the original flavors are retained. For richer flavors, try the paellas or *cazuelas* (seafood casseroles). They are also well known for their salads.

NECOCHEA Taberna Española
Calle 89 360 **Tel** *(02262) 525-126*   **Road Map** *C3*

A restaurant with a lovely family atmosphere, the Taberna is a cozy place to eat. It serves delicious seafood dishes. The paella comes with heaps of mussels and not too much saffron, allowing the fish flavors to come through. They also have a good selection of both red and white wines.

PINAMAR El Viejo Lobo
Avenida del Mar, corner Bunge **Tel** *(02254) 483-218*   **Road Map** *D3*

Acclaimed for its seafood dishes, this spacious restaurant offers a stylish, contemporary dining experience. The main highlights are its *gambas al ajillo* (prawns in garlic) or *pez lenguado con alcaparras* (flatfish in browned butter with caper sauce). There are excellent sea views from the terrace. Note that only Visa cards are accepted.

SAN ANTONIO DE ARECO Almacen de Ramos Generales
Zapiola 143 **Tel** *(02326) 456-376*   **Road Map** *C3*

The *asado* (open air barbecue) is popular here and diners should ask for beef cuts such as *bife de chorizo* (sirloin steak), which can be tastier than the fillet and rump. Try the *conejo al verdeo* (rabbit in spring onions), *txangurro* (Basque seafood stew), or *milanesas* (cutlet of veal or chicken). Desserts include *pastelitos* (deep-fried pastries with quince) and figs in syrup.

SAN ANTONIO DE ARECO Puesto la Lechuza
Calle Arellano & Pasaje de la Riestra 423 **Tel** *(02326) 1540-5745*   **Road Map** *C3*

Formerly a *pulpería* (gaucho saloon and grocery store), this lovely old place serves wonderful *picadas* (large platters of cheese, salami, olives, and peppers in oil) and barbecued meats that are grilled to perfection. The *morcilla* (blood sausage) and the excellent *chorizos* (spicy sausages) are recommended.

SANTA ROSA Club Espanol
Hilario Lagos 237   **Road Map** *C3*

It is worth coming here just to soak up the atmosphere of the old colonial days when criollos of Spanish descent and newly-arrived immigrants met to drink and chat over a dry *manzanilla* sherry. The sherry is still available and the food is great, especially the *milanesas*, the roast chicken dishes, and the flan.

TANDIL Época de Quesos
San Martin, cnr 14 de Julio 704 **Tel** *(02293) 448-750*   **Road Map** *C3*

Built in 1860, this restaurant is often visited by people who just want to see the beautiful building. There is an impressive range of salamis on offer as well as delicious local cheeses. They can be sampled on site or taken away. Ask for a *picada* (pre-meal platter served in small proportions) if you want to try a morsel of everything.

VILLA GESELL El Estribo
Avenida 3, cnr Paseo 109 **Tel** *(02255) 460-234*   **Road Map** *D3*

A much-loved *parrilla*, this place specializes in steak, chicken, and the best kind of offal – salted and grilled until crunchy – but there is plenty to choose from the varied menu, which includes *bondiola* (pork shoulder) in a brown ale sauce and *ensaladas* (salads) in abundance; the Don Pedro dessert must be tried.

ARGENTINIAN MESOPOTAMIA

COLÓN La Estancia
Urquiza 158 **Tel** (03447) 423-312   **Road Map** C2

Warm and atmospheric, La Estancia has brick archways, creaking wooden floorboards, and walls decorated with ranch tools and wild boar and deer trophies collected from hunts in the nearby Parque Nacional El Palmar (see p165). The traditional meat-dominated cuisine is first-rate and the staff are welcoming and friendly.

CORRIENTES La Morocha
Salta esq F J de la Quintana **Tel** (03783) 438-699   **Road Map** C1

Located in the heart of Corrientes's historical barrio, this lovely lime-painted bistro sits on a corner of Plaza 25 de Mayo and is housed within a colonial residence that once belonged to a city governor. The short menu includes homemade pastas, fresh fish, and red meat dishes.

GUALEGUAYCHÚ La Cascada
Avenida Costanera 370 **Tel** (03446) 432-451   **Road Map** C2

Located on the coastal avenue near the town center, this family-oriented parrilla has great atmosphere. Diners can see their beefsteaks being barbecued on the huge open grill. Crisp pizzas are also served, some with daring river fish toppings. Parents can relax in the wine-tasting salon while the kids keep busy in the play area.

MERCEDES Sabor Único Restobar
Avenida San Martín 1240 **Tel** (03773) 420-314   **Road Map** C2

A beautiful historic home is the setting for this restaurant that serves typical Argentinian cuisine. Options include milanesas (breaded veal cutlets), steaks, and burgers as well as homemade pastas. Warm family atmosphere complete with a small play area for children in the outside garden and a patio for outdoor dining. Pets are welcome.

PARANÁ Ristorante Giovanni
Urquiza 1047 **Tel** (0343) 423-0527   **Road Map** C2

One block from Paraná's central plaza, Giovanni offers decent food at a prime location. The menu is extensive and includes pastas, and beef staples, although the wild fish is the chef's specialty and there are almost a dozen surubí (a type of river fish) dishes to choose from. Waiters are friendly, but not very quick.

PUERTO IGUAZÚ El Gallo Negro
Avenida Victoria Aguirre 773 **Tel** (03757) 422-165   **Road Map** D1

A good spot for a long, lazy lunch, El Gallo Negro's best feature is its garden terrace, dotted with rustic wooden benches dressed in crisp white tablecloths and formally arranged tableware. On the menu, the mains are fairly standard, but the tropical desserts are divine.

PUERTO IGUAZÚ La Rueda
Avenida Córdoba 28 **Tel** (03757) 422-531   **Road Map** D1

A favorite with Iguazú's well-heeled residents, La Rueda combines upscale dining with a bustling atmosphere and a subtropical-inspired menu and decor. Native wood furniture abounds and the roof is thatched with tacuara bamboo. The main menu includes mouth-watering river fish options as well as standard parrilla fare. Only American Express accepted.

PUERTO IGUAZÚ Aqva
Avenida Córdoba, esq Carlos Thays **Tel** (03757) 422-064   **Road Map** D1

Quiet and softly lit, Aqva is ideal for romantic evenings. The decor features native woods and stone, and the menu includes caviar starters and exquisite pastas. There is an impressive wine list, and welcome extras include freshly baked bread. It has excellent service with attentive waiters regularly topping up diners' glasses.

ROSARIO Deck del Náutico
Club Náutico de Rosario, Comunidad Floral de Navarra & 104 **Tel** (0341) 426-3352   **Road Map** C2

Housed within Rosario's yacht club, Deck del Náutico is a romantic dining spot with stylish decor and an intimate, candlelit terrace that overlooks Río Paraná. Its menu prioritizes river fish options including the surubí and dorado. It serves seafood and parrilla staples as well.

ROSARIO Ristorante Da Vinci
España 777 **Tel** (0341) 447-7447   **Road Map** C2

Simple pasta dishes, prepared using fresh ingredients and based on regional recipes from Italy, are the house specialty at this city-center eatery. The place also offers some of the best desserts in town. Representations of the namesake maestro's work ornament the walls. The service is quick and the atmosphere relaxed.

SANTA FE Resto España
Calle San Martín 2644 **Tel** (0342) 400-8834   **Road Map** C2

This traditional eatery has belonged to the same family of Spanish descent for over 30 years. Housed in a century-old building, its interior is one of high ceilings, colonnades, stained-glass windows, and wall paintings. A varied menu features regional specialties, and Spanish paella and seafood platters.

CÓRDOBA AND THE ANDEAN NORTHWEST

CACHI Comedor El Aujero
Ruis de los Llanos s/n **Tel** (03868) 1563-8036

Road Map B1

A basic, canteen-like restaurant with blacksmiths' tools on the walls, Comedor El Aujero is the archetypal local eatery. Gauchos from the surrounding area visit this restaurant for barbecued beef and pork and stuffed red peppers, which they wash down with glasses of house wine.

CAFAYATE El Rancho
Toscano 4 **Tel** (03868) 421-256

Road Map B1

Despite the abundance of vineyards, Cafayate is short on good restaurants. El Rancho, however, is consistently good for local corn-based dishes such as *humitas* (steamed corn wraps) and tamales (corn wraps stuffed with meat) and does wonderful grilled goat. Desserts include regional specialities such as white cheese with fruit conserves.

CÓRDOBA La Yaya
Independencia 468

Road Map C2

This popular neighborhood eatery specializes in *comida de campo* (country cooking). Its range of tasty dishes includes *locro criollo* (pork and bean stew), *humita en cazuela* (corn wrap in a stew), and *bondiola de cerdo dorada al romero con puré de manzanas* (pork with rosemary and applesauce).

COSQUIN Parrilla Saint Jean
San Martín 200 **Tel** (03541) 451-059

Road Map B2

Undoubtedly the best steakhouse in town, Parrilla Saint Jean is popular with the locals. The restaurant is mainly known for its exceptionally good grilled meats and hearty wines. The *chorizo* (spicy sausage) especially is tender and full of flavor. The place is always busy so it is best to reserve a table.

LA CUMBRE La Casona del Toboso
Belgrano 349 **Tel** (03548) 451-436

Road Map B2

Housed in a little cottage, La Casona del Toboso is La Cumbre's best known restaurant. Popular with the locals, it is famous for its trout, fresh from the region's rivers and served with mushroom sauce, and excellent goat. They also serve good grills and pastas with ingredients sourced from nearby cooperatives.

MOLINOS Estancia Colomé
Ruta Provincial 53, Km 20 **Tel** (03868) 494-044

Road Map B1

Delicate red meat and fish dishes are on offer at this beautiful and refined restaurant, which gets most of its vegetables from the estate's own organic kitchen gardens. The wine list is excellent and it is worth trying the *bodega's* own top vintages. There are delightful views of the vineyards and across to the Nevada de Cachi.

SALTA El Solar del Convento
Caseros 444 **Tel** (0387) 421-5124

Road Map B1

Salta is generally excellent for Andean food and empanadas (stuffed turnovers), but this restaurant is the best place to come for a huge steak. They also offer a complimentary glass of champagne. The restaurant is spacious and the walls are decorated with local artworks, including handwoven saddle blankets and animal masks.

SALTA José Balcarce
Mitre, corner Necochea **Tel** (0387) 421-1628

Road Map B1

An absolute must-visit for anyone coming to Salta, José Balcarce has chefs who take the best ingredients out of the Andean larder and turn them into innovative and delicious concoctions. Stand-out meals include llama *carpaccio* (thinly sliced raw meat), llama with *tuna* (prickly pear) sauce, and trout with butter and ginger.

SAN MIGUEL DE TUCUMÁN El Fondo
San Martín 846 **Tel** (0381) 422-2161

Road Map B1

One of the best *parrillas* in town, famous for their empanadas, which in this region are often slightly spicy as well as sweet, and steaming bowls of *locro* (stew). There is a salad bar and an excellent wine list which includes the Cabernet-Malbec-Merlot blend. There is also live music during the weekends.

SAN SALVADOR DE JUJUY Manos Jujeñas
Senador Pérez 379 **Tel** (0388) 424-3270

Road Map B1

A small eatery decorated with local crafts and costumes, Manos Jujenas has soft Andean music playing in the background. The restaurant is divided over two levels and serves excellent tamales, *humitas*, and empanadas. There is also live music offered occasionally.

VILLA GENERAL BELGRANO Viejo Munich
Avenida San Martín 362 **Tel** (03546) 463-122

Road Map B2

An Alpine-looking restaurant, this used to be the tavern of choice for survivors of the German battleship *Graf Spee* which sank off the coast of Uruguay in 1939 *(see p183)*. It now keeps up the Teutonic theme with nine types of beer, brewed on site, as well as sauerkraut, German wurst, and cheeses.

Key to Price Guide see p292 **Key to Symbols** see back cover flap

CUYO AND THE WINE COUNTRY

GODOY CRUZ 1884
Belgrano 1188 **Tel** *(0261) 424-3336*   🍴 Ⓥ 🍷 $$$$ **Road Map** *B2*

Argentina's famous chef, Francis Mallman, created this prestigious restaurant in the beautiful surroundings of Bodegas Escorihuela *(see p211)*. Focusing on fresh regional ingredients such as baby goat and lamb, 1884 offers an excellent Patagonian-style menu. It also has a premium regional wine list.

LUJÁN DE CUYO Ruca Malén
Ruta Nacional 7, Km 1059 **Tel** *(0261) 410-6214*   🚶 ♿ 🍴 Ⓥ 🍷 $$$ **Road Map** *B2*

Ruca Malén is known for fine five-course meals, usually beef-based but with alternative entrées such as chicken or fish, paired with generous samples of premium red and white. Reservations are necessary for lunch, served either in the dining room or on a shaded terrace, normally as part of tours and tastings at its namesake *bodega*.

LUJÁN DE CUYO Cavas Wine Lodge
Costaflores s/n Alto Agrelo **Tel** *(0261) 410-6927*   ♿ 🍴 Ⓥ 🍷 $$$$$ **Road Map** *B2*

A romantic candlelit restaurant in a luxury vineyard spa-hotel *(see p282)*, Cavas Wine Lodge offers panoramic views of the Andes. The menu offers beef, trout, and the occasional seafood item, complemented by grilled fresh vegetables. It has a wide selection of regional wines. Open to non-guests by reservation only. Children under 10 not permitted.

MALARGÜE El Bodegón de María
Rufino Ortega and Villegas **Tel** *(02627) 471-655*   🍴 🍷 $$ **Road Map** *B3*

Malargüe is no gourmet mecca, but this unpretentious restaurant delivers quality home-style Italo-Argentinian cooking. The pasta, pizza, beef, and trout are all worthwhile, but the light-crusted *caprese* empanadas are the best items on the menu. It has low-key but engaging rural decor, with pleasant service.

MENDOZA El Gato Que Pesca
Mitre 1538, Chacras de Coria **Tel** *(0261) 496-0320*   ♿ 🍴 Ⓥ 🍷 $$ **Road Map** *B2*

A family-run restaurant, El Gato Que Pesca is easily comparable to the more pricey and sophisticated eateries in Chacras, Mendoza's "gourmet ghetto" area. Specialties include varied crêpes and appetizers, but the menu changes frequently. The inviting decor includes antique household items and the owner's startlingly original paintings.

MENDOZA Facundo
Sarmiento 641 **Tel** *(0261) 420-2866*   ♿ 🍴 Ⓥ $$ **Road Map** *B2*

A well-established grill, the bright and cheerful Facundo has an elaborate salad bar which also offers international dishes such as stuffed chicken breast with mustard sauce. A mixed appetizer plate includes varied cheeses and cold cuts. A restaurant more for friends than romantic diners.

MENDOZA Karma
Peru 1192 **Tel** *(0261) 423-2387*   ♿ 🍴 Ⓥ 🍷 $$ **Road Map** *B2*

A novelty for Mendoza which has few Indian restaurants, Karma in part owes its origins to Brad Pitt and Indian-born Tibetan, Karma Apo Tsang, who came to Cuyo for the filming of *Seven Years in Tibet*. Dishes such as samosas (deep-fried stuffed pastry) and mutton masala are delicious but the spice level has been calibrated to Argentinian palates.

MENDOZA La Albahaca
Espejo 659 **Tel** *(0261) 425-9511*   🍴 Ⓥ 🍷 $$ **Road Map** *B2*

La Albahaca has an excellent mid-range Italo-Argentinian menu, which includes antipasti, risotto, trout, and seafood ravioli. The visual presentation is outstanding and the service assiduous, but the dining room, in a converted private residence, seems a little cramped. Unfortunately, the desserts are not as delicious as the main dishes.

MENDOZA La Marchigiana
Patricias Mendocinas 1550 **Tel** *(0261) 423-0751*   ♿ Ⓥ 🍷 $$ **Road Map** *B2*

Known to everybody in town, this traditional elite Italian restaurant offers great home-made pastas, particularly lasagna, which is the definite star on the menu. They also serve rice, baked fish, and grilled meat, and the wine list is good as well. Despite the imposing design, it is unpretentious with gracious service.

MENDOZA La Sal
Belgrano 1069 **Tel** *(0261) 420-4322*   ♿ 🎵 🍴 Ⓥ 🍷 $$ **Road Map** *B2*

Possibly Mendoza's most sophisticated fusion restaurant, La Sal offers an exclusive dining experience. The decor follows a wicker theme. Their seasonally changing menu includes items such as beef ravioli with mussel butter, herb-marinated chicken breast with pumpkin, and spinach lasagna.

MENDOZA La Tasca de Plaza España
Montevideo 117   🍴 Ⓥ 🍷 $$ **Road Map** *B2*

An informal Spanish restaurant, La Tasca's bright decor is complemented by frequently changing art exhibitions. Along with tapas, the place also serves traditional dishes such as Spanish omelet, seafood items including scallops and razor clams, and a casserole of zucchini, onions, and peppers in cheese sauce.

MENDOZA Naturata Restaurant Vegetariano

🖼️ 🖳 V $$

Don Bosco 73 **Tel** *(0261) 15543-0450*   **Road Map** *B2*

Located in the city center, Naturata is a welcome sight in a country where vegetarian restaurants are rare. A variety of dishes, including savory tarts, *empanadas* (stuffed turnovers), and pastas feature in the daily *tenedor libre* (all-you-can-eat buffet). Food can also be taken away. Open for lunch only.

MENDOZA Azafrán

🚶 ♿ 🖳 V 🖳 $$$

Sarmiento 765 **Tel** *(0261) 429-4200*   **Road Map** *B2*

With casual decor consisting of simple wooden tables and chairs, Azafrán is a pleasant place to dine. It has a pan-Argentinian menu that places more of an emphasis on game dishes, such as wild boar, and uses more herbs and spices in its cooking than most Argentinian restaurants.

MENDOZA Mar y Monte

🖼️ 🖳 🖳 $$$

Darragueira 648, Chacras de Coria **Tel** *(0261) 496-5164*   **Road Map** *B2*

Literally "Sea and Sierra," Mar y Monte merges traditions of Chile's diverse Pacific fish and seafood selection with regional versions of Argentinian standards, including wild game dishes such as *vizcacha* (type of rodent). It has a spacious patio ideal for outdoor dining. It also has a downtown Mendoza branch.

MENDOZA Praga

♿ 🖳 V 🖳 $$$

Leonidas Aguirre 413 **Tel** *(0261) 425-9585*   **Road Map** *B2*

This restaurant has attractive dining rooms with high ceilings and open-air seating facing a small park. The menu includes quality seafood, especially salmon and trout, plus appetizers such as octopus cooked in a Spanish-Mediterranean style. They have a large wine list consisting mainly of white wines.

MENDOZA Francesco

♿ 🖳 V 🖳 $$$$

Chile 1268 **Tel** *(0261) 425-3912*   **Road Map** *B2*

An upmarket, formal Italian restaurant with an extensive menu, Francesco is under the same ownership as La Marchigiana (*see p299*). Specialties include pastas and risotto, as well as fish and red meat dishes. The restaurant also has a huge wine selection. It is advisable to make reservations.

SAN AGUSTÍN DEL VALLE FÉRTIL Rinco's Restó

🖼️ ♿ V 🖳 $$

Rivadavia s/n   **Road Map** *B2*

In an area where the dining experience lags well behind the spectacular scenery, Rinco's Resto has raised the standard of Italo-Argentinian food and also created a warm, inviting ambience in which to dine. The menu's highlights are pastas and meats. It also stocks some good wines.

SAN JUAN Club Sirio Libanés

V 🖳 $$

Entre Rios 33 Sur **Tel** *(0264) 422-3841*   **Road Map** *B2*

In a city with a strong Middle Eastern presence, Club Sirio Libanés is a traditional eastern Mediterranean restaurant with Moorish architecture. The highlights of the diverse buffet and à la carte menu include savory lamb empanadas (stuffed turnovers) with a touch of lemon, falafel, and stuffed grape leaves. The service is efficient and formal.

SAN JUAN De Sánchez

🚶 V 🖳 $$

Rivadavia 61 Oeste **Tel** *(0264) 420-3670*   **Road Map** *B2*

A casual restaurant, De Sánchez offers more than just regional cuisines. Light dishes with visual flair include *pincho de pulpo y langostinos en olio de uva y paprika* (octopus and prawn brochettes brushed with grapeseed oil and paprika). The place also sells magazines, books, and CDs, and Argentinian images decorate the walls.

SAN JUAN Maloca

🚶 ♿ 🎵 $$

Del Bono 321 **Tel** *(0264) 435-2503*   **Road Map** *B2*

Located in the outskirts of the city in a residential neighborhood, Maloca showcases Latin American food from around the continent, including Mexican tacos and Colombian *arepas* (corn bread) rarely found in Argentinian provincial cities. The place has a casual atmosphere but with separate dining areas that give reasonable privacy.

SAN LUIS Serafina

V 🖳 $$

San Martín 510 **Tel** *(02652) 424-977*   **Road Map** *B2*

Serafina is the most diverse and sophisticated restaurant in this small provincial capital. Specializing in grilled meats, most notably mutton, and pastas, they have a long menu and wine list. The dining room, however, is rather cluttered with too many tables placed close together.

SAN RAFAEL El Restauro

🚶 V 🖳 $$

Comandante Salas and Day **Tel** *(02627) 445-482*   **Road Map** *B3*

A well-located restaurant, El Restauro is a step above the others in town for its regional menu of pasta, lamb, pork, and poultry cooked in a gaucho wok. In addition to an ample wine list, it offers local brews of pale ale, amber, and stout. The restaurant is housed in a handsome historic building with high ceilings and other period features.

TUNUYÁN Killka

🚶 ♿ 🖳 V 🖳 $$$$

Finca La Pampa, Los Árboles **Tel** *(02622) 429-570*   **Road Map** *B3*

Part of the stunning Bodega Salentein (*see p282*), Killka is mainly patronized before or after tours and wine tasting. This ultramodern place serves a series of fixed-price lunches with trout and lamb as the specialties. The seating offers views of the vineyards and looming Andes. À la carte dishes can be adapted for vegetarians.

PATAGONIA

BARILOCHE El Mundo
$$
Mitre 759 **Tel** *(02944) 423-461*
Road Map B4

When pro-skier Hugo Francioni quit the slopes in 1992, he converted his house into this upbeat pizzeria. Celebrities, including Jane Fonda and footballer Carlos Tévez, have dropped by since – signed portraits hang as proof from the walls – tempted by over 100 varieties of pizza. Toppings include salmon and wild boar.

BARILOCHE El Boliche de Alberto
$$$
Villegas 347 **Tel** *(02944) 431-433*
Road Map B4

Sizzling, juicy steaks are the order of the day at this classic, family-owned *parrilla*. Owner Alberto's sons, daughters, and their cousins barbecue the beef on the huge flame grill or wait at the tables. The menus come cloaked in cowhide, and the food is authentic and reasonably priced.

BARILOCHE Jau-Ja
$$$
Elflein 148 **Tel** *(02944) 422-952*
Road Map B4

This delightful, popular eatery excels in Lake District specialties, from trout and salmon to Patagonian lamb and venison. The decor is modern/minimalist, the service quick and genuinely cheerful, and the background resounds with the laughter and chatter of fellow diners.

BARILOCHE Kandahar
$$$
20 de Febrero 698 **Tel** *(02944) 424-702*
Road Map B4

It is well worth visiting Kandahar, where the delightfully eclectic decor is a mixture of lime-green walls, velvet drapes, chaises longues, and hanging mannequins. The largely organic menu is limited to eight items, each a traditional Patagonian specialty served with a modern and creative twist.

COMODORO RIVADAVIA Puerto Cangrejo
$$$$
Avenida Costanera 1051 **Tel** *(0297) 444-4590*
Road Map B5

Located in Comodoro Rivadavia's port area, Puerto Cangrejo is the city's most traditional restaurant serving some reputable seafood and offering spectacular ocean views. The king-crab cocktail starters are good, as are the shellfish. It is a very popular place and diners should arrive early on weekends or reserve in advance.

EL BOLSÓN Patio Venzano
$$
Sarmiento & Hube
Road Map B4

Owner Osvaldo built the cypress-wood cabin that houses this romantic little restaurant. The family prepares and serves the meals, dishing up delicious house specialties including fresh trout, smoked or grilled, homemade pastas, and pancakes – the latter big enough to share between two.

EL CALAFATE El Puesto
$$$
Gobernador Moyano & 9 de Julio **Tel** *(02902) 491-620*
Road Map B6

This historical gem was built by an estancia owner in 1940 as an inn for his gaucho workers. Today a bijou family-run restaurant, it serves salmon and wild trout with other regional specialities, each prepared in the original clay oven. It is advisable to arrive early on weekends or to reserve a table in advance.

EL CALAFATE La Tablita
$$$
Coronel Rosales 28 **Tel** *(02902) 491-065*
Road Map B6

In business for over 30 years, this no-frills *parrilla* is a big favorite with local non-vegetarians. Located a short hike away from the town center, and reached by crossing a small bridge over Arroyo Calafate, it serves tender spit-roasted lamb, huge beefsteaks, and generous salads, all at great prices.

EL CALAFATE Pura Vida
$$$
Avenida del Libertador General San Martín 1876 **Tel** *(02902) 493-356*
Road Map B6

Pura Vida is all about relaxed dining, with lakeside views and stylish, homely decor that includes pastel-colored walls and abstract art. The menu offers home-made pastas, stews, and excellent vegetarian dishes, all exquisitely prepared and presented. Pura Vida is just a ten-minute walk from the town center.

EL CALAFATE Casimiro Biguá
$$$$
Avenida del Libertador General San Martín 963 **Tel** *(02902) 492-590*
Road Map B6

This upmarket *parrilla* and wine bar on El Calafate's main street hums with the chatter of satisfied diners. Delectable menu items include king crab, wild boar, and other red meats, prepared according to traditional recipes. Cuban cigars are a post-meal option, to be enjoyed with a quality Italian coffee.

EL CHALTÉN El Bodegón (La Cervecería)
$$$
Avenida San Martín s/n **Tel** *(02962) 493-109*
Road Map A5

This microbrewery is the ideal spot to relax after a hard day's trekking. The ample menu features pizzas, pastas, soups, and the house specialty is a deliciously spicy beef *locro* (stew), ideally washed down with a high quality draught pilsner or a malty Bock beer. It is a great place to meet other travelers.

EL CHALTÉN Estepa

$$$

Cerro Solo, esq Antonio Rojo **Tel *(02962) 493-069***

Road Map A5

A little jewel of a restaurant, Estepa is known for its Patagonian lamb but serves freshwater fish, beef, pizza, and pasta options as well. The atmosphere is snug and cabin-like, and the service is charming. The extras include a varied vegetarian menu and live bossa nova every other Saturday.

ESQUEL Casa Grande

$$$

Roca 441 **Tel *(02945) 15-469-712***

Road Map B4

Cozy and stylish, Casa Grande is a great choice for dining couples and small groups. Set within a family house that dates from 1946, it has some lovely design touches, including light fittings carved from *lenga* wood. The chef's specialty is succulent, slow-roasted Patagonian lamb.

ESQUEL Don Chiquino

$$$

Avenida Ameghino 1641 **Tel *(02945) 450-035***

Road Map B4

The star attraction at this pasta-house is owner, Tito Frede. Storyteller, comedian, and magician, Tito works the floor performing impromptu magic tricks for diners – the "salt trick" is a favorite – while regaling them with stories from his family's history. The pasta is also first-rate.

GAIMAN Gwalia Lan

$$$

M D Jones & Eugenio Tello **Tel *(02965) 15-682-352***

Road Map B4

Homely and inviting, Gwalia Lan is the perfect place to relax after a day braving the Patagonian elements. It has a dimly lit, cavern-like interior characterized by bare-brick archways and walls painted in soft hues. The food is excellent, especially the home-made pastas, which are the chef's specialty.

PUERTO MADRYN Mariscos del Atlántico

$$$

Club Náutico, Avenida Rawson 288 **Tel *(02965) 15-552-500***

Road Map B4

Conjure up an image of an ideal fisherman's restaurant and it would be exactly like the family-run Mariscos del Atlántico where the staff are friendly and the food first-rate. It has ocean views, clapboard walls, and nets hung from the rafters. Try the fresh clams, hand-picked by the male family members on dawn dives in Golfo Nuevo.

PUERTO MADRYN Plácido

$$$

Avenida Roca 506 **Tel *(02965) 455-991***

Road Map B4

To eat at Plácido is to dine in style, with romantic ocean views, super-smooth service, and jazz or bossa nova playing in the background. The extensive menu has everything from seafood to Patagonian lamb and pastas. The outstanding wine list features various vintages, and the very pricey Dom Perignon champagne.

PUERTO MADRYN Vernardino Club del Mar

$$$

Boulevard Brown 860 **Tel *(02965) 474-289***

Road Map B4

On the beach and close to the sea, Vernardino is an ideal lunch or dinner spot. Young, amiable staff ferry regional platters to and from the dining area, which includes an outside terrace with uninterrupted ocean views. There is a kids' play area too, making this a great spot for families.

SAN MARTÍN DE LOS ANDES Ku

$$$

Avenida San Martín 1053 **Tel *(02972) 427-039***

Road Map B4

Snug, rustic, and cabin-like, Ku first opened three decades ago and is now a mainstay of San Martín's culinary scene. The place serves the most delicious desserts in town. Both the warm woody decor and the hearty cuisine, mainly consisting of wild meats, make this an ideal eatery during the ski season.

SAN MARTÍN DE LOS ANDES La Reserva

$$$$

Belgrano 940 **Tel *(02972) 428-734***

Road Map B4

Stylish and elegant, La Reserva's philosophy is "slow food." Prepared in a leisurely fashion, elaborate dishes are sourced from local ingredients and specialties include wild boar and trout. The place is dimly lit and perfect for a romantic evening. There is also an outside terrace for alfresco meals.

SAN MARTÍN DE LOS ANDES La Tasca

$$$$

M Moreno 866 **Tel *(02972) 428-663***

Road Map B4

Family-run La Tasca is part-restaurant and part-treasure trove. Century-old wine casks sit atop the main bar, antique iron stoves provide heating, and one of the cash tills dates from 1916. There is also delicious food on offer, including trout, venison, and tasty home-made pastas, which are also the house specialties.

VIEDMA Capriasca

$$$

Alvaro Barros 685 **Tel *(02920) 426-754***

Road Map C4

A beautifully renovated, century-old corner house in Viedma's city center, Capriasca boasts exquisite architectural detail and highly recommendable regional cuisine, including freshwater fish and shellfish specialities. Friendly service complements an excellent dining experience.

VILLA LA ANGOSTURA Tinto Bistro

$$$$$

Boulevard Nahuel Huapi 34 **Tel *(02944) 494-924***

Road Map B4

Located in the center of town, Tinto Bistro attracts a chic crowd with a menu that leans towards Eastern and Middle Eastern cuisines and includes curries, fish dishes, and salads. The wine list has over 150 wines, with an array of international labels. On Thursdays, after 1am, the restaurant is transformed into a bar with a DJ.

Key to Price Guide *see p292* **Key to Symbols** *see back cover flap*

TIERRA DEL FUEGO AND ANTARCTICA

RÍO GRANDE Sonora
♿ Ⓥ 🍴 $$
Perito Moreno 705 **Tel** *(02964) 423-102* **Road Map** *B6*

Contained within a charming little corner house, this family-run pizzeria serves over 30 different varieties of pizzas. Cheaply priced burgers and tapas options – best shared between a few people – are also on the menu, as is Mexican food. There is bottled Guinness offered alongside the usual Argentinian beers.

RÍO GRANDE Los Troncos
Ⓥ 🍴 $$$
Islas Maluinas 998 **Tel** *(02964) 433-982* **Road Map** *B6*

This traditional *parrilla* (steakhouse) serves classic Argentinian fare. There is a good selection of grilled meats, including *bondiola de cerdo* (pork shoulder) and other cuts on offer. Regional specialties such as fresh trout are also served in addition to a variety of pasta dishes. Closed Mon.

RÍO GRANDE Posada de los Sauces
♿ 🍴 $$$
Elcano 839 **Tel** *(02964) 430-868* **Road Map** *B6*

Río Grande's best dining option, Posada de los Sauces is housed in a namesake inn and offers meat, fish, and pasta mains. The service is prompt and polite, but the best thing about dining here is the opportunity to retire afterwards to the comfortable upstairs bar for post-prandial drinks and chatter.

USHUAIA Tía Elvira
♿ Ⓥ 🍴 $$$
Avenida Maipú 349 **Tel** *(02901) 424-725* **Road Map** *B6*

Housed within a pretty seafront building opposite the port area and run by a family of German descent, Tía Elvira has uncomplicated seafood specialties and some tasty German-inspired desserts, including a very good home-made apple strudel. For better ocean views, ask for a table upstairs. Note that wheelchair access is to downstairs only.

USHUAIA La Cantina Fueguina de Freddy
🍴 $$$$
Avenida San Martín 326 **Tel** *(02901) 421-887* **Road Map** *B6*

The live king crabs in the fish tank at the entrance to this friendly, family-run *cantina* give a good indication of what is on the menu – a seafood bonanza of crab, sea bass, and shellfish specialties. Visitors can wash down their meal with a Patagonian wine or locally brewed beer.

USHUAIA Moustacchio
♿ Ⓥ 🍴 $$$$
Avenida San Martín 298 **Tel** *(02901) 423-308* **Road Map** *B6*

For nearly 40 years, this family-run *parrilla* has served traditional Argentinian meats, including barbecued beefsteak and Patagonian lamb, which diners can watch being spit-roasted over an open fire on the restaurant's main floor. Moustacchio has a long wine list and food prices are reasonable.

USHUAIA Tante Nina
Ⓥ 🍴 $$$$
Gobernador Godoy 15 **Tel** *(02901) 432-444* **Road Map** *B6*

Housed in a smart second-floor location off Ushuaia's coastal avenue, Tante Nina is an upscale seafood restaurant run by a family of chefs. The house specialties include black sea bass and mussels. Broad windows offer fantastic views of Canal Beagle and the service is friendly and professional.

USHUAIA Volver
♿ 🍴 $$$$
Avenida Maipú 37 **Tel** *(02901) 423-977* **Road Map** *B6*

Atmospheric Volver is a throwback to Ushuaia's pioneer past, with wooden floorboards, a roaring open fireplace, fishing nets that hang from the ceiling, and old pots and pans on the walls. The lauded food is just as traditional, with delicious king crab and lamb specialties. It is better to arrive early at this popular eatery.

USHUAIA Gustino
♿ ♿ ♪ Ⓥ 🍴 $$$$$
Maipú 505, 1er Piso, esq Laserre **Tel** *(02901) 430-003* **Road Map** *B6*

This light-filled restaurant, café, and wine bar has an array of dining tables to choose from. The menu focuses on regional seafood and meats and includes dishes such as marinated trout with shaved Parmesan, *pappardelle* with lamb ragoût, and risotto with king crab, shrimp, and mussels. Extensive wine list.

USHUAIA Kaupé
♿ Ⓥ 🍴 $$$$$
Roca 470 **Tel** *(02901) 422-704* **Road Map** *B6*

A short walk up an incline from the city center, Kaupé is a sophisticated restaurant and wine bar. Its gourmet cuisine emphasizes regional ingredients, including *centolla* (king crab), sea bass, and scallops. The wine list is impressive and views across the colorful rooftops to the bay and Canal Beagle are delightful.

USHUAIA Le Martial
♿ ♿ ♪ Ⓥ 🍴 $$$$$
Las Hayas Resort Hotel, Avenida Luis Fernando Martial 1650 **Tel** *(02901) 430-710* **Road Map** *B6*

Housed in the luxurious Las Hayas Resort Hotel *(see p287)*, Le Martial is Ushuaia's most elegant eatery, with wine-red walls, superior furnishings, and beautifully executed cuisine, including mouth-watering delicacies such as baby sea bass. Views of the bay and Canal Beagle are stunning and the wine list is the best in town.

SHOPPING IN ARGENTINA

Shopping is tremendous fun in Argentina and reason enough in itself to visit the country. Foreign visitors will find that prices for locally-produced goods, including luxury buys such as leather items and jewelry, are very reasonable. Added to this is a great variety of shopping centers: in the major cities there are swanky, modern malls, department stores, and exclusive high-fashion boutiques that stock imported goods and brand names. In the country's interior, several small towns are renowned for their colorful and atmospheric artisans' markets that usually take place over the weekends. They sell locally made products that include crafted gaucho paraphernalia and high-quality weavings and ceramics.

A colorful **mate** gourd

The glittering interiors of Galerías Pacífico, Buenos Aires *(see p91)*

OPENING HOURS

In cities, malls usually open from 10am to 10pm daily. Food courts and cinemas within malls stay open later. Street shops usually open from 9am to 8pm on weekdays; most close at 1pm on Saturdays, and remain shut on Sunday. In the small towns of Argentina, store owners usually close for a siesta between 1 and 4:30pm.

HOW TO PAY

Cash is universally accepted, preferably the Argentinian peso. Many places also accept US dollars. Credit cards are widely accepted in cities, unlike small towns in Argentina's interior. Preferred cards are MasterCard and Visa, and to a lesser extent American Express.

TAXES AND REFUNDS

Argentina's local sales tax is called *Impuesto al Valor Agregado* (IVA). The current rate is 21 percent and is included in the advertised price for goods. Visitors are able to reclaim IVA on their purchase when buying products made in Argentina worth AR$70 or more from shops displaying a **Global Refund** logo. Ask for a *factura* (receipt) and a Global Refund cheque when making a purchase. These should be stamped at customs prior to departure, who will then send you to a *puesto de pago* for the refund. These desks are located at several Argentinian airports.

Handicrafts shop in Quilmes, Tucumán *(see p189)*

BARGAINING

Bargaining is much less common in Argentina than in other Latin American countries. Asking the question *Cuanto vale?* (How much is it worth?) usually elicits an accurate response. Only at crafts' markets and antiques shops do vendors sometimes start at a higher price than the one they accept. Visitors may feel confident enough to make a lower offer here, particularly when purchasing a combination of items.

SHOPPING MALLS AND BOUTIQUES

Shopping malls, ranging from modest buildings to plush, air-conditioned establishments, are ubiquitous in Argentinian towns and cities. Some, such as the Galerías Pacífico *(see p91)* mall in Buenos Aires and **El Palacio** in Salta, are housed in lovely, century-old landmark buildings. Many of these malls have multiplex cinemas, food courts, and also play areas for kids.

High-end international brands of clothing, perfume, and jewelry can be found in boutiques on the main avenues in big cities. In Buenos Aires, the trendy neighborhood of Palermo Viejo is known for its chic boutiques run by independent Argentinian designers. Some designers such as **Ricky Sarkany**, **Laura Driz**, and **Bensimon** have shops in Buenos Aires and branches across the other major cities of Argentina.

SPECIALIST STORES

Specialist stores that sell high-quality merchandise produced or manufactured in Argentina's interiors can be found in most cities. *Vinotecas* sell wines from Cuyo and other wine-growing regions, as well as imported spirits and cigars. *Talabarterías* stock products of the Pampas, including gaucho gear, leather-wear, polo shirts, *mate* gourds, and *bombillas* (metal straws). One of the best-known chains is **Cardon**, which has outlets in most cities. For leather specifically, there are *casas de cuero*. Similarly, *casas de lana* sell luxury woolen products, made from both sheep and guanaco wool. In the theater district of Buenos Aires, there are *casas de tango*, which specialize in showy outfits worn by tango performers.

Argentinian antiques are increasingly popular with collectors and dealers from abroad. The major concentrations of antiques shops are in Buenos Aires (*see pp118–21*).

ARTISANS' MARKETS

On weekends, main squares in almost every town in Argentina are taken over by *ferias artesanales* (artisans' markets). These fairs sell good souvenirs and gifts, such as ceramics, *mate* gourds, native weavings, and gaucho ware. The most authentic markets are held in the interior, particularly El Bolsón in Patagonia (*see p240*) and the villages of Quebrada de Humahuaca in the high Andean Northwest (*see pp196–200*).

The wine cellar of Bodega Salentein in Mendoza *(see pp210–11)*

BODEGAS AND CHACRAS

Argentinian wines have a deservedly burgeoning reputation. The best vintages can be acquired at *bodegas*, most of which are concentrated in the Cuyo region. In Mendoza, **Bodega La Rural**, **Bodega y Cavas de Weinert**, **Bodega Salentein**, and **O. Fournier** are some of the best-stocked *bodegas* (*see pp210–11*). In San Juan, **Graffigna Wines** have the best merchandizing facilities. Larger wineries in Mendoza provide a courier service for sending home bulk acquisitions. The charge is US$12 per bottle, at a maximum of 12 bottles per day. *Chacras* (small farms) cluster on the outskirts of several towns in the interior, particularly in Patagonia. Here, visitors can buy organic foods including fruits, honey, cheeses, and beers, all at low prices. In Patagonia, the *chacras* of El Bolsón, Viedma, and Los Antiguos are well known for their produce.

Purmamarca's crafts market, Quebrada de Humahuaca *(see pp196–200)*

What to Buy in Argentina

Shopping is tremendous fun in Argentina given the wide range of beautiful and unique items available. Major cities have modern shopping malls and high-fashion boutiques, while in provincial towns artisans' markets sell everything from beautifully-crafted gaucho gear to high-quality weavings. Prices, including the cost of luxury items, are low compared to those in Europe and the US.

A ceramic item at MALBA

Some of the bigger stores will ship purchases home and, if requested, shop attendants will gift wrap the item.

INDIGENOUS HANDICRAFTS

Visitors will find artisans selling regional handicrafts across the country – woolens made of guanaco and llama wool in Patagonia, the Andean Northwest, and Cuyo and excellent ceramics in the Andean Northwest. Jewelry is another quality Argentinian product and is available in a variety of designs and metals.

Warm woolen gloves

Poncho woven with traditional patterns

Indigenous pattern woven on woolen polo bands

Woven carpet from Purmamarca, Córdoba

Woolens and weavings

Bright handwoven rugs, ponchos, and shawls are on offer, made from a variety of wools, including the rare alpaca and vicuña wools. Indigenous symbolism pervades many of the designs.

Jewelry

Artisanal fairs across Argentina offer exquisite jewelry that is handmade from nickel, silver, or gold with semi-precious stones and indigenous motifs.

Inexpensive silver pendants found all across Argentina

Gold earrings with semi-precious stones

Necklace with gold beads

Metal straw and scoop for herbal tea

Two *mate* gourds

Ceramic item made by indigenous people

Handmade earthen pot

Mate

Mate *drinking is an age-old Argentinian ritual and* mate *gourds range from highly-wrought silver to those crafted from calabash (pumpkin). The* bombilla *(drinking straw) is the main accessory.*

Earthenware

Sold at crafts markets across the Andean Northwest and Argentinian Mesopotamia, ceramics are often embellished with indigenous motifs and patterns dating back millennia.

TRADITIONAL PRODUCTS

Many shops in Buenos Aires sell authentic gaucho ware and items decorated with brightly-colored *fileteado*. Quality and prices can vary from shop to shop, so it is best to look around before buying anything. Traditional gaucho ware may also be found at estancias all across the country, especially in Patagonia.

Fileteado art

Filete *is a flamboyant folk art that has adorned shop fronts, buses, and tango halls in Buenos Aires since the 19th century. It typically sets elaborately designed calligraphy within a stylized border of climbing plants, flowers, or even dragons.*

Wall-hanging embellished with elaborate *fileteado* design

Gaucho ware

Coltskin boots, sombreros, and bombachas *(cotton trousers) are typically worn by the cowboys.* Facones *(knives) and* espuelas *(spurs) are their accessories.*

A typical gaucho hat

Traditional belt worn by cowboys

Well-carved gaucho knife

Traditional spurs

A pair of leather boots

SOUVENIRS

Fine wines and authentic leather goods make interesting souvenirs. Wines are available at any shopping mall in Buenos Aires. However, the best option is to visit a vineyard in the Cuyo region or less well-known vineyards in Salta to buy directly from the *bodegas*. Exotic leather goods are available, mainly in Argentinian Mesopotamia, but visitors have to be careful about fakes.

Wines

Wines are labeled according to region and grape. The signature red grape is Malbec from Mendoza and the Cuyo region. The pick of Argentina's white varieties is Torrontés, particularly the variety grown in Salta.

White wine from José L. Mounier

Red wine made with Malbec grapes

Leather accessories

Most leather goods are hand made from cowhide. Exotic leathers from Argentinian Mesopotamia, used to make luxury gifts, include caiman and lizard leathers.

Belt with *pampa* pattern

Leather handbag made from cow and capybara leathers

Leather dog collars sold commonly in street stores in Buenos Aires

ENTERTAINMENT IN ARGENTINA

The variety of entertainment in Argentina is a reflection both of its rich cultural heritage and the passion of the Argentinians. Tango, the dance that grew out of the immigrant slums of Buenos Aires, is undergoing a vigorous revival, and folkloric music, inextricably linked to the Pampas and native Northwest, is enjoyed across the country. Towns and cities stage classical music recitals, avant-garde plays, and dance productions at festivals or grand, century-old theater venues. Cinema is also extremely popular, and ranges from Argentinian and foreign art house films to the latest Hollywood block-busters. Nightlife buzzes beyond sunrise in cities and beach resorts. Popular sports are followed fanatically and the atmosphere within stadiums can be electric. For annual events throughout Argentina, see pages 40–43.

PRACTICAL INFORMATION

Local newspapers and magazines carry regular listings and advertisements of events. Often, hotels have in-house publications high-lighting programs in the city. Tourist information offices also publish annual calendars of events. **Ticketek** offices in Buenos Aires, Rosario, and Mar del Plata list upcoming events for those cities.

SPECTATOR SPORTS

Argentina's sports stadiums are not to be missed. Apart from the famous ones in Buenos Aires, there are sev-eral outside the capital that are worth visiting, especially when a *clásico* match of *fútbol* (soccer) is being played between two First Division rivals. The popular matches worth watching are ones between **Newell's Old Boys** and **Rosario Central**. Tickets for games can be bought from ticket agencies or directly from stadiums. Standard ticket prices are AR$10–40, but can cost as much as AR$100 especially when it is a clash between top soccer teams. Argentinians are very passionate about equestrian sports, especially *el turf* (horse racing) and polo. Car racing is also popular and the Argentinian round of the World Rally Championship takes place in Córdoba province every May.

BARS AND NIGHTCLUBS

Argentinian cities are famous for their nightlife and visitors can enjoy nights out until sunrise. In most cities there are happy hours from 5 to 9pm although bars and pubs get busy after 10pm, while clubs fill up from around 2am onwards and stay open until dawn. Buenos Aires has the liveliest nightlife *(see p123)*, closely followed by Rosario.

Club Del Vino, a popular nightclub in Palermo

In the summer, bars and clubs in coastal resorts such as Mar del Plata and Pinamar are filled with young vacationers.

CLASSICAL MUSIC AND DANCE

Lovers of classical music enjoy an extensive calendar with Buenos Aires boasting the most concert venues, including Teatro Colón *(see pp72–3)*. There are venues in other cities as well including **Teatro El Círculo** and **Teatro Lavarden** in Rosario, and **Teatro Municipal Colón** in Mar del Plata. Music festivals take place through the year, led by the Festival Internacional de Música Clásica in Ushuaia. Other recommended festivals are the Conciertos en el Bosque in Buenos Aires province, Música Clásica por los Caminos del Vino in Mendoza, where recitals are given in the atmospheric *bodegas* and churches of Mendoza's wine regions.

A polo match at the Polo Argentine Open Championship, Buenos Aires

Poster advertising bands at a music festival, Buenos Aires

Another major attraction is Argentina's most practiced classical dance form, ballet. Julio Bocca, a star performer, has made Argentinian ballet popular with the masses through his company, Ballet Argentino. The company tours the country frequently and is known for staging stunning performances.

FOLKLORIC MUSIC

Mainly found in Argentina's interiors, folkloric music is most popular in the province of Salta. In its namesake capital city, there are several restaurants that offer dinner-and-show packages. A more authentic experience is offered in *peñas*, small clubs that host informal folk-music gatherings where visitors can bring their own instruments. These clubs can be found in towns across the country, especially in Salta. The Festival Nacional de Folklore Cosquín, the biggest folkloric festival in Argentina, is held in Córdoba province and attracts the cream of folkloric talented performers.

THEATER AND FILM

The biggest concentration of theaters in the country is found in Buenos Aires, but other cities such as Rosario, Mendoza, and Córdoba also have important venues with regular performances. During summer, large companies in Buenos Aires switch location to Mar del Plata, where the **Teatro Auditorium** stages grand productions.

Argentina has its own thriving film industry *(see pp32–3)*. There are cinema halls in most towns and modern multiplexes in cities, the biggest chain being **Cinemark**. Art house cinemas such as **Cosmos** survive in Buenos Aires, and Rosario's screenings include Hollywood and Argentinian movies, with a smattering of world cinema. Mar del Plata's Festival Internacional de Cine de Mar del Plata and the Festival Internacional de Cine Independiente in the capital are two of the most important film festivals in Argentina.

CONTEMPORARY MUSIC

Argentina's rock music scene is vibrant and soloists such as Charly García and other local bands enjoy large followings. International groups stage their concerts mainly in football stadiums. Festivals, including Cosquín Rock in Córdoba, and Epecuén Rock and Gesell Rock in Buenos Aires, attract big names. Festival Jazz en Miramar takes place in Buenos Aires province. Smaller concert venues in cities host Argentinian and international jazz and blues musicians.

Musicians performing at Casa Blanca, Buenos Aires

OUTDOOR ACTIVITIES AND SPECIALIZED HOLIDAYS

Trekker trail sign at a park

Argentina's dazzling range of landscapes and good tourist facilities make the country ideal for almost every kind of adventure holiday, from mountaineering and trekking to polo and paragliding. Thanks to the extensive coastline, beautiful lakes, and complex network of rivers and wetlands, visitors have many water-based outdoor options. Come winter, skiing, snowboarding, and ice climbing are offered by tour companies along the Andes from Mendoza to Ushuaia. The country's open landscapes across its interior are ideal for sprawling golf courses. Driving, whether down the lonely roads or through well-developed resorts, can also be fun. For a relaxed holiday, spas, wine tours, and estancias are extremely inviting. The best organizers are local operators who offer subsidized deals.

Cycling along a trail through Parque Nacional Los Arrayanes

CYCLING AND MOUNTAIN BIKING

Argentina's terrain in the Andean regions, ranging from gravel tracks and rocky inclines to undulating foothills and shady copses, has made mountain biking popular. However, only cyclists who can handle gusty winds should cross the Patagonian steppe by bike. Popular with road and mountain bikers are the Lake District and sierras of Córdoba, de la Ventana, and Tandil. Northwest hubs such as Tucumán and Salta have tour agencies that hire out bikes. Local firms such as adventure specialist **Andestrack** in San Martín de los Andes and **Montañas Tucumanas** in San Miguel de Tucumán offer guided and self-guided mountain biking tours. Not many opt to bike down Buenos Aires avenues, but there are highways and long-distance roads for those using racing bicycles.

GOLF

There are more than 240 golf courses in Argentina recognized by **Asociación Argentina de Golf**, ranging from **Lagos de Palermo Municipal Club** in Buenos Aires to the most southerly golf course in the world, the 9-hole **Ushuaia Golf Club** close to Parque Nacional Tierra del Fuego.

The provinces of Neuquén and Río Negro, with their well-forested lakelands at the foot of the Andes, have proved popular with golfers. Just south of Bariloche, the **Llao Llao Hotel and Resort** boasts undulating fairways and challenging holes, while the **Arelauquen Lodge**, also near Bariloche at Lago Gutierrez, organizes golf and polo excursions. The hotel has its own 18-hole course. The Jack Nicklaus-designed **Chapelco Golf and Resort** is a first-class par-72 course near San Martín de los Andes. Argentinian tour companies **Covitour** and **Secontur** create golfing itineraries across the country. In the southern provinces, **Patagonia Golf** can add on fly-fishing trips.

DRIVING HOLIDAYS

Ruta Nacional 40 is legendary (*see p243*) but there are many paved highways and other trunk roads that are also fun to explore.

Off-road driving experiences can be exciting, from bumpy excursions in the Andean high plains to rough drives across salt lakes and down gravel and mud roads. **Movitrak** in Salta offers adventurous off-road driving experiences. Patagonia has also boomed as a driving destination. The Seven Lakes drive between Villa La Angostura and San Martín de los Andes is a great excursion on excellent roads. **Argentina**

A lonely road heading westwards across Patagonia to Perito Moreno

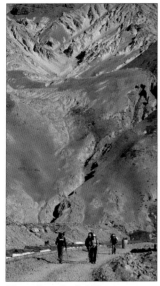

Hikers at Parque Provincial Aconcagua

Vision, in Puerto Madryn, can arrange vehicles for tours. In Córdoba, the **Caravana Club** offers a wide range of 4WD tours across the roads of Traslasierra, while fans of quad biking can also try **Kumbre** in Tandil. Another Argentina-based specialist to contact is **Canal Fun and Nature** in Ushuaia.

WALKING AND CLIMBING

With several beautiful sierras and challenging summits, Argentina is a walker's and climber's heaven.

The Chaltén and Fitz Roy area, Córdoba province, and the sierras of Tandil and de la Ventana offer all levels of challenges. **Huilén Viajes y Turismo** in Villa La Angostura offers a wide range of services for walkers, riders, climbers, and rafters in the lake region. Mendoza has long attracted serious rock climbers and experienced walkers and **Aymará Adventures and Expeditions** offers a package tour for climbers who want to ascend Aconcagua. **Centro Andino Buenos Aires**, a team that plans mountaineering trips, has branches in the capital and in major climbing centers such as Mendoza, Bariloche, and El Chaltén.

SPAS AND LUXURY HOLIDAYS

Famous for its spa, the Park Hyatt *(see p282)* in Mendoza, uses wine-based oils for massages. Llao Llao Hotel and Resort near Bariloche also offers health treatments. In Buenos Aires, many hotels such as Faena Hotel & Universe *(see p275)* have spas that offer a range of treatments. Porteños in the Palermo area use the **Evian Agua Club and Spa**. Argentina's largest spa town is Termas de Río Honda *(see p188)*, said to have "healing" waters.

SKIING AND WINTER SPORTS

The winter sports season starts in early July and lasts until early October. Luxury ski resorts include Las Leñas *(see p219)* in Mendoza province, **Villa Cerro Catedral** near Bariloche, and **Chapelco Ski Resort** near San Martín de los Andes. Managed by local Mapuches is Batea Mahuida near **Villa Pehuenia** in Neuquén. An operator that can arrange ski trips is **Ripio** in the capital. Glacier tours are available through local operators such as **MIL Outdoor Adventure** in Calafate and **Camino Abierto** in Patagonia. For ice climbing, **Compañia de Guias de la Patagonia** in Ushuaia is recommended.

Paraglider at Cerro Otto in Bariloche, Patagonia

IN THE AIR

The wide blue skies in Argentina can be explored by balloon, helicopter, glider, or paraglider. These activities are ideal even for beginners. Bariloche and Córdoba are established centers for all airborne activities, and it is possible to arrange gentle balloon flights across the rolling Pampas. Operators such as Lan & Kramer *(see p273)* in Buenos Aires plan all kinds of flights for learners and more experienced pilots.

TANGO

The tourist industry has attracted dozens of tango operators, from cowboys to expert historians, who can enrich a trip through the lesser known barrios in the capital, where tango was born and evolved. Tango-themed hotels such as **Lina's Tango Guest House** and Mansión Dandi Royal *(see p275)*, as well as major service providers such as **Kallpatour**, can organize tango shows and lessons to be combined with sightseeing trips in Buenos Aires.

WINE AND FOOD

Many vineyards now have organized tours and tasting sessions *(see pp210–11)*. Those in the Mendoza region with an international reputation include Salentein *(see p300)*, **Club Tapiz**, and Cavas Wine Lodge *(see p299)*. **The Grapevine** in Mendoza is good for tours led by knowledgeable, locally-based experts. Other regions are less developed, but **Terra Riojana** is opening doors to fascinating cellars in San Juan and La Rioja. **Arblaster and Clarke**, based in the UK, are highly respected. They plan detailed tours to explore *bodegas* and their exclusive vintages, and can combine tours with trips to Chile and Uruguay. Food trails have just started to become popular. Buenos Aires-based **Alejandro Frango** organizes meals out for individuals and small groups, during which local food delicacies are explained.

WHALE-WATCHING

Península Valdés is one of the world's most famous whale-watching locations. Operators such as **Jorge Schmid**, **Whales Argentina**, and **Tito Botazzi** arrange transport and expert guides to help visitors spot dolphins, killer whales, and porpoises. Southern Right whales, however, are the star attraction. All major international tour operators that feature Argentina in their itineraries offer packages for whale-watching.

Puerto Deseado *(see p229)* is an excellent location for observing porpoises and many other marine species, and almost all tours include the rockhopper penguin colony on Isla Pingüino *(see p229)*. **Darwin Expediciones** is the main operator in the town.

FISHING AND HUNTING

Fly-fishing for trout and salmon is growing in popularity, especially in Patagonia and the Lake District. **Tiempo de Pesca** in San Martín de los Andes arranges river trips. Patagonia Golf offers a variety of fly-fishing tours. Pablo Mazza of **Río Seco** is a well-known expert; the other good local agent is **Skifish**. Argentinian river fishing is also popular and **Pira Lodge** and **Estancia San Alonso**, both in Esteros del Iberá, can arrange boats and guides. Hunting expeditions to exclusive hunting estates and estancias can be organized by **Argentine Adventures**.

Fly-fishing in Río Chimehuin, which flows out of Lago Huechulafuquen

Windsurfing off Playa El Doradillo beach in Puerto Madryn

SAILING AND WINDSURFING

In Bariloche, **Velero Gourmet** offers luxury sailing trips to Victoria Island in Lago Nahuel Huapi. Canal Beagle is popular with sailors and **Rumbo Sur SRL** can organize boats and combine itineraries with land-based excursions. Windsurfing is gaining in popularity in Argentina, and Lago Traful on the Seven Lakes road is a good choice; **Dormis Costa Traful** can arrange windsurf gear as well as kayaking and horse-riding excursions. Waterskiing or speedboating across Río Plata, as well as fishing trips combined with visits to Uruguay, can be arranged by luxury tour agent, **Fueguito**.

RAFTING

There are many grades of white-water rafting in the Andean valleys, with the busy rafting centers located in Bariloche and Mendoza. In the former, **Extremo Sur** and **Aguas Blancas** can organize full-day rafting adventures down Río Manso (which has grades II to IV white-water sections) as well as gentle kayaking trips through the chain of lakes that connect Bariloche with Puerto Montt in Chile. In Mendoza, **Ríos Andinos** – based in the main rafting center, Potrerillos – offers a range of river tours, from moonlit rafting and kayaking to hydrospeed trips.

CRUISES

Buenos Aires and Ushuaia are favorite stopovers for the long-haul luxury cruises that come down from Brazil and the US. For smaller cruises around Canal Beagle and around Cape Horn, try **Témpanos Viajes** in Ushuaia and **Mare Australis**, which has offices in the US. International adventure tour operators, such as **Peregrine Adventures** and **Explore**, hire medium-sized icebreaker and ice-proof ships during the summer to explore the South Atlantic and Antarctica. There are no longer any regular passenger services up Río Paraná, but cruises and fishing voyages around a stretch of this river in Corrientes can also be organized. US-based luxury operator **Exsus** arranges a range of tailor-made river and ocean cruises.

DIVING AND SNORKELING

There have been concerns raised by environmentalists over people swimming with whales, and it is important to check the credentials of anyone offering whale-watching off the Puerto Madryn coast.

However, there are many exciting diving opportunities off the Atlantic coast, in Lago Traful, famous for its submerged forest, Lago Nahuel Huapi, and in the Falkland Islands (Islas Malvinas). In Ushuaia, **Ushuaia Divers** arrange snorkeling and shipwreck dives.

Diver approaches a Southern Right whale off Península Valdés

DIRECTORY

CYCLING AND MOUNTAIN BIKING

Andestrack
www.andestrack.com.ar

Montañas Tucumanas
www.montanas
tucumanas.com

GOLF

Arelauquen Lodge
Opp Lake Gutiérrez,
Bariloche. **Tel** (02944) 476-
110. **www**.arelauquen
lodge.com

Asociación Argentina de Golf
www.aag.org.ar

Chapelco Golf and Resort
www.chapelcogolf.com

Covitour
www.covitour.com

Lagos de Palermo Municipal Club
Ave Tornquist 6397,
Buenos Aires. **City Map** 2
A3. **Tel** (011) 4772-7261.

Llao Llao Hotel and Resort
Ave Bustillo, Bariloche.
Tel (02944) 448-530.
www.llaollao.com

Patagonia Golf
www.patagoniagolf.
com.ar

Secontur
www.secontur.com

Ushuaia Golf Club
Tel (02901) 432-946.

DRIVING HOLIDAYS

Argentina Vision
Puerto Madryn.
Tel (02965) 455-888.
www.argentinavision.com

Canal Fun and Nature
www.canalfun.com

Caravana Club
San Martín 1140, Córdoba.
Tel (03544) 470-261.

Kumbre
www.kumbre.com

Movitrak
www.movitrack.com.ar

WALKING AND CLIMBING

Aymará Adventures and Expeditions
9 de Julio 1023, Mendoza.
Tel (0261) 420-2064.
www.aymaramendoza.
com.ar

Centro Andino Buenos Aires
Rivadavia 1255, Buenos
Aires. **City Map** 5 D5.
Tel (011) 4381-1566.

Huilén Viajes y Turismo
Tel (02944) 495-489.
www.huilenviajes.com.ar

SPAS AND LUXURY HOLIDAYS

Evian Agua Club and Spa
Cerviño 3626, Buenos
Aires. **City Map** 5 F3.
Tel (011) 4807-4688.
www.aguaclubspa.com

SKIING AND WINTER SPORTS

Camino Abierto
www.caminoabierto.com

Chapelco Ski Resort
www.cerrochapelco.com

Compañia de Guias de la Patagonia
Gobernador Campos 795,
Ushuaia. **Tel** (02901) 437-
753. www.compania
deguias.com.ar

MIL Outdoor Adventure
www.miloutdoor.com

Ripio
www.ripioturismo.com.ar

Villa Cerro Catedral
Ave Ant. Argentina Base,
near Bariloche.
Tel (02944) 460-140.

Villa Pehuenia
www.villapehuenia.org

TANGO

Kallpatour
www.kallpatour.com

Lina's Tango Guest House
www.tangoguesthouse.
com.ar

WINE AND FOOD

Alejandro Frango
www.gastrosofia.com

Arblaster and Clarke
www.arblasterand
clarke.com

Club Tapiz
Pedro Molina, Ruta 60
s/n, Maipú, Mendoza.
Tel (0261) 496-0131.

The Grapevine
Galería San Marcos, Local
12, Mendoza. **Tel** (0261)
429-7522. **www**.the
grapevine-winetours.com

Terra Riojana
www.terrariojana.com.ar

WHALE-WATCHING

Darwin Expediciones
www.darwin-
expeditions.com

Jorge Schmid
www.puntaballena.
com.ar

Tito Botazzi
Puerto Pirámides.
Tel (02965) 474-110.

Whales Argentina
www.whalesargentina.
com.ar

FISHING AND HUNTING

Argentine Adventures
www.argentine
adventure.com.ar

Estancia San Alonso
Esteros del Iberá.
Tel (03782) 497-073.

Pira Lodge
www.piralodge.com

Río Seco
Paraguay 647, Buenos
Aires. **City Map** 3 E4.
www.riosecoadventures.
com

Skifish
Palacio 130, Bariloche.
Tel (02944) 431-257.
www.skifish.net

Tiempo de Pesca
Ragussi 26, San Martín de
los Andes. **www**.tiempo
depesca.com

SAILING AND WINDSURFING

Dormis Costa Traful
Ruta 65, Lago Traful.
Tel (02944) 479-005.
www.hosteriavillatraful.
com

Fueguito
www.fueguito.com

Rumbo Sur SRL
www.rumbosur.com.ar

Velero Gourmet
www.sailingpatagonia.
com.ar

RAFTING

Aguas Blancas
www.aguas blancas.
com.ar

Extremo Sur
Morales 765, Bariloche.
Tel (02944) 427-301.
www.extremosur.com

Ríos Andinos
Ruta Internacional 7, Km
55, Potrerillos.
Tel (0261) 429-5030.

CRUISES

Explore
55 Victoria Rd,
Farnborough, UK.
Tel (0044) 870-333-4001.
www.explore.co.uk

Exsus
10 Rockefeller Plaza, New
York City, 10020, USA.
Tel (001) 212-332-4848.
www.exsus.com

Mare Australis
www.australis.com

Peregrine Adventures
8 Clerewater Place,
Thatcham, Berkshire, UK.
www.peregrine-
adventures.com

Témpanos Viajes
San Martín 626 PB,
Ushuaia.
Tel (02901) 436-020.

DIVING AND SNORKELING

Ushuaia Divers
LN Alem 4509, Ushuaia.
www.tierradelfuego.
org.ar

On the Open Range

Many estancias once served as the second homes of rich urbanites and today, some of them offer the most luxurious rural accommodation in the country for tourists. Many activities such as bird-watching, trekking, and polo keep visitors occupied. Aspiring gauchos can gallop across the plains or go on horseback treks while skilled riders can try horse-breaking. During walks in the area, it is possible to see abundant birdlife and spot hares, rheas, skunks, and foxes. On some working estancias, visitors can also help with sheep-shearing, watching over the cattle, and preparing a barbecue. In the evenings, local dance performances as well as engaging storytelling sessions around the campfire can be arranged for visitors.

Visitors going on a horse-riding tour with the help of a guide

GAUCHO FOR A DAY

Argentinian gauchos have always been proud of their legacy and are more than pleased to show visitors how to become a gaucho for a day. In the Pampas, Estancia La Bamba and Estancia El Ombú, both located in San Antonio de Areco *(see p145)*, are well known for their traditional rustic accommodation. Here, visitors can participate in sheep-shearing activities or just watch the gauchos in action.

Working sheep estancias include **Estancia Alice**, otherwise known as El Galpon del Glaciar, near El Calafate, and the isolated **Estancia La Angostura** in Patagonia. The century-old Estancia Monte Dinero *(see p231)*, near Río Gallegos in Patagonia, also offers trekking apart from gaucho activities. **Estancia Río Capitán**, located in southern Patagonia, also organizes wildlife tours.

BIRD-WATCHING, TREKS, AND HORSE-RIDING

Life on an estancia entails being close to nature. Most ranches offer bird-watching as part of their package. Estancia Telken *(see p242)*, near Perito Moreno in Patagonia, is known for bird-watching as is **Estancia Rincón del Socorro** in Esteros del Iberá *(see pp166–7)*. The latter also organizes trekking trips and is a good base to explore the World Heritage Site of Cueva de las Manos.

An excellent option for horse-riding is **Estancia Huechahue** in Neuquén, from where there are expeditions into Parque Nacional Lanín *(see p237)*. In Patagonia, visitors who opt for leisurely horse rides are also treated to views of the region's glaciers and awesome peaks. Some of the well known estancias that offer bird-watching, trekking, and horse-riding are **Estancias La Maipú** and **El Cóndor**, both located on Lago San Martín.

LUXURY ESTANCIAS

Some estancias provide the perfect laid-back getaway. These include **Estancia Cerro de la Cruz** near Tandil, in the Pampas, **Estancias La Oriental**, **Menelik**, and **Los Toldos** in Patagonia. They have in common fine dining, spectacular locations, and personalized service. **Estancia Peuma Hue** is a luxurious stopover for trips into Parque Nacional Huapi *(see pp238–9)*. Hostería Helsingfors *(see p254)* in Los Glaciares and **Hostería Alta Vista** in El Calafate is another excellent option. There are two beautiful estancias in Córdoba – **Estancia El Colibrí**, famous for their wines and haute cuisine, and Estancia La Paz *(see p280)*, once the residence of President Roca. Near Esteros del Iberá is Estancia Rincón del Socorro, which is an ideal place to relax before heading into the preserve.

The well-furnished living room of Estancia Cerro de la Cruz

The vast Estancia El Galpón del Glaciar, near Los Glaciares, Patagonia

OTHER ACTIVITIES

Many estancias boast of excellent in-house libraries. They usually have a good collection of books on the country's culture and include classy coffee-table books as well as classics on rural life, such as Hernandez's *Martín Fierro*. Some estancias arrange for evening dance performances where visitors can watch or participate in lively country dances such as the foot-stamping *chacarera*, the playful *gato*, and the sensous *zamba*. Some estancia owners recount anecdotes around the communal dining table, while others organize formal story-telling sessions. More adventurous visitors can opt for hot air balloon rides that provide magnificent views of the Argentinian countryside.

TOURS AND RESERVATIONS

Many firms help visitors plan tours to Argentina's estancias. International tailor-made tour operator **Last Frontiers** has expert knowledge of horse ranches and arranges stays at exclusive polo estancias. **Arz and Horse** in San Martín de los Andes organizes tours and **Trekking Travel** in Mendoza provides trekking information, and arranges wine tours in the region. **Aves Patagonia** is a good option for trips to ranches across Patagonia, where rare bird species can be found. **Sol Iguazú** and **Yacutinga Lodge** are useful for trips to the Misiones area. A major Argentinian tour operator for activities related to wildlife is **Lihue Expediciones**. UK-based **Naturetrek** offers guidance to estancias and their activities. Some of the grandest ranches can be found in a comprehensive list on the Estancias de Santa Cruz and Estancias Argentinas websites *(see p273)*.

DIRECTORY

GAUCHO FOR A DAY

Estancia Alice
Ruta Provincial 11, near El Calafate. ***Tel*** *(011) 4311-8614.* **www**.estanciaalice.com.ar

Estancia La Angostura
Ruta Nacional 40, near Tres Lagos. ***Tel*** *(02962) 491-501.*

Estancia Río Capitán
Ruta Provincial 35, Patagonia, Province of Santa Cruz. ***Tel*** *(02286) 420-938.*

BIRD-WATCHING, HORSE-RIDING AND TREKS

Estancia El Cóndor
Ruta Nacional 40, Lago San Martin. **www**.cielospatagonicos.com

Estancia Huechahue
A.E 12 –Junin de los Andes, (8371) Neuquén. ***Tel*** *(02972) 491-303.* **www**.huechahue.com

Estancia La Maipú
Maipú 864, Piso 3 Oficina "A", Buenos Aires. **City Map** 3 E4. ***Tel*** *(011) 4901-5591.* **www**.estancialamaipu.com.ar

Estancia Rincón del Socorro
Casilla 45, 3470 Mercedes, Corrientes. ***Tel*** *(03782) 497-172.* **www**.rincondelsocorro.com

LUXURY ESTANCIAS

Estancia Cerro de la Cruz
Ruta Provincial 72, near Sierra de la Ventana. ***Tel*** *(011) 156-1582-449.* **www**.estanciacerrodelacruz.com

Estancia El Colibrí
Camino a Santa Catalina, Km 7, Santa Catalina, Córdoba. ***Tel*** *(03525) 465-888.* **www**.estanciaelcolibri.com

Estancia La Oriental
Junín, Province of Buenos Aires. ***Tel*** *(02362) 15-640-866.* **www**.estancia-laoriental.com

Estancia Los Toldos
Hosteria Cueva de las Manos, Patagonia. ***Tel*** *(011) 4901-0436.*

Estancia Menelik
www.cielospatagonicos.com/english/menelik.html

Estancia Peuma Hue
www.peuma-hue.com

Hostería Alta Vista
Ruta Provincial 15, Km 35, (9405) El Calafate, Santa Cruz. ***Tel*** *(02902) 499-902.* **www**.hosteriaaltavista.com.ar

TOURS AND RESERVATIONS

Arz and Horse
Rudecindo Roca 1020, San Martín de los Andes. ***Tel*** *(02972) 422-597.*

Aves Patagonia
www.avespatagonia.com.ar

Last Frontiers
www.lastfrontiers.com/argentina

Lihue Expediciones
Ave Córdoba 827, Buenos Aires. **City Map** 2 A3. ***Tel*** *(011) 5031-0070.*

Naturetrek
Cheriton Mill, Hants, UK. ***Tel*** *(0044) 1962-733-051.*

Sol Iguazú
www.soliguazu.com.ar

Trekking Travel
www.trekking-travel.com.ar

Yacutinga Lodge
www.yacutinga.com

SURVIVAL
GUIDE

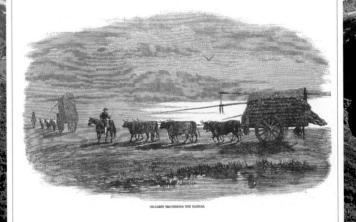

OX-CARTS TRAVERSING THE PAMPAS.

PRACTICAL INFORMATION 318–327

TRAVEL INFORMATION 328–335

PRACTICAL INFORMATION

Mass tourism is a relatively new phenomenon in Argentina, and the quality of the country's tourist infrastructure and services is gradually improving. It is a relatively easy country to travel around in, although tourist facilities may still be limited in its remote rural interiors. All major cities, towns, and resorts have visitor information centers that provide maps and

Information sign in El Calafate, Patagonia

brochures detailing activities, hotels, restaurants, and attractions. Hotel desk staff are usually very helpful and almost everyone on the street will gladly stop to give directions and advice. Contrary to conventional wisdom, visitors are not dogged by bureaucracy and red tape at every step, although it is advisable to carry relevant documentation at all times.

A bustling summer day at Plaza de Mayo, the capital's major tourist hub

WHEN TO GO

Argentina can be visited all year round, except for skiing (June–September) and whale-watching (August–December). Most Argentinians holiday in summer (January–Febuary), a period when Buenos Aires can be humid and popular resorts often crowded. The capital is at its best during spring and autumn.

Climatic conditions vary from region to region: the north is hotter than the south; the west is drier than the east; and the wind rarely stops blowing in Patagonia.

VISAS AND PASSPORTS

Citizens of North America, Australasia, South Africa, Great Britain, and all other Western European countries require no visa to enter Argentina for a stay of up to 90 days. Citizens of other countries should check their status and requirements at their Argentinian embassy or consulate. Visits can be

extended either by visitors presenting their passports at the immigration center or by leaving and re-entering the country. This is usually done by taking the short trip to Uruguay from Buenos Aires. Information on long-term stays for business travelers can be obtained at their local Argentinian embassy. US citizens cannot enter Brazil without a visa, an important consideration when traveling to Iguazú Falls. In case of loss of passport, visitors should inform their embassy.

CUSTOMS INFORMATION

Visitors may enter Argentina from overseas with up to 2 liters of alcoholic beverages, 400 cigarettes, 50 cigars, and 3 fl oz (100 ml) of perfume. For travelers entering from a neighboring country, half these quantities can be brought in. Vegetables, plants, fruits, and other perishable foods are prohibited. Pets must be certified in advance and have all their vaccinations up-to-date. It is important that passengers traveling from tropical countries, where diseases such as cholera or yellow fever are prevalent, carry a vaccination certificate.

TOURIST INFORMATION

The state tourist board in Argentina is the **Secretaría de Turismo y Deportes de la Nación**. Although it may be difficult to find one in the interiors, all major cities have tourist offices that provide maps and brochures, plus information on where to stay and what to see in their area.

Well-equipped tourist information center providing brochures and maps

◁ **A tourist camping at the foothills of the magnificent Mount Fitz Roy**

Visitors on the foredeck of a tour boat, Parque Nacional Los Glaciares

WHAT TO WEAR

For visits to Buenos Aires and central Argentina, visitors should bring light summer clothes and a raincoat for trips taken between November and March. The rest of the year, cold winds, morning frosts, and even snow can bring the temperature down.

During the summer in Patagonia, travelers must take sunblock and clothes that cut out UV rays. Visitors will also need to carry warm winter clothing and harsh weather gear, especially if visiting the mountain areas. The northeast and northwest are in the subtropical region and have hot, humid days and sudden rainstorms. Nights in the Andean high plains are intensely cold all through the year and sweaters or llama wool ponchos are required.

SOCIAL CUSTOMS AND ETIQUETTE

Argentinians are generally courteous but friendly and informal, and have a relaxed attitude towards protocol and etiquette. Depending on age and degree of acquaintance, they greet one another with either a kiss on one cheek or a handshake. It is increasingly fashionable for men to do the former on greeting, but is by no means universal. If in doubt, proffer a hand.

Dress is casual but usually smart – it is better to attend a business meeting in a smart shirt than in a rumpled suit and tie. Everything moves at a slower pace outside the major cities in Argentina, and in hotter regions the afternoon siesta still remains a popular custom.

LANGUAGE

The official language of Argentina is Spanish, spoken by almost everyone in the main cities, towns and interior. Outside the university-educated middle-classes and those who work full-time in the tourism sector, English is not spoken widely. For anyone who is traveling off the beaten track, a smattering of Spanish is a great advantage. Small pockets of native people speak Aimará or Quechua in the northwest, and Guaraní is still strong in Misiones and along the Paraguayan border.

In Buenos Aires, many people still use elements of *lunfardo*, an argot that arose in prisons in the late 19th century that is a mix of Spanish, Italian, and Genovese.

ADMISSION PRICES

Many of the major museums in Argentina's bigger cities are subsidized by the federal or state government and are therefore cheap, and often free, to enter. The admission charge is likely to be in the order of US$1. In the free museums, visitors are encouraged to give a voluntary contribution, essential to the survival of these underfunded institutions. To enter private museums, visitors should expect to pay around US$3 to US$4. Note, however, that most such museums have days (often Wednesday) when admissions are either half-price or free. Entrance to MALBA in Buenos Aires (see pp110–11), for example, is free on Wednesdays.

Cinemas are cheaper Monday through Wednesday. The door charge at nightclubs varies substantially, but is not less than US$4 and can go up to US$20 in the most modern and fashionable venues.

OPENING HOURS

Banks are generally open from 10am to 3pm on weekdays and closed over the weekends. Museums, art galleries, and other cultural venues usually open at 10am and close at 7 or 8pm.

Most supermarkets and shops, including big shopping malls, don't close until 9pm or later. Bars, pubs, and restaurants stay open very late, making nightlife vibrant and lively. In the provinces, many shops and services close in the afternoon for siesta.

Art exhibition space in Museo de Arte Latinoamericano, Buenos Aires

TRAVELERS WITH SPECIAL NEEDS

Although Argentina is yet to develop an efficient tourist infrastructure for disabled travelers, there has been an improvement in recent years. Modern museums, art galleries, and upscale hotels now have access facilities, although it is advisable for visitors to check in advance. An increasing number of buses in the major Argentinian cities have pavement level doors for accompanied wheelchair users.

The **Decthird** tour company specializes in accessible tourism, providing adapted hotel accommodation, tours and transfers, and 24-hour telephone support. **Access-Able Travel Source** and the **Society for Accessible Travel and Hospitality (SATH)** both promote awareness and accessibility for travelers with special needs.

TRAVELING WITH CHILDREN

Argentina is an extremely child-friendly country and youngsters are welcomed everywhere. However, navigating a pushchair over the potholed pavements of Buenos Aires can be stressful. Some cultural differences, should be noted – Argentinian children do not, as a rule, have separate meal times and rarely go to bed before their parents do. Most restaurants and hotels are more child-friendly than their first world

Backpackers trekking through Parque Nacional Los Glaciares, Patagonia

counterparts and will happily bring out a high chair and a child-sized food portion. Many restaurants also have supervised play areas.

SENIOR TRAVELERS

Senior travelers will find no particular problems getting around in Argentina, though the usual common sense precautions regarding safety and medical care apply here as everywhere else. While concession prices are less common here than in first world countries, it never harms to enquire at museums and other tourist sites.

50plus Expeditions is a tourist agency that organizes special tours mainly for groups of senior travelers around Patagonia. They also arrange Antarctic cruises. **ElderTreks** is an adventure travel company that deals exclusively with travelers above the age of 50. They organize a wide variety of

tours around Argentina that focus on wildlife, tango, gaucho experiences, wine tasting, and national parks.

GAY AND LESBIAN TRAVELERS

Buenos Aires competes with Rio de Janeiro for the title of gay capital of Latin America. It has a vibrant and eclectic scene encompassing bars, restaurants, and lodgings. Other big cities also have plenty to offer the gay traveler, and the majority of hotels around the country have no qualms about accommodating gay or lesbian couples. This is still a macho society, however, meaning that gay men have greater visibility than lesbians. The **International Gay and Lesbian Travel Association (IGLTA)** offers a wealth of information on tour agencies and accommodation options.

BACKPACKERS

Argentina has recently been firmly entrenched on the backpacker trail. The number of youth hostels in Buenos Aires has increased and other top destinations such as Salta, Bariloche, and El Calafate are also well served by hostels and budget accommodations. Students who belong to youth hosteling associations may get a discount for lodging, but concessions are not available for transport and other services. Hitchhiking is still a good way to get around the country, though all the usual precautions should be taken.

Senior travelers on a winery tour at Bodega Nieto Senetiner

WOMEN TRAVELERS

It is rare that women travelers, whether in groups or pairs, face problems in Argentina. However, it is advisable to take the usual precautions, including not walking alone late in the evening. If there is a need to take a taxi, it is advisable to call for radio taxis *(see p335)* that come to the doorstep. **Radio Taxi Porteño** and **Radio Taxi del Plata** in Buenos Aires are some popular ones.

Women traveling alone may attract attention although it is usually of the harmless kind. Argentinian men sometimes pass a stream of *piropos* (unsolicited comments or sexual advances), which range from *Que lindaque sos!* (You're lovely!) to *De qué juguetería te escapaste?, ¡muñeca!* (From which toyshop did you escape? You doll!). It is best to ignore them. On beaches, keep to minimum exposure to avoid attention. The **Young Women's Christian Association (YMCA)** has a branch in Buenos Aires that offers basic and comfortable accommodations.

TIME

There is only one time zone in Argentina, though certain provinces, particularly those with large agricultural sectors, occasionally put the clocks back or forwards an hour. Argentina is 3 hours behind

Plugs used across Argentina

GMT during its summer, and 4 hours behind during its winter.

ELECTRICITY

Electricity in Argentina runs on 220 volts and sockets take either two- or three-pronged plugs and these plugs are flat-shaped. Adaptors for foreign appliances can be purchased at *ferreterías* (hardware stores) and major supermarkets. Power outages are usually short lived.

CONVERSIONS

US to Metric
1 inch = 2.54 centimeters
1 foot = 30 centimeters
1 mile = 1.6 kilometers
1 ounce = 28 grams
1 pound = 454 grams
1 pint = 0.6 liters
1 gallon = 3.79 liters

Metric to US
1 millimeter = 0.04 inch
1 centimeter = 0.4 inch
1 meter = 3 feet 3 inches
1 kilometer = 0.6 mile
1 gram = 0.04 ounces
1 kilogram = 2.2 pounds
1 liter = 2.1 pints

DIRECTORY

VISAS AND PASSPORTS

Australia
Tel (011) 4779-3500.
www.argentina.embassy.gov.au

Canada
Tel (011) 4808-1000.
www.cic.gc.ca

UK
Tel (011) 4808-2200.
www.ukinargentina.fco.gov.uk

USA
Tel (011) 5777-4533.
www.argentina.usembassy.gov

TOURIST INFORMATION

Secretaría de Turismo y Deportes de la Nación
www.turismo.gov.ar

TRAVELERS WITH SPECIAL NEEDS

Access-Able Travel Source
Tel (0303) 232-2979.
www.access-able.com

Decthird
Tel (015) 4182-5469.
www.decthird.com

Society for Accessible Travel and Hospitality (SATH)
Tel (0212) 447-7284.
www.sath.org

SENIOR TRAVELERS

50plus Expeditions
Tel (0416) 749-5150.
www.50plusexpeditions.com

ElderTreks
Tel (0416) 588-5000.
www.eldertreks.com

GAY AND LESBIAN TRAVELERS

International Gay And Lesbian Travel Association (IGLTA)
www.iglta.org

WOMEN TRAVELERS

Radio Taxi del Plata
Tel (011) 4505-1111.
www.delplata.com.ar

Radio Taxi Porteño
Tel (011) 4566-5777.

Young Women's Christian Association (YWCA)
Tel (011) 4322-1550.

Visitors seated at tables outside a restaurant, Bariloche

Personal Security and Health

Argentina is relatively safe, however, in popular tourist cities such as Mendoza, Córdoba, Buenos Aires, and other areas, it is experiencing an upsurge of petty theft and assaults. It is therefore best to keep valuables locked away in the hotel safe. There are few health issues. It is advisable to bring prescribed drugs, as well as a first aid kit and water purification tablets when traveling anywhere off the beaten track. If you have a persistent medical condition it may be a good idea to have a doctor's letter translated into Spanish, although most Argentinian doctors will have at least a basic grasp of English.

Traffic jam along a city road, a common sight in Argentina

A Federal policeman in his uniform, Buenos Aires

POLICE

The Federal Police has jurisdiction across Argentina but in reality is active mainly in the capital. Most routine police work in the country is undertaken by the provincial police forces. Visitors may find that local police are not always helpful and the problems afflicting police forces in most developing nations, such as corruption and low salaries, are evident here.

Those who find themselves a victim of, or witness to, a serious crime, must report to their embassy and the relevant law enforcement authority. In Buenos Aires, this is the **Comisaría del Turista**,

which has English-speaking staff. Under no circumstances should you hand over important documents, such as a passport, to a police officer without a witness being present and a receipt provided.

LOST AND STOLEN PROPERTY

There is little point in reporting lost or stolen property to the police unless there is a need to file a *levantar un acta* (official report) for insurance purposes. Visitors will need to do this at the nearest *comisaría* (police station), usually within 24 hours of the robbery. Lost passports and credit cards should be reported as soon as possible to the embassy *(see p321)* and to the card issuer, respectively.

Petty theft is not a major problem in Argentinian cities but visitors must always be on guard particularly in unsafe neighborhoods and when using ATMs outside banking hours. Hotel thefts are rare but it is wise not to leave valuables in the room.

STREET HAZARDS

Not all Argentinian drivers follow road regulations and as a pedestrian it is best to be alert at all times and look carefully while crossing a busy junction. Be prepared for uneven road surfaces and pavements, and flying grit while driving on gravel roads.

Noisy street marches and protests are part of the daily routine in Buenos Aires, although their effect is mainly felt by commuters traveling from the province to the city. Hence, it is safer to always allow for a bit of spare time to reach a destination.

NATURAL DISASTERS

Argentina has had very few large-scale natural hazards that present a threat to human life. Heavy rainstorms result in flooding due to a poor drainage system in some parts of the capital. Earthquakes are a theoretical risk in provinces such as Mendoza and San Juan, which border the Andean range. The last tremor of serious note occured in 1993 in San Juan *(see p216)*. In the unlikely event of an earthquake, it is advisable to move away from electricity poles and high structures.

IN AN EMERGENCY

It is best to call an ambulance in case of an emergency and to go to a state hospital *emergencia* (emergency room) if not covered by medical insurance. Visitors are advised to carry along their medical papers in case the doctor wants to take a look at the prescription.

A police car in Buenos Aires

HOSPITALS AND PHARMACIES

Argentina has two types of hospitals: public and private. The former are usually underequipped and underfunded, although the doctors and nurses are highly qualified as many also work in the private sector. Some well-maintained goverment hospitals are **Hospital Zonal General de Agudos San Roque Manuel B. Gonnet** in La Plata and **Hospital de Urgencias** in Córdoba. Private hospitals are generally of a high standard, offering first-class health services and spotless rooms. These include Buenos Aires's **Hospital Alemán** and **Hospital Británico**. There is also a medical institute exclusively for children called **Hospital de Niños Dr. Ricardo Gutiérrez**.

Some "prescription only" drugs available in more developed countries, such as antibiotics and birth-control pills, can be bought over the counter in Argentina. Most *farmacias* (pharmacies) are open from 9am to 8pm and major cities have 24-hour outlets such as **Farmacity Malabia** and **Farmacity Santa Fe** in the capital and **Farmacia 2001** in Tucumán.

One of the many pharmacies found in Argentina's cities

SERIOUS DISEASES

Malaria or cholera may be found in some rural regions. A more common disease is dengue, a viral illness spread by mosquitos. *Chagas* is a chronic condition transmitted through a blood parasite carried by the cone nose or "kissing bug." It is prevalent in rural parts but the risk of contracting it is miniscule.

MINOR HAZARDS

The most common minor ailments to afflict visitors to Argentina are dehydration and sunstroke. Both of these can easily be avoided by carrying a strong sunscreen, a cap, and bottled water on any excursion or trips to the beach. Tap water is also potable all across the country.

Some serious diseases are carried by insect bites but a nasty rash is by far the most likely irritant a visitor can get. It is wise to keep a good brand of repellent always at hand. Altitude sickness can, in extreme cases, be dangerous but is only an issue for visitors traveling to the Andean highlands.

Food poisoning is rarer here than in most Latin American countries, although the usual common sense precautions apply.

PUBLIC TOILETS

Good public bathrooms are scarce in Argentina and the well-maintained ones are mainly in cities. It is best to use the services of public toilets in the nearest fast food chain, shopping mall, or department store.

TRAVEL AND HEALTH INSURANCE

Visitors traveling to Argentina are advised to purchase private travel insurance that includes full medical coverage. This is useful in case of emergencies which require treatment at private clinics where medical care can be very expensive. Argentina shares no reciprocal health insurance scheme with any other country.

VACCINATIONS

Visitors traveling to remote areas of the country should ensure that their regular immunizations, such as tetanus, are up-to-date. They should also consider having a Hepatitis B vaccination. Except for a few rural areas bordering Bolivia and Paraguay, Argentina is mainly malaria-free.

DIRECTORY

EMERGENCY NUMBERS

Ambulance
Tel 107.

Comisaría del Turista
Avenida Corrientes 436, Buenos Aires. **City Map** 3 E4. *Tel (0800) 999-5000.*

Fire Service
Tel 100.

Police (Buenos Aires and Mar del Plata)
Tel 911.

Police (Argentina)
Tel 101.

HOSPITALS AND PHARMACIES

Farmacia 2001
Monteagudo 501, Tucumán. *Tel (0800) 555-2001.*

Farmacity Malabia
Corrientes 5258, Buenos Aires. **City Map** 4 B5. *Tel (011) 4857-3651.* **www**.farmacity.com

Farmacity Santa Fe
Santa Fe 2822, Buenos Aires. **City Map** 2 B3. *Tel (011) 4821-3000.* **www**.farmacity.com

Hospital Alemán
Avenida Pueyrredón 1640, Buenos Aires. **City Map** 2 B3. *Tel (011) 4827-7000.* **www**.hospitalaleman.com.ar

Hospital Británico
Pedriel 74, Barracas, Buenos Aires. *Tel (011) 4309-6400.* **www**.hospitalbritanico.org.ar

Hospital de Niños Dr. Ricardo Gutiérrez
Sánchez de Bustamante 1330, Buenos Aires. **City Map** 2 A3. *Tel (011) 4962-9232.*

Hospital de Urgencias
Calle Catamarca 441, Córdoba. *Tel (0351) 4341-201.*

Hospital Zonal General de Agudos San Roque Manuel B. Gonnet
Calle 508 btwn 18 & 19, La Plata. *Tel (0221) 484-029-094.*

Banking and Currency

The unit of currency in Argentina is the peso, but US dollars are widely accepted in tourist areas and most supermarket chains. The majority of tourist-oriented hotels, shops, and restaurants accept all major credit cards. Bring cash or traveler's checks in either US dollars or euros; other foreign currencies are not readily exchanged in all banks and will not be accepted as cash. The Argentinian peso slumped in 2002 when it was allowed to float freely on foreign exchanges; before that one peso was pegged to one US dollar. Since then the Argentinian Central Bank's monetary policy is to keep the peso steady at around three pesos to one US dollar.

Visitors changing money at a *casa de cambio* in Córdoba

BANKS AND CASAS DE CAMBIO

Argentina's banks range from the state-run behemoth, **Banco de la Nación Argentina**, to local independent banks, as well as international banks such as **Citibank**. Opening hours are normally from 10am to 3pm on weekdays. Avoid lunch hours to escape long queues. Ask hotel staff for opening hours of the nearest branches.

Casas de cambio (bureaux de change) are generally open longer hours than banks and tend to offer quicker service and better exchange rates in comparison to shops and hotels. It is advisable not to exchange money in a hotel unless there is absolutely no other alternative. Ministro Pistarini International Airport in the capital also has several *casas de cambio*, including the excellent **Banco Piano**.

AUTOMATIC TELLER MACHINES (ATMS)

Most banks have ATMs – look out for the Banelco and Link machines that display the symbol of the card issuer.

Visitors will be charged between US\$1 and US\$5, depending on the bank and the card issuer. Getting change in Argentina is difficult and most vendors blanch at the sight of a 100 peso note, so it is better not to withdraw cash in multiples of 100. Instead, request for 190 pesos rather than 200. For safety reasons, always withdraw money only during business hours, preferably in populated areas such as bank lobbies or shopping malls.

Standard ATM, found across Argentina

TRAVELER'S CHECKS AND CREDIT CARDS

Traveler's checks still remain the safest way of carrying money. However, not all banks exchange them, so it is better to check beforehand

instead of joining the long queue. A better option for exchanging money is at a *casa de cambio*. Their opening hours vary from region to region though they are usually open until at least 6pm. In Buenos Aires, most are situated in the Microcentro, close to where Reconquista and Calles Sarmiento intersect. The commission is around 2 percent, with a minimum service charge of about US\$5. **American Express** traveler's checks can be changed without commission at their office in Retiro.

Credit cards are accepted in most major outlets, but it is wise to ask first, especially in restaurants. The most widely accepted cards are **MasterCard** and **Visa**, followed by American Express. Visitors will have to show a photo ID, if the need arises.

WIRING MONEY

It is advisable to use the facility of wiring money as a last resort. Instead, it is better to go to either **Forex Cambio**, who, like Banco Piano, can also cash foreign checks, or **Western Union**. Charges fluctuate and a minimum fee would be about US\$50. It is advisable to call ahead to check for the best rates.

CURRENCY

The Argentinian peso is divided into 100 centavos. In the 2002 economic crisis a number of provinces issued their own paper money bonds. These are no longer legal tender. Do not accept any note that is not marked "pesos" and check the watermark carefully.

The peso's symbol, AR\$, is easily confused with that of the US dollar (US\$). Assume that a product is priced in pesos unless it is stated otherwise. Always carry small amounts of cash in coins and small denomination bills for tips and minor purchases. Buses only accept coins and taxi drivers are unable to give change for larger denomination notes.

Coins

Centavo coins are in denominations of 5¢, 10¢, 15¢, 25¢, and 50¢. The centavo coins were introduced in 1994, followed by 1 peso. 1¢ was also available but it has been withdrawn from circulation.

| 5 centavos | 10 centavos | 25 centavos |

| 50 centavos | 1 peso |

Bank Notes

In 1992, banknotes were introduced in denominations of AR$2, AR$5, AR$10, AR$20, AR$50, and AR$100. The $1 was replaced by a coin in 1994. The notes usually have images of the country's heroes on one side and, on the other, some of the major events in Argentinian history.

2 pesos

5 pesos

10 pesos

20 pesos

50 pesos

100 pesos

Communications and Media

Stamp featuring the Pampas

Public telephones (*locutorios*) are the cheapest way to make calls in Argentina although cellular phones are now affordable and coverage is excellent. Booths in Internet cafés are far more efficient than payphones on the street. Most major cities and even remote villages have at least one Internet café. The mail service may not be very reliable but it is still cheap and efficient by Latin American standards. Mailboxes are usually the British-style red letter boxes found around street corners. For entertainment, Argentina has five free television channels transmitting numerous programs ranging from documentaries and talk shows to soap operas. The radio is quite popular with Argentinians, featuring breakfast shows and pop music programs.

TELEPHONE NUMBERS

The country code for calling Argentina is 54, followed by an area code, which can be one, two, three, or four digits; for example Buenos Aires's area code is 11 followed by the telephone number. All landline numbers in Buenos Aires have eight digits. Public telephones are found everywhere, but more rarely in remote areas. Public call centers are assigned a cabin with a meter which displays the charged amount. It is better to check at the counter for discounts on international or domestic calls. Pre-paid phonecards can be bought at these call centers to call abroad.

CELL PHONES

Visitors should ask their phone provider at home about international roaming before going abroad. All Argentinian cell numbers begin with 15 and are followed by eight digits. To call cell phones in Buenos Aires from overseas, dial +54 9 11 and the number, leaving out the 15. Some hotels offer a cell phone renting service, but this can be expensive. Visitor centers have companies that offer a similar service, such as **Phonerental** in Buenos Aires.

INTERNET AND FAX

Most Argentinian hotels, hostels, and guesthouses have Internet facilities. Even small villages in the interior have a *locutorio* (Internet café) since most homes do not have personal computers. The hourly rate for broadband access rarely exceeds AR$3. The only disadvantage is that the speed of the connection is slower in small towns than in the cities. Also, the letters on the keyboard may not be the standard Western letters. Printing pages is also quite cheap at less than a US dollar per page. Fax machines are available in most hotels with basic facilities and all *locutorios*. Faxes are normally charged at AR$3 to AR$6 per sheet.

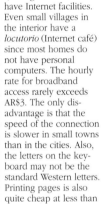

Telephone sign at El Cuyo

MAIL SERVICES

Sending and receiving parcels through the regular mail service in Argentina is not recommended. Registering both letters and parcels improves the odds against pilfering. However, the safest way to send anything abroad is through one of the international courier companies such as **FedEx**, **DHL**, and **UPS**.

The main *oficinas de correos* (post offices) in large towns and cities are open from 8am to 8pm on weekdays and from 8am to 1pm on Saturdays. **Correo Central** *(see p67)* is inexpensive for domestic mail. A *poste restante* (mail holding service) is available at main post offices in the major cities; letters should be addressed to the recipient's name, followed by the words *"Lista de Correos,"* and then by the name and address of the post office. Collecting the mail will cost the recipient around AR$6, and they will need to show ID.

A *locutorio* in the town of El Bolsón, Patagonia

Popular talk show with Argentinian actor Susana Giménez on Telefé

ARGENTINIAN ADDRESSES

Argentinian addresses list the house number after the name of the street. Other useful words to recognize are *departamento* (apartment), *piso* (floor), and *local* (unit). Always include the *código postal* (zip or postal code).

RADIO AND TELEVISION

The majority of Argentinian households have cable television, giving them access to over 70 channels. Some of these are Argentinian channels such as Crónica, a news channel, and others are foreign channels such as Sony. Most hotels in the country also have cable television in the rooms.

There are five free *canales abiertos* (open channels). The state-run Canal 7 specializes in documentaries, live folk music, and panel shows. There is also América, which airs soap operas and panel shows, and Canal 13, with news programs and sitcoms based on US teleserials. Telefé features one of the most famous talk shows in the country with the popular host Susana Giménez.

Radio is quite popular in Argentina. The most listened to radio station is La 100 on 99.9 FM, which plays Latin pop. Some well-known names in radio are Mario Pergolini, Roberto Pettinato, and Fernando Peña, who host breakfast shows that blend conversation and English-language pop and rock.

Almost every city in the country has a local radio station. These small-time stations help visitors in the case of lost possessions by putting out an appeal to recover the property.

NEWSPAPERS AND MAGAZINES

The *Buenos Aires Herald (see p119)* is popular for English-language news and listings in the capital. It dates back to 1876 and is an iconic newspaper whose finest hour was during the 1970s military dictatorship, when it was one of the few press organs to openly criticize the government's rule. The *International Herald Tribune*, *Time*, and *Newsweek* are usually available at larger newsstands and airports.

The two biggest local newspapers are the broadsheet *La Nación* and the tabloid *Clarín (see p122)*. The former is the voice of the country's center-right, while the latter is more populist and with higher production values. Although the newspapers are in Spanish, both papers are worth picking up on a Friday for the listings supplements.

Magazines in Argentina are a mix of homegrown titles and Spanish-language versions of international magazines. Popular gossip magazines are *Gente*, *Caras*, and *Noticias*, which specialize in celebrity news. Fashion magazines include *El Planeta Urbano*, while *D-Mode* is a good guide to clubs and restaurants.

A news *kiosko* at the pedestrianized Calle Florida in Buenos Aires

TRAVEL INFORMATION

Transport infrastructure in Argentina, although still not highly efficient, is much improved. Politicians and bureaucrats have finally woken up to the numerous problems faced by the country's transport network. Now, tourists can arrive at the sleek and modern terminal at Ministro Pistarini International Airport or travel the length and breadth of Patagonia in a comfortable, air-conditioned *micro* (coach). Visitors can opt to arrive in Argentina via the other five countries it shares its borders with or even

Roadside marker on Ruta Nacional 3

choose to come across by sea from Uruguay. With a couple of exceptions, cross-country train journeys are, unfortunately, a thing of the past, so visitors should expect to get around the country mainly by air or by road. Major cities and important tourist destinations across Argentina usually have small airports, and almost all places are accessible by *micro*. The vast majority of rutas nacionales (major highways) are asphalted and operate as turnpikes; rutas provinciales (smaller roads) off the beaten track are often graveled.

ARRIVING BY AIR

All international flights arrive at Buenos Aires's Ministro Pistarini International Airport, usually known as Ezeiza after the area in which it is located. This is 22 miles (35 km) west of the city center. The only exceptions are flights between Buenos Aires and Uruguay, which depart from Aeroparque Jorge Newbery. Ezeiza has two interlinked ter-minals, A and B, the latter used exclusively by Argentina's main airline, **Aerolíneas Argentinas**. Baggage collection and customs operate smoothly, although baggage handlers at Ezeiza airport are notoriously light fingered, so ensure that suitcases are locked and preferably shrink-wrapped.

Signboard at Ministro International Airport

Other airlines that fly to Buenos Aires are **Air France**, **American Airlines**, **Iberia**, **KLM**, **British Airways**, and **Varig**.

AIRPORTS

After Ezeiza, Argentina's most important airport is Aeroparque Jorge Newberry, more commonly known as Aeroparque, located a mile (2 km) from downtown Buenos Aires. This is a hub for domestic flights to provincial airports around the country and to Uruguay.

There are 32 airports in Argentina that receive commercial flights. Apart from these, there are smaller airfields for chartered services. Most airports are located some distance from the population centers they serve, but are generally well connected to them by bus, taxi or *remise* (licensed cab).

AIR FARES

Air fares to Argentina are generally expensive. Prices are high from mid-December through to March, when the demand for tickets out of and into the country is at its highest. Internal flight prices also peak at these times, at Easter, and in June and July. Expect to pay around US$800 for a round-trip flight from the United States, and about double that for a flight from Europe. It is possible to find special deals on the Internet which are significantly cheaper, although the flights are unlikely to be direct.

Fixed date returns are always cheaper than open

The bustling check-in hall at Ministro Pistarini International Airport, Buenos Aires

Tourist coaches parked at the Cristo Redentor near the Chilean border

tickets, though there are often some good offers available on round-the-world tickets. For internal flights, Aerolíneas Argentinas has the largest and most reliable network in the country. Unfortunately, it operates a highly controversial "dual pricing" system, where tourists pay almost three times as much as locals for the same journeys.

PACKAGE DEALS AND ORGANIZED TOURS

Packages for resorts around Argentina can be competitive. There is a lively market for holidays in Argentina from neighboring countries Peru and Chile, and even from Spain, where many tour agencies offer weekend breaks or longer-stay deals. These include flight transfers, accommodation at three- or four-star hotels, with a tango show occasionally thrown in. The most popular destinations for package tour operators are Iguazú, Bariloche, Buenos Aires, the Andean Northwest, and the more obvious tourist towns of Patagonia. The all-inclusive package-holiday concept is, however, not yet very popular in Argentina.

Adventure tour firms offer everything from whale-watching and rafting trips to specialist bird and wildlife holidays (see pp310–15). It is best to contact recommended operators in Europe, North America, and Australasia. They have very high health and safety requirements that are certainly higher than those deemed acceptable

by Argentinian law. It is also useful to visit a local travel agent for detailed and up-to-date information.

ARRIVING BY LAND

Argentina shares its borders with five countries: Paraguay, Bolivia, Brazil, Uruguay, and Chile. It is possible to arrive into Argentina via any of these countries, although it is important to check visa requirements beforehand. Travelers arriving by coach will usually be asked to show their passports at the border. Tourists arriving in their own vehicles may be waved through or subjected to a thorough search of their car, depending largely on the whim of the *gendarme* (border guard) on duty.

ARRIVING BY SEA

Boats from Uruguay arrive at the port terminal Dársena Norte at Avenidas Córdoba and Alicia Moreau de Justo in

Puerto Madero (see p75). There are regular services from Colonia del Sacramento (see p117) and other towns in Uruguay. **Buquebus** is a popular operator. Cruise ships berth at Terminal Benito Quinquela Martín at Ramon Castillo street, near Avenida de los Immigrantes, Puerto Madero.

DIRECTORY

ARRIVING BY AIR

Aerolíneas Argentinas
Ave L N Alem 1134, Buenos Aires. **City Map** 3 E3. **Tel** *(0810) 222-86527.* www.aerolineas. com.ar

Air France
San Martin 344, Buenos Aires. **Tel** *(011) 4317-4711.* www.airfrance.com.ar

American Airlines
Tel *(011) 4318-1111.* www.aa.com

British Airways
Tel *(0800) 666-1459.* www.britishairways.com

Iberia
Tel *(0810) 999-4237.* www.iberia.com

KLM
Tel *(0800) 122-3014.* www.klm.com

Varig
Tel *(0810) 266-6874.* www.varig.com.ar

ARRIVING BY SEA

Buquebus
Ave Ant Argentina 821, Buenos Aires. **City Map** 3 E3. **Tel** *(011) 4316-6500.* www.buquebus. com

Docked passenger boats at Puerto Madero

Domestic Flights

While the idea of crossing Argentina by car holds great appeal, most visitors prefer to travel by air, enabling them to see many of the country's sights during a fortnight's holiday. Most of Argentina's tourist hotspots, such as the Glaciar Perito Moreno and Parque Nacional Iguazú, are well served by flights from and to Buenos Aires, though far less so by flights between one another. Travelers hopping around the country by air, therefore, will become familiar with Buenos Aires's main domestic airport, Aeroparque Jorge Newberry.

The control tower at Mendoza's international airport

People departing for a trip on an Aerolíneas Argentinas flight

DOMESTIC AIRLINES

The number of domestic airlines is expected to grow in line with the Argentinian economy and the expansion of the tourist sector. Presently, Aerolíneas Argentinas *(see p328)* is the country's largest domestic carrier, handling about 80 percent of the total traffic.

Its sister airline is known as Austral, and both are owned by Grupo Marsans. They provide a good flight network across Argentina, linking the capital with 33 destinations.

The main competitors of Aerolíneas Argentinas and Austral are **Lade** and **LAN Argentina**. The former is a state-owned airline operated by the Argentinian military that runs domestic flights to a number of key destinations. LAN Argentina is an affiliate of the LAN group, which operates services to major cities.

Sol Líneas Aéreas, in operation since 2006, is the first regional low-cost airline in Argentina. It serves destinations mainly in the center of the country, such as Rosario and Córdoba, as well as popular Atlantic coastal resorts such as Mar del Plata, Villa Gesell, and Punta del Este in Uruguay. A low-cost airline in Argentina is **Andes Líneas Aéreas**, which has flights from Buenos Aires to Salta. **Baires Fly** planes can carry a maximum of 19 passengers, but it has a flight network for both international and national flights.

RESERVATIONS

Reservations can be made via the websites of various domestic airlines or at their branch offices. Electronic tickets are valid, though paper versions can only be collected by the credit card holder. It is advisable for travelers to carry a print-out of the email sent to them confirming the booking. Visitors who are prepared to spend some time surfing online travel agencies, and are flexible about the days on which they travel, will usually be able to secure discounted fares. Aerolíneas Argentinas and Austral offer by far the greatest choice of flights and destinations, but those searching for a bargain should check with their competitors.

A view of the domestic airport in Buenos Aires, Aeroparque Jorge Newberry

CHECKING IN

Checking in is usually very straightforward. Travelers must have their ticket or flight reference number at hand along with their passports. At Aeroparque Jorge Newberry it is advisable to arrive at least an hour before the departure time, and about 2 hours in advance at provincial airports. Online check-in is possible for travelers with electronic tickets from 36 hours prior to departure time up to two hours before the flight is scheduled to take off. Industrial action by pilots or ground crew is not unknown, so keep an eye on the news.

BAGGAGE RESTRICTIONS

Visitors can carry up to 33 lb (15 kg) on domestic flights with Aerolíneas Argentinas, and up to 44 lb (20 kg) with LAN Argentina. However, both airlines only allow 11 lb (5 kg) as hand luggage. Travelers on hunting trips will have to get a special license to carry firearms.

AIR PASSES AND CONCESSIONARY FARES

Domestic flights in Argentina can, unfortunately, be expensive. Aerolíneas Argentinas offers a discount called Visite Argentina. Those who book a flight from a foreign airport to Ezeiza International Airport and book an onward domestic flight at the same time can secure discounts of between 20 to 30 percent. For example, instead of paying US$272 for a flight from Buenos Aires to Bariloche, the same route will cost only US$189.

LAN's Sudamérica Airpass offers special rates for those who purchase three or more one-way LAN flights within Latin America. The pass must be bought 14 days before the first flight and it is better to check the discount percentage before booking. If arriving in Argentina from another Latin American country or from Spain, it is wise to check the package deals on offer. Up until the age of two, children travel free or with a 90 percent discount and between 2–11 years old, they are charged only 67 percent of the ticket price for adults. There are no special prices for senior citizens or students. Most airlines also offer concessionary fares to groups of more than nine people traveling together.

Passengers waiting by information screens at Jorge Newberry Airport

SHUTTLE SERVICES

There are regular shuttle services between Ezeiza and Aeroparque Jorge Newberry organized by the company **Manuel Tienda León**. These provide air-conditioned buses that seat at least 45 passengers. They organize pick-up and delivery, luggage deposit, special services such as guided tours, and even chauffered limousines.

FLIGHT DURATION CHART
1:15 = Duration in hours: minutes
(This chart does not include layover time)

BUENOS AIRES							
1:10 CÓRDOBA							
2:15	3:15 SALTA						
3:40	4:50	5:55 USHUAIA					
0:55	2:10	3:10	4:35 MAR DEL PLATA				
2:20	3:30	4:35	6:00	3:15 BARILOCHE			
3:13	4:10	3:28	6:53	4:07	5:33 EL CALAFATE		
1:50	3:00	4:05	4:30	2:45	4:10	5:03 MENDOZA	
1:25	2:40	3:40	5:05	2:20	3:45	4:38	3:15 CORRIENTES

Traveling around Argentina

As most airlines charge tourists in American dollars for domestic flights, flying around Argentina is expensive. There are, however, many other safe and convenient options. *Micros* travel virtually everywhere and are usually air-conditioned and comfortable. Traveling within Argentina's towns and cities is convenient, with plenty of taxis and *colectivos* (city buses). It is easy to journey by train from Buenos Aires to surrounding cities although there is no single national railroad network. Visitors can cross to Uruguay by ferry or opt for boat excursions in national parks and along major rivers.

One of Argentina's sleek modern *micros*

MICROS

Long-distance coaches are a great way to get around the country: they are far cheaper than flights and go to more destinations, more frequently. Fares vary according to the season, but expect to pay between AR$120 and AR$250 for a sleeper service to Bariloche or Mendoza from Buenos Aires. As well as the time of year, the price also depends on the type of seat reserved. Most companies offer three options in ascending price order: *semi-cama* (reclining seat), *cama* (seat with a greater reclining angle), and *super cama* (seat that reclines 120 degrees). Air conditioning is usually very efficient so wear extra layers, even if it is hot outside.

Established companies such as **Via Bariloche** and **Andesmar** have efficient on-line booking services that accept all major credit cards. Tickets can be collected or purchased from Buenos Aires's Retiro bus terminal *(see p334)* where all the major companies are based, or from provincial stations. While top operators offer regular services between Argentina's major cities, to get from village to village in the interior, visitors have to take a minibus. Luggage limits can

be checked with the operator, and bags are handled by *maleteros* (porters) who expect a tip of around AR$2.

TRAINS

Only a handful of private and provincial companies operate train services outside of greater Buenos Aires. Among them are **Ferrovías** and **Trenes de Buenos Aires**. However, their trains can be occasionally ill-maintained and uncomfortable. Note too that coach class on some trains may not be heated in winter and can be very cold without a blanket.

There are around six main routes that depart from the capital for destinations such as Mar del Plata, Rosario, and Bahía Blanca. Train

enthusiasts will enjoy a ride on one of the touristy routes traversed by **El Tren del Fin del Mundo**, La Trochita *(see p240)*, **Tren Patagónico**, which links the Atlantic coast with Bariloche, and Salta's amazing Tren de las Nubes *(see p195)*.

FERRIES

Apart from the popular route connecting Buenos Aires with Colonia del Sacramento in Uruguay, there are very few sea-based transport services in Argentina. Buquebus *(see p329)* sells tickets for this trip. Boat excursions, however, are common, including ones along Canal Beagle in Tierra del Fuego, in the Patagonian lakes around Bariloche and San Martín de los Andes, and, most spectacular of all, cruises to Antarctica out of Ushuaia *(see pp264–7)*.

DIRECTORY

MICROS

Andesmar
www.andesmar.com

Via Bariloche
www.viabariloche.com.ar

TRAINS

El Tren del Fin del Mundo
www.trendelfindelmundo.com.ar

Ferrovías
www.ferrovias.com.ar

Trenes de Buenos Aires
www.tbanet.com.ar

Tren Patagónico
www.trenpatagonico-sa.com.ar

People on a train going from Buenos Aires to Tigre

Argentina by Road

For the adventurous of spirit looking for a different kind of holiday experience, there is the option of traveling across Argentina by road. An increasingly popular tourist activity, driving around the country has become much safer and more convenient. Argentina's road network is comprehensive – if a place is listed on a map, it can usually be reached by car or motorbike. Driving offers an intimate view of the country. Roads pass spectacular scenery along the Atlantic coast or run across barren Patagonia where wide open spaces encourage a sense of freedom and adventure.

GENERAL SAFETY

Though paved, most of the country's *rutas nacionales* can be narrow, making over-taking tiring and sometimes dangerous. Windscreen and headlamp guards are essential on the roughly graveled *rutas provinciales* as there is a danger of flying stones. By law, drivers must carry warning triangles, a first-aid kit, and an international driving license. Seat belts must be worn and spare tyres, a car-jack, car pump, wiper blades, and oil must be carried, along with anti-freeze if driving in the south.

It is also important to trust in local knowledge – if someone says that a road is impassable at a particular time of year, it is safer to assume that they know what they are talking about.

RENTING CARS AND MOTORBIKES

Most of the main international hire companies such as **Avis** and **Hertz** have offices in Argentina. Expect to pay between US$40 and US$60 per day depending on the required mileage. Some smaller, local companies offer the same level of service for a significant discount; visitors should ask for details at their hotel or travel agent. By law a person must be at least 21 to hire a car in Argentina. A driving license, passport and, often, a credit card are required. It is crucial that the renting agency hands over the ownership documents for the vehicle, which must be shown at police checkpoints.

OFF-ROAD DRIVING

Conventional wisdom dictates that travelers need a 4WD (four-wheel drive) vehicle with truck-tyre tread to get around Argentina, but that is not always the case. Roads often look worse than they actually are. For off-road driving, however, a solid 4WD vehicle with strong suspension is a must. Maintenance gets more expensive farther away from towns and cities, so it is worth installing extra shock-absorbers and carrying plenty of fuel, before starting out on a long journey.

Distance marker along Ruta Nacional 40

GREAT DRIVES

The 3,100-mile (5,000-km) long trunk road, Ruta Nacional 40, is easily the country's most famous high-way *(see p243)*. However, there are plenty of other routes to satisfy those with a thirst for both adventure and awe-inspiring scenery. If visitors want to get a sense of how enormous, dry, and featureless most of Patagonia is, they can try the fully paved Ruta Nacional 3, which runs down the Atlantic coast. Ruta Nacional 23, on the other hand, running from Ruta Nacional 40 to El Chaltén, is a difficult, high drive with a spectacular backdrop. For the purist road-tripper, Ruta Nacional 25 from Trevelin to Trelew is perfect, with the requisite remote gas stations staffed by friendly local people. Ruta Provincial 9 runs from Buenos Aires to the Bolivian border, following the old Camino Real to the silver mines. It also passes through Quebrada de Humahuaca *(see pp196–200)*.

The journey across South America taken by Che Guevara and his friend, Alberto Granado, in 1952, is becoming an increasingly popular driving route. The famous 8,700-mile (14,000-km) drive was documented in the 2004 biopic *The Motorcycle Diaries*. It is, however, not advisable to try it on a battered Norton 500, as Che and Granado did.

DIRECTORY

RENTING CARE AND MOTORBIKES

Avis
Tel (011) 4378-9640, (0810) 9991-2847. **www**.avis.com.ar

Hertz
Tel (0810) 222-43789. www.milletrentacar.com.ar

Lonely stretch of Ruta Nacional 40 going through Bajo Caracoles, Patagonia

Getting around Buenos Aires

A delightful city for tourists to navigate, Buenos Aires has a good public transport system, one of the cheapest in Latin America, that features an expanding subway and extensive bus routes; taxis and minicabs are also numerous. The city is laid out in the rectangular grid pattern common to most big cities in Latin America, and most areas of interest are concentrated between La Boca in the south and Belgrano in the north, bounded to the east by the river. Porteños are usually very friendly and enjoy helping lost tourists to get back on track.

Passengers on the Subte, South America's oldest subway

THE SUBTE AND OVERLAND TRAINS

The quickest and simplest way to get around the capital is by using the subway, known as the Subte. There are six subway lines (A to E, and H). A one-way ticket to any destination costs AR$0.70. A good tip in this coin-scarce city is to buy a ten-journey ticket for AR$7. The downside of the Subte is that coverage is quite limited when compared with the area covered by the city's extensive bus network. Nevertheless, the subway is a convenient way to travel between the city's main sights.

The overland train network is not the most useful form of public transport for tourists and is thus the least used. Commuter trains going to the mainly affluent northern suburbs are tolerably comfortable, while the ones going to the more impoverished southern suburbs are usually overcrowded and poorly maintained, and not suitable for visitors. Some of the major stations in Buenos Aires include **Retiro Mitre**, **Retiro San Martín**, and **Constitución**.

COLECTIVOS

Colectivos (city buses) cover the entire city of Buenos Aires. There are almost 500 lines with some subdivided into additional numbers according to the route they take. Lines 1 and 2 of the No. 39, for example, travel from La Boca along Avenida Santa Fe to their terminus in Chacarita; Line 3 has the same starting and finishing point but passes through Palermo Viejo. The colored plate at the bottom of the bus windscreen shows its sub-route, if any, and number. Other useful lines include the No. 60, which connects Constitución station with the delta town of Tigre; the No. 93, which travels along one of the city's major thoroughfares, Avenida del Libertador; and the No. 152, which connects La Boca in the south with Belgrano in the north.

The Guía "T" booklet, available at every kiosk, is a useful guide to the city's bus services. The main bus station is in **Retiro**. A single *colectivo* journey to anywhere in the federal capital, or to anywhere in the suburbs provided the journey begins inside the federal capital, costs a flat AR$0.80. Note that the ticket machines accept only coins.

Open-top tourist buses, run by Buenos Aires Bus, are a good way of seeing the sights of the city. Buses depart hourly from 9am to 5:30pm from the corner of Florida and Avenida Roque Sáenz Peña. Visit www.buenosairesbus.com for more information.

DRIVING

Stop sign in Buenos Aires

The legal age to drive a car in Buenos Aires is 17. It is compulsory to wear front seatbelts and children under 10 must sit at the back. The speed limit is 25 mph (40 kmph) and overtaking is done on the left, while right of way is given to cars crossing intersections from the right. Most of the laws are routinely flouted but the legal age is strictly followed. The blood alcohol content limit is 0.05 percent and penalties for drunken driving include the risk of trial and imprisonment if an accident takes place.

WALKING

Buenos Aires is a huge city, but the main areas of tourist interest are fairly compact and easy to get around on foot. The condition of the pavements in most barrios is tolerable, although drivers rarely pay much attention to pedestrians. Also, it is advisable not to wander alone into uncharted territory after dark.

A brightly colored *colectivo*, Buenos Aires

Black and yellow taxi, Buenos Aires

A *remise*

TAXIS AND REMISES

There are many cabs on the streets of Buenos Aires and it is usually easy to find one at any time. Taxis are painted black and yellow and run on meters; *remises*, which are licensed minicabs, look like any other private car. For safety reasons, it is recommended that visitors use either a radio taxi or a *remise*. If a tourist must hail a taxi, it is advisable to make sure that the vehicle is marked with a company name and serial number and that the red *libre* light in the front window is on. A fee must be agreed before setting off when using *remises*. On no account will a driver change anything over a AR$20 peso note, unless agreed upon in advance. Some of the popular *remises* include **Amistax** and **Radio Taxi Premium**. Taxis are not the quickest option during rush hours when traffic jams are common.

DIRECTORY

THE SUBTE AND OVERLAND TRAINS

Constitución Station
Gral Hornos 11. *Tel (011) 4304-0028*.

Retiro Mitre
Ramos Mejia 1430. **City Map** 3 E3. *Tel (011) 4317-4407*.

Retiro San Martín
Ramos Mejia 1430. **City Map** 3 E3. *Tel (0800) 666-358-736*.

COLECTIVOS

Retiro
Ave Ant. Argentina & Calle 10. *Tel (011) 4310-0700*.

TAXIS AND REMISES

Amistax
Tel (011) 4582-7774.

Radio Taxi Premium
Tel (011) 5238-0000.

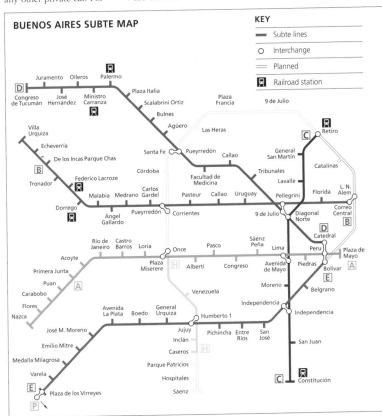

BUENOS AIRES SUBTE MAP

KEY

— Subte lines
○ Interchange
= Planned
▣ Railroad station

General Index

Page numbers in **bold** refer to
main entries

A

Abaporu (Tarsila do Amaral) 111
Abra Pampa 44
Accommodations **270–87**
  apart-hotels 272
  Argentinian Mesopotamia **279**
  bodegas see Bodegas
  boutique hotels 271, 273
  budget accommodation 271
  Buenos Aires **274–7**
  chain hotels 271, 273
  Córdoba and the Andean
    Northwest **280**
  Cuyo and the Wine Country **281–2**
  disabled travelers 273
  estancias see Estancias
  gradings 270
  hospedajes 271
  hosterías see Hosterías
  luxury hotels 270, 271
  national parks and campsites 273
  Pampas **278**
  Patagonia **283–6**
  pensiones 271
  posadas see Hosterías
  pricing and booking 270
  rented apartments 271
  self-catering and cabin complexes
    272
  taxes 270
  Tierra del Fuego and Antarctica **287**
  tipping 273
  youth hostels 273
Addresses 327
Aida (Giuseppe Verdi) 72
Air travel 328, 330–31
Albatross Islet, South Georgia
  (Subantarctic Islands) 265
Almodovar, Pedro 33
Alta Gracia (Córdoba and the Andean
  Northwest) **182**
Aluminé (Patagonia) **236**
  accommodations 283
Alvear Palace Hotel (Recoleta) 96,
  99, 270
Ambrosetti, Juan B. 66
Andean condors 18, 246
  Parque Nacional Quebrada del
    Condorito 183
  Parque Nacional Talampaya
    (Córdoba and the Andean
    Northwest) 185
Andean Northwest 8, 14, 17, 47
  cuisine 290–91
  flora and fauna 18
  landscape 18
  See also Córdoba and the Andean
    Northwest
Andes 13, 18, 134, 153, 203, 242,
  244, 57
  See also Andean Northwest
Angling see Fishing
Antarctica 9, 257, 258, **262–7**
  cruising the Antarctic Peninsula 9,
    258, **266–7**
  cruising the Subantarctic Islands
    264–5
  wildlife **265**
  See also Tierra del Fuego and
    Antarctica
Antiguo Senado de la Confederación
  (Paraná) 162

Antiques see Art and antiques
Antonioni, Michelangelo 31
  Blow-up 31
Archaeology
  Museo de Arqueología de Alta
    Montaña de Salta 192, 194
  Museo de La Plata 142–3
  Parque Nacional Sierra de las
    Quijadas 218
  Quilmes 189
Architecture 8, 30, **34–5**
Argentinian Football Association
  (AFA) 38
Argentinian Mesopotamia 8, 14,
  156–75
  accommodations 279
  Esteros del Iberá 157, **166–7**
  getting around 159
  Parque Nacional Iguazú **172–5**
  region map 158–9
  restaurants 297
Argentinian Republic, creation of 50
Arlt, Roberto 31, 68
Art and antiques
  Feria de San Pedro Telmo (Plaza
    Dorrego) 78
  shopping 118, 120, 121, 305
Art and literature **30–31**
Artisans markets 305, 306.
  See also Markets
Asado 22, 290, 291
Atlantic coast
  landscape and wildlife 19
  resorts see Beach resorts
ATMs 324
Autumn events 42
Avenida 9 de Julio and Obelisco
  (Plaza de Mayo and Microcentro) **70**
Avenida de Mayo (Plaza de Mayo and
  Microcentro) 62

B

Backpackers 320
Bahía Blanca (Pampas) **154**
  accommodations 278
  restaurants 296
Baggage restrictions 331
Bajo Caracoles (Patagonia) **244**
Balcarce (Pampas) **151**
Banco de la Nación (Plaza de Mayo
  and Microcentro) 62, **64–5**
Banks
  banking and currency **324–5**
  opening hours 319
Banquina de Pescadores (Mar del
  Plata) 149
Barenboim, Daniel 16, 72
Bariloche (Patagonia) 9, 35, 221,
  222, **238**
  accommodations 283
  restaurants 301
Bars and clubs 288, 308
  in Buenos Aires 123, 125
Basilíca see Cathedrals, chapels,
  churches, and convents
Batalla de Monte Caseros (Penuti and
  Bernheim) 49
Bath, The (Prilidiano Pueyrredón) 30
Batistuta, Gabriel 16, 39
Battle of Monte Caseros 49, 106
Battle of Tuyutí (Cándido López) 50
Bay of Isles, South Georgia
  (Subantarctic Islands) 265
Beach resorts 8, 137, 138
  Carilo (Pampas) 150

Beach resorts (cont.)
  Chapadmalal (Pampas) 150
  Mar del Plata (Pampas) 137, 138,
    148–9
  Miramar (Pampas) 138, 151
  Necochea (Pampas) 151
  Pinamar (Pampas) 138, 150
  Villa Gesell (Pampas) 138, 150
Belgrano (Buenos Aires) 77, 105, **114**
  See also Palermo and Belgrano
Belgrano, General Manuel 98, 105,
  114, 196, 198
Benoit, Pierre 140
Berni, Antonio 30, 80, 91, 102, 110
  Manifestación 110
Biblioteca Nacional (Recoleta) 97, **103**
Birdlife 18, 19
Bird-watching 314
  Estancia Rincón del Socorro
    (Esteros del Iberá) 167, 314, 315
  Estancia Telken (Patagonia) 242, 314
  Parque Nacional Chaco
    (Argentinian Mesopotamia) 168–9
  Parque Nacional El Rey (Córdoba
    and the Andean Northwest) 201
  Parque Nacional Laguna Blanca
    (Patagonia) 235
  Senda Pozo Verde (Parque
    Nacional El Rey) 201
  See also Andean condors; Birdlife;
    National Parks; Provincial Parks;
    Provincial Reserves; Reserves
Blanqui, Andrés 98, 182
Blow-up (Michelangelo Antonioni) 31
Boat excursions
  Esteros del Iberá 166–7
  Parque Nacional Iguazú 173, 175
  Parque Nacional Los Glaciares 250,
    253, 254
  See also Cruises
Boca Juniors 38, 77, 85, 124
  See also Soccer
Bodegas 134, 190, **210–11**, 272
  Bodega del Fin del Mundo
    (Neuquén) 234
  Catena Zapata (Mendoza) 210
  Cavas de Weinert (Mendoza) 211,
    305
  Cavas Wine Lodge (Mendoza) 210
  Chandon (Mendoza) 210
  Escorihuela (Mendoza) 211
  Familia Zuccardi (Mendoza) 211
  Finca la Rosa (Cafayate) 190
  La Rosa di Michel Torino (Cafayate)
    177
  La Rural (Mendoza) 208, 211, 305
  López (Mendoza) 211
  Nieto Senetiner (Mendoza) 211, 320
  O. Fournier (Mendoza) 305
  Salentein (Mendoza) 210, 305, 311
  Suter (San Rafael) 219
  Valentín Bianchi (San Rafael) 219
  Zapata Agrelo (Luján de Cuyo) 203
  See also Vineyards; Wines
Borges, Jorge Luis 16, 31, 68, 103
  El Aleph 31
  Ficciones 31
Bosque Petrificado José Ormachea
  (Patagonia) **229**
British immigrants 20
  polo 36
  soccer 38–9
Buenos Aires 8, 13, 16, 17, 30, 50,
  56–131, 134
  accommodations 274–7

Buenos Aires (cont.)
architecture 8
Buenos Aires at a Glance 58–9
Cementerio de la Recoleta **100–1**
entertainment 122–5
Farther Afield 116–17, 277, 295
founding of 47
getting around 334–5
immigrants 21
Museo de Arte Latinamericano de
Buenos Aires (MALBA) **110–11**
Palermo and Belgrano *see* Palermo
and Belgrano
Plaza de Mayo and Microcentro
see Plaza de Mayo and Microcentro
Plaza San Martín and Retiro *see*
Plaza San Martín and Retiro
Recoleta *see* Recoleta
restaurants 292–5
San Telmo and La Boca *see* San
Telmo and La Boca
shopping 118–21
Street Finder maps 126–31
Teatro Colón **72–3**
Bustillo, Alejandro 62, 64, 102, 153
Butch Cassidy and the Sundance
Kid **241**

C

Cabildo de Buenos Aires (Plaza de
Mayo and Microcentro) 59, 63, **65**
Cabildo de Salta (Salta) 192, 194
Cachi (Córdoba and the Andean
Northwest) 178, **191**
restaurants 298
Cafayate (Córdoba and the Andean
Northwest) 9, 177, 178, **190**
accommodations 280
restaurants 298
Cafés 123, 288
Café La Biela (Recoleta) 96, **98–9**
Café Tortoni (Plaza de Mayo and
Microcentro) 42, **68**, 123, 125
Confitería Molino (Plaza del
Congreso) 69
Confitería Richmond 88
Caiman 166, 168, 169
Caleta Valdés (Reserva Provincial
Península Valdés) 227
Calle Florida (Plaza San Martín and
Retiro) 88
Calle Necochea (San Telmo and La
Boca) **81**
Camarones (Patagonia) **228**
Camila (Maria Luisa Bemberg) 145
Cambiaso, Adolfo 36, 109
Campero, Juan Fernández 200–1
Campo Argentino de Polo de
Palermo (Palermo) 36, **109**
Campos, Florencio Molina 30, 80, 120
Canal Beagle (Tierra del Fuego) 24,
257, 258, **260**, 312
Canto al Trabajo (Rogelio Yrurtia) **79**
Capilla *see* Cathedrals, chapels,
churches, and convents
Capybara 166, 169
Carcass Island (Falkland Islands) 264
Carilo (Pinamar) 150
Carmen de Patagones (Patagonia) **224**
Carnaval 8, 40, 41, 159, 164
Casa Chorizo 35
Casa de Cambio see Banks
Casa de Cultura (Mercedes) 165
Casa de Gobierno (Corrientes) 168
Casa de Gobierno (La Plata) 141

Casa de Gobierno (La Rioja) 185
Casa de Gobierno (Salta) 192
Casa de la Cultura (Carmen de
Patagones) 224
Casa del Marqués Campero (Yavi) 201
Casa Histórica de la Independencia
(San Miguel de Tucumán) 189
Casa Mínima (San Telmo and La
Boca) 8, **78**
Casa Rosada (Plaza de Mayo and
Microcentro) 60, 61, 62, **64**, 69
Catamarca *see* San Fernando del Valle
de Catamarca
Catedral Metropolitana (Plaza de
Mayo and Microcentro) 62, **65**
Catedral *see* Cathedrals, chapels,
churches, and convents
Cathedrals, chapels, churches, and
convents
Basílica Catedral Santuario Nuestra
Señora del Rosario (Rosario) 160
Basílica de San Francisco (Plaza de
Mayo, Buenos Aires) 63
Basílica Nuestra Señora de Luján
(Luján) 144
Capilla Bethel (Trevelin) 241
Capilla de Santa Barbara (San
Salvador de Jujuy) 198
Capilla Moriah (Trelew) 225
Capilla Vieja (Gaiman) 225
Catedral de la Inmaculada
Concepción (La Plata) 135, 138,
140–1
Catedral de Nuestra Señora del
Valle (Catamarca) 188
Catedral Metropolitana (Plaza de
Mayo, Buenos Aires) 62, **65**
Catedral Municipal (Paraná) 162
Catedral Nuestra Señora de Luján
(Río Gallegos) 231
Catedral San Nicolas de Bari (La
Rioja) 185
Catedral (San Salvador de Jujuy) 198
Catedral (Santiago del Estero) 188
Christ Church, Stanley (Falkland
Islands) 264
Church of the Misión Salesiana (Río
Grande) 256, 261
Convento de San Bernardo
(Salta) 193
Iglesia Catedral (Córdoba) 180
Iglesia Catedral (Salta) 192, 194
Iglesia Catedral (San Luis) 218
Iglesia de la Candelaria y San
Antonio (Humahuaca) 197, 200
Iglesia de la Compañía (Córdoba)
181
Iglesia de Nuestra Señora del Pilar
(Recoleta) 96, **98**
Iglesia de Nuestra Señora del
Rosario y San Francisco (Yavi) 201
Iglesia de San Francisco de Paula
(Uquia) 197, 199
Iglesia de San Ignacio (Manzana de
las Luces, Buenos Aires) 67
Iglesia de Santo Domingo (San
Luis) 218
Iglesia del Santisimo Rosario y
Convento de Santo Domingo
(Plaza de Mayo and Microcentro)
66
Iglesia Matriz (Colonia del
Sacramento) 117
Iglesia Nuestra Señora de las
Nieves (Junín de los Andes) 236

Cathedrals, chapels, churches, and
convents (cont.)
Iglesia Nuestra Señora del Carmen
(Carmen de Patagones) 224
Iglesia Nuestra Señora de los
Milagros (Santa Fe) 162
Iglesia Ortodoxa Rusa (San Telmo
and La Boca) **80**
Iglesia Parroquial Nuestra Señora
de la Merced (Alta Gracia) 182
Iglesia San Francisco (San Salvador
de Jujuy) 198
Iglesia San José (Cachi) 191
Iglesia San José (San José de
Jáchal) 216
Iglesia San Pedro Nolasco de
Molinos (Molinos) 190
Iglesia Santo Domingo (La Rioja)
185
Iglesia y Convento de San
Bernardo (Salta) 193, 195
Iglesia y Convento de San
Francisco (Santa Fe) 162
Iglesia y Convento San Francisco
(Salta) 192, 193, 195
La Inmaculada Concepción
(Belgrano, Buenos Aires)
114
San Nicolás church (Plaza de Mayo
and Microcentro) 70
Templo de la Inmaculada
Concepción (Tandil) 152
Templo de San Francisco
(Mendoza) 207
Catelin, Próspero 100
Cave art 30
Cueva de Las Manos (Patagonia) 9,
30, 243
Parque Provincial Ernesto
Tornquist (Pampas) 153
Cell phones 326, 327
Cementerio de la Chacarita (Palermo
and Belgrano) **115**
Cementerio de la Recoleta (Recoleta)
94, 95, 96, **100–1**
Centro Cultural Ciudad de Buenos
Aires (Recoleta) 95, 96
Centro Cultural Islámico Rey Fahd
(Palermo and Belgrano) 25, **112**
Centro Cultural Recoleta (Recoleta)
95, 96, **98**
Centro Cultural Torquato Tasso (San
Telmo) 79
Centro Cultural Villa Victoria (Mar del
Plata) 149
Centro Naval (Plaza San Martín and
Retiro) **88**
Centro Paleontológico Lago Barreales
(Patagonia) **234–5**
Centro Recreativo Glaciar Martial
(Ushuaia) 260
Cerro Aconcagua (Parque Nacional
Provincial Aconcagua) 9, 212, 213
Cerro Blanco (Parque Provincial
Ernesto Tornquist) 153
Cerro Castor (Tierra del Fuego) 258,
260
Cerro Catedral (Parque Nacional
Nahuel Huapi) 43, 239
Cerro Chenque (Comodoro
Rivadavia) 228
Cerro Cristal (Parque Nacional Los
Glaciares) 254
Cerro de la Gloria (Parque San
Martín) 207

Cerro de la Sociedad Científica (Parque Nacional Lihué Calel) 155
Cerro de la Ventana (Parque Provincial Ernesto Tornquist) 153
Cerro de los Indios (Hipólito Yrigoyen) 244
Cerro de los Siete Colores (Purmamarca) 178, 196, 198
Cerro El Centinela (Tandil) 152
Cerro El Matadero (Tafí del Valle) 189
Cerro El Triunfo (Balcarce) 151
Cerro Martial (Tierra del Fuego) 260
Cerro Morado (Parque Provincial Ischigualasto) 217
Cerro Pabellon (Tafí del Valle) 189
Cerro Piltriquitron (El Bolsón) 240
Cerro San Lorenzo (Hipólito Yrigoyen) 244
Cerro Torre (Parque Nacional los Glaciares) 220, 221, 250, 252
Maestri, Cesare and Egger, Tony **253**
Chacra Don Neno (Los Antiguos) 242
Chacarera 23, 28, 29, 188
Chacras 242, 305
Chacras de Coria (Mendoza) 207
Chamame 28, 116
Chapadmalal (Pampas) **150**
Chapelco Ski Resort (San Martín de los Andes) 236
Che *see* Guevara, Ernesto
Children
    entertainment 124, 125
    traveling with 320
Chinese immigrants 25
Cinema 16, **32–3**, 308, 309
Circuito Inferior (Parque Nacional Iguazú) 172, 173, 174
Circuito Superior (Parque Nacional Iguazú) 173, 174
Círculo Militar (Plaza San Martín and Retiro) 88, 89, **90**
Classical music 16, 308–309
    in Buenos Aires 123, 125
Climate **44–5**
Climbing *see* Hiking and trekking
Cloud forests
    Parque Nacional Baritú 198, 201
    Parque Nacional Calilegua (Córdoba and the Andean Northwest) 198, **201**
    Parque Nacional El Rey (Córdoba and the Andean Northwest) **201**
Clubs *see* Bars and clubs
Colón (Argentinian Mesopotamia) 158, **164**
    accommodations 279
    restaurants 297
Colonia Carlos Pellegrini (Esteros del Iberá) 167
Colonia del Sacramento (Uruguay) 116, **117**
Communications and media **326–7**
Comodoro Rivadavia (Patagonia) **228**
    accommodations 283
    restaurants 301
Condors *see* Andean condors
Confiterías see Cafés
Congress of Tucumán, declaration of Independence 49
Congress of Tucumán, The Declaration of Independence of Argentina from Spain in 1816 (Francisco Fortuny) 49
Conquest of the Desert campaign *see* Conquista del Desierto
Conquista del Desierto 50, 101, 154, 155, 236

Convento *see* Cathedrals, chapels, churches, and convents
Córdoba (Córdoba and the Andean Northwest) 9, 134, 177, **180–81**
    accommodations 280
    Jesuit missions 13, 24, 180–81
    map 180
    restaurants 298
Córdoba and the Andean Northwest **176–201**
    accommodations 280
    getting around 179
    Quebrada de Humahuaca **196–7**
    region map 178–9
    restaurants 298
    Santa Catalina **186–7**
Cordón del Plata (Mendoza) 210
Coronation Island (South Orkney Islands) 265
Correo Central (Plaza de Mayo and Microcentro) 34, **67**
Corrientes (Argentinian Mesopotamia) 17, 19, 158, **168**
    accommodations 279
    restaurants 297
Cortázar, Julio 16, 31
    Las Babas del Diablo 31
Cosquín (Córdoba and the Andean Northwest) **183**
    restaurants 298
Credit cards 304, 324
Cristo Redentor (Córdoba and the Andean Northwest) 184
Cristo Redentor (Cuyo and the Wine Country) **212**
Cruce de Lagos (Patagonia) **239**
Cruises 9, 312, 313
    Canal Beagle 260
    Cruce de Lagos 239
    Cruising the Antarctic Peninsula **266–7**
    Cruising the Subantarctic Islands **264–5**
    See also Boat excursions
Cueva de las Manos (Patagonia) 9, 30, 134, 222, 242, **243**
Currency 324
    crisis 50–51, 67
Cusco School 30, 197
Customs information 318
Cuyo and the Wine Country 8, 9, **202–19**
    accommodations 281–2
    getting around 205
    Mendoza Winery Tour **210–11**
    region map 204–205
    restaurants 299–300
    wines of Mendoza **208–209**
Cycling and mountain biking 310, 313

Dance **28–9**, 308–309
    tango *see* Tango
    venues 122, 125
    See also Teatro Colón
Dante 68
de la Vega, Jorge 111
    Rompecabezas 111
Demarchi, Silvestre 66
Desert campaign *see* Conquista del Desierto
Desire, the 229
Difunta Correa 25, **216**
Dinosaurs 221, **232–3**, 234
    Argentinosaurus huinculensis 232, 233, 235
    Dakosaurus andiniensis 232, 233
    Eoraptor lunensis 217

Dinosaurs (cont.)
    Futalognkosaurus dukei 234
    Giganotosaurus carolinii 232, 233, 235
    Herrerasaurus ischigualastensis 217
    Neuquensaurus 143
    Phorusrhacid 233
    Pterosaur 218
    Titanosaurus 233
    Unenlagia paynemili 234–5
    See also Paleontology
Dirty War 33, 54, 55, 64
    Due Obedience law 55
    Escuela de Mecánica de la Armada (ESMA) (Palermo) 113
    La Historia Oficial (Luis Puenzo) 33
    Madres de la Plaza de Mayo 64
Disabled travelers 273
Diving and snorkeling 312, 313
do Amaral, Tarsila 111
    Abaporu 111
Don Segundo Sombra (Ricardo Güiraldes) 31, 145
Drake Passage 257
Drake, Francis 230
Driving 224
    Argentina by road **333**
    holidays 310, 313
Duarte, Eva *see* Perón, Eva
Durrell, Gerald 201
    Whispering Land, The 201

E

Echeverría, Esteban 31
    Facundo 31
Economy 14, 15
Edificio Kavanagh (Plaza San Martín and Retiro) 35, 88, **91**
Egger, Tony **253**
El Aleph (Jorge Luis Borges) 31
El Beso de la Mujer Arana (Manuel Puig) 31
El Bolsón (Patagonia) 222, **240**
    accommodations 283
    restaurants 298
El Calafate (Patagonia) **247**, 250
    accommodations 284
    restaurants 301
El Caminito (San Telmo and La Boca) 8, 12, 17, 82–3, **85**
El Chaltén (Patagonia) 222, **246**, 250, 252, 253
    accommodations 284
    restaurants 301–2
El Gaucho Martín Fierro see Hernández, José
El Maitén (Patagonia) **240**
El Matadero (Domingo F. Sarmiento) 31
El Trueno Entre Las Hojas (Armando Bo) 32
El Zanjón (San Telmo and La Boca) 34, **78**
Elephant Island (Antarctic Peninsula) 267
Elephant seals 135, 226, 227
Emergencies 322, 323
Endurance, the 265, **267**
Entertainment **308–309**
    bars and clubs *see* Bars and clubs
    in Buenos Aires **122–5**
    children 124
    guides and tickets 122, 308
    film 309
    music and dance 122, 123, 308, 309
    sports 36–7, 124, 308
    tango 123

Entertainment (cont.)
theater 123, 309
See also Equestrian sports
Equestrian sports 8, **36–7**, 308
Feria de Mataderos 116
horse racing 109, 124, 308
polo *see* Polo
Escuela de Mecánica de la Armada
(ESMA) (Palermo and Belgrano)
112–13
Esquel (Patagonia) **241**
accommodations 284
restaurants 302
Estación Retiro (Plaza San Martín and
Retiro) **92**
Estancias 8, 22, 137, 272, 273, **314–15**
activities 138, 314–15
Alice (El Calafate) 247, 314, 315
Alta Vista (El Calafate) 247, 314, 315
architecture 35
Cerro de la Cruz (Pampas) **153**,
314, 315
Colomé (Molinos) 191, 314, 315
El Colibrí (Córdoba) 314, 315
El Condor (Lago San Martín) 246,
314, 315
El Ombú (San Antonio de Areco)
145, 314
Faro Punta Delgada (Reserva
Provincial Península Valdés) 227
Finca la Rosa (Cafayate) 190
gaucho for a day 314, 315
growth of 48
Harberton (Tierra del Fuego) 260,
261
Huechahue (Neuquén) 314, 315
La Angostura (Gobernador
Gregores) 245, 314, 315
La Anita (El Calafate) 247
La Bamba (San Antonio de Areco)
145, 272, 314
La Maipú (Lago San Martín) 246,
314, 315
La Oriental (Patagonia) 244, 314, 315
La Paz (Córdoba) 280, 314
Los Talas (Luján) 144
Los Toldos (Patagonia) 243, 314, 315
luxury estancias 314, 315
Menelik (Patagonia) 244, 314, 315
Monte Dinero (Patagonia) **231**, 314
Nibepo Aike, Lago Roca (Parque
Nacional Los Glaciares) 254
Peuma Hue (Parque Nacional
Huapi) 314
Rincón del Socorro (Esteros del
Iberá) 167, 314, 315
Río Capitan (Gobernador Gregores)
245, 314, 315
Santa Catalina (Córdoba and the
Andean Northwest) 186–7
Santa Isabel, Chapadmalal
(Pampas) 150
Telken (Patagonia) **242**, 243, 314
tours and reservations 315
Viamonte (Río Grande) 261
Esteros del Iberá (Argentinian
Mesopotamia) 8, 18, 157, **166–7**
accommodations 279
birdlife **167**
restaurants
Eva Perón Social Aid Foundation 108
Evita (Alan Parker) 33
Evita *see* Perón, Eva

F

Facundo (Esteban Echeverría) 31
Falkland Islands (Subantarctic
Islands) 9, 264

Falklands War 54, 264
Monumento a los Caídos de
Malvinas (Plaza San Martín and
Retiro) 89, 90
Fantasia (show tango) 26
Faro de Cabo Vírgenes (Reserva
Provincial Cabo Vírgenes) 231
Farther Afield (Buenos Aires) **116–17**
accommodations 277
restaurants 295
Federalists 49, 64, 162, 185
civil war 168
See also Unitarists
Feria de Mataderos (Buenos Aires)
116, 120, 122
Feria *see* Markets
Ferrari, León 102, 111
Sin título 111
Festivals and fairs 23, **40–43**, 309
Ficciones (Jorge Luis Borges) 31
Fileteado 6–7, 8, **67**, 76, 307
Film 32–3
Fishing 312, 313
Junín de los Andes (Patagonia) 236
Lago Cardiel (Patagonia) 245
Lago Fagnano (Tierra del Fuego)
261
Lago Posadas (Patagonia) 244
Parque Nacional Laguna Blanca
(Patagonia) 235
Parque Nacional Lanín (Patagonia)
237
Río Menendez 261
Río Paraná 8, 163
Río Pulmari 236
Río Quillen 236
Flora and fauna **18–19**, 255
See also Wildlife
Folklore music 28, 29, 309
instruments 29
Food 120, 121, **288–91**
Central Argentina and the Pampas
290
everyday fare 290–91
food tours 311
Northeast 291
Northwest 290
Patagonia and Tierra del Fuego 291
See also Restaurants
Football *see* Soccer
Fossils *see* Paleontology
Four Horsemen of the Apocalypse
(Rudolph Valentino) 29
Foz do Iguaçu (Brazil) 175
Freud, Sigmund 113
Fundación Proa (San Telmo and La
Boca) **84–5**

G

Gaiman (Patagonia) 221, 224, **225**
accommodations 284–5
restaurants 302
Galerías Pacífico (Plaza San Martín
and Retiro) 59, 88, **91**, 120, 121, 304
Galtieri, President Leopoldo 64
Gambaro, Griselda 31, 32
Gardel, Carlos 16, 29, 32, 68, 96
tomb at Cementerio de la
Chacarita 115
Gardens *see* Parks and gardens
Garganta del Diablo (Parque Nacional
Iguazú) 153, 172, 174, 175
Garganta del Diablo (Quebrada de
Cafayate) 190
Gauchito Gil 25, **165**
Gaucho culture 8, **22–3**, 136, 137,
146–7
Día de la Tradición 41

Gaucho culture (cont.)
Feria de Mataderos 116
gaucho for a day 314–15
gear 23, 305, 306, 307
Juan Facundo Quiroga 185
Juan Moreira 23
literature 31
sports 37
Gay and lesbian travelers 320, 321
Genoese immigrants 21, 77, 84, 85
German immigrants 17, 20, 21, 84,
150
Glaciar *see* Glaciers
Glaciers 8, 14
Agassiz (Parque Nacional Los
Glaciares) 250, 254
de los Tres (Parque Nacional Los
Glaciares) 252
Huemul (Lago del Desierto) 19, 247
Martial (Ushuaia) 260
Moreno (Parque Nacional Los
Glaciares) 44, 134
Onelli (Parque Nacional Los
Glaciares) 250, 254
Parque Nacional Los Glaciares
(Santa Cruz) 134, 248, **250–5**
Perito Moreno (Parque Nacional
Los Glaciares) 134, 222, 247, 248–9,
250, 251, 254
Piedras Blancas (Parque Nacional
Los Glaciares) 253
Polaco (Parque Nacional Provincial
Aconcagua) 213
Spegazzini (Parque Nacional Los
Glaciares) 134, 250, 254
Torre (Parque Nacional Los
Glaciares) 252
Upsala (Parque Nacional Los
Glaciares) 134, 250, 254
Viedma (Parque Nacional Los
Glaciares) 253, 254
Glory of Don Ramiro, The (Enrique
Larreta) 114
Gobernador Gregores (Patagonia) **245**
Golf 310, 313
Golfo Nuevo (Reserva Provincial
Península Valdés) 226
Goose Green (Falkland Islands) 264
Gualeguaychú (Argentinian
Mesopotamia) 8, 158, **164**
accommodations 279
restaurants 297
Guanacos 13, 155, 217, 222, 226, 228,
244, 245
Guaraní 20, 25, 47, 157, 169, 172
Guevara, Ernesto 33, 182, **183**
Che Guevara Museum (Rosario) 160
Museo del Che Guevara (Alta
Gracia) 182
Güiraldes, Ricardo 31, 145
Don Segundo Sombra 31, 145
Gypsy Cove (Falkland Islands) 264

H

Hang gliding 184, 311
Health **322–3**
Hernández, José 31, 100, 108
Martín Fierro 31, 100, 108, 149
Museo de Arte Popular José
Hernández (Palermo and Belgrano)
108
tomb at Cementerio de la Recoleta
100
Hiking and trekking 134, 311
Cerro Aconcagua (Parque Nacional
Provincial Aconcagua) 9, 212, 213
Cerro Cristal (Parque Nacional Los
Glaciares) 254

Hiking and trekking (cont.)
  Cerro de la Ventana (Parque
    Provincial Ernesto Tornquist) 153
  Cerro Torre 250, 252, 253
  El Chaltén (Patagonia) 222, 246, 250
  estancias 314, 315
  Mount Fitz Roy (Patagonia) 222,
    250, 252
  Parque Nacional Chaco
    (Argentinian Mesopotamia) 168–9
  Parque Nacional Los Glaciares
    (Patagonia) 9, 250–55
  Potrero de la Aguada (Parque
    Nacional Sierra de las Quijadas)
    218
  Sierra de la Ventana (Pampas) 152
Hipódromo Argentino de Palermo
  (Palermo) 37, **109**
Hipódromo de San Isidro 124
Hipólito Yrigoyen (Patagonia) **244**
History **46–55**
  Argentinian Republic, creation of 50
  currency crisis 50–51
  Falklands War 54
  Peróns and Argentina 51, **52–3**, 54
  Wars of Independence 49, 84, 87
Horse racing 109, 308
Horse-riding 138
  at estancias 138, 314, 315
  Sierra de la Ventana 152
  Tafí del Valle 189
  Tandil 152
Hospitals and pharmacies 323
Hosterías 271
  Alta Vista (El Calafate) 247, 314,
    315
  Helsingfors (Parque Nacional Los
    Glaciares) 254
  Monte León (Parque Nacional
    Monte León) 230
Hotels *see* Accommodations
Howler monkey 166, 168, 169
Humahuaca (Quebrada de
  Humahuaca) 197, 198, 200
  accommodations 280
  restaurants
Hunting 312, 313

I

Ice calving **251**, 266
Ice trekking (Parque Nacional Los
  Glaciares) 252, 253
Iguazú Falls (Argentinian
  Mesopotamia) 8, 157, 170–71,
  172–3, 174
Iguazú River 135, 175
Iglesia y Convento de Santo Domingo
  (Plaza de Mayo and Microcentro)
  66
Iglesia *see* Cathedrals, chapels,
  churches, and convents
Immigrants 13, 17, 21, 48, 221
  architecture 34–5
  British *see* British immigrants
  Chinese 25
  Fiesta Nacional del Immigrante
    (Misiones) 40
  French 20
  Genoese 21, 77, 84, 85
  German 17, 20, 21, 84, 150
  Italian *see* Italian immigrants
  Jewish *see* Jewish immigrants
  Museo de la Inmigración (Plaza de
    Mayo and Microcentro) **74–5**
  Spanish *see* Spanish
  Swiss 21
  Welsh *see* Welsh
Incas 47, 199

Independence 49
  Casa Histórica de la Independencia
    (Tucumán) 189
  Congress of Tucumán 49
  Monumento a los Dos Congresos 69
  Wars of Independence 49, 84, 87
Indigenous art and craft 30
  Museo de Artesanía Tradicional
    Folklórica (Corrientes) 168
  Museo y Mercado Provincial de
    Artesanías (Paraná) 162
  pottery 30
  shopping 120, 305, 306
Indigenous peoples 13, 17, **20–21**, 47
  Araucana 66
  Aymara 177
  Colla 20
  Comechingones 177
  Conquista del Desierto 13, 50, 154,
    155, 221, 236
  Fuegian 66
  Guaraní *see* Guaraní
  Huapi 35
  Huarpe 47,203
  Kaweskar 257
  La Ciénaga 143
  Manekenk 257
  Manzaneros 155
  Mapuche *see* Mapuche
  Mocovi 168
  Pampa 47
  Quechua 177
  Querandi 137
  Sanavirones 177
  Selknam 257, 261
  Tehuelche *see* Tehuelche
  in Tierra del Fuego 257
  Toba 168
  Wichí 20, 168
  Yámana 257, 261
Instituto Nacional Eva Perón 108
Internet and fax 326
Iruya (Quebrada de Humahuaca) 197,
  198, 200
Isla Cormorán (San Julián) 230
Isla de los Pajaros (Puerto Deseado)
  229
Isla Grande (Tierra del Fuego) 257
Isla Justicia (San Julián) 230
Isla Las Mangas (Parque Nacional
  Pre-Delta) 162
Isla Martillo (Tierra del Fuego) 261
Isla Martín García (Buenos Aires) 116,
  117
Isla Moreo (Camarones) 228
Isla Pingüino (Puerto Deseado) 229
Isla San Martín (Parque Nacional
  Iguazú) 173, 174
Islas Malvinas *see* Falkland Islands
Isla Victoria (Parque Nacional Nahuel
  Huapi) 239
Italian immigrants 17, 20, 21, 206
  in Córdoba 180
  in La Boca 21
  in Mendoza 208

J

Jardín Botánico (Palermo and
  Belgrano) 105, **107**
Jardín Japonés (Palermo and
  Belgrano) 58, **106–107**
Jardín Zoológico (Palermo and
  Belgrano) **107**, 124
Jesuits 8, 13, 165, 177
  Alta Gracia 182
  architecture 34
  Colegio Nacional de Monserrat
    (Córdoba) 181

Jesuits (cont.)
  Cripta Jesuítica del Noviciado Viejo
    (Córdoba) 181
  evangelical missions 24, 48, 157
  expulsion 48, 67, 181, 182
  Iglesia de la Candelaria y San
    Antonio (Humahuaca) 200
  Iglesia de la Compañía (Córdoba)
    181
  Jesús María (Córdoba and the
    Andean Northwest) 184
  Manzana de las Luces (Córdoba)
    181
  Manzana de las Luces (Plaza de
    Mayo and Microcentro) 24, 63, 66–7
  Museo de Cultura Jesuítica
    Guillermo Furlong (Yapeyú) 165
  Rectorado de la Universidad
    Nacional de Córdoba (Córdoba)
    181, 182
  religious art 30
  San Ignacio Miní (Argentinian
    Mesopotamia) 158, 169
  Santa Catalina (Córdoba and the
    Andean Northwest) 186–7
  Yapeyú 165
Jesús María (Córdoba and the Andean
  Northwest) **184**
Jewish immigrants 17, 20, 21, 24–5
  Museo de la Shoá (Plaza San
    Martín) 93
  Museo Judío de Buenos Aires
    Dr. Salvador Kibrick 70
  Templo de la Congregación
    Israelita (Buenos Aires) 25, 70
Judaism 24–5
Jujuy *see* San Salvador de Jujuy
Junín de los Andes (Patagonia) 221,
  236
  accommodations 285

K

Kavanagh, Corina 91
Kayaking *see* Rafting and kayaking
King George Island (Antarctic
  Peninsula) 267
Kirchner, Cristina Fernandez de 15,
  55
Kirchner, Néstor 55
Kodak Gap (Antarctic Peninsula)
  266
Kuitca, Guillermo 31, 110
  Siete últimas canciones 110

L

La Boca (Buenos Aires) 6–7, 8, 21, 58
  See also San Telmo and La Boca
La Bombonera (San Telmo and La
  Boca) **85**, 122, 124
Lacámera, Fortunato 30
La City (Plaza de Mayo and
  Microcentro) **67**
La Costanera (Rosario) 160
La Cumbre (Córdoba and the Andean
  Northwest) **184**
  restaurants 298
La Dama Boba (Lope de Vega) 71
Lago *see* Lakes
La Historia Oficial (Luis Puenzo) 33
La Hoya ski resort (Esquel) 241
La Inmaculada Concepción
  (Belgrano) 114
La Justicia (Rogelio Yrurtia) 71
Lake District (Patagonia) 222
Lakes 8, 222
  Lago Argentino (Parque Nacional
    Los Glaciares) 247, 250, 251, 254
  Lago Barreales (Patagonia) 234

Lakes (cont.)
Lago Buenos Aires (Los Antiguos) 242
Lago Cardiel (Patagonia) **245**
Lago del Desierto (Patagonia) **246–7**
Lago Escondido (Parque Nacional Lanín) 237
Lago Fagnano (Tierra del Fuego) 261, 287
Lago Huechulafquen (Parque Nacional Lanín) 237
Lago Lácar (Parque Nacional Lanín) 236, 237
Lago Nahuel Huapi (Parque Nacional Nahuel Huapi) 238
Lago O'Higgins *see* Lago San Martín
Lago Posadas (Hipólito Yrigoyen) 244
Lago Puelo (El Bolsón) 240
Lago Roca (Parque Nacional Los Glaciares) 254
Lago San Martín (Patagonia) 245, **246**
Lago Tromen (Parque Nacional Lanín) 237
Lago Verde (Parque Nacional Los Alerces) 241
Lago Viedma (Parque Nacional Los Glaciares) 134, 253
Laguna de los Tres (Parque Nacional Los Glaciares) 252
Laguna Iberá (Esteros del Iberá) 167
Laguna Onelli (Parque Nacional Los Glaciares) 250, 254
Laguna Torre (Parque Nacional Los Glaciares) 252
La Milonga 2 (Diego Manuel Rodríguez) 27
La murga 81
Land and conservation 14
Landscape and wildlife **18–19**, 134
See also Wildlife
Language 319
La Niña Santa (Lucrecia Martel) 33
La Plata (Pampas) 13, 138, **140–43**
accommodations 278
map 141
Museo de La Plata 141, **142–3**
restaurants 296
La Rioja (Córdoba and the Andean Northwest) **184–5**
Larreta, Enrique 114
Glory of Don Ramiro, The 114
La Rural (Palermo and Belgrano) **112**
Las Babas del Diablo (Julio Cortázar) 31
Las Cañitas (Palermo and Belgrano) **113**
Las Islas de los Pajaros (Canal Beagle) 260
Las Leñas (Cuyo and the Wine Country) 9, **219**, 311
La Trochita 240, 241
Laurie Island (South Orkney Islands) 265
Lavalle, General Juan 71, 101, 198
La Virgen de Luján (Luján) 25, 40, 138, 144
La Vuelta de Rocha (San Telmo and La Boca) **84**, 85
Leather goods 305, 307
Legislatura de Buenos Aires (Plaza de Mayo) 63
Lemaire Channel (Antarctic Peninsula) 266
Lezama, José Gregorio 80
Literature 16, **30–31**

Livingston Island (Antarctic Peninsula) 267
Llao Llao (Parque Nacional Nahuel Huapi) 239, 311
López, Cándido 30, 50, 81
Battle of Tuyutí 50
Lorca, Federico García 68
Los Antiguos (Patagonia) **242**
accommodations 285
Los Penitentes (Cuyo and the Wine Country) **212**
accommodations 281
Luján (Pampas) 138, **144**
Luján de Cuyo (Cuyo and the Wine Country) 214–15
restaurants 299

M
Maestri, Cesare **253**
Magellan, Ferdinand 221, 230, 257
Magellanic forest 255
Mail services 326, 327
Maillart, Norbert 67
Palacio de Justicia (Plaza de Mayo) 71
Maimará (Quebrada de Humahuaca) 196, 198, 199
Malargüe 204, **219**
accommodations 281
restaurants 299
MALBA *see* Museo de Arte Latinamericano de Buenos Aires
Malbec wines 9, 209
See also Wines
Manifestación (Antonio Berni) 110
Manzana de las Luces (Córdoba) 181
Manzana de las Luces (Plaza de Mayo and Microcentro) 24, 63, **66–7**
Manzana Histórica (Viedma) 224
Maps
Antarctic Peninsula cruise 266–7
Argentina at a Glance 134–5
Argentina, orientation 10–11
Argentina Region by Region inside front cover
Argentina Road Map inside back cover
Argentinian Mesopotamia 158–9
Buenos Aires at a Glance 58–9
Buenos Aires, Farther Afield 116
Buenos Aires Street Finder 126–31
Buenos Aires Subte 334
Buenos Aires, Greater 11
climate zones 44–5
Córdoba and the Andean Northwest 178–9
Córdoba 180
Cuyo and the Wine Country 204–205
Esteros del Iberá 166–7
Falkland Islands 264
La Plata 141
Mendoza 206
Mendoza Winery Tour 210–11
Palermo and Belgrano 105
Pampas 138–9
Paraná River System 163
Parque Nacional Iguazú 172–3, 174
Parque Nacional Lanín 237
Parque Nacional Los Glaciares 250–51
Parque Nacional Los Glaciares northern sector 253
Parque Nacional Nahuel Huapi 238–9
Patagonia 223
Plaza de Mayo and Microcentro 61
Plaza de Mayo street-by-street 62–3
Plaza San Martín and Retiro 87

Maps (cont.)
Plaza San Martín street-by-street 88–9
Quebrada de Humahuaca 196–7
Recoleta 95
Recoleta street-by-street 96–7
Reserva Provincial Península Valdés 226–7
Rosario 161
San Telmo and La Boca 77
Salta street-by-street 192–3
Tierra del Fuego and Antarctica 258–9
Mapuche 20, 25, 47, 66, 113, 155, 221, 237
Mapuche music **29**
Museo Mapuche (Junín de los Andes) 236
Mar del Plata (Pampas) 8, 137, 138, **148–9**
accommodations 278
restaurants 296
Maradona, Diego 16, 39, 64, 85
Marine wildlife
Antarctica 264, **265**, 267
Museo de Ciencias Naturales y Oceanografía (Puerto Madryn) 225
Parque Nacional Monte León (Patagonia) 230
Reserva Provincial Península Valdés (Patagonia) 226–7
See also Whale-watching
Markets 304, 305, 306
crafts fair, Parque Lezama 80
in Buenos Aires 120, 121
Feria Artesanal (El Bolsón) 240
Feria de Mataderos (Buenos Aires) 116, 120, 122
Feria de San Pedro Telmo (San Telmo) 59, 78, 118, 120, 121
Feria Plaza Francia 118, 120, 121
Martín Fierro (Hernández, José)
Martín, Benito Quinquela 30, 68
Museo de Bellas Artes de La Boca Benito Quinquela Martín 84
Mate 22, 48, 306
Meano, Vittorio 69
Mendoza (Cuyo and the Wine Country) 9, 134, 203, 204, **206–207**, 214–15
accommodations 281–2
map 206
Mendoza Winery Tour **210–11**
restaurants 299–300
wines of Mendoza 203, **208–209**
Mendoza, Garcia de 203
Mendoza, Pedro de 47, 48, 77
Menem, Carlos 15, 55
Mercedes (Argentinian Mesopotamia) 137, 158, **165**
restaurants 297
Mestizo 9, 17, 20
Microcentro *see* Plaza de Mayo and Microcentro
Milonga 22, 26, 123, 125
finding a *milonga* **79**
Ministerio de Economía (Plaza de Mayo) 62
Miramar (Pampas) **151**
accommodations 278
Misiones 17, 19
Mitre, General Bartolomé 67, 144
tomb at Cementerio de la Recoleta 100
Molinos (Córdoba and the Andean Northwest) **190–91**
accommodations 280
restaurants 298

Monumento Natural Bosques
Petrificados (Patagonia) **229**
Monumento Natural Laguna de los
Pozuelos (Córdoba and the Andean
Northwest) **200**
Monuments and statues
Canto al Trabajo (San Telmo) **79**
Monument of José de San Martín
(Plaza San Martín) 87
Monumento al Ejercito Libertador
(Parque San Martín) 207
Monumento a los Caídos de
Malvinas (Plaza San Martín and
Retiro) 89, **90**
Monumento a los Dos Congresos
(Plaza del Congreso) 69
Monumento a los Españoles
(Parque 3 de Febrero) 106
Monumento Nacional a la Bandera
(Rosario) 160
Monumento Primera Misa (Puerto
San Julián) 230
Moreira, Juan **23**
Moreno, Francisco P. 142, 238, 242
Motorcycle Diaries, The 33, 160
Mount El Puntudo (Lago Cardiel) 245
Mount Erebus (Antarctic Peninsula)
266
Mount Fitz Roy (Parque Nacional Los
Glaciares) 18, 222, 246, 247, 250,
252
Museo *see* Museums and galleries
Museums and galleries
admission charges 319
Azotea de Lapalma (Gualeguaychú)
164
Buque Museo Fragata Presidente
Sarmiento (Puerto Madero) 75
Casa de Cultura (Mercedes) 165
Casa del Marqués Campero (Yavi)
201
Casa Histórica de la Independencia
(San Miguel de Tucumán) 189
Centro de Interpretación Histórica
Calafate (El Calafate) 247
Complejo Museográfico Enrique
Udaondo (Luján) 144
El Caminito (San Telmo and La
Boca) **85**
El Fogón de los Arrieros
(Resistencia) 168
Fundación Proa (La Boca) 84–5
Galería de Honor a las Banderas
(Rosario) 160
Gesell Museum, Villa Gesell
(Pampas) 150
Manzana Histórica (Viedma) 224
Museo Antropológico Gobernador
Eugenio Tello (Viedma) 224
Museo Argentino de Ciencias
Naturales Bernardino Rivadavia
(Palermo and Belgrano) **115**
Museo Arqueológico Doctor
Eduardo Casanova (Tilcara) 199
Museo Arqueológico Pio Pablo
Díaz (Cachi) 191
Museo Camín Cosquín (Cosquín) 183
Museo Casa de Ricardo Rojas
(Recoleta) **103**
Museo Casa de Yrurtia (Belgrano)
114
Museo Casa Uriburu (Salta) 193
Museo de Armas de la Nación
(Círculo Militar) 90
Museo de Arqueología Calchaquí
(Cafayate) 190
Museo de Arqueología de Alta
Montaña de Salta (Salta) 192, 194

Museums and galleries (cont.)
Museo de Arte Contemporáneo
Rosario (Rosario) 160
Museo de Arte Decorativo Firma y
Odilo Estévez (Rosario) 160
Museo de Arte Español Enrique
Larreta (Belgrano) 114
Museo de Arte Latinamericano de
Buenos Aires (Palermo and
Belgrano) 35, 105, **110–11**, 319
Museo de Arte Moderno (San
Telmo and La Boca) **79**
Museo de Arte Popular José
Hernández (Palermo and Belgrano)
108
Museo de Artes Plásticas Eduardo
Sívori (Palermo and Belgrano) **106**
Museo de Artesanía Tradicional
Folklórica (Corrientes) 168
Museo de Bellas Artes (Tandil) 152
Museo de Bellas Artes de La Boca
Benito Quinquela Martín (San
Telmo and La Boca) **84**
Museo de Ciencias Naturales y
Oceanografía (Puerto Madryn) 225
Museo de Cultura Jesuítica
Guillermo Furlong (Yapeyú) 165
Museo de Historia Natural (Parque
Provincial Ischigualasto) 217
Museo de la Casa Rosada (Casa
Rosada) 64
Museo de la Ciudad (Plaza de
Mayo and Microcentro) **66**
Museo de la Ciudad Virginia
Choquintel (Río Grande) 261
Museo de la Estación Ferrocarril
(Puerto Deseado) 229
Museo de la Inmigración (Plaza de
Mayo and Microcentro) **74–5**
Museo de la Pasion Boquense (La
Bombonera) 85
Museo de La Plata (La Plata) **142–3**
Museo de la Patagonia Francisco
P. Moreno (Bariloche) 238
Museo de la Policia (La City) 67
Museo de la Shoá (Plaza San
Martín and Retiro) **93**
Museo de la Vid y del Vino
(Cafayate) 190
Museo de los Niños (Buenos Aires)
124
Museo de los Pioneros (Río
Gallegos) 231
Museo de Sitio (Villa El Chocón) **235**
Museo del Área Fundacional
(Mendoza) 207
Museo del Automovilismo Juan
Manuel Fangio (Balcarce) 151
Museo del Che Guevara (Alta
Gracia) 182
Museo del Cine Pablo Cristian
Ducrós Hicken (San Telmo and La
Boca) **79**
Museo del Fin del Mundo
(Ushuaia) 260
Museo del Hombre Chaqueño
Ertivio Acosta (Resistencia) 168
Museo del Instituto Nacional de
Estudios de Teatro (Teatro Nacional
Cervantes) 70, 71
Museo del Mar (Mar del Plata) 148
Museo del Patrimonio (Palacio de
las Aguas Corrientes) 74
Museo del Puerto (Bahía Blanca) 154
Museo Ernesto Soto Avendaño
(Tilcara) 199
Museo Etnográfico (Plaza de Mayo
and Microcentro) **66**

Museums and galleries (cont.)
Museo Evita (Palermo and
Belgrano) **108**
Museo Ferroportuario (Comodoro
Rivadavia) 228
Museo Ferroviario (El Maitén) 240
Museo Ferroviario Roberto Gailán
(Río Gallegos) 231
Museo Folklórico (La Rioja) 184, 185
Museo Folklórico (San Miguel de
Tucumán) 189
Museo Gauchesco Ricardo Güiraldes
(San Antonio de Areco) 145
Museo Gregorio Funes (Córdoba)
180
Museo Histórico del Norte (Salta)
194
Museo Histórico Casa del Virrey
Liniers (Alta Gracia) 182
Museo Histórico de Camarones
(Camarones) 228
Museo Histórico Nacional (San
Telmo and La Boca) 80
Museo Histórico Nacional (San
Telmo and La Boca) **81**
Museo Histórico Nacional del
Cabildo y de la Revolución de
Mayo 65
Museo Histórico Provincial
Brigadier General Estanislao López
(Santa Fe) 162
Museo Histórico Provincial Juan
Lavalle (San Salvador de Jujuy) 198
Museo Histórico Provincial Julio
Marc (Rosario) 161
Museo Histórico Provincial Marqués
de Sobremonte (Córdoba) 181
Museo Histórico Regional Emma
Nozzi (Carmen de Patagones) 224
Museo Histórico Regional (Gaiman)
225
Museo Histórico y Numismático
del Banco de la Nación (Cabildo
de Buenos Aires) 65
Museo Irureta de Bellas Artes
(Tilcara) 199
Museo Jesuítico Nacional de Jesús
María (Jesús María) 184
Museo José Antonio Terry (Tilcara)
199
Museo Judío de Buenos Aires
Dr. Salvador Kibrick 70
Museo Leleque (Patagonia)
241
Museo Manuel de Fella (Alta
Gracia) 182
Museo Mapuche (Junín de los
Andes) 236
Museo Marítimo de Ushuaia
(Ushuaia) 260
Museo Mitre (La City) 67
Museo Muestra Arqueología
(Puerto San Julián) 230
Museo Municipal Cármen Funes
(Plaza Huincul) 235
Museo Municipal de Arte
Hispanoamericano Isaac Fernández
Blanco (Plaza San Martín and
Retiro) **92–3**
Museo Municipal de Arte Juan
Carlos Castagnino (Mar del Plata)
149
Museo Municipal de Arte Moderno
(Mendoza) 206
Museo Municipal de Bellas Artes
Dr. Genaro Pérez (Córdoba) 181
Museo Municipal de Bellas Artes
Juan B. Castagnino (Rosario) 161

Museums and galleries (cont.)
Museo Municipal de Ciencias Naturales Lorenzo Scaglia (Mar del Plata) 148
Museo Municipal de la Ciudad (Rosario) 161
Museo Municipal Ernesto Bachmann (Villa El Chocón) 235
Museo Municipal Mario Brozoski (Puerto Deseado) 229
Museo Municipal (Colonia del Sacramento) 117
Museo Nacional de Arte Decorativo (Palermo and Belgrano) **108–109**
Museo Nacional de Bellas Artes (Neuquén) 234
Museo Nacional de Bellas Artes (Recoleta) 30, 95, 97, **102**
Museo Nacional del Hombre (Palermo and Belgrano) **113**
Museo Nacional del Petróleo (Comodoro Rivadavia) 228
Museo Paleontológico Egidio Feruglio (Trelew) 225
Museo Paraje Confluencia (Neuquén) 234
Museo Portugués (Colonia del Sacramento) 117
Museo Primeros Pobladores (San Martín de los Andes) 236
Museo Provincial de Bellas Artes Emiliano Guiñazú (Mendoza) 207
Museo Provincial de Historia Natural (Santa Rosa) 154–5
Museo Regional Malargüe (Malargüe) 219
Museo Regional Monseñor Fagnano (Río Grande) 261
Museo Regional Municipal El Calafate (El Calafate) 247
Museo Regional Pueblo de Luis (Trelew) 225
Museo Regional Trevelin (Trevelin) 241
Museo Rosa Novak (Puerto San Julián) 230
Museo Salesiano Cardenal Cagliero (Viedma) 224
Museo Sanmartiano (Yapeyú) 165
Museo Tradicionalista (Tandil) 152
Museo Xul Solar (Recoleta) 25, **103**
Museo y Mercado Provincial de Artesanías (Paraná) 162
Museo Yámana (Ushuaia) 260
opening hours 319
Posta de Hornillos (Quebrada de Humahuaca) 196, 198
Provincial History Museum (Santiago del Estero) 188
Pucará de Tilcara (Tilcara) 199
Sarmiento Historical Museum (Belgrano) 114
Solar de los Haedo (Gualeguaychú) 164
Taller y Museo de Platería Criolla y Civil (San Antonio de Areco) 145
World Tango Museum (Café Tortoni) 68
Mountains and puna 18
Music 16, **28–9**, 308–309
Andean 28
chacarera 23, 28, 29, 188
chamame 28, 116
classical 308–309
contemporary 309
cumbia 28, 123
festivals 308
folklore 28

Music (cont.)
Mapuche **29**
pop music 16, 28, 29
rock nacional 16, 28, 29
shopping in Buenos Aires 119, 121
urban rhythms 28
venues 122, 125
zamba 28, 188
See also Folklore music

N
Namuncurá, Ceferino 25, 212
Ñandú 155, 165, 200
See also Rhea
Nant y Fall (Trevelin) 241
National Palace of the Arts *see* Palais de Glace (Recoleta)
National Parks (Parque Nacional) 14, 18, 273
Asociación de Parques Nacionales (Palacio Haedo) 91
campsites 273
Calilegua (Córdoba and the Andean Northwest) **201**
Chaco (Argentinian Mesopotamia) 14, **168–9**
El Palmar (Argentinian Mesopotamia) **165**
El Rey (Córdoba and the Andean Northwest) **201**
Iguazú (Argentinian Mesopotamia) 9, 135, 170–71, **172–5**
Lago Puelo (El Bolsón) 240
Laguna Blanca (Patagonia) **235**
Lanín (Patagonia) **237**
Lihué Calel (Pampas) **155**
Los Alerces (Patagonia) **241**
Los Arrayanes (Patagonia) 238, 310
Los Cardones (Córdoba and the Andean Northwest) 18, **191**
Los Glaciares (Patagonia) 9, 134, 247, **250–55**, 320
Monte León (Patagonia) 14, **230**
Nahuel Huapi (Patagonia) **238–9**
Perito Moreno (Patagonia) 13, 134, **244**
Pre-Delta (Argentinian Mesopotamia) **162**
Quebrada del Condorito (Córdoba and the Andean Northwest) **183**
Río Pilcomayo (Argentinian Mesopotamia) **169**
Sierra de las Quijadas 203, **218**
Talampaya (La Rioja) 176, 177, **185**, 217, 218
Tierra del Fuego (Ushuaia) 19, 258, **261**
See also Provincial Parks; Provincial Reserves; Reserves
Necochea (Pampas) **151**
accommodations 278
restaurants 296
Neko Harbor (Antarctic Peninsula) 266
Neuquén (Patagonia) 17, **234**
accommodations 285
Newspapers and magazines 119, 121, 327
Ngillatún 25

O
Obelisco, Avenida 9 de Julio (Buenos Aires) **70**
Ocampo, Victoria 31
Centro Cultural Villa Victoria (Mar del Plata) 149
Off-road driving 134, 310, 313
Oktoberfest 21, 183

Opening hours 319
banks and *casas de cambio* 319, 324
pharmacies 323
Opera season (Buenos Aires) 42
Outdoor activities **310–15**

P
Pachamama 25, 41, 177, 196, 199
Palacio Noel (Museo Municipal de Arte Hispanoamericano Isaac Fernández Blanco) 92–3
Palacio Barolo (Plaza de Mayo and Microcentro) 35, **68**
Palacio de Correos y Telecomunicaciones *see* Correo Central
Palacio de Gobierno (Plaza de Mayo) 63
Palacio de Gobierno (San Luis) 218
Palacio de Justicia (Plaza de Mayo and Microcentro) **71**
Palacio de la Legislatura (La Plata) 140
Palacio de las Aguas Corrientes (Plaza de Mayo and Microcentro) **74**
Palacio del Correo (Plaza de Mayo and Microcentro) 160
Palacio Haedo (Plaza San Martín and Retiro) 88, 89, **91**
Palacio Municipal (La Plata) 140
Palacio Municipal (Paraná) 162
Palacio Paz *see* Círculo Militar
Palacio San José (Argentinian Mesopotamia) **164**
Palacio San Martín (Plaza San Martín and Retiro) 88, 89, **90**
Palais de Glace (Recoleta) 96, **102**
Paleontology
Centro Paleontológico Lago Barreales (Patagonia) 234
Museo de Historia Natural (Parque Provincial Ischigualasto) 217
Museo de La Plata 143
Museo Municipal Cármen Funes (Plaza Huincul) 235
Museo Municipal de Ciencias Naturales Lorenzo Scaglia 148
Museo Paleontológico Egidio Feruglio (Trelew) 225
Parque Nacional Los Cardones 191
Parque Nacional Sierra de las Quijadas 203, 218
Parque Provincial Ischigualasto 203, 217
Patagonia **232–3**
tourism 232
Villa El Chocón 235
See also Dinosaurs; Petrified forests
Palermo and Belgrano (Buenos Aires) 8, 58, 77, **104–15**
accommodations 277
area map 105
getting around 105
Museo de Arte Latinoamericano de Buenos Aires (MALBA) **110–11**
restaurants 294–5
Villa Freud **113**
Pampas 8, **136–55**
accommodations 278
cuisine 290
flora and fauna 18
getting around 139
landscape 18,134
Mountains of the Pampas **153**
Museo de La Plata **142–3**
region map 138–9

Pampas (cont.)
  restaurants 296
  wetlands 18
Paradise Bay (Antarctic Peninsula) 266
Paragliding 184, 311
Paraná (Argentinian Mesopotamia) 8,
  162
  accommodations 279
  Paraná Delta 116, 117, 163
  Paraná River System 14, **163**
  restaurants 297
Parks and gardens
  Jardín Botánico (Palermo and
    Belgrano) 105, **107**
  Jardín Japonés (Palermo and
    Belgrano) 58, **106–107**
  Jardín Zoológico (Palermo and
    Belgrano) 107, **124**
  Parque 3 de Febrero (Palermo and
    Belgrano) 8, 45, 80, 104, 105, **106**,
    122, 124
  Parque Bernardo O'Higgins
    (Mendoza) 207
  Parque de la Costa (Buenos Aires)
    124
  Parque de la Independencia
    (Rosario) 161
  Parque El Desafío (Gaiman) 225
  Parque Lezama (San Telmo and La
    Boca) **80**
  Parque Miguel Lillo (Necochea) 151
  Parque San Martín (Mendoza) 42, 207
  Parque Temaikén (Buenos Aires)
    124
  Parque Urquiza (Paraná) 162
  Parque Urquiza (Rosario) 160
  Parque Urquiza (Gualeguaychú) 164
  Paseo del Bosque (La Plata) 141
  Parque dos Aves Foz Tropicana
    (Brazil) 175
Parque see Parks and Gardens
Parque Nacional see National Parks
Parque Natural Pinar del Norte (Villa
  Gesell) 150
Parque Provincial see Provincial Parks
Parrillas 288
Pasaje Dardo Rocha (La Plata) 141
Pasaje Juramento (Rosario) 160
Patagonia 8, 9, 3, 19, **220–55**
  accommodations 283–6
  cuisine 291
  getting around 223
  landscape and wildlife 19
  paleontology **232–3**
  Parque Nacional Lanín 236, **237**
  Parque Nacional Los Glaciares **250–
    55**
  Parque Nacional Nahuel Huapí
    238–9
  region map 222–3
  Reserva Provincial Península
    Valdés **226–7**
  restaurants 301–3
  satellite image 10
  Welsh in Patagonia **224**
Pato 36
Pauke, Florian 30
Paz family 89
  tomb at Cementerio de la Recoleta
    101
Paz, José Camilo 90, 101
Peñas 194, 309
  See also Folklore music
Peña, Sáenz, tomb at Cementerio de
  la Recoleta 100
Penguins 135, 265
  Adelie 265, 267
  Chinstrap 265, 267

Penguins (cont.)
  Emperor 266
  Gentoo 261, 267
  King 9, 265
  Macaroni 265, 267
  Magellanic 19, 226, 227, 228, 229,
    230, 231, 261
  Rockhopper 229, 264, 267, 312
Península Valdés (Patagonia) 9, 19,
  221, 226–7
  accommodations 285
  whale-watching 226, 227, 312
Penuti and Bernheim 49
  Batalla de Monte Caseros 49
Peoples **20–21**
Perito Moreno (Patagonia) **242**
  accommodations 285
Perón, Eva 51, 2–3, 64
  Museo Evita (Palermo and
    Belgrano) **108**
  tomb at Cementerio de la Recoleta
    100
Perón, Juan Domingo 16, 24, 51–4, 64
Peronism see Perón, Juan Domingo
Personal security 322–3
Petrified forests 232
  Bosque Petrificado José Ormachea
    (Patagonia) **229**
  Monumento Natural Bosques
    Petrificados (Patagonia) **229**
  See also Paleontology
Pinamar (Pampas) 8, 138, **150**
  accommodations 278
  restaurants 296
Pirámide de Mayo (Plaza de Mayo)
  62, 63
Pismania (Cuyo and the Wine
  Country) **216–17**
Pizza, Birra, Faso (Caetano and
  Stagnaro) 33
Place, Harry see Butch Cassidy and
  the Sundance Kid
Plaza 25 de Mayo (La Rioja) 185
Plaza 25 de Mayo (Rosario) 160
Plaza 25 de Mayo (San Fernando del
  Valle de Catamarca) 188
Plaza 9 de Julio (Salta) 192, 193, 194
Plaza Chile (Mendoza) 206–207
Plaza Cortázar see Plaza Serrano
Plaza de Mayo and Microcentro
  (Buenos Aires) 58, **60–75**, 319
  accommodations 274–5
  area map 61
  flashpoint of history **64**
  getting around 61
  the Peróns 52–3
  restaurants 292
  street-by-street 62–3
  Teatro Colón **72–3**
Plaza del Congreso (Plaza de Mayo
  and Microcentro) 56–7, 58, **69**
Plaza Dorrego (San Telmo and La
  Boca) 59, **78**
Plaza Embajada de Israel (Plaza San
  Martín and Retiro) **93**
Plaza España (Mendoza) 206
Plaza Francia (Recoleta) 96, 97
Plaza Huincul (Patagonia) 234, 235
Plaza Independencia (Mendoza) 206
Plaza Independencia (San Luis) 218
Plaza Intendente Alvear (Recoleta) 97
Plaza Italia (Mendoza) 206
Plaza Lavalle (Plaza de Mayo and
  Microcentro) **71**
Plaza Mariano Moreno (La Plata) 140
Plaza Primero de Mayo (Paraná) 158,
  162
Plaza Pringles (San Luis) 218

Plaza Prospero Molina (Cosquín)
  183
Plaza Rivadavia (Bahía Blanca) 154
Plaza San Martín (Colón) 164
Plaza San Martín (Córdoba) 180
Plaza San Martín (Mendoza) 207
Plaza San Martín (Santa Rosa)
  154
Plaza San Martín and Retiro (Buenos
  Aires) 58, **86–93**
  accommodations 276
  area map 87
  getting around 87
  restaurants 293
  street-by-street 88–9
Plaza Serrano (Palermo and
  Belgrano) **115**
Police 322
Polo 36, 314
  Abierto Argentino de Palermo 36,
    41, 109, 308
Pop music 16, 28, 29
Popular cults 24, 25
Port Lockroy (Antarctic Peninsula)
  262–3, 266
Posta de Hornillos (Quebrada de
  Humahuaca) 196, 198
Practical information **318–27**
Pre-Columbian culture 17, 185, 217
  beliefs 25
  Hornillos Huarpes (Parque
    Nacional Sierra de las Quijadas)
    218
  Museo Antropológico Gobernador
    Eugenio Tello (Viedma) 224
  Museo Arqueológico Doctor
    Eduardo Casanova (Tilcara) 199
  Tilcara 196
  Uspallata (Cuyo and the Wine
    Country) 212
Pre-Hispanic art 30
Presidente Sarmiento (Puerto
  Madero) 75
Provincial Parks (Parque Provincial)
  Aconcagua (Cuyo and the Wine
    Country) 204, **213**
  Ernesto Tornquist (Pampas) 152,
    153
  Ischigualasto (Cuyo and the Wine
    Country) 14, 202, 203, 204, **217**
  Valle Fértil (San Agustín del Valle
    Fértil) 217
Provincial Reserves (Reserva
  Provincial)
  Cabo dos Bahías (Camarones) 228
  Cabo Vírgenes (Patagonia) **231**
  Parque Luro (Santa Rosa) 155
  Península Valdés (Patagonia) **226–7**
  Punta Tombo (Patagonia) **228**
Public holidays 43
Puente Transbordador Nicolás
  Avellaneda (San Telmo and La
  Boca) **84**
Puerto Deseado (Patagonia) **229**, 312
  accommodations 285
Puerto Iguazú 172
  accommodations 279
  restaurants 297
Puerto Madero (Plaza de Mayo and
  Microcentro) 35, **75**
Puerto Madryn (Patagonia) 224, **225**
  accommodations 285
  restaurants 302
  Welsh 221
Puerto Pirámides (Reserva Provincial
  Península Valdés) 226
Puerto San Julián (Patagonia) **230**
  accommodations 286

Pueyrredón, Prilidiano 30, 102
  Bath, The 30
  Retrato de Manuelita Rosas 30, 102
Puig, Manuel 31
  El Beso de la Mujer Arana 31
Puna Jujena (Humahuaca) 200
Punta Delgada (Reserva Provincial
  Península Valdés) 227
Punta Norte (Reserva Provincial
  Península Valdés) 227
Purmamarca (Quebrada de
  Humahuaca) 196, 198, 305
  accommodations 280

Q

Quebrada de Cafayate (Córdoba and
  the Andean Northwest) 9, **190**
Quebrada de Humahuaca (Córdoba
  and the Andean Northwest) 2–3, 9,
  132–3, 134, 177, 178, **196–200**
Quilmes (Córdoba and the Andean
  Northwest) **189**
Quiroga, Juan Facundo **185**
  tomb at Cementerio de la Recoleta
  101

R

Racing and show jumping 37
Radical Party 50, 54–5
Radio and television 327
Radio taxis 321
Rafting and kayaking 312
  Río Aluminé 236
  Río Andinos 312
  Río Jáchal 216
  Río Mendoza, 204, 212
  Río Quequen 151
  See also White-water rafting
Ranches *see* Estancias
Recoleta (Buenos Aires) 58, 77, **94–
103**
  accommodations 276–7
  area map 95
  Cementerio de la Recoleta 94, 95,
  100–1
  dogs of Recoleta **99**
  getting around 95
  restaurants 293
  street-by-street 96–7
Religion **24–5**
Religious art and architecture 30
Remises 335
Reserva *see* Reserves
Reserva Provincial *see* Provincial
  Reserves
Reserves
  Esteros del Iberá (Argentinian
  Mesopotamia) **166–7**
  Monumento Natural Bosques
  Petrificados (Patagonia) **229**
  Monumento Natural Laguna de los
  Pozuelos (Córdoba and the Andean
  Northwest) **200**
  Reserva Ecológica Costanera Sur
  (Plaza de Mayo and Microcentro) **75**
  Reserva Municipal Laguna Nimez
  (El Calafate) 247
  Reserva Natural Caverna de las
  Brujas (Malargüe) 219
  Reserva Natural Integral (Parque
  Provincial Ernesto Tornquist) 153
  Reserva Natural Laguna de
  Llancanelo (Malargüe) 219
  Reserva Natural La Payunia
  (Malargüe) 219
  Reserva Natural Ría del Deseado
  (Puerto Deseado) 229
  See also Provincial Reserves

Resistencia (Argentinian
  Mesopotamia) **168**
Restaurants 288–9, **292–303**
  Argentinian Mesopotamia **297**
  bars and *confiterías* 288
  Buenos Aires **292–5**
  chain restaurants 288
  children 289
  Córdoba and the Andean
  Northwest **298**
  credit cards 289
  Cuyo and the Wine Country
  299–300
  eating hours 288
  Pampas **296**
  parrillas 288, 290
  Patagonia **301–2**
  prices 289
  service charge 289
  smoking 289
  tenedor libre 288, 289,
  Tierra del Fuego and Antarctica **303**
  vegetarian options 289
  wheelchair access 289
  See also Food
Retiro Belgrano (Estación Retiro) 92
Retiro Mitre (Estación Retiro) 92
Retiro San Martín (Estación Retiro) 92
Retiro *see* Plaza San Martín and Retiro
Retrato de Manuelita Rosas (Prilidiano
  Pueyrredón) 30, 102
Revolución de Mayo (1810) 49, 63
  Día de la Revolución de Mayo
  (Buenos Aires) 42
  Monumento a los Españoles
  (Parque 3 de Febrero) 106
Rhea 217, 226, 228
  See also Ñandú
Río Aluminé 236
Río Andinos 312
Río Atuel 219
Río Blanco 252, 253
Río Chuschas 190
Río Conchas 190
Río Cosquín 183
Río de la Plata 58, 80, 116, 137
Río de las Vueltas 246
Río Deseado 229
Río Diamante 219
Río Dulce 188
Río Gallegos (Patagonia) **230–31**
  accommodations 286
Río Grande Valley 196
Río Grande (Tierra del Fuego) 198,
  258, **261**
  accommodations 287
  restaurants 303
Río Iguazú *see* Iguazú River
Río Jáchal 216
Río Limay 234
Río Loro Hausi 190
Río Manso 238
Río Mendoza 212
Río Menendez 261
Río Negro 224
Río Neuquén 234
Río Paraná 157, 158, 159, 160, 163
  Paraná River System **163**
Río Pilcomayo 169
Río Pinturas 243
Río Quequen 151
Río Sali Valley 189
Río San Juan 216
Río Turbio (Patagonia) 230, **247**
Río Uruguay 14, 157, 158, 164
Río Xibi Xibi 198
Rivadavia, Bernardino 49, 100, 115,
  185

Roca, General Julio Argentino
  Conquista del Desierto 50, 101,
  154, 155, 236
  tomb at Cementerio de la Recoleta
  101
Rodriguez, Diego Manuel 27
  La Milonga 2 27
Rompecabezas (Jorge de la Vega) 111
Rosario (Argentinian Mesopotamia)
  134, 158, **160–61**
  accommodations 279
  map 161
  restaurants 297
Rosas, Juan Manuel de 31, 49, 106,
  107, 113, 144
  defeat at the Battle of Monte
  Caseros 49, 106, 144
  campaign against indigenous
  peoples 155
Ruta Nacional 40 245, 310, 333
  Argentina's Loneliest Road **243**
Ryan, James *see* Butch Cassidy and
  the Sundance Kid

S

Sailing and windsurfing 312, 313
Salesian missionaries 24, 257, 261
Salina Grande (Reserva Provincial
  Península Valdés) 227
Salisbury Plain, South Georgia
  (Subantarctic Islands) 265
Salta (Córdoba and the Andean
  Northwest) 9, 19, 30, 135, 177, 178,
  192–5
  accommodations 280
  restaurants 298
  settlement of 47
  street-by-street 192–3
  Train to the Clouds **195**
  wines of Salta 191
Salto San Martín (Parque Nacional
  Iguazú) 173
San Agustín del Valle Fértil (Cuyo and
  the Wine Country) **217**
  accommodations 282
  restaurants 300
San Antonio de Areco (Pampas) 8,
  137, 138, **145**
  restaurants 296
San Cayetano 25
San Fernando del Valle de Catamarca
  (Córdoba and the Andean
  Northwest) 30, **188**
San Ignacio Miní (Argentinian
  Mesopotamia) 24, 30, 156, 157, **169**
  accommodations 279
San José de Jáchal (Cuyo and the
  Wine Country) **216**
San Juan (Cuyo and the Wine
  Country) 9, **216**
  accommodations 282
  restaurants 300
San Luis (Cuyo and the Wine
  Country) **218**
  accommodations 282
  restaurants 300
San Martín de los Andes (Patagonia)
  9, 222, **236**
  accommodations 286
  restaurants 302
San Martín, General José de 180, 185,
  212
  birthplace at Yapeyú 158, 165
  burial at Catedral Metropolitana
  65
  declaration of Independence 49
  Día del Libertador General San
  Martín 43

San Martín, General José de (cont.)
in Mendoza 207
Templete Sanmartiano (Yapeyú) 165
San Miguel de Tucumán (Córdoba and the Andean Northwest) **189**
restaurants 298
San Rafael (Cuyo and the Wine Country) **219**
accommodations 282
restaurants 300
San Salvador de Jujuy (Quebrada de Humahuaca) 20, 198
restaurants 298
San Telmo and La Boca (Buenos Aires) 8, 58, **76–85**
accommodations 275
area map 77
getting there 77
restaurants 292–3
Santa Catalina (Córdoba and the Andean Northwest) **186–7**
Santa Fe (Argentinian Mesopotamia) 158, **162**, 163
restaurants 297
Santa Rosa (Pampas) 8, **154–5**
accommodations 278
restaurants 296
Santiago del Estero (Córdoba and the Andean Northwest) 47, 177, 178, **188**
Sarmiento, Domingo F. 64, 105, 216
El Matadero 31
Sea lions 221, 225, 226, 227, 228
Seals 19, 264, 265, 267
Security **322–3**
Sendero Laguna de los Tres (Parque Nacional Los Glaciares) 252
Sendero Laguna Torre (Parque Nacional Los Glaciares) 252
Sendero Macuco (Parque Nacional Iguazú) 173, 175
Sendero Piedra del Fraile (Parque Nacional Los Glaciares) 253
Senior travelers 320, 321
Shackleton, Ernest 265, 267
Shopping **304–307**
art and antiques 118, 120, 121, 305
artisans' markets *see* Markets
bargaining 304
bodegas 305
boutiques 304, 305, 306
chacras 305
crafts and gifts 118, 121, 306
earthenware 307
fashion 119, 121
fileteado 307
food 120, 121, 305
gaucho ware 305, 306, 307
how to pay 304
in Buenos Aires **118–21**
jewelry 306
leather 305, 307
lingerie and swimwear 119, 121
malls 120, 121, 304, 305, 306
mate 306
music 119
newspapers and books 119
opening hours 304
souvenirs 306
specialist stores 305
tango 304, 305
taxes and refunds 304, 305
what to buy **306–307**
wine 120, 121, 305, 307
woolens and weavings 306
Sierra de Aconquija (Córdoba and the Andean Northwest) 189

Sierra de la Ventana (Pampas) 138, 139, **152–3**
Sierra Las Animas (Pampas) 152
Siete últimas canciones (Guillermo Kuitca) 110
Sin título (León Ferrari) 111
Sistema de Tandilia 152, 153
Sisterna, Benjamin 148
Skiing and winter sports 311, 313
Cerro Castor (Tierra del Fuego) 260
Chapelco Ski Resort (Patagonia) 236
La Hoya (Patagonia) 241
Las Leñas (Cuyo and the Wine Country) 9, 203, 219, 311
Los Penitentes (Cuyo and the Wine Country) 212
Valdelén winter sports complex (Patagonia) 246
Villa Cerro Catedral (Parque Nacional Nahuel Huapi) 239
Snow Hill Island (Antarctic Peninsula) 266, 267
Soccer 16, **38–9**, 124, 308
Social customs and etiquette 319
Society of Jesus *see* Jesuits
Solar, Xul 30, 102, 103
Soldi, Raúl 73
Southern Patagonian Ice Field 253, 254
Southern Right Whale 19, 312
Península Valdés 9, 43, 226–7
Playa El Doradillo (Puerto Madryn) 225
South Georgia (Subantarctic Islands) 265
South Orkney Islands (Subantarctic Islands) 265
South Shetland Islands (Antarctica) 258, 264, 266
Souvenirs 306
Spanish
colonization of Argentina 13, 47–8, 137, 177
immigrants 13, 17, 20
Spas and luxury holidays **311**, 313
Pismanta 216–17
Termas de Río Honda 188
Specialized holidays **310–15**
Sports 16, 308, 309
in Buenos Aires 124, 125
See also Equestrian sports; Polo; Soccer
Spring events 40
Stanley (Falkland Islands) 264
Stolen property 322
Strait of Magellan 18, 257
Subantarctic Islands 264–5
Subtropical forests 19
Sulky competition 37
Summer events 41

T

Tafí del Valle (Córdoba and the Andean Northwest) **189**
accommodations 280
Tandil (Pampas) 138, **152**
accommodations 278
restaurants 296
Tango 6–7, **26–7**, 28, 77, 78, 308, 311, 313
Café Tortoni 68
cinema 29, 32
Club Gricel 79
fantasia or show tango 26
Festival Buenos Aires Tango 41
International Tango Festival (Buenos Aires) 122

Tango (cont.)
the *milonga* 26, **79**
outfits, shopping for 305
Palais de Glace (Recoleta) 102
in pop art 27
shows and classes 79, 123, 125
street tango 26–7, 78
in street art 27
Tango Metropolitan Championship (Buenos Aires) 26
World Tango Championship (Buenos Aires) 43
World Tango Museum (Café Tortoni) 68
Tango Argentino 27
Taxis 335
Teatro *see* Theater
Tehuelche 20, 47, 113, 155, 221
Telephones 326
Templo de la Congregación Israelita (Buenos Aires) 25, **70**
Templo de la Inmaculada Concepción (Tandil) 152
Templo de San Francisco (Mendoza) 207
Termas de Río Hondo (Córdoba and the Andean Northwest) **188**, 311
Theater **32–3**, 309
in Buenos Aires 123, 125
Teatro Abierto (Buenos Aires) 32, 33
Teatro Argentino (La Plata) 140
Teatro Avenida (Plaza de Mayo and Microcentro) **68**, 123
Teatro Catalinas Sur (San Telmo and La Boca) **81**, 123
Teatro Centenario (Colón) 164
Teatro Colón (Plaza de Mayo and Microcentro) 16, 32, 42, 50, 123, **72–3**, 308, 309
Teatro El Círculo (Rosario) 308, 309
Teatro General San Martín (Plaza de Mayo and Microcentro) 32, **74**, 123
Teatro Griego (Mendoza) 209
Teatro Lavarden (Rosario) 308, 309
Teatro Martín Fierro (La Plata) 141
Teatro Municipal Colón (Mar del Plata) 308
Teatro Nacional Cervantes (Plaza de Mayo and Microcentro) **70–71**, 123
Teatro Quintanilla (Mendoza) 206
Tierra del Fuego and Antarctica 9, 41, 135, **256–67**
accommodations 287
cruising Antarctica **264–7**
cuisine 291
getting around 259
region map 258–9
restaurants 303
satellite image 10
Tigre and the Delta (Buenos Aires) 8, **116–17**
Tilcara (Quebrada de Humahuaca) 196, 198, 199
accommodations 280
Time 321
Tipping 273
Tolhuin (Lago Fagnano, Tierra del Fuego) 261
Torre de los Ingleses (Plaza San Martín and Retiro) 86, 89, **92**
Torrontés wines 177, 191, 209, 307
See also Wines
Toucans 19, 175, 201
Tours 329
estancias 314–15
food 311

Tours (cont.)
    Mendoza Winery Tour 210–11
    vineyards 311, 313
    See also Boat excursions; Cruises;
        Estancias
Tourist information 318, 321
Train to the Clouds (Salta) **195**
Trains 332, 334
Travel information **328–35**
    air travel 328, 330–31
    Argentina Road Map inside back
        cover
    arriving by land 329
    arriving by sea 329
    colectivos 332
    ferries 332
    great drives 333
    micros 332
    off-road driving 333
    organized tours 329
    renting cars and motorbikes 333
    safety 333
    Subte and overland trains 334
    taxis and *remises* 332
    trains 332, 334
    travel and health insurance 323
    walking in Buenos Aires 334
Traveler's checks 289, 324
Travelers with special needs 320, 321
Trekking *see* Hiking and trekking
Trelew (Patagonia) 221, **225**
    accommodations 286
Tren de las Nubes *see* Train to the
    Clouds
Tren Ecológico de la Selva (Parque
    Nacional Iguazú) 173, 174
Tres Lagos (Patagonia) **245**
Trevelin (Patagonia) **241**
Tunuyán (Cuyo and the Wine
    Country)
    accommodations 282
    restaurants 300
Twelve Prophets, The (Iglesia de la
    Candelaria y San Antonio,
    Humahuaca) 200
Ty Gwyn tea house (Gaiman) 225
Ty Nain tea house (Gaiman) 225

U

UNESCO World Heritage Sites
    Alta Gracia (Córdoba and the
        Andean Northwest) 182
    Colonia del Sacramento (Uruguay)
        116, 117
    Cueva de las Manos (Patagonia) 9,
        134, 242, 245
    Manzana de las Luces (Córdoba)
        181
    Parque Nacional Iguazú
        (Argentinian Mesopotamia) 135,
        172–5
    Parque Nacional Los Glaciares
        (Patagonia) 134, 247, 250–55
    Parque Nacional Talampaya
        (Córdoba and the Andean
        Northwest) 176, 185
    Parque Provincial Ischigualasto
        (Cuyo and the Wine Country) 217
    Quebrada de Humahuaca
        (Córdoba and the Andean
        Northwest) 196–200
    Reserva Provincial Península Valdés
        (Patagonia) 9, 226–7
    San Ignacio Miní (Argentinian
        Mesopotamia) 24, 30, 156, 158,
        169
    Santa Catalina (Córdoba and the
        Andean Northwest) 186–7

Unión Cívica Radical 50, 54–5
Unitarists 49, 64, 157, 162, 185
    civil war 49, 157, 168
    See also Federalists
Uquia (Quebrada de Humahuaca)
    197, 198, 199
Urquiza, General Justo José 106, 164
Ushuaia (Tierra del Fuego) 9, 257,
    258, 259, **260**
    accommodations 287
    restaurants 303
Uspallata (Cuyo and the Wine
    Country) **212**
    accommodations 282

V

Vaccinations 323
Valentino, Rudolph 29
    Four Horsemen of the Apocalypse 29
Valles Calchaquíes (Córdoba and the
    Andean Northwest) 18, 190
Varela, Adriana 27
Vega, Lope de 68, 71
Verdi, Giuseppe 72
Via Christi (Junín de los Andes) 236
Viceroyalty of the River Plate 30, 48–9
Vicuña 190
Viedma (Patagonia) **224**
    accommodations 286
    restaurants 302
Villa Cerro Catedral (Parque Nacional
    Nahuel Huapi) 239
Villa El Chocón (Patagonia) **235**
    accommodations 286
Villa General Belgrano (Córdoba and
    the Andean Northwest) **183**
    restaurants 298
Villa Gesell (Pampas) 138, **150**
    accommodations 278
    restaurants 296
Villa La Angostura (Parque Nacional
    Nahuel Huapi) 222, 238
    accommodations 286
    restaurants 302
Villa O'Higgins (Chile) 247
Villa Traful (Parque Nacional Nahuel
    Huapi) 238
Villa Ventana (Pampas) 153
    accommodations 278
Vineyards 214–15
    Cafayate 9, 190
    Mendoza 208–11
    San Rafael 219
    tours 210–11, 311
    See also Bodegas; Wine
Visas and passports 318, 321
Visitor information centers 318, 321
Volcán Lanín (Parque Nacional Lanín)
    237
Volunteer Point (Falkland Islands) 264

W

Walking *see* Hiking and trekking 311
War of Spanish Succession 48
War of the Triple Alliance 50, 168
Wars of Independence 49, 84, 87
Waterskiing 312
Weddell Sea 267
Weddell seals 265, 266, 267
Welsh 17, 225
    Eisteddfod festival 40
    Welsh in Patagonia 221, **224**, 241
West Point Island (Falkland Islands)
    264
Wetlands 18
    Reserva Ecológica Costanera Sur 75
    Esteros del Iberá (Argentinian
        Mesopotamia) 166–7

Wetlands (cont.)
    Reserva Natural Laguna de
        Llancanelo (Malargüe) 219
    Reserva Natural Ría del Deseado
        (Puerto Deseado) 229
Whale-watching 134, 312, 313
    Antarctic Peninsula 266
    Península Valdés 226, 227, 312
    See also Whales
Whales 264
    Austral Frank 230
    Blue 142, 265
    Fin 265, 266
    Humpback 265, 266
    Minke 265, 266
    Orca (Killer) 227, 266, 267
    Southern Right *see* Southern Right
        Whale
    See also Whale-watching
What to wear 319
When to go 318
Whispering Land, The (Gerald
    Durrell) 201
White-water rafting 134, 203, 312, 313
    Río Atuel 219
    Río Diamante 219
    Río Jáchal 216
    Río Manso 238
    See also Rafting and kayaking
Wildlife **18–19**
    See also Marine wildlife; National
        Parks; Provincial Parks; Provincial
        Reserves; Reserves
Windsurfing 312, 313
    Chapadmalal 150
    Necochea 151
Wines 311, 313
    Jesuit winery, Jesús María 184
    Malbec 9, 209
    Mendoza Winery Tour **210–11**
    San Juan 9, 216
    shopping 120, 121, 305, 307
    Torrontés 134, 177, 191, 209, 307
    vintages 208
    wines of Mendoza 203, 206, **208–
        209**
    wines of Salta **191**
    See also Bodegas; Vineyards
Winter events 43
    sports *see* Skiing and winter sports
Women travelers 321
World Rally Championship (Córdoba)
    308
World Wide Fund for Nature 14

Y

Yacyreta Dam (Río Paraná) 163
Yapeyú (Argentinian Mesopotamia)
    158, **165**
Yatay palm 157, 164, 165
Yavi (Córdoba and the Andean
    Northwest) **200–1**
Yerba mate 48
Youth hostels 273
Yrurtia, Rogelio 71, **79**, 114
    Canto al Trabajo 79
    La Justicia 71

Z

Zamba 28, 188
Zapala (Parque Nacional Laguna
    Blanca) 235
Zonda wind 203

Acknowledgments

Dorling Kindersley would like to thank the many people whose help and assistance contributed to the preparation of this book.

Main Contributors
Wayne Bernhardson first visited Buenos Aires in 1981 during a military dictatorship. He has contributed to both magazines and newspapers including Trips, National Geographic Traveler, and San Francisco Chronicle.

Declan McGarvey visited Argentina in 1999 and decided to stay after falling in love with the country. Nine presidents later, he remains in Buenos Aires, where he works as a travel writer and editor. He is co-author of Eyewitness Top 10 Buenos Aires, has collaborated on and edited several Time Out guides to Patagonia and Buenos Aires, and has contributed to DK's Where to Go When series.

Chris Moss lived in Argentina for 10 years and commutes there regularly from his home in London. He has written on Latin American topics for the Daily Telegraph, Independent, Guardian, New Internationalist, and Condé Nast Traveller, and is the author of Landscapes of the Imagination: Patagonia (Signal Books).

Fact Checkers
Ariel Waisman, Sofí Saul

Proofreader
Deepthi Talwar

Indexer
Jyoti Dhar

Editorial and Design
Publisher Douglas Amrine
List Manager Vivien Antwi
Managing Art Editor Jane Ewart
Publishing Manager Scarlett O'Hara
Project Editor Alastair Laing
Project Designers Sonal Bhatt, Paul Jackson
Senior Cartographic Editor Casper Morris
Managing Art Editor (jackets) Karen Constanti
Jacket Design Tessa Bindloss
DTP Designer Natasha Lu
Picture Researcher Ellen Root
Production Controller Louise Daly

Design and Editorial Assistance
Hannah Dolan, Alexandra Farrell, Fay Franklin, Anna Freiberger, Margaret McHugh, Mariane Petrou, Susana Smith

DK Picture Library
Emma Shepherd, Romaine Werblow

Additional Photography
Philip Dowell, Mike Dunning, Frank Greenaway, Cyril Laubscher, Richard Leeney, Ian O'Leary, Neil Setchfield.

Special Assistance
DK would like to thank the following for their assistance: Analia Martino at Museo de la Plata, German Maschwitz at Fronterasur, Preeti Pant, Guadalupe Requena and Cintia Mezza at Museo de Arte Latinamericano de Buenos Aires.

Photography Permissions
DK would like to thank the following for their assistance and kind permission to photograph at their establishments:
Alvear Palace Hotel, Ateneo Grand Splendid, Banco de la Nación Argentina, Basílica Nuestra Señora de Luján, Cabildo de Buenos Aires, Café La Biela, Café Tortoni, Catedral de la Inmaculada Concepción, Catedral Metropolitana, Catedral Nuestra Señora del Valle, Cementerio de la Recoleta, Centro Cultural Recoleta, Che Lulu hotel, Congreso Nacional Argentino, Correo Central Argentino, Estancia Cerro de la Cruz, Estancia La Bamba, Estancia Rincón del Socorro, Estación Retiro, Galerías Pacífico, Iglesia de la Compañía, Iglesia de Nuestra Señora del Pilar, Iglesia Parroquial Nuestra Señora de la Merced, Iglesia San Francisco, Instituto Nacional de Estudios de Teatro, Mansión Dandi Royal, Museo Argentino de Ciencias Naturales Bernardino Rivadavia, Museo Casa de Ricardo Rojas, Museo de Arqueología de Alta Montaña de Salta, Museo de Arte Español Enrique Larreta, Museo de Arte Hispanoamericano Isaac Fernández Blanco, Museo de Arte Latinoamericano de Buenos Aires, Museo de Arte Popular José Hernández, Museo de Artes Plastícas Eduardo Sivori, Museo de la Pasion Boquense, Museo de La Plata, Museo de la Shoá, Museo del Mar, Museo del Puerto (Bahía Blanca), Museo Etnográfico (Buenos Aires), Museo Folklórico, Museo Gauchesco Ricardo Güiraldes, Museo Histórico Nacional, Museo Judío de Buenos Aires Dr. Salvador Kibrick, Museo Municipal Carmen Funes, Museo Municipal Ernesto Bachmann, Museo Nacional de Arte Decorativo, Museo Nacional de Bellas Artes, Museo Nacional del Hombre, Museo Paleontológico Egidio Feruglio, Museo Regional Malargüe, Museo Xul Solar, Palacio de las Aguas Corrientes, Palacio San José, Palacio San Martín, Palais de Glace, Parque Nacional Iguazú, Parque Provincial Ischigualasto, Restaurant Notorious, Taller y Museo de Platería Criolla y Civil, Teatro Catalinas Sur, Teatro Municipal General San Martín, Templo de la Congregación Israelita, Villa Gesell.

Picture Credits
t=top; tc=top centre; tr=top right; cla=centre left above; ca=centre above; cra=centre right above; cl=centre left;

c=centre; cr=centre right; clb=centre left below; cb=centre below; crb=centre right below; bl=bottom left; bc=bottom centre; br=bottom right; ftl=far top left; ftr=far top right; fcla=far centre left above; fcra=far centre right above; fcl=far centre left; fcr=far centre right; fclb=far centre left below; fcrb=far centre right below; fbl=far bottom left; fbr=far bottom right.

Every effort has been made to trace the copyright holders, and we apologize in advance for any unintentional omissions. We would be pleased to insert the appropriate acknowledgments in any subsequent edition of this publication.

The publisher would like to thank the following individuals, companies, and picture libraries for their kind permission to reproduce their photographs:
Works of art have been reproduced with the kind permission of the following copyright holders:
MALBA-FUNDACION COSTANTINI / MUSEO DE ARTE LATINOAMERICANO DE BUENOS AIRES: Manifestación, 1934 (Public Demonstration) (Temple on Burlap) 180 x 249 cm by Antonio Berni © José Antonio Berni 110cla; Siete últimas canciones, 1986, de la serie homónima (Last Seven Songs, from the homonymous series) (Acrylic painting on canvas) 141,5 x 226 cm © Guillermo Kuitca 110br; Abaporu, 1928 (Oil on canvas) 85,3 x 73 cm by Tarsila do Amaral © Guillermo Augusto Do Amaral 111tc; Rompecabezas, 1968-1970 (Puzzle) (Acrylic on canvas, 17 panels to be assembled) 100 x 100 cm each panel by Jorge de la Vega © Ramón de la Vega 111crb; Sin título, 1979 (Untitled) (Stainless steel wire and silver weldings) 100 x 40 x 40 cm © León Ferrari 111bc.

AKG-IMAGES: 53br.
ALAMY: Arco Images 29tc, 47bc, 162c, 184bc, 186tl, 186tr, 186br, 187tc, 217cr, /Therin-Weise 201t; Rodolfo Arpia 13c; Purvis Beau 291c; BKWine.com/Per Karlsson 86; Blickwinkel 19br, 79br; Steve Bly 6-7, 40cl; Tibor Bognar 60, 63cr, 170-71; Brianlatino 96tr; James Brunker 237br; Bryan & Cherry Alexander Photography 267bl; Cristina Cassinelli 306bl; Cephas Picture Library 134cl, 203b; Frederic Cholin 36cb; Classic Image 47c; Gary Cook 250cla; Javier Corripio 239crb; CuboImages srl 85br; Tim Cuff 251br; Danita Delimont 5clb, 28cl, 40tc, 42b; David R. Frazier Photolibrary, Inc. 72tr, 172tr, 288br, 290cla, 307br, 330b; Saturno Dona' 5crb, 304tc; Emilio Ereza 306fbl; Javier Etcheverry 35cr, 35bc, 137b, 226br, 255clb; f1 online 20bl; Mark O'Flaherty 209cra; Folio 266clb; Robert Fried 35bl, 35br, 173cra, 239bc, 309bl, 330cla; Fabian Gonzales 289bc; Rodney Griffiths 8bl; Martin Harvey 258bl; Gavin Hellier 248-49; Jeremy Hoare 15tl, 22-3c, 38tr, 72bl, 123tl, 247bc; Chris Howarth 88cl; Imagebroker 38tl, 44bl; Interfoto Pressebildagentur 9br, 133c; Jon Arnold Images Ltd 250clb; Norma Joseph 1c, 8tc, 17tr, 264cl, 307tc; Jupiter Images /Brand X 251tc; Christian Kapteyn 255crb, 255br, 311bc; Lemarco 59cr, 63br, 322tr; LightTouch Images/Colin Harris 265t; MAF 306br; Mary Evans Picture Library 55tl; MB-America 9tl; Network Photographers 59br; A. Parada 36tr; Peter Llewellyn (L) 36cl; Photos-12 29tr; Christopher Pillitz 31br; Popperfoto 38ca, 38-9c, 39cr, 39cb, 39bl, 39bc, 39br, 53cra, 151c; Richard Wareham Fotografie 160br, 161tr, 173crb; Robert Harding Picture Library Ltd 262-63, /Geoff Renner 254b, 267cr; Emiliano

Rodríguez 4-5tc, 20tr, 198cl, 238ca, 238cb; Marcelo Rudini 20crb; Gordon Sinclair 307cb; Paul Springett 253clb, 314cl; Stephen Frink Collection 18clb; Stockbyte 63cra; James Sturcke 241tr, 315tl; Tbkmedia.de 135tr; Angel Terry 87tc; Tom Till 202; Travel Excellence 18cr, 34cl; TravelStockCollection/ Homer Sykes 64clb; Genevieve Vallee 169c; Joan Vendrell 191tr; Simon Vine 255bc; Visual&Written SL 226tr, 230tl; Visions of America/LLC/Joe Sohm 257b; Westend 61 144tl; Wim Wiskerke 35crb, 120b, 288cl; WorldFoto 265crb, 266br, 267tl; Anna Yu 307ca.
ARCHIVO GENERAL DE LA NACIÓN: 32br.
ARCHIVOLATINO: Diego Giudice 37tl.

JADD CHENG: 112br.
CORBIS: 136; Theo Allofs 227tl; Yann Arthus-Bertrand 172cl, 175tr; Bettmann 29cb, 52bc, 53tl, 53c, 53cb, 54tc, 54clb, 54bl, 113bl; Marcello Calandrini 135br; Corbis Sygma 33tr, /Diego Goldberg 55bc, 103c; Pablo Corral V 72cla, William Coupon 29bl; Owen Franken 21br; Diego Giudice 37tr, 163ca; Jon Hicks 117br, 318cl; Dave G. Houser 53bc; Hulton-Deutsch Collection 52clb; Bob Krist 266cla; Michael Lewis 28crb, 208-209c; Eduardo Longoni 291tl; Craig Lovell 62cl, 77tc; Francesc Muntada 227cra; Diego Lezama Orezzoli 117tr; Hubert Stadler 3c; 306fbr; Anthony John West 13b; Zefa/Hugh Sitton 22tr.
GERALD CUBITT: 239cra.

DK IMAGES: Philip Dowell 19bc.

FRANK LANE PICTURE AGENCY: Minden Pictures/ Konrad Wothe 222cl.
FRONTERASUR.COM: 306ca, 306cr, 307bl, 307bc.

GETTY IMAGES: 39crb; AFP Photo 29br, /Pedro Armestre 29crb, /Daniel Garcia 28tr, /Jeff Haynes 37br, /Juan Mabromata 43tc, /Mauricio Lima 37cr; AFP Photo/Staff/Roland Magunia 27bt; AFP Photo/ Stringer 52bl; AFP Photo/Stringer/Mayela Lopez 16tr, /Juan Mabromata 27bl; Hulton Archive /Nobby Clark 31tr, /Stringer/Keystone 52br, 52-53c, 253br; Science Faction /Louie Psihoyos 232-33c, 233tl; Minden Pictures, /Flip Nicklin 312br; Stocktrek Images 10bl; Stone /Andrea Booher 22br; Time & Life Pictures / Mansell 267br, /Hart Preston 51tc, /Frank Scherschel 32cra, /Stringer/Thomas D. McAvoy 52cl.

JAIME TORRES OFFICE: 26cr.
JON ARNOLD IMAGES LTD: Walter Bibikow 256.
LATIN PHOTO: Rodrigo Buezas 36bl; Fernando Calzada 17b, 20br, 20-21c, 25tr, 26tr; Silvina Enrietti 42tr; German Falke 19cb, 20clb, 22bl, 74cr, 157b, 163cl, 169tc, 172tl, 245br; Miguel Fleitas 18cl; Carlos Ortiz Fragala 42tl, 209bl; Christian Heit 21cr; Guillermo Jones 62tr, 165br; Norberto Lauria 40br, 306cl; Enrice Limbrunner 22cla; Patrick Lüthy 21tr, 101tl; Maria Menegazzo 11br; Mule 67tr; Patricio Murphy 35cla; Pepe Pride 39tl; Diego Ivo Piacenza 117cl, 163crb, 163bl; Nicolas Pousthomis 20cl; Pronatura 192tr; Pablo Rey 327tl; Aznarez Soledad 55crb; Sub.coop/ Juan Vera 15bc.
LEBRECHT MUSIC & ARTS PHOTO LIBRARY: E.Comesana 73tl.
PATRICK LIOTTA: 27cr.
ALEJANDRO LIPSZYC: 26br.
LONELY PLANET IMAGES: Chris Barton 230bc; Krzysztof Dydynski 12, 308cr; Andrew Peacock 320bl.

MARY EVANS PICTURE LIBRARY: 51crb.
MASTERFILE: T. Ozonas 41bc.
MUSEO DE LA PLATA: 142ca, 142cl.
NATIONAL GEOGRAPHIC IMAGE COLLECTION: Damnfx 232br.

NATURAL VISIONS: Richard Coomber 155tr.
NATURE PICTURE LIBRARY: Ross Couper-Johnston 166tl, 166br; Luiz Claudio Marigo 167br; Pete Oxford 19cla. Odyssey Productions, Inc.: Robert Frerck 21cra, 22c, 28bl, 34tr, 58cl, 59tl, 63tl, 73cla, 73br, 94; Russell Gordon 23tl.

JOSHUA ONG: 73cr.
IGNACIO OTHEGUY: 154br.

PHOTOGRAPHERS DIRECT: David Alayo 16bl; Andres Perez Moreno Photography 239tc; Archivolatino/ Diego Giudice 32bl; CFW Images/Rachel Tisdale 195crb; Emiliano Rodríguez Photography /Emiliano Rodríguez Ruiz de Gauna 76; Fotoscopio /Gustavo Di Pace 26cl, 27tl, 73tl,197bl; Javier Etcheverry Photography 232tr; Dale Mitchell 19cl; Lebrecht Music & Arts Photo Library /Elbie Lebrecht 50clb; Sylvia Cordaiy Photo Library Ltd /Sylvia Cordaiy 252b; Fotozonas.com /Tomeu Ozonas 45br.
PHOTOLIBRARY: Cephas Picture Library Ltd 177b, / Andy Christodolo 208br, /Kevin Judd 208cl, 214-15; Foodanddrink Photos 209c; Iconotec /H.FougFre 14b,132-33; Index Stock Imagery,Inc. /Garry Adams 200tl; Jon Arnold Travel /Peter Adams 8c; Jtb Photo Communications Inc 135cr; Mary Evans Picture Library 269c; Mauritius /Michael Obert 156; Medio Images /Photodisc 56-7; Nordic Photos /Chad Ehlers 104; Oxford Scientific Films /Colin Monteath 220, 255c, 316-17; Photodisc /Glen Allison 4br, 82-3; Photononstop /Yvan Travert 221b, /Marc Vérin 178bl, 268-69; Michael Runkel 176.
PHOTOSHOT: Nhpa /Thomas Kitchin & Victoria Hurst 18fcrb; Kevin Schafer 19crb.
PRODUCCIONES CENTAURO: 23bl.

REDFERNS MUSIC PICTURE LIBRARY: Jon Lusk 27tr; Philip Ryalls 26clb.
REUTERS: Marcos Brindicci 36-37c, 43br, 124tl, 308bl; Viktor Korotayev 33br; Enrique Marcarian 23cra, 38bl; Handout/ Rodolfo Coria 233br; STR New 160cl.
DIEGO MANUEL RODRIGUEZ: 29cr.

SOUTH AMERICAN PICTURES: 28-9c; Tony Morrison 146-47; Frank Nowikowski 113tr.

HANNE THERKILDSEN: 79tl.
THE BRIDGEMAN ART LIBRARY: Military encampment of the governor Jeronimo Matorras during the Gran Chaco campaign (oil on canvas), Cabrera, Tomas (18th century)/Museo Histórico Nacional, Buenos Aires, Argentina, Index /The Bridgeman Art Library 46; The Congress of Tucumán – Declaration of the Independence of the United Provinces of Río and the Plata on 9th July 1816 (colour litho), Fortuny, Francisco (19th century) (after)/Private Collection, Index/The Bridgeman Art Library 49tr; The Battle of Monte Caseros in April 1852, printed by C. Penuti and Alejandro Bernheim (litho), Uruguayan School (19th century)/Museo Histórico Nacional Casa Rivera, Montevideo, Uruguay, Index /The Bridgeman Art Library 49cb; Shield of the Confederation of Argentina (colour litho), Argentinian School, (19th Century) / Private Collection, /The Bridgeman Art Library 49br; Battle of Tuyutí, from the paintings depicting the Triple Alliance War, 1866 (oil on canvas), López, Cándido (1840-1902) /Museo Histórico Nacional, Buenos Aires, Argentina, Index/The Bridgeman Art Library 50t; The Arrival of General Juan Facundo Quiroga (1790-1835) in Madrid on the 24th June 1820 (colour litho), French School, (19th century) / Bibliotheque des Arts Decoratifs, Paris, France, Archives Charmet 185crb.
THE GRANGER COLLECTION, NEW YORK: 7c, 48t, 50bc, 56c, 107bc, 317c.
THE PICTURE DESK: The Art Archive /Museo Naciónal de Bellas Artes Buenos Aires /Gianni Dagli Orti 30br; The Kobal Collection /Historias/Progress 33tl, /MGM 31c, / Paramount 32cl, /La Pasionaria/ Maria Gowland 33cr.

JUSTIN TYLER: 109br.

EMMA WERNER DE OLIVER: 186clb, 187bl, 187br.
WIKIPEDIA, THE FREE ENCYCLOPEDIA: 27cl, 27clb, 33cl, 38cl, 49bl, 51bl, 52tr, 155bc.
WINE REPUBLIC ARGENTINA: Richard Gordon 209br.

Front Endpaper: ALAMY: BKWine.com /Per Karlsson bc; Tibor Bognar cr; Tom Till tl; CORBIS: ftr; Jon ARNOLD IMAGES LTD: Walter Bibikow cl; ODYSSEY PRODUCTIONS, INC.: Robert Frerck br; PHOTOGRAPHERS DIRECT: Emiliano Rodríguez Photography /Emiliano Rodrígucz Ruiz de Gauna fcr; PHOTOLIBRARY: Mauritius /Michael Obert tr, Michael Runkel ftl, Nordic Photos /Chad Ehlers fbr, Oxford Scientific Films /Colin Monteath fcl.

Jacket images: Front: CORBIS: GALEN ROWELL DK IMAGES: Linda Whitwam bl. Back: DK IMAGES: Demetrio Carrasco bl; Linda Whitwam clb; Nigel Hicks tl; GETTY IMAGES: George Haling cla. Spine: DK IMAGES: Linda Whitwam.

All other images © Dorling Kindersley
For further information see: www.dkimages.com

Phrase Book

In Argentina, waves of immigration at the end of the 19th century and at the beginning of the 20th century (especially from Italy, but also from France and Spain) influenced the way people spoke. The variant of Spanish spoken in Argentina is known as *rioplatense*. "Ll" and "y" are both pronounced like English "sh" as in "she", as opposed to the "y" sound in Castilian Spanish. The "s" sound can become like an "h" when it occurs before another consonant or at the end of a word as in "tres" – "treh"; it may be omitted altogether, as in "dos" – "do". As in other Latin American countries, "c" and "z" are often pronounced as "s", as opposed to "th" in Castilian Spanish.

In an Emergency

Help!	**¡Socorro!**	*sokorro*
Stop!	**¡Pare!**	*pareb*
Call a doctor!	**¡Llamen un médico!**	*shamen oon medeeko*
Call an ambulance	**¡Llamen a una ambulancia**	*shamen a oona amboolans-ya*
Police!	**¡Policía!**	*poleesee-a*
I've been robbed	**Me robaron**	*meb rrobaron*
Where is the nearest hospital?	**¿Dónde queda el hospital más cercano?**	*dondeb keda el ospeetal mas sairkano*
Could you help me?	**¿Me puede ayudar?**	*meb pwedeb a-shoodar*

Communication Essentials

Yes	**Sí**	*see*
No	**No**	*no*
Please	**Por favor**	*por fabor*
Pardon me	**Perdone**	*pairdoneb*
Excuse me	**Disculpe**	*deeskoolpeb*
I'm sorry	**Lo siento**	*lo s-yento*
Thanks	**Gracias**	*gras-yas*
Hello!	**¡Buenas!**	*bwenas*
Good day	**Buenos días**	*bwenos dee-as*
Good afternoon	**Buenas tardes**	*bwenas tardes*
Good evening	**Buenas noches**	*bwenas noches*
Night	**Noche**	*nocheb*
Morning	**Mañana**	*man-yana*
Tomorrow	**Mañana**	*man-yana*
Yesterday	**Ayer**	*a-shair*
Here	**Acá**	*aka*
How?	**¿Cómo?**	*komo*
When?	**¿Cuándo?**	*kwando*
Where?	**¿Dónde?**	*dondeb*
Why?	**¿Por qué?**	*por keb*
How are you?	**¿Qué tal?/¿Cómo va?**	*keb tal/komo ba*
Very well, thank you	**Muy bien, gracias**	*mwee byen gras-yas*
Pleased to meet you	**Encantado/mucho gusto**	*enkantado/ moocho goosto*

Useful Phrases

Fine!	**¡Qué bien!**	*keb b-yen*
Do you speak a little English?	**¿Habla un poco de inglés?**	*abla oon poko deb eengles*
I don't understand	**No entiendo**	*no ent-yendo*
Could you speak more slowly?	**¿Puede hablar más despacio?**	*pwedeb ablar mas despas-yo*
I agree/OK	**De acuerdo/bueno**	*deb akwairdo/bweno*
Let's go!	**¡Vámonos!**	*bamonos*
How do I get to/ which way to..?	**¿Cómo se llega a...?/ ¿Por dónde se va a...?**	*komo se sbega a/por dondeb seb ba a*
¡Qué piola!	**keh pyola**	*That's great!*

Useful Words

large	**grande**	*grandeb*
small	**pequeño**	*peken-yo*
hot	**caliente**	*kal-yenteb*
cold	**frío**	*free-o*
good	**bueno**	*bweno*
bad	**malo**	*malo*
sufficient	**suficiente**	*soofees-yenteb*
open	**abierto**	*ab-yairto*
closed	**cerrado**	*serrado*
entrance	**entrada**	*entrada*
exit	**salida**	*saleeda*
full	**lleno**	*sheno*
right	**derecha**	*dairecha*
left	**izquierda**	*eesk-yairda*

straight on	**(todo) recto**	*(todo) rrekto*
over	**arriba**	*arreeba*
quickly	**pronto**	*pronto*
early	**temprano**	*temprano*
late	**tarde**	*tardeb*
now	**ahora**	*a-ora*
soon	**ahorita**	*a-oreeta*
less	**menos**	*menos*
much	**mucho**	*moocho*
in front of	**delante**	*delanteb*
opposite	**enfrente**	*enfrenteb*
behind	**detrás**	*detras*
first floor	**segundo piso**	*segoondo peeso*
ground floor	**primer piso**	*preemair peeso*
lift	**ascensor**	*asensor*
bathroom	**baño**	*ban-yo*
women	**mujeres**	*moobaires*
men	**hombres**	*ombres*
toilet paper	**papel higiénico**	*papel eeb-yeneeko*
camera	**cámara**	*kamara*
batteries	**pilas**	*peelas*
passport	**pasaporte**	*pasaporteb*
visa	**visa**	*beesa*
tourist card	**tarjeta turística**	*tarbeta tooreesteeka*
thief	**chorro**	*chorro*
lazy	**atorrante**	*atorranteb*
bar	**boliche**	*boleecheb*
idiot	**boludo**	*boloodo*
cop	**cana**	*kana*
to tease	**cargar**	*kargar*
money	**guita**	*geeta*
bride	**cioma**	*koyma*
to eat	**morfar**	*morfar*
kid	**pibe**	*peebeb*
mess	**quilombo**	*keelombo*
driver's license	**registro**	*rebeestro*
shanty town	**villa miseria**	*beesha meesair-ya*
to nick, to steal	**afanar**	*afanar*
to get frightened	**achicarse**	*acheekarseb*
No way	**¡Ni en pedo!**	*nee en pedo*
to put up with	**bancar**	*bankar*
girl/woman	**mina**	*meena*

Health

I don't feel well	**Me siento mal**	*meb s-yento mal*
I have a stomach ache	**Me duele el estómago**	*meb dweleb el estomago*
headache	**la cabeza**	*la kabesa*
He/she is ill	**Está enfermo/a**	*esta enfairmo/a*
I need to rest	**Necesito decansar**	*neseseeto deskansar*

Post Offices and Banks

I'm looking for a	**Busco una**	*boosko oona*
Bureau of change	**casa de cambio**	*kasa deb kamb-yo*
What is the dollar rate?	**¿A cómo está el dolar?**	*a komo esta el dolar*
I want to send a letter	**Quiero enviar una carta**	*k-yairo emb-yar oona karta*
postcard	**postal**	*postal*
stamp	**estampilla**	*estampee-sba*
to draw out money	**sacar dinero**	*sakar deenairo*

Shopping

I would like/want...	**Me gustaría/quiero...**	*meb goostaree-a/k-yairo*
Do you have any...?	**¿Tiene...?**	*t-yeneb*
expensive	**caro**	*karo*
How much is it?	**¿Cuánto cuesta?**	*kwanto kwesta*
What time do you open/close?	**¿A qué hora abre/ cierra?**	*a ke ora abreb/ s-yairra*
May I pay with a credit card?	**¿Puedo pagar con tarjeta de crédito?**	*pwedo pagar kon tarbeta deb kredeeto*

Sightseeing

beach	**playa**	*pla-sba*
castle, fortress	**castillo**	*kastee-sho*
guide	**guía**	*gee-a*
motorway	**autopista**	*owtopeesta*
road	**carretera**	*karretaira*
street	**calle, callejón**	*ka-sheb, ka-shebon*
tourist bureau	**oficina de turismo**	*ofeeseena deb tooreesmo*
town hall	**municipalidad**	*mooneeseepaleedad*

Getting Around

When does it leave?	¿A qué hora sale?	a keh ora saleh
When does the next train/bus leave for...?	¿A qué hora sale el próximo tren/ autobús a...?	a keh ora saleh el prokseemo tren/ owtoboos a
customs	aduana	aduana
Could you call a taxi for me?	¿Me puede llamar un taxi?	meh pwedeh shamar oon taksee
port of embarkation	puerta de embarque	pwairta deh embarkeh
boarding pass	tarjeta de embarque	tarbeta deh embarkeh
car hire	alquiler de autos	alkeelair deh owtos
bicycle	bicicleta	beeseekleta
rate	tarifa	tareefa
insurance	seguro	segooro
petrol station	estación de nafta	estas-yon deh nafta
garage	garage	garabeh
I have a flat tyre	Se me pinchó una goma	seh meh peencho oona goma

Staying in a Hotel

I have a reservation	Tengo una reserva	engo oona rresairba
Are there any rooms available?	¿Tiene habitaciones disponibles?	yones deesponeebles
single/double room	habitación sencilla/ doble	abeetas-yon sensee-sha/dobleh
twin room	habitación con camas gemelas	abeetas-yon kon kamas hemelas
shower	ducha	doocha
bath	bañadera	ban-yadaira
I want to be woken up at...	Necesito que me despierten a las...	neseseeto keh meh desp-yairten a las
warm/cold water	agua caliente/fría	agwa lak-yenteh agwa
soap	jabón	babon
towel	toalla	to-a-sha
key	llave	shabeh

Eating Out

I am a vegetarian	Soy vegetariano	soy behetar-yano
fixed price	precio fijo	pres-yo feeho
glass	vaso	baso
cutlery	cubiertos	koob-yairtos
Can I see the menu, please?	¿Me deja ver el menú, por favor?	me deha ber el menoo por fabor
The bill, please	la cuenta, por favor	la kwenta por fabor
I would like	Quiero un poco	k-yairo oon poko
some water	de agua	deh agwa
breakfast	desayuno	desa-shoono
lunch	almuerzo	almwairso
dinner	comida	komeeda

Menu Decoder See also pp290–91

bife de chorizo a caballo	beefeh deh choreeso a kabasho	char-grilled sirloin steak with two fried eggs on top
bife de chorizo	beefeh deh choreeso	char-grilled sirloin steak
bife de lomo	beefeh deh lomo	char-grilled fillet steak
centolla	sentosha	spider crab
chimichurri	cheemeechoorree	hot sauce
choripán	choreepan	pork sausage sandwich
churrasco	choorrasko	char-grilled rump steak
churrasco a caballo	choorrasko a kabasho	char-grilled rump steak with two fried eggs on top
matambre	matambreh	pork flank or skirt steak
mollejas	moshehas	sweetbreads
torta de humita	torta deh oomeeta	yellow sweet pumpkin and sweet corn mixed with cheese, onion and red pepper
arroz	arros	rice
atún	atoon	tuna
azúcar	asookar	sugar
bacalao	bakala-o	cod
bizcochuelo	beeskochwelo	cake
camarones	kamarones	prawns
carne	karneh	meat

cebolla de chip	sebo-ya de cheep	spring onion
		bread roll
huevo	webo	egg
jugo	boogo	fruit juice
langosta	langosta	lobster
leche	lecheh	milk
mantequilla	mantekee-sha	butter
marisco	mareesko	seafood
pan	pan	bread
papas	papas	potatoes
pescado	peskado	fish
pollo	po-sho	chicken
postre	postreh	dessert
potaje	potabeh	soup
roseta	rroseta	bread roll
sal	sal	salt
salsa	salsa	sauce
sopa	sopa	soup
té	teh	tea
vinagre	beenagreh	vinegar
zapallito	sapa-sheeto	courgette

Time

minute	minuto	meenooto
hour	hora	ora
half-hour	media hora	med-ya ora
quarter of an hour	un cuarto	oon kuarto
Monday	lunes	loones
Tuesday	martes	martes
Wednesday	miércoles	m-yairkoles
Thursday	jueves	hwebes
Friday	viernes	b-yairnes
Saturday	sábado	sabado
Sunday	domingo	domeengo
January	enero	enairo
February	febrero	febrairo
March	marzo	marso
April	abril	abreel
May	mayo	ma-sho
June	junio	boon-yo
July	julio	hool-yo
August	agosto	agosto
September	septiembre	sept-yembreh
October	octubre	oktoobreh
November	noviembre	nob-yembreh
December	diciembre	dees-yembreh

Numbers

0	cero	sairo
1	uno	oono
2	dos	dos
3	tres	tres
4	cuatro	kwatro
5	cinco	seenko
6	seis	says
7	siete	s-yeteh
8	ocho	ocho
9	nueve	nwebeh
10	diez	d-yes
11	once	onseh
12	doce	doseh
13	trece	treseh
14	catorce	katorseh
15	quince	keenseh
16	dieciséis	d-yeseesays
17	diecisiete	d-yesees-yeteh
18	dieciocho	d-yes-yocho
19	diecinueve	d-yeseenwebeh
20	veinte	baynteh
30	treinta	traynta
40	cuarenta	kwarenta
50	cincuenta	seenkwenta
60	sesenta	sesenta
70	setenta	setenta
80	ochenta	ochenta
90	noventa	nobenta
100	cien	s-yen
500	quinientos	keen-yentos
1000	mil	meel
first	primero/a	preemairo/a
second	segundo/a	segoondo/a
third	tercero/a	tairsairo/a
fourth	cuarto/a	kwarto/a
fifth	quinto/a	keento/a
sixth	sexto/a	seksto/a
seventh	séptimo/a	septeemo/a
eight	octavo/a	oktabo/a
ninth	noveno/a	nobeno/a
tenth	décimo/a	deseemo/a

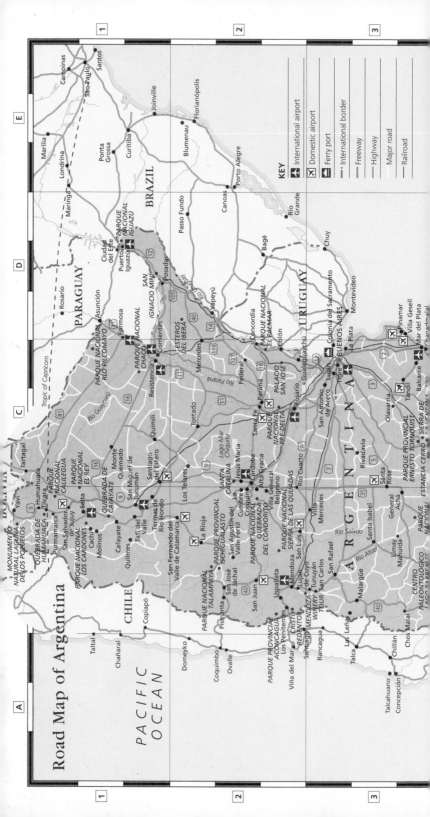

Road Map of Argentina